Foreword

All anthologists are fallible. Those whose choices are restricted to the files of a particular magazine face additional hazards. For one thing, they can choose only from what has already been chosen. For another, when a considerable time span is covered, a question comes up: Should the book be simply a collection of what the editors think is excellent, or should some consideration be given to the historical record—some attempt made to reflect the temper of a particular time, the styles of a particular period, the attitudes of a particular decade? In the end, we were persuaded that we could honor the other considerations without departing from the criterion of excellence. We would like to believe that these nine hundred poems broadly represent almost a half-century of poetry and are among the best poems that appeared in *The New Yorker* between 1925 and 1969.

The contents of this book are arranged in what may strike the reader at first as an odd way. The poems are printed alphabetically by title. We tried other arrangements, but this one seemed, finally, to provide the most variety and therefore to be truer to the way poems actually appear in *The New Yorker* week after week. For the convenience of the reader, there is an index in which the poems are arranged alphabetically by author.

Sometimes a poet changes the title of a poem before including it in a book. Sometimes he revises a poem. All the poems here are reprinted in the original versions published in *The New Yorker*.

The Editors

Contents

(Poems arranged alphabetically by title)

[vii]

Contents

Contents

Contents

Contents

Contents

Contents [xxiii]

The New Yorker
Book of Poems

A

ABOVE THE ARNO

My room in Florence was the color of air.
Blue the stippled wall I woke to,
the tile floor white except where
shadowed by the washstand and my high
bed. Barefoot, I'd go to the window to look
at the Arno. I'd open the broad shutters like a book,
and see the same scene. But each day's sky,
or night, dyed it a different light.

The turbid river might be lizard-green, or gray,
or yellowish like the stucco *palazzi*
on the opposite quay.
Boys would be angling with long, lank
poles, sitting on the butts of them, dangling
legs from the paved bank;
they wore handkerchiefs, the corners knotted,
for caps against the strong

sun, and had their dogs along;
the dogs, brown-and-white spotted,
had to lie quiet. But I never saw anything
jerk the lines of the yellow poles.
The boys smoked a lot, and lazed in the sun.
Smaller ones dove and swam in the slow, snaking Arno
right under the sign that read, "PERICOLO!
DIVIETO DI BAGNARSI."

Over Ponte Santa Trinità, fiacres would go,
or a donkey-hauled cart, among the auto
and popping scooter traffic. Freckled-gray
blinkered horses trotted the red-and-black
carriages in which the richer tourists rode.
(A donkey looks like a bunny under its load,
with its wigwag ears and sweet expression;
the workman-driver flicks

a string whip like a gadfly over it.)
I'd hear hoof clops and heel clicks
among hustling wheels on the bridge. It curved
like a violin's neck across the Arno,
and had two statues at each end—
white, graceful, a little funny.
One, a woman, had lost her head, but strode
forward holding her basket of fruit just the same.

You could see Giotto's Tower in my "book" and
the gold ball on top of Brunelleschi's Dome
and the clock with one hand
on the campanile of the Palazzo Vecchio,
and a blue slice of the Apennines the color of my room.
One day I slept all afternoon—
it was August and very hot—and didn't wake
until late at night,

or rather, early morning.
My mind was fresh—all was silent.
I crossed the white tiles, barefoot,
and opened the book of the shutters
to faint stars, to a full Arno,
starlight fingering the ripples. Gondola-slim
above the bridge, a new moon held a dim
circle of charcoal between its points.

Bats played in the greenish air,
their wing joints
soft as moths' against the bone-gray *palazzi* where
not a window was alight,
the doorways dark as sockets.
Each of the four statues so white
and still,
rose, somnambulistic, from its hill

of stone above the dusky slide
of the river. On my side,
a muscular, round-polled
man—naked behind—hugged a drape
against him, looking cold.
His partner, fat,
in short toga and hat
made of fruit, leaned a hand on a Horn

of Plenty. On the opposite bank, in torn
sweeping robes, a Signora

bore sheaves of wheat along her arm.
And, striding beside her, with stately charm
in her broken flounces, the Headless One
offered her wealthy basket, chin
up—though I had to imagine
chin, face, head, headdress, all.

Then a tall
tower began to tell "F O U R,"
and another, with different timbre, spelled it
a minute later. Another mentioned it for the third time
in harsh bronze and slow.
Still another, with delicate chime,
countered and cantered it. By now, the sky had turned
della Robbia-blue, the Arno yellowed silver.

I stood between the covers of my "book" and heard
a donkey's particular heels,
like syllables of a clear, quick word,
echo over the Arno. Then came the scrape-clink
of milk cans lowered on cobbles. And with the moon still
there, but transparent, the sky began to fill
with downy clouds—pink
as the breasts of Botticelli's Venus—foretinting dawn.

—MAY SWENSON

THE ACCOUNTANT IN HIS BATH

The accountant dried his imperfect back
As he stood in the sinking water,
"In ten years' time I'll be dead as cork,
No sooner, no later.

"Numbers display more muscle every day;
They multiply while I'm asleep.
When I fall to pieces they won't even see;
They'll keep on adding each other up.

"I know the numbers; each has a color—
Twenty-three is olive green.
Five's a comedian (all have characters),
One is God, and eight's the Queen.

"But I was never envious of numbers,
Watching them replace each other;

Like the grim wolves, not one remembers
His fading father.

"Passionless, lean, their armies march,
Invade more ledgers, take more men alive,
But they're not free to run or lurch
Each to his private grave."

Patches of water shrank inside the bath.
Confident in the immortal numbers,
He heard his wife's amazing laugh;
"I love her," he said as he pulled on his pajamas.

                                       —ADRIAN MITCHELL

THE ACTOR

Say you were the kid who could not sleep
In the new house in the north, with the wind
Flapping roof shingles, window banging softly
And tub humming for rain, the outside soft with moon,
And the man in the door looking into that softness—

Would you not follow? Out to the road
To hunch along the dark fringe as he walks
In a trance through the years rising like sand,
Falling back to leave him quickened
With each step, until he finds the old road
Leading to a concrete slab poured and forgot
By someone with a cottage in his head.

You crouch in fern and northern orchids.
He climbs onto the gray square,
Bows to the footweeds, and begins
A monologue. As he intones old names,
The man he was lives with his friends
In the shape of bulbs in the night
And posters curling in basements.

You are afraid for him, for yourself,
For all those players who rehearse their lines
In the trees beyond the city. As he
Storms with mad verse the indifferent air,
Something like night moves through the weeds.

                                       —THOMAS SNAPP

AN ADDRESS TO THE VACATIONERS AT CAPE LOOKOUT

The whole weight of the ocean smashes on rock;
the sun hounds the night; gulls ravel the edge.
Here it is better to allow for what happens, all of it—
the part assumed, the lie that keeps a rendezvous
with proof, the wickerwork that disguises the iron.
This place is too real for that blame
people pin on each other, for honor or dishonor.
    Have you noticed how uninvited
    anything pure is? Be brave—there is such a thing
    as helping history get on with its dirty work.

When the home folk tell you goodbye,
they shouldn't *bid* you goodbye that corrupted, wise way,
or burden you with too great a gift; and I
wouldn't burden you, except with one great gift:
the cold, the world that spins in cold space—
to be able to walk away, not writhe in regret
or twist in the torture bush. After all,
there is such a thing as justice in friendship.
    Have you noticed how uninvited
    anything pure is? Here something big lifts us
    outside, scorns our bravery or fear.

What disregards people does people good.

                         —WILLIAM STAFFORD

ADMIRAL

Admiral, the prisoner of your giant's
Strength, I spent my leisure in the brig,
Devising arms against your eminence
And arsenal of law, absurdly bent
To open war on my inconsequence.

Your might, the quarry of my rich abuse,
Refused to settle in a human face,
But rose in visionary interviews
To constellate my firmament with bright
Insignia whose stars shone to accuse.

But when, as though in parody of grace,
The amnesty of your indifference

Fell upon my crime, how commonplace
That long impenitence appeared! How dull
The sulky freedom yawning in my face!

Now, compounded by neglect, my debts
Assail their creditors, and, Admiral,
Your far agenda, year by year, forgets
My reckoning, though each oblivious night
Shoulders aloft your golden epaulets.
                                        —JOHN ALEXANDER ALLEN

ADVICE TO A PROPHET

When you come, as you soon must, to the streets of our city,
Mad-eyed from stating the obvious,
Not proclaiming our fall but begging us
In God's name to have self-pity,

Spare us all word of the weapons, their force and range,
The long numbers that rocket the mind;
Our slow, unreckoning hearts will be left behind,
Unable to fear what is too strange.

Nor shall you scare us with talk of the death of the race.
How should we dream of this place without us—
The sun mere fire, the leaves untroubled about us,
A stone look on the stone's face?

Speak of the world's own change. Though we cannot conceive
Of an undreamt thing, we know to our cost
How the dreamt cloud crumbles, the vines are blackened by frost,
How the view alters. We could believe,

If you told us so, that the white-tailed deer will slip
Into perfect shade, grown perfectly shy,
The lark avoid the reaches of our eye,
The jack-pine lose its knuckled grip

On the cold ledge, and every torrent burn
As Xanthus once, its gliding trout
Stunned in a twinkling. What should we be without
The dolphin's arc, the dove's return,

These things in which we have seen ourselves and spoken?
Ask us, prophet, how we shall call

Our natures forth when that live tongue is all
Dispelled, that glass obscured or broken,

In which we have said the rose of our love and the clean
Horse of our courage, in which beheld
The singing locust of the soul unshelled,
And all we mean or wish to mean.

Ask us, ask us whether with the worldless rose
Our hearts shall fail us; come demanding
Whether there shall be lofty or long standing
When the bronze annals of the oak-tree close.

—RICHARD WILBUR

ADVICE TO COLONEL VALENTINE

To fall in love, though classically human,
Is comic if a girl or an old man,
Pathetic if a boy or an old woman.

Love remains decent for how long? The nation
Allows each female thirty years, tacks on
Ten more for males intent on procreation.

Your decent years, you say, have lapsed? The comic
Come crowding, yet love gnaws you to the quick
As once when you were fifteen and pathetic?

Dye your hair, do you ask? Dress natty,
Swing an aggressive cane, whistle and lie?
That would indeed be to act comically.

Friend: honor your gray hairs, keep out of fashion—
Even if a foolish girl, not yet full grown,
Confronts you with a scarcely decent passion.

—ROBERT GRAVES

AEGEAN

Where only flowers fret
And some small passionate
Bird sings, the trumpets sounded yes-
    terday.

The famous ships are gone,
Troy fades, and the face that shone—
Fair Helen, in her tower—could not
    stay.

Where are the temples set
Their gods would not forget,
The trophies, and the altars? Echo,
    say.
There's no one any more
But Echo on the shore,
And Echo only laughs and runs away.

Though still the olive glows
Like silver, and the rose
Is glittering and fresh, as in their
    day,
No witnesses remain
Of battles on the plain
And the bright oar and the oar spray.

—Louis Simpson

AFTERGLOW

Sunset is always disturbing
whether theatrical or muted,
but still more disturbing
is that last desperate glow
that turns the plain to rust
when on the horizon nothing is left
of the pomp and clamor of the setting sun.
How hard holding on to that light, so tautly drawn and different,
that hallucination which the human fear of the dark
imposes on space
and which ceases at once
the moment we realize its falsity,
the way a dream is broken
the moment the sleeper knows he is dreaming.

—Jorge Luis Borges

(*Translated from the Spanish by Norman Thomas di Giovanni*)

AFTER GREECE

Light into the olive entered
And was oil. Rain made the huge, pale stones
Shine from within. The moon turned his hair white
Who next stepped from between the columns,
Shielding his eyes. All through
The countryside were old ideas
Found lying open to the elements.
Of the gods' houses, only
A minor premise here and there
Would be balancing the heaven of fixed stars
Upon a Doric capital. The rest
Lay spilled, their fluted drums half sunk in cyclamen
Or deep in water's biting clarity
Which just barely upheld me

The next week, when I sailed for home.
But where is home—these walls?
These limbs? The very spaniel underfoot
Races in sleep, toward what?
It is autumn. I did not invite
Those guests, windy and brittle, who drink my liquor.
Returning from a walk, I find
The bottles filled with spleen, my room itself
Smeared by reflection onto the far hemlocks.
I some days flee in dream
Back to the exposed porch of the maidens
Only to find my great-great-grandmothers
Erect there, peering
Into a globe of red Bohemian glass.
As it swells and sinks I call up
Graces, Furies, Fates, removed
To my country's warm, lit halls, with rivets forced
Through drapery, and nothing left to bear.
They seem anxious to know
What holds up heaven nowadays.
I start explaining how in that vast fire
Were other irons—well, Art, Public Spirit,
Ignorance, Economics, Love of Self,
Hatred of Self, a hundred more,
Each burning to be felt, each dedicated
To sparing us the worst; how I distrust them
As I should have done those ladies; how I want
Essentials: salt, wine, olive, the light, the scream—
No! I have scarcely named you,
And look, in a flash you stand full-grown before me,
Row upon row, Essentials,
Dressed like your sister caryatids,
Or tombstone angels jealous of their dead,
With undulant coiffures, lips weathered, cracked by grime,
And faultless eyes gone blank beneath the immense
Zinc-and-gunmetal northern sky.
Stay then. Perhaps the system
Calls for spirits. This first glass I down
To the last time
I ate and drank in that old world. May I
Also survive its meanings, and my own.

—JAMES MERRILL

AFTER READING A CHILD'S GUIDE
TO MODERN PHYSICS

If all a top physicist knows
About the Truth be true,
Then, for all the so-and-sos,
Futility, and grime
Our common world contains,
We have a better time
Than the Greater Nebulae do
Or the atoms in our brains.

Marriage is rarely bliss
But, surely, it would be worse
As particles to pelt
At thousands of miles per sec
Around a universe
In which a lover's kiss
Would either not be felt
Or break the loved one's neck.

Though the face at which I stare
While shaving it be cruel,
Since year after year it repels
An aging suitor, it has,
Thank God, sufficient mass
To be altogether there,
Not an indeterminate gruel
Which is partly somewhere else.

Our eyes prefer to suppose
That a habitable place
Has a geocentric view,
That architects enclose
A quiet, Euclidean space—
Exploded myths, but who
Would feel at home a-straddle
An ever-expanding saddle?

This passion of our kind
For the process of finding out
Is a fact one can hardly doubt,
But I would rejoice in it more
If I knew more clearly what
We wanted the knowledge for—
Felt certain still that the mind
Is free to know or not.

It has chosen once, it seems,
And whether our concern
For magnitude's extremes
Really becomes a creature
Who comes in a median size,
Or politicizing nature
Be altogether wise,
Is something we shall learn.

—W. H. AUDEN

AFTER THE LAST BULLETINS

After the last bulletins the windows darken
And the whole city founders readily and deep,
Sliding on all its pillows
To the thronged Atlantis of personal sleep,

And the wind rises. The wind rises and bowls
The day's litter of news in the alleys. Trash
Tears itself on the railings,
Soars and falls with a soft crash,

Tumbles and soars again. Unruly flights
Scamper the park, and taking a statue for dead

Strike at the positive eyes,
Batter and flap the stolid head

And scratch the noble name. In empty lots
Our journals spiral in a fierce noyade
Of all we thought to think,
Or caught in corners cramp and wad

And twist our words. And some from gutters flail
Their tatters at the tired patrolman's feet
Like all that fisted snow
That cried beside the long retreat

Damn you, damn you! to the emperor's horse's heels.
Oh none too soon through the air white and dry
Will the clear announcer's voice
Beat like a dove, and you and I

From the heart's anarch and responsible town
Rise by the subway-mouth to life again,
Bearing the morning papers,
And cross the park where saintlike men,

White and absorbed, with stick and bag remove
The litter of the night, and footsteps rouse
With confident morning sound
The songbirds in the public boughs.

—RICHARD WILBUR

AFTER THE PERSIAN

I do not wish to know
The depths of your terrible jungle:
From what nest your leopard leaps
Or what sterile lianas are at once your serpents' disguise and home.

I am the dweller on the temperate threshold,
The strip of corn and vine,
Where all is translucence (the light!),
Liquidity, and the sound of water.
Here the days pass under shade
And the nights have the waxing and the waning moon.
Here the moths take flight at evening;
Here at morning the dove whistles and the pigeons coo.
Here, as night comes on, the fireflies wink and snap

Close to the cool ground,
Shining in a profusion
Celestial or marine.

Here it is never wholly dark but always wholly green,
And the day stains with what seems to be more than the sun
What may be more than my flesh.

—LOUISE BOGAN

AGAINST SEASONS

Why should we praise them, or revere
The stations of the Zodiac,
When every unforgiving year
Drives us hence and calls us back?

The expectations we invent
Drift bodiless on the drifting air,
And who conceives them but must
    rent
The dark apartment of despair?

Days come and go, and we suppose
The future will bring something big;

But season after season throws
Rhomboids of sunlight on the rug.

They say a heavenly horn will blow;
They say we must not be afraid;
But they are fools for saying so.
Endless meridians swing and fade;

All bodies in their orbits go;
The sky has nothing left to give.
We in this clash of circles know
Only the vicious ones we live.

—ROBERT MEZEY

THE AGE OF SHEEN

I never see the colored boats of night
Jewelling the dull river, breaking their light
Upon it, without thinking of that age
Of sheen when the long poems are written,
The oblique books read until the exotic midges
Of the deep hours caper upon the page,
When there is time for the unlikely love,
And the mind, luxuriant in its sheath,
Wears the time shiningly, having no thought
Of the river, and the irony underneath.

—DOROTHY HUGHES

ALCOHOLIC

He was like the Lord drunk
at the sight of the world
and the size of his shadow
on top, like a newspaper blown
by the wind against a bush.
The green fields were his youth
where he and his mad companions
flew over the barefooted earth
in love. Compassion
for friends killed by the war
is marked as the village there
where the land pauses.
Then comes the wild forest,
the vacant cabin,
the birches decaying,
the half-rotten hemlocks,
the disasters of middle age,

a second life worse than the first,
the ever-present hint of collapse,
the great tree falling,
the world burned by sunlight
into a ball,
into cheap, green glass,
into nothing at all,
and him with no words,
no love,
drunk,
drunk at the sight of his shadow
and the spot shining there
where the light
reflects a toy marble
lying
by chance
on the kitchen floor.

—F. D. Reeve

ALMANAC

The hammer
struck my nail
instead of nail.
A moon flinched
into being.
Omen-black, it
began its trail.

Risen from horizon
on my thumb
(no longer numb
and indigo),
it waxed yellow,
waned to a sliver
that now sets white,
here at the rim
I cut tonight.

I make it disappear
but try to mark
its voyage

over my little
oval ceiling—
cloudless, pink again,
and clear.

In the dark
quarter-inch
of this moon,
before it arrived
at my nail's tip,
did an unmanned airship
dive 200 miles
to the hem of space
and vanish?

At the place
of Pharaoh Cheops'
tomb (my full moon
floating yellow),
was a boat
for ferrying souls

to the sun disclosed
in a room sealed
5,000 years?

Reaching whiteness,
this moon-speck waned
while an April
rained. Across the
street, a vine

crept over brick
up 14 feet.

Was it then
that Einstein
(who said there is
no hitching post
in the universe),
at 76, turned ghost?

—MAY SWENSON

ALONE

what a word and I thought it would
    be
less disrespectful
old rotten tooth hanging on
there is no radius for this

so here I am
with the rusty motor of hope
sticking out of the sand like a dead
    arm
well it lasted
long enough it lasted until it was over

it ground the corn and did the dishes
and when it started to break down
where could I hide the pieces
with that repairman
looking at my uncouth hair
while I handed him tools always
the wrong one

now I can watch bushes
running their fingers over the legs

of strangers and say why not
let them have whatever
they get out of it

under the shadows are more
shadows and under those shadows
is nothing

I have my work to do
inventing new memories
and keeping verbs in the proper mood
somebody has to
and if I walk my defeated secrets
like a dog what's that to you
who left by way of the mirror
still believing that rain shows mercy

when how many times did I tell you
the fireflies are naked and cold
in the rags of their light

—RICHARD SHELTON

AMAGANSETT BEACH REVISITED

I

Once more I move among you, dear familiar places,
Pale shores, pale dunes, long burdened by my long love of you—
The sun strikes the great glass of ocean a glancing blow,
The waves are kneeling in the sun-dazzled spaces.
June is upon us: earth and sea
Are thronged with tidal life; the mackerel now
Swarm the Atlantic shallows; from some bough
Inland, the red-winged blackbird sounds his "fleur-de-lis"—
Life, that lifts up
In the green woodland the day-lily's cup,
Wakes in my heart once more;
Imagination spreads wide wings in me.
The blue road of the sea,
The void sea-road that runs
From here to the horizon, now—as once
In earlier summers when I strode along,
Measuring to the sea's rhythm the rhythms of my song—
Beckons imagination on.

II

All afternoon, I have pressed
Eastward, toward Amagansett. In the west,
The sun grazes the rim. Two sandpipers
Companion me now along the way—
They skirt the surges, keeping just out of reach
Of the advancing and receding foam.
It is early evening; we have come
To the broad shelf of Amagansett beach.
In the enormous dome
Seaward, the horizon is garlanded
With tender clouds; the hollow shell
Of heaven is luminous; the exhausted, pale
Waters exhale
A vast oceanic odor, a sea-soft breath.
Sundown. A sense of absence and of vacancy.
While there is still daylight,
A faint moon-path appears upon the sea;
While yet the living light prevails
Against the encroaching night,
The tenuous light of memory
Sets its cold seal upon
All that is gone—
On the now vanished day,
On the now vanished past.

—JOHN HALL WHEELOCK

THE AMBROSIA OF DIONYSUS AND SEMELE

Little slender lad, toad-headed,
For whom ages and leagues are dice to throw with,
Smile back to where, entranced, I wander,
Gorged with your bitter flesh,
Drunk with your Virgin Mother's lullaby.

Little slender lad, lightning-engendered,
Grand master of magicians,
When pirates stole you at Icaria
Wild ivy gripped their rigging, every oar
Changed to a serpent, panthers held the poop,
A giant vine sprouted from the mast crotch,
And overboard they plunged, the whey-faced crew!

Lead us with your song, tall Queen of Earth!
Twinned to the god, I follow comradely
Through a first rainbow limbo, webbed in white,
Through chill Tyrrhenian grottoes, under water,
Where dolphins roll among their marble rocks,
Through sword-bright jungles, tangles of unease,
Through halls of fear, ceilinged with incubi,
Through blazing treasure chambers walled with garnet,
Through domes pillared with naked Caryatids—
Then mount at last on wings into pure air,
Peering down with regal eye upon
Five-fruited orchards of Elysium,
In perfect knowledge of all knowledges.

And still she drowsily chants
From her invisible bower of stars.
Gentle her voice, her notes come linked together
In intricate golden chains paid out
Slowly across brocaded cramoisy,
Or unfold like leaves from the jade-green shoot
Of a rising bush whose blossoms are her tears . . .
Oh, whenever she pauses, my heart quails
Until the sound renews.

Little slender lad, little secret god,
Pledge her your faith in me,
Who have ambrosia eaten and yet live.
                                        —ROBERT GRAVES

AMNESIAC

No use, no use, now, begging Recognize!
There is nothing to do with such a beautiful blank but smooth it.
Name, house, car keys,

The little toy wife—
Erased, sigh, sigh.
Four babies and a cocker!

Nurses, the size of worms, and a minute doctor
Tuck him in.
Old happenings

Peel from his skin.
Down the drain with all of it!
Hugging his pillow

Like the red-headed sister he never dared to touch,
He dreams of a new one—
Barren, the lot are barren!

And of another color.
How they'll travel, travel, travel, scenery
Sparking off their brother-sister rears

A comet tail!
And money the sperm fluid of it all.
One nurse brings in

A green drink, one a blue.
They rise on either side of him like stars.
The two drinks flame and foam.

O, sister, mother, wife,
Sweet Lethe is my life.
I am never, never, never coming home!

—SYLVIA PLATH

AMSTERDAM LETTER

Brick distinguishes this country,
And broad windows—rather, rectangles
Of wide and glittering scope—
And cabbages.
Cattle a specialty, and cheese, storks—if they are not all dead

Or abandoned—and flowers, oh, flowers!
Some say as well, quick humor.
Is it a specimen of humor that a cabdriver proposes to marry me?
The speaking of English is at least general.
I have spoken as well a little Dutch with an old Frisian lady.
How affable she was, amusing and helpful!
(They *are* helpful and affable, and their far too occasional teams of horses
Wear rosettes by the ears.)
Aside from that, and above all, the dense, heavy, fragrant sky
And rich water, a further extension of color—
The sky a low window over this twining of green water and bridges—
And the sedate, gabled houses pressed closely together
And bicyclists, six abreast or more,
Whirling round corners like swallows.
How quiet they are! Even the trolleys!
While the trains seem to glide like sleighs on runners
So that after those many places dedicated, it would seem, to clatter,
The absence of it becomes an active delight in itself.

The delight is in part, of course, the lovely dividing of the city
By those ancient and ripe-green canals, and the mixed fragrance
Of the River Amstel and roasting coffee,
And the bravura of carved animal heads, the elegance of panels,
And those panes of violet and panes flushed yellow
(To transmit the effect of sunlight in winter)
That alternate the pure meaning of glass
With the blindness of shutters closed over warehouse windows,
And that Gothic German-French sense of the arabesque and the scroll,
The urn and the garland of leaves.

As for that delicacy of manner, that responsiveness to many,
That prevalence of what seems self-possessed, contained, and easy—
I am speaking of those who went out of their way
To lead me to Rembrandt's house
(Which in his lifetime he lost),
Of the woman at the Cantine,
Of the Madame, too, in the Zeedijk,
Amiable conversationalists
Who did not make me feel stupid
Because I would never speak their language,
Who by a manner suggested
What I have no word for—
Unfeigned it is and unblighted,
That "generous, free disposition"
That so strongly confirms
A fitness of things,
As do also the upright geraniums,

All of which, by the elm-dark canals
(Where dogs on the loose loped up to me
With cold, wet noses
And ducks paddled under the Seven Arches
And the gilt swan rode on the crest of the fortified tower),
Offered some measurable glimpse of what
There, by the water beds
And the ancient, calmed passions of their reflections,
Informed me as the moon does,
Which was in part the pleasure of learning
Those words that I did from the old Frisian woman—
Horse, sky, cow, tree, thank you, I mean,
Beauty, and love.

—JEAN GARRIGUE

ANGEL AND STONE

In the world are millions and millions of men, and each man,
With a few exceptions, believes himself to be at the center,
A small number of his more or less necessary planets careering
Around him in an orderly manner, some morning stars singing together,
More distant galaxies shining like dust in any stray sunbeam
Of his attention. Since this is true not of one man or of two
But of ever so many, it is hard to imagine what life must be like.
But if you drop a stone into a pool, and observe the ripples
Moving in circles successively out to the edges of the pool, and then
Reflecting back and passing through the ones that continue to come
Out of the center over the sunken stone, you observe it is pleasing.
And if you drop two stones, it will still be pleasing, because now
The angular intersections of the two sets form a more complicated
Pattern, a kind of reticulation regular and of simple origins.
But if you throw a handful of sand into the water, it is confusion,
Not because the same laws have ceased to obtain, but only because
The limits of your vision in time and number forbid you to discriminate
Such fine, quick, myriad events as the angels and archangels, thrones
And dominations, principalities and powers are delegated to witness
And declare the glory of before the lord of everything that is.

Of these great beings and mirrors of being, little at present is known,
And of the manner of their perceiving not much more. We imagine them
As benign, as pensively smiling and somewhat coldly smiling, but
They may not be as we imagine them. Among them there are some who count
The grassblades and the grains of sand by one and one and one,
And number the raindrops, and memorize the eccentricities of snowflakes.
Some of the greater ones reckon and record the tides of time,
Distinguishing the dynasties of mountains, races, cities

As they rise, flower, fall, to whom an age is as a wave,
A nation the spray thrown from its crest, while one, being charged
With all the crossing moments, the comings together and drivings apart,
Reads in the chromatin its cryptic scripture as the cell divides;
And one is the watcher over chance events and the guardian of disorder
According to the law of the square root of *n*, so that a certain number
Of angels or molecules shall fall in irrelevance and be retrograde.

So do they go, those shining creatures, counting without confusion,
And holding in their slow, immeasurable gaze all the transactions
Of all the particles, item by atom, while the pyramids stand still
In the desert and the deermouse huddles in his hole and the rain falls
Piercing the skin of the pool with water in water and making a million
And a million designs to be pleasingly latticed and laced and interfused
And mirrored to the lord of everything that is by one and one and one.

—HOWARD NEMEROV

ANNIVERSARY

Where were we in that afternoon? And where
is the high room now, the bed on which you laid your hair
as bells beat early in the still air?

A two o'clock of sun and shutters. Oh, recall
the chair's angle—a stripe of shadow on the wall—
the hours we gathered in our hands, and then let fall.

Wrist on wrist, we relive memory: shell of moon
on day sky, two o'clock in lazy June—
and twenty years gone in an afternoon.

—RICHMOND LATTIMORE

ANOTHER KIND OF BURNING

The south wind's molded by a spine of hill—
tree-dense, Appalachian—that from miles of woods
brings the scent of another kind of burning,
the fume of life, hair-thin, wrist-thick,
that last season's and the one before's and before that's
leaves resurrect,

and all the creeks composed of decomposings
comb the hillsides, shape roads. Three meet

where Back Creek crosses under a low
highway bridge. Among those who died here
was a boy

already caught by the same Heraclitean flux:
a father at sixteen in his mother-in-law's house,
driven out by women, driving too fast,
met at this crossroads
by the triple goddess.

The tracks of burning on the macadam's
what's left—that and
the wrist-thin, unbroken neck
of an infant now fatherless
in fact.

—RUTH FOX

ANOTHER YEAR COME

I have nothing new to ask of you,
Future, heaven of the poor.
I am still wearing the same things.

I am still begging the same question
By the same light,
Eating the same stone,

And the hands of the clock still knock without entering.

—W. S. MERWIN

ANTS AND OTHERS

Their spare, fanatic sentry comes
across the miles of afternoon
and finds us out—our single crumb
left dozing in a yellowed spoon—
sets up his wireless, reports
to Brown Shirts, comrades, pantry
        thieves.
(Their army goes like coffee grounds
down doorknobs, drains, up balconies
we meant to guard from minor lusts,
but lacked the key or missed the
        time.)

Defenseless now, the last crust leans
beside a cup. The brown knots climb,
as neat as clocks. I feel the heat
of other lives, and hungers bent
on honeycombs that are not there,
and do not ask what sweet is meant
for which of us, there being such
        need
of loaves and fishes everywhere.

—ADRIEN STOUTENBURG

ANTWERP: MUSÉE DES BEAUX-ARTS

Rubens, de Vos, Memling—room after room
Of imperious and crusted flesh, luxuriantly
Spread under cavaliers and Christs, under eyes
Of students scrutinizing the texture of tombs.
The oyster light and dedicated thought
Create their own life, placidly sensuous,
Away from the glitter and moan of the port.

Outside, in wafer-thin air, women hurry by,
Flesh no longer proud, and shapeless with suffering
Or boredom, or both. Banana boats
Hoot over cobbled streets, inscribe in pale sky
Their steamy messages. But only hidden under
Paint, centuries down in these cavernous rooms,
Do the senses, passionate as thunder,
Stretch themselves out and, like boats passing the boom
At sunset, reach open sea—a spiritual south.

—ALAN ROSS

APPALACHIAN FRONT

Panther lies next to Wharncliffe
and Wharncliffe next to Devon
and Devon next to Delorme.
In each a single fisherman casts
in the slow, black water of the Big
    Sandy.
Catfish is the whisker lurking
behind the bobbing cork.
He lives, it seems, in dense night
from day to day until the fisherman
from Wharncliffe pulls him out
to be fried in tin-roof, tarpaper shacks
from there to Matewan.

Politicians call this valley
a depressed area.

But, under the sun, my heart
will not have it so.
Straight up from the brackish water,
up the mountainside,
green pointed trees
as close as bird's wings
grow fierce and clean,
and then for miles beside the tracks
the river moves faster over the rocks
and the water isn't black at all—
only the silt underneath.
The water over the rocks
is running clear and cold and pure.

—ROBERT LEWIS WEEKS

AQUARIUM

The old fish fiddle with their fins and glide.
As if I had their water in my eyes,
    My body skates from side to side
Before the glass square that defines their motion,

And wonders how they moralize
The evened edges of their narrowed ocean.

What rich escapes, through black walls greenly weeded,
From pirate shark, flounder, or captain squid,
  Must plank the brain no longer needed!
Nights—to give plausibility, even ground,
  To what in fluider days they did—
They flee in one-eyed angles round and round.

Once the sly currents of the Gulf flowed cool
And fanned their gills with luminous information;
  The wit of drains in a heated pool
Alone selects them now. All's bright and blank
  In the captive phase of evolution.
Ecology is different in a tank.

Here, in asparagus light, schooled to the turns,
The management providing every dish,
  They drill their fins around the ferns
And take a gurgling pleasure in the glare.
  They know: the style, it is the fish.
Their side of the glass, water is everywhere.

—George T. Wright

THE ARCTIC OX

(derived from "golden fleece of the arctic,"
an article in the "atlantic monthly," by john j. teal, jr.,
who rears musk oxen on his farm in vermont)

To wear the arctic fox
you have to kill it. Wear
  qiviut—the underwool of the arctic
    ox—
pulled off it like a sweater;
your coat is warm, your conscience
      better.

I would like a suit of
qiviut, so light I did not
  know I had it on, and in the
course of time another,
since I had not had to murder

the "goat" that grew the fleece
that grew the first. The musk ox
  has no musk and it is not an ox—
illiterate epithet.
Bury your nose in one when wet.

It smells of water, nothing else,
and browses goatlike on
  hind legs. Its great distinction
is not egocentric scent
but that it is intelligent.

Chinchillas, otters, water rats,
and beavers keep us warm.
    But think! A "musk ox" grows six
        pounds
of *qiviut*; the cashmere ram,
three ounces—that is all—of *pashm*.

Lying in an exposed spot,
basking in the blizzard,
    these ponderosos could dominate
the rare-hairs market in Kashan, and
        yet
you could not have a choicer pet.

They join you as you work,
love jumping in and out of holes,
    play in water with the children,
learn fast, know their names,
will open gates and invent games.

While not incapable
of courtship, they may find its
    servitude and flutter too much
like Procrustes' bed,
so some decide to stay unwed.

Camels are snobbish
and sheep unintelligent,
    water buffaloes neurasthenic,
even murderous,
reindeer seem overserious.

Whereas these scarce *qivies*,
with golden fleece and winning ways,
    outstripping every fur bearer—
there in Vermont quiet—
could demand Bold Ruler's diet:

Mountain Valley water,
dandelions, carrots, oats;
    encouraged as well, by bed
made fresh three times a day,
to roll and revel in the hay.

Insatiable for willow
leaves alone, our goatlike
    qivi-curvi-capricornus
sheds down ideal for a nest.
Songbirds find *qiviut* best.

Suppose you had a bag
of it; you could spin a pound
    into a twenty-four- or five-
mile thread—one, forty-ply,
that will not shrink in any dye.

If you fear that you are
reading an advertisement,
    you are. If we can't be cordial
to these creatures' fleece,
I think that we deserve to freeze.
                                      —MARIANNE MOORE

ARIA

Music lifting and falling,
Waiting itself below,
The bowl at the base of the fountain
Spilling the overflow
In streams of silk and silver
To runnels underground.
The music is more like water
In pattern than in sound.

Moreover, hear this music
And see this water rise
In light almost more brilliant
Than that of Paradise,
Light beyond light, revealing
No fleck of time, no trace
Of cloud, no bar of shadow
To mark the dial's face.

The double rush and cadence
Of intricate delight,
Music lifting and falling,
Like water, pure and bright,

And light, beyond all radiance,
Intense, complete, profound,
No cloud on the golden mountain,
No shade on the golden ground.

—ROLFE HUMPHRIES

THE ARMADILLO—BRAZIL

This is the time of year
when almost every night
the frail, illegal fire balloons appear.
Climbing the mountain height,

rising toward a saint
still honored in these parts,
the paper chambers flush and fill with
        light
that comes and goes, like hearts.

Once up against the sky it's hard
to tell them from the stars—
planets, that is—the tinted ones:
Venus going down, or Mars,

or the pale green one. With a wind,
they flare and falter, wobble and toss;
but if it's still they steer between
the kite sticks of the Southern Cross,

receding, dwindling, solemnly
and steadily forsaking us,
or, in the downdraft from a peak,
suddenly turning dangerous.

Last night another big one fell.
It splattered like an egg of fire
against the cliff behind the house.
The flame ran down. We saw the pair

of owls who nest there flying up
and up, their whirling black-and-white
stained bright pink underneath, until
they shrieked up out of sight.

The ancient owls' nest must have
        burned.
Hastily, all alone,
a glistening armadillo left the scene,
rose-flecked, head down, tail down,

and then a baby rabbit jumped out,
short-eared, to our surprise.
So soft!—a handful of intangible ash
with fixed, ignited eyes.

Too pretty, dreamlike mimicry!
O falling fire and piercing cry
and panic, and a weak mailed fist
clenched ignorant against the sky!

—ELIZABETH BISHOP

ARSENIC

I THE FIRST LETTER

They will be telling you soon who you are,
The importunate, slovenly, younger thinkers—
But only because they are young. From afar,
You may hear certain familiar voices,
Romantic but growing increasingly dim,

Express themselves in some thirty sounds
Out of a possible twenty thousand;
The terraces will be swinging in place
With their few discordant violins, the lamps
Hissing with gas, the smell of an old
Shoebox suddenly tainting the wharf—
Or could the sky's incredible liquor
Be responsible for the odor of
A set of ancient mah-jongg tiles
You found in your mother's closet once?
What are they doing here on the coast?
They are lustreless now from disuse and the sun.

> *"I have taken a sufficient dose and still*
> *Feel nothing, a slight burning sensation,*
> *But no smell of garlic, the telltale sign.*
> *Strange. And several seconds have passed.*
> *No pain. But for those who follow, I note*
> *That the phone will appear farther away . . ."*

II THE SECOND LETTER

Now they will tell you your favorite words,
Symbols gone sickly with use—such as
Gull   blue   ocean   house—
Are no longer possible. And they're right.
You *have* been a bit of a fool. You have
Been feeling your way
When you should have gone straight
To the heart of the matter. Which is what?
To have looked humiliation full
In the face instead of walking around
It, like a dog chained to a pole . . .

For instance, a letter arrived this week,
Saying
> *"You're not expressing yourself.*
> *It's hard to know who you are."*

These facts
Are relevant:
I have never killed.
I have loved three times—
Possibly four.
I have two suits
I will never wear.

The mornings are bad,
But by evening I'm
Myself again.

Do you know me now, Miss Mandarin?
You of the scented, mauve-lined page
Who tell me that you were once a nun
But now, when a sailor stalks the streets,
You feel the old magic welling up,
The thing most of all you're afraid to lose?
Don't tell me *you're* the one who wrote
Three hundred times on a warehouse wall
"Don't knock love!" If so, I shake
Your hand still blue from chalk . . .

III The Third Letter

But there it is. One word
Used up already. Blue.
And here's another, thinly disguised:

Meanwhile the sea, a hundred yards away,
Already bored with its literary career,
Is beating itself up, again, again,
And, sick of the moon's attentions every night,
Is carving a sandbar farther out
Behind which it hopes to draw its skirts
And thus avoid the shore's vulgar display.
It's deluded, of course. It isn't very bright.
But it's beautiful. Which, around here, is right.

Now I am going back to the house
For a drink. From the upper porch, I see
A gull go by on the steadiest wings
You ever saw. If a scavenger's
That gorgeous, what will they say of me?
There's something to be said for everything,
For garbage, for instance, in this case.

> *"I've been meaning to write much sooner but*
> *Something has kept me from saying just*
> *What I wanted to . . . Are you well? Does J.*
> *Still wake each night and need comforting?*
> *I think, perhaps, that the lack of love,*
> *Yes, love . . . I feel you no longer*
> *Love, sincerely, with a thousand thoughts . . ."*

Starlight, dear walk, when this view is
Nothing but emptied space and snow,
When no foot breaks its silences,
What faces, guests will then arrive
Frantic with their reasons to live?

—HOWARD MOSS

THE ARTIST

Mr. T
        bareheaded
                in a soiled undershirt
his hair standing out
        on all sides
                stood on his toes
heels together
        arms gracefully
                for the moment
curled above his head!
        Then he whirled about
                bounded
into the air
        and with an entrechat
                perfectly achieved
completed the figure.
        My mother
                taken by surprise
where she sat
        in her invalid's chair
                was left speechless.
"Bravo!" she cried at last
        and clapped her hands.
                The man's wife
came from the kitchen:
        "What goes on here?" she said.
                But the show was over.

—WILLIAM CARLOS WILLIAMS

THE ASIANS DYING

When the forests have been destroyed their darkness remains
The ash the great walker follows the possessors
Forever
Nothing they will come to is real

Nor for long
Over the watercourses
Like ducks in the time of the ducks
The ghosts of the villages trail in the sky
Making a new twilight

Rain falls into the open eyes of the dead
Again again with its pointless sounds
When the moon finds them they are the color of everything

The nights disappear like bruises but nothing is healed
The dead go away like bruises
The blood vanishes into the poisoned farmlands
Pain the horizon
Remains
Overhead the seasons rock
They are paper bells
Calling to nothing living

The possessors move everywhere under Death their star
Like columns of smoke they advance into the shadows
Like thin flames with no light
They with no past
And fire their only future

—W. S. MERWIN

AS I WAS GOING TO SAINT IVES

As I was going to Saint Ives
In stormy, windy, sunny weather,
I met a man with seven wives
(The herons stand on the swift water).

One drinks her beer out of his can
In stormy, windy, and bright weather,
And who laughs more, she or her man?
(The herons stand still on the water.)

One knows the room his candle lit,
In stormy, lightning, cloudburst weather,
That glows again at the thought of it
(Two herons still the swift water).

His jealous, wild-tongued, Wednesday's wife—
In dreepy, wintry, wind-lashed weather

—What's better than that ranting strife?
(Two herons still the roaring water.)

There's one whose mind's so like his mind
In streaming wind or balmy weather,
All joy, all wisdom seem one kind.
(The herons stand in the swift water.)

And one whose secret mazes he
In moon-swept, in torrential weather
Ransacks, and cannot find the key
(Two herons stand in the white water).

He'll think of none save one's slim thighs,
In heat and sleet and windy weather,
Till death has plucked his dreaming eyes
(Two herons guard the streaming water).

And when to Saint Ives then I came
In fairest, rainiest, windiest weather,
They called his shadow by my name.
(The herons stand in the quick water.)

And the one whose love moves all he's done,
In windy, warm, and wintry weather,
—What can he leave but speaks thereon?
(Two herons still the swift water.)
                                    —Daniel G. Hoffman

ASPECTS OF ROBINSON

Robinson at cards at the Algonquin; a thin
Blue light comes down once more outside the blinds.
Gray men in overcoats are ghosts blown past the door.
The taxis streak the avenues with yellow, orange, and red.
This is Grand Central, Mr. Robinson.

Robinson on a roof above the Heights; the boats
Mourn like the lost. Water is slate, far down.
Through sounds of ice cubes dropped in glass, an osteopath,
Dressed for the links, recounts an old Intourist tour.
—Here's where old Gibbons jumped from, Robinson.

Robinson walking in the Park, admiring the elephant.
Robinson buying the *Tribune*, Robinson buying the *Times*. Robinson

Saying, "Hello. Yes, this is Robinson. Sunday
At five? I'd love to. Pretty well. And you?"
Robinson alone at Longchamps, staring at the wall.

Robinson afraid, drunk, sobbing. Robinson
In bed with a Mrs. Morse. Robinson at home;
Decisions: Toynbee or luminal? Where the sun
Shines, Robinson in flowered trunks, eyes toward
The breakers. Where the night ends, Robinson in East Side bars.

Robinson in Glen-plaid jacket, Scotch-grain shoes,
Black four-in-hand, and oxford button-down,
The jewelled and silent watch that winds itself, the brief-
Case, covert topcoat, clothes for spring, all covering
His sad and usual heart, dry as a winter leaf.

—WELDON KEES

ASPECTS OF SPRING IN GREATER BOSTON

Stirring porch pots up with green-fingered witchcraft,
from ditch-delicious outskirt trailing moon-struck
cats, with twitch of toad, of mummied broomstalk,
hag Spring in a wink blacks the prim white magic
of winter-wimpled Boston's every mate-sick
splinter of spinster landscape.
                                        Under the matchstick
march of her bridgework, giggling, the Lady Mystic
twitches her sequins coyly, but the calls
of her small tugs entice no geese. Canals
take freight; the roads throw up stiff hands; and the Charles
arches. Spring comes like a life raft smack to the waters
of Walden, or like a butt-slap.
                                        And yet she loiters.
Where is song while the lark in winter quarters
lolls? What's to solace Scollay's drugstore-floaters
and sing them to their dolls? and yet,
                                        strange musics—
migrant melodies of exotic ozarks—
twitter and throb where the bubble-throated jukebox
lurks iridescent by these lurid newsracks.
Browser, leafing here, withhold your wisecracks—
tonight, in public, straight from overseas,
her garish chiaroscuro turned to please
you and her other newsstand devotees,
the quarter-lit Diana takes her ease.

So watch your pockets, cats, hang onto your hearts,
for when you've drunk her glitter till it hurts—
Curtain. Dark scurries to dark. Full-feasted
Spring, like an ill bird, settles to the masthead
of here and there an elm. The streets are misted.
A Boston rain, archaic and monastic,
cobbles the blacktop waters, brings mosaic
to dusty windshields, to the waking, music.

—George Starbuck

THE ASPEN AND THE STREAM

The Aspen:

Beholding element, in whose pure eye
My boughs upon a ground of heaven lie—
O deep surrendered mind, where cloud and stone
Compose their beings and efface your own,
Teach me, like you, to drink creation whole
And, casting out myself, become a soul.

The Stream:

Why should the water drink,
Blithering little tree?
Think what you choose to think,
But lisp no more at me.

I seek an empty mind.
Reflection is my curse.
Oh, never have I been blind
To the damned universe,

Save when I rose in flood
And in my lathered flight
So fouled myself with mud
As to be purged of sight.

The Aspen:

Your water livens me, but not your word,
If what you spoke was what I thought I heard.
But likely I mistook you. What with the claims
Of crow and cricket teaching me their names,
And all this lilt and shifting in my head,
I must have lost the drift of what you said.

THE STREAM:
There may be rocks ahead
Where, shivered into smoke
And brawling in my bed,
I'll shred this gaudy cloak;

Then, dodging down a trough
Into a rocky hole,
I'll shake the daylight off
And repossess my soul

In blackness and in fall,
Where self to self shall roar
Till, deaf and blind to all,
I shall be self no more.

THE ASPEN:
Out of your sullen flux I shall distill
A gayer spirit and a clambering will,
And reach toward all about me, and ensnare
With roots the earth, with branches all the air—
Even if that blind groping but achieves
A darker head, a few more aspen leaves.

—RICHARD WILBUR

AT DELFT

IN MEMORY OF JOHANNES VERMEER

The clocks begin, civicly simultaneous,
　　And the day's admitted. It shines to show
How promptness is poverty, unless
　　Poetry be the result of it. The chimes
Stumble asunder, intricate and dense,
　　Then mass at the hour, their stroke
In turn a reminder—for if one dances,
　　One does so to a measure. And this
Is a staid but dancing town, each street
　　Its neighbor's parallel, each house
A displacement in that mathematic, yet
　　Built of a common brick. Within,
The key is changed; the variant recurs
　　In the invariable tessellation of washed floors,
As cool as the stuffs are warm, as ordered
　　As they are opulent. White earthenware,
A salver stippled at its lip by light,

The light itself, diffused and indiscriminate
On face and floor, usher us in,
　The guests of objects: as in a landscape,
All that is human here stands clarified
　By all that accompanies and bounds. The clocks
Chime muted underneath domestic calm.

—Charles Tomlinson

AT THE FISHHOUSES

Although it is a cold evening,
down by one of the fishhouses
an old man sits netting,
his net, in the gloaming almost invisible,
a dark purple-brown,
and his shuttle worn and polished.
The air smells so strong of codfish
it makes one's nose run and one's eyes water.
The five fishhouses have steeply peaked roofs
and narrow, cleated gangplanks slant up
to storerooms in the gables
for the wheelbarrows to be pushed up and down on.
All is silver: the heavy surface of the sea,
swelling slowly as if considering spilling over,
is opaque, but the silver of the benches,
the lobster pots, and masts, scattered
among the wild jagged rocks,
is of an apparent translucence
like the small old buildings with an emerald moss
growing on their shoreward walls.
The big fish tubs are completely lined
with layers of beautiful herring scales
and the wheelbarrows are similarly plastered
with creamy iridescent coats of mail,
with small iridescent flies crawling on them.
Up on the little slope behind the houses,
set in the sparse bright sprinkle of grass,
is an ancient wooden capstan,
cracked, with two long bleached handles
and some melancholy stains, like dried blood,
where the ironwork has rusted.

The old man accepts a Lucky Strike.
He was a friend of my grandfather.

We talk of the decline in the population
and of codfish and herring
while he waits for a herring boat to come in.
There are sequins on his vest and on his thumb.
He has scraped the scales, the principal beauty,
from unnumbered fish with that black old knife,
the blade of which is almost worn away.

Down at the water's edge, at the place
where they haul up the boats, up the long ramp
descending into the water, thin silver
tree trunks are laid horizontally
across the gray stones, down and down
at intervals of four or five feet.

Cold dark deep and absolutely clear,
element bearable to no mortal,
to fish and to seals . . . One seal particularly
I have seen here evening after evening.
He was curious about me. He was interested in music;
like me a believer in total immersion,
so I used to sing him Baptist hymns.
I sang him "A mighty fortress is our God."
He stood up in the water and regarded me
steadily, moving his head a little.
Then he would disappear, then suddenly emerge
almost in the same spot, with a sort of shrug
as if it were against his better judgment.
Cold dark deep and absolutely clear,
the clear gray icy water . . . Back, behind us,
the dignified tall firs begin.
Bluish, associating with their shadows,
a million Christmas trees stand   —
waiting for Christmas. The water seems suspended
above the rounded gray and blue-gray stones.
I have seen it over and over, the same sea, the same,
slightly, indifferently swinging above the stones,
icily free above the stones,
above the stones and then the world.
If you should dip your hand in,
your wrist would ache immediately,
your bones would begin to ache and your hand would burn
as if the water were a transmutation of fire
that feeds on stones and burns with a dark-gray flame.
If you tasted it, it would first taste bitter,
then briny, then surely burn your tongue.
It is like what we imagine knowledge to be:

dark, salt, clear, moving, utterly free,
drawn from the cold hard mouth
of the world, derived from the rocky breasts
forever, flowing and drawn, and since
our knowledge is historical, flowing, and flown.

—ELIZABETH BISHOP

AT YEARSEND

Now winter downs the dying of the year,
And night is all a settlement of snow;
From the soft street the rooms of houses show
A gathered light, a shapen atmosphere,
Like frozen-over lakes whose ice is thin
And still allows some stirring down within.

I've known the wind by waterbanks to shake
The late leaves down, which frozen where they fell
And held in ice as dancers in a spell
Fluttered all winter long into a lake;
Graved on the dark in gestures of descent,
They seemed their own most perfect monument.

There was perfection in the death of ferns
Which laid their fragile cheeks against the stone
A million years. Great mammoths overthrown
Composedly have made their long sojourns,
Like palaces of patience, in the gray
And changeless lands of ice. And at Pompeii

The little dog lay curled and did not rise
But slept the deeper as the ashes rose
And found the people incomplete, and froze
The random hands, the loose unready eyes
Of men expecting yet another sun
To do the shapely thing they had not done.

These sudden ends of time must give us pause.
We fray into the future, rarely wrought
Save in the tapestries of afterthought.
More time, more time. Barrages of applause
Come muffled from a buried radio.
The Newyear bells are wrangling with the snow.

—RICHARD WILBUR

AUBADE: LAKE ERIE

When sun, light-handed, sows this Indian water
With a crop of cockles,
The vines arrange their tender leafage
In the sweet shadows of an artificial France.

Awake, in the frames of windows, innocent children
Loving the blue, sprayed leaves of childish life
Applaud the bearded corn, the bleeding grape,
And cry,
"Here is the hay-colored sun, our marvellous cousin,
Walking in the barley,
Turning the harrowed earth to growing bread,
And splicing the sweet, wounded vine.
Lift up your hitchhiking heads
And no more fear the fever,
You fugitives and sleepers in the fields;
Here is the hay-colored sun!"

And when their shining voices, clean as summer,
Play, like church bells, over the field,
A hundred dusty Luthers rise from the dead, unheeding,
Search the horizon for the gap-toothed grin of factories,
And grope, in the green wheat,
Toward the woodwinds of the Western freight.
                                        —THOMAS JAMES MERTON

THE AUGSBURG ADORATION

Mozart, Goethe, and the Duke of Wellington
Spent the night at the Drei Mohren; so did we.
Did the Duke of Wellington find by his bed
Two bananas and two sugar-cubes, as we did?
Did the sparrows cheep, cheep, cheep to get the sugar?

And did Mozart sleep, next night, beside the highest
Spire in all the world—unfinished then? Ulm's emblem
Is a sparrow holding in its beak a straw.
You can buy it, in chocolate, at the bakeries.

Did Goethe see, among the cobblestones, the Roman
Manhole-covers marked SPQR? For the breath
Of those letters, the Senate and the People

Lived for us, indomitable as the sparrows
The bread-eating cats stalked in the ruins of Rome.

Travellers, we come to Rome, Ulm, Augsburg,
To adore something: the child nursing at the stone
Breast beside a stone ox, stone ass, a flesh-and-blood
Sparrow who nests in the manger. The Three Kings
Bring him stones and stones and stones, the sparrow
Brings a straw. The years have worn away the stone,
But the bird cramming food into the beseeching
Mouth in its nest of rubbish, is as perfect
As when the child first said of Mozart, Goethe,
And the Iron Duke: *One of them shall not fall*
On the ground without your Father. They have fallen
And the sparrow has not fallen. The straw-bearing
Sparrow at Ulm, at Augsburg, is indistinguishable
In its perfection from the sparrow who brought straw
To its nest, food to its young, in Rome, in Nazareth—
The green Forum's sparrows are the sparrows of home.

—RANDALL JARRELL

AVALANCHE

The drift descends like rattling dust
from stem and bough and lofty weed,
flaps in the wind, stamps on the deck,
litters the eaves with seed and spore
and pods as dry as old canoes,
until the house creaks in the flow
sent down to us by teeming hills.

All day, all year, and in cold dreams
I fight an avalanche of lives
swarming in silk, brooding in bark,
intent on sprouting anywhere—
along the sink, beneath the door,
out of the chimney's leafless mouth,
from every wrinkle, crack, or pore,
armpit or furrow, crevice or gut,
and the grit of eyelids closed too long.

I wake up often in the dark,
alerted by a sudden field
of thistles pressed against a wall,

and smell the heat of each dry torch,
or hear beneath my silent desk
the wild cucumber's spiny purse
drag an inch forward, pause, and
    scrape
another step. I try for sleep,
but the pillow has its nettles up,
the room is rank with sweat and
    thorn.

Each dawn, each day, I rise and dress,
clutch clumsy tools, use my own
    hands
to rake the dross from lilac beds,
spy out odd corners, scour and sweep,
uproot all vines that choke the lives
I want to keep; and yet I know
how soon, some night, the drift will
    flow,
pile up, and fill my seedless eyes.

—ADRIEN STOUTENBURG

AWAKING

After night, the waking knowledge—
The gravel path searching the Way;
The cobweb crystal on the hedge,
The empty station of the day.

So I remember each new morning
From childhood, when pebbles amaze.
Outside my window, with each dawn-
    ing,
The whiteness of those days.

The sense felt behind darkened walls
Of a sun-drenched world, a lake
Of light, through which light falls—
It is this to which I wake.

Then the sun shifts the trees around,
And overtops the sky, and throws
House, horse, and rider to the ground,
With knock-out shadows.

The whole day opens to an O,
The cobweb dries, the petals spread,
The clocks grow long, the people go
Walking over themselves, the dead.

The world's a circle, where all moves
Before after, after before,
And my aware awaking loves
The day—until I start to care.

—STEPHEN SPENDER

B

THE BABIES

Let us save the babies.
Let us run downtown.
The babies are screaming.

You shall wear mink
and your hair shall be done.
I shall wear tails.

Let us save the babies
even if we run in rags
to the heart of town.

Let us not wait for tomorrow.
Let us drive into town
and save the babies.

Let us hurry.
They lie in a warehouse
with iron windows and iron doors.

The sunset pink of their skin
is beginning to glow.
Their teeth

poke through their gums
like tombstones.
Let us hurry.

They have fallen asleep.
Their dreams
are infecting them.

Let us hurry.
Their screams rise
from the warehouse chimney.

We must move faster.
The babies have grown into their
    suits.
They march all day in the sun without
    blinking.

Their leader sits in a bulletproof car
    and applauds.
Smoke issues from his helmet.
We cannot see his face—

we are still running.
More babies than ever are locked in
    the warehouse.
Their screams are like sirens.

We are still running to the heart of
    town.
Our clothes are getting ragged.
We shall not wait for tomorrow.

The future is always beginning now.
The babies are growing into their
    suits.
Let us run to the heart of town.

Let us hurry.
Let us save the babies.
Let us try to save the babies.

—MARK STRAND

[43]

A BABY TEN MONTHS OLD
LOOKS AT THE PUBLIC DOMAIN

Somewhere near the end of a snow-
    shoe trail
In a craggy waste where Standard Oil,
Even, won't stake its claim
To a rocky part of the public domain,
This latest baby of ours gets a last
    portion
Of the national parks belonging to
    everyone.

There where early snowflakes visit,
And government rules prohibit
The shooting of dwindling herds,
Our baby says "Mine!" for his first
    word.

One surviving part of a divided world
Belongs, in a vague way, to our child.

A few fought-over acres on the sur-
    face—
And, I suppose, a vast cone of space
Stretching up forever—are his by
    birth.
He sits in our front yard and gazes
Out where his little herd grazes,
Northwest in the direction
Of his cosmic section.

          —WILLIAM STAFFORD

BAHAMAS

Where are we,
Mary, where are we?
They screen us and themselves
With tree-lined lanes

And the gardens of hotels though we
    have travelled
Into the affluent tropics. The harbors
Pierce all that. There are these islands

Breaking the surface
Of the sea. They are the sandy peaks
Of hills in an ocean

Streaked green by their shoals. The
    fishermen
And the crews from Haiti
Tide their wooden boats out

In the harbors. Not even the guitar-
    ists,
Singing the island songs
To the diners,

Tell of the Haitian boats,
Which bear their masts, the tall
Stripped trunks of trees

(Perhaps a sailor,
Barefoot on the ragged deckload
Of coconuts and mats, leans

On the worn mast) across the miles
Of the Atlantic, and the blinding
    glitter
Of the sea.

          —GEORGE OPPEN

BALDPATE POND

Touring the old miles again
we are, it's October here,
good for a drive at night;

good time to be out; wind's
down; everything is quiet;
pretty cold; but let's stop a

minute anyway—the air is so
clear. Come on, now, and let's
forget the passionate symbol.
There doesn't have to be any-

thing unusual in the scene.
It's what's been here all the
time, isn't it? Oh, then perhaps

you are remembering. Exactly
what, though? The demands of May?
July's answer? That spurt in

September? Well, look around then;
here's something good—here's
armistice. Take it tonight; on

any nights like this, you'd
be a fool not to.

The half-moon lights the lake,
the hills are gleaming faintly,
the apples hang from the trees.

O you, dying of love for this
world, you, learning—at the age of,
say, 50—that Love is impossible,

stop there!
        O stop there, we're

on to those tricks: philosophers
and syllogisms and even what's
left possible-impossible for their
crazy songs . . . Another minute
    here?

It will be enough.
              —E. F. WEISSLITZ

THE BALLAD OF LONGWOOD GLEN

That Sunday morning, at half past ten,
Two cars crossed the creek and entered the glen.

In the first was Art Longwood, a local florist,
With his children and wife (now Mrs. Deforest).

In the one that followed, a ranger saw
Art's father, stepfather, and father-in-law.

The three old men walked down to the cove;
Through tinkling weeds Art slowly drove.

Fair was the morning, with bright clouds afar.
Children and comics emerged from the car.

Silent Art, who could stare at a thing all day,
Watched a bug climb a stalk and fly away.

Pauline had asthma, Paul used a crutch;
They were cute little rascals but couldn't run much.

"I wish," said his mother to crippled Paul,
"Some man would teach you to pitch that ball."

Silent Art took the ball and tossed it high.
It stuck in a tree that was passing by—

And the grave green pilgrim turned and stopped.
The children waited, but no ball dropped.

I never climbed trees in my timid prime,
Thought Art—and forthwith started to climb.

Now and then his elbow or knee could be seen
In a jigsaw puzzle of blue and green.

Up and up Art Longwood swarmed and shinned,
And the leaves said *yes* to the questioning wind.

What tiaras of gardens! What torrents of light!
How accessible ether! How easy flight!

His family circled the tree all day.
Pauline concluded, "Dad climbed away."

None saw the delirious celestial crowds
Greet the hero from earth in the snow of the clouds.

Mrs. Longwood was getting a little concerned.
He never came down. He never returned.

She found a few coins at the foot of the tree.
The children grew bored. Paul was stung by a bee.

The old men walked over and stood looking up,
Each holding five cards and a paper cup.

Cars on the highway stopped, backed, and then,
Down a rutted road, waddled into the glen.

And the tree was suddenly full of noise:
Conventioners, fishermen, freckled boys.

Anacondas and pumas were mentioned by some,
And all kinds of humans continued to come:

Tree surgeons, detectives, the fire brigade.
An ambulance parked in the dancing shade.

A drunken rogue with a rope and a gun
Arrived on the scene to see justice done.

Explorers, dendrologists—all were there,
And a strange, pale girl with gypsy hair.

And from Cape Fear to Cape Flattery
Every paper had "MAN LOST IN TREE."

And the sky-bound oak (where owls had perched
And the moon dripped gold) was felled and searched.

They discovered some inchworms, a red-cheeked gall,
And an ancient nest with a new-laid ball.

They varnished the stump, put up railings and signs;
Rest rooms nestled in roses and vines.

Mrs. Longwood, retouched, when the children died
Became a photographer's dreamy bride.

And now the Deforests, with *four* old men,
Like regular tourists, visit the glen,

Munch their lunches, look up and down,
Wash their hands, and drive back to town.

—VLADIMIR NABOKOV

BALLAD OF THE MOUSE

A mouse the trap had slapped on, but not caught,
stood in the floor,
bloody-whiskered, in the curious light
snapped on from the kitchen door.

Grooved in the gray skull-fur
where the steel spring banged him,
blood from his ears, and one of two bead-black eyes
popped almost out, and hanging,

looking his bad luck, he skeered through doors,
rooms, halls, waddled along walls,

was exposed behind dressers,
hobbling with the load of his pain through falls,

bumps, skids, until the portable (peaches-
can) prison (from the trash sack) fell
into place, changing the hellishly lighted chambers
to a pleasurably blackened cell

as comfortable as his hole, but showing
a scar of light around the rim.
A shirt cardboard slid under—moving floor—
and gathered him

into the lurch and claw-slipping tilt and
ride of air, and bore
him giddy, sloping, and scratching
out the back door

to the yellow-porch-lit and midnight lawn,
and slid free his small terror
into the matty, spiny grass that held him like rails.
Shadowy, his executioner,

choosing (over drowning or crushing)
the doubtful love of a gun,
loomed over him, unready, tall. Unsteadily
he tried to run and the world blurred, un-

til he sat gathering his shakes in the grass blades.
The long-barrelled (.22, target) revolver lowered
to arm's length
from the panting, furred bird-ribs not yet dead,

and aimed, and fired—
six irregular shots
that drove deep their thunderous metal seeds
into the earth in spots

all around the tiny breath
they were meant for, spurting up yellow-brown
fountains of dirt
as before some palace, circus: forest, pillars, a kind of crown

in the noise and light of the murdering storm.
That poor marksman, love,

                clicked, quietly
                ticked, reloading, far, far, far above

                the withered and dumb and dirt-daubled mouse.
                Then light and leaden rain
                stomped down again, and one blind iron tear
                flooded all the sap of his pain

                into the earth along with it, leaving—
                indistinguishable in the churned-up lawn—
                a flattened and sucked-out pelt
                of half-buried once-mouse, now mouse-gone.

                In the yellow-gloomed arena, death's main drag, beyond
                which stars still leaked
                the light of heaven onto woods
                and hills the echoes had crashed and streaked

                and rolled across from farm to farm,
                in the ochre fungus of death, gun-handed, stone,
                stood the hunter, victor—
                tall, foolish, furious; alone.

                                                —ROBERT WALLACE

BALLADE OF ENGLAND

Where are now, in coign or crack,
The golden schedules that we made
Before the windows all went black,
Before the barren cannonade?
The magic word has been mislaid,
The page is missing from the book;
Having looked and looked, we are
        afraid
That there is nowhere left to look.

Open the shutters front and back,
Look up and down the esplanade;
Bill and Silas, Neil and Jack
Have vanished with the cavalcade

Of the befuddled and betrayed,
Whose cherished time the demon
        took.
We wait in vain, their faces fade,
And there is nowhere left to look.

Santa Claus has lost his sack.
Where are the toys we learnt to
        trade—
The dilettante bric-a-brac,
The ideologies of jade?
Where are the pompoms and the
        braid,
The trinkets of the private nook?

We have looked for them in sun and shade
And there is nowhere left to look.

ENVOI
My friend, the horses that we played
Have failed to answer to the book;
We looked to see our fortunes made,
But there is nowhere left to look.

—LOUIS MACNEICE

A BAROQUE WALL-FOUNTAIN IN THE VILLA SCIARRA

Under the bronze crown,
Too big for the head of the stone cherub whose feet
A serpent has begun to eat,
Sweet water brims a cockle and braids down

Past spattered mosses, breaks
On the tipped edge of a second shell, and fills
The massive third below. It spills
In threads then from the scalloped rim, and makes

A scrim or summery tent
For a faun-ménage and their familiar goose.
Happy in all that ragged, loose
Collapse of water, its effortless descent

And flatteries of spray,
The stocky god upholds the shell with ease,
Watching about his shaggy knees
The goatish innocence of his babes at play;

His fauness all the while
Leans forward slightly, into a clambering mesh
Of water-lights, her sparkling flesh
In a saecular ecstasy, her blinded smile

Bent on the sand floor
Of the trefoil pool, where ripple-shadows come
And go in swift reticulum,
More addling to the eye than wine, and more

Interminable to thought
Than pleasure's calculus. Yet since this all

Is pleasure, flash, and waterfall,
Must it not be too simple? Are we not

More intricately expressed
In the plain fountains that Maderna set
  Before St. Peter's—the main jet
Struggling aloft until it seems at rest

In the act of rising, until
The very wish of water is reversed,
  That heaviness borne up to burst
In a clear, high, cavorting head, to fill

With blaze, and then in gauze
Delays, in a gnatlike shimmering, in a fine
  Illumined version of itself, decline,
And patter on the stones its own applause?

If that is what men are,
Or should be, if those water-saints display
  The pattern of our *areté*,
What of these showered fauns in their bizarre,

Spangled, and plunging house?
They are at rest in fullness of desire
  For what is given, they do not tire
Of the smart of the sun, the pleasant water-douse,

And riddled pool below,
Reproving our disgust and our ennui
  With humble insatiety.
Perhaps Saint Francis, who lay in sister snow

Before the wealthy gate,
Freezing and praising, might have seen in this
  No trifle but a shade of bliss—
That place of tolerable flowers, that state

As near and far as grass,
Where eyes become the sunlight, and the hand
  Is worthy of water: the dreamt land
Toward which all hungers leap, all pleasures pass.
                                        —RICHARD WILBUR

BARROOM MATINS

Popcorn, peanuts, clams, and gum—
We whose Kingdom has not come
Have mouths like men but still are
          dumb,

Who only deal with Here and Now
As circumstances may allow;
The sponsored program tells us how.

And yet the preachers tell the pews
What man misuses God can use:
Give us this day our daily news

That we may hear behind the brain
And through the sullen heat's mi-
          graine
The atavistic voice of Cain:

"Who entitled you to spy
From your easy heaven? Am I
My brother's keeper? Let him die."

And God, in words we soon forget,
Answers through the radio set,
"The curse is on his forehead yet."

Mass destruction, mass disease—
We thank thee, Lord, upon our knees
That we were born in times like these,

When, with doom tumbling from the
          sky,
Each of us has an alibi
For doing nothing. Let him die.

Let him die, his death will be
A drop of water in the sea,
A journalist's commodity.

Pretzels, crackers, chips, and beer—
Death is something that we fear,
But it titillates the ear.

Anchovy, almond, ice, and gin—
All shall die though none can win;
Let the *Untergang* begin.

Die the soldiers, die the Jews,
And all the breadless, homeless
          queues.
Give us this day our daily news.

—Louis MacNeice

BATHING SONG

For some, the sea:
To battle and vault
Over the sleazy waves with their cocky crests,
The cut and slash of salt.
But for me
The alkaline river, the mild and ale-brown river:
To rock and rest
In the shallows and hear the hiss of the willows is best.

The yammering trees
Must speak for the wind,
And so on the noisy hill the word goes by

With a waterfall sound.
But below, at peace,
Is the havering river, the devious, dawdling river,
Where now I lie
And, floating, follow the lazy yachts of the sky.

—ANNE RIDLER

BATHTUBS

Scoops in the sea rock full of natural water,
used petrol drums, old oaken buckets oversized,
glossy ceramics, thermal springs, potholes—

anything serves: the Soochow tub, majestic,
fed with hot pitchers, the Scythian, steamed in mist
of hemp, the social clusters of the Japanese.

Have cargoes: Thoughtful omphalopsychite,
the athlete's sluice of sweat, the foreman's Saturday night.
A siren leers through the conniving foam,

advertising come-hither or soaps for sale.
Kings come to it or, in the Mycenaean
asaminthys, Homer's heroes scrubbed by queens.

I had for boat once an old brown tin bathtub
tabbed with twin ears for soap and plugged with a cork,
and sailed on a small pond until it drowned.

The Three of Gotham used, I think, a bathtub.
Poppaea brimmed her tub with donkey's milk.
Lady Godiva mistook one for a horse.

My dreamboats sail by night such perilous seas.
In the middle of the salon and the dressed people,
I, in my bathtub, dreading I may be noticed.

Better I like, above the dwindling earth,
to fly my hip-winged old flat-bottomed bathtub
through slippery space, and past the floating stars.

—RICHMOND LATTIMORE

BATTLE PROBLEM

A company of vessels on the sea,
Running in darkness like a company
Of stars or touchless martyrs in the fields
Above, or a wan school beneath its keels,
Holds a discrete deployment.

               Men who ride
In the ships are borne by no calculable tide;
Hurtled untouched, untouching, side by side
They sit at table, sleep in beds, keep shops
In marvellous spirals that reconcile the ship's
Way and the world's, the spinning and ellipse.
They hardly feel the weather; they do not feel
The ships around them or the planets wheel.
Trusting the several forces that direct
Things parallel, they will not intersect.

Moved by safe appetites, like the older stars,
The saints, and certain migratory creatures,
Older men conn the darkened ships at sea
In not the usual sense of company.

                    —WILLIAM MEREDITH

THE BEAR ON THE DELHI ROAD

Unreal, tall as a myth,
by the road the Himalayan bear
is beating the brilliant air
with his crooked arms.
About him two men, bare,
spindly as locusts, leap.
One pulls on a ring
in the great soft nose; his mate
flicks, flicks with a stick
up at the rolling eyes.

They have not led him here,
down from the fabulous hills
to this bald alien plain
and the clamorous world, to kill
but simply to teach him to dance.

They are peaceful both, these spare
men of Kashmir, and the bear
alive is their living, too.
If, far on the Delhi way,
around him galvanic they dance,
it is merely to wear, wear
from his shaggy body the tranced
wish forever to stay
only an ambling bear
four-footed in berries.

It is no more joyous for them
in this hot dust to prance
out of reach of the praying claws
sharpened to paw for ants
in the shadows of deodars.

It is not easy to free
myth from reality
or rear this fellow up
to lurch, lurch with them
in the tranced dancing of men.

—EARLE BIRNEY

BEARS

Wonderful bears that walked my room all night,
Where have you gone, your sleek and fairy fur,
Your eyes' veiled and imperious light?

Brown bears as rich as mocha or as musk,
White opalescent bears whose fur stood out
Electric in the deepening dusk,

And great black bears that seemed more blue than black,
More violet than blue against the dark—
Where are you now? Upon what track

Mutter your muffled paws that used to tread
So softly, surely, up the creakless stair
While I lay listening in bed?

When did I lose you? Whose have you become?
Why do I wait and wait and never hear
Your thick nocturnal pacing in my room?
My bears, who keeps you now, in pride and fear?

—ADRIENNE CECILE RICH

BEAUTY IN TROUBLE

Beauty in trouble flees to the good angel
  On whom she can rely
To pay her cab fare, run a steaming bath,
  Poultice her bruised eye;

Will not at first, whether for shame or caution,
  Her difficulty disclose,
Until he draws a checkbook from his plumage,
  Asking how much she owes

(Breakfast in bed: coffee and marmalade,
   Toast, eggs, orange juice,
After a long, sound sleep—the first since when?—
   And no word of abuse);

Loves him less only than her saintlike mother;
   Promises to repay
His loans and most seraphic thoughtfulness
   A millionfold one day.

Beauty grows plump, renews her broken courage,
   And, borrowing ink and pen,
Writes a newsletter to the evil angel
   (Her first gay act since when?):

The fiend who beats, betrays, and sponges on her,
   Persuades her white is black,
Flaunts vespertilian wing and cloven hoof,
   And soon will fetch her back.

Virtue, good angel, is its own reward:
   Your dollars were well spent.
But would you to the marriage of true minds
   Admit impediment?

                                        —ROBERT GRAVES

THE BEAVER'S STORY

The violent praise the destructive rites of the hawk;
A kingly deceit has the snake,
Vigilant, sinuous in leaves,
Coiled in a pattern of envy,
With a tongue of venom.

Deep forests protect the weak and provoke the strong.
Like a tree, antlers spring
From the velvet head of the elk.
Wolves hunt in a pack.
Ferocious bears have their cave in rock.

I would impose a form on the barbarous wilderness.
I do not trust the trees.
I trust my own teeth
To move them to my design
Away from this carpentry of death.

Flying out of the sunset, stiff, petalled lilies to pluck,
Flamingoes alight on the lake.
I study their stilted reflection.
At dawn they are gone.
In the reeds, the industrious moorhen,

So early building a nest where those fires were banked,
Knows already by instinct
How high, when the long rains come,
The water will flood, whose calm
Shall make the unwary succumb.

This benevolent water deceives who will not use it.
It speaks in my language, tacit.
In a climate of fear and conflict,
A secret architect,
I carry the plans of the city.

I construct where hostile conditions hold others in bondage.
I fell, and measure to usage,
Turning the course of the river,
Dragging logs of my labor
To uphold the measure of life.

Against wild nature I set the cool and Athenian;
A metrical city is mine:
Lanes in harmony laid
From the central beat of the blood.
I do not sprawl. I saw to the level of need.

—Vernon Watkins

THE BED

Your clothes of snow and satin and pure blood
Are surplices for many sacraments
Full of woven musk of birth and death,
Full of the wet wildflower breath of marriages,
The sweat, the slow mandragora of lust;

Meadow of sleep, table of sour sickness,
Infinite road to travel, first of graves,
Your square and subtle presence rules the house,
And little winging hurts of everyday
Clutch at your white skirt and are comforted.

What matter if you are wise or if you know?
A third of life is yours, all that we learn
We tell you, and you dream us night by night.
We take your advice, confess in sharp detail,
Add to your knowledge, yet can teach you nothing.
"Lie here," you say, and whomever we bring you, sad,
Ashamed, or delighted, you take in the spirit we give.

Let me not know too much, and let your soul
Not lead me farther on than sleep and love,
For her I marry is more white than you.
Some day, as if with ancient torches stand
And fill the walls with fires around her head,
And let your gown be fresh as April grass,
And let your prothalamium be sweet.

—Karl Shapiro

BEETLE ON THE SHASTA DAYLIGHT

Hills moved. I watched their shadows
riding by like names said
only once. The oaks turned round
and leaves ran past my head.

It was all reeling back where
the old disasters hung between
locked doors stitching the air,
unheard, as if they'd never been.

And the sun came falling through
the window of the train; it filled
my lap, slid down my arms into
the aisle, a blazing river spilled

inside. I found her in the shallow
light, wearing her skeleton
strapped smooth over her belly,
wallowing on her back, alone.

Some little Pequod spitting, mast-
        heads
tufted with joints like unfleshed frogs,
lame as a butterfly spread
on a pin. And from the thrashing legs

hooks caught at nothing, casting
and casting in the air, her
bent and beaded feelers lashing
until the threads would have to tear.

Pharaohs watched her push her dung
        ball
on the sand the way the sun
rolled slowly over heaven, saw
how she hatched her children

out of that roundness, called her Life.
They made her image out of stone,
greener than stems, to celebrate
the ornamental lake a queen

had built, to mark a lion hunt
or even marriage. They sent
her gleaming in the tombs of all
the dead so they might rise again.

I didn't touch her; slipping a marker
from my book under her back,
I turned my wrist down gently, set her
right. A piece of the whole shook

world turned up. Alive! She was
amazed to flex herself, to feel
the sun along her side like juice,
to have her front legs wheel

her forward, arched in a priestly
benediction. Oh, she was tight. She
        served
her concentrated self, and neatly.
Her eyes glittered out of her head.

Lightly she went and steady down
the aisle. Not any landscape she
remembered. Yet she was sure of
        home,
composed her dark wherever she
        might be

creeping. I waved her well. Saw
that she left no furrow in the floor.
But someone got up, swelling out
of his seat, and raised his foot before

my hand could drop, and put it down
and passed into the next car
and was gone. There was no sound
but the train's sound. Far

down the tracks, the sun rolled over.
I had to sit there after that
and look at California moving
backward, pressing my face flat

against the glass until it froze
to my skin. All afternoon
I looked out at the hills, those
trees with the light crawling down

their branches like white beetles
and the sky lurching among
the leaves, the shape of it tilting
at me crushed under the sun.

—SHIRLEY KAUFMAN

BEFORE DAWN

(TO OLD FRIENDS)

Flippantly,
In the cinemas past sleep,
Their faces bloat—moons
On this skyline of wakefulness—
But they never speak. No need.
I've had the script
Before.

Let the brittle leaves
Scratching by below
Keep up the exquisite
Harmony.

My Lord, if I
Yield now at last,
Pray, turn to the soul—
As old men afraid
With sickness turn
To the Almighty's

Safety kit in terror
Of their sixtieth year—

Then let me be
Content with what will be,
And sleep. . . .

But the leaves left over
Scratch with claws at graves
Where rain and weeds
Would have surely made
Good earth, I thought. . . .

Did I wake them,
The whole set, to settle
Our old scores, and suffer
Their silence: Monica
And Mary, her mother, or Harry.
Or Jill, and Jill's brother?

As she of Carthage
In the shades below
Turns from a barren land,
Each turns from me,
Who flung firebrands
Into our granaries
Days without end.

But try, perhaps try
To take it to the Lord in prayer—
Miscreant in a whited sepulchre
With old men suddenly
Chewing our sins
Thick as rhinoceros skins,
In dead, repentant air.

Or better, have it out
In a weather, perhaps, of friends—

(God save this rout of leaves
Cascading up the drive!)
Sleep again, or wake all over
With an old incurable
Abscess of thought.
No knife, no surgeon
To cut it off.

Oh, I'll have it out
Now with all of them!
Have it out, fool!
Make their mouths
Talk, smile, wince,
As you did once—
Over and over again.

—HORACE HAMILTON

BEFORE THE CASHIER'S WINDOW
IN A DEPARTMENT STORE

1

The beautiful cashier's white face has risen once more
Behind a young manager's shoulder.
They whisper together, and stare
Straight into my face.
I feel like grabbing a stray child
Or a skinny old woman
And diving into a cellar, crouching
Under a stone bridge, praying myself sick,
Till the troops pass.

2

Why should he care? He goes.
I slump deeper.
In my frayed coat, I am pinned down
By debt. He nods,
Commending my flesh to the pity of the daws of God.

3

Am I dead? And, if not, why not?
For she sails there, alone, looming in the heaven of the beautiful.
She knows
The bulldozers will scrape me up
After dark, behind

The officers' club.
Beneath her terrible blaze, my skeleton
Glitters out. I am the dark. I am the dark
Bone I was born to be.

4

Tu Fu woke shuddering on a battlefield
Once, in the dead of night, and made out
The mangled women, sorting
The haggard slant-eyes.
The moon was up.

5

I am hungry. In two more days
It will be Spring. So: this
Is what it feels like.

—James Wright

BENDIX

This porthole overlooks a sea
Forever falling from the sky,
The water inextricably
Involved with buttons, suds, and dye.

Like bits of shrapnel, shards of foam
Fly heavenward; a bedsheet heaves,

A stocking wrestles with a comb,
And cotton angels wave their sleeves.

The boiling purgatorial tide
Revolves our dreary shorts and slips
While Mother coolly bakes beside
Her little jugged apocalypse.

—John Updike

BETWEEN TWO WORLDS

The stripped almond of the plane is gone,
veering against an anchored moon.
Cloud waste spews out over the red
tiles of Belgium. You beat a tympanum
of cloud; I drum deserted cobblestones.

Now into your moving star I toss
my calendar, the shadow of a house,
and normal days. We meet as two gulls
might, in a cinema of sky, the green sea
under, the green eye of the sea scanning
the alternate shores of night.

This starry field is ours to trace.
Between the hour and zero hour,

tideless as in an aquarium,
the virginal water clocks unwind,
the luminous frescoes smile and sway,
and in that lambent medium
tomorrows bite off yesterday.

—ROSEMARY THOMAS

BEYOND THE HUNTING WOODS

I speak of that great house
Beyond the hunting woods,
Turreted and towered
In nineteenth-century style,
Where fireflies by the hundred
Leap in the long grass.
Odor of jessamine,
And roses, canker-bit,
Recall the famous times
When dame and maiden sipped
Sassafras or wild
Elderberry wine
While far in the hunting woods
Men after their red hounds
Pursued the mythic beast.

In all that great house finding
Not one living thing,
I ask it of a stranger,
Or of the wind or weather,
What charm was in the wine
That they should vanish so,
Ladies in their stiff
Bone and clean of limb,
And over the hunting woods
What mist had maddened them
That gentlemen should lose
Not only the beast in view
But Belle and Ginger, too,
Nor home from the hunting woods
Ever, ever come?

—DONALD JUSTICE

BIG, FAT SUMMER—AND THE LEAN AND HARD

I

And she aloof to laughter—till I don't know
How many times more open and gross
We played with puckers of the sea, or bent
Our backs, inconsequentially, to the sky's

Largely permissive kiss, before we knew
Either faithful blandness, her blue heaviest
Shadow.
            Or first saw, one insatiable day
Crammed with jewel-like small ires and oar-

Strokes, we were the prodigious: she
Throve of her dulcet reign. For whenever
Through the faintest aperture she emerged
And like a greater noontide swept the scene—

Salaam! Salaam! Pitched to our knees,
Savoring eyes rolled nearly inward,
We made the beach at once a bout
Between so much—as we fought to smother

Blinks and gasps, till blazing, whooping
Tempests of laughter lost the game—
That never a day but the sun fell dead
Blithely toasting our Queen of Dismay

While she, with consummate justice, looked away.

II

And when, soon as recovered, at day's end,
In those rose-petalled hours of troubled,
Delicate issue between sunlight and rock,

Gaily we followed her white purse
Down and down dark twists of streets
Straight to the smoky pits of the bazaars,
It seemed as if we clambered up and up—

Agile as the wild goats—past cleavages
And bloated bright sick rays to the dimmest
Summit of our understanding. If so
Sardly looking down we saw her

—Rather pinpointing a heaven—
Demurely, almost stodgily, wedged in
To another whole feast of indifference, was it not
Parts of us, and very well roasted, too,

She fed on there so daintily? Oh, lady, lady—
In your vast hours of igneous jubilee
That burned away our small talk—who could not see
What clear-around-the-clock dilated blurts

And deliberate piggeries we made our hearts?

III

Still, any nostrum azure our mirth invented
In sport of her—no joking—was it such harm?
Where mountains in all license stood her honor,

Surely she could not mind if early mornings,
Sorely rising, we biked in a brush of bodies

Until, aching, prostrate, we pounded the ground
On peaks of merriment she could not climb.

Or, where the sea's low downstreet shoulder hailed
All day our cracking wise by breaking up,
If, any evening, as pointedly in cantinas
—Dauntless yawns stupendously suppressed—

Once more by starlight we buckled and convulsed.
And yet, some afternoons, on obsessive sands,
Heating such bronze-cold trances of vacation
Our frostier side cares never blew away,

As we had supposed, at the lightest chafing,
We found our limits. If only from how often,
Thigh by forgotten thigh, we lay almost
Like objects of no known provenance or use

For all our stipulation of wrecked display.

IV

We stared. No misery flushed that unwavering
Sky. Yet after her careful dimity had bought
Bolt upon bolt of bright-striped stuff for awnings,

And actually as if unveiling an excellence
Even vaster in aspect, tented she sat,
We might have cried, had any cloud sailed by,
"We are almost as virginal—ohaw—

As if it were Spring with us today!"
Nor made that dying a laugh, a flick of thumb
To nose, so much from perplexity for her
—Mysterious *mère* of all our vinegar—

As for our lean, hard-glutted days alone;
Knowing, under motionless brows,
                                        as eyes
Met like the flesh of flagons lifted still,
Agony had so much become our meat

We suffered the open, insensate—O heavy air!—
For all we stripped to heady collars of surf
Or shipped on commodious sands whatever pleasure
Of the moment as august as sorrow burned.

                                        —FREDERICK BOCK

THE BIG NASTURTIUMS

All of a sudden the big nasturtiums
Rose in the night from the ocean's bed,
Rested awhile in the light of the morning,
Turning the sand dunes tiger red.

They covered the statue of Abraham Lincoln,
They climbed to the top of our church's spire.
"Grandpa! Grandpa! Come to the window!
Come to the window! Our world's afire!"

Big nasturtiums in the High Sierras,
Big nasturtiums in the lands below;
Our trains are late and our planes have fallen,
And out in the ocean the whistles blow.

Over the fields and over the forests,
Over the living and over the dead—
"I never expected the big nasturtiums
To come in my lifetime!" Grandpa said.

—Robert Beverly Hale

THE BIGHT

ON MY BIRTHDAY

At low tide like this how sheer the water is.
White crumbling ribs of marl protrude and glare
and the boats are dry, the pilings dry as matches.
Absorbing, rather than being absorbed,
the water in the bight doesn't wet anything,
the color of the gas flame turned as low as possible.
One can smell it turning to gas; if one were Baudelaire
one could probably hear it turning to marimba music.
The little ochre dredge at work off the end of the dock
already plays the dry perfectly off-beat *claves*.
The birds are outsize. Pelicans crash
into this peculiar gas unnecessarily hard,
it seems to me, like pickaxes,
rarely coming up with anything to show for it,
and going off with humorous elbowings.
Black-and-white man-of-war birds soar
on impalpable drafts
and open their tails like scissors on the curves
or tense them like wishbones, till they tremble.

The frowsy sponge boats keep coming in
with the obliging air of retrievers,
bristling with jackstraw gaffs and hooks
and decorated with bobbles of sponges.
There is a fence of chicken wire along the dock
where, glinting like little plowshares,
the blue-gray shark tails are hung up to dry
for the Chinese-restaurant trade.
Some of the little white boats are still piled up
against each other, or lie on their sides, stove in,
and not yet salvaged, if they ever will be, from the last bad storm,
like torn-open, unanswered letters.
The bight is littered with old correspondences.
Click. Click. Goes the dredge,
and brings up a dripping jawful of marl.
All the untidy activity continues,
awful but cheerful.

—ELIZABETH BISHOP

THE BIRDS

It is difficult to imagine how vulnerable they are,
these sleek heads, yellow-eyed
(an observer would call them round- or pear-shaped).
They dip into grass, somehow
chirrup while holding a worm in one corner of
a beak,
make waddling through milkwort
irresistible
(and not funny).
The feeling my skin gets is
iridescent,
nothing in me except what shines on the outside,
granite splintered
with light.
I understand their pleasure
at putting one claw after another
in identical gestures
(or using their wings
to cross the quick spring clouds in this
suburban acre of thick
traffic and skinny trees).
The weight of my body belongs
to the earth and moves
up and down.

The sun lifting my hair
drives me west
when it sinks
into a darkness full of wind
and the bones of sparrows.

—DAVID POSNER

A BIRTHDAY CANDLE

Thirty today, I saw
The trees flare briefly like
The candles on a cake,
As the sun went down the sky,
A momentary flash,
Yet there was time to wish

Before the light could die,
If I had known what to wish,
As once I must have known,
Bending above the clean
Candlelit tablecloth
To blow them out with a breath.

—DONALD JUSTICE

BIRTH OF A GREAT MAN

Eighth child of an eighth child, your wilful advent
     Means, as they say, more water in the stew.
Tell us: Why did you choose this year and month
     And house to be born into?

Were you not scared by Malthusian arguments,
     Proving it folly at least, almost a sin,
Even to poke your nose around the door—
     Much more, come strutting in?

Yet take this battered coral in proof of welcome.
     We offer (and this is surely what you expect)
Few toys, few treats, your own stool by the fire,
     Salutary neglect.

Watch the pot boil, invent a new steam engine;
     Daub every wall with inspirational paint;
Cut a reed pipe, blow difficult music through it;
     Or become an infant saint.

We shall be too shorthanded for interference
     While you keep calm and tidy and never brag.
But evade the sesquipedalian school inspector
     With his muzzle and his bag!

—ROBERT GRAVES

THE BLACK ANGEL

All matronly in her stoop, her wings canted
At an odd angle,
This angel must have seemed
Ridiculous and tender once—
Like a Wedgwood goddess or a Gibson girl,
And as white as a bar of soap.

Whether it be the weather or the work
Of parasites,
A blackness more profound
Than any ever come upon
Has come upon the lady where she stands.
I cannot meet her eye,

But stand beneath her on this little mound,
Turn, and read such names
As Gingerich, Miller, Yoder—
The early settlers of our town.
I picture them in their Sears, Roebuck dresses,
Their boots, their broad-brimmed hats.

Were they like little children in their beds
Who start from sleep
To find the light put out
And know that there is something there—
A kind of mowing as of restless wings—
And do they sleep late here?

Where are the people as beautiful as poems,
As calm as mirrors,
With their oceanic longings—
The idler whom reflection loved,
The woman with the iridescent brow?
For I would bring them flowers.

I think of that friend too much moved by music
Who turned to games
And made a game of boredom,
Of that one too much moved by faces
Who turned his face to the wall, and of that marvellous liar
Who turned at last to truth.

They are the past of what was always future.
They speak in tongues,
Silently, about nothing.

They are like old streetcars buried at sea,
In the wrong element, with no place to go. . . .
I will not meet her eye,

Although I shall, but here's a butterfly,
And a white flower,
And the moon rising on my nail.
This is the presence of things present,
Where flying woefully is like closing sweetly,
And there is nothing else.

—Henri Coulette

BLACKBERRYING

Nobody in the lane, and nothing, nothing but blackberries,
Blackberries on either side, though on the right mainly,
A blackberry alley, going down in hooks, and a sea
Somewhere at the end of it, heaving. Blackberries
Big as the ball of my thumb, and dumb as eyes
Ebon in the hedges, fat
With blue-red juices. These they squander on my fingers.
I had not asked for such a blood sisterhood; they must love me.
They accommodate themselves to my milk bottle, flattening their sides.

Overhead go the choughs in black, cacophonous flocks—
Bits of burnt paper wheeling in a blown sky.
Theirs is the only voice, protesting, protesting.
I do not think the sea will appear at all.
The high green meadows are glowing, as if lit from within.
I come to one bush of berries so ripe it is a bush of flies
Hanging their blue-green bellies and their wing panes in a Chinese screen.
The honey fust of the berries has stunned them; they believe in Heaven.
One more hook, and the berries and bushes end.

The only thing to come now is the sea.
From between two hills a sudden wind funnels at me,
Slapping its phantom laundry in my face.
These hills are too green and sweet to have tasted salt.
I follow the sheep path between them. A last hook brings me
To the hills' northern face, and the face is orange rock
That looks out on nothing, nothing but a great space
Of white and pewter lights, and a din like silversmiths
Beating and beating at an intractable metal.

—Sylvia Plath

BLACK JESS

He was no good. Somewhere
in the dreary, lost log of his days
shines the discovery of a fluid
that makes two and two five and—
what is more to the point—black white. And Jesse,
obtuse to the advantages
of being a free (black) man in a free country,
grew addicted to his pigment-thinner
and applied it so liberally
he dissolved.
The precipitate—that is,
Jesse's social remains—
turned up on a small hummock
in Long Island Sound,
not far from the police station,
as the gull flies, but distant—
thanks to a moat
of navigable water—
by some eight hundred years
of littoral law.
He erected upon this rock
a castle, roofed over
with mumbling flaps of corrugated tin,
walled with the same, portcullised
with a shred of tarp, vented
with a smoke hole, and fortified
against the eternal siege of frost and famine
with a fire pit
and a pile of rags. My father,
who'd admired Jesse in better days
(Jess had been chef at a club),
would drive down to the water's edge
some Sundays and wave Jess ashore
for a basket of staples. Otherwise
it was *moules au rien* for Jesse. His competitors
on an open market were seagulls,
a thieving, contumacious lot,
who preyed upon Jesse's mussels, often
adding insult to injury by dropping
and cracking them on his roof. The
effect was acoustically perfect,
since Jesse, for all such purposes,
resided in a tin drum. What
was worse, Jesse couldn't run out in time
to capture the mussel before the seagull got it

and carried it off, gargling "Help! Help!"
through its clamped bill. The Shorefront
Homeowners' Association
viewed dimly Jesse's castle—
or, rather, too plainly
for good taste, having slowly over seven years
encrusted its bleak and heron-haunted point
with a solid carapace of Cadillac,
concrete, and splitlevelranchstyle dwellings—
and, in solemn session, resolved
to expunge the eyesore. Jesse,
of course, was not represented, but afterward
received a deputation from the mainland,
apprising him of the sense-of-the-meeting
and suggesting he remove reasonably
without forcing recourse to law.
Jesse agreed to move but,
upon later consideration,
bethought that circumstance had beached him
about as far out as he could go,
and beyond was open water. Though dietetically
a seagull, he could not swim, nor fly,
and his boat leaked . . . Therefore he remained.
The police harbor patrol a week later
secured a beachhead on Black Jess—
as the kids called it by now—
breached through the citadel, and found the king
recovering from a vintage Sneaky Pete
he'd traded some quahogs for. They gave him three
days to dismantle and retire. But four
days passed and Jess remained. My father,
for whom Jesse in better days
had prepared a certain immortal plank steak,
had arisen and, in the name of Art,
questioned the morality—and legal right—
of the police. Thus you might say
Jesse owed his deliverance to a cow
he had done no favors for. The Shorefront
Homeowners' Association authorized
its lawyer to call the Coast Guard—
since the waters were navigable—
and a second landing was made, this time
under the American Flag. But Jesse,
on advice of counsel (my father),
stayed where he was. It appeared
the Coast Guard had trespassed
on the U.S. Army Corps of Engineers.

The Coast Guard was not convinced, possibly
for the reason that the District Captain
was a cousin of the secretary
of the Homeowners' Association.
But the U.S. Army Corps of Engineers,
like Neptune, was not to be bearded
in its own rivers-and-harbors. The affair
went to Washington and turned up
on the docket of the United States Supreme Court.
The Court opined Jesse had squatter's rights
anyway, by virtue of seven years *in situ*
on an island in federal waters, and the Shorefront
Homeowners' Association
had only one appeal left—to God—
for his removal. Well,
Jesse's no longer on his rock. The Lord,
in His infinite mercy to the Shorefront
Homeowners' Association,
sent down a plague upon the mussels
that had hung off the tidewater rocks
like dark grapes. They disappeared,
and Jesse went with them. I don't know where.
That April his tin tent was struck
by a committee of volunteers; nothing
remains of Jesse—except the name,
Black Jess, which you may find
one day in the marine atlases of the world to designate
a dot on Long Island Sound.

—PETER KANE DUFAULT

THE BLIND SHEEP

The Sheep is blind; a passing Owl,
A surgeon of some local skill,
Has undertaken, for a fee,
The cure. A stump, his surgery,
Is licked clean by a Cat; his tools—
A tooth, a thorn, some battered
     nails—
He ranges by a shred of sponge,
And he is ready to begin.
Pushed forward through the gaping
     crowd,
"Wait," bleats the Sheep. "Is all pre-
     pared?"
The Owl lists forceps, scalpel, lancet—

The old Sheep interrupts his answer:
"These lesser things may all be well,
But tell me, friend, how goes the
     world?"
The Owl says blankly, "You will find
     it
Goes as it went ere you were blinded."
"What?" cries the Sheep. "Then take
     your fee,
But cure some other fool, not me.
To witness that enormity
I would not give a blade of grass.
I am a Sheep, and not an Ass."

—RANDALL JARRELL

BLUE FLAG

Blue as the blowpipe's petal of flame,
the flag, afloat at the crest of the wave
of its leaves, unfurls an ephemeral crown,
three-tiered, nine-rayed, and girdled with jade.

Sealed, to begin with, in tissue, and stuck
to the stem in a curve like a locust's wing,
it rides into light in this envelope lean
as a leaf, too thin to hold a thing,

it would seem, till it opens and shows a ship-
in-a-bottle surprise: slim as a moth
at birth stands an elegant spindle, sea purple
and patched with gold, that turns, no sloth

so slow, to a lily of chiselled gauze.
In curves as sharp as if carved with scalpels
from paper-thin slices of stone inked in,
pen-fine, with damson lines like the marble's

veins, it spreads its spurs. It shows
its colors in yellow carpets plumed
with plush for the feet of the bee as she feels
her way over azure bridges and perfumed

paths, through tunnels down to the well-hid
wells where the diamond drop of nectar
is. All this to bring, spring
after spring, the seed to the bud to the flower

to the bee, again, again, and again
with undiminished *esprit*, to bear,
once more, the same lambent form as before,
jewel-winged, a weld of blue fire and air.

                                        —DOROTHY DONNELLY

THE BLUEFLY

Five summer days, five summer nights,
The ignorant, loutish, giddy bluefly
Hung without motion on the cling peach,
Humming occasionally, "O my love, my fair one!"
As in the Canticles.

Magnified one thousand times, the insect
Looks farcically human; laugh if you will!
Bald head, stage-fairy wings, blear eyes,
A caved-in chest, hairy black mandibles,
    Long spindly thighs.

The crime was detected on the sixth day.
What then could be said or done? By anyone?
It would have been vindictive, mean, and whatnot
To swat that fly for being a bluefly,
    For debauch of a peach.

Is it fair, either, to bring a microscope
To bear on the case, even in search of truth?
Nature, doubtless, has some compelling cause
To glut the carriers of her epidemics—
    Nor did the peach complain.

                                    —ROBERT GRAVES

BLUES FOR AN OLD BLUE

Beneath this tent, clutching this glass of beer,
Wearing pajama pants and a funny hat,
I, Buzzy Bigelow, class of '24,
Tilt on a folding chair and mourn my fate.
Though never one to moan to hell or heaven,
I mourn here, on a camp chair in New Haven.

My sentiment has justice. Note the paunch
Under these purple stripes, or cite the dead
They said could not be here today for lunch.
Such ironies are cheap. Is it I who died,
Too young for one war, too old for another?
Why did I ever come? Why did I bother?

It was to ogle the class millionaire,
Sneer at the failure, shake the Senator's hand,
Though a stranger. The class crook did not appear.
But gone! gone is the one I came to find,
Mature at twenty, perpetually at leisure,
Witty, athletic, smart in a blue blazer.

There are the customary offerings:
Parade to the ball game, the boys slightly stiff,

And after that the Singing of Old Songs—
But Bigelow, '24, has had enough.
Perched on a rickety chair, he wipes his glasses,
Watches the hours go by, and mourns his losses.

—WALKER GIBSON

BONE CHINA

Out of these thin, thin cups I drink pale tea,
  Brown as a moorland stream, and not much hotter.
A ghostly Chinaman is watching me,
  And, by his side, a ghostly English potter.

The latter mixed bone ash with China clay;
  Strange how a thinner cup lasts so much longer.
He drank the same drink, though he called it tay,
  And drank it nearly boiling, and much stronger.

The former used to mouth impromptu verse
  By the Pavilion of the Serious Seeker—
By moonlight, too, and by the hour; what's worse,
  The tea he drank was hot but even weaker.

The tea I drink is like my hostess, pale,
  And too refined, and could be somewhat warmer.
I'd rather ply my latter ghost with ale
  Or drink rice wine by moonlight with my former.

—R. P. LISTER

THE BONES OF INCONTENTION

I

In a Southern garden Lucinda sits.
Apricots ripen in her apron.
Her voice lessens the afternoon's
    sunless,
Painful heat with kindness.
Simon fans himself with a wing
And speaks only to complain.
Can you remember? Has it rained
In August?
It is a kind of truth, that the sky
Is a china plate; it descends like a china
Plate. Here are willows, giving no
    shade.
But pale, Babylonian weeping. Garden
Birds sleep without landing,
And awake an inch above the oven.
Can you remember? Has it rained
In August?
Why do you remain outdoors? Is it not
Cooler in the house? Is it not
Cooler in the tulip cellar?

II

My dog turns the corner, speaking
          Greek.
He is happy, for it is raining.
Cats and dogs come out into it,
          turning
Their human faces up.
The garden steams, the roof steams.
Lights are off in the house
And everyone is at the windows

Watching the rain. But Lucinda
Remains in her chair, still speaking.
Simon's upstairs, afraid of God's Au-
          gust rain.
The summer afternoon takes out its
          bones
And builds a fragrant bamboo garden
Around Lucinda. Laughing like Vene-
          tian blinds.
Why do you remain outdoors?

—ROBERT DAVID COHEN

BONE THOUGHTS ON A DRY DAY: CHICAGO

Walking to the Museum
Over the Outer Drive,
I think, before I see them
Dead, of the bones alive.

Bird bone may be breakable, but
Have you ever held a cat's jaw shut?
Brittle as ice.

Take mice:
The mouse is a berry; his bones mere seeds.
Step on him once and see.

How perfectly the snake smooths over the fact
He stings sharp beads around that charmer's neck!

You mustn't think that the fish
Choke on those bones, or that chickens wish.

The wise old bat
Hangs his bones in a bag.

Two chicks in tandem ride a bike,
Unlike
That legless swinger of crutches, the ostrich.

Only the skull of a man is much of an ashtray.

Each owl
Turns on a dowel.

When all the other tents are struck, an old
Elephant pitches himself on his own poles.

But as for *my* bones—
Tug of a toe, blunt-bowed barge of a thighbone,
Gondola-squadron of ribs, and the jaw scow—
They weather the swing and storm of the flesh they plow,
Out of conjecture of shore, one jolt from land.

I climb the museum steps like a beach.
There, on squared stone, some cast-up keels bleach.
Here, a dark sea speaks with white hands.

—GEORGE STARBUCK

BONNARD: A NOVEL

The tea party at Le Cannet. Just as we arrived it began,
a downpour, and kept on.
This might have been the time
before: Charles-Xavier playing Scriabin études, all the others
at the open window.
A landscape—lawn, garden,
strawberry patch, Japanese footbridge, barges moving on the river
beyond—as in Verlaine
behind a mist of rain,
and the regular noise of the rain on tens of thousands of leaves:
such is the prose that wears
the poem's guise at last.
White cats, one in almost every chair, pretend not to be watching
young Jean worry the dog.
Lucie, damp, dashes in
dishevelled from the forest, dumping out a great bag of morels
on the table; the white
cloth will surely be spoiled,
but the mushrooms look iridescent, like newly-opened oysters
in the raindark air, blue
by this light. Calling it
accidental is only declaring that it exists. Then tea
downstairs, Jean opening
the round pantry window,
the smell of wet soil and strawberries with our cinnamon toast. All
perception is a kind

of sorting out—one green
from another, parting leaf from leaf—but in the afternoon rain
signs and shadows only,
the separate life renounced,
until that resignation comes, in which all selfhood surrenders . . .
Upstairs, more Scriabin
and the perfect gestures
of Lucie and Jean playing ball with the dog. All the cats are deaf.
Steady rain. The music
continues, Charles-Xavier
shouting over the notes, ignoring them, "Beatitude teaches
nothing. To live without
happiness and not wither—
there is an occupation, almost a profession." Take the trees—
we could "contrive to do
without trees," but not leaves,
Charles-Xavier explains from the piano, still playing, "we require
their decorum that is
one of congestion, till
like Shelley we become lewd vegetarians." Apprehensive
about the rain, I ask
Jean to order a closed
carriage for Simone. The doctor frowns—a regular visitor
these days?—and frightens her,
eying Lucie's mushrooms;
his diagnosis: toadstools. Scriabin diminishes. Is the dog
lost? Jean rushes outside.
Punishment of the dog:
he is forbidden the strawberry patch. Darker now. One candle
is found for the piano,
and the music resumes
with Debussy, a little sphere of yellow in the sopping dusk.
The river's surface looks—
is it the rain?—like the sea
in shallows; this moment is an instance of the world becoming
a mere convenience,
more or less credible,
and the old questions rise to our lips—but have we spoken a word?—
before we remember,
prompted by the weather
probably, or the time of day, that we already know something;
we are not new-born, then.
What is it that we know?
The carriage comes at last, but it is an open carriage, merely
hooded. We crowd under,
fending off the last drops
with a violet golf-umbrella Charles-Xavier has somehow

managed for us. A slow
cold drive under the trees,
Simone balancing the suspect mushrooms in her lap. I tell her
it is not dangerous;
we cannot die, but are
in this light or lack of it—trees dripping, the green sky fraudulent—
much less individuals
than we hope or fear to be.
Once home, we shall have a little supper of Lucie's fresh-picked morels.

—RICHARD HOWARD

BOY AT TARGET PRACTICE: A CONTEMPLATION

I

Each time, greenbones, you pressed the neat trigger,
You punched a new horizontal into the air.
In all of ever, those lines had not been there.

In the tumbling can, those sudden, dark-rimmed holes
With revengefully sharp edges were new bits
Of subtraction; never had other bullet hits

Made them. And when, glancing from jarred stone,
A pellet went all waspy into the sky,
That was a new parabola, a new cry.

II

Now, getting caught, I think, by a sudden knowing
That everything's unique in the world's swarm
Of things is like getting caught with nothing warm

Around you, outside when summer clouds are hailing.
It feels uncomfortable—useless, too.
We need to make ourselves (and commonly do)

Protective outer garments of fat and fuzzy
Generalization; that's the way to obscure
From the ends of our nerves those sharp peltings of pure

Facts, real facts. Of course, we can't destroy them.
Not you or I or the wisest man of us
Can live with them. But aren't they marvellous?

—W. R. MOSES

BOY IN ICE

O river, green and still,
By frost and memory stayed,
Your dumb and stiffened glass divides
A shadow and a shade.

In air, my shadow's face
Its winter gaze lets fall
To see beneath the stream's bright
        bars
That other shade in thrall.

A boy, time-fixed in ice,
His cheeks with summer dyed,
His mouth a rose-devouring rose,
His bird throat petrified.

O fabulous and lost,
More distant to me now
Than rock-drawn mammoth, painted
        stag,
Or tigers in the snow,

You stare into my face,
Dead as ten thousand years,
Your sparrow tongue sealed in my
        mouth,
Your world about my ears.

And till our shadows meet,
Till time burns through the ice,
Thus frozen shall we ever stay
Locked in this paradise.

—Laurie Lee

BOY-MAN

England's lads are miniature men
To start with, grammar in their shiny hats,
And serious; in America who knows when
Manhood begins? Presidents grin and hug,
And while the suave King waves and gravely chats,
America wets on England's old green rug.

The boy-man roars. Worry alone will give
This one the verisimilitude of age.
Those white teeth are his own, for he must live
Longer, grow taller than the Texas race.
Fresh are his eyes, his darkening skin the gauge
Of bloods that freely mix beneath his face.

He knows the application of the book
But not who wrote it; shuts it like a shot.
Rather than read, he thinks that he will look;
Rather than look, he thinks that he will talk;
Rather than talk, he thinks that he will not
Bother at all; would rather ride than walk.

His means of conversation is the joke,
Humor his language, underneath which lies

The undecoded dialect of the folk.
Abroad, he scorns the foreigner; what's old
Is worn, what's different bad, what's odd unwise.
He gives off heat and is enraged by cold.

Charming, becoming to the suits he wears,
The boy-man, younger than his eldest son,
Inherits the state; upon his silver hairs
Time, like a panama hat, sits at a tilt
And smiles. To him the world has just begun
And every city waiting to be built.

Mister, remove your shoulder from the wheel
And say this prayer, "Increase my vitamins,
Make my decisions of the finest steel,
Pour motor oil upon my troubled spawn,
Forgive the Europeans for their sins,
Establish work, that values may go on."

—KARL SHAPIRO

THE BREAK

As in a dream of flood from which we rose intact but alone

Or in worse days held a child high overhead (let me see his face
one more time) as we went down

Or in that other life spoke golden words and sang and floated
and wished we had not died insane

Or further still wept finding no body to receive our drowning rays
as yet unborn,

Now burn, lungs, in the fierce flood, breathe
the strange element in this living time;
breathe; burn; and change.

—E. N. SARGENT

BREAKWATERS

Elms are bad, sinister trees.
Falling, one leaf too many,
they kill small boys in summer,
tipped over by a crow's foot,
bored with the business of leaves.

An uneasiness attends
dead elms—timber for coffins,
ammunition boxes. And
breakwaters. Bolts open sores
of orange rust in their flanks,

and yet there is loveliness.
Ultimate green of eelgrass
soothes with the comfort of hair
all the tiny agonies
that crawl in hidden places

and sing when the tide is low
and death is not imminent,
scrabbling in an eczema
of pink and white barnacles
and mussels of midnight blue.

Terrifying as altars,
by night black, a sea-Stonehenge.
Filigrees of little wracks
dance on them at high water
in a devil dance. They change.

Their male look lasts a few tides;
when the reek is washed away
and the stubble is shaven,
on a tall September night,
the sea will take his new brides.

In his calm he will lap them,
then batter their waists away,
emphasize their Celtic heads.
And when they are old and raddled,
thin, thin as a Belsen arm,

they will stand bare and skinny
and their stringent hard old hearts
will disregard his knocking.
Dour, malignant to the core,
they will try to outlive him.

—TED WALKER

THE BRICK

By itself and from a distance,
    its redness is cinnabar and hard,
    contusing the air.
It thrusts away space with a small,
  brute displacement,
    and yet it is there—contained.
It lines its lines with and against
  and in
    the great box of the sky
    through all the unperceived lami-
      nations
of reality.

Put it nearer
  and it impinges on the air
  with angular assertion.
It invades all contours,
  breaks down the continuum,
  thrusts itself into the molds
of height and weight and latitude.
Its shadow is its own:
  a procrustean block
  wedged out of tetragon black-
  ness.

Nine inches from the eye,
  it contradicts itself,
  changes its gender,
  burgeons with tiny inconsisten-
    cies
of texture:
  the smoothness is not smooth,
  the redness is more than red,
  the hardness is vulnerable.
It is feminine in the loss of its
  muscular and total squareness.
Here the gravity of its presence
  is passive,
  waits for the support
  of the ground on which it lies.
Here it is inert,
  virginal and fecund,
  anxious
  with an internal myriad
  movement—
  the prey of forces.
And millions of atoms
  are its children.

—PAUL ROCHE

BROBDINGNAG

The owls roost like gray lamps up there
above the firebreak and weeds,
where we never venture after dark—
wicks of ears blowing in a fir-black wind,
eyes (rounder and simpler than our own)
staring down at this estate
toward the picture window we cannot close
to any viewer, wise bird or beast.

We bought for privacy here,
but shadows become, in the electric glare
of anniversaries or games,
improbable animals on a visible wall:
giraffes on hassocks or in easy chairs,
fauns shuffling cards, blue apes and swans
waltzing across the rumpus room
until they splash from the ceiling and fall
like mammoth commas in a bed.

Even after hours, shadows may sprawl,
larger than life, on a drunken field.
I have no fear for these, but fear
when the wind is high, and bats are few,
how some sad, dwindling shape of ours
could creep through silver husks of fog
and seem, to those above, a smaller thing
than we conceive ourselves to be:
more mouse than giant, more creature than man,
and vulnerable to watching beaks.

Still though they are,
with talons shut around a waving branch,
they could drift down.
I have wakened often from a cold dream
and smelled the smoke beneath their wings
and seen their eyes, this side of the pane,
hot and intent with a strange love
for what they can light upon and keep.

—ADRIEN STOUTENBURG

THE BROKEN HOME

Crossing the street,
I saw the parents and the child
At their window, gleaming like fruit
With evening's mild gold leaf.

In a room on the floor below,
Sunless, cooler—a brimming
Saucer of wax, marbly and dim—
I have lit what's left of my life.

I have thrown out yesterday's milk
And opened a book of maxims.
The flame quickens. The word stirs.

Tell me, tongue of fire,
That you and I are as real
At least as the people upstairs.

My father, who had flown in World War I,
Might have continued to invest his life
In cloud banks well above Wall Street and wife.
But the race was run below, and the point was to win.

Too late now, I make out in his blue gaze
(Through the smoked glass of being thirty-six)
The soul eclipsed by twin black pupils, sex
And business; time was money in those days.

Each thirteenth year he married. When he died
There were already several chilled wives
In sable orbit—rings, cars, permanent waves.
We'd felt him warming up for a green bride.

He could afford it. He was "in his prime"
At three score ten. But money was not time.

When my parents were younger this was a popular act:
A veiled woman would leap from an electric, wine-dark car
To the steps of no matter what—the Senate or the Ritz Bar—
And bodily, at newsreel speed, attack

No matter whom—Al Smith or José Maria Sert
Or Clemenceau—veins standing out on her throat

As she yelled *War mongerer! Pig! Give us the vote!*,
And would have to be hauled away in her hobble skirt.

What had the man done? Oh, made history.
Her business (he had implied) was giving birth,
Tending the house, mending the socks.

Always the same old story—
Father Time and Mother Earth,
A marriage on the rocks.

One afternoon, red, satyr-thighed
Michael, the Irish setter, head
Passionately lowered, led
The child I was to a shut door. Inside,

Blinds beat sun from the bed.
The green-gold room throbbed like a bruise.
Under a sheet, clad in taboos,
Lay whom we sought, her hair undone, outspread,

And of a blackness found, if ever now, in old
Engravings where the acid bit.
I must have needed to touch it
Or the whiteness—was she dead?
Her eyes flew open, startled strange and cold.
The dog slumped to the floor. She reached for me. I fled.

Tonight they have stepped out onto the gravel.
The party is over. It's the fall
Of 1931. They love each other still.

SHE: Charlie, I can't stand the pace.
HE: Come on, honey—why, you'll bury us all!

A lead soldier guards my windowsill:
Khaki rifle, uniform, and face.
Something in me grows heavy, silvery, pliable.

How intensely people used to feel!
Like metal poured at the close of a proletarian novel,
Refined and glowing from the crucible,
I see those two hearts, I'm afraid,
Still. Cool here in the graveyard of good and evil,
They are even so to be honored and obeyed.

. . . Obeyed, at least, inversely. Thus
I rarely buy a newspaper, or vote.
To do so, I have learned, is to invite
The tread of a stone guest within my house.

Shooting this rusted bolt, though, against him,
I trust I am no less time's child than some
Who on the heath impersonate Poor Tom
Or on the barricades risk life and limb.

Nor do I try to keep a garden, only
An avocado in a glass of water—
Roots pallid, gemmed with air. And later,

When the small gilt leaves have grown
Fleshy and green, I let them die, yes, yes,
And start another. I am earth's no less.

A child, a red dog roam the corridors,
Still, of the broken home. No sound. The brilliant
Rag runners halt before wide-open doors.
My old room! Its wallpaper—cream, medallioned
With pink and brown—brings back the first nightmares,
Long summer colds, and Emma, sepia-faced,
Perspiring over broth carried upstairs
Aswim with golden fats I could not taste.

The real house became a boarding school.
Under the ballroom ceiling's allegory,
Someone at last may actually be allowed
To learn something; or, from my window, cool
With the unstiflement of the entire story,
Watch a red setter stretch and sink in cloud.

                                             —JAMES MERRILL

BUCKDANCER'S CHOICE

So I would hear out those lungs—
The air split into nine levels,
Some gift of tongues of the whistler

In the invalid's bed: my mother,
Warbling all day to herself
The thousand variations of one song;

It is called Buckdancer's Choice.
For years, they have all been dying
Out, the classic buck-and-wing men

Of travelling minstrel shows;
With them also an old woman
Was dying of breathless angina,

Yet still found breath enough
To whistle up in my head
A sight like a one-man band—

Freed black, with cymbals at heel,
An ex-slave who thrivingly danced
To the ring of his own clashing light

Through the thousand variations of
    one song
All day to my mother's prone music,
The invalid's warbler's note,

While I crept close to the wall,
Sock-footed, to hear the sounds alter,
Her tongue like a mockingbird's break

Through stratum after stratum of a
    tone
Proclaiming what choices there are
For the last dancers of their kind,

For ill women and for all slaves
Of death, and children enchanted at
    walls
With a brass-beating glow underfoot,

Not dancing but nearly risen
Through barnlike, theatrelike houses
On the wings of the buck and wing.

—JAMES DICKEY

BULLFROG

With their lithe, long, strong legs,
Some frogs are able
To thump upon double-
Bass strings, though pond water deadens and clogs.

But you, bullfrog, you pump out
Whole fogs full of horn—a threat
As of a liner looming. True
That, first hearing you
Disgorging your gouts of darkness like a wounded god,
Not utterly fantastically, I expected
(As in some antique tale depicted)
A broken-down bull up to its belly in mud,
Sucking black swamp up, belching out black cloud

And a squall of gudgeon and lilies.
                                        A surprise
Now, to see you, a boy's prize,
No bigger than a rat, with all dumb silence
In your little old woman hands.

—TED HUGHES

BUMS, ON WAKING

Bums, on waking,
Do not always find themselves
In gutters with water running over
        their legs
And the pillow of the curbstone
Turning hard as sleep drains from it.
Mostly, they do not know

But hope for where they shall come
        to.
The opening of the eye is precious,

And the shape of the body also,
Lying as it has fallen,
Disdainfully crumpling earthward
Out of alcohol.
Drunken under their eyelids
Like children sleeping toward Christ-
        mas,

They wait for the light to shine
Wherever it may decide.

Often it brings them staring
Through glass in the rich part of
        town,
Where the forms of humanized wax
Are arrested in midstride
With their heads turned, and dressed
By force. This is ordinary, and has
        come

To be disappointing.
They expect and hope for

Something totally other:
That while they staggered last night
For hours, they got clear,
Somehow, of the city; that they
Have burst through a hedge and are
        lying
In a trampled rose garden,

Pillowed on a bulldog's side,
A watchdog's, whose breathing

Is like the earth's, unforced—
Or that they may, once a year
(Any dawn now), awaken
In church, not on the coffin boards
Of a back pew, or on furnace-room
        rags,
But on the steps of the altar

Where candles are opening their eyes
With all-seeing light

And the green stained glass of the
        windows
Falls on them like sanctified leaves.
Who else has quite the same
Commitment to not being sure
What he shall behold, come from
        sleep—
A child, a policeman, an effigy?

Who else has died and thus risen?
Never knowing how they have got
        there,

They might just as well have walked
On water, through walls, out of
        graves,
Through potter's fields and through
        barns,
Through slums where their stony pil-
        lows
Refused to harden, because of
Their hope for this morning's first
        light,

With water moving over their legs
More like living cover than it is.

                              —JAMES DICKEY

THE BURGLAR OF BABYLON

On the fair green hills of Rio
There grows a fearful stain:
The poor who come to Rio
And can't go home again.

On the hills a million people,
A million sparrows, nest,
Like a confused migration
That's had to light and rest,

Building its nests, or houses,
Out of nothing at all, or air.
You'd think a breath would end
them,
They perch so lightly there.

But they cling and spread like lichen,
And the people come and come.
There's one hill called the Chicken,
And one called Catacomb;

There's the hill of Kerosene,
And the hill of the Skeleton,
The hill of Astonishment,
And the hill of Babylon. *

Micuçú* was a burglar and killer,
An enemy of society.
He had escaped three times
From the worst penitentiary.

They don't know how many he mur-
dered
(Though they say he never raped),
And he wounded two policemen
This last time he escaped.

They said, "He'll go to his auntie,
Who raised him like a son.
She has a little drink shop
On the hill of Babylon."

He did go straight to his auntie,
And he drank a final beer.
He told her, "The soldiers are
coming,
And I've got to disappear.

"Ninety years they gave me.
Who wants to live that long?
I'll settle for ninety hours,
On the hill of Babylon.

"Don't tell anyone you saw me.
I'll run as long as I can.
You were good to me, and I love you,
But I'm a doomed man."

Going out, he met a *mulata*
Carrying water on her head.
"If you say you saw me, daughter,
You're just as good as dead."

There are caves up there, and hide-
outs,
And an old fort, falling down.
They used to watch for Frenchmen
From the hill of Babylon.

Below him was the ocean.
It reached far up the sky,
Flat as a wall, and on it
Were freighters passing by,

Or climbing the wall, and climbing
Till each looked like a fly,
And then fell over and vanished;
And he knew he was going to die.

He could hear the goats *baa-baa*-ing,
He could hear the babies cry;
Fluttering kites strained upward;
And he knew he was going to die.

* According to some, Micuçú (mē-cóo-sóo) is short for *mico sujo* (dirty marmoset). Ac-
cording to others, and more likely, it is the folk name of a deadly snake, in the north.

A buzzard flapped so near him
  He could see its naked neck.
He waved his arms and shouted,
  "Not yet, my son, not yet!"

An Army helicopter
  Came nosing around and in.
He could see two men inside it,
  But they never spotted him.

The soldiers were all over,
  On all sides of the hill,
And right against the skyline
  A row of them, small and still.

Children peeked out of windows,
  And men in the drink shop swore,
And spat a little *cachaça*
  At the light cracks in the floor.

But the soldiers were nervous, even
  With tommy guns in hand,
And one of them, in a panic,
  Shot the officer in command.

He hit him in three places;
  The other shots went wild.
The soldier had hysterics
  And sobbed like a little child.

The dying man said, "Finish
  The job we came here for."
He committed his soul to God
  And his sons to the Governor.

They ran and got a priest,
  And he died in hope of Heaven
—A man from Pernambuco,
  The youngest of eleven.

They wanted to stop the search,
  But the Army said, "No, go on,"
So the soldiers swarmed again
  Up the hill of Babylon.

Rich people in apartments
  Watched through binoculars

As long as the daylight lasted.
  And all night, under the stars,

Micuçú hid in the grasses
  Or sat in a little tree,
Listening for sounds, and staring
  At the lighthouse out at sea.

And the lighthouse stared back at him,
  Till finally it was dawn.
He was soaked with dew, and hungry,
  On the hill of Babylon.

The yellow sun was ugly,
  Like a raw egg on a plate—
Slick from the sea. He cursed it,
  For he knew it sealed his fate.

He saw the long white beaches
  And people going to swim,
With towels and beach umbrellas,
  But the soldiers were after him.

Far, far below, the people
  Were little colored spots,
And the heads of those in swimming
  Were floating coconuts.

He heard the peanut vender
  Go *peep-peep* on his whistle,
And the man that sells umbrellas
  Swinging his watchman's rattle.

Women with market baskets
  Stood on the corners and talked,
Then went on their way to market,
  Gazing up as they walked.

The rich with their binoculars
  Were back again, and many
Were standing on the rooftops,
  Among TV antennae.

It was early, eight or eight-thirty.
  He saw a soldier climb,
Looking right at him. He fired,
  And missed for the last time.

He could hear the soldier panting,
  Though he never got very near.
Micuçú dashed for shelter.
  But he got it, behind the ear.

He heard the babies crying
  Far, far away in his head,
And the mongrels barking and
    barking.
  Then Micuçú was dead.

He had a Taurus revolver,
  And just the clothes he had on,
With two contos in the pockets,
  On the hill of Babylon.

The police and the populace
  Heaved a sigh of relief,
But behind the counter his auntie
  Wiped her eyes in grief.

"We have always been respected.
  My shop is honest and clean.
I loved him, but from a baby
  Micuçú was always mean.

"We have always been respected.
  His sister has a job.
Both of us gave him money.
  Why did he have to rob?

"I raised him to be honest,
  Even here, in Babylon slum."
The customers had another,
  Looking serious and glum.

But one of them said to another,
  When he got outside the door,
"He wasn't much of a burglar,
  He got caught six times—or more."

This morning the little soldiers
  Are on Babylon hill again;
Their gun barrels and helmets
  Shine in a gentle rain.

Micuçú is buried already.
  They're after another two,
But they say they aren't as dangerous
  As the poor Micuçú.

On the fair green hills of Rio
  There grows a fearful stain:
The poor who come to Rio
  And can't go home again.

There's the hill of Kerosene,
  And the hill of the Skeleton,
The hill of Astonishment,
  And the hill of Babylon.

—Elizabeth Bishop

BURNING MOUNTAIN

No blacker than others in winter, but
The hushed snow never arrives on that slope.
An emanation of steam on damp days,
With a faint hiss, if you listen some places;
Yes, and if you pause to notice, an odor,
Even so near the chimneyed city—these
Betray what the mountain has at heart. And all night,
Here and there, popping in and out of their holes
Like groundhogs gone nocturnal, the shy flames.

Unnatural, but no mystery.
Many are still alive to testify
Of the miner who left his lamp hanging
Lit in the shaft and took the lift and never
Missed a thing till, halfway home to supper,
The bells' clangor caught him. He was the last
You'd have expected such a thing from:
The worrying kind, whose old-womanish
Precautions had been a joke for years.

Smothered and silent, for some miles the fire
Still riddles the fissured hill, deviously
Wasting and inextinguishable. They
Have sealed off all the veins they could find,
Thus at least setting limits to it, we trust.
It consumes itself, but so slowly it will outlast
Our time and our grandchildren's, curious
But not unique; there was always one of these
Nearby, wherever we moved, when I was a child.

Under it, not far, the molten core
Of the earth recedes from its thin crust,
Which all the fires we light cannot prevent
From cooling. Not a good day's walk above it,
The meteors burn out in the air to fall
Harmless in empty fields, if at all.
Before long, it practically seemed normal,
With its farms on it, and wells of good water,
Still cold, that should last us, and our grandchildren.

—W. S. MERWIN

BY CANOE THROUGH THE FIR FOREST

Into the slain tons of needles,
On something like time and dark
          knowledge
That cannot be told, we are riding
Over white stones, forward through fir
          trees,
Following whatever the river
Through the clasping of roots follows
          deeply.

As we go inward, more trunks
Climb from the edge of the water

And turn on the banks and stand
          growing.
The nerves, in the patches of tree-
          light
On the ripples, can feel no death,
But shake like the wings of angels

With light hard pressed to keep up,
Though it is in place on each feather.
Heavy woods in one movement
          around us
Flow back along either side,

Bringing in more essential curves;
Small stones in their thousands turn
   corners

Under water and bear us on
Through the glittering, surfacing wing-
   beats
Cast from above. As we pass over,
As we pass through each hover of
   gold,
We lift up our blades from the water,
And the blades of our shoulders,

Our rowing muscles, our wings,
Are still and tremble, undying,
Drifting deeper into the forest.
Each light comes into our life

Past the man in front's changed hair,
Then along the wing-balancing floor,

And then onto me and one eye,
And into my mouth for an instant.
The stones beneath us grow rounder
As I taste the fretted light fall
Through living needles to be here
Like a word I can feed on forever,

Or believe like a vision I have
Or want to conceive out of greenness.
While the world fades, it is *becoming*.
As trees shut away all seeing,
In my mouth I mix it with sunlight.
Here, in the dark, it is *being*.

—JAMES DICKEY

BY THE BRIDGE

I recall, before the banks
sank in this wilderness of rains,
clear waters of the Wild Brooks
torrented atop white rocks
worn smooth and slabbed, with a sun
in bubbles splintered over them.

I stood on this bridge and saw
the waters mix; the confluence,
too, of sparrows and shadow
the length of the long hedgerow,
and finches strung on fences
like bright beads on an abacus.

There were sounds of quietness
not listened for but heard
among beds of watercress
where, with eyes of gentleness
and hocks sucking soft hot mud,
some patient herd always waded.

Every close-cropped pasture, lush
with marsh marigold, was quiet
with an intermittent hush

of leaves in a delicate ash
when the wind unentwined
and not a cricket fidgeted.

Whatever the stream bore down
from unaccountable hills
in the misted distance passed on
to gaze at dark reflections
in the deep blue calm of pools
below the drop of the falls.

All ugliness, all violence
passed away. Through the stone piers
of the bridge's permanence,
uprooted trees in remonstrance
brushed eely green streamers
of silkweed, pulled to the weir

beyond. Even when the great storm
broke, massive banks drained
vast cargoes away; but a dam
of blackened branches jammed
across the stream and all poured
over. Still the lands lie under flood

and no quietness of sound
is heard now in the silence
seeping from the vanished ground.
Violated, broken things find
islands to rot upon. The dance
of the multiple suns is done.

—TED WALKER

BY THE RIVER EDEN

I

Never twice that river
Though the still turning water
In its dark pools
Mirrors suspended green
Of an unchanging scene.

Frail bubbles revolve,
Break in rippling falls,
The same, I could believe,
Each with its moment gone,
I watched in former years,

Ever reforming maze
Of evening midge's dance,
Swifts that chase and scream
Touching in their low flight
The picture on the stream.

Heart is deceived,
Or knows what mind ignores:
Not the mirroring flux
Nor mirrored scene remain
Nor the rocky bed
Of the river's course,

But shadows intangible
That fade and come again.
Through their enduring forms
The glassy river runs;
All flows save the image
Cast on that shimmering screen.

II

Beside the river Eden
Some child has made her secret garden
On an alder strand
Marked out with pebbles in the sand
Patterned with meadow flowers,
As once I did, and was.

My mother, who from time past
Recalls the red spots on the yellow mimulus
That nodded in the burn
Talking as it ran to her alone,
Was that same child—
To eighty years between she gives little thought.

And hers, bedridden,
Mused on an old cracked darkened picture of a salmon-river
Painted in Paradise so long ago
None living ever saw those tumbling waters flow.
By her imagination made miraculous,
Water of life poured over its faded varnished stones.

All is one, I or another,
She was I, she was my mother,
The same child for ever
Building the same green bower by the same river
In her far and near unfading meadows of remembered summer.

III

The lapwing's wavering flight
Warns me from her nest,
Her wild sanctuary—
Dark wings, white breast.
The Nine Nicks have weathered,
Lichened slabs tumbled;
In sand under roots of thyme
Bone and feather lie,
The ceaseless wind has blown;
But over my gray head
The plover's unageing cry.

—Kathleen Raine

BY THE SALTINGS

When the wind is in the thrift
gently, down by the saltings
at dawn when the vapors lift;

and pattering sanderlings
run from you rather than fly
across the sandflat screaming;

before the runnels drain dry
among the sea-lavender
and sun severs sea from sky;

there is time enough under
any listing low-tide hull
of your choosing to wonder

at the force of it to pull
you to its shelter, alone
as you are and as fearful

as some crab beneath some stone.

—TED WALKER

C

CADENZA

The violinist's shadow vanishes.

The husk of a grasshopper
Sucks a remote cyclone and rises

The full bare throat of a woman walk-
ing water
The loaded estuary of the dead

And I am the cargo
Of a coffin attended by swallows

And I am the water
Bearing the coffin that will not be
silent

The clouds are full of surgery and col-
lisions
But the coffin escapes—a black dia-
mond

A ruby brimming blood
A turquoise beating its shores

A sea that lifts swallow wings and
flings
A summer lake open

Sips and bewilders its reflection
Till the sky shuts back like a burned
land to its spark

A bat with a ghost in its mouth
Struck at by lightnings of silence.

Blue with sweat, the violinist
Crashes into the orchestra, which
explodes.

—TED HUGHES

CAGES

As cages, think of department stores and certain zoos
(Think of thinking) where,
Safe from hawks, the talking mynas and cuckoos
Contrive a reasonable rapport.
One could wax Whitmanesque, trapped in rhetorics
And vistas, thinking of all
The different kinds of cages there are.
But the principle is the same. Webster
Says: "An enclosure or box

[97]

Furnished with metal
Bars for confining birds, or

Other animals." The language, a likelier
Cage, is explicit and unspirited,
Allotting slight area for thought to stir
And move about, allowing no room
For doubt. A little boy at the zoo
Once asked his mother if the other
Animals would all turn out
As the zebras did
If kept too long in cages. He little knew
The truth of it. Captives always, more
Or less, carry a residuum

Of captivity forever after, in
The form of mental process, scar, and attitude,
As obvious as if worn upon the skin.
For there is much of camouflage and stratagem
In living, in imprisonment in the safest
Sanctuaries, whose innocently deceiving
Walls restrain and hide
The amphibian and the quadruped,
The orangutan, bird collection, wildebeest,
All of whom, before leaving,
The little boy would get to see, in time.

—MARVIN SOLOMON

THE CALCULATION

A man six feet tall stands on a curb, facing a light suspended
fifteen feet above the middle of a street thirty feet wide. He
begins to walk along the curb at five m.p.h. After he has been
walking for ten seconds, at what rate is the length of his shadow
increasing?—*A problem posed by my calculus instructor, Penn
State, 1946.*

Facing a streetlight under batty moths
And June bugs ratcheting like broken clock springs,
I stand, for the sake of a problem, on the curb—
Neither in grass nor gutter—while those wings
Switch down the light and patch my undershirt.

I turn half right. My shadow cuts a hedge,
Climbs through a rhododendron to a porch,

And nods on a window sill. How far it goes
I leave to burglars and Pythagoras.
Into the slanting glare I slant my watch,

Then walk five miles per hour, my shoes on edge
In a practiced shuffle past the sewer grid,
Over the gold no-parking-or-pausing zones,
And into the clear—five seconds—into dirt,
Then over a sawhorse studded with lanterns,

And, at the tenth, I stiffen like a stump
Whose lopped head ripples with concentric figures,
Note the location of my other head
In a garden, but keep trundling forward,
Ignoring Doppelgängers from moon and lawn-lamp,

My eyes alert now, levelling my feet,
Seeing my shadow sweeping like a scythe
Across the stalks of daisies, barking trees
And scraping up the blistered weatherboard
To the eaves of houses, scaling the rough shingles.

At fifteen seconds, in a vacant lot,
My head lies on a board. I count it off.
I think back to the garden, and I guess,
Instructor, after fifteen years of sweat,
It was increasing five feet plus per second.

At the start, I could have fallen, turned around,
Or crossed to the very center of confusion,
My shadow like a manhole, no one's length,
Or the bulb itself been broken with a shot,
And all my reckoning have gone unreckoned.

But I was late because my shadow was
Pointing toward nothing like the cess of light,
Sir, and bearing your cold hypotenuse—
That cutter of corners, jaywalker of angles—
On top of my head, I walked the rest of the night.

—DAVID WAGONER

CALENTURE

He never lives to tell,
but other men bring back the tale

of how, after days of gazing at the sea
unfolding itself incessantly and greenly—
hillsides of water crested with clouds of foam—
heavy with a fading dream of home,
he climbs aloft one morning and, looking down,
cries out at seeing a different green,
farms, woods, grasslands, an extending plain,
hazy meadows, a long tree-fledged horizon,
swallows flashing in the halcyon sun,
his ship riding in deep rippling grain,
the road well-known to him, the house, the garden,
figures at the gate, till, dazed by his passion,
he suddenly climbs down and begins to run.
Stunned by his joy, the others watch him drown.

Such calenture, they say,
is not unknown in lovers long at sea,

yet such a like fever did she make in me,
this green-leaved summer morning, that I,
seeing her confirm a wish made lovingly,
felt gate, trees, grass, birds, garden glimmer over,
a ripple cross her face, the sky quiver,
the cropped lawn sway in waves, the house founder,
the light break into flecks, the path shimmer,
till, seeing her eyes clear and true at the center,
I walked toward her on the flowering water.

—ALASTAIR REID

THE CALIFORNIANS

Beautiful and blond they come, the Californians,
Holding their blond beautiful children by the hand;
They come with healthy sunlight in tall hair;
Smiling and empty they stride back over the land.

Tanned and tempting, they reverse the pioneer
And glide back to Atlantic shores from their state,
And shows on Broadway have tall, oh, very tall girls,
To replace the shorter kind we generate.

California men put airplanes on like shoes
To swoop through the air they beautifully advertise,
And the women of California are splendid women,
With nothing, nothing, nothing behind their eyes.

Oranges, movies, smiles, and rainless weather,
Delightful California, you spread to our view,
And the whitest teeth, the brownest, most strokable shoulders,
And a hateful wish to be empty and tall like you.

—THEODORE SPENCER

CALM WINTER SLEEP

Sleep, calm winter sleep, the rides are woollen
Over the dreaming roots, thick snow in sunlight
Is sugar under the trees, wool or sugar,
Immaculate, crystalline, soft. All night this has fallen:

All night, like flaws in the night, under a singing
Steady moon, flutter of whirling frost-flakes
Settling in light packed cumulus has drifted
Into the copses, by the twig-sieves sifted.

We wake to this: from the bedroom window we see,
Leaning flank by flank in pajamas and nightgown,
Its levelling laydown on the unregular earth;
We speak of this coldness with our joined warm breath—

As distance instructs us we think of the seamless snow
As a bride's dress hiding a rough brown secret body
In sleep, calm winter sleep, before the firegroom
Melts with one spring and lets her rivers go.

So distance says; but after oats and bacon,
The children mufflered, we venture and pass the wicket,
And how complicated the snow is, how alive a surface
As through all the flamboyant frettings of the thicket

The weak pale arrows of St. Lucy's sun
Yellow as an old apple strike in a brandished handful
Defining a paving crazed with mysterious blue;
With breezed shelving and with crisscrossed various

Other arrows of thrush-foot marking this mantle
Fitter for convict than bride; and with giddy drip-holes

Under the holly pointels, and deep in the bush
The nap worn through already in umber stipples!

Last night we spoke of the Bomb, of the perilous statesmen,
And those who shiver in tents, who are all our proper
Concern; this morning we laugh and look into the snow.
Have you forgotten your childhood that you grieve so?

Have you remembered your childhood that you grieve so?
It is not to explore too closely the heart's motions
Makes us quite wise: what dies is what's dissected.
Only I know that sometimes when least expected

What must be happiness is suddenly found,
Quite pointlessly, by following some small thing
Like the linked arrows of a bird, unguessed-at
In what from the window was one great trackless ground—

Though in the next night, under the silver eyeball
Of the bathed night-mistress, out of the castled west
The confetti's tourbillons again will bluster
And lay our happiness waste-wide with the rest.

—HILARY CORKE

THE CALYX OF THE OBOE BREAKS

The calyx of the oboe breaks,
silver and soft the flower it makes;
and next, beyond, the flute-notes seen,
now are white and now are green.

What are these sounds, what daft
      device,
mocking at flame, mimicking ice?
Musicians, will you never rest
from strange translation of the breast?

The heart, from which all horrors
      come,
grows like a vine, its gourd a drum;
the living pattern crawls and climbs,
eager to bear all worlds and times;

trilling leaf and tinkling grass
glide into darkness clear as glass;
then the musicians cease to play,
and the world is waved away.

—CONRAD AIKEN

THE CAMPUS

I work to music on the radio.
The one discordant note comes from growling
Dogs up on the hill; police brought them
To find a satyr after dark who tries

Climbing in windows, waiting behind trees.
The trees are too thin. I suppose he sees
A skirt flutter over the hill, then runs toward it.
The echo of his steps drops dead on the grass,
The logic he meant to push gets tangled in his feet
And flaps like a loose cord inside his windy skull.
Smooth skin reflects the moon, his trousers crackle
Like dry leaves. His hands perform a game
On the victim. He can bite her lips,
Stifle the cry, kiss, jump away.
He may want to kill her out of pure joy.
Probably his wish sails in a child's park,
Traces a flower with a red crayon.
It's easy to imagine his young body,
Tough-limbed, hairy, lurching from side to side,
Panting to get out of the dark—

                    By day
The campus here is pleasant. Health Science,
The Art Forum, throw cantilevers at
The broad steps of the Non-Sectarian Chapel.
The rituals of this climate keep us busy.
Men trim the privets, move snowplows in winter.
Bells whine every quarter of an hour, domestic,
Complacent; but beyond the clock tower at times,
When the wind is cold and the night falls early,
A question bangs in our heads like an old door
That will not stay closed, for all our knowledge.
                                    —DAVID POSNER

CANAAN

She is committed to the earth and the earth
Is plighted forever to her.
The wilderness is prone to her.
The hopeful race of all the earth is
Betrothed to her, pleasant ground of expectation,
Lambent country of Canaan.

Jordan heaved his banks away.
Jordan's valley bubbled over
High between these opposites.
He rose by night; he dipped by day.
He dipped down for the hosts of the wilderness
And for the silver country of Canaan.

The men of the wilderness at Jordan's ford
Lifted the Ark of the Covenant on their shoulders.
Jordan fled for all his worth.
Jordan-bed lay smitten to dry boulders.
The wilderness bore the Ark of the Lord
Of all the earth
Into the holy country of Canaan.

Canaan's the land where the wilderness landed.
Therefore I am not altogether confounded
Still to discover a wilderness in her.
Jordan shed his ways, lifted up the river;
Canaan's husbanded
Now with a ploughing sword, she is anointed
With burning torrents, bridal country—
Canaan of loss.
There goes that leviathan in his glory;
But here dissembles that wilderness. Fowl and beast
Have no more wonderful identity.
The tribes of the pomegranates and the tribes of the yeast,
The families of rubies and the families of grass
Are one to another as waste and waste
In the arms of Canaan of silver dross.

But I am not altogether confounded that
So immanent and green and promised a land
Confounds me with seeming not what she seemed;
Seeing the hopeful race is covenanted
Not less to Canaan
Than Canaan to her promised wilderness;
Seeing default of this double covenant, seeing
Treachery to the warm harvest, no gathering in
Of the pearly vines of Canaan.
The same thing over and over again.
In this I am not altogether bewildered.

No year is twice the same, or has occurred
Before. We bandy by the name of grief
Grief which is like no other. Not a leaf
Repeats itself, we only repeat the word.

       January, as usual, frigid. As before,
       A silent stir in February. More
       Of a stir in March. Activity
       In April, as previously.
       May, as usual, abundant. As before,
       A superfluity in June. Greenery galore

Thereafter, as always. The season exults,
But never the same season warily
Secretes the same petal from the same
Pod of a single bud. The circumstances are
Everywhere novel. The results
Only appear similar.

Time lacks experience. Therefore I am not quite
Confounded by history,
Being of the hopeful race of the earth,
Promised to promise, a mystery to mystery,
By which I am not altogether mystified,
Since she is plighted to me, a wilderness, and I to
The silver country of Canaan.

—MURIEL SPARK

CAPE ANN: A VIEW

Tropic of ice—
the sea a razor-line toward Spain.
This house I rented on the first of June
already hums with bees about their pueblos,
and from a bare deck rotted by the sun
I see bird islands and the snow-patched slopes
where sea gulls hold their raucous councils.
In single file,
as if they had pried apart the whaleback rock
that shoulders my front door, late irises
shuck off their thin rag-paper wrappings
and stand like roosters while their petals blow.

Again the fond summer comes to a grim edge
off which, this morning, one gray lobsterman
goes trolleying from float to float
and stops at each, his bubbling motorboat
adrift, to rake the sea.
Becalmed, he hauls a shower to his knees,
measures his catch in ounces and in inches,
and, patient, throws out almost everything.
He swings about,
steadfast, his motor muttering, as if with hope,
and fades like a dead soul, still standing up.

A rusty lilac knocks against a shingle;
the old GE refrigerator champs and snores.
When echoes echo in too many rooms,

I go downstairs, compelled to open doors
as if someone stood waiting there . . .
Cold sun steps in. There's little to surprise
a stranger in this neighborhood.

Whoever lives here must be gone for good;
his lavish water colors bleed and sag,
his breadbox is unhinged, his tacked-up wall map
of the zodiac's washed brown with rain;
his pantry shelf keeps one white plate—on it
someone once painted a high-buttoned shoe;
upstairs, there's a wan piece of *art nouveau*
and a black sweater gone in the right sleeve.

My relics, fallen among his,
lean on the shelves of a long afternoon.
A trapezoid of light goes crabwise on the floor,
the bees with Yo-yo spoolings lift and sink
on the still air, and, in a thrust of gold,
a spider's little partly finished net
abstracts the heart of treachery.

The evening, at first screened in clear pastels,
soon washes out in a romantic clamor.
Gulls on a fishhouse roof,
spaced perfectly, a wing apart, observe
these last annunciations of the visible.
The stars come thick; and, as I move
toward sleep within the sleep of walls
that may recall my tenancy, fish, lion,
scorpion, and ram climb the important track
from whose solicitous and shining grace
a name descends on the anonymous.

—John Malcolm Brinnin

CARE

Most that I know but one
Make me better than I am,
Freer and more intent,
Glad and more indolent.
What shall I think of you,
Who make me worsen?

Is it a hate I have,
And if so, what is hate

That makes me reprobate
By expectation?
Or do I learn your lack,
Not mine, and give it back

As mine, the empty lack as mine
That makes me worsen?
And if you do misread
Me in your own need,

Why do I care whose is
The botched lesson?

Because I think if one
Should bring to my mind disdain

So near destruction,
I think that I should be
Crying out, Help me!
Help me.

—JOSEPHINE MILES

CATARACT

I

The lashes of my eye are clipped away,
the eyelids pinned back with
diamond hatpins.
Tomcats pad in; their tiger tails
don't show under those starched smocks.
Grinning like balloons, they rise
and nudge the ceiling. They have been trained
to pick cobwebs from human eyes.

I lie under the beam of God's kilowatts,
a cloud of opium raining down like soot.
A well, murky with hoarded reflections,
is uncovered. Will they find me there—
with the drowned woodchuck, the white-eyed snake?

I've watched a glacier grinding
through the tumid ranges of the brain,
dropping silt
over my inner eye. Words flick
out of the haze like angry birds,
or crawl, wings torn off,
peeping feebly. . . .
But I cannot remember what saints and martyrs
have said under far worse circumstances.

II

When I was nine, strapped down
by nightmares, I screamed for
my sleeping father. Big as the hunter's moon,
he loomed in his nightshirt.
"Father, please chase those cats out of
the poppy trees, kick them into the dark
where I can't hear them hissing
'She . . . She . . .'
Don't let their prickers slip, Daddy!
Light a cigar."

I see the shadow of ivy on a plaster wall,
yellow roses climbing, my son's chestnut thatch
polished by a barn lantern—
don't let the blackbirds in the window!
A hand is turning the white doorknob.

God, dear, I am not ready. I am ashamed
to entertain you here at the beginning,
at the bottom of the well.
All I have for tea are these mud pies,
rich with stone raisins, pressed into rusted
cake tins. I set them out to dry, a row a day,
when the sun was hot on my gingham back,
and I pulsed like a tree toad in June,
mixing sweets, baking cakes,
enough, more than enough, for everyone.

—MARGORET SMITH

CAT GODDESSES

A perverse habit of cat goddesses—
Even the blackest of them, black as coals
Save for a new moon blazing on each breast,
With coral tongues and beryl eyes like lamps,
Long-leggèd, pacing three by three in nines—
This obstinate habit is to yield themselves,
In verisimilar love ecstasies,
To tatter-eared and slinking alley toms
No less below the common run of cats
Than they above it—which they do for spite,
To provoke jealousy, not the least abashed
By such gross-headed, rabbit-colored litters
As soon they will be happy to desert.

—ROBERT GRAVES

THE CCC

CCC campers near West Cummington
In the middle thirties built a sensible dam,
Considering the river—three strong piles
Of squarish field stones, rescued from old walls,
Held solid by concrete; between these piers,
Two slabs of tightly banded logs, let down
To make a pool in summer, taken up

In October when the after-swimming air
Would be too cold even if the water wasn't,
Then dropped back into place in middle June
When the ice-floed floods from springs of melting snow
Had reached the larger rivers and the sea.
I swam there seldom as a boy; the place
Seemed tame and dull compared to other parts
Of the same river, natural, undammed.
I liked much better what the CCC
Had done upcountry: stands of spruce and fir
Planted in rambling patterns, some my height,
Some more, some less, all young and growing,
Handsome and sturdy in the midsummer air.
But I thanked the CCC boys most of all
For what they did at Windsor Jambs, a gorge
Of rapids and waterfalls—they let it be
Essentially as it was, as today it is,
Neither cutting nor planting trees atop its sides,
Sweeping no needles up, breaking no rocks,
Letting the water fall as waters will.
They took away nothing. All they thought to add
Was a series of sturdy posts along the edge
Of its cliffs, above sheer drop-offs—thick brown posts
Connected by three strands of stout steel rope,
Which, as I walked, I could run my hand along
Like an electric train, adding my game
To the natural beauty into which I gazed.
When I went back, at twenty, after the war,
I found the tent floors rotting, the dam unused,
The pines far taller than I, growing on,
But the Jambs the same, and every post still strong.
Only the rust on the ropes, which stopped my hands
From feeling extended echoes, showed that here,
Even here, in time, like all things, time would change
And make forgotten the works of the CCC.

—THOMAS WHITBREAD

THE CEMETERY AT ACADEMY, CALIFORNIA

I came here with a young girl
once who perched barefoot on her
family marker. "I will go
here," she said, "next to my sister."
It was early morning and
cold, and I wandered over

the pale clodded ground looking
for something rich or touching.
"It's all wildflowers in the spring,"
she had said, but in July
there were only the curled cut
flowers and the headstones blanked ou

on the sun side, and the long
shadows deep as oil. I walked
to the sagging wire fence
that marked the margin of the
place and saw where the same ground,
festered here and there with reedy
grass, rose to a small knoll
and beyond where a windmill
held itself against the breeze.
I thought I heard her singing on
the stone under the great oak,
but when I got there she was
silent and I wasn't sure
and was ashamed to ask her,
ashamed that I had come here
where her people turned the earth.

Yet I came again, alone,
in the evening when the leaves
turned in the heat toward darkness
so late in coming. There was
her sister, there was her place

undisturbed, and relatives and
friends, and other families
spread along the crests of this
burned hill. When I kneeled
to touch the ground it seemed like
something I had never seen,
the way the pale lumps broke down
to almost nothing, nothing
but the source of what they called
their living. She, younger now
than I, would be here someday
beneath the ground my hand combed.
The first night wind caught the leaves
above, crackling, and on
the trunk a salamander
faded in the fading light.
One comes for answers to a
place like this and finds even
in the darkness, even in
the sudden flooding of the
headlights, that in time one comes
to be a stranger to nothing.

—Philip Levine

CHAIR, DOG, AND CLOCK

That's the queer life, *said the chair,*
The chair that came from Ireland,
That's the queer life!
Twenty-five guineas they paid on the dot,
But now that I'm got,
Do they treat me with proper respect? They do not.
His grim, gross hams in his blue-serge suit—
Too much!
And her bloody great rawboned corsets
(Saving your presence) spiked as a ploughman's boot—
Well, of course, it's
Not what I'm used to at all.
I've a thoroughly delicate sense of touch,
Said the chair,
Stuck in a Tudorbethan hall
With a bogus Broadwood and a Paisley shawl,
Not what I'm used to at all, at all,
Not what I'm used to at all.

Have I told you the tale of my life? (You have, *said the dog*.)
Well, I'll tell you again, *said the chair*.
I was born—yes I recall
Exactly where.
In a lovely wood of Limerick
The branch I was that bore the birds,
The soft salt air—(Skip that! *said the dog*.)
I will that. I will swallow my words.
Let us hop two hundred years. (Good show! *said the dog*.)
Twenty-five guineas they paid and they looked at my legs.
Well, well, I thought, well, well;
All things come to him that endures,
All things proceed in their due rotation—
High time you returned the compliment,
For it's often enough I have looked at yours
(For I take what you might call
A basic view of the human situation).
Oh, the little round bottoms of children like cherries
That found me too hard and as broad as a bath!
The fresh young hips of a girl!
And two sometimes
Sat in me then,
A boy and a girl, *that* I remember,
Making of rhymes,
Changing of kisses,
Eating of berries—
That was the best.
By broad maternal acres blessed,
I grinned and bore it. And then the wrinkled,
The puckered shanks of the threshold-haunters I knew,
Dry and tetchy as timbers, too—
That's the queer view,
Said the chair, the Irish chair,
That's the queer view!
And breeches and bockers and trews
And bustles and panniers in various manners
(Though never a crinoline,
For I wasn't sufficiently broad in the beam)—
The lot—
I knew them all and they're none of them news.
(Do they treat me with proper respect? They do not.)
I can tell you the mode and the social code
And the very day that knickers came in,
Ah, sure I can, praise God,
Said the chair,
The chair with three legs in the eighteenth century
And one in the Brompton Road.

Never thee mind, *said the dog,*
The china dog from Stafford,
Never thee mind!
All's grand for the likes of you.
These flowers of flesh they come and go:
At babytime they briskly blow;
Boyflower hangs his head with dew;
Like flags they are shaken out in summer,
But, oh, the winter wind
Comes cutting round the corner quick
And mister of his petals skinned
Lies pithless in the snow.
Toward their proper ends they grow;
Hang on, you'll see it through.
But I, dad, that's another kettle,
Said the dog with painted whiskers,
Perched on the back of a Mummerset settle,
Staring all day down the gullet of doom
While a daft, starved skivvy with a broom
And a streamlined Hoover with fathoms of flex
Is supposed to be sweeping the room
And looks very much more like sweeping the decks!
It's a dent or a scratch or a worm for thee
But a shove and a dustpan for me, old dear,
A shove and a dustpan for me.
If I could break this china sleep,
Said the dog, the Staffordshire dog,
Sharp on these china paws I'd creep,
Deep with these china claws I'd dig
Under this Beautiful Home a big
Big hole, down down,
Tunnel it, kennel it under the ground
Till the house came crump with a sniggering sound
And hammered her in like a nail,
Said the dog,
The dusty dog with a supercilious grin
And a crack in the tip of his tail.

Dig dog, *said the clock,*
Dig dog dig dog dig dog,
Said the clock.
Then they all came in and the clock said,
ONE TWO THREE you're dead.

                                            —HILARY CORKE

CHANGE OF ADDRESS

When the ring gleamed white and your chair hugged the edge of it,
and I led an elephant into the tent
with my skin like gold lamé, and black mesh snaking
the length of my legs, and hair of pomaded waves curling red
to the waist; when I leaped to the back of the elephant,
scaling his five thousand wrinkles,
yes, feeling his huge bones lurch
and the canvas ripping up
night near my neck (and all the lights blazing);
when I slid down his hairy trunk
to lie flat in the sawdust under the five-cloved foot,
waiting, with the old silk handkerchief over my face—
did you think you were at a circus?

Or the year I wore purple velvet and a torn wedding veil
with a little blue fan spread over my pale thighs,
and hovered near the ceiling pouring tea (and good omens
were predicted when the oatmeal cookies were passed),
and you cried out: the recipe, the recipe!
And then when I hitched a ride on that Spanish rooster, waving
goodbye with one hand, the other holding tight to his blazing
comb, and seven candles burned on the wedding canopy—
did you think it was a painting you were looking at?

You can tear up your lecture notes now, erase every phone
number under my name, and go shopping in someone else's suitcase.
I've changed my address again. And don't waste your money
on bilingual road maps. After a six-day ocean voyage,
a train ride, and three Métro transfers, you'd only find nights
where the breath churns to snow after dark,
and a bench with a man making blankets of his arms, his wife
in her black wool nightgown, and a three-legged cat
in her lap. And then, would you recognize me?

—Kathleen Fraser

CHARITY OVERCOMING ENVY

(LATE-FIFTEENTH-CENTURY TAPESTRY, FLEMISH OR FRENCH, IN THE BURRELL
COLLECTION, GLASGOW ART GALLERY AND MUSEUM)

Have you time for a story
(depicted in tapestry)?
Charity, riding an elephant,
stands on a "mosaic of flowers," facing Envy,

the flowers "bunched together, not rooted."
Envy, on a dog, is worn down by obsession,
his greed (since of things owned by others
he can only take *some*). Crouching uneasily
in the flowered filigree, among wide weeds
   indented by scallops that swirl,
daisies, pink harebells, little flattened-out
sunflowers, thin arched coral stems, and—
   ribbed horizontally—
slivers of green, Envy, on his dog,
   looks up at the elephant,
cowering away from her, his cheek scarcely scratched.
He is saying, "O Charity, pity me, Deity!
   O pitiless Destiny,
   what will become of me,
maimed by Charity—*Caritas*—sword unsheathed
over me yet? Blood stains my cheek. I am hurt."
In chest armor over chain mail, a steel shirt
to the knee, he repeats, "I am hurt."
The elephant, at no time borne down by self-pity,
   convinces the victim
that Destiny is not devising a plot.

The problem is mastered—insupportably
tiring when it was impending.

Deliverance accounts for what sounds like an axiom.

The Gordian knot need not be cut.

                    —MARIANNE MOORE

CHERRYLOG ROAD

Off Highway 106
At Cherrylog Road, I entered
The '34 Ford without wheels,
Smothered in kudzu,
With a seat pulled out to run
Corn whiskey down from the hills,

And then, from the other side,
Crept into an Essex
With a rumble seat of red leather,

And then, out again, aboard
A blue Chevrolet, releasing
The rust from its other color,

Reared up on three building blocks.
None had the same body heat;
I changed with them inward, toward
The weedy heart of the junk yard,
For I knew that Charlotte Holbrook
Would escape from her father at noon

And would come from the farm
To seek parts owned by the sun
Among the abandoned chassis,
Sitting in each in turn
As I did, leaning forward,
As in a wild stock-car race

In the parking lot of the dead.
Time after time, I climbed in
And out the other side, like
An envoy or movie star
Met at the station by crickets.
A radiator cap raised its head,

Become a real toad or a kingsnake,
As I neared the hub of the yard,
Passing through many states,
Many lives, to reach
Some grandmother's long Pierce-
            Arrow
Sending platters of blindness forth

From its nickel hubcaps
And spilling its tender upholstery
On sleepy roaches,
The glass panel in between
Lady and colored driver
Not all the way broken out,

The back-seat phone
Still on its hook.
I got in as though to exclaim,
"Let us go to the orphan asylum,
John; I have some old toys
For children who say their prayers."

I popped with sweat as I thought
I heard Charlotte Holbrook scrape
Like a mouse in the Southern-state
            sun
That was eating the paint in blisters
From a hundred car tops and hoods.
She was tapping like code,

Loosening the screws,
Carrying off headlights,
Sparkplugs, bumpers,

Cracked mirrors and gear knobs,
Getting ready, already,
To go back with something to show

Other than her lips' new trembling
I would hold to me soon, soon,
Where I sat in the ripped back seat
Talking over the interphone,
Praying for Charlotte Holbrook
To come from her father's farm

And to get back there
With no trace of me on her face
To be seen by her red-haired father,
Who would change, in the squalling
            barn,
Her back's pale skin with a strop,
Then lay for me

In a bootlegger's roasting car
With a string-triggered 12-gauge shot-
            gun
To blast the breath from the air.
Not cut by the jagged windshields,
Through the acres of wrecks she
            came,
With a wrench in her hand,

Through dust where the blacksnake
            dies
Of boredom, and the beetle knows
The compost has no more life.
Someone outside would have seen
The oldest car's door inexplicably
Close from within.

I held her and held her and held her,
Convoyed at terrific speed
By the stalled, dreaming traffic around
            us,
So the blacksnake, stiff
With inaction, curved back
Into life, and hunted the mouse

With deadly overexcitement,
The beetles reclaimed their field
As we clung, glued together,

With the hooks of the seat springs
Working through to catch us red-
      handed
Amidst the gray, breathless batting

That burst from the seat at our backs.
We left by separate doors
Into the changed, other bodies
Of cars, she down Cherrylog Road,

And I to my motorcycle,
Parked like the soul of the junk yard

Restored, a bicycle fleshed
With power, and tore off
Up Highway 106, continually
Drunk on the wind in my mouth,
Wringing the handlebars for speed,
Wild to be wreckage forever.

—JAMES DICKEY

CHESAPEAKE

I

Nature most calm is often a crisis.
I remember a bay day,
creaseless, ruffleless,
land out of sight out of mind,
when the aimlessness
of my eyes, hands, dreams, work, art
rose up in my throat and smote me,
and I cried for wind. . . .

Wind high,
bay gray and white,
the avenging angel's
enormous
wings over us:
it rained a spray of
dross cold; sails grew; boat heeled;
lungs filled with danger;
our bodies blessed and bent
to servitude,
you a slave
to the tiller, I
slave to your prescience.
Lord, Lord give us clearance.

II

Lost souls haunt rivers.
In a light wind,
by moon,
they can keep you as half-wakeful
as the boat that sways always
on its anchor
back and forth,

and your light dreams
bring you up short
on your body;
you rise and cry out,
"Where am I?"
The ghosts recede to shore.
Next morning, old stumps
abandoned by pioneers
are covered by
large silent birds.

This bay is not rhetorical:
modestly
it receives its rivers,
except at Annapolis
where Severn, South, Magothy
swirl and pull off
a small naval battle.
Otherwise, patiently
receiving all tributes of waters,
it slumbers and waits
for the storms to ride across its
      stretches,
for the wind to call out the changes
that set the nun buoys nodding
and all the bells and gongs
to dire scolding.
A bay is an infold,
a withholding
between prosaic land
and cannibal ocean.

At bay, at bay!
How many a day's journey
across the whims of water
to find headway!
Lighthouse and land ho.
It's moving that counts.

—GERTA KENNEDY

CHILD

Child of the season of adventure, child of the heart
Running forever in the landscape of happiness,
That long autumn strangely free of frost,
    where stars hang low
    like the ripe fruits they are
    and the wild geese gather slowly
    (one waits over the house still, with rich wings)
In the fires of the late sun,

There is no child like you in that country where the third
            litters of wild animals start
To show small golden faces: chipmunk-mask no larger than a fingertip,
          rabbit small enough to spend the whole
            winter of youth in the earth, a press
Of tiny snakes guarded by something lying like a stick across the path
                (except for the markings).
In all that country you are the only one

Laughing and calling with human voice along the roads,
    you are the only one with intricate hands to tear old vines apart
And fearless feet to tread them, the only one with a small caress
To bring smiles, to bring milk into an abandoned breast, and
    into the cave of the breast a bright thing
Far away won

That grows and grows like the wildbird over the house or low stars
          or the earth-warmed litter in its hole.
Child, poem and poet, you are most golden
    you are the most golden of all.

—E. N. SARGENT

THE CHOICE

I have known one bound to a bed by wrist and ankle,
Scarred by the whips of a wasting ache,
Who, at the point of entering of the needle,
Looked once around to take
The final view, then spoke;
The echo of that terribly witty joke
Pursued the surgeon to his home in Kew,
Deafened a nurse all night, and leaden lay
On the heart of a thick-skinned anesthetist
Long after they'd dispatched his ended clay.

That one lies in Oxford and is its earth.
Also, a bright-eyed woman in Germany,
In a sightless trap, far below ground,
Of which another held the key,
Surveyed without visible alarm
Or twitching of a pinioned arm
The instruments set out upon a table;

Then from her mouth there flowed a resolute
Stream of satire deliciously edged until
The tormentor tormented stopped it with a boot.

She fell as ash, not bones, in Herzen fields.
All brave men breathe her when the wind
Blows east from Danube. And Tom Caine,
When the Imperial was mined
And water had flooded all but the wireless room,
Spoke without audible gloom
From fifty fathoms down for fifteen hours
To his messmates on land, told several stories,
Then to a doctor carefully described
Asphyxiation's onset and his doom.

He is grown water and surrounds the pole.
If ever you dip a cup in any sea
Tom Caine is in it somewhere. On the whole
Men die asleep or else disgracefully;
But not all men. Perhaps we are never,
By any average mountain, wood, or river,
More than a heart's breadth from the dust
Of one who laughed with nothing left to lose.
Who saw the joke beneath the mammoth's foot?
And what shall I choose, if I am free to choose?

—HILARY CORKE

CHORUS OF THE UNBORN

We, the unborn,
The yearning has begun to plague us,
The shores of blood broaden to re-
  ceive us;
Like dew we sink into love
But still the shadows of time lie like
  questions
Over our secret.

You who love,
You who yearn,
Listen, you who are sick with parting:
We are those who begin to live in
  your glances,
In your hands which are searching the
  blue air—

We are those who smell of morning.
Already your breath is inhaling us,
Drawing us down into your sleep,
Into the dreams which are our earth,
Where night, our black nurse,
Lets us grow
Until we mirror ourselves in your eyes,
Until we speak into your ear.

We are caught
Like butterflies by the sentries of your
  yearning—
Like birdsong sold to earth—
We who smell of morning,
We future lights for your sorrow.

—NELLY SACHS

(Translated from the German by Ruth Mead and Matthew Mead)

CHRIST CHURCH MEADOWS, OXFORD

(AN AMERICAN SCHOLAR, RETURNED TO HIS OWN COUNTRY AFTER TWO YEARS AT
OXFORD, SPEAKS)

I

Often I saw, as on my balcony
  I stirred the afternoon into my tea,
Enamelled swards descending to the *Thames*,
  Called *Isis* here, and flowers that were gems,
Cattle in herds, and great senescent trees,
  Through which, as Pope predicted, ran the breeze.
Ad sinistram, where limpid *Cherwell* flows,
  Often I saw the punts of gallant beaux,
Who sang like shepherds to each gentle love
  Quaint tales of *Trojan* warriors to prove
That loving *Maidens* are rewarded here
  With bastards and with pints of watered beer.
Here, too, I saw my countrymen at large,
  Expending *Kodachrome* upon a barge;
From chauffeured *Car* or touring *Omnibus*,
  They leered at me, calling me "them," not "us;"
A jutting woman came to me and said,
  "Your *Highness*, can those big white geese be fed?"

"*Yankee* go home," I snarled. "Of course the *Swans*
Are bred to disregard *Americans*."
She fainted then, beside two *Christ Church* porters,
Who cast her, as I told them, on the waters.

II

"Stop it. Pastiche
Reveals attrition.
Define! Define! The Meadows
Want definition."

"King Charles, King James,
Flying here, went
For walks in refuge, free
From Parliament."

"Yes, yes. To name
Their past is pleasant.
What of the Meadows now?
What of the present?"

"I think they are stuffed,
Like birds which are dead,
Stored in the Sunday parlor,
And visited."

—DONALD HALL

CHRISTMAS EVE

(AUSTRALIA, 1943)

The wind blows hot. English and foreign birds
And insects different as their fish excite
The would-be calm. The usual flocks and herds
Parade in permanent quiet out of sight,
And there one crystal like a grain of light
Sticks in the crucible of day and cools.
A cloud burnt to a crisp at some great height
Sips at the dark condensing in deep pools.

I smoke and read my Bible and chew gum,
Thinking of Christ and Christmas of last year,
And what those quizzical soldiers standing near
Ask of the war and Christmases to come,
And, sick of causes and the tremendous blame,
Curse lightly and pronounce Your serious name.

—KARL SHAPIRO

THE CHURCH OF SAN ANTONIO DE LA FLORIDA

(GOYA PANTHEON)

A cleaning woman opened the rusty door
and, taking our pesetas, led us down
a narrow, dust-filled hall (the wicker chairs
were chewed by rats) into the sun-propped vault.
Only his body lay there, marble-stored.
Some skull-geographer, to map renown,
cut off his head and hid it from the years.
Above, his paintings soared without a fault.
We sprained our necks, squatting on the floor.

For once, the angels seemed half-real and phrased
in human terms, like that small, beetled friar
framed in the central arch, who taught to men
how time, and the end of time, may be undone
and justice rouse the dead. The tomb was blazed
in light and flowers, and kittens frisked and gyred
among the leaves and withered cyclamen.
Between the cats, the frescoes, and the sun,
we spent three hours, indolent with praise.

His mind went, in the end. Upon his walls
he thumbed the dreams that horrified his bed,
those visions we call black. In one long room,
deep in the Prado, tourists still may see
howling Time devour his children's heads;
the fight with clubs upon a mountain col—
two cripples on their knees, their staves upthrown
in contest for their brothers' charity;
the Witches' Mass of human animals.

Painter, you are a lucky man to lie,
though shorter by a head, here in this dome
made sacred by the years, by art sublime,
where human angels crowd the ceiling stones
to hear the truth arise and testify,
and tombs of flowers seem a kittens' home—
though underneath squats dark and naked Time,
chewing on the splinters of your bones,
and through the walls run rats with small, red eyes.

—PAUL PETRIE

CICADA

I lay with my heart under me,
under the white sun,
face down to fields
and a life that gleamed
under my palm like an emerald hinge.
I sheltered him where we lay alive
under the body of the sun.
Trees there dropped their shadows
like black fruit,
and the thin-necked sparrows came
crying through the light.

At my life line I felt
his bent, bright knee
work like a latch.
He was safe with me
in the room my round bones made—

or might have been—
but he sang like a driven nail
and his skinless eyes looked out,
wanting himself as he was.

Wisdom was imprecise,
my hand's loose judgment dark.
Some jewel work straining in his thigh
broke like a kingdom.
I let him go,
a jackstraw limping to the dynamo
of hunger under the hungering sun
and the world's quick gizzard.
High noon hummed,
all parts in place—
or nearly so.

—ADRIEN STOUTENBURG

A CIRCLE

Adam and Eve, like us,
Stood up to watch the sun;
Like us, Eve and Adam
Lay down under the moon.

Like Adam and Eve, we ask
Our questions of the sun;
And lie, like Eve and Adam,
Unanswered under the moon.

—THEODORE SPENCER

CIRCLE OF STRUGGLE

This morning, when I had to kill
a mouse to free it
from my trap,
I remembered the rat's gnawed foreleg
my father made me see—sheer bone
protruding from a thin
clenched paw. And this was our se-
        cret,
father's and mine, kept
from mother, safe in her kitchen
for years.
        When he died at the verge
of my manhood, she fled north
with me. There I learned the seasons
in a long strange year.

I saw the crippled trees
crumple into colors, shedding
their brilliant disease of leaves
that left the branches dead
and trembling in the snow-white
        wind,
magical and stark
between streetlamps and starlight.

I learned to set out traps
for muskrats, mink, and rabbits—
        declaring
I would never marry, never.
And each dawn of the long first winter,
silent in the moonlight, I hiked through

the frost-bright, mysteriously
dreamlike sleeping trees
that jutted like black bone
from wounded snow. Alone among
the creatured drifts and banks
piled up in the months between
my father's death and my
own beating flesh,
I was fearful and desirous
of the gray silent wolves
a crushed thing's single shriek
could summon from the dark.

With my strong Confederate bayonet
I'd pry slick frozen steel apart,
freeing stiff legs severed
in my traps. Now and then
a worthless skin.
   One morning
early in the wind and while
the blowing moon still wobbled,
jostling the dark fixed trunks
of night, I heard a chain snap tight.
Then beating wings. Something white
was fumbling at the base of the trees.

Like snow rising from snow,
a silver fox locked
in its talons, the great white owl
  rose—
then fell, dragged back by the trapped
  weight.
Dazzled by the brightening
air, its lunar eyes blazed
in their mask of blind snow
as I tripped on ice, reared
to meet its stare. It challenged:
I froze.
   White breast wide
with the heavy wings of a warrior
angel, it dipped the hook of its beak
in slow deliberation
and stole a vivid eye from the skull,
then turned to me. Impatient,
in an outburst of brilliance,
it battered up
out of the snow, blindly clumsy at
  first,

then—transfigured by the high light
  of ascent—aglide
and glowing
   in the pale soaring sky.

Wet blood, bright
in the decomposing snow,
wound in a desperate
circle of struggle, round
and round the strict radius
of the staked chain.

All around me the horizon tensed
for dawn, encircling my vision
with the limits of a saw-toothed land
sharp against the sky,
and, from this trap's dead center,
I looked up at the fatal stars
so innocent in their slow prison
of seasons and hours.

This morning, when I
sent my wife and daughter from the
  room,
they fled as if to witness death
were death itself. *Am I to die?*
—this accusation in their fear
has followed me until
I feel as if my own is the small
nodding skull I've crushed,
and mine the one bright eye
staring from its ruin.
   So I
am the child again, facing your can-
  dor,
knowing this time you must die,
your face pass into my face,
mine into others. What
shall I tell them, father? What can
we tell to these strangers
we have made from our love?

Somewhere,
in the belly of the owl and the earth,
we all stare incessantly from
darkness to darkness soaring.
     —WILLIAM PITT ROOT

CITY SONGS

I

What if the ways be stone,
  What if the many pass?
We are to lie alone
  Behind a curtained glass.

What if the wheels be swift,
  What if the horns be loud?
Here is the corner; lift
  Your lashes out of the crowd.

Let them flutter and crawl
  To the nineteenth window up.
We are to light a small,
  Circular fire and sup.

Two yellow lamps, and a blue
  Circular flame to start.
After we can do
  With darkness, heart on heart.

II

Think no less of all his pain
  Because he told it in a room.
The song he sang and the refrain
  Are old as air, and dark as doom.

Such an old unhappiness
  Was not for half the sky to hear.
Walls remember our distress;
  Floors are pitiful of fear.

The winds receive our song and go.
  His was kept, and is the same

As when you held your forehead low
  To catch the syllables that came.

Think no less of any word
  Because it filled a little room.
That night is gone, but we have heard
  Eternal singing in a tomb.

III

She keeps one instant to herself
  Before the day comes back and
    climbs
To her tired lap, as it has done
  And yet will do these million times.

Afternoon will lead the same
  Old five unaltering hours around:
Hoofs and wheels and peopled dust,
  And an intolerable gray sound.

All returns; but not the dawn,
  That when it comes is neat and
    new.
It is her one own moment, saved
  And cooled for her with timeful
    dew;

It is the instant when she lies
  And slowly smiles at something
    strange—
A going footstep, light and small,
  That was a child; and he was
    Change.

—MARK VAN DOREN

CITY WITHOUT WALLS

"Those fantastic forms, fang-sharp,
Bone-bare, that in Byzantine painting
Were a shorthand for the Unbounded
Beyond the Pale, unpoliced spaces
Where dragons dwelt and demons roamed,

"Colonized only by ex-worldlings,
Penitent sophists, and sodomites,
Are visual facts in the foreground now,
Real structures of steel and glass:
Hermits, perforce, are all today,

"With numbered caves in enormous jails,
Hotels designed to deteriorate
Their glum already corrupted guests,
Factories in which the functional
Hobbesian Man is mass-produced.

"A key to the street each convict has,
But the Asphalt Lands are lawless marches
Where gangs clash and cops turn
Robber barons: reckless he
Who walks after dark in that wilderness.

"But electric lamps allow nightly
Cell meetings where subcultures
May hold palaver, like-minded,
Their tongues tattooed by the tribal jargon
Of the vice or business that brothers them:

"And mean cafés to remain open
Where, in bad air, belly-talkers,
Weedy-looking, work-shy,
May spout unreason, some ruthless creed
To a dozen dupes till dawn break.

"Every workday Eve fares
Forth to the stores her foods to pluck,
While Adam hunts an easy dollar:
Unperspiring at eventide
Both eat their bread in boredom of spirit.

"The weekend comes that once was holy,
Free still but a feast no longer,

Just time out, idiorrhythmic,
When no one cares what his neighbor does:
Now newsprint and network are needed most.

"What they view may be vulgar rubbish,
What they listen to witless noise,
But it gives shelter, shields them from
Sunday's Bane, the basilisking
Glare of Nothing, our pernicious foe.

"For what to Nothing shall nobodies answer?
Still super-physiques are socially there,
Frequently photographed, feel at home,
But ordinary flesh is unwanted:
Engines do better what biceps did.

"And soon computers may expel from the world
All but the top intelligent few,
The egos they leisure be left to dig
Value, virtue from an invisible realm
Of hobbies, sex, consumption, vague

"Tussles with ghosts. Against Whom
Shall the Sons band to rebel there,
Where Troll-Father, Tusked-Mother
Are dream-monsters like dinosaurs
With a built-in obsolescence?

"A Gadgeted Age, yet as unworldly
As when faintly the light filtered down
On the first men in Mirkwood,
Waiting their turn at the water hole
With the magic beasts who made the paths.

"Small marvel, then, if many adopt
Cancer as the only offered career
Worth-while, if wards are full of
Gents who believe they are Jesus Christ
Or guilty of the Unforgivable Sin:

"If arcadian lawns where classic shoulders,
Baroque bottoms make beaux gestes
Is too tame a dream for the dislocated,
If their lewd fancies are of flesh debased
By damage, indignities, dirty words:

"If few now applaud a play that ends
With warmth and pardon the word to all

As, blessed, unbamboozled, the bridal pairs,
Rustic and oppidan, in a ring-dance
Image the stars at their stately bransels:

"If all has gone phut in the future we paint,
Where, vast and vacant, venomous areas
Surround the small sporadic patches
Of fen and forest that give food and shelter,
Such home as they have, to a human remnant,

"Stunted in stature, strangely deformed,
Numbering by fives, with no zero,
Worshipping a juju *General Mo*,
In groups ruled by grandmothers,
Hirsute witches who, on winter nights,

"Fable them stories of fair-haired elves
Whose magic made the mountain dam,
Of dwarves, cunning in craft, who smithied
The treasure hoards of tin cans
They flatten out for their hut roofs. . . .

"Still moneyed, immune, stands Megalopolis:
Happy he who hopes for better,
What awaits Her may well be worse."

Thus I was thinking at three A.M.
In mid-Manhattan till interrupted,
Cut short by a sharp voice:

"What fun and games you find it to play
Jeremiah-*cum*-Juvenal.
Shame on you for your *Schadenfreude!*"

"My!" I blustered. "How moral we're getting!
A pococurante? Suppose I were,
So what, if my words are true."

Thereupon, bored, a third voice:
"Go to sleep now for God's sake!
You both will feel better by breakfast time."
                                        —W. H. AUDEN

CLAIR DE LUNE

Powder and scent and silence. The young dwarf
Shoulders his lute. The moon is Levantine.
It settles its pearl in every glass of wine.
Harlequin is already at the wharf.

The gallant is masked. A pressure of his thumb
Communicates cutaneous interest.·
On the smooth upward swelling of a breast
A small black heart is fixed with spirit gum.

The thieving moment is now. Deftly, Pierrot
Exits, bearing a tray of fruits and coins.
A monkey, chained by his tiny loins,
Is taken aboard. They let their moorings go.

Silence. Even the god shall soon be gone.
Shadows, in their cool, tidal enterprise,
Have eaten away his muscular stone thighs.
Moonlight edges across the empty lawn.

Taffeta whispers. Someone is staring through
The white ribs of the pergola. She stares
At a small garnet pulse that disappears
Steadily seaward. Ah, my dear, it is you.

But you are not alone. A gardener goes
Through the bone light about the dark estate.
He bows, and, cheerfully inebriate,
Admires the lunar ashes of a rose,

And sings to his imaginary loves.
Wait. You can hear him. The familiar notes
Drift toward the old moss-bottomed fishing boats:
"Happy the heart that thinks of no removes."

The song drifts across water, and the sound
Of water sings by the Cytherean shore,
And the stone god of morning will restore
The rose to the vast processions of its ground.

—ANTHONY HECHT

CLAMMING

I go digging for clams every two or three years
Just to keep my hand in (I usually cut it),
And whenever I do so I tell the same story: how,
At the age of four,
I was trapped by the tide as I clammed a vanishing sandbar.
It's really no story at all, but I keep telling it
(Seldom adding the end, the commonplace rescue).
It serves my small lust to be thought of as someone who's lived.

I've a war, too, to fall back on, and some years of flying,
As well as a staggering quota of drunken parties,
A wife and children; but somehow the clamming thing
Gives me an image of me that soothes my psyche
As none of the louder events—me helpless,
Alone with my sand pail,
As fate in the form of soupy Long Island Sound
Comes stalking me.

My youngest son is that age now.
He's spoiled. He's been sickly.
He's handsome and bright, affectionate and demanding.
I think of the tides when I look at him.
I'd have him alone and seagirt, poor little boy.

The self, what a brute it is. It wants, wants.
It will not let go of its even most fictional grandeur,
But must grope, grope down in the muck of its past
For some little squirting life and bring it up tenderly
To the lo and behold of death, that it may weep
And pass on the weeping, keep it all going.

Son, when you clam,
Watch out for the tides, take care of yourself,
Yet no great care,
Lest you care too much and talk too much of the caring
And bore your best friends and inhibit your children and sicken
At last into opera on somebody's sandbar.
When you clam, Son,
Clam.

—REED WHITTEMORE

A CLASSIC WAITS FOR ME

(WITH APOLOGIES TO WALT WHITMAN, PLUS A TRIAL MEMBERSHIP IN THE
CLASSICS CLUB)

A classic waits for me, it contains all, nothing is lacking,
Yet all were lacking if taste were lacking, or if the endorsement of the right man
     were lacking.
O clublife, and the pleasures of membership,
O volumes for sheer fascination unrivalled.
Into an armchair endlessly rocking,
Walter J. Black my president,
I, freely invited, cordially welcomed to membership,
My arm around John Kieran, Hendrik Willem van Loon, Pearl S. Buck,
My taste in books guarded by the spirit of William Lyon Phelps
(From your memories, sad brothers, from the fitful risings and callings I heard),
I to the classics devoted, brother of rough mechanics, beauty-parlor technicians,
     spot welders, radio-program directors
(It is not necessary to have a higher education to appreciate these books),
I, connoisseur of good reading, friend of connoisseurs of good reading everywhere,
I, not obligated to take any specific number of books, free to reject any volume,
     perfectly free to reject Montaigne, Erasmus, Milton,
I, in perfect health except for a slight cold, pressed for time, having only a few
     more years to live,
Now celebrate this opportunity.
Come, I will make the club indissoluble,
I will read the most splendid books the sun ever shone upon,
I will start divine magnetic groups,
    With the love of comrades,
      With the life-long love of distinguished committees.

I strike up for an Old Book.
Long the best-read figure in America, my dues paid, sitter in armchairs everywhere,
     wanderer in populous cities, weeping with Hecuba and with the late Wil-
     liam Lyon Phelps,
Free to cancel my membership whenever I wish.
Turbulent, fleshy, sensible,
Never tiring of clublife,
Always ready to read another masterpiece provided it has the approval of my presi-
     dent, Walter J. Black,
Me imperturbe, standing at ease among writers,
Rais'd by a perfect mother and now belonging to a perfect book club,
Bearded, sunburnt, gray-neck'd, astigmatic,
Loving the masters and the masters only
(I am mad for them to be in contact with me),
My arm around Pearl S. Buck, only American woman to receive the Nobel Prize
     for Literature,
I celebrate this opportunity.

And I will not read a book nor the least part of a book but has the approval of the Committee,
For all is useless without that which you may guess at many times and not hit, that which they hinted at,
All is useless without readability.
By God! I will accept nothing which all cannot have their counterpart of on the same terms (89¢ for the Regular Edition or $1.39 for the De Luxe Edition, plus a few cents postage).
I will make inseparable readers with their arms around each other's necks,
By the love of classics,
By the manly love of classics.

—E. B. WHITE

THE CLEARING

Above this bramble-overarched long lane,
Where an autochthonous owl flits to and fro
In silence,
Above these tangled trees—their roots encumbered
By strawberries, mushrooms, pignuts, flowers' and weeds'
Exuberance—
The planetary powers gravely observe
With what dumb patience
You stand at twilight in despair of love,
Though the twigs crackling under a light foot
Declare her immanence.

—ROBERT GRAVES

CLOSING TIME

At midnight, flaking down like chromium
Inside the tavern, light slips off the bar
And tumbles in our laps. The tumbler, falling
Off the edge of the table, goes to pieces
As quick as mercury around our shoes.
Good night to shuffleboard and countercheck.
The last ball bearing pins its magnet down
And sinks into a socket like the moon.

Over the rings around our eyes, the clock
Says time to decipher wives, husbands, and cars
On key chains swinging under bleary light.
Good night to folding friends on the parking lot
As parallel as windows in a wallet.

Lined up like empties on the curb, good night
To all who reach the far side of the street,
Their eyelids pressed as tight as bottle caps.

Good night to those with jacks as openers,
Those whose half-cases chill their pelvises,
And those with nothing on tap all day tomorrow,
Who wind up sleeping somewhere cold as stars,
Who make the stairs and landings but not doors,
Those in the tubs or hung on banisters,
Those with incinerators in their arms,
Whose mouths lie open for another one.

Good night to drivers driven by themselves
To curve through light-years at the straightaway.
Good night to cloverleaf and yellow-streak,
To all those leading sheriff's deputies
Over soft shoulders into power poles,
The red-in-the-face whose teeth hang down by nerves,
The far-afield, the breakers of new ground
Who cartwheel out of sight, end over end.

—DAVID WAGONER

THE CLOWN

"Practically all you newspaper people,"
The Clown said, "get it badly mixed up
With sentimental junk, but you are a chap

"With an intelligent face. I am not crying
On the inside. I am no brave faker.
On the contrary, I am a simple laugh,

"And the laugh pretends to be about
Nothing in particular, and not the answer
To anyone's extremely difficult question.

"Nor do I pretend that the world is really,
In its deep center, utterly charming
And lovely as a joke, or that it feels good

"To be crucified. Laughter is the sign
Of an emotion that is like other emotions
But more transient and less related

"To the problems of the man who displays it.
It is my specialty, and all laughs
Are mad laughs. I realize that I could argue

"That these red polka dots are spots
Of blood, and that I laugh to explain them,
But any reason is a false reason;

"Polka dots are as crazy as polka dots,
Or as the light heart itself,
Which suddenly laughs in the shuttered room

"That is real and unhappy, where the old
Without chances talk to the young without hope.
Men dying of cancer, even,

"Lift for a second in their hollow bodies
No hope, but a lightness like air.
They don't stay lifted. (What will stay lifted?)

"If even for men dying, there is my madness,
Who puts me out of work?" The Clown
Cartwheeled across the dressing room, and bowed.

—DONALD HALL

CODA

Love is not worth so much;
I regret everything.
Now, on our backs,
in Fayetteville, Arkansas,
the stars are falling
into our cracked eyes.

With my good arm,
I reach for the sky
and let the air out of the moon.
It goes whizzing off
to shrivel and sink
in the ocean.

You cannot weep;

I cannot do anything
that once held an ounce
of meaning for us.
I cover you
with pine needles.

When morning comes,
I will build a cathedral
around our bodies.
And the crickets,
who sing with their knees,
will come there
in the night to be sad
when they can sing no more.

—JAMES TATE

COLD FIRE

Through water, his own waterfall
furthering, the electric eel
loops downward into a drowned pool
of himself. Snowfall and storm coil
to the same fold, invisible
as sleep. He is their shepherd. Whole

oceans above him turn and spool

silver from valleys. A slow wheel
tears you from me, love—beautiful
as the sea. And when your eyes, all
depth and breadth of the world's blue
        soul,
fill, do I flicker there like coal?

—GEORGE STARBUCK

COLLOQUY

In the broken light, in owl weather,
Webs on the lawn where the leaves end,
I took the thin moon and the sky for cover
To pick the cat's brains and descend
A weedy hill. I found him grovelling
Inside the summerhouse, a shadowed bulge,
Furred and somnolent. "I bring,"
I said, "besides this dish of liver and an edge
Of cheese, the customary torments,
And the usual wonder why we live
At all, and why the world thins out and perishes
As it has done for me, sieved
As I am toward silences. Where
Are we now? Do we know anything?"
Now, on another night, his look endures.
"Give me the dish," it said.
I had his answer, wise as yours.

—WELDON KEES

COME OUT INTO THE SUN

Come out into the sun and bathe your eyes
In undiluted light. On the old brass
Of winter-tarnished grass,
Under these few bronze leaves of oak
Suspended, and a blue ghost of chimney smoke,
Sit and grow wise
And empty as a simpleton.

The meadow mouse, twitching her nose in prayer,
Sniffs at a sunbeam like celestial cheese.
Come out, come out into the sun
And bask your knees,

And be an acolyte of the illumined air.
The weathercock, who yesterday was cold,
Today sings hallelujah hymns in gold.

Soon the small snake will slip her skin
And the gray moth, in an old ritual,
Unseal her silk cocoon.
Come shed, shed now, your winter-varnished shell
In the deep diathermy of high noon.
The sun, the sun, come out into the sun,
Into the sun, come out, come in.

—ROBERT FRANCIS

COMING BACK TO AMERICA

We descended the first night from Europe   riding the ship's sling
Into the basement. Forty floors of home weighed on us. We broke through
To a room, and fell to drinking madly with all those boozing, reading
The Gideon Bible in a dazzle of homecoming scripture   Assyrian armies
The scythes of chariots blazing like the windows of the city   all cast
Into our eyes in all-night squinting beams of unavoidable violent glory.
There were a "million dollars in ice cubes" outside our metal door;
The dead water clattered down hour after hour as we fought with salesmen
For the little blocks that would make whole our long savage drinks.
I took a swaying shower, and we packed the whole bathroom of towels into
Our dusty luggage, battling paid-for opulence with whatever weapon
Came to hand. We slept; I woke up early, knowing that I was suffering
But not why. My breath would not stir, nor the room's. I sweated
Ice in the closeness   my head hurt with the Sleep of a Thousand Lights
That the green baize drapes could not darken. I got up, bearing
Everything   found my sharp Roman shoes   went out   following signs
That said SWIMMING POOL. Flashing bulbs on a red-eyed panel, I passed
Through ceiling after ceiling of sleeping salesmen and whores, and came out

On the roof. The pool water trembled with the few in their rooms
Still making love. This was air. A skinny girl lifeguard worked
At her nails; the dawn shone on her right leg in a healthy, twisted flame.
It made me squint   slick and lacquered with scars   with the wild smoky city
Around it   the great breath to be drawn above sleepers   the hazy
Morning towers. We sat and talked. She said a five-car wreck
Of taxis in Bensonhurst had knocked her out and taken her kneecap
But nothing else. I pondered this   the sun shook off a last heavy
Hotel   and she leapt and was in the fragile green pool as though
I were still sleeping it off eleven floors under her; she turned in a water
Ballet by herself   graceful   unredeemable   her tough face exactly
As beautiful and integral as the sun come out of the city. Vulnerable,

Hurt in my country's murderous speed, she moved   and I would have taken
Her in my arms in water throbbing with the passion of travelling men,
Unkillable, both of us, at forty stories in the morning   and could have
Flown with her   our weightlessness preserved by the magic pool drawn from
Under the streets   out of that pond   passing over the meaningless
Guardrail   feeling the whole air pulse like water sleepless with desperate
Lovemaking   lifting us out of sleep into the city summer dawn
Of hundreds of feet of gray space spinning with pigeons now under
Us   among new panels of sun in the buildings blasting light silently
Back and forth across streets between them: could have moved with her
In all this   over the floods of glare raised up in sheets   the gauze
Distances where warehouses strove to become   over the ship I had ridden
Home in riding gently   whitely   beneath. Ah, lift us, green
City water, as we turn the harbor around with our legs   lazily changing
The plan of the city with motions like thistles   like the majestic swirling
Of soot   the winged seed of pigeons   and so would have held her
As I held my head   a-stammer with light   defending it against the terrible
Morning sun of drinkers   in that pain, exalting in the blind notion
Of cradling her somewhere above ships and buses   in the air like a water
Ballet   dancing deep among the dawn buildings in a purely private
Embrace of impossibility   a love that could not have been guessed:
Woman   being   idea   temple dancer   tough girl from Bensonhurst
With a knee rebuilt out of sunlight   returned-to amazement   O claspable
Symbol   the unforeseen on home ground   the thing that sustains us forever
In other places!

—James Dickey

COMMUNICATION TO THE CITY FATHERS OF BOSTON

> Dear Sirs: Is it not time we formed a Boston
> Committee to Enact a Dirge for Boston?
>
> When New York mushrooms into view, when Boston's
> townspeople, gathered solemnly in basements,
> feel on their necks the spider webs of bombsights,
> when subway stops grow ripe with fear like beesnests
> making a honey-heavy moan, whose business
> will it be then to mourn, to take a busman's
> holiday from his death, to weep for Boston's?
>
> When dust is scattered to her bones, when grieving
> thunderheads add hot tears, when copper grapevines
> clickety-clack their telegraphic ragtime
> tongues at the pity of it, how in God's name
> will rhymesters frying in their skins in garden

bowers on Brattle Street concoct a grave-song
grave and austere enough for such a grieving?

Move we commit some song, now, to the HOLD files
of papers in romantic places. Helpful
of course to cram our scholars with hog's headfuls
of Lowells, khaki-cap them, ship them wholesale
to Wake or Thule—some safe base, where heartfelt
terror may milk them of a tear. But hell's fire,
what'll they have on us in all those HOLD files?

You want some rewrite man to wrap up Boston
like garbage in old newsprint for the dustbin?
The Statehouse men convivial at Blinstrub's,
the Milk Street men, the men of subtler substance
squiring Ledaean ladies to the swan boats,
the dockers, truckers, teen-age hotrod bandits—
what could he make of them, to make them Boston?

Or even make of me, perched in these Park Street
offices playing Jonah like an upstart
pipsqueak in raven's clothing—First Mate Starbuck
who thinks too much? Thinking of kids at bus stops
exchanging dirty footnotes to their Shakespeares,
while by my window the Archbishop's upstairs
loudspeaker booms redemption over Park Street.

Thinking of up the hill the gilded Statehouse
where just this year I watched the plaster faces
of Sacco and Vanzetti waved on flannel
arms until duly banned from the empanelled
pain of a State's relentlessly belated
questioning of itself. (Last year, the Salem
witches; next year, if next year finds a Statehouse . . . ?)

Thinking of Thor, Zeus, Atlas. Thinking Boston.
Thinking there must be words her weathered brownstone
could still rewhisper—words to blast the brassbound
brandishers on their pads—words John Jay Chapman
scored on her singlehanded, words Sam Adams,
Garrison, Mott, Thoreau blazed in this has-been
Braintree-Jamaica-Concord-Cambridge-Boston.

There were such men. Or why remember Boston?
Strange how not one prepared a dirge for Boston.

—GEORGE STARBUCK

THE COMPANIONS

There used to be gods in everything, and now they're gone.
A small one I remember, in a green-gray stone,
Would watch me go by with his still eyes of a toad,
And in the branch of an elm that hung across the road
Another was; he creaked at me on windless days.
Now that he's gone I think he might have wanted praise
For trying to speak my language and getting that far at least
Along on the imitation of a speaking beast.

Maybe he wanted help, maybe they all cried out
As they could, or stared helpless to enter into thought
With "read me," "answer me," or "teach me how to be
Whatever I am, and in return for teaching me
I'll tell you what I was in you, how greater far
Than I are seeking you in fountain, sun, and star."
That's but interpretation, the deep folly of man
To think that things can squeak at him more than things can.

And yet there came those voices up out of the ground
And got into my head, until articulate sound
Might speak them to themselves. We went a certain way
Together on that road, and then I turned away.

I must have done, I guess, to have grown so abstract
That all the lonely summer night's become but fact,
That when the cricket signals I no longer listen,
Nor read the glowworms' constellations when they glisten.

—Howard Nemerov

THE COMPOST HEAP

Think from how many trees
Dead leaves are brought
To earth on seed or wing,
How many traceries
Their silence wrought
Before the stubborn spring.
The stuff of life made these;
It was not thought.

Then Earth, where spirits tread,
Turns in her sleep
And keeps a magic round.

Children of the dead
Run, run and leap,
Where all is common ground,
And the cunning thread
Of time they keep.

All that is fit to praise
Where twined limbs cross
Grows from such a bed.
Fear no dearth of days,
For life will toss
As many as are sped;

Only in other ways
We count our loss.

Think, where the dancers tread
And mourners weep,
All is common ground.

Where life and leaf are shed,
The rose will keep
Both light and substance sound,
That holy fire being fed
By the compost heap.

—VERNON WATKINS

CONNAIS-TU LE PAYS?

I have discovered a country
where the pages of books are all
margins and the calendar is frozen
in a wall of ice. Its mirrors are kept
in cages and covered at night.

I cross its border by way
of the labyrinth in the radiator.
The doors close behind me.

The guards at the gate of the prin-
cipal
city are dangerous. Also
the porter who hangs on the wall
like a silver knife. As for the troll
who once lured me under the bridge,
I blame him for everything.

There is no map of the city
but I know my way.
When I get to my room,
the others are waiting: the child
with tiny blue fish in her hair,
the ghost with a flashlight,
the prince who died of a bloody

nose and the angel who guards him,
the white nun dragging
her long black shadow.

I show them the sand I have
smuggled in my shoes, and my letters
written on dry grass.
I bring them a yellow wax
flower in a green pot.
We celebrate the silence.

At night, when it rains, we paint
a small fire on the wall
and sit before it, drinking
from cups made of buttons.
We drink to the present which is
eternal. We drink to the delicate
shells which grow in the garden,
to salt rising up
from the earth like smoke,
to another safe journey.

Outside, the water is moving
past in search of some
low place to lie down.

—RICHARD SHELTON

CONSOLATION IN WAR

Happy the dead!
If we do ill,
They will not know we lied.
Happy the dead!
If we do well,
Their death is justified.

—LEWIS MUMFORD

THE CONSTANT LOVER

I have continued to seek her
In the most unlikely places—
Even in the arms of women!

Most men, as they grow older,
Are able to generalize,
But I can't—not even about women.

For it's only her I love.
The shape of two brown eyebrows

Demands all my fidelity.

So I write poems,
And so my life passes,
But she is changeless

And seems more beautiful as time
  passes.

—Louis Simpson

THE CORNER KNOT

I was a child and overwhelmed: Mozart
Had snatched me up fainting and wild at heart
To a green land of wonder, where estranged
I dipped my feet in shallow brooks, I ranged
Rough mountains, and fields yellow with small vetch:
Of which, though long I tried, I could not fetch
One single flower away, nor from the ground
Pocket one pebble of the scores I found
Twinkling enchanted there. So for relief
"I'll corner-knot," said I, "this handkerchief,
Faithful familiar that, look, here I shake
In these cool airs for proof that I'm awake."
I tied the knot, the aspens all around
Heaved, and the riverbanks were filled with sound;
Which failing presently, the insistent loud
Clapping of hands returned me to the crowd.
I felt and, fumbling, took away with me
The knotted witness of my ecstasy,
Though flowers and streams were vanished past recall,
The aspens, the bright pebbled reach and all.

But now grown older, I suspect Mozart
Himself had been snatched up by curious art
To my green land: estranged and wild at heart
He too had crossed the brooks, essayed to pick
That yellow vetch with which the plains are thick;
And being put to it (as I had been)
To smuggle back some witness of the scene,

Had knotted up his cambric handkerchief
With common music, rippling, flat and brief;
Then, home again, had sighed above the score
"Ay, a remembrancer, but nothing more."

        —ROBERT GRAVES

CORTEGE FOR COLETTE

(THE PALAIS ROYAL GARDENS)

Minister of birds, islands, and pools,
Familiar of shade by the hushed walk of sedges,
Collector of grasses, seed-heavy and bent,
Who gather the violet seed and the grape
(Known to the moonmen and the green fever),
All receipts and brews, felicitous cures
Under sinewy roofs and streets of the root . . .

Genius, moreover, of gardens,
The bowknot, the crescent, and square,
And as many circular knots, and that pruning art
The shears do so well with the snail,
Tender and trainer of fountains,
Benefactor of box, quincunx, and yew,
Mathematician of the parterres
By a lapful of sparrows,

I have heard, I have come by these arches and urns,
All the classical battery of forms
Through the rectangular perspectives
Down the long galleries that end in the windows.
Closed are the gates. The calm is great
In the dark, where the small waters blow.
There is a sense of a slow sailing out
As a sudden wind tries a few leaves.
A part of a cloud interrupts the passage
Of the knobbed moon.

And I do not think the garden is what it was.
Like a promise departed, the rectangular perspectives
Down the long galleries end in the windows,
Stop with the shutters.
Should I speak I would not be heard
There where the moon slowly sails on,
For where might there be another speech

Such as signs give, and omens,
Such as sense has in those dreams
For which there is no translation except
In the absolutely unheard music about, perhaps, to be given,
Like a part of the secret sky broken off
Just at the surface where it crowds
With those vaguely summoned to take the long turns of the dance?

But let me not (standing outside these gardens,
These oblong gardens, behind closed gates,
Where only some sliver of water sighs,
Spilling over and over into its pool,
Where under the yellow light of the lamps
Only a cat walks, and it is late for the arcades
Out of the gardens to keep their own life,
And for low doors opening into mossed courts),
Let me not, to the diminished perspectives
Hovered with ivy where an urn sits,
                                        declare
That a part of the world having gone back into itself,
A meaning is thereby lost,
The disappearance of which torments us,
For it was not subtle but gross.

Amidst all this matching of flowers and shapes,
This tending of borders, this cutting by trowels,
Though compelled to pay close attention and not to walk blindly,
As if in a massacre of petals,

Let me know
That that of which you were the great witness lives,
That the torn butterfly will not leave the page,
Pierced by the light you gave,
That, by the power not to forget
Profoundly connecting with the root,
You brought by its weight some perfected whole
Of a part of the self into flower,
Who lightly go to the grave,
Having expended all you could give.

I do not speak of the corruption of ivy,
Of absence where presence dwells,
Of darkness where there is love.
Let me be mute as a child about death,
Address the invisibles—
For whom your genius, like a delicate beast
Training your heart,
To your sense giving lessons,

Led you out of the one world
Into the many countries of dreams and illusions—

And simply lift up the flower,
Simply salute the cloud,
From the cat to the horse by way of the dragon,
To some striped sky by way of the bird,

That it be borne, your body,
In the arms of young men, round and round,
And, to the march blown by bugles,
That the dark iron of its velvet vow
Shock through the blood some understanding
Just as surpassing as perfume when the touched body
Gives forth the divine humors of rain, leaves, and love.

—JEAN GARRIGUE

THE COT

I stopped in a sidestreet surplus shop, just south of Yorkville,
a holy, antic basement where a butterfish in a bowl and a fierce Sahara cat,
a rarity in Manhattan, were guardians of wilderness relics: ancestral
buttons, bones of lizards, aggregations of driftwood and coral, remaindered
shells. More autumn museum than shop. Its gentle keeper—
in his time, I imagine, an explorer, hunting guide, or harbor tugboat captain—
kept for noon naps an outlandish cot in a corner, an antique of extinct
canvas and bandied wooden legs, quaint for terrace sleeping
and catching October faiths from the river winds.
                    Kind to young voyagers, the keeper
decreed a just price, and, amidst uprisings of dust, the wild desert cat's
        protestations,
we dismantled the cot, which I carried home in a cab.
And I was warm enough on the cot, curled up like a pioneer,
like a mountain hunter, in a Western roll of blankets.
In the ambient winds were chances of change, scents of East River deities,
and there were more stars than usual for Manhattan, restless and cold,
as stars should be in October; but it was the windows I carefully wondered at,
their lights, by distance, quite warm and wicked, the dangerous shades
slightly drawn, to a wilderness watcher, on what promises of color
and surprise. And although I knew well that, for a quick faith before
sleep, the least stars are better, I kept to my choice of lights until the last
windows went out, when, having little knowledge, for all my pretensions, of dark,
I moved back to my own bed, leaving the wilderness prayer cot (still good for naps
        at noon)
adrift in true night with the stars, the river winds, and the abstract faiths of Oc-
    tober.

—GROVER AMEN

CÔTE D'AZUR

Since my life's been spent
In a passionate attachment
For someone
From the age of one;
Since my time's been lost
Waiting for the post
Or telephone;
Since I have grown
Up from hand to mouth
On love
And have thoroughly enjoyed the not altogether to be despised,
If not notorious, glory of my youth;
Since I can or will not change,
Where should I range
When body falters and beauty dies—
When I must meet old age,
I, no sage?

God grant my sight fade with my eyes
When mirrors are not kind.
God send me a foolish wambling man,
Also purblind.
For him I'll cake on rouge and powder
And wear a parrot on my shoulder.
We'll be absurd—
Two old birds—
Treasonous to grandparenthood,
Rightly scorned by all the good
Who cackle and play cards,
Gossip, and decry the moderation
Of the younger generation.
When candlelight recalls romance,
He'll make a wobbly amorous advance
(Both of us a little merry
From too much sherry),
But I shall have a fan
And tap his hand
And say "Come, come!"
And send him home—
Both relieved to stop play-acting
When the part gets too exacting.

—KATHERINE HOSKINS

THE COUNTERSHADOW

In daylight, even,
walking that same
suburban street
I take back home
at night, I mind
how I repeat
myself past lamp-
posts, drunken with
the countershadow
that I drag, feet-
first, closing on
my heels until,
within the arc
beside me, I
surpass myself,
to lunge across
the curb and, two-
lengths tall, race
leaning, up the
trapezoidal squares,
as if to chart
some progress or
intent that, half-
way to the public
light, dissolves
in dark cement.

—PHILIP BOOTH

COUPLE

I remember them, man and wife, in their little car,
Submitting to combustion cautiously.
It stood austerely upright, flecked with tar,
And jarred by highways, slightly weak of knee—
An elderly spinster wearing a yellow brooch.
Its doors were yellow, with yellow hood and wheel:
A pumpkin incompletely turned to coach.
They always spoke of it as "the automobile."

They sat upon its springs with folded hands,
Nodding to one another when it started—
They, too, of indeterminate date and style
But incorruptible, unbribed, unbartered.
They carried on uninteresting conversation
In earnest tones, unable to be silent
Above the engine's cough, its loud abrasion.
Outside their lives, the world, now grown more violent,
They viewed through tinted lenses on the nose
And saw each other through two sets of glass
In astigmatic monochrome of rose.
The roads were vague, long parlors pink with gas.

At night, they sat in stuffy rooms and listened
To titters in the street, where schoolgirls pilfered
The secrets of their beaus; their glasses glistened,
Round shields of moonlight, sensually silvered.
He sat like granite in the dark and weighed

His weight, and waited for illumination;
She in her veiled volcanic ashes grayed.
Sometimes she stroked the dark in inspiration,
And a lost creature stirred inside her bones,
But nothing came of it; she turned to leather
While he talked on in long-familiar tones.
They were two spinsters, skirting death together.

But then their yellow car coughs in my mind,
And I, caught in the stress of my own strife,
Recall their elegance in pumpkin's rind.
Some compromise is possible with life.

—WALTER STONE

THE COUPLE

A Greek ship
Sails on the sea
Carrying me past
The islands
Into an unknown
Island where
The burros
Are sleeping, houses
Are white, and brown
Honey is sold in
The general store. That's
Me up on the hill,
Living with the
Man I'm going
To marry—there
We are—he plays
The violin
But never practices,
I fold and unfold
The nylon blouses
I brought from
America and put
Them neatly in
A drawer. It is
Time to go out.
We explore the island
And at the same time
Argue about
Getting married.
We walk close to

The sea, which happens
To knock our eyes
Out with its blue. An
Old lady, call her a
Witch, passes us by and
Asks us the way to
The post office.
We continue on the rocks,
Walking by the sea. "I bet
We look married," I say,
And turn my eyes from
The sea. "Only to
An old lady
Going to mail
Letters at the post
Office," he replies.
And begins to weep.
Not one snorkel
Will float
Us under the sea,
To the schools of fish
Who are enjoying
Their mateless
Existence, or
Take us away from
Our troubles. The
Young girl folds
Up her blouses and
Begins to pack.
The young man

Picks up his fiddle
And places it
Back into
The imitation
Alligator case.
The island
Now is sinking
Beneath the blue sea.

The life plot thickens.
Wait.
We have forgotten
Our footsteps.
We must
Cover them up
To
The post office.

—SANDRA HOCHMAN

THE CRACK

There is a private tension that endears
the opposed split sides of a granite block;
some deep affinity decides the rock
when the first fault or wavering edge appears,
and the grained flaw grows jaggeder as it nears
the face that someone beat upon or broke
in art or anger. Sometimes at such a crack
all holds; so luck, so lovingly, coheres.

I saw a Lipchitz Mother straining once
to embrace the air, made jagged by her grace,
and Lipchitz said that he had meant the stone
merely to test his tools, but had begun
serious work on staring at a face
his hammer had laid bare by luck alone.

—MICHAEL GOLDMAN

CRANE

One day, when childhood tumbled the spongy tufts
Banking the naked edge of our bottom lands,
A shadowy sand-hill crane
Arose from Rocky Spring with a flipping fish,
A speckled rainbow,
Speared in her slim black bill.
She offered her wings in sluggish waves,
Wading impossibly up the slapping waters,
And ascended the crystal floods.

Under that dark ark,
Two grappling anchors of dangling legs
Rolled away so smoothly the eye forgot them
Until that tall, ungainly crane

Lay in the sky like a dream.
Her snaking head
Pivoted vaguely over our deep, green valley
And straightened to kiss the horizon.
Fish and crane
Swam through the white bowl of blue air,
Spinning outward upon
Mountainous heights and their soft, mysterious pulleys.

My naked shoulders ached for the tumbling clouds,
And my shivering legs
Thrashed through those mossy fishing meadows,
Over the rose-pebbled bottoms,
And churned in the chilled and iridescent spawn
Of the crane's pool.
Clamped and flexed in the vise of their beating wings
Now flaring astride the brassy eye of the sun,
I gasped like a fish
Hung out in the harsh and sudden air,
And flipped, past sparkling regions, underground.

—JOSEPH LANGLAND

CREPE DE CHINE

When she gives a "psychic reading,"
which isn't likely to be more than once—at the most twice—a day,
a set of Oriental glass chimes
    suspended from the ceiling of her
    tackily exotic little "parlor,"
announces that a client has entered.

She calls out hoarsely "*Un moment*"
    but keeps the customer waiting two or three minutes
before she emerges from her shadowy living quarters with an air of
indifference and fatigue.

    Invariably she is dressed,
        or you might say costumed,
in lavender or rose-colored crepe de Chine
        shadowy as the room from which she emerges,
and this crumpled apparel is not redeemed
        by her string of dimly opalescent beads.

Usually she will condescend to say "*Bonjour*" to the client,
    almost as if she were expelling

her last breath,
and after this ominous greeting she will mumble something unintelligible.
"What?"
"Nothing. Sit down."

She will then have, or affect to have, a little attack
of asthma.
"The dampness of these old houses," she will mutter.
And yet, despite all this atmosphere of fakery,
the reading will be honest, sometimes distressingly so.

"I am afraid that you have waited too long to consult
a competent physician."
"Your idea that you are loved is altogether mistaken."
"Your employment—I mean the business in which you're engaged—
is in so precarious a state that I can only advise you
to give it up or liquidate it,
and retire to an inexpensive foreign place, perhaps some unfashionable
town in Mexico.
Of course I am sorry
to give you this information, but the truth is something
for which there is no substitute."

When the unnerved client has paid her the variable fee
and returned to the relative comfort
of the street's weather,
The Crepe-de-Chine,
as she is called in "The Quarter,"
must drink a bit of brandy
to assuage her true distress, her headache, and her exhaustion . . .
—TENNESSEE WILLIAMS

CREW PRACTICE ON LAKE BLED, IN JUGOSLAVIA

(FOR MY SON, JOHN)

I'd wave the gnats away and try
to tell you, *no one is more dear,*
unable to tell, or think why

and justify our life besides,
hardly in touch. As like that shell
fanning water, our shadow glides

down to the dark bottom, beneath
consideration nearly. . . . Past
the feudal castle, with each breath

striding much like a galley or
a leggy water bug, it drops
airs, ages lost in the Great War,

the Austro-Hungarian Empire
and pine island astern—where still
an alpine church upholds its spire

but holds it, also, upside down
in the water mirror, as though
gravity dragged images down

and drained them off. So many
    lives. . . .
Caretakers raking the far shore
burn off a winter of wet leaves;

the column of smoke bows. Swallows
blow over all day, hurried through
our sunset like following harrows

until the sky yields. In wide, dim rings
they orbit, and come back as bats
stroking raggedly on damp wings

(as will the dark, frantic for more,
beat circles over the lamplit
footpath, still darker than before),

equipment in perfect order.

Whenever overtaken, I
duck, nor trust anyone's radar,

not even theirs. Then, when I look
at what comes true, or listen, hard
by the flat tension of a lake

while gooseflesh rises, recalling
how the coxswain's regular bark
marked time, forced rising and falling,

or out of habit dream on Proust,
how little we know or love, those
we know the best and love the most,

then, man to man, this heartless view
tempts me almost to tell a lie,
and wish you better than I do.

                —James Scully

THE CRITICS

With difficulty the ship was built,
Launched with more difficulty still;
The workmen were intractable,
The cradle was a rotten one,
The harbor had clogged up with silt—
And then the barnacles fastened on.
         —Theodore Spencer

THE CROSSING

The stream
piles out of the pile-
up of earth—
we call them mountains.

It
runs west to east,
roughly, or
from where it starts in the
pileup of earth, it runs
ESE
    to be very exact. &

in spring the birds cross it
                    heading north.

Thousands and thousands of birds
heading north cross it heading
north.
                    Singing   . It makes everyone
                    very happy. The
            stream is reasonably happy by itself
                    running ESE
                                        as it does
                    & is basically unaffected
            by all those migrations
    of thousands and thousands of birds.
                            —PAUL BLACKBURN

CROSSING KANSAS BY TRAIN

The telephone poles   gather about
have been holding their   a waterhole. This
arms out   is Kansas. The
a long time now   mountains start here
to birds   just behind
that will not   the closed eyes
settle there   of a farmer's
but pass with   sons asleep
strange cawings   in their workclothes.
westward to   —DONALD JUSTICE
where dark trees

CROSSING THE PARK

Crossing the park to see a painting
Somebody painted of the park—
One that I once found more enchanting
Than the park itself—I stopped to look

At the cocksure pigeons, mincing on gravel,
The trees, each reading its own green book,
And felt the amphibian nerve and muscle
Of life quiver like a tuning fork,

Then steady itself to evoke some distant,
Wordless country existing still,
Growing louder on what was silent,
Its wild, sad energy visible

In hundreds of forms of pulsing shadow
Boned by the light, and then formed again
By the light—to the right, an imperfect meadow,
To the left, a sleeping, unfinished man—

Forms never to be composed so neatly,
Finished, framed, and set out to view
As the painting that hung in the nearby gallery
In permanent green, in abiding blue,

For any vision must mean that something
Is being omitted; being discrete
By making the possible seem like one thing
Means lopping the head off or the feet,

Or leaving a leaf out or one wave
Of that merciless connoisseur, the sea,
Or pretending the body exists for love,
Or forgetting the pictures of misery

That are found in the news each day, that spell
Out fortunes each night across the sky:
The terrible kingdoms of the small,
The crystal ball of every eye.

The sun relinquished the sky. In slow
Inches the shade climbed up the trees.
Too late to get where I started to,
I watched their metamorphoses

Gradually give up the light
Till there was nothing more to give
To leaves and lives whose forms dispute
Those parks, those paintings in which I live.

—Howard Moss

CRUCIFORM

Here, in the sand, where someone laid him down,
The one known human signature is clear.
Whether woman or man, white-skinned or brown,
Whether the outflung arms were so for fear
Or agony or weariness or shame,
Here, in one line athwart another line,
Is briefly written the one, mutual name,

A savior's or a thief's, or yours or mine.
Dunes sifted undersea long since have borne
This selfsame cross, small and anonymous;
Tan deserts that the wind has not yet worn
Will print this symbol. And not one of us
But then, or some day, could lie down and fit
Our desolate arms and bodies into it.

—WINIFRED WELLES

THE CRUSE

Joy and the soul are mates, as heart and sorrow;
The soul has portal difficult and narrow,
Being a vessel oddly wrought, a cruse
Which, proffered sorrow, always must refuse.

The heart's more open and allows despair,
Fluid importunate and not so rare.
The soul for joy is shaped, the heart for ruth,
And love's the only oil that flows in both.

—LOUISE TOWNSEND NICHOLL

THE CURRENT

Down the dawn-brown
River the charcoal woman
Swept in a boat thin
As the old moon.
White tremblings darted and broke
Under her hat's crown.
A paddle stroke
And she was gone, in her wake
Only miniature
Whirlpools, her faint,
Ritualistic cries.

Now up the stream,
Urging an unwilling
Arc of melon rind
Painted red to match
His wares, appeared
The meat vendor.

The young, scarred face
Under the white brim
Glowed with strain
And flamelike ripplings.
He sat in a cloud of flies.

If, further on,
Someone was waiting to thread
Morsels of beef
Onto a green
Bamboo sliver
And pose the lean brochette
Above already glowing
Embers, the river,
Flowing in one direction
By moon, by sun,
Would not be going
To let it happen yet.

—JAMES MERRILL

THE CUTTING EDGE

Even the spring water
couldn't numb the slash
of that green rock
covered with river lace.
Slowly the blood spread
from under the flap of skin
that winked open; deep in
my foot, for a second, I saw
something holding back,
and I sat down in the water
up to my waist in water,
my pockets filling with it.
I squeezed the green rock,
pressed it to my cheeks,
to my eyelids. I did not
want to be sick or faint
with children looking on,
so I held to the edge of the stone
until I came back.

That was a year ago.
I threw the stone away
as though I could banish it
from creation; I threw
it into the dry reeds,
where it could do no harm,
and dragged myself bleeding
up the hillside and drove home.

I forgot the stone
drying among burned reeds
in October; I forgot
how cold this place got
when the winds came down the
         pass,
and how, after the late rains,
the first pale ice-plants dot
the slopes like embroidery,
then larkspur, myrtle, and the great,

bellowing, horned blooms
that bring summer on.

Huddling to where it fell,
like a stunned animal,
the stone stayed. I kneel
to it and see how dust
has caked over half of it
like a protruding lip
or a scab on no cut
but on a cutting edge.
It comes away from the ground
easily, and the dry dirt
crumbles, and it's the same.
In the river its colors
darken and divide
as though stained; the green
patterning I thought lace
is its own, and the oily shine
comes back, and the sudden smell
of dizziness and sweat.

I could take it home
and plant it in a box;
I could talk about
what it did to me
and what I did to it,
or how in its element
it lives like you or me.
But it stops me, here
on my open hand,
by being a stone, and I send
it flying over the heads
of the fishing children,
arching alone above
the dialogue of reeds,
falling and falling toward water,
somewhere in water to strike
a conversation of stone.

—PHILIP LEVINE

D

DAEDALUS

My son has birds in his head.

I know them now. I catch
the pitch of their calls, their shrill
cacophonies, their chitterings, their
    coos.
They hover behind his eyes, and
    come to rest
on a branch, on a book, grow still,
claws curled, wings furled.
His is a bird world.

I learn the flutter of his moods,
his moments of swoop and soar.
From the ground, I feel him try
the limits of the air—
sudden lift, sudden terror—
and move in time to cradle
his quivering, feathered fear.

At evening, in the tower,
I see him to sleep, and see

the hooding over of eyes,
the slow folding of wings.
I wake to his morning twitterings,
to the *croomb* of his becoming.

He chooses his selves—wren, hawk,
swallow, or owl—to explore
the trees and rooftops of his heady
    wishing.
Tomtit, birdwit.
Am I to call him down, to give him
a grounding, teach him gravity?
Gently, gently.
Time tells us what we weigh, and
    soon enough
his feet will reach the ground.
Age, like a cage, will enclose him.
So the wise men said.

My son has birds in his head.

—Alastair Reid

THE DAEMON

Must I tell again
In the words I know
For the ears of men
The flesh, the blow?

Must I show outright
The bruise in the side,

The halt in the night,
And how death cried?

Must I speak to the lot
Who little bore?
It said "Why not?"
It said "Once more."

—Louise Bogan

[155]

DAFYDD AP GWILYM RESENTS THE WINTER

(FREELY ARRANGED FROM THE PROSE TRANSLATION BY NIGEL HESELTINE)

Across North Wales
The snowflakes wander,
A swarm of white bees.
Over the woods
A cold veil lies.
A load of chalk
Bows down the trees.

No undergrowth
Without its wool,
No field unsheeted;
No path is left
Through any field;
On every stump
White flour is milled.

Will someone tell me
What angels lift
Planks in the flour-loft
Floor of heaven,
Shaking down dust?
An angel's cloak is
Cold quicksilver.

And here below
The big drifts blow,
Blow and billow
Across the heather
Like swollen bellies.
The frozen foam
Falls in fleeces.

Out of my house
I will not stir
For any girl,
To have my coat
Look like a miller's,
Or stuck with feathers
Of eider down.

What a great fall
Lies on my country!
A wide wall, stretching
One sea to the other,
Greater and grayer
Than the sea's graveyard.
When will rain come?

—ROLFE HUMPHRIES

THE DAGGER

A dagger rests in a drawer.
It was forged in Toledo at the end of the last century.
    Luis Melián Lafinur gave it to my father, who
    brought it from Uruguay. Evaristo Carriego once
    held it in his hand.
Whoever lays eyes on it has to pick up the dagger and
    toy with it, as if he had always been on the lookout
    for it. The hand is quick to grip the waiting hilt,
    and the powerful obeying blade slides in and out
    of the sheath with a click.
This is not what the dagger wants.
It is more than a structure of metal; men conceived it

and shaped it with a single end in mind. The dag-
ger that last night knifed a man in Tacuarembó
and the daggers that rained on Caesar are in some
eternal way the same dagger. The dagger wants
to kill, it wants to shed sudden blood.
In a drawer of my writing table, among draft pages and
old letters, the dagger dreams over and over its
simple tiger's dream. On wielding it the hand
comes alive because the metal comes alive, sensing
itself, each time handled, in touch with the killer
for whom it was forged.
At times I am sorry for it. Such power and singlemind-
edness, so impassive or innocent its pride, and the
years slip by, unheeding.

—JORGE LUIS BORGES
(Translated from the Spanish by Norman Thomas di Giovanni)

DAISIES OF FLORENCE

Bambini picking daisies in the new spring grass
Of the Boboli Gardens
Now and now and now in rosy-petalled fingers hold
The multitude of time.
To the limits of the small and fine florets innumerable of white and gold
They know their daisies real.

Botticelli with daisies from the timeless fields of recollection scatters
That bright Elysium or Paradise
Whose flowers none can gather,
Where spirits golden immortal walk forever
With her who moves through spring after spring in primavera robed,
Ripening the transient under her veil.

—KATHLEEN RAINE

DAKOTA: FIVE TIMES SIX

Nobody painted Mrs. Aherne's store
And, standing at a corner where dry wind
Sanded it, all its boards turned bone-gray finally,
And by the time I visited, untended,
The barbershop next door—where Mr. Mack

Told jokes I smiled at, fearing all the while
The flyspecked Lucky Tiger on the wall,
Out of the corner of my six year's eye—
I could remember it no other color.

I can remember now, at five times six,
Her dress—beyond the crystal candy jars,
Behind the smeary counter glass—was gray
(Dyed gray, maybe, not weathered, but gray as
The siding of her store); so were her hair
And eyes, even the tarnished silver brooch
That pinched her dress tight at the withered throat.

Dakota six knew bone-gray when he saw it:
Cows often died in fields of only dust,
So did farmhouses with their eyes poked out.
I can remember bone-gray, bleached-board gray
Better than rainbows—there it seldom rained.

But Mrs. Aherne sold taste rainbows at
Two for one cent, and from her shelves rained sugar.

—JOSEPH HANSEN

DAMOCLES

Death never troubled Damocles,
  Nor did the incertitude
When the sword, swung by a light
    breeze,
  Cast shadows on his food—
    "A thread is spun
    For every son,"
Said he, "of Pyrrha's brood."

But great Zeus cursed him, nonethe-
    less,
  With vision to deplore
The end of that day's childishness,

And he could eat no more:
    His fame would float
    Through anecdote
Into dead metaphor.

Then orators from every land,
  Caught by the same disease,
With thump of fist or saw of hand
  Or sinking to their knees,
    Would madly boom
    Of the world's doom
And swords of Damocles.

        —ROBERT GRAVES

THE DARK AND FALLING SUMMER

The rain was full of the freshness
    and the fresh fragrance of darkening grapes.
The rain was as the dark falling of hidden
And fabulous plums ripening—great blue thunderheads moving slowly.
The dark air was possessed by the fragrance of freshness,
By a scattered and confused profusion until,
After the tattering began, the pouring-down came,
And plenitude descended, multitudinous.
Everywhere was full of the pulsing of the loud and fallen dusk.

—DELMORE SCHWARTZ

A DAY IN THE CITY

(BOSTON—NEW YORK)

I. A TASTE OF QUEENS

The dead in Queens lean westward from their stones,
Bidding granitic and marmoreal
Adieux to their descendants, who go west
A better way across the bridge to lodge
Like unspent bullets in high offices
And spiring living rooms up in the air.
Low grow the tenant cabins—stucco, brick,
Half-timbered, double-numbered—where the quick
Who were not fast enough groom their feat sons
To leap the river and, for love or money,
Fall stunningly upon the stony city.
Here Maple Towers ("Now Renting 3-Rm. Apts.")
Now towers without a tree, its swimming pool
A blue oasis in the asphalt plain
Where caravans of Carey buses ply
From Flushing to their caravanserai
In that gray fret of city over there,
Bearing us strangers straight to our desire.

II. THE AMAIR TOWER

Amair, whose lightfoot jets transship today
Across the Pole to where tomorrow starts,
I do not like your *pied-à-terre*, which squats,
Arrived and immemorial, upon
Diminished traces of that lovely gray

Novembrist town bespoke by the old school
Who specialized in rainy afternoons
Enclosing incandescent *thés dansants,*
From which the singles and the couples went
On by tall lemon cab to their affairs
Down at the Café Brevoort or upstairs
Above the Plaza's titles and palms. Now I
Am escalated to a mezzanine
From which I will be launched into an air—
Which fifty stories circulate—as rare
As the rich breath of couchant unicorns
Or levant chairmen at the dormant board,
Whose low end I will sit at and, like Molly,
Bloom into smiles and, yes, say yes to folly.

III. High Places

Sitting in conference with the president,
I am at first a trifle hesitant
To pierce his thin-skinned sphere with my harsh voice
And possibly dissipate his corporate choice
Of fruitwood furniture and cosmic view—
Look! Look! Canarsie! Inwood! Greenpoint! Kew
Gardens! United Nations Plaza!—true
Embodiment of everything that's ex-
Travagant in American life but sex,
Which is supplied in minims by Miss Hatch
Outside his office door to each fresh batch
Of clients, underlings, and impressees,
Who, on his bounty, sail the seven seas
Of his blue, black, calm, manic, angry moods,
This king of men and emperor of goods.
We talk across two tankards of his pale
Impeccable imported English ale,
Which break out in a fine cold sweat, like me,
In his stern presence. Can my dim words be
Reaching their destination? Yes, sir. He
Nods in his waking sleep and sanctifies
My views in every echelon of eyes.

IV. East Forty-second Street

Acutely, the late sun interrogates
The street held in its custody, casting
New light on western faces, shadowing
Each subject with the long arm of the law
Of relativity, gilding the back,
Benighting the east front of everyone.
In front of Longchamps, on a burning brass

Standpipe stained orange by sundown, a tall green
Girl worth her weight in meadows, orchards, trees
Sits waiting for her date to claim her long,
Cool fall champaign, capped by black scuds of curls,
And stage a pastoral with her as Phyllis
And him as Colin, awkward, forward, witty,
Against the pre-cast forest of the city.

—L. E. Sissman

DAY ON KIND CONTINENT

I
All Day

All day the light wind blew on the house
Where my baby was asleep, and I read
The Gilgamesh at the open window,
Thinking matchless deeds for him.
The soldiers came at noon to build
Bridges, their hammers came to my house,
"Cold voices," I thought, "in air."
And my baby slept silent all day,
And my wife sang fever songs all day.

The soldiers were burning a hillside
For roads. The air shook for all
The birdless, rising heat. Being the kind
Of man I am, I could not hate them.
With the light wind, smoke blew on my house.

At three o'clock my wife began trombone
Practice in the bedroom. The baby's fists
Fell open and closed, but he could not scream,
Being so kind. I listened—the distance
That lay between my window and the hillside
Moving off, moving off. Her playing
Was effortless and beautiful, surrounding
The small house.

Soon I fell asleep, the setting sun in my palm
Saying, "As if, as if," as if I were a child-
Dreamer with a wish just before sleep. My
Wife fell asleep, too, her lovely mouth pressed
About the trombone's mouth. My son
Fell asleep to her breathing's song.

The soldiers were putting out the fires,
As if to say "Thank you." Gilgamesh, "two-thirds
God and one-third man," was putting out the sun,
Moved by the kindness that moves the birds.

II
The Dream

We are going to another valley,
Wrapped in ribbons, along the grass river,
To find pasture in the valley
For our simple sheep.

The kind currents in the water,
The currants of the cool jars—
And in my mind's orchard of wind—
We are going to another valley.

Light follows the obedient sheep,
Wherever they are led, by pressing
Fragrant hands in the warm wool.
Light is deity of the service trees.

That the hawk tilts and glides
Is a truth, that the hawk wants to kill
My lamb is no truth, as
We are going to another valley.

As watch to the East, I stood,
Seeing rain as distant as sky
Over a valley. I went up unhurt
And came down unhurt.

A god spends the night blessing
A barren woman, and a boy
Is born at Random, in grass.
To say we are going to another valley

Is a good and simple truth.
The sheep need pasture, sun, and shade.
We neither shear them nor burn them,
Nor do we eat them, being kind.

They tend to themselves, and gently ask
That we tend to ourselves, and we
Exchange small gifts when a season turns.
The sky is clear and very patient overhead.

—Robert David Cohen

D.C.

The bad breed of the natives with their hates
That border on a Georgian night,
The short vocabulary, the Southern look
That writes a volume on your past, the men
Freeholders of the city-state, the women
Polite for murder—these happen to be;
The rest arrive and never quite remain.

The rest live with an easy homelessness
And common tastelessness, their souls
Weakly lit up by blazing screens and tales
Told by a newspaper. Holidays, the vast
Basilicas of the railroad swallow up
Hundreds of thousands, struggling in the tide
For home, the one identity and past.

The noble riches keep themselves, the miles
Of marble breast the empty wind,
The halls of books and pictures manufacture
Their deep patinas, the fountains coldly splash
To the lone sailor, the boulevards stretch out
Farther than Arlington, where all night long
One living soldier marches for the dead.

Only the very foreign, the very proud,
The richest, and the very poor,
Hid in their creepy purlieus white or black,
Adore this whole Augustan spectacle,
And chancelleries perceive the porch of might
Surmounted by the dome in which there lies
No Bonaparte, no Lenin, but a floor.

Yet those who govern live in quaintness, close
In the Georgian ghetto of the best;
What was the simplest of the old becomes
The exquisite palate of the new. Their names
Are admirals and paternalists, their ways
The ways of Lee, who, having lost the slaves,
Died farther South, a general in the wrong.

—KARL SHAPIRO

DEAD CENTER

(AN ELEGY)

A thin fox
sidled by with his stingy shadow.
Bees hung in air,
each like a chandelier;
hot pine pinched my nostrils.

You sat up in bed
wrestling with the fox's silence—
it isn't time, it isn't time.
I looked at your face with the sharp
    regret
a mother feels for her child

sleeping after the day's war.

They broke flowers on your coffin,
knowing you weren't there. The sun
    came out
and all your faces flared for a mo-
    ment;
you weren't there.
I'll beat my poem into a trap
for the stingy fox, to prove
that you were here.

—RUTH WHITMAN

A DEAD LEAF

Today, the first dead leaf in the hall
Is surprised, taking on its second nature,
To find that trees are forms of furniture;
The earliest message to arrive from winter,
It's too far gone, indoors or out,
To eat the sun or drink the water,
And I, I am more desperate than ever,
Reading the memoirs that Madame Blank
Keeps sending on in thick installments.
Twelve publishers have firmly declined. . . .
(Thank God! For I am thinly disguised
As yet another form of furniture:
My name is Harrod—a character
Who at one point rather stupidly remarks,
"Only a Fool could love King Lear.")
Madame would hate these opening lines;
She is against both cadence and meter.

Armories, windows,
Days and weeks
Of peering out, then drawing back—
Is there enough artillery
To blast the gossips of this block?
Paranoia is a border line

Without a country on either side.
That fortress of brownstones across the way
Is money talking
With nothing to say.

Rectitude and impropriety!
I have given them both up,
And settled for a sleazy mysticism,
Befuddled rain and poisoned mist;
Sometimes I'm so depressed I think
It's *life* that's the anesthetist.
But then I wake quite sane, as if
A bicycle race were about to start:
I'm in the park, the sun is bright,
Water ravishes the eye, and soon
I've won the race, I've made my mark!
Then, once again, the telephone
Is my one lifeline out of the dark.

I'm sick of being obsessed by B.,
Whose muffled cryptograms grow hoarse
Explaining themselves, outwitting me.
Does that mean this? Does this mean that?
Temperamental unclarity!

This week, drinks and dinner with M.
Lunch with L. Dinner with P.
A party for C.'s new Argentine.
Handel on Thursday. A *vernissage*.
Next week, drinks and dinner with M.
Tuesday I think I'll watch TV.

To retire from it all! To sit and sit
In a wheelchair, old, in Central Park,
Only a lens that drinks the sun,
Or on a bench in southern France,
The first cassis at four o'clock. . . .

August was green, November brown.
Someday soon I'll awake to see
The world go white from head to toe,
A tablecloth at first, and then
A slab of pockmarked travertine—

The first snow.
                                —HOWARD MOSS

DEAD OF WINTER

The city shuffles through the snow, the whirling snow, and I, indifferent
To cold, remember how he looked, the casket much too small, the grief a
Discomfort buried under triumphs of survival—memories
Of snowdrifts hollowed out, as I am hollowed out, a snowman
Dissolving into frozen sunlight, caving into dust,
A drift of words, iambic flights of migratory
Goodbyes, a dead-of-winter funeral, the earth
Too stiff to weep, the open grave a trenchant
Disclosure. Nothing lasts and nothing lives
Forever; even now the city
Disintegrates in gusts of snow,
The words revolve like poems
Around a solitude
Of empty feelings,
Around myself,
Until, dead,
Alone,
I,
Alive,
Begin to
Feel tears run down
My face, the plowed-up
Drifts melting into slush.
An alley cat, emerging,
Shakes off paralysis, accepts
The warm, triumphant sun; the pigeons,
A flock in flight, discover crusts of bread
Among old ladies blinking through the park, as
Regrets give way to tremblings underground, murmurings,
And I, delivered from despair, rejoice, remember
How, snowbound, schools were closed, toboggans hurtled down the street,
A snowball slowly rolled across the yard became a beach ball—
Bright colors spinning into golden suns, reflective moons, as words
That whirl become a warm embrace, a dance of birds across an open
Astonishment of sky, and I, I think of you, I think that you know why.

—ANTHONY TOWNE

DEAR MEN AND WOMEN

(IN MEMORY OF VAN WYCK BROOKS)

In the quiet before cockcrow when the cricket's
Mandolin falters, when the light of the past
Falling from the high stars yet haunts the earth
And the east quickens, I think of those I love—
Dear men and women no longer with us.

And not in grief or regret merely but rather
With a love that is almost joy I think of them,
Of whom I am part, as they of me, and through whom
I am made more wholly one with the pain and the glory,
The heartbreak at the heart of things.

I have learned it from them at last, who am now grown old
A happy man, that the nature of things is tragic
And meaningful beyond words, that to have lived
Even if once only, once and no more,
Will have been—oh, how truly—worth it.

The years go by: March flows into April,
The sycamore's delicate tracery puts on
Its tender green; April is August soon;
Autumn, and the raving of insect choirs,
The thud of apples in moonlit orchards;

Till winter brings the slant, windy light again
On shining Manhattan, her towering stone and glass;
And age deepens—oh, much is taken, but one
Dearer than all remains, and life is sweet
Still to the now enlightened spirit.

Doors are opened that never before were opened,
New ways stand open, but quietly one door
Closes, the door to the future; there it is written,
"Thus far and no farther"—there, as at Eden's gate,
The angel with the fiery sword.

The Eden we dream of, the Eden that lies before us,
The unattainable dream, soon lies behind.
Eden is always yesterday or tomorrow,
There is no way now but back, back to the past—
The past has become paradise.

And there they dwell, those ineffable presences,
Safe beyond time, rescued from death and change.

Though all be taken, they only shall not be taken—-
Immortal, unaging, unaltered, faithful yet
To that lost dream world they inhabit.

Truly, to me they now may come no more,
But I to them in reverie and remembrance
Still may return, in me they still live on;
In me they shall have their being, till we together
Darken in the great memory.

Dear eyes of delight, dear youthful tresses, foreheads
Furrowed with age, dear hands of love and care—
Lying awake at dawn, I remember them,
With a love that is almost joy I remember them:
Lost, and all mine, all mine, forever.

—JOHN HALL WHEELOCK

THE DEATH ROOM

Look forward, truant, to your second childhood.
The crystal sphere discloses
Wallpaper roses mazily repeated
In pink and bronze, their bunches harboring
Elusive faces, under an inconclusive,
Circling, spidery ceiling craquelure,
And, by the window frame, the well-loathed, lame,
Damp-patch, crosspatch, sleepless L-for-Lemur,
Who, puffed to giant size,
Waits jealously till children close their eyes.

—ROBERT GRAVES

THE DECEPTRICES

Because they are not,
they paint their lips
and dress like whores.

Because they are uncertain,
they put on the bold
looks of experience.

This is their youth, too
soon gone, too soon
the unalterable conclusion.

—WILLIAM CARLOS WILLIAMS

THE DELTA

There are men making death together in the wood

We have not deserved this undergrowth
We have not merited this mud
O Jesus this mud

There are men making death together in the wood

My sergeant lies in a poisoned shadow
My friend has choked on a flower
The birds are incontinent in their terror

There are men making death together in the wood

They have taken my hands away
And they have hidden me from the moon
Pain makes decisions all around me

There are men making death together in the wood

The fish are puzzled among darkening knots of water
The ancient stairways of light ·sway and spill
The ferns are stained with the yellow blood of stones

There are men making death together in the wood

We have hidden the children for safety beneath the water
And the children are crying to us through the roots of the trees
They are soft pebbles without number
And they fill the streams

And the moon appears to watch now white with grief

See them now
Pilgrimming unwilling into dying
Unburdened now of blood
Their hurt bodies soaked with the dusk
See the reluctant file

In a line he leads them
In a long slow line

They leave us over the hill
They are grass
They are dust

They are shed stone
Cold as the moon

And the widow moon above
Is cold and white
And will let no lovers in tonight
   —MICHAEL DENNIS BROWNE

DESTROYING ANGEL

In this cool corner where dark stars of ivy
Make deep green heaven and the boles of holly
Are writhen with its hairy arms I sit,
Out of unseasonably hot September,
With book and deck chair. The noon-centered sun
Burns on the leafage and with golden pointels
Thrusts at the crevices, most being turned
By polished bucklers but the slippery few
Thin-showered between; so on the floor of mold
Swim watery sovereigns trembling in the dance
The seldom breeze makes, and, upon my page,
One like a spotlight glides from *freſshe* to *fayre*,
To *Laura* and other words of peace, *Diana*,
Daphnis, and all that history-buried rout
In Sidney's English. . . . Now in the cage of boughs,
The shadow-blackbird hops, the notes are fleeting:
The great bride opens and the sparkling groom
Comes winged with summer, and those cherubs lie
Locked in each alley; now the sweet hay
Goes tanned in barn-sheaves, but alone and green
I float withdrawn in moistness, and the cool
Is coiled like shawls about me, icy-blue.
Sheer plenitude. What antique world is this
Of still demeanor? *Wherefore, ſaid this Ladye,*
Conſider what Flours do lye aboute your feete,
Holeſome or nooxious? Ladye, there are none;
It is too dark, this is the garden's crypt
And suckles cryptogams—one stands before me,
Leaden-buff upon its obscene pillar,

A foot from my foot. I observe upon it
A green fly like an emerald pinhead crawling,
"*Aphis*, a common and most troublesome pest."
This toadstool is (I note the ruptured volva)
"Fool's-mushroom, Deathcap, or Destroying Angel,
Amanita phalloides, summer, in woods,
A deadly killer." Does that answer your question,
Ladye, are we there now? *Marke this Lorde's endeavor,*
Shee faid, and thanke him for't. Accepted kindly;
And the still nymph of silence like a statue
Stands bare before me, open, shielding nothing,
With hands dangling, not even the hair lifted
In passing air, transparent. . . . I might be
A man of any century now, although
Six hundred yards away the petroled highroad
Bears the rude complex engines of our shame,
And the sharp wristwatch ticking at my pulse
Half weds me to them. Ladye, we are in any
Summer of England and your eyes in mine
Promise a paradise of wells. So lead me.

And then the spotlight douses; even in that
Widest and even in that bluest heaven,
The black clouds come like fate's hands out of nothing,
Clenching the squeezed sun. Sudden blind and dazed
On a pink page in livid script I read now:
Soe reaching out his arme, his falfchion in it,
Meaning with that blow to have cleaved Amphialus
He ftrake with rage. The oother nimblie fhunned it:
Nay, thou fhalt not, he faid, thou Atomie.
A gust that's more a coldness of the blood
Than moving air trembles the inward branches. . . .
Last evening in the roses, with a squirt
I sprayed destruction on Amphialus,
Aphis, and other garden knights in green,
Turning the jointings of their little armor.
Shall not my hour come? Mushroom, cloud, and Atomie,
Fool's-mushroom, Deathcap, and Destroying Angel,
From Asia's heart or from New Mexico springing,
Nooxious, deadly killer, summer, in woods,
Spore-scattering of intolerable evil
Unguessable in Arcadia, the evergreen
From the world's birth shall be everblack and all,
Ladye, Aphis, Amphialus, and I,
Returned to chaos. . . . Though the shadow passes,
And sovereigns waltz once more, that coldness lingers;

The day is sour, my watch a time bomb, and
When, Aphis, you and I confront in roses,
Which is the pest and which the gardener?
We archers shoot our arrows at the sun—
Nay then, ʃhee ʃaid, do thus and I am done.
                              —HILARY CORKE

DIALOGUE

Oh father, answer me,
Why, why must money be?
The stones along the shore,
The leaves upon the tree

Are worth as much and more.
Why must we labor for
Our greasy greenery
When such fine things are free?

The leaf, alas, will die
And crumble in your hand,
And the stone's color dry
To dullness on the sand.

And only money, son,
Retains its character
When withered in the sun
Or dried in the salt air.

. . .
                              —HOWARD NEMEROV

THE DIAL TONE

A moment of silence first, then there it is;
But not as though it only now began
Because of my attention; rather, this:
That I begin at one point on its span
Brief kinship with its endless going on.

Between society and self it poses
Neutrality perceptible to sense,
Being a no man's land the lawyer uses
Much as the lover does. Charged innocence,
It sits on its own electrified fence,

Is neither pleased nor hurt by race results,
Or by the nasty thing John said to Jane,
Is merely interrupted by insults,
Devotions, lecheries; after the sane
And mad hang up at once, it will remain.

Suppose that, in God, a black bumblebee
Or colorless hummingbird buzzed all night,

Dividing the abyss up equally,
And carried its neither sweetness nor its light
Across impossible eternity.

Now take this hummingbird, this bee, away;
And, like the Cheshire smile without its cat,
The remnant hum continues on its way,
Unwinged, able at once to move and wait,
An endless freight train on an endless flat.

Something like that, some loneliest of powers
That never has confessed its secret name.
I do not doubt that if you gave it hours,
And then lost patience, it would be the same
After you left that it was before you came.

—HOWARD NEMEROV

DINOSAURS

We cannot trap them in our zoos, oh, no!
They seem to haunt us everywhere we go:
where deer tracks punctuate the forest paths,
they lumber through to dirty up the snow
and bring the highway and the telegraph;
through aisles of Shopwells pterodactyls skim;
they wedge between our actions and our dreams
and throw their shadows on our movie screens;
brontosaurs thump through private rooms
where Siamese delicately purl
between the porcelains, immune to gun-
smoke. They are the blocks of buildings we pile
up, the spreading empires of the history books
that edge along the spine of our preserves,
making us nervous though they have no nerves.
Bearing in bulk the weight they lack in wit,
they are our steady progress and the lack of it.

—CAROLYN STOLOFF

DISTANCES

On the hill's top we stood
　Neck back to see which star
Stood farthest; we had heard
　Some lights made turns so far
Through such deep space no man
　Knew of them; we had read
Some lights could not be known.
　"But they are nearer," I said,
"Than I to this my brother,
　The dark boy of my lies,
Than him the great stars bend over
　In inches from my eyes."

Indeed, man may not pierce
　Those bending circles, might
Conceivably not reach
　Even that first dome's light;
Yet this dark friend, my brother,
　Sets close to me his face,
And I could force that outer
　Sky before the space
That bars me from him. Eyes
　Look on me as I start
My hand to him. He says
　Nothing. I depart.

　　　　　　　　　　—JEREMY KINGSTON

THE DIVINE INSECT

Already it's late summer. Sunbathers go
Earlier now. Except for those who lie
Dazed between sea-music and radio,
The beach is bare as the blue bowl of the sky,
Where a cloud floats, solitary and slow.

Inland, when the slant evening sunbeams touch
Leaves, long obscured in tunnelled shade, to flame,
The divine insect, for I called him such,
Begins his high, thin music. To my shame,
I never learned what he was, who owe him so much.

Listening to his faint song, so pure, so dim,
I made my poems; he was mystery's decoy—
Something far and lost, just over the rim
Of being, or so I felt, and, as a boy,
I wove fantastic notions about him.

Throughout long evenings and hushed midnights when
Grasshoppers shrilled, his barely perceptible note
Wound on like a thread of time, while my pen
Made its own scratchy music as I wrote.
The divine insect and I were comrades then.

I could pass through that minuscule sound, it seemed to me,
As through a fine tube, getting smaller and still more small,

Until I was smaller than nothing—then, suddenly,
Come to the other end of the tube, and crawl
Out, into glittering infinity.

For if by travelling west you shall come east,
Or, as Einstein has it, the continuum
Curves on itself, may we not through the least
Come to the largest, and so finally come
Back where we were, undiminished and unincreased?

These few green acres where so many a day
Has found me, acres I have loved so long,
Have the whole heaven of stars for crown, and stay
Unspoiled by that. Here, in some thrush's song,
I have heard things that took my breath away.

It is a country out of the world's ken;
Time has no power upon it. Year on year,
Summer unfolds her pageant here again;
I have looked deep into all being here
Through one loved place, far from the storms of men.

Here often, day and night, there will be heard
The sea's grave rhythm, a dark undertone
Beneath the song of insect or of bird,
Sea-voices by sea-breezes landward blown,
And shudder of leaves by the soft sea-wind stirred.

In the jade light and gloom of woodland walks,
The spider lily and slender shinleaf stand,
The catbird from his treetop pulpit talks
The morning up, and, in the meadowland,
The velvet mullein lift their woolly stalks.

The world grows old. Ageless and undefiled
These stay—meadow and thicket, wood and hill.
The green fly wears her golden dress, the wild
Grape is in bloom, the fork-tailed swallow still
Veers on the wind as when I was a child.

And in mid-August, when the sun has set
And the first star out of the west shows through,
The divine insect, as I call him yet,
Begins his faint, thin note, so pure, so true,
Putting me ever deeper in his debt.

—JOHN HALL WHEELOCK

DIVISION

During the winter she began
  to notice things coming apart,
  dividing with no special plan
  into slabs and rounds. At the heart
of the wind that blew in the street,
  below the lengths of tan coffee
  smell, and river, and oily, sweet
  burning chicken bubbled the tree-
  sour flavor of wine. In the round,
  barking throats of dogs, stone teeth
    ground.

When she went inside, the heads,
  the arms, the eyes rained down on
    her
in a shower of sound; the reds,
  the deep bone grays were a blur
of noise—so loud that the ends

of her fingers became smooth and
    numb.
She could only speak to her friends,
she found, in a long, narrow hum
of transparent sound.

                              One evening,
moving quickly, simply trying
to make things whole, she got
    naked
onto an uptown bus, and would
not be hidden, would not be led;
and when they dragged her off, she
    could
see the lean tree of their arms
    spread
out and could hear each color they
    said.

—JOHN RATTI

THE DOUBLE

On other cloudy afternoons,
You will be sitting here or pacing
The rooms, your restless words
Unuttered. I put you there now
So the drama may continue, with pop-
    lars
Invoking the wind outside, the lamp-
    light
Slowly focussing to a pencil point.
Here, it is murdering an angel
In the very center of everywhere. This
    same

Joy shall be yours, drawing the blood
    out
Among these mazes that continue
Always, under the aspects
Of a cloudy day.
                    Mysterious the mazes
Of those afternoons through which
The red leaves sweep, your own hand
Tracing joyfully there another life
To live you on afternoons like this.

—IRVING FELDMAN

DREAM

<small>(AFTER COMING ON JEROME S. SHIPMAN'S COMMENT *
CONCERNING ACADEMIC APPOINTMENTS FOR ARTISTS)</small>

The committee—now a permanent body—
    formed to do but one thing,
discover positions for artists, was worried, then happy,
rejoiced to have magnetized Bach and his family
"to Northwestern," besides five harpsichords
    without which he would not leave home.
For his methodic unmetronomic melodic diversity
contrapuntally appointedly persistently
    irresistibly Fate-like Bach—find me words.

Expected to create for university
    occasions, inventions with wing,
was no problem after stiff master-classes (stiffer in Germany) . . .
each week a cantata; chorales, fugues, concerti!
  Here, students craved a teacher and each student worked.
    Jubilation! Re-rejoicings! Felicity!
    Repeated fugue-like, all of it, to infinity.
    (Note too that over-worked Bach was not irked.)

Haydn, when he had heard of Bach's billowing sail,
begged Prince Esterházy to lend him to Yale.
Master-mode expert fugue-al forms since, prevail.

    Dazzling nonsense . . . I imagine it? Ah! nach
    enough. J. Sebastian—born at Eisenach:
    its coat-of-arms in my dream: BACH PLAYS BACH!

                    —MARIANNE MOORE

THE DREAM

I

I met her as a blossom on a stem
Before she ever breathed, and in that dream
The mind remembers from a deeper sleep:
Eye learned from eye, cold lip from sensual lip.
My dream divided on a point of fire;
Light hardened on the water where we were;

---

* *Encounter*, July, 1965.

A bird sang low; the moonlight sifted in;
The water rippled, and she rippled on.

II

She came toward me in the flowing air,
A shape of change, encircled by its fire;
I watched her there, between me and the moon;
The bushes and the stones danced on and on;
I touched her shadow when the light delayed;
I turned my face away, and yet she stayed.
A bird sang from the center of a tree;
She loved the wind because the wind loved me.

III

Love is not love until love's vulnerable.
She slowed to sigh, in that long interval.
A small bird flew in circles where we stood;
The deer came down, out of the dappled wood.
All who remember, doubt. Who calls that strange?
I tossed a stone, and listened to its plunge.
She knew the grammar of least motion, she
Lent me one virtue, and I live thereby.

IV

She held her body steady in the wind;
Our shadows met, and slowly swung around;
She turned the field into a glittering sea;
I played in flame and water like a boy
And I swayed out beyond the white sea foam;
Like a wet log, I sang within a flame.
In that last while, eternity's confine,
I came to love, I came into my own.

—THEODORE ROETHKE

A DREAM OF GOVERNORS

The deepest dream is of mad governors.—*Mark Van Doren.*

The Knight from the world's end
Cut off the dragon's head.
The monster's only friend,
The Witch, insulting, fled.
The Knight was crowned and took
His Lady. Good and gay,

They lived in a picture book
Forever and a day.

Or else: When he had sat
So long, the King was old
And ludicrous and fat.

At feasts, when poets told
How he had shed the blood
Of dragons long ago,
He thought, Have I done good
To hear that I did so?

The chorus in a play
Declaimed, "The soul does well
Keeping the middle way."
He thought, That city fell;
Man's life is founded on
Folly at the extreme;
When all is said and done,
The City is a dream.

At night, the King alone
Went to the dragon's cave.

In moonlight, on a stone,
The Witch sat by the grave.
He grasped her by the hand
And said, "Grant what I ask!
Bring evil on the land
That I may have a task!"

The Queen has heard his tread;
She shuts the picture book.
The King stands by the bed.
In silence, as they look
Into each other's eyes,
They see a buried thing
That creeps, begins to rise,
And spreads the dragon's wing.

—LOUIS SIMPSON

DREAMSCAPE IN KÜMMEL

Upward through crystal in a kümmel bottle
a bare sprig branched into the vacancy,
and I was climbing, fly-size, in that subtle,
odd liqueur, up a flavor tree
on limbs so brittle that I thought I'd fall.

I held on helpless, lost, like dwindled Alice,
calling through thick, sweet emptiness for aid,
while all the bulging faces through the glass
dream or womb I hung in smiled and made
wavering pantomimes of friendliness.

And it was easy for the ones outside
to toast my plight with their complacent *crème*;
they only tasted from the other side,
sipping tiny samples on a stem,
the loneliness that I was drowning in.

—HAROLD WITT

DREAMS OF WATER

1

An odd silence
Falls as we enter
The cozy ship's bar.

The captain, smiling,
Unfolds his spyglass
And offers to show you

The obscure shapes
Of certain islands
Adrift in the offing.

I sit in silence.

2

People in raincoats
Stand looking out from
Ends of piers.

A fog gathers,
And little tugs,

Growing uncertain

Of their position,
Start to complain
With the deep and bearded

Voices of fathers.

3

The season is ending.
White verandas
Curve away.

The hotel seems empty,
But, once inside,
I hear a great splashing.

Behind doors,
Grandfathers loll
In steaming tubs,

Huge, unblushing.

—DONALD JUSTICE

DROPPING YOUR AITCHES

. . . *an* was formerly usual before an unaccented syllable be-
ginning with *h* (*an historical* work), but now that the *h* in
such words is pronounced the distinction has become pedantic,
& *a historical* should be said and written.—*From* A Dictionary
of Modern English Usage, *by* H. W. *Fowler.*

Stopping at an otel with an Ibernian
   Name or else an Elvetian,
He sat in a lobby with an exangular
   Outline, Roman or Grecian,
Furnished for the season with an ibis-
     cus
   Potted, or an ydrangea.
With an Avana between his lips,
   He did not feel a stranger.
Just then an ysterical female,
   An Erodias or an Ypatia,
But vastly too respectable

For an etaira or a geisha,
   In an abiliment foreign and wild,
   A Turkish or an Ispanic,
Approaching him, made an arangue
   That put him in a panic.
She seemed a creature of environment
   Not good, or of an eredity
Ill-judged, an aruspex out of her
     mind,
   Or an Egelian oddity.
For himself, he was neither an Ercu-
     lean

Form, an Ephaestus or an Yperion.
He wished her an armonious exit
  But prompt into the empyrean.
He puffed and he puffed and she dis-
    appeared,
  Either by an allucination
(An ypothesis not untenable)
  Or an ydraulic manipulation.
Those who don't drop their aitches
    will think

The whole thing an yperbole,
An Omeric fiction, an eroic way
  Of playing the ostrich verbally.
But those who consider the aitch to
    be
  Something purely metaphorical
Will swallow the story hook, line, and
    sinker
  As a true confession, an istorical.

—Joseph Warren Beach

THE DRUNKARDS

I

Notions of freedom are tied up with drink.
Our ideal life contains a tavern
Where man may sit and talk or just think,
All without fear of the nighted wyvern;
Or yet another tavern where it appears
There are no No Trust signs, no No Credit,
And, apart from the unlimited beers,
We sit unhackled, drunk, and mad to edit
Tracts of a really better land where man
May drink a finer, ah, an undistilled wine
That subtly intoxicates without pain,
Weaving the vision of the unassimilable inn
Where we may drink forever without owing,
With the door open, and the wind blowing.

II

The noise of death is in this desolate bar,
Where tranquillity sits bowed over its prayer
And music shells the dream of the lover,
But when no nickel brings this harsh despair
Into this loneliest of homes,
And of all dooms the loneliest yet,
When no electric music breaks the beat
Of hearts to be doubly broken but now set
By the surgeon of peace in the splint of woe,
Pierces more deeply than trumpets do
The motion of the mind into that web
Where disorders are as simple as the tomb
And the spider of life sits, sleep.

—Malcolm Lowry

DURING DECEMBER'S DEATH

The afternoon turned dark early;
The light suddenly faded;
The dusk was black although elsewhere the first star in the cold sky whistled;
And I thought I heard the fresh scraping of the flying steel of boys on roller
    skates
Rollicking over the asphalt in 1926,
And I thought I heard the dusk and silence raided
By a calm voice commanding consciousness:
Wait: wait: wait as if you had always waited
And as if it had always been dark
And as if the world had been from the beginning
A lost and drunken ark in which the only light
Was the dread and white of the terrified animals' eyes.
And then, turning on the light, I took a book
That I might gaze upon another's vision of the abyss of consciousness—
The hope, and the pain of hope, and the patience of hope, and its torment, its
    astonishment, its endlessness.

—Delmore Schwartz

THE DUSK OF HORSES

Right under their noses, the green
Of the field is paling away
Because of something fallen from the
    sky.

They see this, and put down
Their long heads deeper in grass
That only just escapes reflecting them

As the dream of a millpond would.
The color green flees over the grass
Like an insect, following the red sun
    over

The next hill. The grass is white.

There is no cloud so dark and white at
    once;
There is no pool at dawn that deepens

Their faces and thirsts as this does.
Now they are feeding on solid
Cloud, and, one by one,

With nails as silent as stars among the
    wood
Hewed down years ago and now rot-
    ten,
The stalls are put up around them.

—James Dickey

DYING: AN INTRODUCTION

> Always too eager for future, we
> Pick up bad habits of expectancy.
> —*Philip Larkin.*

I. RING AND WALK IN

Summer still plays across the street,
An ad-hoc band
In red, white, blue, and green
Old uniforms
And rented instruments;
Fall fills the street
From shore to shore with leaves,
A jaundiced mass
Protest against the cold;
I slip on ice
Slicks under powder snow and stamp my feet
Upon the doctor's rubber mat,
Ring and Walk In
To Dr. Sharon's waiting room—
For once, with an appointment,
To nonplus
Ugly Miss Erberus.
Across from other candidates—
A blue-rinsed dam
In Davidows, a husk
Of an old man,
A one-eyed boy—I sit
And share their pervigilium.
One *Punch* and two
Times later comes the call.

II. PROBABLY NOTHING

Head cocked like Art, the *Crimson* linotype
Operator, Dr. Sharon plays
Taps on my game leg, spelling out the name,
With his palpating fingers, of my pain.
The letters he types are not visible
To him or me; back up the melting pot
Of the machine, the matrix dents the hot
Lead with a letter and another; soon a word,
Tinkling and cooling, silver, will descend
To be imposed upon my record in
Black-looking ink. "My boy, I think," he says,
In the most masterly of schoolish ways,

In the most quiet of all trumps in A
Flat, "this lump is probably nothing, but"—
A but, a buzz of omen resonates—
"I'd check it anyway. Let's see when I
Can take a specimen." Quiet business
With the black phone's bright buttons. Sst, ssst, st:
An inside call. In whispers. Over. Out.
"Can you come Friday noon? We'll do it then."
I nod I can, and pass the world of men
In waiting, one *Life* further on.

III. O.P.O.R.

Undressing in the locker room
Like any high school's, full of shades
In jockstraps and the smell of steam,
Which comes, I guess, from autoclaves,
And not from showers, I am struck
By the immutability,
The long, unchanging, childish look
Of my pale legs propped under me,
Which, nonetheless, now harbor my
Nemesis, or, conceivably,
Do not. My narcissistic eye
Is intercepted deftly by
A square nurse in a gas-green gown
And aqua mask—a dodo's beak—
Who hands me a suit to put on
In matching green, and for my feet
Two paper slippers, mantis green:
My invitation to the dance.
I shuffle to the table, where
A shining bank of instruments—
Service for twelve—awaits my flesh
To dine. Two nurses pull my pants
Down and start shaving. With a splash,
The Doctor stops his scrubbing-up
And walks in with a quiet "Hi."
Like hummingbirds, syringes tap
The Novocain and sting my thigh
To sleep, and the swordplay begins.
The stainless-modern knife digs in—
Meticulous trencherman—and twangs
A tendon faintly. Coward, I groan.
Soon he says, "Sutures," and explains
To me he has his specimen
And will stitch up, with boundless pains,
Each severed layer, till again

He surfaces and sews with steel
Wire. "Stainless." Look how thin it is,
Held in his forceps. "It should heal
Without a mark." These verities
Escort me to the tiring room,
Where, as I dress, the Doctor says,
"We'll have an answer Monday noon."
I leave to live out my three days,
Reprieved from findings and their pain.

IV. PATH. REPORT

Bruisingly cradled in a Harvard chair
Whose orange arms cramp my pink ones, and whose black
Back stamps my back with splat marks, I receive
The brunt of the pathology report,
Bitingly couched in critical terms of my
Tissue of fabrications, which is bad.
That Tyrian specimen on the limelit stage
Surveyed by Dr. Cyclops, magnified
Countless diameters on its thick slide,
Turns out to end in -oma. "But be glad
These things are treatable today," I'm told.
"Why, fifteen years ago—" a dark and grave-
Shaped pause. "But now, a course of radiation, and—"
Sun rays break through. "And if you want X-ray,
You've come to the right place." A history,
A half-life of the hospital. Marie
Curie must have endowed it. Cyclotrons,
Like missile silos, lurk within its walls.
It's reassuring, anyway. But bland
And middle-classic as these environs are,
And sanguine as his measured words may be,
And soft his handshake, the webbed, inky hand
Locked on the sill and the unshaven face
Biding outside the window still appall
Me as I leave the assignation place.

V. OUTBOUND

Outside, although November by the clock,
Has a thick smell of spring,
And everything—
The low clouds lit
Fluorescent green by city lights;
The molten, hissing stream
Of white car lights cooling
To red and vanishing;
The leaves,

Still running from last summer, chattering
Across the pocked concrete;
The wind in trees;
The ones and twos,
The twos and threes
Of college girls,
Each shining in the dark,
Each carrying
A book or books,
Each laughing to her friend
At such a night in fall;
The two-and-twos
Of boys and girls who lean
Together in an A and softly walk
Slowly from lamp to lamp,
Alternatively lit
And nighted; Autumn Street,
Astonishingly named, a rivulet
Of asphalt twisting up and back
To some spring out of sight—and everything
Recalls one fall
Twenty-one years ago, when I,
A freshman, opening
A green door just across the river,
Found the source
Of spring in that warm night,
Surprised the force
That sent me on my way
And set me down
Today. Tonight. Through my
Invisible new veil
Of finity, I see
November's world—
Low scud, slick street, three giggling girls—
As, oddly, not as sombre
As December,
But as green
As anything:
As spring.

                                        —L. E. Sissman

E

EARLINESS AT THE CAPE

The color of silence is the oyster's color
Between the lustres of deep night and dawn.
Earth turns to absence; the sole shape's the sleeping
Light—a mollusk of mist. Remote,
A sandspit hinges the valves of that soft monster
Yawning at Portugal. Alone wakeful, lanterns
Over a dark hull to eastward mark
The tough long pull, hidden, the killing
Work, hidden, to feed a hidden world.
Muteness is all. Even the greed of the gulls
Annulled, the hush of color everywhere
The hush of motion. This is the neap of the blood,
Of memory, thought, desire; if pain visits
Such placelessness, it has phantom feet.
What's physical is lost here in ignorance
Of its own being. That solitary boat,
Out fishing, is a black stroke on vacancy.
Night, deaf and dumb as something from the deeps,
Having swallowed whole bright yesterday, replete
With radiance, is gray as abstinence now.
But in this nothingness, a knife point: pleasure
Comes pricking; the hour's pallor, too, is bladed
Like a shell, and as it opens, cuts.
—Babette Deutsch

EARTH AND FIRE

All do not seek the exalted fire;
All do not let the moment bless.
And yet what so rewards desire,
So nourishes? Confess:
He's wrong who toils for less.

Measure the ground and weigh its
    yield,

Changing the crops while seasons
    turn.
Yet who can say a barren field
Where the dry brambles burn
Brings not the best return?

Then the fine breath of wintry air
Answers the crisp and stubborn earth.

Without the exaltation there
Uniting death and birth,
What is a man's song worth?

Earth's natural order brings a wealth

Of promise, bounty, and regret.
Through changes he alone has health
And writes off all the debt
Whose heart on heaven is set.

—VERNON WATKINS

EARTH TREMOR IN LUGANO

Open the window on the high
Balcony whose frail white grate
Glows with geranium flames against a
    sky
Of blue as soft as soot, and overhangs
The grand piano of the lake,
Dropping its coals of petals that
The winds of summer shake
With sudden bangs.

A sound of water
Drops like stones
And with a clatter
Smashes the aspidistras in
The stunned courtyard.

A smattering of tiles
Drops past the window
Like red snow,
The bed seems
To thump down steps,
And the portrait of a nun,

Worked in shivery sequins,
Frantically shakes its head at us
From the flaking wall.

We sit up in bed, and this
Makes the balcony outside
The creepered window rend
Its wrought-iron scrollwork,
Which, with a smothered crash,
Drops into a tree in a shower of
Blossom and birds.

After the balcony,
Our brass bed flops
Into the accommodating tree.

We lie there waiting for the firemen,
And staring up at the house that
    wears
Telephone wires like a shawl.

—JAMES KIRKUP

THE EDGE OF DAY

The dawn's precise pronouncement
    waits
With breath of light indrawn,
Then forms with smoky, smut-red lips
The great O of the sun.

The moldering atoms of the dark
Blaze into morning air;

The birdlike stars droop down and
    die,
The starlike birds catch fire.

The thrush's tinder throat strikes up,
The sparrow chips hot sparks
From flinty tongue, and all the sky
Showers with electric larks.

And my huge eye a chaos is
Where molten worlds are born;
Where floats the eagle's flaming
    moon,
And crows, like clinkers, burn;

Where blackbirds scream with comet
    tails,
And flaring finches fall,

And starlings, aimed like meteors,
Bounce from the garden wall;

Where, from the edge of day, I spring
Alive for mortal flight,
Lit by the heart's exploding sun
Bursting from night to night.

—LAURIE LEE

ELEGY

The gnu up at the zoo
Has closed his eyes in death;
He was a very patient gnu
Who never made too much to-do
Until he was out of breath.
Few there were understood him,
Very few understood him.
Now he is gone
I mourn alone
That most untimely death.

The ape who had no shape
Went over the hill today;
He always wanted to escape
Until he discovered a way—
And he closed his eyes
In sheer surprise

When he found he was dead, they
    say.
Many there are will mourn him,
Many who once did scorn him,
And some there are will pray.

I pray every day
For all things that draw breath:
For the ape and the gnu
Up at the zoo,
For the turtledove and the tiger too,
I pray with every breath.
But chiefly for myself I pray,
And for the staring fish that may
Not close their eyes by night or day—
No, not even in death.

—JOHN HALL WHEELOCK

ELEGY: E. W.

Ah, comic officer and gentleman,
Kneeling on stone and falling through the air
In R.M. battle dress, sitting a horse,
Marrying gentry, getting a divorce,
Rushing the Season up to Town, and then
Reclusing it in Zomerzet again,
Rising above your station, taking train
From it to the interior of the brain,
Sending up slyly your establishers,
Turning the world off with a click, a curse
From your stark armory of bolted words,
Mimicking to the life, the death, the fools
Through whose void headpieces Britannia rules

Her residue, impersonating an
Irascible, irrational old man
Full of black humors and still darker flights
Beyond aphotic shores on jetty nights
To madness real or bogus, telling all
To a confessor in a grated stall
And stepping shriven, bent, and arrogant
From holy mutter into worldly cant,
Embracing traces of the English past
In all their fossil arbitrariness,
Embodying Highgate's mezzo sentiment
And Mayfair's sopranino *ton,* and yet,
As well, the ground bass of Commercial Street,
You wrote us, first and last, in permanent
Ink and perduring words, a testament
Of how it was in our uneven years:
Laughter in bed, our long index of fears,
Bad manners, time killed callously, a war
Always impending, love abandoned for
Short-term investments, and at long term's end
Aloneness's monolith on every hand.

Ironic officer and gentleman,
We say goodbye with a slight tear perhaps
Ironic in intent also, although
As grave and serious at heart as you.

—L. E. SISSMAN

ELEGY IN A THEATRICAL WAREHOUSE

They have laid the penthouse scenes away, after a truly phenomenal run,
And taken apart the courtroom, and the bright, shiny office, and laid them all
    away with the cabin in the clearing, where the sun slowly rose through a
    smashing third act.
And the old family mansion on the road above the mill has been gone a long
    time,
And the road is gone,
The road that never did lead to any mill at all.

The telephone is gone, the phone that rang and rang and never did connect with
    any other phone,
And the great steel safe, where no diamonds ever were.
They have taken down the pictures, portraits of ancestors lost and unclaimed, that
    hung on the massive walls,
And taken away the books that reached the study ceiling,
The rows and rows of books bound in leather and gold, with nothing, nothing,
    nothing inside,

And the bureaus and the chests that were empty to the brim,
And the pistols that brought down so many, many curtains with so many, many
   blanks.

Almost everything is gone,
Everything that never held a single thing at all.

—KENNETH FEARING

THE ELM SPEAKS

I know the bottom, she says. I know it with my great tap root.
It is what you fear.
I do not fear it; I have been there.

Is it the sea you hear in me,
Its dissatisfactions?
Or the voice of nothing that was your madness?

Love is a shadow.
How you lie and cry after it!
Listen. These are its hooves. It has gone off, like a horse.

All night I shall gallop thus, impetuously,
Till your head is a stone, your pillow a little turf,
Echoing, echoing.

Or shall I bring you the sound of poisons?
This is rain now, this big hush.
And this is the fruit of it: tin-white, like arsenic.

I have suffered the atrocity of sunsets.
Scorched to the root,
My red filaments burn and stand, a hand of wires.

Now I break up in pieces that fly about like clubs.
A wind of such violence
Will tolerate no bystanding; I must shriek.

The moon, also, is merciless; she would drag me
Cruelly, being barren.
Her radiance scathes me. Or perhaps I have caught her.

I let her go. I let her go,
Diminished and flat, as after radical surgery.
How your bad dreams possess and endow me!

I am inhabited by a cry.
Nightly it flaps out,
Looking, with its hooks, for something to love.

I am terrified by this dark thing
That sleeps in me;
All day I feel its soft, feathery turnings, its malignity.

Clouds pass and disperse.
Are those the faces of love, those pale irretrievables?
Is it for such I agitate my heart?

I am incapable of more knowledge.
What is this, this face
So murderous in its strangle of branches?

Its snaky acids hiss.
It petrifies the will. These are the isolate, slow faults
That kill, that kill, that kill.

—SYLVIA PLATH

THE EMPTY HOUSE

Then, when the child was gone,
I was alone
In the house, suddenly grown huge.
  Each noise
Explained itself away
As bird, or creaking board, or mouse,
Element or animal.
But mostly there was quiet as after
    battle
Where round the room still lay
The soldiers and the paintbox and the
    toys.
But when I went to tidy these away,
I felt my mind swerve:
My body was the house,
And everything he'd touched, an ex-
    posed nerve.

—STEPHEN SPENDER

THE ENDING

(TOKYO: A WOMAN SPEAKS)

Should I not be ashamed
to lie on this brocade-covered bed
making these terrible noises out of my mouth,
like a shot rabbit or a dog hit by a car?

I go on screaming. I am not ashamed,
for are we also not animals,
born in another's blood, dying in our own?

I have been this way since yesterday noon.
It was precisely noon.
After looking at your posed face looking
toward that other woman posing by the pond,
I could do nothing but look at my foolish watch,
steadily ticking as if time were important.

In that garden where trees and blades of grass
were put in a careful order, she was a wholly
artificial creature, trying to be
more fluid than water, more supple than fish.
The day disintegrated around my feet.
I stamped the pieces into the soft ground.

Looking up at the burning sun, I opened
my eyes wide and silently screamed, "Blind me!"

The unmoved sun merely
put a dark dazzle inside my head.
I looked again at my watch,
whose tick was a second pulsebeat on my wrist,
as if I really had somewhere to go,
as if there were really anyplace I could go.

A distant bell struck twelve times, telling the world
my love had just drowned in the pond.

Sunlight and time dripped out of my eyes.
I saw you suddenly in your full nature,
the tenderly tended, artificial man,
bones brilliant as porcelain,
eyes blue enamel baked in your head,
your face a fan opened to prove
every line of the landscape painted there.

Now I weep, in a woman's way,
less for the loss of love
than for the revolting view of your weakness,
naked there in the sun,
the little boy, whining for one more kite.

I scream. I am not ashamed.

And yet this evening, at the hot window,
I felt that the horrible sun had set
not in the sky but there on my consumed hands
still burning from their final touch of you.

—PAUL ENGLE

ENDLESS

Under the tall black sky you look out of your body
lit by a white flare of the time between us
your body with its touch its weight smelling of new wood
as on the day the news of battle reached us
falls beside the endless river
flowing to the endless sea
whose waves come to this shore a world away.

Your body of new wood your eyes alive barkbrown of treetrunks
the leaves and flowers of trees stars all caught in crowns of trees
your life gone down, broken into endless earth
no longer a world away but under my feet and everywhere
I look down at the one earth under me,
through to you and all the fallen
the broken and their children born and unborn
of the endless war.

—Muriel Rukeyser

THE END OF THE PARADE

The sentence undulates,
raising no song;
it is too old, the
words of it are falling
apart. Only percussion
notes continue
with weakening
emphasis what was once
all honeyed sounds
full of sweet breath.

—William Carlos Williams

ENGLISH BEACH MEMORY: MR. THUDDOCK

Outside that bulbous Babylon
    Of sepia-faced princes who played cricket,
    Of prophetesses on vacation with enormous sleeves and shaven dogs whimper-
        ing in woollen coats,
    Of ancient actors who had grown masks with beaks;
In short, outside the Hotel Superb,

Motionless for hours sat Mr. Thuddock
On the box of his cab of black leather,
 Its varnish split by age
 Into crinkling saurian wrinkles—
  A vessel, it seemed, floating high in air,
  A black vessel poised on an asphalt mirage,
  Cupping the sky high up above the sea,
And he,
  An idol in a top hat,
  With tilted eyebrows and face impassive.

With his whip upright beside him,
Its lash pendent in the air,
He might resemble, too, an angler
On a day of summer, in a clearing over a pool,
As he baited his hook with his voice, warm and wheedling,
  "Cab, sir?" "Cab, m'lady?"
As he waited so patiently for those cold fish, the customers, to bite,
To issue timidly from the depths, weedy with gilding,
And fin their way past the palm trees and the porters.

Sooner or later he would land them,
 Then trundle his precious load of fringes, laces, flounces, Pomeranian dogs,
 The cab rumbling o'er seaside aerial bridges
(Fragile and glistening as those of the spider), vibrant,
Spanning the far-down green tumuli of the treetops.
 An idol was he then again,
 Clad in the bold gold robes of the sunlight,
 Or a pagod, perhaps, conveying other idols to safety,
 Idols in search of salt air to embalm
 Their centuries of convalescence.

In the winter,
 The shut cab would rock in the wind
 And would smell of oats and of beer,
 But the jobs were few;
And Mr. Thuddock would sit in the cabmen's red-tiled temple,
Eating eggs, consuming steamy air,
For later he must wait under the flat yellow windows
Of the enormous night for hours;
Then the rain would tattoo upon the black drum of his top hat,
Or, till he threshed his arms and shifted it,
The snow would lie upon his shoulders
As tonight it lies so lightly
On the cold granite slab that covers his bones.

       —Osbert Sitwell

THE ENIGMA

Mine will last though others fall to dust.
He began to row across the flaming lake.
Acrid fumes were sweet as the unexplained.
Tears ran down his face all day
As on those whirling came, as come they must.
In his gutted heart bell's memories would break.

Mine will stay though others live in hate.
The lake was vile with forms tormenting mind,
The fumes through tears were dear reality.
They came believing but they faded in the maze
As he rode on time's mystery of fate.
Change as they would, there was no other kind.

Mine will survive though others fall to dust.
He neared the dark escarpment and white pall,
Crying in a wilderness of forms,
His head fiery, his heart hearing ancient bells.
They came to judgment, as come all must,
He thought he felt the meaning of the fall.

It had to do with struggles in the night,
With breakless Adam and still breakless Eve,
The ever oncome, the will to row in fire,
Bells bringing memories of helps long gone.
Though he hailed them, hurled them out of sight,
His would survive, though never to him cleave.

—Richard Eberhart

THE ENIGMA VARIATIONS

Lying in the dark music,
thinking of faceless friends,
or those kept whole but marred
by envy or turned self-hate,
and Father's upturned face
fishing the lily ponds
of pain, alone, the moon
bandaging his head,

and all good children grown
up to the four winds,
tears move upon my face
like half notes on a sheet,
and I would be a grave
walked on by stones to keep
even a moldering faith,
though time is the heart of music.

—Paul Petrie

ENNUI

GLACIER ACCIDENT KILLS SKI PARTY; ONE BODY STILL MISSING—*Headline.*

Trapped me in ice. No, not one chink is gaping.
How many eons now before I melt?
I wait the shattering kiss the sun withheld
And long to join the free and jumping dead.
My walls turn all things blue, through which I see
Blue generations born and die, escaping
In happy twirling ghost-swarms, all but me,
The only ghost on earth with wings unspread.

Outside, my bodiless sisters frisk and dive.
I'd show them speed, could I but get away.
Alas, alas, the snows that froze me dead
Have sealed me in my old lugubrious clay,
The only ghost on earth who isn't gay.
When I consider all that waits ahead—
Years, years of boredom in my icy bed,
No books to read and not one game to play—

Sometimes I almost wish I were alive.

—PETER VIERECK

EPILOGUE FOR A MASQUE OF PURCELL

Beast and bird must bow aside,
Grimbald limp into the wings,
All that's lovely and absurd,
All that dances, all that sings

Folded into trunks again—
The haunted grove, the starlit air—
All turns workaday and plain,
Even the happy, happy pair.

Harpsichord and trumpet go
Trundling down the dusty hall.
That airy joy, that postured woe,
Like the black magician's spell,

Fall in pieces round us now
While the dancer goes to lie

With the king, and need not know
He will jilt her by-and-by.

We were young once and are old;
Have watched the dragon die before;
Knew the innocent and bold,
Saw them through the cardboard door

Kiss the guilty and afraid,
Turning human soon enough.
We have wept with the betrayed,
Never known them die for love.

Yet, since nothing's done by halves
While illusion's yet to do,
May we still forgive ourselves,
And dance again when trumpets blow.

—ADRIENNE CECILE RICH

ERRANTRY

The baby wades alone across the lawn,
Intrepid, with his golden head upright,
Each step a stubbing, as though riding on

Stilts already at a giant's height;
Then down he plunks on his great snowy seat
Of diaper in the ant's land, in the sunlight

Hot on the smudgy toes of both his feet.
Rages of infancy! How he could cry!
But man's attempt he loves and will repeat,

Surging and teetering, with impassioned eye,
To reach the wildwood lilac shade, and enter
Under the Persian leaves where the kittens lie,

Green-eyed, bedizened, at the dappled center.
—Robert Fitzgerald

ESSAY ON LUNCH

Quick lunch! quick lunch! the neon cries, and I,
Dismayed by an eating on the fly,
As you perhaps anticipate, reply:
Slow lunch! With beer, meat, gravy, pudding, pie.
Who is it that, for lunch, could really wish
A little salad, on a little dish?
Or a cup of soup, lukewarm for gulping quick?
Or candy bar? Or ice cream on a stick?
Or hot dog gobbled at a hot-dog stand?
Or Coke, or Pepsi, or some other brand?
Our lunches, like our jets, designed for speed,
Hardly begin to meet the nation's need.
Not so the workingman, whose noon repast
Is seldom eaten light, and never fast.
The foreman's whistle calls him from his spade
To one full hour recumbent in the shade,
Where, as the sweat cools on his honest brow,
He leisurely attacks his honest chow.
His back against a tree in perfect ease,
He takes enormous bites of bread and cheese—
A clear reproof to that white-collar class
That will not trust its pants to God's green grass.

The mighty sandwiches of beef and ham,
Of peanut butter, apple butter, jam,
Three hard-boiled eggs, six pickles, followed by
A huge and oozing slab of lemon pie,
Prepare the workingman to undertake,
Refreshed and braced, a chunk of chocolate cake.
We'll leave him here as he removes his shoes
And curls up underneath his tree, to snooze.
    Our drugstore fare must all the more displease
When we reflect on lunches overseas,
Where every Frenchman is a skilled gourmet,
And Spaniards take siestas every day.
The German waitress, seeing one sit down,
Makes for one's table, not with pad and frown
And tiny glass of water (as done here)
But with a stalwart, smiling stein of beer,
Assuming—and why not?—that anyone
Would gladly have his *Mahlzeit* thus begun.
She brings then loads of heavy German food,
Promoting heavy German lassitude,
And many a German, after such a snack,
Spends many an afternoon flat on his back.
    Far as we are, a long and liquid span,
From lunch by such a European plan,
Far as we are, as well, from workingmen,
By habit, on a bourgeois regimen,
This is the best advice you'll get from me:
Pack heavy lunch pails—or pack two or three—
And take them to your offices, and eat
In quantity and leisure. Prop your feet
(Shoeless, of course) against the window sill,
And let the hasty hustle, if they will.

                   —WALKER GIBSON

ESTUARY

As the image of the sun
after the blinding moment
lasts on the closed lids violet
an instant, and color comes
across the tight eye's darkness
though the source of light has gone,

so when I take the low lane
between the fields of barley,

with the slither of a sea
wind sucking the sun-cracked husks,
to gaze at the sunken hulks
of ships as they flake at noon

in the lapped inlet, I can
recall that, with the tiderace
of boyhood just begun, once
I ran down the jetty steps,

stubbing up pebbles, and stopped
to stare at a bark broken

in three across the open
mud flat, each part with a mast
still and splintering spars, fast
in banks of sand. And though I
remember the terror my
eyes saw treading the decks on

that bright morning with the wind
light now—the wind that had
          smashed
that great ship fallen, awash
like driftwood, ribbed in fitful

patches of water—yet still
I would wish to be alone

with the loneliness of then:
and free to make my horrors
walk the boards beyond the shore
at the bidding of my will
only, with the power, as well
as to make, to efface them

by turning to see the men
with bright-bandanna faces
gladdening the noonday as
they picked the purple winkles
like scatterings of damsons
with salt dried like bloom on them.

—TED WALKER

THE ETERNAL RETURN

Along how many Main Streets have I walked,
Greeting my friends, commenting on the weather,
Carrying bundles, wondering as I talked
If the brown paper bags would hold together—

At Christmastime with white breath blowing thin,
In spring when garden tidings are exchanged,
In autumn with the darkness closing in
And all the winter's work to be arranged.

Wherever I have lived—and many places
Have briefly seemed my permanent abode—
The shops on Main Street and the passing faces,
Beyond all history and change of mode,

Remain the same. And if, while on a walk,
I should encounter people who belong
In Main Streets of my past, I'd stop to talk
Without suspecting anything was wrong.

Even if I met someone who was dead,
I would discount the fact as in a dream.

Here things that lie behind are still ahead,
And calendars less final than they seem.

External accidents of time and space
Become, on Main Street, but illusory errors,
As all my incarnations, face to face,
Repeat themselves like people in two mirrors.

I greet acquaintances unchanged as I,
Stop for a moment, comment on the weather,
And at the corner, as I say goodbye,
Pray God my paper bundles hold together.
— ROBERT HILLYER

ETERNITIES

"I'm rich,"
said
Irish
derby,
slopping
a drink
on the floor.
"So I've always
missed
the pleasures
of the poor."

"Taste his spit!"
said the sawdust.
"It's a scandal
and a shame."

"Naught but outer limbo,"
said the roach
on his way
to the door,
said the roach
on his way,
on his fraught-filled
way, on his fraught-
filled way to the door,
and toward
a stair of his own.

(When he reached
the cracked enamel
in the kitchen
of his pad,
he made a
tour
of quarters,
leaving molecules
like pennies
on the oilcloth
of the poor—
five molecules
of Scotch
on every
plate.)

But the fumes had drunk
his mind to stuff,
and roachie slept
an emperor's sleep,
dreaming of previous lives,
in derby hats,
when he had slopped
the whiskey
to the floor,
crying for the pleasures
of the poor.
— NORMAN MAILER

ET QUID AMABO NISI QUOD AENIGMA EST

Then watching the unposed beggars pose
I saw the subjects that occasion offered him
doubtless never intrigued the master
as they intrigue us:
Harvest, the Kermesse, Justitia, Skating.
He took down suffering—and those insanely
rush-hour comments on where some action was—
first as a means to chaffer his betters, those
lumpish onlooker burghers, too often viewed
at a distance.
                    Obviously, though, he was
moved by dolts; the highly sketchable maimed;
the cloaks in which you feel fleas mincing
and see where rats, by night, nibble. Just what
inner occasion let him see things—
                    things as they were—
is not clear; only that he needed them.

Take "Blind Peasant, Begging"—the dazzled eye,
wild stare of a winter deer begging food or
safe passage from where he's been cornered. But
smiling, incongruously—a wily smile,
up-to-no-good, you think. Yet the whole body
in rapt and freehold peace. Not ignorance, this
indifference to the pains which make him up.

            Or take all these little fellows
clumping about with hats over their eyes
all looking squashed, like dwarfs, chin flush with chest
and neck sinking its root in shoulder thew:
this swirl of dying dancers might have been called
"Ataraxy Among the Accident-Prone"
or "Survival Through Indifference, As Seen
in the Peasants of Breughel."
                                After so many
scrapes as patently planed their knotty faces
the living showed through; lives, like their profiles,
gathered a certain definition from
cold fires and dry trenchers. Chill days grew light
and marvellous when each got circumscribed,
like three-time losers the second time around.

I thought of others: people I knew, whose smiles
stolidly flickered like home movies; some who
displayed lapsed attitudes, say, toward going out
in the rain (without coat or rubbers) all day;

the crowded minds, decreeing against the crowd,
or sailing alone at night in rising weather.

Madness may well
be a crowded mind. But fury comes to the
stripped life. The soul that would survive its strife
grows
accident-prone, carefully careless
with its flesh. —Not the stink, taste,
the sore of having been so wanting long,
the dizzy or the colic of haste

it is the *against*,
the gainsaying of the hap bidding
hapless to death's gain: deathward, weighted,
wearied sunless, the cringing, the hulk strange
of a presence, a space change, a win time dons
when you gag in the gorge of the timing,
the falling, the false surrender:
sleeping in doorways, sailing alone at night,
who wryly bear their limps, their abdominal
pains, all mornings after, hanging and hanging,
lousy shirts, the pocked forearm, and scarred wrist.

—STEPHEN SANDY

EVENING

I called him to come in,
The wide lawn darkened so.
Laughing, he held his chin
And hid beside a bush.
The light gave him a push;
Shadowy grass moved slow.
He crept on agile toes
Under a sheltering rose.

His mother, still beyond
The bare porch and the door,
Called faintly, out of sound,
And vanished with her voice.
I caught his curious eyes
Measuring me, and more—
The light dancing behind
My shoulder in the wind.

Then, struck beyond belief
By the child's voice I heard,

I saw his hair turn leaf,
His dancing toes divide
To hoofs on either side,
One hand become a bird.
Startled, I held my tongue
To hear what note he sang.

Where was the boy gone now?
I stood on the grass, alone.
Swung from the apple bough,
The bees ignored my cry.
A dog roved past, and I
Turned up a sinking stone,
But found beneath no more
Than grasses dead last year.

Suddenly, lost and cold,
I knew the yard lay bare.
I longed to touch and hold
My child, my talking child,

Laughing or tame or wild,
Solid in light and air,
The supple hands, the face
To fill that barren place.

Slowly, the leaves descended,
The birds resolved to hands;
Laugh, and the charm was ended,
The hungry boy stepped forth.
He stood on the hard earth,
Like one who understands

Fairy and ghost, but less
Our human loneliness.

Then, on the withering lawn
He walked beside my arm.
Trees and the sun were gone,
Everything gone but us.
His mother sang in the house,
And kept our supper warm,
And loved us, God knows how,
The wide earth darkened so.

—James Wright

AN EVENING OF RUSSIAN POETRY

". . . seems to be the best train. Miss Ethel Winter of the
Department of English will meet you at the station and . . ."
—*From a letter addressed to the visiting speaker.*

The subject chosen for tonight's discussion
is everywhere, though often incomplete:
when their basaltic banks become too steep,
most rivers use a kind of rapid Russian,
and so do children talking in their sleep.
My little helper at the magic lantern,
insert that slide and let the colored beam
project my name or any such like phantom
in Slavic characters upon the screen.
The other way, the other way. I thank you.

On mellow hills the Greek, as you remember,
fashioned his alphabet from cranes in flight;
his arrows crossed the sunset, then the night.
Our simple skyline and a taste for timber,
the influence of hives and conifers,
reshaped the arrows and the borrowed birds.
Yes, Sylvia?

"Why do you speak of words
when all we want is knowledge crisply browned?"

Because all hangs together—shape and sound,
heather and honey, vessel and content.
Not only rainbows—every line is bent,
and skulls and seeds and all good worlds are round,
like Russian verse, like our colossal vowels:

those painted eggs, those glossy pitcher flowers
that swallow whole a golden bumblebee,
those shells that hold a thimble and the sea.
Next question.

"Is your prosody like ours?"

Well, Emmy, our pentameter may seem
to foreign ears as if it could not rouse
the limp iambus from its pyrrhic dream.
But close your eyes and listen to the line.
The melody unwinds; the middle word
is marvellously long and serpentine:
you hear one beat, but you have also heard
the shadow of another, then the third
touches the gong, and then the fourth one sighs.

It makes a very fascinating noise;
it opens slowly, like a grayish rose
in pedagogic films of long ago.

The rhyme is the line's birthday, as you know,
and there are certain customary twins
in Russian as in other tongues. For instance,
love automatically rhymes with blood,
nature with liberty, sadness with distance,
humane with everlasting, prince with mud,
moon with a multitude of words, but sun
and song and wind and life and death with none.

Beyond the seas where I have lost a sceptre,
I hear the neighing of my dappled nouns,
soft participles coming down the steps,
treading on leaves, trailing their rustling gowns.
And liquid verbs in *ahla* and in *ili*,
Aonian grottoes, nights in the Altai,
black pools of sound with "l"s for water lilies.
The empty glass I touched is tinkling still,
but now 'tis covered by a hand and dies.

"Trees? Animals? Your favorite precious stone?"

The birch tree, Cynthia, the fir tree, Joan.
Like a small caterpillar on its thread,
my heart keeps dangling from a leaf long dead
but hanging still, and still I see the slender
white birch that stands on tiptoe in the wind,

and firs beginning where the garden ends,
the evening ember glowing through their cinders.

Among the animals that haunt our verse,
a species of *Luscinia* comes first:
scores of locutions mimicking its throat
render its every whistling, bubbling, bursting,
flutelike or cuckoolike or ghostlike note.
But lapidary epithets are few;
we do not deal in universal rubies.
The angle and the glitter are subdued;
our riches lie concealed. We never liked
the jeweller's window in the rainy night.

My back is Argus-eyed. I live in danger.
False shadows turn to track me as I pass
and, wearing beards, disguised as secret agents,
creep in to blot the freshly written page
and read the blotter in the looking glass.
And in the dark, under my bedroom window,
until, with a chill whirr and shiver, day
presses its starter, warily they linger
or silently approach the door and ring
the bell of memory and run away.

Let me allude, before the spell is broken,
to Pushkin, rocking in his coach on long
and lonely roads: he dozed, then he awoke,
undid the collar of his travelling cloak,
and yawned, and listened to the driver's song.
Amorphous sallow bushes called *rakeety*,
enormous clouds above an endless plain,
songline and skyline endlessly repeated,
the smell of grass and leather in the rain.
And then the sob, the syncope (Nekrassov!),
the panting syllables that climb and climb,
obsessively repetitive and rasping,
dearer to some than any other rhyme.
And lovers meeting in a tangled garden,
dreaming of mankind, of untrammelled life,
mingling their longings in the moonlit garden,
where trees and hearts are larger than in life.
This passion for expansion you may follow
throughout our poetry. We want the mole
to be a lynx or turn into a swallow
by some sublime mutation of the soul.

But to unneeded symbols consecrated,
escorted by a vaguely infantile
path for bare feet, our roads were always fated
to lead into the silence of exile.

Had I more time tonight I would unfold
the whole amazing story—*neighukluzhe,
nevynossimo*—but I have to go.

What did I say under my breath? I spoke
to a blind songbird hidden in a hat,
safe from my thumbs and from the eggs I broke
into the gibus brimming with their yolk.

And now I must remind you, in conclusion,
that I am followed everywhere and that
space is collapsible, although the bounty
of memory is often incomplete:
once in a dusty place in Mora county
(half town, half desert, dump mound and mesquite)
and once in West Virginia (a muddy
red road between an orchard and a veil
of tepid rain) it came, that sudden shudder,
a Russian something that I could inhale
but could not see. Some rapid words were uttered—
and then the child slept on, the door was shut.

The conjuror collects his poor belongings—
the colored handkerchief, the magic rope,
the double-bottomed rhymes, the cage, the song.
You tell him of the passes you detected.
The mystery remains intact. The check
comes forward in its smiling envelope.

"How would you say 'delightful talk' in Russian?"
"How would you say 'good night'?"

　　　　　　Oh, that would be:
*Bezsonnitza, tvoy vzor oonyl i strashen;
lubov moya, otstoopnika prostee.*
　　　　　　　　　　—VLADIMIR NABOKOV

EX-BASKETBALL PLAYER

Pearl Avenue runs past the high-school lot,
Bends with the trolley tracks, and stops, cut off
Before it has a chance to go two blocks,
At Colonel McComsky Plaza. Berth's Garage
Is on the corner facing west, and there,
Most days, you'll find Flick Webb, who helps Berth out.

Flick stands tall among the idiot pumps—
Five on a side, the old bubble-head style,
Their rubber elbows hanging loose and low.
One's nostrils are two Ss, and his eyes
An E and O. And one is squat, without
A head at all—more of a football type.

Once, Flick played for the high-school team, the Wizards.
He was good—in fact, the best. In '46,
He bucketed three hundred ninety points,
A county record still. The ball loved Flick.
I saw him rack up thirty-eight or forty
In one home game. His hands were like wild birds.

He never learned a trade; he just sells gas,
Checks oil, and changes flats. Once in a while
As a gag he dribbles an inner tube,
But most of us remember anyway.
His hands are fine and nervous on the lug wrench.
It makes no difference to the lug wrench, though.

Off work, he hangs around Mae's luncheonette.
Grease-gray and kind of coiled, he plays pinball,
Smokes those thin cigars, nurses lemon phosphates.
Flick seldom says a word to Mae, just nods
Beyond her face toward bright applauding tiers
Of Necco Wafers, Nibs, and Juju Beads.

—JOHN UPDIKE

EXIT, PURSUED BY A BEAR

Chipmunk chewing the Chippendale,
Mice on the Meissen shelf,
Pigeon stains on the Aubusson,
Spider lace on the delf.

Squirrel climbing the Sheraton,
Skunk on the Duncan Phyfe,

Silverfish in the Gobelins
And the calfbound volumes of *Life*.

Pocks on the pink Picasso,
Dust on the four Cézannes,
Kit on the keys of the Steinway,
Cat on the Louis Quinze.

Rings on the Adam mantel
From a thousand bygone thirsts,
Mold on the Henry Millers
And the Ronald Firbank firsts.

The lion and the lizard
No heavenly harmonies hear

From the high-fidelity speaker
Concealed behind the Vermeer.

Jamshid squats in a cavern
Screened by a waterfall,
Catered by Heinz and Campbell,
And awaits the fireball.

—OGDEN NASH

F

FABLE

There is an inevitability
(Said the tumbling bat)
In certain human relationships
(Said the hot, red fox)
Over which character
(Said the cat on the back fence)
And morality
(Said the mink)
Have little or no control
(Said the cod as he wiggled his tail),
Especially when those who are concerned
Possess neither (sang the nightingale).

—NORMAN HARRIS

FAIRGROUND

Thumping old tunes give a voice to its whereabouts
long before one can see the dazzling archway
of colored lights, beyond which household proverbs
cease to be valid,

a ground sacred to the god of vertigo
and his cult of disarray: here jeopardy,
panic, shock are dispensed in measured doses
by foolproof engines.

As passive objects, packed tightly together
on roller coaster or ferris wheel, mortals
taste in their solid flesh the volitional
joys of a seraph.

Soon the roundabout ends the clumsy conflict
of Right and Left: the riding mob melts into
one spinning sphere, the perfect shape performing
the perfect motion.

Mopped and mowed at, as their train worms through a tunnel,
by ancestral spooks, caressed by clammy cobwebs,

grinning initiates emerge into daylight
as tribal heroes.

Fun for Youth who knows his libertine spirit
is not a copy of Father's, but has yet to
learn that the tissues which lend it stamina,
like Mum's, are bourgeois.

Those with their wander-years behind them who are rather
relieved that all routes of escape are spied on,
all hours of amusement counted, requiring
caution, agenda,

keep away:—to be found in coigns where, sitting
in silent synods, they play chess or cribbage,
games that call for patience, foresight, maneuver,
like war, like marriage.

—W. H. AUDEN

FAIRY STORY

Hunt, hunt again. If you do not find it, you
Will die. But I tell you this much: it
Is not under the stone at the foot
Of the garden, or by the wall by the fig tree.
I tell you this much to save you trouble, for I
Have looked. I know. Hurry, for

The terror is, all promises are kept.

Even happiness.

—ROBERT PENN WARREN

FAITHFULLY TINYING AT TWILIGHT VOICE

faithfully tinying at twilight voice
of deathless earth's innumerable doom:
againing (yes by microscopic yes)
acceptance of irrevocable time

particular pure truth of patience heard
above the everywhereing fact of fear;
and under any silence of each bird
who dares to not forsake a failing year

—now, before quite your whisper's whisper is
subtracted from my hope's own hope, receive
(undaunted guest of dark most downwardness
and marvellously self diminutive

whose universe a single leaf may be)
the more than thanks of always merest me
                              —E. E. CUMMINGS

FALL COMES IN BACK-COUNTRY VERMONT

(1. ONE VOTER OUT OF SIXTEEN)

Deader they die here, or at least
Differently, deeper the hole, and after
The burying, at night, late, you
Are more apt to wonder about the drainage

Of the cemetery, but you know that you needn't, for
Here's all hills anyway, or mountain, and the hole
Standard, but if no drainage problem, yet
You may still wake with a kind of psychic

Twitch, as when the nerves in the amputee's
Stump (a saw did it, no doubt) twitch and wonder
How that which has gone off and set up
As a separate self is making out, and whether

It repents of its rashness and would like
To come back and crawl into bed and be
Forgiven, and even though you, like me,
May forget the name of the dead, in the dark you

Can't help but remember that if there are only
Sixteen voters and one dies that leaves only
Fifteen, and no doubt you know the story
Of how it began, how he laid his axe down, then

Just sat on a log, not saying a word, till
The crew knocked off for the day, and never
Came back (it was cancer) and later you'd see him
Sit on the porch in the sun and throw bread

To the chipmunks, but that was last year, and now
There's the real-estate sign in the yard, and the grass

Not cut, and already one window knocked out,
For the widow's heartbroken and gone, and the bed

Is stripped to the mattress, and the bedpan
Washed with ammonia and put on a high shelf,
And the stuffed lynx he shot now all night glares
At the empty room with a feral vindication,

And does not forgive, and thinks with glee
How cancer is worse than a .30-30, and

(2. THE BEAR AND THE LAST PERSON TO REMEMBER)
It is well the widow is gone, for here winter's
Not made for a woman lone, lorn, and slow-foot,
And summer already sinks southward, and soon
All over the state the summer people

Will put the lawnmower in the red barn, drain
The plumbing, deny the pain of that heart-pinch
They cannot define, and get out the suitcase
To pack, for last night, in moonlight and high

On the mountain, I heard the first bear-hoot,
As the bear that all day had stripped bushes of the last
Blueberries, felt that hot itch and heaved
Up his black, hairy man-height in moonlight,

Lifted the head and curled back the black lip
To show the white moon-gleam of tush, and the throat
Pulsed in that call that is like the great owl's,
But more edged with anguish, and then far off,

From a ruined orchard, by the old cellar hole,
In the tang and the tawny air-taste of the apple-
Night, the she-bear, too, rises,
And the half-crushed apple, forgotten, falls

From the jaw gone slack in that moment before
Her utterance, and soon now, night after night,
On the mountain the moon-air will heave with that hunger,
So that, in that hour, the boys of the village

Come out, climb a ridge and reply, and when
Off on the mountain that hoot comes, and nearer,
The girls with them shiver and giggle, not quite
Daring to face that thought that from dark now,

Hot-breathed and hairy, earth-odored and foam-flecked,
Rises, and they want to go home, all but one,
Who feels that the night cannot breathe, and who soon,
On the raw mattress, in that house, will cry

Out, but the house is empty, and
Through the window where once the lace curtains hung
And a green shade was but is not,
The moonlight now pours like God, and the sweat

Of her effort goes ice, for she remembers,
So struggles to thrust off that weight that chokes her,
Thrusts herself up on that mattress and, gasping
In that ice and ice-iron of moonlight, with

What breath in that dishevelment
Is possible, says, "But here—it was here—
On this bed that he died, and I'll catch it and die"—
But does not, comes back, comes back until snow flies,

And many years later will be the last person
To remember his name who there on that bed

(3. The Human Fabric)
Had died, but for now let us take some comfort
In the fact that the fifteen surviving voters,
Remembering his name, feel, in the heart,
Diminished, for in this section death

Is a window gone dark and a face not seen
Anymore at the P.O., and in the act
Of rending irreparably the human fabric,
Death affirms the fact of that fabric, so what

If at night, in first snow, the hunters pass—
Pale clerks and mechanics from Springfield and Hartford,
With red caps and rifles and their pitiful
Blood lust and histrionic maleness—and passing,

Throw out from the car the empty bourbon
Bottle to lie in the snow by the For
Sale sign, and snow covers the bottle, will cover
The sign itself, and then the snowplow

Will pile up the banks as high as the eaves,
So that skiers who sing past in sports cars at dusk

Cannot see it, nor singing, need yet to know
The truth which at last they will come to need,

That life is of life paradigm, and death
The legend of death, nor need ever to know

(4. AFTERWARD)

That all night, eaves-high, the snow will press
Its face to the black ice of glass and, by
The white light its own being sheds, stare
Into that trapped cubicle of emptiness which

Is that room, but by that time I
Will not be here, in another place be,
And in my bed, not asleep, will endeavor
To see in my mind the eagle that once,

Above sunset, above the mountain in Stratton,
I saw—on thinnest air, high, saw
Lounging—oh, look!—it turns and, turning,
Shoulders like spray that last sun-gleam before

The whistling down-plunge to the mountain's shade.
I touch the hand there on the pillow.

—ROBERT PENN WARREN

FALLING

A 29-year-old stewardess fell . . . to her death tonight when she
was swept through an emergency door that suddenly sprang
open . . . The body . . . was found . . . three hours after the
accident.—*The Times.*

The states when they black out and lie there rolling   when they turn
To something transcontinental   move by   drawing moonlight out of the great
One-sided stone hung off the starboard wing tip.   Some sleeper next to
An engine is groaning for coffee   and there is faintly coming in
Somewhere the vast beast-whistle of space. In the galley with its racks
Of trays   she rummages for a blanket   and moves in her slim tailored
Uniform to pin it over the cry at the top of the door.   As though she blew

The door down with a silent blast from her lungs   frozen   she is black
Out finding herself   with the plane nowhere and her body taking by the throat
The undying cry of the void   falling   living   beginning to be something
That no one has ever been and lived through   screaming without enough air
Still neat   lipsticked   stockinged   girdled by regulation   her hat

Still on   her arms and legs in no world   and yet spaced also strangely
With utter placid rightness on thin air   taking her time   she holds it
In many places   and now, still thousands of feet from her death   she seems
To slow   she develops interest   she turns in her maneuverable body

To watch it. She is hung high up in the overwhelming middle of things   in her
Self   in low body-whistling wrapped intensely   in all her dark dance-weight
Coming down from a marvellous leap   with the delaying, dumfounding ease
Of a dream of being drawn   like endless moonlight to the harvest soil
Of a central state of one's country   with a great gradual warmth coming
Over her   floating   finding more and more breath in what she has been using
For breath   as the levels become more human   seeing clouds placed honestly
Below her left and right   riding slowly toward them   she clasps it all
To her and can hang her hands and feet in it in peculiar ways   and,
Her eyes opened wide by wind, can open her mouth as wide   wider   and suck
All the heat from the cornfields   can go down on her back with a feeling
Of stupendous pillows stacked under her   and can turn   turn as to someone
In bed   smile, understood in darkness   can go away   slant   slide
Off tumbling   into the emblem of a bird with its wings half-spread
Or whirl madly on herself   in endless gymnastics in the growing warmth
Of wheatfields rising toward the harvest moon. There is time to live
In superhuman health   seeing mortal unreachable lights far down   seeing
An ultimate highway with one late priceless car probing it   arriving
In a square town   and off her starboard arm the glitter of water catches
The moon by its one shaken side   scaled, roaming silver   My God it is good
And evil   lying in one after another of all the positions for love
Making   dancing   sleeping   and now cloud wisps at her   no
Raincoat   no matter   all small towns brokenly brighter from inside
Cloud   she walks over them like rain   bursts out to behold a Greyhound
Bus shooting light through its sides   it is the signal to go straight
Down like a glorious diver   then feet first   her skirt stripped beautifully
Up   her face in fear-scented cloths   her legs deliriously bare   then
Arms out   she slow-rolls over   steadies out   waits for something great
To take control of her   trembles near feathers   planes head-down
The quick movements of bird-necks turning her head   gold eyes   the insigh
eyesight of owls blazing into the hencoops   a taste for chicken overwhelming
Her   the long-range vision of hawks enlarging all human lights   of cars
Freight trains   looped bridges   enlarging the moon racing slowly
Through all the curves of a river   all the darks of the Midwest blazing
From within. A rabbit in a bush turns white   the smothering chickens
Huddle   for over them there is still time for something to live
With the streaming half-idea of a long stoop   a hurtling   a fall
That is controlled   that plummets as it wills   turns gravity
Into a new condition, showing its other side like a moon   shining
New Powers   ·   there is still time to live on a breath made of nothing
But the whole night   time for her to remember to arrange her skirt
Like a diagram of a bat   tightly it guides her   she has this flying-skin

Made of garments   and there are also those sky-divers on TV   sailing
In sunlight   smiling under their goggles   swapping batons back and forth
And He who jumped without a chute and was handed one by a diving
Buddy. She looks for her grinning companion   white teeth   nowhere
She is screaming   singing hymns   her thin human wings spread out
From her neat shoulders   the air beast-crooning to her   warbling
And she can no longer behold the huge partial form of the world   now
She is watching her country lose its evoked master shape   watching it lose
And gain   get back its houses and peoples   watching it bring up
Its local lights   single homes   lamps on barn roofs   if she fell
Into water she might live   like a diver   cleaving   perfect   plunge

Into another   heavy silver   unbreathable   slowing   saving
Element: there is water   there is time to perfect all the fine
Points of diving   feet together   toes pointed   hands shaped right
To insert her into water like a needle   to come out healthily dripping
And be handed a Coca-Cola   there they are   there are the waters
Of life   the moon packed and coiled in a reservoir   *so let me begin*
To plane across the night air of Kansas   opening my eyes superhumanly
Bright   to the dammed moon   opening the natural wings of my jacket
By Don Loper   moving like a hunting owl toward the glitter of water
One cannot just fall   just tumble screaming all that time   one must use
It   she is now through with all   through all   clouds   damp   hair
Straightened   the last wisp of fog pulled apart on her face like wool   revealing
New darks   new progressions of headlights along dirt roads   from chaos

And night   a gradual warming   a new-made, inevitable world of one's own
Country   a great stone of light in its waiting waters   hold   hold out
For water: who knows when what correct young woman must take up her body
And fly   and head for the moon-crazed inner eye of Midwest imprisoned
Water   stored up for her for years   the arms of her jacket slipping
Air up her sleeves to go   all over her? What final things can be said
Of one who starts out sheerly in her body in the high middle of night
Air   to track down water like a rabbit where it lies like life itself
Off to the right in Kansas? She goes toward   the blazing-bare lake
Her skirts neat   her hands and face warmed more and more by the air
Rising from pastures of beans   and under her   under chenille bedspreads
The farm girls are feeling the goddess in them struggle and rise   brooding
On the scratch-shining posts of the bed   dreaming of female signs
Of the moon   male blood like iron   on what is really said by the moan
Of airliners passing over them at dead of Midwest midnight   passing
Over brush fires burning out in silence on little hills   and will wake
To see the woman they should be   struggling on the rooftree to become
Stars.   For her the ground is closer   water is nearer   she passes
It   then banks   turns   her sleeves fluttering differently as she rolls
Out to face the east, where the sun shall come up from wheatfields   she must
Do something with water   fly to it   fall in it   drink it   rise

From it   but there is none left upon earth   the clouds have drunk it back
The plants have sucked it down   there are standing toward her only
The common fields of death   she comes back from flying to falling
Returns to a powerful cry   the silent scream with which she blew down
The coupled door of the airliner   nearly   nearly losing hold
Of what she has done   remembers   remembers the shape at the heart
Of cloud   fashionably swirling   remembers she still has time to die
Beyond explanation. Let her now take off her hat in summer air the contour
Of cornfields   and have enough time to kick off her one remaining
Shoe with the toes   of the other foot   to unhook her stockings
With calm fingers, noting how fatally easy it is to undress in midair
Near death   when the body will assume without effort any position
Except the one that will sustain it   enable it to rise   live
Not die   nine farms hover close   widen   eight of them separate, leaving
One in the middle   then the fields of that farm do the same   there is no
Way to back off   from her chosen ground   but she sheds the jacket
With its silver sad impotent wings   sheds the bat's guiding tailpiece
Of her skirt   the lightning-charged clinging of her blouse   the intimate
Inner flying-garment of her slip in which she rides like the holy ghost
Of a virgin   sheds the long wind-socks of her stockings   absurd
Brassière   then feels the girdle required by regulations squirming
Off her: no longer monobuttocked   she feels the girdle flutter   shake
In her hand   and float   upward   her clothes rising off her   ascending
Into cloud   and fights away from her head the last sharp dangerous shoe
Like a dumb bird   and now will drop in   SOON   now will drop

In like this   the greatest thing that ever came to Kansas   down from all
Heights   all levels of American breath   layered in the lungs   from the frail
Chill of space to the loam where extinction slumbers in corn tassels   thickly
And breathes like rich farmers counting   will come among them after
Her last superhuman act   the last slow careful passing of her hands
All over her unharmed body   desired by every sleeper in his dream:
Boys finding for the first time their loins filled with heart's blood
Widowed farmers whose hands float under light covers to find themselves
Arisen at sunrise   the splendid position of blood unearthly drawn
Toward clouds   all feel something   pass over them as she passes
Her palms over *her* long legs   *her* small breasts   and deeply between
Her thighs   her hair shot loose from all pins   streaming in the wind
Of her body   let her come openly   trying at the last second to land
On her back   This is it   THIS
                         All those who find her impressed
In the soft loam   gone down   driven well into the image of her body
The furrows for miles flowing in upon her where she lies very deep
In her mortal outline   in the earth as it is in cloud   can tell nothing
But that she is there   inexplicable   unquestionable   and remember
That something broke in them as well   and began to live and die more
When they walked for no reason into their fields to where the whole earth

Caught her   interrupted her maiden flight   told her how to lie   she cannot
Turn   go away   cannot move   cannot slide off it and assume another
Position   no sky-diver with any grin could save her   hold her in his arms
Plummet with her   unfold above her his wedding silks   she can no longer
Mark the rain with whirling women that take the place of a dead wife
Or the goddess in Norwegian farm girls   or all the backbreaking whores
Of Wichita. All the known air above her is not giving up quite one
Breath   it is all gone   and yet not dead   not anywhere else
Quite   lying still in the field on her back   sensing the smells
Of incessant growth try to lift her   a little sight left in the corner
Of one eye   fading   seeing something wave   lies believing
That she could have made it   at the best part of her brief goddess
State   to water   gone in head first   come out smiling   invulnerable
Girl in a bathing-suit ad   but she is lying like a sunbather at the last
Of moonlight   half-buried in her impact on the earth   not far
From a railroad trestle   a water tank   she could see if she could
Raise her head from her modest hole   with her clothes beginning
To come down all over Kansas   into bushes   on the dewy sixth green
Of a golf course   one shoe   her girdle coming down fantastically
On a clothesline, where it belongs   her blouse on a lightning rod:

Lies in the fields   in *this* field   on her broken back as though on
A cloud she cannot drop through   while farmers sleepwalk without
Their women from houses   a walk like falling toward the far waters
Of life   in moonlight   toward the dreamed eternal meaning of their farms
Toward the flowering of the harvest in their hands   that tragic cost

Feels herself go   go toward   go outward   breathes at last fully
Not   and tries   less   once   tries   tries   AH, GOD—

—James Dickey

THE FALLS

The pretty girls of the fall
　　are not all so barren as these
　　　　that fly down on the north of the mind
　　　　　　through the eye of the south, the red
　　　　　　radishes of their bare knees
　　　　　　　　advertising the onset of sleep.

Bears do not hibernate; they sleep
　　away a lardy intoxication,
　　　　and their ladies give them the nod
　　　　　　inside the cave of retreat
　　　　　　　　or under the leaves a call
　　　　　　　　　　summoning the naked beast.

Some women are scared by beasts,
  some animals by clumsy calls.
   Some daughters make their fathers fall.
    Some eyes shoot through the mind
    like the north wind, then sleep.
     Some minds, dying, drop to their knees.

But the prettiest fall of all
  is my own in a gesture of love
   as I arc through the heaven of death
    and the angels blow my body on,
     and I head for the heart of a girl
      on the soft white breast of the world.

                               —F. D. REEVE

FAMILIAR FACES, LONG DEPARTED

Where are the dear domestics, white and black,
Who stayed for years or hastened to repack,
Diverse as weather, changeful as the wind,
And kind to children overdisciplined?
No more the stifled giggle on the stairs,
The scornful flounce when Madam put on airs,
The sympathetic heart beneath the starch
When boys who loved to dance were trained to march.
The subject round which every talk revolved,
The servant problem, is at last resolved.

The Huldas, Bridies, Posies, and Francines
Are now the happy servants of machines.
Time clocks have superseded bells, and wages
Rise with the pointer in the pressure gauges.
The hands that knew such varied skills prepare
The lean assembly line's unvaried fare,
To make the things that serve as their replacement
In every function from third floor to basement
And heartlessly supplant with a device
The youth who brought romance as well as ice.

The house is shaken by the whining hum
That Nature most abhors, the vacuum.
Freed from the mute reproval of the maid,
Talk has grown loose and manners have decayed.
Damask and finger bowls are empty names,
At breakfast time the toast leaps up in flames,

The cocktail hour expands, the dinner shrinks;
Now no one needs to care what Bridget thinks.
All in prefabricated ruin lies—
And Ganymede gives notice in the skies.

—ROBERT HILLYER

FAMILY EVENING

With banked fire to mark the occa-
    sion,
We launch the evening, and all board
For the Happy Isles of Sweet Con-
    cord—
And the crew so trained to protest no
    word.

But our envy will follow the early bird
Who contrives to excuse herself the
    trip;
Whereafter none may part but be
The rat leaving a sinking ship.

—DAN HUWS

A FANTASY OF LITTLE WATERS

The cirrus bow of surf is blown
Into the color of the sky;
And rootless, vaguely yellowish,
A protoplasmic jellyfish,
Sporting one dark spot, floats by,
Suspended like a burnt-out sun. . . .

One evening, when our daughter
    turns
The faucet on, we'll kiss her hands
Until they shiver with deep concerns,
Unearthed, straying where she stands;
And she will shake the feeling off,
Shaking her hair at all the bother

Of fixing it, and hear a cough
Drifting from a distant room
Like little waters, and will assume
It wasn't she, it was another.

With fingers grown from coral shelves,
One morning those clear hands will
    groom
Loose strands, the veins of platinum
Distend, their blowzy breaths become
The clouds flooding her nails; the
    comb
Fathoming her flowing selves.

—JAMES SCULLY

A FAR CRY AFTER A CLOSE CALL

For if they do these things in a green tree what shall be done
in the dry?—*Luke* 23:31.

Nuns, his nieces, bring the priest in the next
Bed pralines, not prayers for the next world,
    But I've had one look myself
    At *that* one (looking

Back now, crammed in the convalescent ward,
With the invisible man opposite

        Sloshing most of the Black Sea
            Around in his lungs,

While the third patient coughs and borrows *Time*).
No one turned over when I was wheeled in;
        The efficient British nurse
            Snipped off my soggy

Trousers and put me right, "sure as Bob's your
Uncle." The water roared and ran away,
        Leaving only words to stock
            My mind like capsules

Crowding a bottle. Then the lights blew up,
Went out, someone was going through My Things
        While I rowed—rowed for my life
            Down the rubber floor—

But the waves failed me. The hallway heaved where I
Foundered and turned in my doctor's dry hands
        To sovereign selflessness.
            Meaning had melted.

"*Mon corps est moi*," Molière said. They're more than that,
This monster the body, this miracle
        Its pain—when was I ever
            Them, when were they me?

At thirty-three, what else is there to do
But wait for yet another great white moth
        With eager, enlarging eyes
            To land on my chest,

Slowly, innocently choking me off?
The feelers stir while I lie still, lie here
        (Where on earth does it come from,
            That wind, that wounding

Breath?), remembering the future now,
Foreseeing a past I shall never know,
        Until the little crisis
            Breaks, and I wake.

For as Saint Paul sought deliverance from
The body of this death, I seek to stay—
        Man is mad as the body
            Is sick, by nature.

                        —RICHARD HOWARD

FAREWELL TO NARCISSUS

Farewell to Narcissus, who mistook
his face in the brine brook
for another looking back,
for a lover, a kissing and caressing
    brother.

He's gone in his own grave, sealed as
    stone
in his own rapt look, alone
as a bird in a mirror, flown
off forever from the hunter and the
    weather.

The brain like a trigger then is locked
in an echo; thought is rocked
in its own cradle; blood is blocked.

The camel is bigger than the eye of
    the needle.

Narcissus is seduced by his own look.
His heart skips back and forth
from earth to water, south to north,
captured in the crooked brook, the
    sweet serenader.

A last farewell to the fluttered en-
    counter.
If it ever mattered,
the fond fool is flattered.
Nothing now shall leave, now nothing
    more shall enter.

                —ROBERT HORAN

FAREWELL VOYAGING WORLD!

It was the departure, the sun was risen,
the light came across the flat sea, the yellow blades
fell like swords on the small white houses
the half hoisted sail creaked on the ship
the seagulls hovered in circles and cried
on the foredeck the sailors stood at the capstan

the moving light made the land look as if it were moving
the houses shifted the windows changed
cocks crew and the hens strutted into the street
and you went down the path of shells, carrying
a box on your shoulder a bundle in your hand
I followed hearing ahead the sound of your feet

but you carried also the invisible
you carried also the unspoken
what we could not say what we had not said
what we had not lived and could never live
what we had lived but could not be forgotten
where will you remember it where again will you sit down

at a little foreign table reading a paper
the news a month old and our hearts a month dead
with a strange clock above you and a bird in a cage

chirping in another language
but not yet now it is still the daybreak
look they are hoisting the sail and singing

the moving light makes the land seem to move
it is we who are going away and not you
we take away with us an indecipherable heritage
time is broken in our hands
it is we who leave you here in a motionless ship
as we begin the immeasurable circle

say goodbye to us make your farewells
the earth is leaving you the earth is going
never again shall we come to this permanent ship
or you everlasting with your box on your shoulder
it will always be daybreak with us, the beginning,
we shall never be older or wiser or dead.

—CONRAD AIKEN

FATHER FATHER SON AND SON

Sweet father   I have shrunk a bit
I think I know
although I think you see me grow
and so I do
although although
sweet father

I can tell when it began
Before I was a full grown man
I was a child   the child was
and then I thought and now I know
and so apparently I grow
sweet father

How far to go   How far to go
All clocks agreed the child ran slow
and so it did   a little man
before the hours began to know
the time before a cock could crow
or I woke up   sweet father

Before the hours began to know
I ran easily if slow
according to the clock   and still out-
    ran it

which left me large   which made you
    small
I saw you ticking on a wall
stricken with time   sweet father

I learned the minutes pain by pain
I saw them pass and come again
I watched how fear wound up and
    struck
I learned what discipline it took
to tick   You could not falter
on your wall   sweet father

You could not falter on your wall
With steady hands you measured out
the world on which all clocks agreed
that bound and rounded every sense
into the fixed circumference
of time and need   sweet father

When I was large and you were small
I still had room inside one head
for any other world instead
of one   the one on which all clocks
    agree

the one that I have grown to see
outgrow me in our time   sweet father

It grew in me with time until
what was inside and once a part
outgrew me and stood out
locked and common under a vault of
    sky
that shall not open

while the habitual clock it ticks in
    me

It ticks   I measure now what I can
    see
who see you leaving time behind
sweet father   I would stop
to see you in eternity
but my enormous children crawl
I must not falter on my wall

                                        —Jon Swan

FENCE WIRE

Too tight, it is running over
Too much of this ground to be still
Or to do anything but tremble
And disappear left and right,
As far as the eye can see,

Over hills, through woods,
Down roads, to arrive at last
Again where it connects,
Coming back from the other side
Of animals, defining their earthly
        estate

As the grass becomes snow
While they are standing and dream-
        ing
Of grass and snow.
The winter hawk that sits upon its
        post,
Feeling the airy current of the wires,

Turns into a robin, sees that this is
        wrong,
Then into a boy, and into a man who
        holds
His palm on the top tense strand
With the whole farm feeding slowly
And nervously into his hand.

If the wire were cut anywhere
All his blood would fall to the ground
And leave him standing and staring

With a face as white as a Hereford's.
From years of surrounding grain,

Cows, horses, machinery trying to
        turn
To rust, the humming arrives each
        second,
A sound that arranges these acres
And holds them high-strung and en-
        thralled.
Because of the light, chilled hand

On the top thread tuned to an E,
Like the low string of a guitar,
The dead corn is more
Balanced in death than it was,
The animals more aware

Within the huge human embrace
Held up and borne out of sight
Upon short, unbreakable poles
Wherethrough the ruled land intones
Like a psalm—properly,

With its eyes closed,
Whether on the side of the animals
Or not, whether disappearing
Right, left, through trees or down
        roads,
Whether outside, around, or in.

                                        —James Dickey

FERN

Here is the fern's frond, unfurling a gesture,
Like a conductor whose music will now be pause
And the one note of silence
To which the whole earth dances gravely—

A dancer, leftover, among crumbs and remains
Of God's drunken supper,
Dancing to start things up again.
And they do start up—to the one note of silence.

The mouse's ear unfurls its trust,
The spider takes up her bequest,
And the retina
Reins the Creation with a bridle of water.

How many went under? Everything up to this point went under.
Now they start up again
Dancing gravely, like the plume
Of a warrior returning, under the low hills,

Into his own kingdom.

—Ted Hughes

FIGURES OF AUTHORITY

Everyone grows younger; my thinning hair
drops from the shears of someone—is it my son?—
who yesterday smelled old and formidable
when I entered the seamy male world of my father.
Even now, I sometimes feel a twitch of fear
with only the razor's edge between me and death.

The doctor who delivered me—felled by death
aeons ago—was stern, had graying hair,
and knew old-fashioned remedies for fear,
such as rough treatment for a gentle son.
Love then was mere indulgence in a father.
Doctors today find *me* formidable.

But where is the dentist who is not formidable,
whose warning word is not harbinger of death?
Decay, decay! Dark symbol of the father
even as he bends a dazzling shock of hair

and wholesome smile over his aging son—
his in a bond as old as blood and fear.

Others, of course, deliver one from fear
and bugaboo time. Is history formidable
when one's instructed by its youngest son,
a Fulbright fellow? And is one nearer death
than he, so obviously civilization's heir
he makes one feel like civilization's father?

The psychiatrist is everybody's father,
who surfaces our deeps of filial fear,
our twisted love, and does not turn a hair.
Is nothing, then, sacred or formidable
to him, who reads within our life our death?
Presumptuously, I yearn to call him son.

When I was a child believing myself a son
of God, taught by a reverend balding Father,
I accepted—yes, almost desired—death;
it was life I looked upon with childish fear.
Now life seems pleasant, not formidable,
and they may have their heaven. God is here

in the eyes of the latest son, who does not fear
his father (who finds *him* formidable—
a taste of death, yet look! he has such hair!).

—Edward Watkins

THE FIGURES ON THE FRIEZE

Darkness wears off, and, dawning into light,
they find themselves unmagically together.
He sees the stains of morning in her face.
She shivers, distant in his bitter weather.

Diminishing of legend sets him brooding.
Great goddess-figures conjured from his book
blur what he sees with bafflement of wishing.
Sulking, she feels his fierce, accusing look.

Familiar as her own, his body's landscape
seems harsh and dull to her habitual eyes.

Mystery leaves, and mercilessly flying
the blind fiends come, emboldened by her cries.

Avoiding simple reach of hand for hand,
which would surrender pride, by noon they stand
withdrawn from touch, reproachfully alone,
small in each other's eyes, tall in their own.

Wild with their misery, they entangle now
in baffling agonies of why and how.
Afternoon glimmers, and they wound anew—
flesh, nerve, bone, gristle in each other's view.

"What have you done to me?" From each proud heart,
new phantoms walk in the deceiving air.
As the light fails, each is consumed apart,
he by his ogre vision, she by her fire.

When night falls, out of a despair of daylight,
they strike the lying attitudes of love,
and through the perturbations of their bodies
each feels the amazing, murderous legends move.

—ALASTAIR REID

FILLING STATION

Oh, but it is dirty!
—this little filling station,
oil-soaked, oil-permeated
to a surprising, over-all
black translucency.
Be careful with that match!

Father wears a dirty,
oil-soaked monkey suit
that cuts him under the arms,
and several quick and saucy
and greasy sons assist him
(it's a family filling station),
all quite thoroughly dirty.

Do they live in the station?
It has a cement porch

behind the pumps, and on it
a set of crushed and grease-
impregnated wickerwork;
on the wicker sofa
a dirty dog, quite comfy.

Some comic books provide
the only note of color—
of certain color. They lie
upon a big dim doily
draping a taboret
(part of the set), beside
a big hirsute begonia.

Why the extraneous plant?
Why, oh why, the table?
Why, oh why, the doily?

(Embroidered in daisy stitch
with marguerites, I think,
and heavy with gray crochet.)

Somebody embroidered the doily.
Somebody waters the plant,
or oils it, maybe. Somebody

arranges the rows of cans
so that they softly say:
ESSO—SO—SO—SO
to high-strung automobiles.
Somebody loves us all.

—Elizabeth Bishop

FINDING THEM LOST

Thinking of words that would save him, slanting
Off in the air, some cracked, some bent;
Finding them lost, he started saying
Some other words he never meant.

The green went back and forth in waves
As if his heart pumped out the lawn
In blood, not grass. A bench sailed down,
Becoming the bench he sat upon,

Staring out at the crazy garden,
With its women washed out to milky shades,
Or pressed through the trees' accordion,
While the past jerked past in lantern slides,

Badly lit, of images unbidden—
Faces, arms, and forgotten eyes
That, peeping through the leaves, half hidden,
Turned on and off like fireflies.

Fire and flies. *That* was it,
He thought, as the nurse bloomed, coming, coming
Straight through a tree to hold his hand.
Holding hers, he felt blood drumming

Through the twined bones of where they met.
It was three months the stubborn grass
Wouldn't rise up to meet his foot,
Or, rising up, caught him unawares.

How to get back to pure imagination,
He asked the nerves of work and love,
And both networks of such importance
He dreamed them. But what was he dreaming of?

Sleep, it was sleep, that found him napping
When the delicious dew of sweat

Brought forth the baby he'd been hiding
Wrapped in his skin, maybe his heart.

And what the mirror gave back was him
Finally, tired and very old.
"My life, begin . . ." But it didn't, wouldn't,
Though grass was grass and no bench sailed

Down to a garden to support him
And no one walked through a tree to hold
His hand. But a green lawn pulses in him.
Home, he still dreams of going home.

—Howard Moss

FINGERNAIL SUNRISE

The salt wave sings
Before, beyond, and under time, and along the long sand falls,
Dinted with brilliant things
Coiled or broken, deaf to the wild birds' calls.

Pause and look down.
The flash we saw in the distance now becomes for us a shell,
Spun from the loom of waters to its own
Stillness and inward music; mark it, where it fell.

Stilled at the core
Of sky and water, skimmed by shag and oystercatchers flown,
Leaving the print of talons on the shore
Of daylight, and the shore of all that's known,

Thought ends in this.
A hundred footprints now arrive at this fine skin of horn
Divining daybreak here by artifice,
Fingernail sunrise, rifted sky reborn.

Should a man die,
Leaving a fingered skein, though never of this workmanship,
Certain and cold, and be outlasted by
Such art, who then might hear the speaking lip,

Unseen, confess,
"Here, in the heart of color, in the tidewrack of the sea,

This mask of mine, for winds to dry and waters to caress,
Shuts history out, till turned by its own key"?

The half is written,
Split like a shell, silvered with pearl, now death has overlaid it,
Secret, beautiful, and forgotten,
Mute, remembered alone by him who made it.

—VERNON WATKINS

FIREWORKS

Not guns, not thunder, but a flutter of clouded drums
That announce a fiesta: abruptly, fiery needles
Circumscribe on the night boundless chrysanthemums.
Softly, they break apart, they flake away, where
Darkness, on a svelte hiss, swallows them.
Delicate brilliance: a bellflower opens, fades,
In a sprinkle of falling stars.
Night absorbs them
With the sponge of her silence.

—BABETTE DEUTSCH

FIRST DEATH IN NOVA SCOTIA

In the cold, cold parlor
my mother laid out Arthur
beneath the chromographs:
Edward, Prince of Wales,
with Princess Alexandra,
and King George with Queen Mary.
Below them on the table
stood a stuffed loon
shot and stuffed by Uncle
Arthur, Arthur's father.

Since Uncle Arthur fired
a bullet into him,
he hadn't said a word.
He kept his own counsel
on his white, frozen lake,
the marble-topped table.
His breast was deep and white,
cold and caressable;

his eyes were red glass,
much to be desired.

"Come," said my mother,
"Come and say goodbye
to your little cousin Arthur."
I was lifted up and given
one lily of the valley
to put in Arthur's hand.
Arthur's coffin was
a little frosted cake,
and the red-eyed loon eyed it
from his white, frozen lake.

Arthur was very small.
He was all white, like a doll
that hadn't been painted yet.
Jack Frost had started to paint him
the way he always painted

the Maple Leaf (Forever).
He had just begun on his hair,
a few red strokes, and then
Jack Frost had dropped the brush
and left him white, forever.

The gracious royal couples
were warm in red and ermine;
their feet were well wrapped up

in the ladies' ermine trains.
They invited Arthur to be
the smallest page at court.
But how could Arthur go,
clutching his tiny lily,
with his eyes shut up so tight
and the roads deep in snow?

—ELIZABETH BISHOP

THE FIRST OF ALL MY DREAMS

the first of all my dreams was of
a lover and his only love,
strolling slowly (mind in mind)
through some green mysterious land

until my second dream begins—
the sky is wild with leaves; which dance
and dancing swoop (and swooping
        whirl
over a frightened boy and girl)

but that mere fury soon became
silence: in huger always whom
two tiny selves sleep (doll by doll)
motionless under magical

foreverfully falling snow.
And then this dreamer wept: and so
she quickly dreamed a dream of spring
—how you and i are blossoming

—E. E. CUMMINGS

FIRST THINGS FIRST

Woken, I lay in the arms of my own warmth and listened
To a storm enjoying its storminess in the winter dark
Till my ear, as it can when half asleep or half sober,
Set to work to unscramble that interjectory uproar,
Construing its airy vowels and watery consonants
Into a love speech indicative of a proper name.

Scarcely the tongue I should have chosen, yet, as well
As harshness and clumsiness would allow, it spoke in your praise
Kenning you a godchild of the Moon and the West Wind,
With power to tame both real and imaginary monsters,
Likening your poise of being to an upland county,
Here green on purpose, there pure blue for luck.

Loud though it was, alone as it certainly found me,
It reconstructed a day of peculiar silence
When a sneeze could be heard a mile off, and had me walking
On a headland of lava beside you, the occasion as ageless

As the stare of any rose, your presence exactly
So once, so valuable, so very new.

This, moreover, at an hour when only too often
A smirking devil annoys me in beautiful English,
Predicting a world where every sacred location
Is a sand-buried site all cultured Texans "do,"
Misinformed and thoroughly fleeced by their guides,
And gentle hearts are extinct like Hegelian bishops.

Grateful, I slept till a morning that would not say
How much it believed of what I said the storm had said
But quietly drew my attention to what had been done—
So many cubic metres the more in my cistern
Against a leonine summer—putting first things first:
Thousands have lived without love, not one without water.

                                          —W. H. Auden

FISH

I am fish:
I swim in your kindness. Fat,
silvery, veined with tears
strange to your outer waters, yet
I am home from my fears.

And my sea?
What sea clamors its old
birth of my blood? What wish
of mine against my own chemistry
is magic? I am cold;

I am cold in my veins;
there flows in my net of inner water
an old call. Let me not wish
to house in these domains;
no daughter

of your ocean am I.
Born to strange salt, listen, I must go
back. Will you hear my longing cry
that to your sea I know
I am no flesh?

                                          —Emily Townsend

FIVE BIRDS RISE

Your mind lies open like the map of rivers
Scored in the palm of our accomplished death;
Five birds rise, soaring out of timbered valleys
That guard this world incorporate of our breath;
But when I lie with you
The dusty angels huddle to the ground
And fiery whirlblasts twist the senses round.

Your heart is troubled like the broken water
Of Garple, where it leaves the moors behind
And pours, dishevelled by high rocks and shingle,
Over five holy falls and then lies blind,
Circling and whirled about
In beer-brown pools where trout savage the flies—
A flick-knife killing, sudden as your eyes.

Your body is a wood where I have built
Five leaky huts to keep my shadows in;
Brown falling leaves have curtained all the air
And livid colors move beneath the skin,
Proving that I have sown
Some death in you that withers all your grain
While it consumes the substance of my own.

—WILLIAM HAYWARD

A FIXTURE

Women, women,
women, women
in a department store,
with hats on
(hats in *it*)
and shoes on
(shoes in *it*),
dresses, coats, gloves
on (and *in*
all the departments);

in the lobby
(in a niche)
between two glass
revolving doors
(sluff, sluff,

sluff, sluff),
rubber bottoms
of whirling doors
(flick, flick,
click, click),
women in, women out,

sits a nun;

in the mid-whirl
(a station),
white, black, wooden
(a fixture),
holding a wooden
cup, she sits
between the glitter

of double doors,
her hexagonal
glasses glittering
over glassy fixed
eyes, a garter snake
of black beads (wooden?)
catching light,
crawling (clicking)
up her draped, fixed,
short, carved black
knees (thighs)—

her white hat (hood)
a head cover,
her shoes, short, black,
flat (foot covers),
her dress a black
curtain (cape)
over a longer curtain shape;

she is the best dressed.
                                        —MAY SWENSON

FLEE ON YOUR DONKEY

Ma Faim, Anne, Anne, Fuis sur ton âne. . . .—*Rimbaud.*

(JUNE 1962)

Because there was no other place
to flee to,
I came back to the scene of the disordered senses,
came back last night at midnight,
arriving in the thick June night
without luggage or defenses,
giving up my car keys and my cash,
keeping only a pack of Salem cigarettes
the way a child holds on to a toy.
I signed myself in where a stranger
puts the inked-in X's—
for this is a mental hospital,
not a child's game.

Today an interne knocks my knees,
testing for reflexes.
Once I would have winked and begged for dope.
Today I am terribly patient.
Today crows play blackjack
on the stethoscope.

Everyone has left me
except my muse,
that good nurse.

She stays in my hand,
a mild white mouse.

The curtains, lazy and delicate,
billow and flutter and drop
like the Victorian skirts
of my two maiden aunts
who kept an antique shop.

Hornets have been sent.
They cluster like floral arrangements on the screen.
Hornets, dragging their thin stingers,
hover outside, all knowing,
hissing: *the hornet knows.*
I heard it as a child
but what was it that he meant?
The hornet knows!
What happened to Jack and Doc and Reggy?
Who remembers what lurks in the heart of man?
What did the Green Hornet mean, *he knows?*
Or have I got it wrong?
Is it the Shadow who had seen
me from my bedside radio?

Now it's *Dinn, Dinn, Dinn!*
while the ladies in the next room argue
and pick their teeth.
Upstairs a girl curls like a snail;
in another room someone tries to eat a shoe;
meanwhile an adolescent pads up and down
the hall in his white tennis socks.
A new doctor makes rounds
advertising tranquillizers, insulin, or shock
to the uninitiated.

Six years of such small preoccupations!
Six years of shuttling in and out of this place!
Oh, my hunger! My hunger!
I could have gone around the world twice
or had new children—all boys.
It was a long trip with little days in it
and no new places.

In here,
it's the same old crowd,
the same ruined scene.

The alcoholic arrives with his golf clubs.
The suicide arrives with extra pills sewn
into the lining of her dress.
The permanent guests have done nothing new.
Their faces are still small
like babies with jaundice.

Meanwhile,
they carried out my mother
wrapped like somebody's doll, in sheets,
bandaged her jaw and stuffed up her holes.
My father, too. He went out on the rotten blood
he used up on other women in the Middle West.
He went out, a cured old alcoholic
on crooked feet and useless hands.
He went out calling for his father
who died all by himself long ago—
that fat banker who got locked up,
his genes suspended like dollars,
wrapped up in his secret,
tied up securely in a straitjacket.

But you, my doctor, my enthusiast,
were better than Christ;
you promised me another world
to tell me who
I was.

I spent most of my time,
a stranger,
damned and in trance—that little hut,
that naked blue-veined place,
my eyes shut on the confusing office,
eyes circling into my childhood,
eyes newly cut.
Years of hints
strung out—a serialized case history—
thirty-three years of the same dull incest
that sustained us both.
You, my bachelor analyst,
who sat on Marlborough Street,
sharing your office with your mother
and giving up cigarettes each New Year,
were the new God,
the manager of the Gideon Bible.

I was your third-grader
with a blue star on my forehead.

In trance I could be any age,
voice, gesture—all turned backward
like a drugstore clock.
Awake, I memorized dreams.
Dreams came into the ring
like third-string fighters,
each one a bad bet
who might win
because there was no other.
I stared at them,
concentrating on the abyss
the way one looks down into a rock quarry,
uncountable miles down,
my hands swinging down like hooks
to pull dreams up out of their cage.
Oh, my hunger! My hunger!

Once,
outside your office,
I collapsed in the old-fashioned swoon
between the illegally parked cars.
I threw myself down,
pretending dead for eight hours.
I thought I had died
into a snowstorm.
Above my head
chains cracked along like teeth
digging their way through the snowy street.
I lay there
like an overcoat
that someone had thrown away.
You carried me back in,
awkwardly, tenderly,
with the help of the red-haired secretary
who was built like a lifeguard.
My shoes,
I remember,
were lost in the snowbank
as if I planned never to walk again.

That was the winter
that my mother died,
half mad on morphine,
blown up, at last,
like a pregnant pig.
I was her dreamy evil eye.
In fact,
I carried a knife in my pocketbook—

my husband's good L. L. Bean hunting knife.
I wasn't sure if I should slash a tire
or scrape the guts out of some dream.

You taught me
to believe in dreams;
thus I was the dredger.
I held them like an old woman with arthritic fingers,
carefully straining the water out—
sweet, dark playthings,
and above all mysterious
until they grew mournful and weak.
Oh, my hunger! My hunger!
I was the one
who opened the warm eyelid
like a surgeon
and brought forth young girls
to grunt like fish.
I told you,
I said—
but I was lying—
that the knife was for my mother . . .
and then I delivered her.

The curtains flutter out
and slump against the bars.
They are my two thin ladies
named Blanche and Rose.
The grounds outside
are pruned like an estate at Newport.
Far off, in the field,
something yellow grows.

Was it last month or last year
that the ambulance ran like a hearse
with its siren blowing on suicide—
Dinn, dinn, dinn!—
a noon whistle that kept insisting on life
all the way through the traffic lights?

I have come back
but disorder is not what it was.
I have lost the trick of it!
The innocence of it!
That fellow-patient in his stovepipe hat,
with his fiery joke, his manic smile—
even he seems blurred, small and pale.

I have come back,
recommitted,
fastened to the wall like a bathroom plunger,
held like a prisoner
who was so poor
he fell in love with jail.

I stand at this old window
complaining of the soup,
examining the grounds,
allowing myself the wasted life.
Soon I will raise my face for a white flag,
and, when God enters the fort,
I won't spit or gag on his finger.
I will eat it like a white flower.
Is this the old trick, the wasting away,
the skull that waits for its dose
of electric power?

This is madness
but a kind of hunger.
What good are my questions
in this hierarchy of death
where the earth and the stones go
Dinn! Dinn! Dinn!
It is hardly a feast.
It is my stomach that makes me suffer.

Turn, my hungers!
For once make a deliberate decision.
There are brains that rot here
like black bananas.
Hearts have grown as flat as dinner plates.
Anne, Anne,
flee on your donkey,
flee this sad hotel,
ride out on some hairy beast,
gallop backward pressing
your buttocks to his withers,
sit to his clumsy gait somehow.
Ride out
any old way you please!
In this place everyone talks to his own mouth.
That's what it means to be crazy.
Those I loved best died of it—
the fool's disease.

—ANNE SEXTON

FLIGHT

One bails out into space
Each morning. Distance

Is nothing: a subway stop,
A walk uphill. The Russian, well-equipped,

Trod space as though man had been twirling there
Always, a bauble on the chandelier

Of the firmament; attached by a beanie
Headdress, Leonov was fully

Aware that should the cord break
It would take

No time for him to die, or go
On into limbo—

A man-made satellite. But he was
Under the proud eye of the world—unlike Goya's

Madman circling Toledo—
Like a Barnum and Bailey missile

With no intent
Of destruction, lent

Terror only from his own terror,
Who rode the air

Hellbent, though no one thought to look up.
A boy stepped

Into one car
Not the next, one segment of the river

Of the subway, and entered upon his death
As much by chance as by the icepick in his brain, the wealth

Of his unlived good years
Spent in a moment. All our fear

Of the unknown, revulsion at brutality
Casts us out to the outer spaces of the mind, whence we

Will return only with time,
Realizing of him

That nothing is the same as one young man, one son,
One good bet, gone.

—Barbara Howes

A FLOCK OF GUINEA HENS SEEN FROM A CAR

The lute and the pear are your half sisters,
The mackerel moon a full first cousin,
And you were born to appear seemly, even when running on
        guinea legs,
As maiden-formed, as single-minded as raindrops,
Ellipses, small homebodies of great orbits (little knots
        at the back like apron strings),
Perfected, sealed off, engraved like a dozen perfect
        consciences,
As egglike as the eggs you know best, triumphantly
        speckled . . .
But fast!
Side-eyed with emancipation, no more lost than a string
        of pearls are lost from one another,
You cross the road in the teeth of Pontiacs
As over a threshold, into waving, gregarious grasses,
Welcome wherever you go—the Guinea Sisters.

Bobbins with the threads of innumerable visits behind you,
As light on your feet
As the daughters of Mr. Barrett of Wimpole Street,
Do you ever wonder where Africa has fled?
Is the strangeness of your origins packed tight in those
        little nutmeg heads, so ceremonious,
                partly naked?
Is there time to ask each other what became of the family
                wings?
Do you dream?
Princess of Dapple,
Princess of Moonlight,
Princess of Conch,
Princess of Guinealand,
Though you roost in the care of S. Thomas Truly, Rt. 1
(There went his mailbox flying by),
The whole world knows you've never yet given up the secret
        of where you've hidden your nests.

—Eudora Welty

FLY IN DECEMBER

In an old, dark house—
where the thick light held us
bowled in glass—

looping from nowhere, furious, he
      came
pirouetting, hurling
a black, drunken aim,

zanging, unzipping the halves of the
      air
all afternoon and evening,
singing black in eye and ear

at the dog, at me, at the light,
flinging,
bitter, rude, a piece of night,

or, overhead, rode invisibly
in the terrier's shouldered, worried
      glance
on some vague journey

through doors into the other rooms,
back, wrestling
whatever angel he held, or doom:

death, the sweetness gone, the loss of
      summer.

At midnight, he stopped
suddenly, letting the windows remem-
      ber

the late snow falling to and fro
again, the furry
stars that burn in lovely agonies as
      they go

beyond our tiny night.
Vile
star—breath—flower!—knot

that won't pull loose to dying,
does he see
at last what is always too late for de-
      riding

perched somewhere, dumb,
watching in a hundred eyes or—
      blind?—
having let it come?

Whatever.
      In the old, dark house
we have settled down for the night,
somehow, the three of us.

                              —ROBERT WALLACE

FOREIGN AFFAIRS

We are two countries girded for the war,
Whisking our scouts across the pricked frontier
To ravage in each other's fields, cut lines
Along the lacework of strategic nerves,
Loot stores; while, here and there,
In ambushes that trace a valley's curves,
Stark witness to the dangerous charge we bear,
A house ignites, a train's derailed, a bridge
Blows up sky-high, and water floods the mines.
Who first attacked? Who turned the other cheek?
Aggression perpetrated is as soon
Denied, and insult rubbed into the injury
By cunning agents trained in these affairs,

With whom it's touch-and-go, don't-tread-on-me,
I-dare-you-to, keep-off, and double-dare.
Tempers could sharpen knives, and do; we live
In states provocative
Where frowning headlines scare the coffee cream
And doomsday is the eighth day of the week.

Our exit through the slammed and final door
Is twenty times rehearsed, but when we face
The imminence of cataclysmic rupture,
A lesser pride goes down upon its knees.
Two countries separated by desire!—
Whose diplomats speed back and forth by plane,
Portmanteaus stuffed with fresh apologies
Outdated by events before they land.
Negotiations wear them out: they're driven mad
Between the protocols of tears and rapture.

Locked in our fated and contiguous selves,
These worlds that too much agitate each other,
Interdependencies from hip to head,
Twin principalities both slave and free,
We coexist, proclaiming "Peace!" together.
Tell me no lies! We are divided nations
With malcontents by thousands in our streets,
These thousands torn by inbred revolutions.
A triumph is demanded, not moral victories
Deduced from small advances, small retreats.
Are the gods of our fathers not still daemonic?
On the steps of the Capitol
The outraged lion of our years roars panic,
And we suffer the guilty cowardice of the will,
Gathering its bankrupt slogans up for flight,
Like gold from ruined treasuries.
And yet, and yet, although the murmur rises,
We are what we are, and only life surprises.

—STANLEY KUNITZ

FOR HANI, AGED FIVE, THAT SHE BE BETTER ABLE TO DISTINGUISH A VILLAIN

Fox flees the farm in a red rogue dazzle
as the barnyard breaks, wakes, each screech pitched
to a dying cackle. Hackles-high, the riled roosters cry
for their raped regal roost, for their favorite gone, but for her gory
feathers. All hens cluck; ducks flap, quack, waddle; geese honk,

gabble; even the eggs rattle. As the horse snorts,
the sow grunts in her puddle; the slow cow moans low at the fuddle;
and the dogs yap, snap at the hogs in a fearful muddle. But the fox is
fled, the hen, as we know, dead. The farmer swears,
tears his hairs, but for what? Not for the fox,
not for that rake's hens and cocks; he blames the loud weasel.

Easy enough to put the blame, but more is the shame
if the choice is wrong. Truth has tricks, before long plays the devil,
and we are betwixt and between what is and what might
have been. To get the facts of nefarious acts,
we must be free of predilections, preconceptions, disproportions,
and distortions; we must be various, vicarious.
We must be fox, hens and cocks, geese and ducks, cows and
sows, hogs and dogs, and horse, of course, and farmer.
If we can doubt, we can figure out (and even that, like a nine-lived cat,
is doubtful, too). The wholly true is known to few, not to many,
perhaps not to any; and all our gains are made with brains
and taking pains, which is magical, tragical, funny.

—Gene Baro

FORM WAS THE WORLD

The boy looked out of eyes like Euclid's eyes.
Form was the world. Precision of part to part
Was just and perfect. The flint's form, the penny's bright size,
Troubled the nerves with knowledge of pure art.

The grooving of separate things together,
Perception of arched, waved, round,
Was more than the pride of blue weather.
The turn of the wheel to the ground

Or the curl of a dropped apple rind
Struck home as much joy and wonder
As the high walk of the wind,
As the roll and flow of thunder.

I remember it thinly now . . .
                          Brain's weariness is mine
Because, spontaneous, I no longer feel
My breath caught up at the strict and valid line,
Or stare at the right rondure of the wheel.

—Maurice English

FOR NICHOLAS, BORN IN SEPTEMBER

You bring the only changes to this season.
Once more, Gomorrah has enjoyed its harvest;
old cards, discarded dominoes and chips
lie scattered on the patio; the beach
is quiet, half of its shells brought home to fade
like negatives. For miles the day is empty,
given to gulls that slide along the wind
and stab the shore. And I recall the way
so many autumns came. Bulbs on a cord
tottering upside down like icicles
above the wooden bandstand, a scarf of sand,
curling, begins to bury the cement.

We used to play there, in and out like moths
among the dancers, but more often owls,
perching along the edge of night, we'd screech
and try to disapprove of what we saw.
Our parents told us that before the war
the town was better, and certainly, with time,
things would improve; their dignity was silence,
and summers lean and lifeless as the winter
afternoons. Now you have proved the future
falls in slow progressions of the present.
The night the season ended, on Labor Day,
campfires roasted strings of unsold oysters
they'd given to us free. We'd watch sparks lift
across the fire, then finally disappear.
By morning the dancers were no longer there.

For two weeks after Labor Day, we'd spot
great herds of porpoises leap up the coast
in rain and ride out like September clouds.
Always, before, it was the saddest month,
the beach and water one monotonous sea
of careless stirrings and transparencies,
the cool breezes turning the white drifts gray.

Today, I saw a red oak tree—the one
they planted when the war was won—its leaves,
stubborn as winter, clawing in the wind
as if to tear it down. The tree in time
collapsed among the barren, upright elms,
but watching it drop here reminded me
how soon the days adjusted to the fall

and settled in to wait like seeds till June,
when porpoises return, salting the tides.

My first-born, the eighteenth of September
of my only season, you have risen
like a sapling among these barren trees.
Each day I watch you spread the deepest roots
in our common soil; I touch you with my hand,
veined and strong as a leaf. This time I feel
a wind I never knew blow through my bones.

—Tod Perry

FOR THE MARSH'S BIRTHDAY

As a father to his son, as a friend to his friend,
Be pleased to show mercy, O God.
—*The Bhagavad-Gita.*

I was alone once, waiting
For you, what you might be.
I heard your grass birds fluting
Down a long road to me.
Wholly for you, for you,
I was lonely, lonely.

For how was I to know
Your voice, or understand
The Irish cockatoo?
Never on sea or land
Had I heard a voice that was
Greener than grass.

Oh, the voice lovelier was
Than a crow's dreaming face,
His secret face that smiles
Alive in a dead place.
Oh, I was lonely, lonely;
What were the not to me?

The not were nothing, then.
Now, let the not become
Nothing, and so remain,
Till the bright grass birds come
Home to the singing tree.
Then let them be.

Let them be living, then,
They have been dead so long.
Love, I am sick of pain
And sick with my longing,
My Irish cockatoo,
To listen to you,

Now you are all alive
And not a dream at all;
Now there are more than five
Voices I listen to
Call, call, call, call, call, call,
My Irish cockatoo.

—James Wright

FOR THE RAIN IT RAINETH EVERY DAY

(TO WILLIAM GRAVES, AGED 8)

Arabs complain—or so I have been told—
Interminably of heat, as Lapps complain
Even of seasonable Christmas cold;
Nor are the English yet inured to rain
Which still, my angry William, as of old
Streaks without pause your birthday windowpane.
But you are English too;
How can I comfort you?

Suppose I said, "Those gales that eastward ride
(Their wrath portended by a sinking glass)
With good St. George of England are allied"?
Suppose I said, "They freshen the Spring grass;
Arab or Lapp would envy a fireside
Where such green-fingered elementals pass"?
No, you are English too;
How could that comfort you?

—ROBERT GRAVES

THE FOSSILS

I

In the cliff over the frog pond
I clawed in the flagmarl and stones,
crushed up
lumps half grease half dust:
atrypas came out,
lophophyllidiums casting shadows,
corals bandaged in wrinkles,
wing-shaped allorismas,
sea-lily discs . . .
that did not molder into dust
but held.

Night rose up
in black smoke, making me blind.
My fingertips rubbed
smooth on my brain, I knelt in the
dark, cracking
the emptiness:
poking up spirifers into flying black
dust,

letting sylvan remains slither through
my fingers,
whiffing the glacial roses,
feeling the pure absence of the
ephemera . . .
And shall I have touched
the ornithosuchus, whose wings
try, not to evade earth, but to press
closer on it?

II

While Bill Gratwick flapped, pranced,
and called the dances,
lightheaded
as a lizard on hind legs I sashayed
with Sylvia, of the woods, as wood-
winds
flared and crackled in the leaves,
Sylph-ia, too, of that breeze
for whom even the salamander re-
kindles wings;

and I danced the 18th Century
        shoulder-rub
with Lucy,
my shoulder blades starting to glitter
on hers as we turned, sailbacks
in laired and changing dance,
our faces
smudged with light from the finger-
        tips of the ages.

III
Outside, in dark fields,
I pressed the coiled
ribs of a fingerprint on a stone:
first light in the flesh.

Over the least fossil
day breaks in gold, frankincense, and
        myrrh.

—GALWAY KINNELL

FRAU BAUMAN, FRAU SCHMIDT, AND FRAU SCHWARTZE

(SCENE: A GREENHOUSE IN MY CHILDHOOD)

Gone the three ancient ladies
Who creaked on the greenhouse ladders,
Reaching up white strings
To wind, to wind
The sweet-pea tendrils, the smilax,
Nasturtiums, the climbing
Roses, to straighten
Carnations, red
Chrysanthemums; the stiff
Stems, jointed like corn,
They tied and tucked—
These nurses of nobody else.
Quicker than birds, they dipped
Up and sifted the dirt;
They sprinkled and shook;
They stood astride pipes,
Their skirts billowing out wide into tents,
Their hands twinkling with wet;
Like witches they flew along rows,
Keeping creation at ease;
With a tendril for needle
They sewed up the air with a stem;
They teased out the seed that the cold kept asleep—
All the coils, loops, and whorls.
They trellised the sun; they plotted for more than themselves.

I remember how they picked me up, a spindly kid,
Pinching and poking my thin ribs
Till I lay in their laps, laughing,
Weak as a whiffet;
Now, when I'm alone and cold in my bed,

They still hover over me,
These ancient leathery crones,
With their bandannas stiffened with sweat,
And their thorn-bitten wrists,
And their snuff-laden breath blowing lightly over me in my first sleep.

—THEODORE ROETHKE

FRÄULEIN READS INSTRUCTIVE RHYMES

OUTSIDE HELP FOR PARENTS WHO MAY HAVE FORGOTTEN HERR DOKTOR
HOFFMAN'S "DER STRUWELPETER"

First hear the story of Kaspar the rosy-cheeked.
Once he was round and fat; he ate his dinner up.
Then see, on Monday night nothing will Kaspar eat.
Tuesday and Wednesday, *nein!* Kaspar throws down his cup.
Watch him shrink to a stick crying *nicht!* all that week.
Sunday he whispers *nicht* and falls down dead.
Now they must bury him; in the black earth he's meek.
And by his grave they leave Kaspar his meat and bread.
    Therefore, says Fräulein, slicing the sauerbraten,
    Eat what I fix for you. See what can happen?

Next prances Friedrich the terrible-tempered.
He pulls the wings from flies; he wrings the chickens' necks.
See with a long horsewhip how in this picture he
Lashes the maid, who cries into her handkerchief.
Wait, *aber*, all is well. Here the big dog comes in.
Angry black dog bites his knee and holds fast.
Now the Herr Doktor pours Friedrich bad medicine.
Downstairs, the napkined dog eats Friedrich's liverwurst.
    Child, says Fräulein, clicking her thimble cup,
    Good, *ja*, be good, or the dog comes to eat you up.

Now look at Konrad the little thumb-sucker.
Ach! but his poor mama cries when she warns him
The tailor will come for his thumbs if he sucks them.
Quick he can cut them off, easy as paper.
Out goes the mother and *wupp!* goes the thumbkin in.
Then the door opens. Enter the tailor.
See in the picture the terrible tongue in
His grinning red mouth! In his hands the great shears.
Just as she told him, the tailor goes *klipp und klapp.*
Eight-fingered Konrad has learned a sad lesson.
    Therefore, says Fräulein, shaking her chignon,
    Suck you must not or the tailor will chop!

Here is smart Robert the flying boy, bad one.
Hui! How the storm blows and coughs in the treetops.
Mama has told him today he must stay in,
But Robert slips out with umbrella and rain cap.
Now he is flying. The wind sucks and pulls him.
See, he is carried up, smaller and smaller.
His cap flies ahead of him; no one can help him.
Therefore, says Fräulein, smoothing her collar,
Mind me, says Fräulein. God stands up in Heaven.
See how He watches? He snatches the bad ones.
                                    —MAXINE W. KUMIN

FRESHMEN

My freshmen
settle in. Achilles
sulks; Pascal consults
his watch; and true
Cordelia—with her just-washed hair,

stern-hearted princess, ready to defend
the meticulous garden of truths in her high-school notebook—
uncaps her ballpoint pen.
And the corridors drum:
give us a flourish, fluorescence of light, for the teachers come,

green and seasoned, bearers
of the Word, who differ
like its letters; there are some
so wise their eyes
are birdbites; one

a mad, grinning gent with a golden tooth, God knows
he might be Pan, or the sub-
custodian; another
is a walking podium, dense
with his mystery—high

priests and attachés
of the ministry; kindly
old women, like unfashionable watering places;
and the assuming young, rolled tight as a City
umbrella;

thought-salesmen with samples cases,
and saints upon whom

merely to gaze is like Sunday—
their rapt, bright,
cat-licked faces!

And the freshmen wait;
wait bristling, acned, glowing like a brand,
or easy, chatting, munching, muscles lax,
each in his chosen corner, and in each
a chosen corner.

Full of certainties and reasons,
or uncertainties and reasons,
full of reasons as a conch contains the sea,
they wait: for the term's first bell;
for another mismatched wrestle through the year;

for a teacher who's religious in his art,
a wizard of a sort, to call the role
and from mere names
cause people
to appear.

The best look like the swinging door
to the opera just before
the Marx Brothers break through.
The worst—debased,
on the back row,

as far as one can go
from speech—
are walls where childish scribbling's been erased;
are stones
to teach.

And I am paid to ask them questions:
Dare man proceed by need alone?
Did Esau like
his pottage?
Is any heart in order after Belsen?

And when one stops to think, I'll catch his heel,
put scissors to him, excavate his chest!
Watch, freshmen, for my words about the past
can make you turn your back. I wait to throw,
most foul, most foul, the future in your face.

—BARRY SPACKS

THE FRIEND OF THE FOURTH DECADE

When I returned with drinks and nuts, my friend
Had moved to the window seat, back to the view.

The clear central pane around which ran
Smaller ones, stained yellow, crimson, blue,

Framed our country's madly whipping flag,
Its white pole above roofs, the sea beyond.

That it was time for the flag to be lowered shed
Light on my friend's tactful disinvolvement—

Or did he feel as punishment somehow
Those angry little stripes upon his shoulders?

A huge red sun flowed positively through
Him in spots, glazing, obscuring his person

To that of Anyman with ears aglow,
On a black cushion, gazing inward, mute.

After dinner he said, "I'm tired of understanding
The light in people's eyes, the smells, the food.

(By the way, those veal birds were delicious.
They're out of Fannie Farmer? I thought so.)

Tired of understanding what I hear,
The tones, the overtones; of knowing

Just what clammy twitchings thrive
Under such cold flat stones

As We-are-profoundly-honored-to-have-with-us
Our This-street-has-been-torn-up-for-your-convenience.

As for what I catch myself saying,
Don't believe me! I *despise* Thoreau.

I mean to learn, in the language of where I am going,
Barely enough to ask for food and love.

"Listen," he went on. "I have this friend—
What's that face for? Did you think I had only one?

You are my oldest friend, remember. Well:
This new friend collects stamps. I now spend mornings

With a bowl of water and my postcard box.
Cards from all over. God! Those were the years

I never used to throw out anything.
Each card then soaks five minutes while its ink

Turns to exactly the slow formal swirls
Through which a phoenix flies on Chinese silk.

These leave the water darker but still clear,
The text unreadable. It's true!

Cards from my mother, my great-uncle, you!
And the used waters deepen the sea's blue.

"I cannot tell you what this does to me.
Scene after scene's immersion and emergence

Rinsed of the word. The Golden Gate, Moroccan
Dancing boys, the Alps from Interlaken,

Fuji, the Andes, Titian's Venus, two
Mandrills from the Cincinnati zoo—

All *that* survives the flood, as does a lighter
Heart than I have had in many a day.

Salt lick big as a fist, heart, hoard
Of self one grew up prizing above rubies—

To feel it even by a grain dissolved,
Absolved I mean, recipient with writer,

By water holy from the tap, by air that dries,
Of having cared and having ceased to care . . ."

I nodded and listened, envious. When my friend
Had gone where he was going, I tried it, too.

The stamp slid off, of course, and the ink woke.
I watched my mother's *Dearest Son* unfurl

In blue ornate brief plungings-up:
Almost a wild iris taking shape.

I heard oblivion's thin siren singing,
And bore it bravely. At the hour's end,

I had my answer. Chances are it was
Some simple matter of what ink she used,

And yet her message remained legible,
The memories it stirred did not elude me.

I put my postcards back upon the shelf.
Certain things die only with oneself.

"You should see Muhammed's taxi," wrote my friend.
"Pure junkyard Bauhaus, angular, dented white,

It trails a wedding veil of squawking dust.
Each ride is worth your life—except I'm just

Not afraid. I'm not.
Those chiefly who discern us have the juju

To take our lives. Bouncing beside Muhammed,
I smile and smoke, am indestructible.

Or else I just can't picture dying
On foreign soil. These years are years of grace.

The way I feel towards home is . . . dim.
Don't worry, I'll go back. Honeymoons end.

Nor does the just man cheat his native earth
Of its inalienable right to cover him."

Finally a dung-and-emerald oasis,
No place I knew of. "Here," he wrote on the back,

"Individual and type are one.
Do as I please, I *am* the simpleton

Whose last exploit is to have been exploited
Neck and crop. In the usual bazaar,

Darker, more crisscrossed than a beggar's palm,
Smell of money draws them after me,

I answer to whatever name they call,
Drink the sweet black condescending dregs,

Try on their hungers like a shirt of flame
(Well, a sports shirt of flame) whereby I've been

Picked clean, reborn each day increasingly
Conspicuous, increasingly unseen."

Behind a door marked DANGER
(This is a dream I have about my friend),

Swaddlings of our whole civilization,
Prayers, accounts, long priceless scroll,

Whip, hawk, prow, queen, down to some last
Lost comedy, all that fine writing

Rigid with rains and suns,
Are being gingerly unwound.

There. Now the mirror. Feel the patient's heart
Pounding—dear God, this once—

Till nothing moves but to a drum.
See his eyes darken in bewilderment—

No, in joy—and his lips part
To greet the perfect stranger.

—JAMES MERRILL

FROM CANTO CXIII

Then a partridge-shaped cloud over dust storm.
The hells move in cycles,
         No man can see his own end.
The Gods have not returned. "They have never left us."
         They have not returned.
Cloud's processional and the air moves with their living.
Pride, jealousy, and possessiveness
         3 pains of hell
and a clear wind over garofani
         over Portofino 3 lights in triangulation
Or apples from Hesperides fall in their lap
         from phantom trees.

The old Countess remembered (say 1928)
                    that ball in St. Petersburg
and as to how Stef got out of Poland. . . .
                    Sir Ian told 'em help
                              would come via the sea
(the black one, the Black Sea)
                              Pétain warned 'em.
And the road under apple-boughs
                    mostly grass-covered
And the olives to windward
                              Kalenda Maja.
Li Sao, Li Sao, for sorrow

        but there is something intelligent in the cherry-stone
Canals, bridges, and house walls
                              orange in sunlight
But to hitch sensibility to efficiency?
                    grass versus granite,
For the little light and more harmony
Oh God of all men, none excluded
and howls for Schwundgeld in the Convention
                              (our Constitutional
                              17 . . . whichwhat)
Nothing new but their ignorance,
                              ever perennial
Parsley used in the sacrifice
        and (calling Paul Peter) 12%
        does not mean one, oh, four, 104%

Error of chaos. Justification is from kindness of heart
        and from her hands floweth mercy.
As for who demand belief rather than justice.
And the host of Egypt, the pyramid builder,
        waiting there to be born.
No more the pseudo-gothic sprawled house
                    out over the bridge there
                    (Washington Bridge, N.Y.C.)
                    but everything boxed for economy.
That the body is inside the soul—
        the lifting and folding brightness
        the darkness shattered,
                    the fragment.
That Yeats noted the symbol over that portico
                              (Paris).
And the bull by the force that is in him—
        not lord of it,
                    mastered.

And to know interest from usura
(Sac. Cairoli, prezzo giusto)
    In his sphere is giustizia.
In mountain air the grass frozen emerald
    and with the mind set on that light
        saffron, emerald,
           seeping.
"but that kind of ignorance" said the old priest to Yeats
  (in a railway train) "is spreading everyday from the schools"—
to say nothing of other varieties.
Article X for example—put over, and 100 years to get back
          to the awareness of
        (what's his name in that Convention).
And in thy mind beauty,
        O Artemis.
As to sin, they invented it—eh?
      to implement domination
eh? largely.
    There remains grumpiness,
      malvagità
Sea, over roofs, but still the sea and the headland.
And in every woman, somewhere in the snarl is a tenderness,
        A blue light under stars.
The ruined orchards, trees rotting. Empty frames at Limone.
And for a little magnanimity somewhere,
And to know the share from the charge
      (scala altrui)
God's eye art 'ou, do not surrender perception.

And in thy mind beauty. O Artemis
    Daphne afoot in vain speed.
When the Syrian onyx is broken.
    Out of dark, thou, Father Helios, leadest,
but the mind as Ixion, unstill, ever turning.

                —Ezra Pound

FROM THE WINDOW DOWN

I follow from my window down
The paths my children's feet have
    mown,
Running to the rim of bank
Where I stood once. Yarrow is rank,

St.-John's-wort straggles at the verge;
The paths like past and future
    merge
In a single child, myself or mine,
Poised there a season out of time.

And blown like the burrowing swal-
    low, he
Shall next in time drop down to sea,
Dropping below my sight to find
Salt desolation. I am blind;

Another watched me so. I gaze
And see myself a child, and raise
That head that I held so before
The bank undid me to the shore.

—Louis O. Coxe

FRONT STREET

I

The moon's little skullcap,
Dry divinity,
Has brought all color
Into question:
What is your skin now—
Lime or gray?
It has a kind of phosphorescent shine.
Fluorescent? Is that what I mean?
There are no words to describe it.

II

That greasy tug
Might be a spy,
That flashing lens
A trained binocular.
A death rattle has obsessed the tree
And a strangling sound the harbor
    water,
Which keeps saying, "Don't count on
    me!"—
As if we were such fools
To count on it ever!

III

I'm sorry the sick palms are so run-
    down,
That Front Street, which used to be
    so gay,
Looks like the street of a plague-
    ridden town—
Empty, apprehensive, dirty.
Do not go down the steps into the
    boat.
A storm is coming.
Can't you hear the wind?
Do you think I enjoy being arbitrary?

Do what I say.
Or else we'd better say goodbye right
    now.

IV

Why did I bring you to Front Street?
    Because
The boats are here,
In case we have to make a quick get-
    away.
All right. Call it irrational fear.
The Jews in Germany, one year be-
    fore
They saw the handwriting on the
    wall,
Would have thought you mad
If you'd told them where
They'd all end up. Think of Oedipus
A second before
The blind seer
Opened his mouth.
No. We're not going back.
We're going some place. Anywhere.
Somewhere we can be, temporarily,
    safe.

V

You think nature's a left-handed com-
    pliment?
A French one's more like it;
I could have told you, twenty years
    ago,
It's a dirty dig. Think of a time,
Five years, or one,
When people weren't at each other's
    throats.
Everywhere there are miles of files

With our names typed in them, yours
    and mine.
The point is to be invisible
Or blinding, nothing in between—
Famous or anonymous . . .
But it's much too late for people like
    us.

VI

O.K., O.K. We'll go back to the
    house.

A false alarm?
What a child you are!
Remember when we get back into
    town,
And the sun's shining, oh, so bright,
And everything seems so right, so fine,
So permanent,
Front Street will be waiting at our
    backs.

              —HOWARD MOSS

THE FROZEN HERO

The air of the museum
Warns "Do not touch." Propped still,
The divine statues wear
Sleep that could spring and kill.

That sinewy warrior, king,
Has waked, and stares in stone.
His eyes are beyond fear.
He ages; his mind is gone.

With a dead tongue he cools
The whispering visitors;
Around his niche, his cave,
The riveted city towers.

Around his marble arms
That crushed the fierce demon,
How cold through finicking glass
The atoms of light pour down.

Fabulous, finished and stripped,
For a great fall he stands:
He held up state and sky;
Hard time is on his hands.

He sees his shadow, nothing,
Etched on the scholar's book;

Pressed with the print of death,
He is praised, but cannot speak.

But yet his majesty moves:
Stealing, hidden and still,
When midnight melts the walls,
He slips his pedestal.

O now he leaps to life
In shafts deeper than rock;
In rooms no city roofs
This conqueror cleaves the dark.

Magnificent in the night
He slays his spectral foes,
He wastes the astonished earth
And wounds the still shadows.

Bent, blind, he walks in blood;
Striding in sleep, nightmares,
Beyond the darkest pole,
He freezes, but still endures.

His proud arms, perilous thews,
Stiffen in silent stone.
The slow light threads his hands
That thrashed the lost dragon.

           —THOMAS H. VANCE

THE FRUIT OF THE TREE

With a wall and a ditch between us, I watched the gate-legged dromedary
Creak open from her sleep and come headfirst toward me
As I held out three rust-mottled, tough pears, the color of camels.
When I tossed one, she made no move to catch it. Whatever they eat
Lies still and can wait: the roots and sticks, the scrag ends of brambles.

She straddled, dipping her neck; gray lips and lavender tongue,
Which can choose the best of thorns, thrust the pear to her gullet.
Choking, she mouthed it; her ruminating jaw swung up,
Her eyes lashed out. With a groan she crushed it down,
And ecstasy swept her down into the ditch, till her chin

And her pointed, prolonged face sat on the wall. She stared
At me, inventor and founder of pears. I emptied my sack.
She ate them painfully, clumsy with joy, her withers trembling,
Careless of dust on the bitten and dropped halves, ignoring flies,
Losing herself in the pit of her last stomach.

When she gazed at me again, our mouths were both deserted.
I walked away with myself. She watched me disappear;
Then, with a rippling trudge, went back to her stable
To snort, to browse on hay, to remember my sack forever.
She'd been used to having no pears, but hadn't known it.

Imagine the hostile runners, the biters of burnouses,
Coughers and spitters, whose legs can kick at amazing angles—
Their single humps would carry us willingly over dunes
Through sandstorms and the swirling djinn to the edges of oases
If they, from their waterless, intractable hearts, might stretch for pears.

—David Wagoner

THE FUNDAMENT IS SHIFTED

The call is for belief,
As once for doubt.
The old firm picture wavers
As if in water,
Like a thing off-centered.
The fundament is shifted by a hairsbreadth;
What next we hear
May be the crack of doom—

Or be, instead,
Resurrection-horn blowing full A.

The physicist
In his high country of transparent landscape,
Who sees the mountains building, the chill growing
In the sun's flame-pit, dissolution snipping
Infinitesimal threads as grain flees grain
Under the beat of the wind and the rain and the sea,
He now, earth's cautious man,
Hazards a blinding guess that he is seeing
—Sprinkled apart, here, there, in the erst-failing cosmos—
Sun-creation raging in its might,
Rising to replace.

And others still,
Outrunning reach of dim-lit eye, make probe
Of modes of being more intense, and powers
Inchoate, dark, glimpsed to be lost again.

Men quail before such newness.
If less hinged upon it
We were less bleak-minded,
Would dare to trust our weight
On what is weightless,
And, like the astronaut,
With open eye
Step out on empty space as on a shelf,
Above the plane of falling.

And not fall.

—ABBIE HUSTON EVANS

THE FURNACE OF COLORS

Who half asleep, or waking, does not hear it:
Drone where the bees swarm, sky of the cornflower,
Blaze of a water lily, music of the reapers—
Lithe bodies moving continually forward
Under the heat haze?

Dust drops from campions where the hedge is hottest;
Foxgloves and grasses tremble where a snake basks,
Coiled under brilliance. Petals of the burnet rose

Flash there, pulsating. Do the gold antennae
Feel for the white light?

All that is made here hides another making;
Even this water shows a magic surface.
Sky is translated; dragonfly and iris
Rise from the gray sheath; unremembered shadows
Cling, where the bloom breaks.

Yet not that bloom, nor any kind of foliage,
Cup, sheath, or daystar, bright above the water,
Clustered forget-me-nots tufted on the stream's bank,
Not one recalls the virginals of April
Heard, when the wood grieved.

Waking entranced, we cannot see that other
Order of colors moving in the white light.
Time is for us transfigured into colors
Known and remembered from an earlier summer,
Or into breakers

Falling on gold sand, bringing all to nothing.
Fire of the struck brand hides beneath the white spray.
All life begins there, scattered by the rainbow;
Yes, and the field flowers, these deceptive blossoms,
Break from the furnace.

—VERNON WATKINS

FURNITURE

there are youngsters now
younger than I, moving as nomads
through the makeshift camping
          grounds

who do not hope for what was
expected: the catalog comforts
of minor success

nor do they imagine
changelessness, that what they en-
          counter
remains

whose parents
in the suburbs, in the small
midwestern towns

have set down heavy houses on the
          land
& filled them
with a weight of furnishings, & in a
          manner
held them down

but not their children: who dreamed
          of Indians
tracking.
& move lightly, from city
to city

exchanging
adornments; themselves the only
shelter they have found

—PHYLLIS HARRIS

G

GAME RESUMED

My locker, green steel,
hung on its hooks a row
of old shorts and T-
shirts, sneakers down at the heel
I wore eight years ago,
still there waiting for me.

Rectangular pit, white
walls flooded in light
are still and always the same.
Why did I ever let go?
Old men can play this game.
Legs slow,
eyes unsharpen, but the wrist
still drives the shape of play,
where the antagonist
is partner. Fadeaway
backhand to front wall
drops softly into place,

as turn by turn we chase
the black sinewy ball,
and, by twos and fours, our deep
drives and corner slants
weave the pattern we keep
turn by turn like a dance.

So, after half an hour,
and after eight years or more
elapsed, after the shower,
we are what we have been,
back where we were before
on the bench at the green
and steel locker, on whose wall
the shirts and the outworn ball
on the corner of the shelf
held, these years between
(forgotten and unseen),
my self.

—RICHMOND LATTIMORE

THE GARDENER

Father, whom I knew well for forty years,
Yet never knew, I have come to know you now—
In age, make good at last those old arrears.

Though time that snows the hair and lines the brow
Has equalled us, it was not time alone
That brought me to the knowledge I here avow.

[265]

Some profound divination of your own
In all the natural effects you sought
Planted a secret that is now made known.

These woodland ways, with your heart's labor bought,
Trees that you nurtured, gardens that you planned,
Surround me here, mute symbols of your thought.

Your meaning beckons me on every hand;
Grave aisles and vistas, in their silence, speak
A language which I now can understand.

In all you did, as in yourself, unique—
Servant of beauty, whom I seek to know,
Discovering here the clue to what I seek.

When down the nave of your great elms I go
That soar their Gothic arches where the sky,
Nevertheless, with all its stars will show,

Or when the moon of summer, riding high,
Spills through the leaves her light from far away,
I feel we share the secret, you and I.

All these you loved and left. We may not stay
Long with the joy our hearts are set upon:
This is a thing that here you tried to say.

The night has fallen; the day's work is done;
Your groves, your lawns, the passion of this place
Cry out your love of them—but you are gone.

O father, whom I may no more embrace
In childish fervor, but, standing far apart,
Look on your spirit rather than your face,

Time now has touched me also, and my heart
Has learned a sadness that yours earlier knew,
Who labored here, though with the greater art.

The truth is on me now that was with you:
How life is sweet, even its very pain,
The years how fleeting and the days how few.

Truly, your labors have not been in vain;
These woods, these walks, these gardens—everywhere
I look, the glories of your love remain.

Therefore, for you, now beyond praise or prayer,
Before the night falls that shall make us one,
In which neither of us will know or care,

This kiss, father, from him who was your son.

—John Hall Wheelock

GENEVA

In this town, in the blurred and snowy dawn,
under humped eaves, in a lopsided house
built, it would seem, by gnomes, in the first
and hushed snowlight, in the snowy hush,
an alarm clock catches and trills time on its tongue
like a clockwork rooster. Silence. And then another
begins to burr in the attic, its small bell
nibbling at the edges of awareness.
So the day speaks. Sleep is left like fallen snow
on the tumbled, snow-white bed in which I wake.
    And then the bells begin their wrangling preamble
to the hour, giving tongue, tumbling
one over the other, faltering, failing, falling
like snow on the white pillow. Their gold tongues wag
with time. (They are rung, it would seem, by gnomes.)
Now, in the town, the day is on its way.
    Snowfalls nibble at the windows. In the great
assembly halls, bells ring
along the marble lobbies, calling the delegates in
to the long tables of words, where, crouched
like watchmakers, they worry away
the agendas of the world, their tongues ticking
like mechanisms, and in the earphones
the voices of interpreters trill their small alarms.
    Time, gentlemen. Time is what they are telling.
The snow melts silently, the watchsprings twitter.
What was the question? Bells
calling time obscure the answer.
(Clocks speak the only universal language,
the only one which does not need translation.)
Eyes on the snow, we listen.
The words roll on like bells
marking time; they fall and fade like snow,
leaving their meaning in a watery
residue. The diplomats pace the halls,

watching the clock, attentive to alarms.
All these words telling time fall thick as snowflakes.
We wait for the conclusion of the clock,
which never comes, except in intervals
of silence. So, the bells assume our time.
Now, in the town, something is ticking away.
(Gnomes can be glimpsed at night, in pools of lamplight,
peering through glass at something small and precious,
ticking, and probably gold.)
In this town of telling, we grow old
in a tumble of bells, and over us all,
in the continuum,
time falls, snow falls, words fall.

—ALASTAIR REID

GETTING THROUGH

I wrote the postcard to you and went out
Through melting snow to mail it. Old Miss Tree
Buttonholed me at the corner with something about
Today being our last chance. Indeed? Well, well,
Not hers and mine, I trusted gallantly,
Disengaging her knuckle from my lapel.

First thing on entering the Post Office,
I made out through my pigeonhole's dim pane
An envelope from you. Cheered up by this,
Card between teeth, I twirled the dials; they whirred
But the lock held. One, two, three times. In vain.
At the stamp window I called for Mr. Bird,

Our friendly Postmaster. Not a soul replied.
Bags of mail lay in heaps, lashed shut, the late
Snowlight upon them. When at last I tried
To avail myself of the emergency stamp machine,
A cancelled 20-franc imperforate
From Madagascar slid out, mocking, green.

Nerves, I thought, wishing more than ever, now,
You had not gone away, considering mailing
My card unstamped, presuming that somehow . . .
What's this! Your envelope lies at my feet,

Ripped open, empty, my name trickling, paling
From snow tracked in by me. Outside, Main Street

Is empty—no: a Telephone Company truck.
Why, I can phone! The mere sound of my voice
Will melt you, help decide you to come back.
But as I hurry home a water drop
Stops me, then little rainbow husks of ice.
There at the shivering telephone pole's top

Two men in rubber boots are cutting wires
Which heavily dangle from a further pole.
(Oh, May Day ribbons! Child our town attires
As Queen in tablecloth and paper crown,
Lurching down Main Street blindly as a mole!)
When the last wire is severed I lurch down

The street myself, my blankness exquisite.
Beyond a juniper hedge sits Mrs. Stone,
Mute on her dazzling lawn. Bracing to sit
In such fresh snow, I brightly call. Her hard
Gaze holds me like amber; I drop my own,
And find I cannot now read the postcard

Still in my grasp, unspotted and uncrushed.
My black inkstrokes hover intensely still
Against the light—starlings gunshot has flushed
That hover one split second, so, then veer
Away for good. The trees weep, as trees will.
Everything is cryptic, crystal-queer.

The stationery store's brow drips, ablaze
Where the pink sun has struck it with the hand
Of one remembering after days and days—
Remembering what? I am a fool, a fool!
I hear with joy, helpless to understand,
Cries of snow-crimson children leaving school.

      —JAMES MERRILL

THE GHOST

What makes permeable the ghost?
Madam, you haunt me but a young month old
And already I see the gray clock through your breasts
And, when I hold you, air

Is in my fingers or cold water at most.
How little rubbing wears the brave nap bare;
You are like old flags of honor hung in naves
Through which we see the stained glass and the vault.
Why, all goes thin and savor flies the salt.

And you in April were sure flesh in my arms;
In May,
Only an eddying in the furniture.
And who can say but time's philosopher
Whether this fading in the lover's palms
Grieves or relieves him? Only I note this much,
That there are those who spring from a rare stem
And grow more strange and solid at each touch—
Whom I have known, but you were not of them.

—HILARY CORKE

THE GHOST OF AN EDUCATION

Muzzy with drink, I let my humor recline
By the river border, watching satire dip,
First as a summer streamer, next a whip
Cracked at the surface, then a fishing line
Pulling the past reluctant from its bed
In vague and tangled shapes. Odd fish, half-dead
Bogies, and old disguises worn no longer
Dripped up, now honest scarecrows. Admiration
Saw last an ancient horrifying conger,
The long lie that was my education.

Assurance gone, satire began to quiver
Till it broke, and the thing hauled up fell back in the river,
Where it lives, with the price of my freedom on its head,
Scaring strangers, slowing the current, fouling the bed.

—JAMES MICHIE

GHOSTS

Never to see ghosts? Then to be
haunted by what is, only—to believe that glass
is for looking through, that rooms, too, can be empty,
the past past, deeds done,
that sleep, however troubled, is your own?
Do the dead lie down, then? Are blind men blind?
Is love in touch alone? Do lights go out?

And what is that shifting, shifting in the mind?
The wind, the wind?

No, they are there. Let your ear be gentle.
At dawn or owl cry, over doorway or lintel,
theirs are the voices moving night toward morning,
the garden's grief, the river's warning.
Their curious presence in a kiss,
the past quivering in what is,
our words odd-sounding, not our own—
how can we think we sleep alone?

What do they have to tell? If we can listen,
their voices are denials of all dying,
faint, on a long bell tone, lying
beyond sound or belief, in the oblique
last reach of the sense through layers of recognition. . . .
Ghost on my desk, speak, speak.

—ALASTAIR REID

THE GIFT OF SONG

Let men take note of her, touching her shyness,
How grace informs and presses the brocade
Wherein her benefits are whitely stayed,
And think all glittering enterprise and highness
Of blood or deed were yet in something minus,
Lacking the wide approval of her mouth,
And to betoken every man his drouth
Drink, in her name, all tankards to their dryness.

Wanting her clear perfection, how many tongues
Manifest what no language understands?
Yet as her beauty evermore commands
Even the tanager with tiny lungs
To flush all silence, may she by these songs
Know it was love I looked for at her hands.

—ANTHONY HECHT

GIRANDOLE

In the dark at first, we see things in their sleep,
like seeds locked up in pods, cocoons, and burs,
each with its sphinx's face persuading us,
"Our looks are black, but we're really beauties. Wait

and see." And we do till, one day, some dove of a dawn
comes in on a pink wing, singing "Wake up!"

Then there's a stir—an unfolding, unfurling, undoing
of knots, shaking off of shells, as infants outgrow
their eggs, the roe spills over in silver, and out
of each buried bean a green head butts itself free,
and the rose goes, or the snail, on its way, unrolling
its roundest corolla. Oh, the view opens up to our eye!

And see what baroque embellishments ensue
as throngs of things take shape and place in space:
the fantail vine hung with the golden horde
of its hundred gourds, and, bright in its broken shell,
a pomegranate's swarm of garnets; moonshine,
pine-tree waves, and skies all mackerel scallops.

Once a fortunate friction ignites the fuse—presto!
Chrysalids burst into blue, the firework-flowers
go up in sparks, the fountain towers, and the story's told.
Breaking through clouds, the sun leaps forth and we see
for ourselves: the blackbird's gold, and the world—what a sight!—
is a girandole, a ring of things—all lights.

—DOROTHY DONNELLY

THE GLASS BLOWER

Canaries were his hobby.
Upstairs in the attic, with his knobby
hands, he put up small-gauge wire stalls;
copper gauze, from the slant roof to the floor,
huddled the birdflock in their drowsy ark.
There were a hundred or more
that sat on crusted bars, their claws locked tight—
upright albino bats, until the night-
time came. When he groped up the stairs the light
blazed and they awoke.
The hungry bodies quickened.
A few flew at the screen, but every dark
reflection glided skillfully on the walls
behind the gold wheelings—wheels of a clock
chirping every second on the second.

Gradually it unwound.
And going to work, a Jonah's underground,

he'd disappear into a warehouse: punch in,
check orders, stir a batch of sand, start
the wheel grinding out his daily payload
of undistracted art—
and shape a universe, a toy glass ball
one shakes, seeing the plastic snowflakes fall
within a pool, upon a parasol
of plastic (underneath,
a woman and a man
were frozen in their strolling). And the haloed,
high-stooled glass blower, leaning over a Bunsen
burner, at a wooden bench, would breathe
in thin glass straws a string of glass balloons.

They were sold—the rare
canaries, then pigeons, chickens, and a pair
of guinea pigs. Experiments, they arrived
and left, like courses in a covered dish.
He even bred, in an aquarium,
rainbow-colored fish;
then, streaked with orange scars, the slim swordtails
cut a wakeless way, and the milky sails
of angelfish, razor-thin, edged trails
of tendril over rock;
the snails neither sank
nor swam, but stuffed their pinkish horns with scum.
He also stocked black mollies. Short-lived,
their bulbous heads and tapering bodies, black
tear-shapes, cruised the bottom of the tank.

Lightheaded bubbles swirled
surfacewise. Wound in a filmy world,
a fetus feeding on its inmost part,
he'd circle bar to bar each night, without
going far, but staggering home stone blind,
his pockets inside out.
Fleeced, he made the cellar workshop a cage
of pipes and copper coils, trying to gauge
the distillation and advancing age
of alcohol. Ferment-
ing, dribbling from the lips,
he would sit wall-eyed with his wheeling mind
among odd junk. Near a dog-eared sea chart,
a bottle made a toppled monument
preserving remnants of a model ship.

—JAMES SCULLY

THE GLASS TOWN

A church tower crowned the town,
double in air and water,
and over anchored houses
the round bells rolled at noon.
Bubbles rolled to the surface.
The drowning bells swirled down.

A sun burned in the bay.
A lighthouse towered downward,
moored in the mirroring fathoms.
The seaweed swayed its tree.
A boat below me floated
upside down on the sky.

An underwater wind
ruffled the red-roofed shallows
where wading stilt-legged children
stood in the clouded sand,

and down from the knee-deep harbor
a ladder led to the drowned.

Gulls fell out of the day.
The thrown net met its image
in the window of the water.
A ripple slurred the sky.
My hand swam up to meet me,
and I met myself in the sea.

Mirrored, I saw my death
in the underworld in the water,
and saw my drowned face sway in
the glass day underneath—
till I spoke to my speaking likeness,
and the moment broke with my
    breath.

—Alastair Reid

GLORY,

it spreads, the campaign—carried on
by long-distance telephone,
        with Saint Diogenes
            supreme commander.
        At the fifty-ninth minute
            of the eleventh hour, a rescuer

makes room for Mr. Carnegie's
music hall, which by degrees
        became (becomes)
            our music stronghold
        (accented on the "né," as
            perhaps you don't have to be told).

Paderewski's "palladian
majesty" made it a fane;
        Tchaikovsky, of course,
            on the opening
        night, 1891;
            and Gilels, a master, playing.

With Andrew C. and Mr. R.,
"our spearhead, Mr. Star"—

in music, Stern—
        has grown forensic,
and by civic piety
        has saved our city panic;

rescuer of a music hall
menaced by the "cannibal
        of real estate"—bulldozing potentate,
            land-grabber, the human crab
        left cowering like a neonate.

As Venice "in defense of children"
has forbidden for the citizen,
        by "a tradition of
            noble behavior,
        dress too strangely shaped or scant,"
            posterity may impute error

to our demolishers of glory. Cocteau's "Preface
to the Past" contains the phrase
        "When very young my dream
            was of pure glory."
        Must he say "was" of his "light
            dream," which confirms our glittering story?

They need their old brown home. Cellist,
violinist, pianist—
        used to unmusical
            impenetralia's
        massive masonry—have found
            reasons to return. Fantasias

of praise and rushings to the front
dog the performer. We hunt
        you down, Saint Diogenes—
            are thanking you for glittering,
        for rushing to the rescue
            as if you'd heard yourself performing.
                                    —MARIANNE MOORE

THE GLOVE

In its absence it has become beautiful,
    my black-leather, my rabbit fur-lined glove,
given over to the foreignness of strangers,

    of mad dogs thieving away to the deep woods
        with my lost glove. I imagine even
the hunger of hobos and the coveted taste

    of leather in their infamous mulligan stews.
        I consider my lost glove. I consider
the copulation of rabbits, the precise instant

    of conception of that hapless mother's son
        who would inhabit my lost glove. I think
of the busy, unknowable chain of commerce,

    the wholesale and the retail of my lost glove.
        And today I leave my home uncertain
which will effect attention to itself—the one

    gloved hand or the one gloveless. I revisit
        my itinerary of the night before:
Huffy's Sinclair, the Eagle Mart, and Tic-Toc Lounge;

    no one has seen my lost glove. Later I find it
        grease-stained behind the cash register of
the Campus Grill. I pull it on, my slipped skin,

    and it fits like a good metaphor in that
        fortuitous gathering of elements:
cowhide, rabbit fur, the five fingers of my hand.

                                            —HAROLD BOND

THE GOLDFISH WIFE

It is Monday morning
And the goldfish wife
Comes out with her laundry
To shout her message.
There! Her basket glistens
In the sun and shines—
A wicker O. And see how
The goldfish wife touches
The clothes, her fingers

Stretching toward starch,
The wind beating her hair
As though all hair
Were laundry. Come,
Dear fishwife, golden
In your gills, come tell
Us of your life and be
Specific. Come into our lives—
Where no sun shines and no

Winds spill
The laundry from the rope—
Come on the broomstick of a
Widow-witch, fly

From the empty clotheslines
Of the poor
And teach us how to air
Our lives again.

—SANDRA HOCHMAN

GOLGOTHA

Gray fur collars on a steel limb,
The welders, keeping hands warm
Inside their sheet-plastic cocoon,
Weave the new dorm
Late into night. It's deadlined
For April. According to plan,
The chewed hill's to be redefined,
And seedlings, to a man,
Stood up in ranks against blight,
Green lawn unrolled,
Brick walls, adolescently bright,
Sprayed to look old.

In my locked childproof basement
        workroom,
Furnace vapors
Chase their own tails in the gloom,
I face ungraded papers,
An iron door in a brick wall
A kick could splinter
Diking the ashes of all
Our hearths of winter,
Half-hear a slow thrash of bedsheets,
A mouse scratch, taking chances
At the trap. Down the spine of my
        Keats
Mildew advances.

Cramped   hand,   an   unrecognized
        name:
How Youth Is Shafted
By Society . . . now I know him,
They got him. Drafted.
Through vines in a gnarled neutral
        zone,
A locust nation,
With flamethrowers chewing, moves
        on
About slow defoliation.
Interesting idea, says my pen
To a John Bircher—liar, liar!
Shots rattle. No, the stuffed lion's
Brass eyeballs in the dryer.

I take out trash, not to read more.
Torn gift wraps, Christmas-tree rain.
Lift can cover on a white horde
Writhing. Lean rain
Blown to bits by the murderous wind
Has it in for you, finger and face,
Drives   through   every   hole   to   your
        brain,
Taking over the place
As though it had been there before,
Had come back in its own hour,
Snow gaining ground in the dark yard,
The mad in absolute power.

—X. J. KENNEDY

GOODBYE TO REGAL

(LONDON, 1959)

In forgiving mood, this sultry July afternoon,
The last lingering child will be gone
From the gates of Regal Secondary Modern School,
A school most teachers gratefully shun.

The intimate daily struggle so calmly ends,
Without victory to either side.
Goodbye to the staff, and to the boys more sadly,
And the girls most sadly, I have replied.

And a friend offers congratulations, echoing
The complaints I should have kept unsaid:
"By God, you must be glad to leave." My children,
For his ignorance I could strike him dead.

—DANIEL HUWS

GOODBYE TO SERPENTS

Through rain falling on us no faster
Than it runs down the wall we go
          through,
My son and I shed Paris like a skin
And slip into a cage to say goodbye.
Through a hole in the wall
Of the Jardin des Plantes
We come to go round

The animals for the last time;
Tomorrow we set out for home.
For some reason it is the snakes
To which we seem to owe
The longest farewell of our lives.
These have no bars, but drift
On an island held still by a moat,

Unobstructedly gazing out.
My son will not move from watching
Them through the dust of cold water,
And neither will I, when I realize
That this is my farewell
To Europe also. I begin to look
More intently than I ever have.

In the moat one is easily swimming
Like the essence of swimming itself,
Pure line and confident curve,
Requiring no arms or legs.
In a tree, a bush, there is one

Whose body is living there motion-
          less,
Emotionless, with drops running down,

His slack tail holding a small
Growing gem that will not fall.
I can see one's eyes in the brush,
As fixed as a portrait's,
Gazing into, discovering, forgetting
The heart of all rainfall and sorrow.
He licks at the air,

Tasting the carded water
Changed by the leaves of his home.
The rain stops in midair before him
Mesmerized as a bird—
A harmony of drops in which I see
Towers and churches, domes,
Capitals, streets like the shining

Paths of the Jardin des Plantes,
All old, all cold with my gaze
In glittering, unearthly fascination.
I say, "Yes! So I have seen them!
But I have brought also the human,
The presence of self and of love."
Yet it is not so. My son shifts

Uneasily back and away, bored now,
A tourist to the bitter end,

And I know I have not been moved
Enough by the things I have moved
    through,
And I have seen what I have seen

Unchanged, hypnotized, and percep-
    tive:
The jewelled branches,

The chandeliers, the windows
Made for looking through only when
    weeping,
The continent hazy with grief,
The water in the air without support
Sustained in the serpent's eye.

      —JAMES DICKEY

THE GRACEFUL BASTION

A white butterfly
in an August garden,
light as it may seem

among the zinnias
and verbenas,
fragile among the red

trumpeted petunias,
is ribbed with steel
wired to the sun

whose triumphant power
will keep it safe,
free as laughter,

secure against
bombardments no more
dangerous to its

armored might than if
the cotton clouds
should merely fall.

    —WILLIAM CARLOS WILLIAMS

THE GRANDSON

There goes the grandson, run off to the beach!
It's *me!* Canary trolleys in a daze
round a corner, parade through blocks of days
like walking on eggs. Spirited out of reach . . .

At each wand's live tip, a stunning wheel leads
blue electrical sparks. They jump the wire—
meteorites, confetti of dying fire.
Clang. Clang. Turned off, then, in flourishing weeds.

I whistled toward the sea . . . *a manikin
whose pores pinked and closed, a glowing disease.*
Evenings, I fell in with the cool sea-breeze
while secret fevers riffled through my skin. . . .

Aeons ago! Now everything depends.
Tugged inside-out like a sweater, all seams,
one is less definite. A cinder. Age seems
a matter of finding yourself at loose ends.

I make for anarchy, the final coup.
But who goes there? What cast-off human fate
runs away to sea? I see. I see! Wait,
wait for me, dear old days! I'm coming too.

                                    —JAMES SCULLY

GRANITE AND STEEL

Enfranchising cable, silvered by the sea,
　　of woven wire, grayed by the mist,
　　and Liberty dominate the Bay—
　　her feet as one on shattered chains,
　　once whole links wrought by Tyranny.

Caged Circe of steel and stone,
　　her parent German ingenuity.
　　"O catenary curve" from tower to pier,
　　implacable enemy of the mind's deformity,
　　of man's uncompunctious greed,
　　his crass love of crass priority,
　　　　just recently
obstructing acquiescent feet
about to step ashore when darkness fell
　　without a cause,
as if probity had not joined our cities
　　in the sea.

"O path amid the stars
crossed by the seagull's wing!"
"O radiance that doth inherit me!"
—affirming inter-acting harmony!

Untried expedient, untried; then tried;
　　sublime elliptic two-fold egg—
way out; way in; romantic passageway
first seen by the eye of the mind,
then by the eye. O steel! O stone!
Climactic ornament, double rainbow,
as if inverted by French perspicacity,
　　John Roebling's monument,
　　German tenacity's also;
　　composite span—an actuality.

                                    —MARIANNE MOORE

GRASSE: THE OLIVE TREES

Here luxury's the common lot. The light
Lies on the rain-pocked rocks like yellow wool
And around the rocks the soil is rusty bright
From too much wealth of water, so that the grass
Mashes under the foot, and all is full
Of heat and juice and a heavy jammed excess.

Whatever moves moves with the slow complete
Gestures of statuary. Flower smells
Are set in the golden day, and shelled in heat,
Pine and columnar cypress stand. The palm
Sinks its combs in the sky. This whole South swells
To a soft rigor, a rich and crowded calm.

Only the olive contradicts. My eye,
Travelling slopes of rust and green, arrests
And rests from plenitude where olives lie
Like clouds of doubt against the earth's array.
Their faint dishevelled foliage divests
The sunlight of its color and its sway.

Not that the olive spurns the sun; its leaves
Scatter and point to every part of the sky,
Like famished fingers waving. Brilliance weaves
And sombres down among them, and among
The anxious silver branches, down to the dry
And twisted trunk, by rooted hunger wrung.

Even when seen from near, the olive shows
A hue of far away. Perhaps for this
The dove brought olive back, a tree which grows
Unearthly pale, which ever dims and dries,
And whose great thirst, exceeding all excess,
Teaches the South it is not paradise.

      —RICHARD WILBUR

A GREET

a great

man
is
gone.

Tall as the truth

was who: and
wore his (mountains
understand

how) life

like a (now
with
one sweet sun

in it, now with a

million
flaming billion kinds
of nameless

silence) sky;
—E. E. CUMMINGS

THE GREAT BEAR

Even on clear nights, lead the most supple children
Out onto hilltops, and by no means will
They make it out. Neither the gruff round image
From a remembered page nor the uncertain
Finger, tracing that image out, can manage
To mark the lines of what ought to be there,
Passing through certain bounding stars until
The whole massive expanse of bear appear
Swinging, across the ecliptic, and although
The littlest ones say nothing, others respond,
Making us thankful in varying degrees
For what we would have shown them: "There it is!"
"I see it now!" Even "Very like a bear!"
Would make us grateful. Because there is no bear,

We blame our memory of the picture. Trudging
Up the dark, starlit path, stooping to clutch
An anxious hand, perhaps the outline faded
Then; perhaps, could we have retained the thing
In mind ourselves, with it we might have staged
Something convincing. We easily forget
The huge, clear, homely dipper that is such
An event to reckon with, an object set
Across the space the bear should occupy;
But, even so, the trouble lies in pointing
At any stars. For one's own finger aims
Always elsewhere; the man beside one seems

Never to get the point. "No! The bright star
Just above my fingertip." The star,

If any, that he sees beyond one's finger
Will never be the intended one. To bring
Another's eye to bear in such a fashion
On any single star seems to require
Something very like a constellation
That both habitually see at night;
Not in the stars themselves but in among
Their scatter, perhaps, some old familiar sight
Is always there to take a bearing from.
And if the smallest child of all should cry
Out on the wet black grass because he sees
Nothing but stars, though claiming that there is
Some bear not there that frightens him, we need
Only reflect that we ourselves have need

Of what is fearful (being really nothing),
With which to find our way about the path
That leads back down the hill again, and with
Which to enable the older children, standing
By us, to follow what we mean by "This
Star," "That one," "The other one beyond it."
But what of the tiny, scared ones?—Such a bear—
Who needs it? We can still make do with both
The dipper that we always knew was there
And the bright, simple shapes that suddenly
Emerge on certain nights. To understand
The signs that stars compose, we need depend
Only on stars that are entirely there
And the apparent space between them. There

Never need be lines between them, puzzling
Our sense of what is what. What a star does
Is never to surprise us as it covers
The center of its patch of darkness, sparkling
Always, a point in one of many figures.
One solitary star would be quite useless,
A frigid conjecture, true but trifling,
And any single sign is meaningless
If unnecessary. Crab, bull, and ram,
Or frosty irregular polygons of our own
Devising, or, finally, the Great Dark Bear
That we can never quite believe is there—
Having the others, any one of them
Can be dispensed with. The Bear, of all of them,

Is somehow most like any one, taken
At random, in that we always tend to say
That just because it might be there, because
Some Ancients really traced it out, a broken
And complicated line, webbing bright stars
And fainter ones together, because a bear
Habitually appeared, then even by day
It is for us a thing that should be there.
We should not want to train ourselves to see it.
The world is everything that happens to
Be true. The stars at night seem to suggest
The shapes of what might be. If it were best,
Even, to have it there (Such a great bear!
All hung with stars!), there still would be no bear.

—JOHN HOLLANDER

GREAT CENTRAL RAILWAY, SHEFFIELD VICTORIA TO BANBURY

"Unmitigated England"
　Came swinging down the line
That day the February sun
　Did crisp and crystal shine.
Dark red at Kirkby Bentinck stood
　A steeply gabled farm
Mid ash trees and a sycamore
　In charismatic calm.
A village street—a manor house—
　A church—then, tallyho!,
We pounded through a housing scheme
　With telly masts a-row,
Where cars of parked executives
　Did regimented wait
Beside administrative blocks
　Within the factory gate.
She waved to us from Hucknall South
　As we hooted round a bend
From a curtained front-room window did
　The diesel driver's friend.
Through cuttings deep to Nottingham
　Precariously we wound;
The swallowing tunnel turned the train
　To London's Underground;

Above the fields of Leicestershire
　On arches we were borne,
And the rumble of the railway drowned
　The thunder of the Quorn;
And silver shone the steeples out
　Above the barren boughs;
Colts in a paddock ran from us
　But not the solid cows;
And quite where Rugby Central is
　Does only Rugby know—
We stopped to watch the station wait
　And sadly saw it go.
By now the sun of afternoon
　Showed ridge and furrow shadows,
And shallow, unfamiliar lakes
　stood shivering in the meadows.
Is Woodford church or Hinton church
　The one I ought to see?
Or were they both too much restored
　In 1883?
I do not know. Toward the west
　A trail of glory runs,
And we leave the old Great Central line
　For Banbury and buns.

—JOHN BETJEMAN

THE GREAT SCARF OF BIRDS

Ripe apples were caught like red fish in the nets
of their branches. The maples
were colored like apples,
part orange and red, part green.
The elms, already transparent trees,
seemed swaying vases full of sky. The sky
was dramatic with great straggling V's
of geese streaming south, mare's-tails above them;
their trumpeting made us look up from golf.
The course sloped into salt marshes,
and this seemed to cause the abundance of birds.

As if out of the Bible or science fiction,
a cloud appeared, a cloud of dots
like iron filings which a magnet
underneath the paper undulates.
It dartingly darkened in spots,
paled, pulsed, compressed, distended, yet
held an identity firm: a flock
of starlings, as much one thing as a rock.
One will moved above the trees
the liquid and hesitant drift.

Come nearer, it became less marvellous,
more legible, and merely huge.
Like dutiful Lot, I turned my back.
Later, I lazily looked around.

The rise of the fairway above and behind us was tinted,
so evenly tinted I might not have noticed
but that at the rim of the delicate shadow
the starlings were thicker and outlined the flock
as an inkstain in drying pronounces its edges.
The gradual rise of green was vastly covered;
I had thought nothing in nature could be so broad but grass.

And as
I watched, one bird,
prompted by accident or will to lead,
ceased resting; and, lifting in a casual billow,
the flock ascended as a lady's scarf,
transparent, of gray, might be twitched
by one corner, drawn upward and then,
decided against, negligently tossed toward a chair.
Melting all thought, the southward cloud withdrew into the air.

—JOHN UPDIKE

THE GREEN AND THE BLACK

Il te fauldra de vert vestir, c'est la livrée aux amoureux.
—*Fifteenth-century French song.*

"Colors," she said, "are never so fine
As when they're worn for fancy's sake
To tell a tale, or go like wine
To your heart and your head,
And there overtake
Blood, mind, and soul, unravishèd."

"Colors," I said, "are all very well
When a color means to both one
       thing:
Red is the fire that burns in Hell,

And gray is a sad tomorrow;
But why is green the spring,
When desire is black like sorrow?"

"Green," she said, "is just for love.
Will you make it black, then, also?"
"Blue is for fools and the sky above,
And man, man is a strange thing
Of sun and shadow,
All colors in a fountain changing."

—ANTHONY BAILEY

THE GREEN SHEPHERD

Here sit a shepherd and a shepherdess,
He playing on his melancholy flute;
The sea wind ruffles up her simple dress
And shows the delicacy of her foot.

And there you see Constantinople's wall
With arrows and Greek fire, molten lead;
Down from a turret seven virgins fall,
Hands folded, each one praying on her head.

The shepherd yawns and puts his flute away.
It's time, she murmurs, we were going back.
He offers certain reasons she should stay . . .
But neither sees the dragon on their track.

A dragon like a car in a garage
Is in the wood, his long tail sticking out.
Here rides St. George, swinging his sword and targe,
And sticks the grinning dragon in the snout.

Puffing a smoke ring, like the cigarette
Over Times Square, Sir Dragon snorts his last.
St. George takes off his armor in a sweat.
The Middle Ages have been safely passed.

What is the sail that crosses the still bay,
Unnoticed by the shepherds? It could be

A caravel that's sailing to Cathay,
Westward from Palos on the unknown sea.

But the green shepherd travels in her eye
And whispers nothings in his lady's ear,
And sings a little song, that roses die,
Carpe diem, which she seems pleased to hear.

The vessel they ignored still sails away
So bravely on the water, Westward Ho!
And murdering, in a religious way,
Brings Cortez to the Gulf of Mexico.

Now Portugal is fading, and the state
Of Castile rising purple on Peru;
Now England, now America grows great—
With which these lovers have nothing to do.

What do they care if time, uncompassed, drift
To China, and the crew is a baboon?
But let him whisper always, and her lift
The oceans in her eyelids to the moon.

The dragon rises crackling in the air,
And who is god but Dagon? Wings careen,
Rejoicing, on the Russian hemisphere.
Meanwhile, the shepherd dotes upon her skin.

Old Aristotle, having seen this pass,
From where he studied in the giant's cave,
Went in and shut his book and locked the brass
And lay down with a shudder in his grave.

The groaning pole had gone more than a mile;
These shepherds did not feel it where they loved,
For time was sympathetic all the while
And on the magic mountain nothing moved.

—Louis Simpson

H

THE HABEAS CORPUS BLUES

In the cathedral the acolytes are praying;
in the tavern the teamsters are drinking booze;
in his attic at dusk the poet is playing,
the poet is playing the Habeas Corpus Blues.

The poet refers the black keys to the white,
he weaves himself a shroud of simple harmonics;
across the street a house burns; in its light
he skeins more skillfully his bland ironics.

All down the block the windows bloom with faces,
the paired eyes glisten in the turning glare;
and the engines throb, and up the ladder races
an angel, with a helmet on his hair.

He breaks the window in with a golden axe,
crawls through the smoke, and disappears forever;
the roof slumps in, and the whole city shakes,
the faces at the windows say *Ah!* and *Never!*

And then the hour; and near and far are striking
the belfry clocks; and from the harbor mourn
the tugboat whistles, much to the poet's liking,
smoke rings of bronze to the fevered heavens borne.

And the hydrants are turned off, the hose rewound;
no longer now are the dirty engines drumming;
the fireman's broken body at last is found,
the fire is out, the insurance man is coming.

And in the cathedral the acolytes are praying,
and in the tavern the teamsters are drinking booze;
while, in his attic, the poet is still playing,
the poet is playing the Habeas Corpus Blues.

—CONRAD AIKEN

HALF

Half of a clasping of the hands
is better, long love understands,
than none. So, in her bed, let her,
at arm's reach from my own, get her
sleep untouched by my demands,
as innocent as when from England's
ferry (fifty years!) she stands
before me, my far, far better

half of a clasp.
At our ages, twenty-one and
sixteen, in the Gare du Nord, bands
were born that, when I met her
first, we didn't know a letter
of—the A's, much less the amper-
      sand's,
half of a clasp.

—HAWLEY TRUAX

HALF-BENT MAN

Haunts me the lugubrious shape
Of a half-blind, burly, old
Man, half bent to earth,
Who on the Princeton campus
Spears stray papers with a nail-
Ended stick, lurching, walking
Crankily, true scavenger
Ridding the earth of detail
And debris, always evident,
A bent man, the true condition,
Half-blind, but cleansing life,
Putting trash in a burlap bag,
He moves as it seems to me

With a profound, heavy purpose,
I am haunted by his life
As towers, books, professors, ideas
Mingle in a world beyond him,
But it is his dark, own burdens
In his bent, half-seeing, weary attitude
I claim as man's and mine,
And O blind-man, rag-picker,
Paper-picker, cleanser of domains,
I shall not betray your meaning
As time bends us to the earth
And we pick what gems and scraps
There are from magnificence.

—RICHARD EBERHART

HAPPINESS OF 6 A.M.

Now you come again
Like a very patient ghost,
Offering me Zen records,
A discourse on the stomach
As the seat of the soul,
Your long white neck to kiss.
The tiger's eye that is
Your favorite jewel

Shines in your hand.
Wanting to, I can't conjure
You up, not a touch.
Unbidden, you cross a thousand miles
To say, "This is the gift
I was going to give you forever."

—HARVEY SHAPIRO

A HARVEST TO SEDUCE

Upon the tree of time
The fruit looms high,
The fruit so fair to pluck!
The hour's late and black.
The time-tree quivers,
Loosens, and delivers
The midnight crop.

Twelve drop,
A harvest to seduce,

Lacking joy or juice.

Beware the vain lament,
The hunger for what's spent.
This is dead-sea fruit
And ashes to the taste.
Quash it with your foot.
What is past is past.

—MELVILLE CANE

HEAD COUPLES

We come together once more, we four, in the center,
Bow and turn single, searching each other's eyes
With brief glances, reading answers to questions unuttered,
Sharing our secret, declaring our silent surprise.
Right and left through, we swing to opposite places
And watch with formal faces while others repeat
Our movements, as though their wills and not the music
Imposed the pattern we had exposed for their feet.
We advance and they retreat in dignified measure;
As they come forward, we part and drop behind;
Thus, in symmetrical circles, although independent,
Our lives, in a slow quadrille, have intertwined.

—WILLIAM H. MATCHETT

HEAVY HEAVY HEAVY

Who winds the clumsy flower clock now, I wonder,
And opens the minaret in Waterworks Park
For bird's-eye views of captive fern and reindeer?
"Heavy heavy heavy hangs over thy head,"
The flower clock said,
"What shall ye do to redeem it?"

Do conch shells hum in shingled bungalows
Where stop-streets subdivide eternity?
Has the crutch bloomed in St. Bartholomew's?

Crazy as preachers, running all night long,
I wonder if streetcars still go off their trolleys,
Trailing brimstone, tolling cling and clang?
"Heavy heavy heavy hangs over thy head,"
The trolley car said,
"What shall ye do to redeem it?"

And there were sea gulls that far from the sea!
Once, I recall, on the soft river air,
Like a hovering Holy Ghost, one talked to me.
It was a night in spring, when ice floes rolled
Like foggy castles in the melting rain.
"Heavy heavy heavy hangs over thy head,"
The ice floe said,
"What shall ye do to redeem it?"

I called it my home town, I guess, although
Constantinople seems more plausible.
I wonder if the night-shift lights still glow
Like sea fires in a shipwrecked neighborhood.
I wonder if some still-eyed ten-year-old
Goes sidewise on the sea floor as I did.
"Heavy heavy heavy hangs over thy head,"
The night lights said,
"What shall ye do to redeem it?"

Must time so rage behind that I still go
Face-down forever toward some small event?
And does my echo know what once I knew?
"Heavy heavy heavy hangs over thy head,"
The echo, echoing, said,
"What shall ye do to redeem it?"

                                    —JOHN MALCOLM BRINNIN

HENGEST CYNING

THE KING'S EPITAPH

Beneath this stone lies the body of Hengist
Who founded in these islands the first kingdom
Of the royal house of Odin
And glutted the screaming eagle's greed.

THE KING SPEAKS

I know not what runes will be scraped on the stone
But my words are these:

Beneath the heavens I was Hengist the mercenary.
My might and my courage I marketed to kings
Whose lands lay west over the water
Here at the edge of the sea
Called the Spear-Warrior;
But a man's might and his courage can
Not long bear being sold,
And so after cutting down all through the North
The foes of the Briton king,
From him too I took light and life together.
I like this kingdom that I seized with my sword;
It has rivers for the net and the oar
And long seasons of sun
and soil for the plough and for husbandry
And Britons for working the farms
And cities of stone which we shall allow
To crumble to ruin,
Because there dwell the ghosts of the dead.
But behind my back I know
These Britons brand me traitor,
Yet I have been true to my deeds and my daring
And to other men's care never yielded my destiny
And no one dared ever betray me.

—JORGE LUIS BORGES
(*Translated from the Spanish by
Norman Thomas di Giovanni*)

THE HERDS

Climbing northward
At dusk when the horizon rose like a hand I would turn aside
Before dark I would stop by the stream falling through black ice
And once more celebrate our distance from men

As I lay among stones high in the starless night
Out of the many hoof tracks the sounds of herds
Would begin to reach me again
Above them their ancient sun skating far off

Sleeping by the glass mountain
I would watch the flocks of light grazing
And the water preparing its descent
To the first dead

—W. S. MERWIN

HERON

He comes down to the shadow
that he left in the shallow
last night. Imperturbable,
pickerel in their stations
barely shift, invulnerable
with him. His feet know these stones.

There are other ways than this:
there are ways only he knows.
In a rickyard where rats are,
he could circle, coil his neck,
and, with wings at the trail, thrash
　　　straw,
and spike what he cared to spike.

And there will happen a time
once more for the cheap, random
kill; for striding dikes in March,
rictus agape, wanton, lewd
with his swagger in some ditch,
randy for the taste of toad.

That is for spring. Lethargy
attends easy victory
now. He would slump on his glut,
lumpish with sloth, his wings
lifting, if they lifted, to a flight
without the rhythms of once.

So, while the painted Carolina
duck squat in sets, like china
on the calico water
of dawn, a thick glaze of sleep
on them, the great gray hoarder
of his want, ravening, keeps

the tensile shadow of neck
in readiness round the rock
under him and, ignoring
the trees where woodpeckers drum
out his hunger, bides, waiting
for the shoal he knows will come.

—TED WALKER

HIGH WIND AT THE BATTERY

The corner bank has lost a great window.
Pete's lunch counter has shattered glass
sitting in its booths.
All the flags are straining horizontally
and the huge crane at Water Street is nodding

because down here at the toe-end of Manhattan
the February winds are howling,
having left the Plain States a few days ago
but not the least bit tired from the trip.

Feeling none too safe in my loft
tucked between tall buildings,
I look up quickly at each shudder of a window,
at every lash of the loose aerial against the glass.

The pigeons, whose roaring coos wake
me up all the time, are keeping quiet
and nervous in several corners. There are

a couple of them outside my bathroom not even
being sexy—apprehensive as hell.

We're always being surprised by weather in this city,
always unprepared for anything natural,
like a rainstorm or blizzard or now this wild wind—
living so much behind walls and travelling around in tunnels.

But I have to admit the wind does excite me.
I'm sorry I'm not at the top of one of these buildings
so I could see things blowing around,
the water arching its back at being rubbed the wrong way,
smoke from ships' stacks looping in every direction.

As a matter of fact, wind like this means
that for a short time the air will be fresher,
that the city is getting a needed dusting—
means that we're that much nearer to slow-coming spring.

—RALPH POMEROY

A HILL

In Italy, where this sort of thing can occur,
I had a vision once—though you understand
It was nothing at all like Dante's, or the visions of saints,
And perhaps not a vision at all. I was with some friends,
Picking my way through a warm, sunlit piazza
In the early morning. A clear fretwork of shadows
From huge umbrellas littered the pavement and made
A sort of lucent shallows in which was moored
A small navy of carts. Books, coins, old maps,
Cheap landscapes, and ugly religious prints
Were all on sale. The colors and noise,
Like the flying hands, were gestures of exultation,
So that even the bargaining
Rose to the ear like a voluble godliness.
And then, when it happened, the noises suddenly stopped,
And it got darker; pushcarts and people dissolved,
And even the great Farnese Palace itself
Was gone, for all its marble; in its place
Was a hill, mole-colored and bare. It was very cold,
Close to freezing, with a promise of snow.
The trees were like old ironwork gathered for scrap
Outside a factory wall. There was no wind,
And the only sound for a while was the little click
Of ice as it broke in the mud under my feet.

I saw a piece of ribbon snagged on a hedge,
But no other sign of life. And then I heard
What seemed the crack of a rifle. A hunter, I guessed;
At least I was not alone. But just after that
Came the soft and papery crash
Of a great branch somewhere unseen falling to earth.

And that was all, except for the cold and silence
That promised to last forever, like the hill.

Then fingers came through, and prices, and I was restored
To the sunlight and my friends. But for more than a week
I was scared by the plain bitterness of what I had seen.
All this happened about ten years ago,
And it hasn't troubled me since, but at last, today,
I remembered that hill; it lies just to the left
Of the road north of Poughkeepsie, and, as a boy,
I stood before it for hours in wintertime.

—ANTHONY HECHT

HIROSHIGE

JAPANESE WOOD-BLOCK PRINT MASTER (1797–1858)

Print, with his hand, his eye, was more than print,
And color more than color,
As the green of that Chinese vase—
Cool as a brimming pond one thousand years—
As poem, paint, sound, or cut of stone
Outglows its master.

That samurai is surely fast alive
In his hunched and silhouetted dozing, assback,
In the blur of fog, on the hump-backed
Bridge.
           And the carvèd runners,
On my west wall, in a marvel of rain,
They slant into a shower of wind,
Their burden heavy, the hill steep;
Black tree-shadows leap behind the road.

Rain pleased this master whether falling,
Falling upon a dark, walled island keep,
Or drenching beggar boys at play, or in sleep

In grasses by a baked summer road.
Their shriek, clear, echoes down my western hall.

Sun, wind, and star wined and pleased
Him, in the prism of his largeness,
With his bags of color, on his sketching walks,
Who rendered composed and perfect
A hawk's arc
Above a distant snow-locked plain, star-stippled
Where men slept at the foot of frozen fires,
Where perhaps one gray woman, at point
Of earliest morning, squawked
Cold talk of dreams to the frosty spirits of air.

But rising through the colors of his stories
(As a horseman approaching in forests of falling leaves),
The samurai moves; he rocks
In all odd angles in his doze,
Past twin hanging towers of smoke
From anyone's embers,
Past the sea wall dripping water, and slow,
Approaching with sleep in his eyes for a hundred years
The gate of stone, the lantern burning waxen,
And, in the hollow, the dream-hung,
The fog-blurred grave.

—MARK M. PERLBERG

HISTORY LESSON

The young eyes leave the volume and stray out,
Weeping for greatness gone, but half in pride
That they have been the witness; they alone
May estimate the blank since wisdom died.

They wind among the water towers and pierce
The many moonwhite roofs, like gravestones laid
On courage; one far sepulchre of souls.
The city is long silent; not a maid

Expects upon her window any more
The tap of steel, the leather-handed love.
She has gone in forever; nor do clouds
Burst into fiery grief and clash above.

The eyes return, and words march on again
With the proud tramp of yesterday's green earth.

Brown are the branches now, and spent the sap
Of the well mind that guessed the body's worth.

So one across the room, observing, smiles.
And sleeps; for this is how the creatures grow:
Dim months of pain from out their little past;
Then lighted strength; and then the letting go.

—MARK VAN DOREN

HITCHHIKER

Each man to his forced march; this is mine.
In the end, everything runs out, runs
Under the wheels—a bandage unwinding
On the center line. Sometimes when my ribs clang
Like a metal signpost at the edge of town,
And so much of the dark I cannot shut out
Crawls with me into my sleeping bag,
I try to think where the owl goes.
For years now my life has taken
No sharp turns, no climb, no detour,
But moves in neutral down
This smooth tar lane, one way.

The towns en route, the festooned, blazing towns,
Are they dreams in my sleep, vanished
On waking? Even so, watching that white line
Grow thin and luminous,
I feel the moon's hub unhinge from center
And roll berserk.

—JACK MARSHALL

THE HOLE IN THE SEA

It's there
in the hole of the sea
where the solid truth lies,
written and bottled,
and guarded by limp-
winged angels—
one word under glass,
magnified by longing
and by the light tricks
of the moving man

in the moon.
Nights, that word shows,
up from the bottle,
up through the water,
up from the imaginable.
So that all who cannot
imagine, but yearn toward
the word in the water,
finding it smaller
in the hole in the sea,

rest there. If no one
has drowned quite
in the hole of the sea,
that is a point
for theology. "Blame God
when the waters part,"
say sailors and Hebrews;
blame God, who writes us,
from His holy solution,

not to be sunk,
though all our vessels
convey black messages
of the end of the world.
So goes the story,
the storybook story, so goes
the saleable story:
Courage is in that bottle,
the driest thing there is.

—MARVIN BELL

THE HOLES

Suddenly I remember the holes,
suddenly I think of a man with no entrances,
no exits, the closed man, with feelers or claws
so sensitive that he can tell
what rock is, or flesh, water, or flame.
Where does everything go when it comes in?
What should I do with the pure speech of cells
where we find ourselves?
The river flies, the dusk crawls into the ground,
the streets get up and leave,
the sun recklessly feeds our blood.
We could be crouching on the branch, we could be
gnawing the brown feathers and thighs of a new animal,
we could be plotting under the ice while others dream.
But I want the infinite man who sleeps
in my veins to rise, I want to hear
the thin buzzing that floats out of my chest
like an arm of locusts making terrible decisions.
Sometimes I want to die because of this.

—STEPHEN BERG

HOMECOMING—MASSACHUSETTS

After the satyr's twilight in the park
Where the Greek children burn among the bushes,
And past the Roman wall where icons are
Beside the hospital's white Renaissance,
I stroll across the Indian burial—
A glacial till on a Mesozoic ledge—
And come again to Mrs. Quinan's hedge.

Everything I have known here is dark.
The fruit we pilfered from her rustling trees
Is gone, and the trees are gone. She will not damn
Our thieving souls again. Her fishwife's tongue
That was a legend and a merriment
Was throttled by a cancer, a cross, a stone,
On a darker night than this. I turn alone

Onto the pavement, knowing we grow old
In any thought. My life waits on this street.
I walk it back from memory, a legend
Of mineral, vegetable, fish, fowl, and flesh,
Saurian, savage, satyr, Roman, clerk—
And Mrs. Quinan's imp, who died like her,
Leaving a faint distaste and then no taste
On a street of centuries. Good friends, good friends,
Nothing in our beginnings knows our ends.

—JOHN CIARDI

HOME REVISITED: MIDNIGHT

I am the shadow in the shadow of the wicker.
The wicker is the shadow in the shadow of the vine.
I sat here when? Ago. Blinked at the flicker
Of a falling star. Said the moon: *Be mine.*
Said the star: *Will be.* And then, and now and then,
The shadow in the shadow is the shadow of Again.

And went away. Or came. What happened? O
It is June again and moony. *Song, song,
So-ong,* the crickets. And *blop, blop, b-lop,*
The frogs. And *ago, ago, ago*
Says the rational man in the shadow. (This is his sop
To the passionate man in the song.) O do I belong
To that rational man? To that passionate, singing man?
Which body shall I wear to memory
When I arise from shadow?

Shall I cry Mother or write prose?
Turn Catholic or blow my nose?
If I rise and go inside,
My dead setter will have died:
"Here, Tug, here, Tug, here on the lawn,
Here in the shadow." Tug is gone
To watch my shadow being born.

I was the center at the center of the shadow.
I am the shadow at the center of the thought.
The house behind me is a house I know.
At every sill and step the house forgot
All but *song, so-ong,* and *blop, b-lop.*
That music is because it cannot stop.

For the center of the music is another music
And the center of the center is a stir.
And what is time that visited my father
With worms and roses and religious physic
And gave his house to me to sit and gather
Shadow at the center of the music of the stir?
—And a rational man? And a passionate, singing man?
And now,
     and then,
          a third, an invisible man
Singing and trusting and distrusting the song
At the center of the center where the shadows throng?

                    —JOHN CIARDI

HOMING PIGEONS

Among left trucks, mailbags, churns,
sometimes in Sunday depots
we glimpse, through dirt-pearled win-
    dows
of a stopping train, square wicker
crates crammed with homing pigeons.
We keep afloat a feather

of memory blown in the air
of our drab compartment.
Singly, over open sea, sheer
from our instrumented course,
we have watched them, confident
beyond their wings' will, cross.

And have thought, outward bound
in sunshine, of the attic
loft where they always land,
their fanciers waiting, alone.
All their lives are goings back
from places where they have not flown.

Alien they seem. Yet
in their brief apportionment
of flight—a timed parole—
is sensed a homing force that drives
us back from all our fanciful
hoverings beyond our lives.

For there are wants kept caged on
    roofs
of the mind's tenements
that coo for us through the dusk,
always hungering, their ruffs
up. They strut their insistence
that we bring them all they ask—

so little: grain enough
to soothe them through the night
they will roost out in sleep.
Or multiply in. If,
neglectful, we forget
their feed, they grate the coop

floor, madden for full crops
and flight. We must indulge
their greed, let them fatten
as they will, some perhaps
surfeiting till they gorge
their death. But few. And in

those interims between
living as we seem to be
and dreaming what we are,
we come to the cage, unseen.

We stroke them as they crowd the
    wire
while we fumble for the key,

then loose them to the corridor
we trust them to, of sanctioned air.
Vigilant, we watch them take
turn after turn beyond us till,
wheeling on the thread of our will,
they clatter back in the hanging dark.

—Ted Walker

THE HORATIANS

Into what fictive worlds can imagination
translate you, Flaccus, and your kin? Not the Courts of
    Grand Opera, that *galère*
    of lunatics, power-famished

or love-ravenous, belting out their arias,
nor the Wards of Buffa, either, where abnormal
    growths of self-love are excised
    by the crude surgery of a

Practical Joke. Perhaps the only invented
story in which your appearance seems credible
    is the Whodunit: I can
    believe in one of you solving

a murder which has the professionals baffled,
thanks to your knowledge of local topography.
    In our world all of you share
    a love for some particular

place and stretch of country, a farm near Tivoli
or a Radnorshire village: what the Capital
    holds out as a lure, a chance
    to get into Society,

does not tempt you, who wry from crowds, traffic-noises,
blue-stockings and millionaires. Your tastes run to
    small dinner-parties, small rooms,
    and the tone of voice that suits them,

neither truckle nor thrasonical, but softly
certain (a sound wood-winds imitate better

than strings), your most worldly wish
a genteel sufficiency of

land or lolly. Among those I really know, the
British branch of the family, how many have
found in the Anglican Church
your Maecenas who enabled

a life without cumber, as pastors adjective
to rustic flocks, as organists in trollopish
cathedral towns. Then, in all
labyrinthine economies

there are obscure nooks into which Authority
never pokes a suspicious nose, *embusqué* havens
for natural bachelors
and political idiots,

Zoological and Botanical Gardens,
museum-basements displaying feudal armor
or old coins: there, too, we find
you among the custodians.

Some of you have written poems, usually
short ones, and some kept diaries, seldom published
till after your deaths, but most
make no memorable impact

except on your friends and dogs. Enthusiastic
Youth writes you off as cold, who cannot be found on
barricades, and never shoot
either yourselves or your lovers.

You thought well of your Odes, Flaccus, and believed they
would live, but knew, and have taught your descendants to
say with you: "As makers go,
compared with Pindar or any

of the great foudroyant masters who won't stop to
amend, we are, for all our polish, of little
stature, and, as human lives,
compared with authentic martyrs

like Regulus, of no account. We can only
do what it seems to us we were made for, look at
this world with a happy eye,
but from a sober perspective."

—W. H. Auden

HORATIAN VARIATION

A tractor now is an essential
On every Sabine farm.
Torn myrtle round a differential
Loses its charm.

I hate the Persian apparatus.
My timid spirit blenches
When bleak Modernity throws at us
Her monkey wrenches.

But I observe, as shadows lengthen
And corpse-cold dews are forming,
That rust works still, which does not
        strengthen
Chilled steel. How warming!

So mope not. Let us rather think
That Times may turn Saturnian.
Visit my shack! We'll dream we drink
The true Falernian.

—LEONARD BACON

HOTEL PARADISO E COMMERCIALE

Another hill town:
another dry Cinzano in the sun.
I couldn't sleep in that enormous echo—
silence and water music, sickly street lamps
neither on nor off—a night
of islands and forgotten languages.

Yet morning, marvellously frank, comes up
with bells, with loaves, with letters
distributed like gifts. I watch a fat priest
spouting grape seeds, a family weeping
in the fumes of a departing bus.

This place is nowhere
except on the map. Wheels spin the sun,
with a white clatter shutters are shut to,
umbrellas bloom in striped and sudden groves.
The day's away, impossibly the same,
and only minutes are at all important—
if women by a wall,
a lean dog, and a cheerful humpback
selling gum and ball-points
are important. My glass is empty.
It is Wednesday. It is not going to rain.

Observation
without speculation. How soon
the eye craves what it cannot see,
goes limpid, glazed, unanswerable,

lights on a pigeon walking in a circle,
hangs on a random shadow,
would rather sleep.

How old am I?
What's missing here? What do these people
feed on, that won't feed on them? This town
needs scrolls, celestial delegations,
a swoon of virgins, apostles in apple green,
a landscape riding on a holy shoulder.

The morning stays.
As though I keep an old appointment,
I start by the cats' corridors (*Banco di Roma*,
wineshops, gorgeous butcheries)
toward some mild angel of annunciation—
upstairs, most likely, badly lit,
speaking in rivets on a band of gold.

Praise God, this town keeps one
unheard-of masterpiece to justify
a million ordinary mornings
and pardon this one.

—JOHN MALCOLM BRINNIN

THE HOUNDED LOVERS

Where shall we go?
Where shall we go
  who are in love?

Juliet went
to Friar Laurence's cell,
  but we have no rest.

Rain water lies
on the hard-packed ground,
  reflecting
the morning sky,

But where shall we go?
We cannot resolve ourselves
  into a dew

Or sink into the earth.
Shall we postpone it
  to Eternity?

The dry heads
of the goldenrod,
  turned to stiff ghosts,

Jerk at their dead
stalks, signalling hieroglyphs
  of grave warning.

Where shall we go?
The movement of benediction
  does not turn back
the cold wind.

—WILLIAM CARLOS WILLIAMS

HOUSE GUEST

The sad seamstress
who stays with us this month
is small and thin and bitter.
No one can cheer her up.
Give her a dress, a drink,
roast chicken, or fried fish—
it's all the same to her.

She sits and watches TV.
No, she watches zigzags.
"Can you adjust the TV?"
"No," she says. No hope.
She watches on and on,
without hope, without air.

Her own clothes give us pause,
but she's not a poor orphan.
She has a father, a mother,
and all that, and she's earning
quite well, and we're stuffing
her with fattening foods.

We invite her to use the binoculars.
We say, "Come see the jets!"
We say, "Come see the baby!"
Or the knife grinder who cleverly
plays the National Anthem
on his wheel so shrilly.
Nothing helps.

She speaks:"I need a little
money to buy buttons."
She seems to think it's useless
to ask. Heavens, buy buttons,

if they'll do any good,
the biggest in the world—
by the dozen, by the gross!
Buy yourself an ice cream,
a comic book, a car!

Her face is closed as a nut,
closed as a careful snail
or a thousand-year-old seed.
Does she dream of marriage?
Of getting rich? Her sewing
is decidedly mediocre.

Please! Take our money! Smile!
What on earth have we done?
What has everyone done
and when did it all begin?
Then one day she confides
that she wanted to be a nun
and her family opposed her.

Perhaps we should let her go,
or deliver her straight off
to the nearest convent—and wasn't
her month up last week, anyway?

Can it be that we nourish
one of the Fates in our bosoms?
Clotho, sewing our lives
with a bony little foot
on a borrowed sewing machine,
and our fates will be like hers,
and our hems crooked forever?

                                        —Elizabeth Bishop

HOW

How can I tell you
how I need our bitter
weary chance meeting of life?

In the fading light of evening
this sadness will dissolve.
Then you are left with yourself
and the dark-eyed water of morning.

Ice sheathes the stalks.
The bleached herbs of the field are frost.
A few blackberry vines shine like blood.

It snows. I wait.
The noise of snow falling on stones and of air falling on trees
is the same.
The air loosens.

I hear the silence of night. I hear what is unsaid.
It is summer within, it is the coughing of a crow—
crow calling to crow. I hear when he calls.

A few weeds and dry leaves lift above the white surface.
It is as if I have come to an open window.

—S. J. Marks

HOW TUESDAY BEGAN

Don't let me lose you,
lady. We're jogging up
First Avenue in the sun,
nursing morning with
our habits.
I must have boarded before
you, where the bus stops
and the dusty nightgowns
beckon from Orchard St.
I must have pulled out
my book, peeled off my gloves,
and settled among the fumes
for a poem or two,
my habit.
I didn't see you,

black, filling the aisle
with your green housedress,
lowering each part of you
gently, in front of me,
maybe heaving a sigh, your
sorrow and habit.

Still, my eyes pulled
sideways. Someone old
moved without moving,
veins, vague eyes resisting
the aisle in front
of her, a journey
to be mastered upright,
seat by seat.

We rolled with the bus,
easy as rubber lifeboats
on troubled water.
But she hung to the same
space, sensing the movement
around her, sinking
in her own flesh.
Then you reached out, lady,

and pulled her in
beside you.
You were fading
and full of troubles, lady,
and you saw her drowning
and you reached out
and said, "I don't see
so good myself."

—Kathleen Fraser

HUGHIE AT THE INN
OR, ADVICE FROM A TAPSTER

Is it not fine to fling against loaded dice
Yet to win once or twice?
To bear a rusty sword without an edge
Yet wound the thief in the hedge?
To be unhorsed, and drown in horrid muck,
And in at the death, by luck?
To meet a masked assassin in a cape,
And kill him, and escape?
To have the usurers all your fortune take,
And a bare living make
By industry, and your brow's personal sweat?
To be caught in the bird-net
Of a bad marriage; then to be trepanned
And stranded on foreign land?
To be cast into a prison damp and vile,
And break bars with a blunt file?
To be cut down from gallows while you breathe
And live, by the skin of your teeth?
To defy the tyrant world, and at a pinch
To wrest from it an inch?
To engage the stars in combat, and therefrom
Pluck a hair's breadth of room?
Is it not fine, worthy of Titans or gods,
To challenge such heavy odds?
But no, but no, my lad;
'Tis cruel chance gone mad;
A stab in the back; a serpent in the breast;
And worst that murders best.
Such broad and open affronts to fear and pain
Breed maggots in the brain:
They are not valour, but the merest rash
Rubbish and balderdash.

Fortune's a drab, and vice her native soil,
And the button's off her foil.
Season your ale, now these long nights draw in,
With thought to save your skin:
Be provident, and pray for cowardice
And the loaded pair of dice.

—ELINOR WYLIE

HUNTER'S MOON

An airborne dragon-
fly, brash with first frost,
buzzed me where I lay
in the open, still,
considering a
juniper lap and
vein of clouds.
    Floating
like seaweed or a
mote down the eye's film,
he stained the sky with
four mica-seamed wings,
just able to hold

onto his outrigged
eyes, spying—a head?
—a stone?
    Circling or,
in the sunless air,
coasting, he hovered,
the wing whirr missing,
flaking, taking me
again—his insect
candor!—and again
for a window, a
door, a sun-banked stone,
or any warm thing.

—STEPHEN SANDY

HURDY-GURDY MAN IN WINTER

He touches, and the wheel of time goes round.
Oh, listen—nothing's in the world so strong.
The larks of ragtime lovers come to ground.
This carrion moment makes men feel they're wrong.

And see the children crowding round the cart,
The sordid cart, where love in memory's lap
Sucks at the bubbling spring designed to start
Remorseful coins to fill the beggar's cap.

He leans on sound as on a ramp of air,
Floating his tunes through doors and window tops,
Tipping up pomp, upsetting habit's chair,
Catching the silver penny where it drops.

What cities feel his battering ram of tune
Break their defenses with nostalgic ease,

Breaching the walls of day that seemed immune,
Painting the dark with sunset poverties.

Rattling a cup, he saunters to waylay
The rich, whose conscience he makes insecure.
Down the long, captivated street he'll play.
The starlike snowflakes lend him strange allure.

His monkey, chained and dressed in exile's cloak,
Leaps up and, crouching on the organ's rim,
Frowns at the shapes that pass, whose breath is smoke;
The sun may turn its wheel, but not for him.

Here comes his master, croupier of the town,
Counting his coins like snowflakes on a bag.
He rakes their mysteries in and puts them down,
The missing bridegroom and the midnight hag.

—Vernon Watkins

HYMN TO PROUST

For you Time past could not forget
   Nor alter what had been—
And Time has still its lost Odette
   And Love its Albertine.

We worship under different names
   The figures of the past,
Like characters from Henry James—
   But not designed to last.

For we know many a Charlus still
   And many a Verdurin,
Gilberte as Swann and de Forcheville,
   And M. Legrandin.

Each, an ambiguous Saint-Loup,
   Carries Françoise within,
And sex comes to its Waterloo
   In Jealousy, not Sin.

For all know Vinteuil's little phrase,
   The brilliant Balbec day,
The Méséglise and Guermantes' ways,
   The grayness of Combray.

Each one has tasted as a child
   Madeleines dipped in tea
And loves that drove the reason wild
   But set the fancy free.

—Gavin Ewart

I

i
never
guessed any
thing (even a
universe) might be
so not quite believab
ly smallest as perfect this
(almost invisible where of a there of a) here of a
rubythroat's home with its still
ness which really's herself
(and to think that she's
warming three worlds)
who's ama
zingly
Eye

—E. E. CUMMINGS

THE ICE SKIN

All things that go deep enough
Into rain and cold
Take on, before they break down,
A shining in every part.
The necks of slender trees
Reel under it, too much crowned,
Like princes dressing as kings,

And the redwoods let sink their
      branches
Like arms that try to hold buckets
Filling slowly with diamonds

Until a cannon goes off
Somewhere inside the still trunk

And a limb breaks, just before mid-
      night,
Plunging houses into the darkness
And hands into cupboards, all seeking
Candles, and finding each other.
There is this skin

Always waiting in cold-enough air.
I have seen aircraft, in war,
Squatting on runways,
Dazed with their own enclosed,
Coming-forth, intensified color
As though seen by a child in a poem.
I have felt growing over
Me, in the heated death rooms

Of uncles, the ice
Skin, that which the dying

Lose, and we others,
In their thawing presence, take on.
I have felt the heroic glaze

Also, in hospital waiting
Rooms—that masterly shining,
And the slow weight that makes you
            sit
Like an emperor, fallen, becoming
His monument, with the stiff thorns
Of fear upside down on the brow,
An overturned kingdom;

Through the window of ice,
I have stared at my son in his cage,
Just born, just born.

I touched the frost of my eyebrows
To the cold he turned to
Blindly, but sensing a thing.
Neither glass nor the jagged
Helm on my forehead would melt.
My son now stands with his head
At my shoulder. I

Stand, stooping more, but the same,
Not knowing whether
I will break before I can feel,

Before I can give up my powers,
Or whether the ice-light
In my eyes will ever snap off
Before I die. I am still,
And my son, doing what he was taught,
Listening hard for a buried cannon,
Stands also, calm as glass.

—James Dickey

IF IN BEGINNING TWILIGHT

if in beginning twilight of winter will stand

(over a snowstopped silent world) one
spirit serenely truly himself; and

alone only as greatness is alone—

one (above nevermoving all nowhere)
goldenly whole, prodigiously alive
most mercifully glorying keen star

whom she-and-he-like ifs of am perceive

(but believe scarcely may) certainly while
mute each inch of their murdered planet grows
more and enormously more less: until
her-and-his nonexistence vanishes

with also earth's
                    —"dying" the ghost of you
whispers "is very pleasant" my ghost to

—E. E. Cummings

IF I SHOULD DIE BEFORE I WAKE

Accidents will happen—still, in time,
The rigors of mortality may chill
The racing channels of the blood, and spin
Around the brain a cold and opaque skin.
Then, one might not remember pain so well;
One could sit back, and life, if not sublime,
Would be a sleep to dream pleasantly in,
Embellishing the heroics of one's prime.

But this is wishful thinking; generally,
The hardening of the arteries portends
A loosening of control, weakness of will,
And a wrecked body, frail, susceptible
To every shock. There is no second wind
Or childhood, but an alien infancy,
And life is a strangling thing, and pitiful,
And inches on, feeling that it must be.

But worse than the sphincter's failure or wry tricks
Of the steadfast heart, the worms of time embed
Their jaws most ravenously into the fork
Where the warm blood of man and woman works
The power of human love to a pale thread,
And sever the fine filament, all that protects
Against the lonely, labyrinthine dark.
What does age trade the body for its sex?

A pity, but longevity is cruel.
When he was eighty, impotent Sophocles said,
"This well-loved instrument is finally out of tune.
Well, I am old, and have my work." And soon
Wrote the "Colonus;" but when he went to bed,
He wept bitterly, being neither stoic nor fool;
His genitals were withered as a prune.
"It's better," he said, "to have never been born at all."

Consider dying young: think of the day
Greece wept hard Leonidas and his boys,
Who butchered at the pass and weren't unnerved
By whispering arrows or whatever served
A Spartan soldier in keeping a soldierly poise
And stiff, prone posture. For us, the apogee
Of youthful martial and sexual prowess lives
On the tiny slope where that silent battalion lay.

I think of Stanley Ketchel, whose cool love
And subsequent early death preserved his youth
And left his classic body middleweight slim;
Graceful and powerful we remember him,
His battering fists telling the brutal truth.
But there are countless tales. It is enough
To guess the fate of vigorous life and limb
And lose them young in grandiose roughstuff.

Ah, if only Aurora had thought to ask
For something more, for supple muscles, say,
And a tireless heart to keep the flesh and blood
Rosy as well as living for the good
Of her fair-haired boy, who hated the endless day.
But she did not. He waited for the dusk,
Who left him a narrow shadow in his bed
And deathless eyes bright in his bitten mask.

The image of an old man's ugly phiz
Drifts in the gloom, wearing a dreadful smile.
Regard this absurd ghost, as he goes by:
Was he not thoughtless once as you and I
Of what must happen in a little while,
Who now despairs that he is come to this?
Let him go. We choose our time to die.
Come, Love, come close, and murder me with a kiss.

                                        —Robert Mezey

ILL MET BY ZENITH

Like Stephen Vincent Benét, I have fallen in love with American names;
Indeed, I even go so far as to call our own Tems the Thames.
Why, then, am I saddened by the appearance of so many American names on the
    roster of the Metropolitan Opera?
Well, not because I am as flighty as a butterfly, flutteriest member of the order of
    Lepidopera.
No, it is because of my affection for the gentle dean of opera commentators, Mil-
    ton Cross,
Without whose sonorous Saturday synopses my radio during the singing season
    would be a total loss.
Here is the ultimate interpreter of a libretto,
A man who can get two "r"s and three "t"s into his pronunciation of "Rigoletto,"
A host both knowledgeable and suave,
Impeccable in his differentiation between the Italian "c" and double "c" as in his

virtuosity with German *"achs"* and umlauts, and French nasals and accents
both *aigus* and *graves.*
He savors each name like a vintage rare and mellow;
I love to taste with him such delectabilities as Loretta Di Franco, Raina Kabai-
vanska, Gabriella Tucci, Biserka Cvejic, Gabor Carelli, Pekka Nuotio,
Arturo Sergi, Anselmo Colzani, Mario Sereni, Tito Gobbi, Elfego Esparza,
Cesare Siepi, Giorgio Tozzi, and Ezio Flagello.
I adore with him the exotic bouquet of other labels that the Metropolitan cellars
have a prodigious store of,
Such as Ludmila Dvorakova, Lili Chookasian, Ruza Pospinov, Gaetano Bardini,
Carlo Bergonzi, Flaviano Lobò, Bonaldo Giaiotti, and, of course, Nicola
Ghiuselev and Nicolai Ghiaurov.
An easy chair, an open fire, a radio tuned to an opera with a cast of foreign artists,
and Maestro Cross in there really giving—
Boy, that's living!
But, O Beverly Bower, O Phyllis Curtin, O Grace Bumbry, Jean Fenn, Laurel
Hurley, Shirley Love, Nell Rankin, Nancy Williams, and Evelyn Lear,
I grant that each of you is a delight to hear,
And O James King, Jess Thomas, William Walker, Robert Merrill, Richard Tucker,
William Dooley, George London, Jerome Hines, and Norman Scott,
I grant that each of you is an artiste supreme—but names worthy of my idol's
talents you have not!
O Rudolf Bing,
When casting, remember one thing:
None does more than Milton can
To justify the Met to man.

—OGDEN NASH

IMAGES

Again this morning trembles on the swift stream the image of the sun,
Dimmed and pulsing shadow insubstantial of the bright one
That scatters innumerable as eyes these discs of light scaling the water.
From a dream foolish and sorrowful, I return to this day's morning,
And words are said as the thread slips away of a ravelled story:
"The newborn have forgotten the great burden of pain
That world has endured before you came."
A marble Eros sleeps in peace unbroken by the fountain,
Out of what toils of ever-suffering love conceived?

Only the gods can bear our memories.
We, in their lineaments serene
That look down on us with untroubled gaze,

Fathom our own mind and what it is,
Purified from the blood we shed, the deaths we die.

How many tears have traced those still unfading presences
Who on dim walls depict spirit's immortal joy?
They look from beyond time on sorrow upon sorrow of ours,
And of our broken many our whole truth one angel tells,
Ingathers to its golden abiding form the light we scatter,
And winged with unconsuming fire our shattered image reassembles.

My load of memory is almost full,
But here and now I see once more mirrored the semblance of the radiant source
Whose image the fleet waters break but cannot bear away.

—KATHLEEN RAINE

I'M HERE

(OLD LADY ON THE WAY TO SLEEP)

I

Is it enough?—
The sun loosening the frost on December windows,
The glitter of wet in the first of morning,
The sound of voices, young voices, mixed with sleigh bells,
Coming across snow in early evening?

Outside, the same sparrows bicker in the eaves.
I'm tired of tiny noises:
The April cheeping, the vireo's insistence.
The prattle of the young no longer pleases.
Behind the child's archness
Lurks the bad animal.

How needles and corners perplex me!
Dare I shrink to a hag,
The worst surprise a corner could have,
A witch who sleeps with her horse?
Some fates are worse.

II

I was queen of the vale—
For a short while,
Living all my heart's summer alone,
Ward of my spirit,
Running through high grasses,
My thighs brushing against flower crowns;

Leaning, out of all breath,
Bracing my back against a sapling,
Making it quiver with my body;
At the stream's edge, trailing a vague finger;
Flesh-awkward, half alive,
Fearful of high places, in love with horses;
In love with stuffs, silks,
Rubbing my nose in the wool of blankets;
Bemused; pleased to be;
Mindful of cries:
The meaningful whisper,
The wren, the catbird.

So much of adolescence is an ill-defined dying,
An intolerable waiting,
A longing for another place and time,
Another condition.

I stayed, a willow to the wind.
The bats twittered at noon.
The swallows flew in and out of the smokeless chimneys.
I sang to the edges of flame,
My skin whiter in the soft weather,
My voice softer.

III

I remember walking down a path,
Down wooden steps toward a weedy garden,
And my dress caught on a rose briar.
When I bent to untangle myself,
The scent of the half-opened buds came up over me.
I thought I was going to smother.

In the slow coming out of sleep,
On the sill of the eyes something flutters,
A thing we feel at evening, and by doors,
Or when we stand at the edge of a thicket,
And the ground chill comes closer to us,
From under the dry leaves,
A beachy wetness.

The body, delighting in thresholds,
Rocks in and out of itself.
A bird, small as a leaf,
Sings in the first
Sunlight.

And the time I was so sick—
The whole place shook whenever I got a chill—
I closed my eyes and saw small figures dancing,
A congress of tree shrews and rats
Romping around a fire,
Jumping up and down on their hind feet,
Their forepaws joined together like hands;
they seemed very happy.

    In my grandmother's inner eye,
    So she told me when I was little,
    A bird always kept singing.
    She was a serious woman.

IV

My geranium is dying, for all I can do,
Still leaning toward the last place the sun was.
I've tried I don't know how many times to replant it.
But these roses: I can wear them by looking away.
The eyes rejoice in the act of seeing, and the fresh afterimage,
Without staring like a lout or a moping adolescent,
Without commotion.

Look at the far trees at the end of the garden.
The flat branch of that hemlock holds the last of the sun,
Rocking it, like a sun-struck pond,
In a light wind.

    I prefer the still joy:
    The wasp drinking at the edge of my cup;
    A snake lifting its head;
    A snail's music.

V

What's weather to me? Even carp die in this river.
I need a pond with small eels. And a windy orchard.
I'm no midge of that and this. The dirt glitters like salt.
Birds are around. I've all the singing I would.
I'm not far from a stream.
It's not my first dying.
I can hold this valley,
Loose in my lap.
In my arms.

    If the wind means me,
    I'm here!
    Here.

                        —THEODORE ROETHKE

IN A DARK TIME

I

In a dark time, the eye begins to see.
I meet my shadow in the deepening shade;
I hear my echo in the echoing wood—
A lord of nature weeping to a tree.
I live between the heron and the wren,
Beasts of the hill and serpents of the den.

II

What's madness but nobility of soul
At odds with circumstance? The day's on fire!
I know the purity of pure despair,
My shadow pinned against a sweating wall.
That place among the rocks—is it a cave,
Or winding path? The edge is what I have.

III

A steady storm of correspondences!
A night flowing with birds, a ragged moon,
And in broad day the midnight come again!
A man goes far to find out what he is—
Death of the self in a long, tearless night,
All natural shapes blazing unnatural light.

IV

Dark, dark my light, and darker my desire.
My soul, like some heat-maddened summer fly,
Keeps buzzing at the sill. Which I is *I*?
A fallen man, I climb out of my fear.
The mind enters itself, and God the mind,
And one is One, free in the tearing wind.

—THEODORE ROETHKE

IN AND OUT

I. SEVERANCE OF CONNECTIONS, 1946

1. CIVIS

Walking the town as if I owned it all—
Each lilac leafing out in Brattle Street,
Each green vane in the hollow square guarding
The gargoyles on Memorial Hall, each inch
Of rubber tubing in the Mallinckrodt
Chemical Laboratory, each
Particle who would learn and gladly teach,
Each English bicycle chained to its rack,

Each green bag humping on its scholar's back,
Each tally for a Cambridge traffic death,
Each boyish girl who makes you catch your breath,
Each Argyle sock, each Bursar's bill, each ounce
Of shag, each brick, each doctorate—as if
I owned the entire spring-wound town, I walk
Up the north path to University Hall.

2. MAGISTER

The Master's teeth squeak as he sprinkles me
(Too hot to handle) with a mist of spit
That dries quite coolly. "Edwards, I've got some
Rough news for you." In his glazed, padded, blue,
Old double-breasted serge suit and his bat-
Wing bow tie (navy, with pink polka dots),
He lets me have it right between the eyes,
His aces on the table, man to boy.
"Look, if there's one thing I can't tolerate
It's smart guys that won't work. The deans are soft
On geniuses. Not me. What we need more
Of is Midwestern athletes who get C's."
He stands up to reveal that his brown vest
Is perfectly misbuttoned. "Now, don't think
That I'm the least bit sorry about you.
I'm sorry for your mother and your dad.
You let them down. Now, you get out of here
And do something worthwhile. Work with your hands.
Stick with it two years. Maybe they'll take you back.
O.K., fella? That's it. Now let's shake."
We shake. I shake in secret with the shame of it.

3. EXILIUM

The ghost goes south, avoiding well-worn ways
Frequented by his friends. Instead, he slips
Into loose shadows on the sunless side
Of the least-travelled street. But even there
One with a bony finger points him out
And pierces him with questions. Zigzagging,
He hedges hastily back to his route,
Which leads on past his windows, tendrilly
Embraced already by the outriders
Of summer's ivy, past his pipes and books
And dirty shirts and mother's picture, past
The dining hall where his name is still good
For a square meal, no questions asked, and past
The common room which is too good for him.
Across the Drive his beast heaves into view:
A monster boathouse lolling on the bank

Of the high river, backside in the water.
Inside, he greets the landlord's black-haired daughter,
Miss Jacobs, with a nod, and goes upstairs
To put his chamois-seated crew pants on.
Then, past the ranks of Compromises, he
Walks out to the land's end of the long float,
Selects his Single, and stands out to sea.

II. A HOME AWAY FROM HOME, 1947

1. ONE O'CLOCK

With gin, *prosciutto*, and Drake's Devil Dogs
In a brown-paper bag, I climb the Hill
On Saturday, the thirty-first of May,
Struck by the sun approaching apogee,
Green comments issued by the Common trees,
Mauve decadence among magnolias,
The moving charcoal shadows on the brown
Stone of the moving brownstone where I live,
And a spring breath of Lux across the Charles.
My key mutters the password; I step in
To the dense essence of an entire past:
Rugs, chicken, toilets, Lysol, dust, cigars.
Through that invisible nerve gas (which leads
In time to total incapacity),
I climb the two flights to my little flat.

2. TWO-THIRTY

Done with the Devil Dogs, I take the brush
Out of the tooth glass and decant my first
Gin of the afternoon. In half an hour
She will be here. All is in readiness:
The bedspread taut, the ashtrays wiped, a glass
Swiped from the bathroom down the hall, a small
Plate of *prosciutto* canapés. Now Fu
Manchu reclines at ease in his hideaway,
While his nets, broadcast, sweep their victim in
To an innocuous address on Pinckney Street.
Now Lou the Loser uses all his ten
Thumbs to count up the minutes till she comes,
Or till (more likely, with his luck) she never shows.
The gin sets up a tickle in my toes.
I blow my nose. The room is hot. A fly
Does dead-stick landings on my neck. She's late.

3. THREE-TEN, *et seq.*

The doorbell rings. I barrel down the stairs
To meet the coolest copy I have seen
Of Sally on the steps. Up in my room,

I fix her gin and secretly survey
This manifestation by which I have so
Astoundingly been visited: a girl.
She walks on her long legs, she talks out loud,
She moves her hand, she shakes her head and laughs.
Is this mechanical marvel to be mine?
Quite paralyzed, I nod and nod and nod
And smile and smile. The gin is getting low
In my tooth glass. The hour is getting on.
Gin and adrenalin finally rescue me
(With an assist from Sally) and I find
My lips saluting hers as if she were
My stern commanding officer. No fool,
She puts us on an equal footing. Soon
My strategies and tactics are as toys
Before the gallop of her cavalry
That tramples through my blood and captures me.

4. Five-Fifty

Later, as racy novels used to say—
Later, I turn to see the westering sun
Through the ailanthus stipple her tan side
With yellow coin dots shaped to fit her skin.
This Sally now does like a garment wear
The beauty of the evening; silent, bare,
Hips, shoulders, arms, tresses, and temples lie.
I watch her as she sleeps, the tapering back
Rising and falling on the tide of breath;
The long eyelashes lying on her cheek;
The black brows and the light mouth both at rest;
A living woman not a foot away.

The west wind noses in at the window,
Sending a scent of soap, a hint of her
Perfume, and the first onions of the night
Up the airshaft to where I lie, not quite alone.

                                        —L. E. Sissman

IN AN OLD HOUSE

In an old house with many fireplaces
That my father took me long ago to visit,
A stairway from the first floor to the third
Slanted, dark, inwalled without a landing.
Nothing else charmed me like that climbable closet

Built, I thought, for one who would have explored
The shuddery penetralia of caves.
"For servants," they told me, after all my guesses,
Who crept between the scrubbing and the mending
And had a story left out of their lives.

—SPENCER BROWN

IN AN OLD ORCHARD

In an old orchard, which the wasps and flickers
alone husband,
under aging trees—
their gentle lanes of gnarled and worm-eaten silence
paved with rank, rotting rubies and
ants milling cider in the sticky grass—

here's fruit most sweet, most stolen, where the ruin
of a fiftieth fall
dapples with leaves,
sun, shards, shadows some famished household,
long ladderless, still pitifully gathering all
windfalls onto its damp lap of graves.

—PETER KANE DUFAULT

INCIDENT ON A FRONT NOT FAR FROM
CASTEL DI SANGRO

There was a sound of hunting in the mountains
That came back dark and dangerous to the ears
Of those who crouched among the broken fountains:

The wounded wirecutter with his biting shears,
The trembling captain with his telephone,
The corporal with the ten-cent photos of his dears.

They all were lost and each one was alone.
Their uniforms were merely a disguise
That kept the naked earth from knowing naked bone.

"Shellshock. No Visitors," said the captain's eyes.
He was himself an isolation ward;
The sun and air and scenery were lies,

And if one wanted truth one had to guard
Oneself from all realities like men,
Yet men were always present. Truth came hard,

Especially when time and time again
The same huge shell exploded in his head,
And arms of strangers opened and, embracing, took him in.

The telephone he carried had been dead
For many hours—ever since *They* found
His battery with a salvo and had dyed the casings red.

It was dissolved from any further sound—
Mechanical foetus, with a broken cord
From which the wires jutted like bone chips in a wound.

The captain shivered, crouched, and spoke no word
To those beside him. His blue eyes were glazed,
And had he spoken they would not have heard.

For they, who once had looked, condemned, or praised,
Were caught up in the earthquake of the age,
Saw mount and man gape wide, and were amazed.

The wirecutter's wound was like a page
In some red book the world would always read.
It made him feel half pity and half rage:

Pity—that he'd been wounded and could bleed;
Rage—that the wounded statues had not bled.
Half-formed, he felt the marble's *having* and his need.

Beside him lay a smashed Apollo's head.
He kicked it, and it rolled from him and caught
Against a cart whose occupants had fled.

Which was the living world, and which was not?
Upon the cold, cracked face there was a leer.
It was too high a price, but safety had been bought.

Immobile, lost between the far and near,
The corporal stared. A picture of his wife
And children was the object of a fear

That made him clutch the coppers of his life,
And dimmed his eyes and covered them with water,
And burned his vitals like a kiss or knife.

He studied the pale face of his one daughter
And then the smiling face of his one son:
These images had led him through the country of the mortar

What had been done was done and would stay done.
He tucked the pictures in his helmet, grinning.
Whatever the outcome of the war, he'd won.

The captain was the one who was not winning;
He felt more war than went on in the town.
For him a peace would never be beginning.

Far from a lake or sea a man can drown,
Or smother in a universe of air.
Among the hosts of earth he weeps alone.

And thus these finally rose beneath the glare
And moved, automatons, beyond their night,
Doomed, yet unmastered, toward the waiting Stair,

And so they came, each one, into the light,
Among the broken statues and the fountains' drouth.
Sun struck the broken columns for its own delight.

Their words had all gone silent in the mouth,
Their feet had all grown weary in the race,
The needle of the compass at last was pointing south.

And each one, with a century in his face,
Turned and strode from the elemental guns,
Through streets whose rubble was a marble lace,

And through pellucid dust that met the sun's
Acclaiming rays and traced the sullen war's
Sign on the suicide corporal and the other ones . . .

Dust on the corporal's stripes, the captain's bars,
Dust on the wounded wirecutter's gauze,
And dust that sifted toward the unseen, unmoved stars.

—HARRY BROWN

IN DEFENSE OF SUPERFICIALITY

Respect all surfaces. The skater is
Safe until his superficiality
Fails. A bridge, the frailest,
Is better than the abyss. The green earth's pleasant,
Very pleasant, isn't it? Don't dig.
Friendship and love are surfaces. Respect them.

All surfaces are smooth seas, and the ship
Moves to music: the sea is shimmering strings,
The sun strums golden wires, and the wind sings.
All mariners must be dancers to such minstrelsy
Until the prow too curious probes too deep
And music ends and light ends, but the sea
Goes on and on and in the whirlpool's round
The dancers go on dancing without sound.

Accept this final bubble,
From one drowned.

—ELDER OLSON

INDIANS

Margaret mentioned Indians,
And I began to think about Indians—

Indians once living
Where now we are living—

About Indians. Oh, I know
About Indians. Oh, I know

What I have heard. Not much,
When I think how much

I wonder about them,
When a mere mention of them,

Indians, starts me. I
Think of their wigwams. I

Think of canoes. I think
Of quick arrows. I think

Of things Indian. And still
I think of their bright, still

Summers, when these hills
And meadows on these hills

Shone in the morning
Suns before this morning.

—JOHN FANDEL

IN EVENING AIR

I

A dark theme keeps me here,
Though summer blazes in the vireo's
    eye.
Who would be half possessed
By his own nakedness?
Waking's my care—
I'll make a broken music, or I'll die.

II

Ye littles, lie more close!
Make me, O Lord, a last, a simple
    thing
Time cannot overwhelm.
Once I transcended time
A bud broke to a rose,
And I rose from a last diminishing.

III

I look down the far light
And I behold the dark side of a tree
Far down a billowing plain,
And when I look again,
It's lost upon the night—
Night I embrace, a dear proximity.

IV

I stand by a low fire
Counting the wisps of flame, and I
    watch how
Light shifts upon the wall.
I bid stillness be still.
I see, in evening air,
How slowly dark comes down on what
    we do.

—THEODORE ROETHKE

INFIRMITY

I

In purest song one plays the constant fool
As changes shimmer in the inner eye.
I stare and stare into a deepening pool
And tell myself my image cannot die.
I love myself; that's my one constancy.
Oh, to be something else, yet still to be!

II

Sweet Christ, rejoice in my infirmity;
There's little left I care to call my own.
Today they drained the fluid from a knee
And pumped a shoulder full of cortisone;
Thus I conform to my divinity
By dying inward, like an aging tree.

III

The instant ages on the living eye;
Light on its rounds, a pure extreme of light,
Breaks on me as my meagre flesh breaks down—

The soul delights in that extremity.
Blessed the meek; they shall inherit wrath;
I'm son and father of my only death.

IV

A mind too active is no mind at all;
The deep eye sees the shimmer on the stone;
The eternal seeks, and finds, the temporal,
The change from dark to light of the slow moon.
Dead to myself, and all I hold most dear,
I move beyond the reach of wind and fire.

V

Deep in the greens of summer sing the lives
I've come to love. A vireo whets its bill.
The great day balances upon the leaves;
My ears can hear the bird when all is still;
My soul is still my soul, and still the Son,
And knowing this, I am not yet undone.

VI

Things without hands take hands: there is no choice—
Eternity's not easily come by.
When opposites come suddenly in place,
I teach my eyes to hear, my ears to see
How body from spirit slowly does unwind
Until we are pure spirit at the end.

—THEODORE ROETHKE

IN HER SONG SHE IS ALONE

Followed the bird in the long forest where it cried,
From paths stepped into the stone shade,
Where the quick, frightened song was heard
Taking its beauty from that solitude,
Its heightened calling rising in the wood.

No path led; hard to discover
Direction with light lost in the leaves' stir.
The only sounds were bird and the lost river
Sunk under fern and flowing under
Root and foot; then sang again, farther, farther.

Nothing lovelier than that lonely call,
Bare and singular, like a gull,
And three notes or four, then that was all.

It drew up from the quiet like a well,
Waited, sang, and, vanishing, was still.

And tall the night came down the limbs,
The trunks descending, and the stems,
To darkness gathered where she comes:
The pool. And by those growing streams
I listened, beyond mourning, for her wings.

                                        —JON SWAN

IN INDIA

In India, the people form among the trees
With a rubbery quiet; on farthest roads
Surround you with a rubbery tread.
I stand in their circles of wonder like a light
Shining in eyes grown vague with centuries
Of stunned obedience and heartbreaking loads.
Not tall, I tower above them by a head;
Pale, I pass through their never-ending night.

A crow came to my window by the sea
At four o'clock in the Taj Mahal Hotel;
He cocked his eye and when I turned my back
Flew to my tea tray with a hideous clack
Of beak and claws, turning over the tea
And making off with the cake. The crow did well,
For down below me, where the street was black
With white-clad Hindus, what was there to take?

And foreigners say the poverty is the cause,
Thinking that gold can cure the old disease,
Thinking that oil can make the old wheel turn.
I see a new landmark on the long skyline,
An edifice of seamless stone and glass
Topped by the great word *Standard* in the skies.
Toward the Arabian Sea I watch it burn
And, being American, feel that it is mine!

And still the native voices, soft as sand,
Cry "Master, Master!" as a professional saint
Might roll his eyes and faint into his god
In the middle of traffic. Still they call aloud
"Sahib, Master!" and hold out their hand.
And lovely women with a moon of paint

Daubed on their foreheads shake hands and fade
Into silence, bowing with a praying bow.

These beautiful, small millions turn to stone
Before your eyes, become soft sculpture swarming up
The slant of temples, where their thighs protrude
Half out of joint, the angles of their arms
Twist in voluptuous torsion, and their bones
Fold into symbols pliable as rope.
The walls are sluggish with their multitude
Of gods and dancers and half-human forms.

But are they gods or droppings of the gods?
Is this the mire in which they all submerge,
This bog of holiness which ingurgitates
Prophet and hero, turning them to stone?
Which are the deities, which the human clods?
Or in this jungle do they truly merge?
And where is Reason in this hive of faith—
The one god missing from this pantheon?

I see a new god carved in fresh relief,
The brown saint in the shining spectacles
Who took the hand of the untouchables,
Who wove all India from a skein of thread.
Now he and all their spinning wheels are gone,
For a young Hindu, under whose homespun
Lay a revolver, knelt and, in good faith,
Received his blessing and then shot him dead.

—KARL SHAPIRO

IN LOVE WITH THE BEARS

To see them coming headstrong
battering the air
home to Goldilocks and three chairs
three bowls of porridge
three beds
taking the steps three at a time
barging into the rooms
this is what I grew up on
three bears with nothing to do
no terror of woods   each with

a small anger toward usurpers
that easy knowledge of something
taken and not returned
something broken and not fixed
something pressed
in which the hump still lay

Now years later I love them for what
they are
the common stutter of their fears

the worse stutter of their deeds
capable of being neighbors
capable of running for a short ways
essentially speechless
their fur hooked by thorns

wearing shabby coats
and passing in the street
sometimes glad to greet me
sometimes afraid to meet me with
their eyes

—GREG KUZMA

IN MEMORIAM: A. C., R. J. O., K. S.

The sky widens to Cornwall. A sense of sea
    Hangs in the lichenous branches and still there's light.
The road from its tunnel of blackthorn rises free
    To a final height.

And over the west is glowing a mackerel sky
    Whose opal fleece has faded to purple pink.
In this hour of the late-lit, listening evening, why
    Do my spirits sink?

The tide is high and a sleepy Atlantic sends
    Exploring ripple on ripple down Polzeath shore.
And the gathering dark is full of the thought of friends
    I will see no more.

For where's Anne Channel, who loved this place the best,
    With her tense blue eyes, and her shopping bag falling apart,
And her racy gossip and 1920 zest,
    And that warmth of heart?

Where's Roland easing his most unwieldy car,
    With its load of golf clubs, backwards into the lane?
Where's Kathleen Stokes with her Sealyhams? There's Doom Bar.
    Bray Hill shows plain.

For this is the turn, and the well-known trees draw near.
    On the road their pattern in moonlight fades and swells.
As the engine stops, from two miles off I hear
    St. Minver bells.

What a host of stars in a wideness still and deep!
    What a host of souls, as a motor bike whines away,
And the silver snake of the estuary curls to sleep
    In Daymer Bay.

—JOHN BETJEMAN

IN MEMORIAM: ERNST TOLLER

The shining neutral summer has no voice
To judge America or ask why a man dies.
And the friends who are sad and the enemies who rejoice

Are chased by their shadows lightly away from the grave
Of one who was egotistical and brave,
Lest they think they can learn without suffering how to forgive.

What was it, Ernst, that your shadow unwittingly said?
O did the child see something horrid in the woodshed
Long ago? Or had the Europe that took refuge in your head

Already been too injured to get well?
O for how long, like the swallows in that other cell,
Had the bright little longings been flying in to tell

About the big and friendly death outside,
Where people do not travel, occupy, or hide;
No towns like Munich; no need to write?

Dear Ernst, lie shadowless at last among
The other campaigners who existed till they'd done
Something that was an example to the young.

We are lived by powers we pretend to understand:
They arrange our loves; it is they who direct at the end
The sickness, the enemy bullet, or even our hand.

It is their tomorrow hangs over the earth of the living
And all we wish for our friends: but existence is believing
We know for whom we mourn, and who is grieving.

                                                        —W. H. AUDEN

IN MONTECITO

In a fashionable suburb of Santa Barbara,
Montecito, there visited me one night at midnight
A scream with breasts. As it hung there in the sweet air
That was always the right temperature, the contractors,
Who had undertaken to dismantle it, stripped off
The lips, let the air out of the breasts.

                                                                    People   disappear
Even in Montecito. Greenie Taliaferro,
In her white maillot, her good figure almost firm,
Her old pepper-and-salt hair stripped by the hairdresser
To nothing and dyed platinum—Greenie has left her Bentley.
They have thrown away her electric toothbrush; someone else slips
The key into the lock of her safety-deposit box
At the Crocker-Anglo Bank; her seat at the cricket matches
Is warmed by buttocks less delectable than hers.
Greenie's girdle is empty.

                                    A scream hangs there in the night—
They strip off the lips, let the air out of the breasts,
And Greenie has gone into the Greater Montecito
That surrounds Montecito like the echo of a scream.

                                                        —RANDALL JARRELL

IN PRAISE OF ANTONIONI

They travelled like a blue pencil against the stars
defining lopsided circles
they travelled together like a postcard like that
she had no exact home no trauma to address on her manila leaves
as she cried daily the stubborn wish
coming back the bandit tugging her satin elbows
only another mansion iceberg warnings across the canal
mannikin check silhouette a drunk teetering under the lanterns
only a peevish change of heart sham of wig dress style
only her love was responsible and undecided
undulating along a troubled coast with baggage-fatigue
the gulls ominous maybe he swore muttered
confessed gesturing sheepishly to the islands
she was fresh from the grounds
father never asked after their explanations
a bowed nun interrupted recessing the belltower steps
to pray stooped beside the abbey's peeling frescoes
a worn matron glowered at their privilege
uneasy and shamed makeshift tourists at a stopover quarter
conspicuously arrogant and sloppy like his extravagance
impatient he monitored the ticker and complained
whitewashed constructions decomposed the horizon
a cold pile of salt blocks in the alarmed weather she shivered
he swept her up suddenly out of bed and exclaimed
it was then just only then for that purpose
lazy curtains billowed far away a train
terminal bells floating her to him safely

his hair oil his leather his pungency
his mouth by her lobes charming beggar
the tiny pink portable radio squawked plopped over brashly
she sighed for his luxury humming and combing
foreknown the shower curtain slid delicious and indolent over his hard back
they excited a new feat far away a train
terminal bells floating him away to a game room
staircase earrings abruptly volcanoes murmured
of summer and evening through the palms
over her bereavement dishevelled sheets curtains pillows
carpets garments rumpled hastily loose in the wind
asphalt baked fans swept slowly late dusty and urban
the window cooled lifting their long ban siesta
gong and cocktails a muted interval of calls from the street
and outward where he goes already keened and silent
roughly over the sorrow of her companion
she laughed ironically to the bare walls
the traffic was ravenous rigid squinting he sat
hammers pummelling the body the car jerked
mangy ogling peasants wet their lips and whistled
footmen advanced from the mansion lemon whistles shrilled
a tangle of circus streamers fluttered onto the furniture
the trio redoubled its inertia from the chimneys
entertained the lawn feasting lazily by the guesthouse groves
no way to end it immobile under the pool statuary
feebly looking for it indoors timid lavender paused wilting and gracious
sea-green blandished haunted eyes and panted weak and gregarious
the refrain tickled until it ached
eventually it came it came for them together
they travelled together like a postcard like that
raked tousled harrowed it would fail shabbily
or persist in unseasonable heat enervating and suave
the limousine's anonymous silence
over the cleared squared demolition areas
she tried to say it often she tried
but it evaded her shrugs filtered through arbitrary blondes and brunettes
bare sunburned arms extended gratefully for the decanters in the sunset
the notes and ribbons and tokens she would fall in the garden
wanting him just only that for that purpose
aimless sincere and good
good for him flaring almost a woman with jealousy
wounded stern and brown she would soothe his fickle confusions
orange and brown his face almost predictably exasperated
and uncertain his ambition stencilled mouth
hard and beloved with willful indifference
to the scenery of the bitter fountains all of them
he would change she would follow

he would complain of their glamor
he would change she would follow his parabolas
against the stars defining it
in the darkness under the searchlights.

—STEPHEN HOLDEN

INSIDE OUT

I walk the purple carpet into your eye,
carrying the silver butter server,
but a truck rumbles by,
  leaving its black tire prints on my foot,
and old images—
  the sound of banging screen doors on hot afternoons
  and a fly buzzing over Kool-Aid spilled on the sink—
flicker, as reflections on the metal surface.

Come in, you said,
inside your paintings, inside the blood factory, inside the
old songs that line your hands, inside
eyes that change like a snowflake every second,

inside spinach leaves holding that one piece of gravel,

inside the whiskers of a cat,

inside your old hat, and most of all inside your mouth where you
grind the pigments with your teeth, painting
with a broken bottle on the floor, and painting
with an ostrich feather on the moon that rolls out of my mouth.

You cannot let me walk inside you too long
inside the veins where my small feet touch
bottom.
You must reach inside and pull me
like a silver bullet
from your arm.

—DIANE WAKOSKI

THE INSOMNIACS

The mystic finishes in Time,
The actor finds himself in Space,
And each, wherever he has been,
Must know his hand before his face,

Must crawl back into his own skin
As in the darkness after crime
The thief can hear his breath again,
Resume the knowledge of his limbs

And how the spasm goes and comes
Under the bones that cage his heart.

So, we are fairly met, grave friend—
The meeting of two wounds in man.
I, gesturing with practiced hand,
I, in my great brocaded gown,
And you, the fixed and patient one,
Enduring all the world can do;
I, with my shifting masks, the gold,
The awful scarlet, laughing blue,
Maker of many worlds, and you,
Worldless, the pure receptacle.

And yet your floating eyes reveal
What saint or mummer groans to
    feel:
That finite creatures finally know
The damp of stone beneath the knees,
The stiffness in the folded hands,
A duller ache than holy wounds,
The draught that never stirs the sleeve
Of glazed evangelists above
But drives men out from sacred calm
Into the violent, wayward sun.

My voice commands the formal stage;
A jungle thrives beyond the wings—
All formless and benighted things
That rhetoric cannot assuage.
I speak a dream and turn to see

The sleepless night outstaring me.
My pillow sweats; I wake in space;
This is my hand before my face;
This is the headboard of my bed
Whose splinters stuff my nightmare
    mouth;

This is the unconquerable drouth
I carry in my burning head.
Not my words nor your visions mend
Such infamous knowledge. We are
    split,
Done into bits, undone, pale friend,
As ecstasy begets its end.
As we are spun of rawest thread,
The flaw is in us; we will break.
O dare you of this fracture make
Hosannas plain and tragical,

Or dare I let each cadence fall
Awkward as learning newly learned,
Simple as children's cradle songs,
As untranslatable and true,
We someday might conceive a way
To do the thing we long to do:
To do what men have always done,
To live in time, to act in space,
Yet find a ritual to embrace
Raw towns of man, the pockmarked
    sun.

—ADRIENNE CECILE RICH

INSTEAD OF A JOURNEY

Turn like a top, spin on your dusty axis
Till the bright metal shines again, your head
Hums, and the earth accelerates,
Dizzy, you drop
Into this easy chair you drowse in daily.
Sit there and watch the walls assume their meaning,
The Chinese plate assert its blue design,
The room renew itself as you grow still.
Then, after your flight and fall, walk to the garden

Or at the open window taste return:
Weather and season, clouds at your vision's rim,
Love's whims, love's habitation, and the heart
By one slow wheel worn down, whetted to gladness.

—MICHAEL HAMBURGER

IN THE EGYPTIAN MUSEUM

Under the lucent glass,
Closed from the living air,
Clear in electric glare
That does not change or pass,
Armlet and amulet
And woven gold are laid
Beside the turquoise braid
With coral flowers inset.

The beetle, lapis, green,
Graved with the old device,
And linen brown with spice,
Long centuries unseen,
And this most gracious wreath
Exiled from the warm hair
Meet now the curious stare—
All talismans of death.

All that the anguished mind
Most nobly could invent
To one devotion bent,
That death seem less unkind;
That the degraded flesh,
Grown spiritless and cold,
Be housed in beaten gold,
A rich and rigid mesh.

Such pain is garnered here
In every close-locked case,
Concentrate in this place
Year after fading year,
That, while I wait, a cry
As from beneath the glass
Pierces me with *Alas
That the beloved must die!*

—JANET LEWIS

IN THE ELEGY SEASON

Haze, char, and the weather of All Souls':
A giant absence mopes upon the trees:
Leaves cast in casual potpourris
Whisper their scents from pits and cellar-holes.

Or brewed in gullies, steeped in wells, they spend
In chilly steam their last aromas, yield
From shallow hells a revenance of field
And orchard air. And now the envious mind

Which could not hold the summer in my head
While bounded by that blazing circumstance

Parades these barrens in a golden trance,
Remembering the wealthy season dead,

And by an autumn inspiration makes
A summer all its own. Green boughs arise
Through all the boundless backward of the eyes,
And the soul bathes in warm conceptual lakes.

Less proud than this, my body leans an ear
Past cold and colder weather after wings'
Soft commotion, the sudden race of springs,
The goddess' tread heard on the dayward stair,

Longs for the brush of the freighted air, for smells
Of grass and cordial lilac, for the sight
Of green leaves building into the light
And azure water hoisting out of wells.

                    —RICHARD WILBUR

IN THE FIELD

This field-grass brushed our legs
Last night, when out we stumbled looking up,
   Wading as through the cloudy dregs
      Of a wide, sparkling cup,

   Our thrown-back heads aswim
In the grand, kept appointments of the air,
   Save where a pine at the sky's rim
      Took something from the Bear.

   Black in her glinting chains,
Andromeda feared nothing from the seas,
   Preserved as by no hero's pains,
      Or hushed Euripides',

   And there the Dolphin glowed,
Still flailing through a diamond froth of stars,
   Flawless as when Arion rode
      One of its avatars.

   But none of that was true:
What shapes that Greece or Babylon discerned
   Had time not slowly drawn askew
      Or like cat's cradles turned?

And did we not recall
That Egypt's north was in the Dragon's tail?
    As if a form of type should fall
    And dash itself like hail,

    The heavens jumped away,
Bursting the cincture of the zodiac,
    Shot flares with nothing left to say
    To us, not coming back

    Unless they should at last,
Like hard-flung dice that ramble out the throw,
    Be gathered for another cast.
    Whether that might be so

    We could not say, but trued
Our talk a while to words of the real sky,
    Chatting of class or magnitude,
    Star-clusters, nebulae,

    And how Antares, huge
As Mars' big roundhouse swing, and more, was fled
    As in some rimless centrifuge
    Into a blink of red.

    It was the nip of fear
That told us when imagination caught
    The feel of what we said, came near
    The schoolbook thoughts we thought,

    And faked a scan of space
Blown black and hollow by our spent grenade,
    All worlds dashed out without a trace,
    The very light unmade.

    Then, in the late-night chill,
We turned and picked our way through outcrop stone
    By the faint starlight, up the hill
    To where our bed-lamp shone.

    Today, in the same field,
The sun takes all, and what could lie beyond?
    Those holes in heaven have been sealed
    Like rain-drills in a pond,

    And we, beheld in gold,
See nothing starry but these galaxies

Of flowers, dense and manifold,
  Which lift about our knees—

White daisy-drifts where you
Sink down to pick an armload as we pass,
  Sighting the heal-all's minor blue
    In chasms of the grass,

And strews of hawkweed where,
Amongst the reds or yellows as they burn,
  A few dead polls commit to air
    The seeds of their return.

We could no doubt mistake
These flowers for some answer to that fright
  We felt for all creation's sake
    In our dark talk last night,

Taking to heart what came
Of the heart's wish for life, which, staking here
  In the least field an endless claim,
    Beats on from sphere to sphere

And pounds beyond the sun,
Where nothing less peremptory can go,
  And is ourselves, and is the one
    Unbounded thing we know.

—RICHARD WILBUR

IN THE MUSEUM

Small and emptied woman, you lie here a thousand years dead,
your hands on your diminished loins, flat in this final bed,
teeth jutting from your unwound head, your spiced bones black and dried.
Who knew you and kissed you and kept you and wept when you died?
Died you young? Had you grace? *Risus sardonicus* replied.
Then quick I seized my husband's hand while he stared at his bride.

—ISABELLA GARDNER

IN THE NIGHT

Out of my window late at night I gape
And see the stars but do not watch them really,
And hear the trains but do not listen clearly;
Inside my mind I turn about to keep
Myself awake, yet am not there entirely;
Something of me is out in the dark landscape.

How much am I then what I think, how much what I feel,
How much the eye that seems to keep stars straight?
Do I control what I can contemplate
Or is it my vision that's amenable?
I turn in my mind; my mind is a room whose wall
I can see the top of but never completely scale.

All that I love is, like the night, outside,
Good to be gazed at, looking as if it could
With a simple gesture be brought inside my head,
Or in my heart, but my thoughts about it divide
Me from my object. Now, deep in my bed,
I turn and the world turns on the other side.

—Elizabeth Jennings

IN THE PUBLIC GARDENS

In the Public Gardens,
    To the airs of Strauss,
Eingang we're in love again
    When ausgang we were aus.
The waltz was played, the songs were
        sung,
    The night resolved our fears;
From bunchy boughs the lime trees
        hung
    Their gold electroliers.
Among the loud Americans

Zwei Engländer were we,
    You so white and frail and pale
    And me so deeply me;
I bought for you a dark-red rose,
    I saw your gray-green eyes,
As high above the floodlights,
    The true moon sailed the skies.
In the Public Gardens,
    Ended things begin;
Ausgang we were out of love
    Und eingang we are in.

—John Betjeman

IN THE SNAKE PARK

A white-hot midday in the Snake Park.
Lethargy lay here and there in coils,
And here and there a neat obsidian head
Lay dreaming on a plaited pillow of its own
Loops, like a pretzel or a truelove knot.

A giant python seemed a heap of tires;
Two Nielsen's vipers looked for a way out,
Sick of their cage and one another's curves;
And the long ring snake brought from Lembuland
Poured slowly through an opening like smoke.

Leaning intently forward, a young girl
Discerned in stagnant water on a rock
A dark-brown shoestring or discarded whiplash,
Then read the label to find out the name,
Then stared again. It moved. She screamed.

Old Piet Vander leaned with us that day
On the low wall around the rocky space
Where amid broken quartz that cast no shade
Snakes twitched or slithered, or appeared to sleep,
Or lay invisible in the singing glare.

The sun throbbed like a fever as he spoke:
"Look carefully at this shrub with glossy leaves."
Leaves bright as brass. "That leaf on top
Just there, do you see that it has eyes?
That's a green mamba, and it's watching *you*.

"A man I once knew did survive the bite,
Saved by a doctor running with a knife,
Serum and all. He was never the same again.
Vomiting blackness, agonizing, passing blood,
Part paralyzed, near gone, he felt

"(He told me later) he would burst apart.
But the worst agony was in his mind—
Unbearable nightmare, worse than total grief
Or final loss of hope, impossibly magnified
To a blind passion of panic and extreme distress."

"Why should that little head have power
To inject all horror for no reason at all?"

"Ask me another, and beware of snakes."
The sun was like a burning glass. Face down,
The girl who screamed had fallen in a faint.
                                        —WILLIAM PLOMER

IN TIME LIKE AIR

Consider the mysterious salt:
In water it must disappear.
It has no self. It knows no fault.
Not even sight may apprehend it.
No one may gather it or spend it.
It is dissolved and everywhere.

But out of water into air
It must resolve into a presence,
Precise, and tangible, and here.
Faultlessly pure, faultlessly white,
It crystallizes in our sight
And has defined itself to essence.

What element dissolves the soul
So it may be both found and lost,
In what suspended as a whole?

What is the element so blest
In which identity can rest
As salt in the clear water cast?

Love in its early transformation,
And only love, may so design it
That the self flows in pure sensation,
Is all dissolved and found at last
Without a future or a past,
And a whole life suspended in it.

The faultless crystal of detachment
Comes after, cannot be created
Without the first intense attachment.
Even the saints achieve this slowly;
For us, more human and less holy,
In time like air is essence stated.
                                        —MAY SARTON

IOWA

Air as the fuel of owls. Snow
unravels, its strings slacken. Creamed

to a pulp are those soft gongs
clouds were. The children

with minds moist as willow pile
clouds purely in their minds; thrones

throng on a bright mud strangely
shining. And here

chase a hog home as a summer sun
rambles over the ponds, and here run

under a sky ancient as America with
its journeying clouds. All their hands

are ferns and absences. Their farm
    homes
on their hills are strangely childlike.
                                        —MICHAEL DENNIS BROWNE

I PAINT WHAT I SEE

(A BALLAD OF ARTISTIC INTEGRITY)

"What do you paint, when you paint on a wall?"
  Said John D.'s grandson Nelson.
"Do you paint just anything there at all?
"Will there be any doves, or a tree in fall?
"Or a hunting scene, like an English hall?"

  "*I paint what I see,*" *said Rivera.*

"What are the colors you use when you paint?"
  Said John D.'s grandson Nelson.
"Do you use any red in the beard of a saint?
"If you do, is it terribly red, or faint?
"Do you use any blue? Is it Prussian?"

  "*I paint what I paint,*" *said Rivera.*

"Whose is that head that I see on my wall?"
  Said John D.'s grandson Nelson.
"Is it anyone's head whom we know, at all?
"A Rensselaer, or a Saltonstall?
"Is it Franklin D? Is it Mordaunt Hall?
"Or is it the head of a Russian?"

  "*I paint what I think,*" *said Rivera.*

  "*I paint what I paint, I paint what I see,*
    "*I paint what I think,*" *said Rivera,*
  "*And the thing that is dearest in life to me*
  "*In a bourgeois hall is Integrity;*
    "*However . . .*
  "*I'll take out a couple of people drinkin'*
  "*And put in a picture of Abraham Lincoln;*
  "*I could even give you McCormick's reaper*
  "*And still not make my art much cheaper.*
  "*But the head of Lenin has got to stay*
  "*Or my friends will give me the bird today,*
    "*The bird, the bird, forever.*"

"It's not good taste in a man like me,"
  Said John D.'s grandson Nelson,
"To question an artist's integrity
"Or mention a practical thing like a fee,
"But I know what I like to a large degree,

"Though art I hate to hamper;
"For twenty-one thousand conservative bucks
"You painted a radical. I say shucks,
   "I never could rent the offices—
   "The capitalistic offices.
"For this, as you know, is a public hall
"And people want doves, or a tree in fall,
"And though your art I dislike to hamper,
"I owe a *little* to God and Gramper,
   "And after all,
   "It's *my* wall . . ."

   "We'll see if it is," said Rivera.
               —E. B. WHITE

IRISH HOTEL

This is the last hotel
And the last light on the sea.
A mind whitewashed and stripped
   clean to the salt
Wind, its eyes
Have the narrow watchfulness of the
   builder—
Wary, because alone. Sleepless, dis-
   creet,
Distracted through its panes of dia-
   mond lead,
The desk clerk is the sea's proprietor
For a moment. Our entry now
Builds a fire in the grate beneath his
   stare.

Usually the weather's kinder, he says.
   But lies,
Believing the rocks out there are mo-
   ments of sun;
The lights in his eyes are sea-moons,
They have no pupils. The wind
Has gouged headland and sky
With the lines of his forehead. Deep-
   er inland

Is the time he dreams of: pools of
   trout,
Hills, a lake-bed, castle-ruins, and
   towns.

Better to here tell him the wind'd
   blown us here
Than that we've come
Poring over his stone floors for a
   home
Unlike any he knows.
Creation is cold—
His coat of tweed covers difficult
   bones;
When bad food and a cold bed
Bring day up over the horizon, the
   sea
An infinite black still, or a vague puz-
   zle of gray across
His features, he knows
We must leave. Though, for a night
His wet wind grows on us like skins,
And he wouldn't guess our strangers'
   minds' need
To love his rocks' black bodies,

The iodine of his bruised sand
Spread over the soiled bones of distant
    farms his mind

Dwells on. If tomorrow's sunrise
Gives us back the world of photo-
    graphs—
Castles, perfect, and towns teeming
    with life's

Human mice—he is not at odds
With our broken beginnings. There
His roof of shaved black slate,
The diamond-panes of his eyes,
His ankles of thick rough stone would
    become
Our hard bed of dreams, his sea flaw-
    less.

                    —DAVID WEVILL

IRRECONCILABLES

How to explain that on the day
we knew disease had invaded her
who had brought us into the world,
that death had cornered her like a
    weapon
she would not escape for long,
the winter sun spread vastly
and with utter ease
giving sharpness to each thing,
making all things stand out
as usually they don't:
a line of ships rooted like rocks,
and people in the frozen streets
free and light as the breath
that clung to them like clouds.

Along the edge of the cold sky
a strip of deep lavender ran
like a streamer in a wind
pulled by an invisible string,

and the water in the port
made over by days of cold
looked chopped but permanent, as if
the sea were chunks of bottleglass.

And everywhere surfaces
giving off the winter sun
in a sort of game of catch,
throwing at each the light

that each received, so that
the effect was a jubilation,
a juggler's feat so fast,
so intricate a trick, the full
extent of its multifarious display
escaped our eyes. But the sense
that it was there, and that
it meant not to deceive
but to reveal a joy
did not elude us.

Yet we were driving to get to her
who we feared might soon be gone.
And how were we to reconcile
exuberance with what we were about?

That a car was taking us
to the condition we call death,
that extinction could occur
when the day showed itself
in a display so bright
it seemed a game of light,
that disappearance should
make sense when all about us
objects we could not name
flared up in a cold winter sun
and shone until we had to turn
from them as from a flame,
nothing in us could reconcile,
nothing in us could explain.

                    —ARTHUR GREGOR

IT WAS THE LAST OF THE PARADES

It was the last of the parades;
    The sergeant said, "Dismissed!"
You waved across the crowd of heads,
    We hugged and laughed and
        kissed;
And time was happy in our beds
    But turning on the wrist.

The banners fly, the bugles blare,
    Again the soldiers come.
Oh, pull the window down, my dear,

Shut out that windy drum!
The real heroics are right here
    At home, and it's a slum.

I tremble like a truck on grades,
    You're fatter in the flanks.
My God, who used my razor blades?
    Those kids are worse than tanks.
That rub-a-dub old music fades.
    Another war? No thanks.

—Louis Simpson

THE IVORY TOWER

Who knows through what mysterious tensions these
Strange pinnacles of personality
Are held in place? The crazy structure sprawls
Over a territory not prepared
For architecture. Here a turret sags
Into the sand; there, on a rock, one tower
Stands up beyond its place in the design,
And gargoyles counterbalance random shifts
From equipoise, or flying buttresses,
As late as yesterday, were improvised
Hastily over space to clutch a wall.

Some years ago this efflorescent structure
Could have been simplified, even rebuilt,
According to a modern analyst,
With low walls all of glass to gulp the sun,
And the interior plain as everyday.
But now it is too late—one column shifted,
One bit of tracery removed, yes, even
One tendril of this ivy vine clipped off,
And the whole delicately balanced thing
Would crash around our ears. It is fantastic,
But best left as it is. And, by the way,
I note it has outlasted all the bombings.

—Robert Hillyer

J

JAKE'S WHARF

Days like this, off Jake's, the August fog
scales up on millpond mornings. Harbor gulls
float quiet as class boats in the leaning tide
(a gray gull rides the spar buoy on one leg
at noon); by four, blown home, they stand parade
on Jake's streaked roof, and summer moors as sou'west
smoke furls in across the Camden Hills.

Come Labor Day, these weather breeders end:
Jake's brightwork dinghies hauled, the mackerel sky
floods schools of rainsqualls on the wharf; September
tides wash through the boat shed where the wind
backs in northeast; three driven days, the timber
creaks, no boat puts off, and only the fish hawks,
cast from bent fir, fish down the spume-lined Bay.

There is another weather then, a day
swung hard northwest, when every island spruce
stands sharpened in the wind's cold lens and rises,
like Blue Hill, in arctic clarity;
now lobstermen set traps where each wave blazes
in the splintered sun; upriver, seals
lie ledged across the tidal Bagaduce.

Days after these ebb gray without a thaw.
For some few men the winter sea is farmland
and frontyard: off Jake's, they drag for scallops,
hand-line cod, and tie up cold where tar
and marline flavor talk that mends the traps.
Time closes in, like snow on cradled yachts,
now "people from away" have driven inland.

These are the weathers Jake knew to weather out
and wait for, slow in the wood-stove warmth of his shop
where, days like this, he used to steam-bend oak,

[349]

or bend to plank a skiff, with his weather eye out
for a high March sky. But now, to a snow-swirl wake
of gulls, his lobster boat swings cold at the mooring;
the wharf leans seaward in the ebb-tide chop.

—PHILIP BOOTH

THE JEALOUS LOVERS

When he lies in the night away from her
the backs of his eyelids burn.
He turns in the darkness as if it were an oven.
The flesh parches and he lies awake
thinking of everything wrong.

He remembers the name of a man
and a weekend before they loved each other.
His mind in its tight corner
watches a scene by the ocean last summer.
Or is it next summer he watches?

In the morning when he goes to meet her,
his heart struggles at his ribs
like an animal trapped in its burrow.
Then he sees her running to meet him,
red-faced with hurry and cold.

She stumbles over the snow.
Her knees above orange knee-socks
bob in a froth of the hems
of skirt and coat and petticoat.
Her eyes have not shut all night.

—DONALD HALL

THE JERSEY MARSH

Under the financier's
Gaze from the tower window
Turned on a west of rich
Farms and dairy meadows,
New York Bay's a gold
Fire that hides
These thirty miles in shadow.
Trestle on trestle over
Channel on channel, trains

Grind to desolate,
Brief stops in blackened grass.
What do dismounting riders
Do, toting their lunch pails here,
There, stragglers into the under-
Growth who disappear?
No ticketers, no yard
Hands; the railroad shacks'
Bolts are covered with rust.

No cars, no lots. Peeled
Billboards miles apart
Promoting last year's
Carryalls and beer
Brands that have effervesced
Forever; gray sky fritters
Along with smoke, but what
Factories are scattered
Have been shut. Power
Turrets blur into cattails
Miles on end. Rectangles
Of matted yellow reed,

Cranes pulled up, but no
Workers. And nothing has
Been built or cleared away;
Surrounding grass produces
Regional stench but doesn't
Decay. Democratic,
The marsh is kept, a link
Between commerce and agri-
Culture, reminding a grateful
Border population
How they no longer have
Much to do with each other.

—DAVID GALLER

JESU, JOY OF MAN'S DESIRING

(CHORALE FROM CANTATA NO. 147, BY J. S. BACH, ARRANGED
FOR PIANO BY MYRA HESS)

Ivory in her black, and all intent
Upon the mirror of her instrument,
Doubling her beauty to the eye and ear,
My Muse arranged this in a distant year.

I thought my longing then could not abide
The discipline to place me at her side
Whose love and art were joined without defect,
Luxurious touch and sway of intellect.

Korê and lady, Myra, downward glancing
Over the hand that sings to the hand dancing,
Breathe and be present now the shades grow still.
Sweet air, be figured at your mistress' will.

As he of Brandenburg hummed in his heart,
The tenor and the alto, part by part,
Mounted in joy amid the tranquil choir
To dwell but tenderly on man's desire.

Softly that note fell, for the baby burning
Under the wintry sign of his sojourning,
The westward star, lay upon Eden's breast
Where husbandman and hunter seek to rest.

So voices woke from every falling voice,
Bidding the Gentile and the Jew rejoice,

With all that generations may conceive,
In Miriam, who is the grace of Eve.

Had she not borne the seed of the Lord God
To ripen in her splendid belly's pod?
And who but sages of the fragrant East
Dared his epiphany, adorned the feast?

And how but in the Cyprian's tongue went round
The tidings of great joy upon that ground
And peaceful glory promised in the air?
Holy became the rose our bodies bear.

So ran Kapellmeister's hymn unending,
So dreamed the maiden on his word attending,
So, as I cherished her in my degree,
The page of ancient music fell to me.

Now life has turned and all seems far and late,
I find this luminous, and meditate
To praise again, though East and West are wild,
The girl, the singing, and the Christmas child.

                                              —ROBERT FITZGERALD

JOURNEY TO THE INTERIOR

I

In the long journey out of the self
There are many detours, washed-out interrupted raw places
Where the shale slides dangerously
And the back wheels hang almost over the edge
At the sudden veering, the moment of turning.
Better to hug close, wary of rubble and falling stones:
The arroyo cracking the road, the wind-bitten buttes, the canyons,
Creeks swollen in midsummer from the flash flood roaring into the narrow valley,
Reeds beaten flat by wind and rain,
Gray from the long winter, burnt at the base in late summer;

Or the path narrowing, winding upward
Toward the stream with its sharp stones,
The upland of alder and birch trees,
Through the swamp alive with quicksand,
The way blocked at last by a fallen fir tree,
The thickets darkening, the ravines ugly.

II

I remember how it was to drive in gravel,
Watching for dangerous downhill places where the wheels whined beyond eighty;
When you hit the deep pit at the bottom of the swale
The trick was to throw the car sideways and charge over the hill, full on the throt-
    tle,
Grinding up and over the narrow road, spitting and roaring—
A chance? Perhaps. But the road was part of me, and its ditches,
And the dust lay thick on my eyelids (who ever wore goggles?),
Always a sharp turn to the left past a barn close to the roadside,
To a scurry of small dogs and a shriek of children,
The highway ribboning out in a straight thrust to the North
To the sand dunes, and fish flies hanging, thicker than moths,
Dying brightly under the street lights sunk in coarse concrete,
The towns with their high pitted road crowns and deep gutters,
Their wooden stores of silvery pine and weather-beaten red courthouses,
An old bridge below with a buckled iron railing, broken by some idiot plunger,
Underneath, the sluggish water running between weeds, broken wheels, tires,
    stones.

And all flows past:
The cemetery with two scrubby trees in the middle of the prairie;
The dead snakes and muskrats, the turtles gasping in the rubble;
The spiky purple bushes in the winding dry creek bed;
The floating hawks, the jack rabbits, the grazing cattle—
I am not moving but they are—
And the sun comes out of a blue cloud over the Tetons,
While, farther away, the heat lightning flashes.

I rise and fall in the slow sea of a grassy plain,
The wind veering the car slightly to the right,
Whipping the line of white laundry, bending the cottonwoods apart,
The scraggly windbreak of a dusty ranch house.

I rise and fall, and time folds
Into a long moment;
And I hear the lichen speak,
And the ivy advance with its white lizard feet—
On the shimmering road,
On the dusty detour.

III

Between the rising and the falling,
Between the lifting and the relinquishing,
Between the swung rope of the bell
And the full peal of sound across the field over the broad valley,

Between the first trembling of the wren's throat and the burst of song from the
    hedgerow,
In the moment of time when the small drop forms but does not fall,
I have known the heart of the sun—
In the dark and light of a dry place,
In a flicker of fire brisked by a dusty wind.
I have heard, in a drip of leaves,
A slight song
After the midnight cries.
I see the flower of all water, above and below me, the never-receding,
Moving, unmoving in a parched land, white in the moonlight,
The soul at a stillstand,
At ease after rocking the flesh to sleep,
Petals and reflections of petals mixed on the surface of a glassy pool,
And the waves flattening out when the fishermen drag their nets over the stones.

I rehearse myself for this:
The stand at the stretch in the face of death,
Delighting in surface change, the glitter of light on waves.
And I roam elsewhere, my body thinking,
Turning toward the other side of light,
In a tower of wind, a tree idling in air,
Beyond my own echo,
Neither forward nor backward,
Unperplexed, in a place leading nowhere.

As a blind man, lifting a curtain, knows it is morning,
I know this change:
On one side of silence there is no smile;
But when I breathe with the birds,
The spirit of wrath becomes the spirit of blessing,
And the dead begin from their dark to sing in my sleep.

                                    —THEODORE ROETHKE

JOURNEY TOWARD EVENING

Fifty, not having expected to arrive here,
Makes a bad traveller; grows dull, complains,
Suspects the local wine, dislikes the service,
Is petulant on trains,
And thinks the climate overestimated.
Fifty is homesick, plagued by memories
Of more luxurious inns and expeditions,
Calls all lakes cold, all seas
Too tide-beset (for Fifty is no swimmer),

Nor, moving inland, likes the country more,
Believes the hills are full of snakes and brigands.
The scenery is a bore,
Like the plump, camera-hung, and garrulous trippers
Whose company henceforward he must keep.
Fifty writes letters, dines, yawns, goes up early
But not to sleep. He finds it hard to sleep.

—Phyllis McGinley

JUAN'S SONG

When beauty breaks and falls asunder
I feel no grief for it, but wonder.
When love, like a frail shell, lies broken,
I keep no chip of it for token.
I never had a man for friend
Who did not know that love must end.
I never had a girl for lover
Who could discern when love was over.
What the wise doubts, the fool believes—
Who is it, then, that love deceives?

—Louise Bogan

JUGGLER

A ball will bounce, but less and less. It's not
A lighthearted thing, resents its own resilience.
Falling is what it loves, and the earth falls
So in our hearts from brilliance,
Settles, and is forgot.
It takes a sky-blue juggler with five red balls

To shake our gravity up. Whee, in the air
The balls roll round, wheel on his wheeling hands,
Learning the ways of lightness, alter to spheres
Grazing his finger ends,
Cling to their courses there,
Swinging a small heaven about his ears.

But a heaven is easier made of nothing at all
Than the earth regained, and still and sole within
The spin of worlds, with a gesture sure and noble,
He reels that heaven in,

Landing it ball by ball,
And trades it all for a broom, a plate, a table.

Oh, on his toe the table is turning, the broom's
Balancing up on his nose, and the plate whirls
On the tip of the broom! Damn, what a show, we cry:
The boys stamp, and the girls
Shriek, and the drum booms,
And all comes down, and he bows and says goodbye.

If the juggler is tired now, if the broom stands
In the dust again, if the table starts to drop
Through the daily dark again, and though the plate
Lies flat on the tabletop,
For him we batter our hands
Who has won for once over the world's weight.

—RICHARD WILBUR

JULY IN INDIANA

The wispy cuttings lie in rows
                where mowers passed in the heat.
A parching scent enters the nostrils.

Morning barely breathed before
              noon mounted on tiers of maples,
fiery and still. The eye smarts.

Moisture starts on the back of the hand.

Gloss and chrome on burning cars fan out
cobwebby lightning over children
              damp and flushed in the shade.

Over all the back yards, locusts
buzz like little sawmills in the trees,
              or is the song ecstatic?—rising
rising until it gets tired and dies away.

Grass baking, prickling sweat, great blazing tree,
magical shadow and cicada song
              recall
those heroes that in ancient days, reclining
on roots and hummocks, tossing pen-knives,

delved in earth's cool underworld
and lightly squeezed the black clot from the blade.

Evening came, will come with lucid stillness
                    printed by the distinct cricket
and, far off, by the freight cars' coupling clank.

            A warm full moon will rise
out of the mothering dust, out of the dry corn land.
                                —ROBERT FITZGERALD

THE JUNK SHOP

The pride of wrights, the joy of smiths abide
            In fallen things—
            In tattered carpetings,
    In blackamoors and chamber pots.
Useless, they stay there in their show of pride
        Under the naked watts.

Is that not childhood in the corner there,
            Color and riot
        So dark now, and so quiet?
    To linger there would be unwise.
What if the tongues of wagons beat the air,
        And dolls opened their eyes?

O milliners, I see you in the hats
            Your deftness made,
        Imprisoned in their shade.
    I mark the cartwheel and the sailor,
The toque, the cloche—these are your habitats,
        Eternity your jailer.

The shoe forsaken is essential last.
            The cobbler fled
        Barefooted with the dead;
    His cunning stayed upon the sole.
Poor boot, your consolation is your past—
        Now broken, you are whole.

Medusa must have looked upon these clocks,
            They are so still,
        With no time left to kill.
    They are like chimneys without lamps,

Or keys forever separate from their locks;
They are like cancelled stamps.

Ah, this is the imperium of things,
Things in themselves.
These crammed and dusty shelves
Contain us in the things we wrought.
These bronze, unbarbered heads are not our kings
But subjects of our thought.

—HENRI COULETTE

K

KINDNESS

Your kindness is no kindness now;
It is unkindness to allow
My unkind heart so to reveal
The difference that it would conceal.
If I were, as I used to be,
As kind to you as you to me,
Or if I could but teach you how
To be unkind, as I am now,
That would be kindness of a kind—
To be again of a like mind.

—Catherine Davis

THE KINGDOM

Where have they led you, into what disguise,
Those not so sobering realities?
The body bears them, being dutiful.
Only the eyes grow vacant. The soul
Walks from a window, unsatisfied at home.
He will wait for his kingdom.

It is true that the eye that feeds on what
It sees is not much darker, shut.
Still, why condemn it or turn from the view?
Nor was the ear made only for listening to,
But for, and through. Yet, to be secure,
The soul locks each door.

The rooms of recognition are unused!
The ghost is restless, an unwilling guest,
Ageing. The disappointed eye receives
Visions of his white and bitter loves.
He listens to silence. This is his kingdom.
He is not at home.

—Jon Swan

THE KING IN MAY

The rich king of a rainy country,
my country is fertile and
        wretched with rain;
all May it has rained.

My bodyguard, thirty-seven hand-picked illusions
in waistcoats of pearl,
        are no consolation.
My palace is a dissatisfaction.
Rain clatters on it like warm vinegar
on a sullen chalice. All day
my queen (who is getting old)
lies inert as a key on a platter
        of fur
and thinks of the same thing.

Warm rain in May; my avenues are
        crowded with green.
Once it was a windy May, the high
white rubble of clouds; now,
        so much dirty laundry.
The nights are unbearable; all my world
is a hot cloister.

This wet plague is destroying me.
I am becoming a vegetable
        of stiff gold.
        —MICHAEL DENNIS BROWNE

THE KITE

It rises over the lake, the farms,
The edge of the woods,
And, like a body without arms
Or legs, it swings
Blind and blackening in the moonless
        air.
The wren, the vireo, the thrush
Make way. The rush
And flutter of wings
Falls through the dark
Like a mild rain.
We cover our heads and ponder

The farms and woods that rim
The central lake.
A barred owl sits on a limb,
Silent as bark.
An almost invisible
Curtain of rain seems to come nearer.
The muffled crack and drum
Of distant thunder
Blunders against our ears.

A row of hills appears.
It sinks into a valley

Where farms and woods surround a
    lake.
There is no rain.
It is impossible to say what form
The weather will take.
We blow on our hands,
Trying to keep them warm,
Hoping it will not snow.
Birds fly overhead.

A man runs by
Holding the kite string.
He does not see us standing dark
And still as mourners under the sullen
    sky.
The wind cries in his lapels. Leaves
    fall
As he moves by them.
His breath blooms in the chill,
And, for a time, it seems that small
White roses fill the air,
Although we are not sure.

Inside the room
The curtains fall like rain.
Darkness covers the flower-papered
    walls,
The furniture and floors
Like a mild stain.
The mirrors are emptied, the doors
Quietly closed. Asleep
In the heavy arms of a chair,
The man runs by and does not see
    us
Out in the freezing air
Of the dream he is having.
The beating of wings and the wind
Move through the deep,
Echoing valley. The kite
Rises over the lake,
The farms, the edge of the woods
Into the moonless night
And disappears.
And the man turns in his chair,
Slowly beginning to wake.

—MARK STRAND

THE KRANKENHAUS OF LEUTKIRCH

The forest nuns, who sheltered us and healed
with charms and science our unfinished frames,
spelled us with some effluvium of the sense
from their own childhoods' wonderment concealed
behind the robe, the veil, the snowy shield.
We knew no tongues; we only knew their names,
identities, and smiles, could not communicate.
Yet all is of a piece; some essence still comes through
from the house, the sisters, and, outside the gate,
the gloom, the wizard world of pines, the great,
the haunted and inhabited and enthralled
interminable Württembergerwald,
and I remember what I never rightly knew,
as in a harbored memory, not quite mine—
that German mind whose gothic dreams divine
the Kobold of the stream, the burnished Ritterling
the sylvan witch who sings behind her door,
the chilly Jungfrau of the sevenfold spring,
and psychic mannikins who, with folded wing,
sit on the mushroom circles of the forest floor.

—RICHMOND LATTIMORE

L

LA BAGARÈDE

I

I take the dogs into
town and buy *chèvre* and a *bâtard*.
Back at La Bagarède I eat
this little meal in the dusk
and sit a long time, until

the Swan grows visible, trailing
her indicated wings down the horizon,
and Orion
begins to stalk the last nights of the
    summer.

II

The black
water I gulp from the spring-fed pool
hits my brain at its root. And
I can hear
the giant, dark blooms of sunflowers
crackling open. And in the sky
the seventh
of the Sisters—the one who hid
for shame
at having loved one who dies—is shin-
    ing.

—Galway Kinnell

LACHESIS

Soul lonely comes and goes; for each our theme
We lonely must explore, lonely must dream
A story we each to ourselves must tell,
A book that as we read is written.

Our life a play of passion, says Raleigh's madrigal,
"Only we die, we die;" but older wisdom taught
That the dead change their garments and return,
Passing from sleep to sleep, from dream to dream.

In that life we dream, says Calderón, each soul
Is monster in the labyrinth of its own being.
Macbeth had his desire, an idiot's tale;
Yet the three fabulous spinners he had seen
Making from evil cause evil to come.

Oedipus' crime was greater, the murdered king
Where the three stories met being his father; yet,

Blind when he saw, he came, a beggar and blind,
Honoring their mystery to the gods
Whose life we die, living their death.

Dark lives are shades that make the picture bright,
Plotinus parabled; some born to sweet delight
And some to endless night, but all are safe
As through those sweet or deadly dreams we pass—
Lost travellers all, Blake said; and Plato taught

That we ourselves have chosen what will befall.
In the Book of the Dead, the people of dreams,
By will and by compulsion drawn to birth,
Live as punishment what each to live desires:
We are ourselves the evil dreams we suffer.

In what mind everlasting all is known,
Or in mind everlasting all forgotten
God knows, or maybe does not know, the Veda says;
Yet a few have seen the curtain drawn and tell
With Juliana that all is well.

But what of the little bloodstained hand
Not all the bitter waves can wash,
Or the betraying hand, dipped in the dish,
Predestined from the beginning of the world,
And yet not guiltless, not forgiven?

"Needs must these things be;" and you and I,
My love, must suffer patiently what we are,
These parts of guilt and grief we bear
Who must about our necks the millstone bear.

                                                                —KATHLEEN RAINE

LA DONNA È PERPETUUM MOBILE

Nice Mrs. Eberle early had been told
That speech, not silence, was authentic gold:
In conversation there must be no pause
When guests are present, even one's in-laws;
Especially with strangers, one must chatter
Continuously—on whatever matter;
And as for thoughts, there never need be any
Conceivably worth anybody's penny.

I meet the lady often. . . . Rat-tat-tat!
Her tongue is loosed before I tip my hat;
After a burst of saturation talk,
My spirit battered, I resume my walk.
Met at a party, she'll rush up with questions,
Answer herself with whirlwinds of suggestions,
Move on to others, talking—there she is,
Now here, now there, a self-replying quiz.

Mention a place (say, India) where you've been;
She tells of books she's read, of plays she's seen,
All about India, and a man she knew
Who lived a hermit's life in Timbuktu—
Oh, that's not India! But there was a swami,
Heavenly-looking, though a little balmy.
"I'd love to see Iran," she says. "Would you?"
She recalls the Persian Show in London, too,
And that reminds her of "'My Persian Rose,"
Sung when she was a child—here's how it goes!
She'd *love* to see the Taj Mahal, but guesses
Most places in the East are horrid messes;
Even in peacetime, food in Asia's bad,
But she loves curry. Do I? Yes. She's glad.

And so it goes and goes, and flows and flows—
A stream, as though she were a verbal hose,
Of things she's heard, of things she thinks she knows.
Could I but choke her, cut her head off clean,
I mean—well, really, that's *just* what I mean.

—Irwin Edman

THE LADY IN THE BARBERSHOP

Finally, among the bottles shining,
The manicurist makes a fine thing
Of her hair—black satin horse's tail
Insatiably growing from her frail
Oriental skull—she braids a coronet
Out of the dark wave. The muse of wet
Wavering lines tightly wound to a net

Of form makes measures men must forget
Because so soon changed, not out of regret,
Or rearing back, or forgetfulness,
But for simple delight black tress on tress
Can be changed. This garden of herself
Spread on her bed at night is her pelf
And her dream, and is a dream itself:

Sargasso where a lingering sea-sylph
Floats downward with seaweed into a gulf
Of great naked rock that is safe and alone
Shining there like some lesser moon.
She makes her appeal to the starlit hours
That draw the tides of this dream: "O Powers
Of night, when I wake and the flowers

Of my hair, seen here, where baldness glowers,
Neither sun nor moon, but the thing that sours
Men and is unknown--let it be seen
On their heads' deracinated heaven,
And let it be my hair that is given,
And my head riven. The world is bald,
Not just they, yet they need to be told."

But the flaming swords of Times Square
Break with the morning on her black hair,
And her mirror is a wilderness of fires
Unsought, like inconsequent desires
Of men. Who has followed her home or has
Gloried in watching her aqueous
Mild glittering among bottles and mirrors

Is on her mind then. How sad the scars
On the head that thinks, "It was, it was!"
The no-faced moon near each cuticle
She will cut in the day is strange, is cruel
As unknown pale privacy
Of stones in a cemetery
And forgotten as they. But "To be, to be"

Each dying filigree seems to sigh,
And as it falls she thinks, "It must hate me."
What to make of this hell where men are wise
That the world falling past their eyes
Will not come again, yet is owned by her?
Ah, all her bright imaginings blur
When she looks in the mirror and sees her hair.

Who can think of justice when it is clear
Celebration is the only thing one can bear?
She sweeps herself up into the line
Of darkness that is her discipline.

—RAPHAEL RUDNIK

THE LAKE

The light that labored to an early fall
Fell in the woods like rain, secret and spare,
And where the autumn road ran to a sprawl
At the lake's edge, four geese blundered into air—
Seeming to pluck my breath in foil of wings
That scooped the gathering dark, and in their ache
For height to take a rhythm from the springs
The heart feeds—from their feeding at the lake,
That lake where autumn calls in Brant, and Blue,
The Whistler Swan, all game and under gun,
Doomed and in wild beauty dear, those few
In pride that preen before the death of sun.
Upward with unseen purchase still they foil
The fallen heart with height as still they quest
For other feeding, one dark more to coil
Around them, perfect still until the last.

—LOUIS O. COXE

THE LAKE

Better disguised than the leaf insect,

A sort of subtler armadillo,
The lake turns with me as I walk,

Snuffles at my feet for what I might drop or kick up,
Sucks and slobbers the stones, snorts through its lips

Into broken glass, smacks its chops.
It has eaten several my size

Without developing a preference—
Prompt, with a splash, to whatever I offer.

It ruffles in its wallow, or lies sunning,
Digesting old, senseless bicycles

And a few shoes. The fish down there
Do not know they have been swallowed,

Any more than the girl out there, who over the stern of a rowboat
Tests its depth with her reflection.

How the outlet fears it—dragging it out,
Black and yellow, a maniac eel,

Battering it to death with sticks and stones!

—TED HUGHES

LAMENT FOR LOST LODGINGS

> Do you remember an Inn, Miranda?
> —From *"Tarantella," by Hilaire Belloc.*

Yes, do you remember an Inn,
Miranda,
Where chairs rocked, creaking,
On the long veranda,
Where beds were elderly
To match the plumbing,
But the manager smiled at our coming?

Far from the highway where the traffic muttered,
It was clapboarded white,
It was greenly shuttered.
There peace descended
When night began,
And we paid by American plan.

Remember the lobster redder than the wine,
The breakfast dining room
That closed at nine,
The wavy mirrors
In the first-floor Women's,
The waitresses all from Smith or Simmons?
And the crickets loud
But the busboys louder,
And the reek of the leek
In the weekly chowder,
And the carefree luggage
That porters brought in,
And the baths you could launch a yacht in?

Nevermore, Miranda, nevermore.
Only the faceless,
Duplicated door
Of a thousand motels
From Taos to Truro,
With television built in the built-in bureau.

Only the wallpaper, self-assertive,
And the dusty coming,
And the going, furtive,
And the Howard Johnson's
For a meal, en masse,
And the clink of the drink
In the toothbrush glass.
Only the guests, neither gentlemen nor ladies
But Monsieur the Buick
Or Madame Mercedes,
And the fee in advance,
And the sleeping pill
For the traffic roaring at the sill.

Let me fly to an Inn, like a sword to its scabbard,
Where the crickets cry
And the walls are clapboard.
Till I find a rocker
On a long veranda,
I'll motor no more, Miranda.

—Phyllis McGinley

LANDSCAPE OF SCREAMS

At night when dying proceeds to sever all seams
the landscape of screams
tears open the black bandage.

Above Moriah, the falling off cliffs to God,
there hovers the flag of the sacrificial knife,
Abraham's scream for the son of his heart,
at the great ear of the Bible it lies preserved.

O hieroglyphs of screams
engraved at the entrance to death.

Wounded coral of shattered throat flutes.

O, O hands with finger vines of fear,
dug into wildly rearing manes of sacrificial blood—

Screams shut tight with the shredded mandibles of fish,
woe tendril of the smallest children
and the gulping train of breath of the very old,
slashed into seared azure with burning tails.

Cells of prisoners, of saints,
tapestried with the nightmare pattern of throats,
seething hell in the doghouse of madness
of shackled leaps—

This is the landscape of screams!
Ascension made of screams
out of the bodies' grate of bones,

arrows of screams, released
from bloody quivers.

Job's scream to the four winds
and the scream concealed in Mount Olivet
like a crystal-bound insect overwhelmed by impotence.

O knife of evening red, flung into the throats
where trees of sleep rear blood-licking from the ground,
where time is shed
from the skeletons in Hiroshima and Maidenek.

Ashen scream from visionary eye tortured blind—

O you bleeding eye
in the tattered eclipse of the sun,
hung up to be dried by God
in the cosmos—

> —NELLY SACHS
> (*Translated from the German by Michael Roloff*)

LARGE BAD PICTURE

Remembering the Strait of Belle Isle or
some northerly harbor of Labrador,
before he became a schoolteacher
a great-uncle painted a big picture.

Receding for miles on either side
into a flushed, still sky

are overhanging pale-blue cliffs
hundreds of feet high,

their bases fretted by little arches,
the entrances to caves
running in along the level of a bay
masked by perfect waves.

On the middle of that quiet floor
sits a fleet of small black ships,
square-rigged, sails furled, motionless,
their spars like burned matchsticks.

And high above them, over the tall cliffs'
semitranslucent ranks,
are scribbled hundreds of fine black birds
hanging in "n"s, in banks.

One can hear their crying, crying,
the only sound there is
except for occasional sighing,
as a large aquatic animal breathes.

In the pink light
the small red sun goes rolling, rolling,
round and round and round at the same height
in perpetual sunset, comprehensive, consoling,

while the ships consider it.
Apparently they have reached their destination.
It would be hard to say what brought them there,
commerce or contemplation.

—Elizabeth Bishop

LAST THINGS

I

I paused in a garden alley of cypress and rose, resembling Paradise;
But I had come as a stranger to that place
And my thought was (and already it is so)
"This garden will be as other gardens gone
Where I have said, 'Here let me stay.' "
For now and now and now moves on
Though none perceives the present come or go
Carrying bird from sheltering tree more swiftly than wings.

The self in exile is the wandering mind
Travelling without rest through times and places.
We cannot lengthen the conscious moment by one heartbeat,
Sense-bound, travel the great sphere where all is present;
Paradise, lost to us, that very place we are,
Outcast beneath the tree whose fruits we gather.

There is a mind whose here is everywhere, whose now all time,
And sometimes we know with its knowledge, in dream or waking:
Is that mind ours, veiled by continual forgetting?
Are we its thoughts astray?
The old, whose souls like ripened seed after the fall of flower
Shake loose from body to be sown anew, or harvested,
Seem at times to be present in past presents
As a shell held to the ear carries the sound of waves
Breaking on distant sands still wet from an ebbing tide;
And I already in early morning sometimes wake
Upon the threshold of some long past day—
A tree stands on the brink of light
White with blossom as once beside a house long desolate.

It is said that body is soul's sepulchre
From whose sleep of oblivion the dead shall rise,
Consciousness from enshrouding flesh and blood stripped bare;
"For is not memory that dread Book of Judgment"—
The poet with the Sybil testifies—
"In whose pages indelible all is written?"
What sanctuary, what labyrinthine garden then shall hide
Self from self-knowledge, self-condemned?
We are ourselves those regions we must inherit,
The places of our sorrow await us in our past
Where like the opium-eater we must dream
Back down the long corridors of time
In vanished cities walking with the dead.

Some have with Blake and with the visionary of Patmos cried
"Come," desiring only that day's glory,
When the last blade of grass and particle of dust shall rise
Out of the past to be forever what it is,
Each in its own time and place within the abiding sphere.
Remembrance to the just is Paradise regained,
And not one sparrow fallen,
Or leaf or star shaken from the abundant tree.

But who, knowing the end with the beginning
Of earth's dust and ashes, and love betrayed,
Shall not wake with a cry at all man must remember?

II

All is judged,
The shadow by the leaf,
Flower by star,
The great tree by its seed.
The perfect is not in time
Where all is marred;

But lucid forms
Cast their images
Upon our waters:
Their faces, veiled or radiant, are always beautiful,
For we imagine them;
They are the aspects of our wisdom.
They bring us messages, intellections,
Impart a mystery,
Could tell us more, if we could hold their gaze.

They play on delicate instruments of joy,
Or cry in harmony the chord of creation,
Tone and overtone,
And when their trumpets sound,
The doom of the world is a great music
Wrecking our images on its waves.

From regions of the mind forgotten,
The frontiers of our consciousness invading,
The Pantocrator raises no hand of power,
When all is judged,
The shadow by the real
Being in recollection what it is,
We what we are.

—KATHLEEN RAINE

LATE DANDELIONS

The dandelions, wrecked on their stems
in a carnage of tentacles, conduits, and hoses,
clock-faces timed for a morning's explosion
that triggers the wire in the crabweed with its dynamite charges,
and detonates roses,

are a judgment. Crowding the clover and fern,
something demoniac, a gross Babylonian brass
hammered in sunburst and pentacle, Medusan or Coptic by turns,

a puffball of plumage on its way to a savage transfigurement,
is struck down in the grass

and time is made human again. Oh, angel
of process, who arranges the sequences
and interprets the seasons, how you wrestled
that night with the dandelion's changes, the wormwood
and work of mutation no watcher has followed,

the fiend in the bag of the mushroom, the corolla's
untimely unreason that forces its ores into feathers,
ravaged the tuft in the bubble, blew a planet away,
leaving only a space where seed after seed gathered,
and a scarab aloft on the stem revelation had hollowed!

—Ben Belitt

LATE LIGHT

when leaving with your loving in my veins
lightfooting over all the wintry walks
I saw my beautiful bawdy city shining
and across the way
a baby plunked asleep on the father's shoulder
flatted as though he were the earth
and gravity
his meat and bone
as you are mine:
how grave I grow eating that meat
in the midst of laughter moving:
I see your all most precious truth
moving to death
eyes dimmer than they were
drinking against me thirstily
the whole man wearing as the days bear down
but yourself
shining as never before:

and when you knelt one day in your heavy coat
and I looked down on that head and counted
all seventeen gray hairs
and tenderness ran like a heavy tide at sea
and drowned you though you did not know it
all dice were cast

—Barbara Bellow Watson

LATE REFLECTIONS

Old and sick, you turn away from mirrors, whether
They show the mocking face years have stained and withered
Or reflection quails at the coward's mean gesture.
Images of body and soul. What is the soul?
A feather blown by odd weathers of shine, of shade.
And the body? Is shaper and shape of the soul.
Sick, the pair live by the clock in a placeless time;
Old, they live in a futureless place, where odors
And a few fragrances are lingering features.
Hard to remember, the shape before it was fixed
As it will be in death, and as hard to believe
The remembered was once pure possibility.
In our grandparents' days, not blind superstition
But the love that illumines reason required that,
After a death in the house, mirrors be covered.

—Babette Deutsch

A LATE SPRING

Childheart, time alone is not enough.
Life waits. Oversized snowflakes start to fall
Past the spring deadline. . . .

    This morning, driving home for Easter,
I saw two mares the color of burnt chestnuts
Browsing in a sloping meadow.
Ankle-deep in the fresh snow,
They walked awkwardly about in it, and hesitated—
Sore-thumb, Negro horses in a world of light,
A mirage of low-lying cotton blossom
Cushioning their hooves.

You could almost hear
Lost gods breathing in the earth. . . .
And, one following the other, sway-backed,
They nudged the soft snow,
Their flexible lips and barely opened teeth
Seizing the sweet grass, the withered needle-stalks,
The roots shaken with water and dirt
Torn from a long sleep.

—James Scully

THE LEGEND OF SUCCESS, THE SALESMAN'S STORY

The legend of success, the salesman's story,
Was finished in the shadows of the day.
Then Peter spoke: "There also is a glory
In failure, in a virtue cast away.
The optimistic fellow in your story
Comes home; my heroes march the other way.

"My first is Courage, and God only knows
His name. I saw his picture once, a death
By Brady—in the Devil's Den—old clothes
And an enormous gun; his only wreath
Dry nettles. But, I tell you, his repose
Was large. He made the silence hold its breath.

"My next is Knowledge. Tie an empty can
To a dog's tail, and hear the welkin howl.
One afternoon in Eden, there began
The terror and the journey of his soul—
Adam or Ishmael, the running man . . ."
He fiddled with his pipe and filled the bowl.

"My third is Magic. He had got the hang
Of words. That age has vanished out of speech,
But in Fitzgerald's fable, as they sang,
The sirens still were fading on the beach.
He glittered and collapsed, a paper bang
At the last party given by the rich."

He lit his pipe. "The other side of glory
Is dark—and still it beckons, like Cathay.
The satisfaction of a happy story
Leaves me nowhere to go."
                              "Well, anyway,"
The salesman said, "I like a happy story.
But each one to his taste, I always say."
                                        —Louis Simpson

LE HIBOU ET LA POUSSIQUETTE

Hibou et Minou allèrent à la mer
Dans une barque peinte en jaune-canari;
Ils prirent du miel roux et beaucoup de sous
Enroulés dans une lettre de crédit.
Le hibou contemplait les astres du ciel,

Et chantait, en grattant sa guitare,
"O Minou chérie, ô Minou ma belle,
O Poussiquette, comme tu es rare,
    Es rare,
    Es rare!
O Poussiquette, comme tu es rare!"

Au chanteur dit la chatte, "Noble sieur à deux pattes,
Votre voix est d'une telle élégance!
Voulez-vous, cher Hibou, devenir mon époux?
Mais que faire pour trouver une alliance?"
Ils voguèrent, fous d'amour, une année et un jour;
Puis, au pays où le bong fleurit beau,
Un cochon de lait surgit d'une forêt,
Une bague accrochée au museau,
    Museau,
    Museau,
Une bague accrochée au museau.

"Cochon, veux-tu bien nous vendre pour un rien
Ta bague?" Le cochon consentit.
Donc ils prirent le machin, et le lendemain matin
Le dindon sur le mont les unit.
Ils firent un repas de maigre et de gras,
Se servant d'une cuillère peu commune;
Et là sur la plage, le nouveau ménage
Dansa au clair de la lune,
    La lune,
    La lune,
Dansa au clair de la lune.

—Francis Steegmuller

LEMONS

I

Scented, cool, and marble dark
the basilica. My unerring words
of benediction echo in the dome.
Under the banners, mumbling lips
of the brown, untouchable poor
moisten with fealty as I pass.
Great brass double doors swing
toward the morning, the sun
shuddering above the piazza
like a struck gong. A clangor
of hot light hovers on rinds
of faces close as a tub of lemons.

And I walk with a learned humility
under the portico, am seen,
and, after a dark ovation
of rising, multitudinous birds,
clapping begins—heavy, hard, dry—
from cupped palms of practiced ap-
    plauders.

II

I fall awake. Acclamations
of rain are bursting—English
rain, sporadic, spontaneous,

containing silences. The room
is possessed of an after-scent
of spilt, lemon-blossom talc.
I feel the simper of my dream
about my satisfied mouth; listening
in the resonant emptiness
of an unlit, narrow stair-well,
I mutter it slack. Dispassionate,
I look toward the city,
its sky awash with ceaseless neon.
Over fields planked with standing
    water
I see the cathedral floodlit
among houses where many lie
with many they have left, awake
without the disturbance of words.

III

Comfortably, behind my lids,
I watched the recurrent boy
leave a house of cheap, flaked brick.
It is Sunday. He does not need
the lemon his mother had him smell
through the nausea of going to school;
yet he carries it past emplacements
of guns laid up in idleness
to a camouflaged hangar
too huge for its Tiger Moth.
Up a rumbling of oil-drums

and a stack of yellow chocks
he climbs, reaches for the truss,
walks along the under-wing,
and, while he recites against the si-
    lence,
shrilly, into the shadowless dark
of the roof, cloudbursts of pigeons
pour out and up into the day.

IV

In a long, undreamable
gallery of unfinishing glass
in the sleep I cannot sleep,
I might stop the perfect birds
at will in the rumorless air;
listen to a subtlety of water
tapping upon lemon leaves
unmolested by any weather;
there would be warmth, latently cool
with ripening astringency;
and, in that plain, unechoing hall,
I should cast exactitudes of truth
in words offering homage
due to time, remembering
how a broken, boyish pontiff
lay on his actual pillow,
tired in an unbegun morning
ugly with February's drift.

—TED WALKER

LEMUEL'S BLESSING

Let Lemuel bless with the Wolf, which is a dog without a mas-
ter, but the Lord hears his cries and feeds him in the desert.
—*From "Jubilate Agno," by Christopher Smart.*

You that know the way,
Spirit,
I bless your ears, which are like cypresses on a mountain
With their roots in wisdom. Let me approach.
I bless your paws and their twenty nails, which tell their own prayer
And are like dice in command of their own combinations.
Let me not be lost.
I bless your eyes, for which I know no comparison.
Run with me like the horizon, for without you

I am no more than a dog lost and hungry,
Ill-natured, untrustworthy, useless.

My bones together bless you like an orchestra of flutes.
Divert the weapons of the settlements and lead their dogs a dance.
Where a dog is shameless and wears servility
In his tail like a banner,
Let me wear the opprobrium of possessed and possessors
As a thick tail properly used
To warm my worst and my best parts. My tail and my laugh bless you.

Lead me past the error at the fork of hesitation.
Deliver me

From the ruth of the lair, which clings to me in the morning,
Painful when I move, like a trap;
Even debris has its favorite positions, but they are not yours—

From the ruth of kindness, with its licked hands;
I have sniffed baited fingers and followed
Toward necessities not my own: it would make me
An habitué of back steps, faithful custodian of fat sheep—

From the ruth of prepared comforts, with its
Habitual dishes sporting my name, and its collars and leashes of vanity—

From the ruth of approval, with its nets, kennels, and taxidermists;
It would use my guts for its own rackets and instruments, to play its own games
        and music;
Teach me to recognize its platforms, which are constructed like scaffolds;
From the ruth of known paths, which would use my feet, tail, and ears as curios,
My head as a nest for tame ants,
My fate as a warning.

I have hidden at wrong times for wrong reasons.
I have been brought to bay. More than once.
Another time, if I need it,
Create a little wind like a cold finger between my shoulders, then
Let my nails pour out a torrent of aces like grain from a threshing machine;
Let distance be nothing to me,
Fatigue, weather, habitation, the old bones, finally,
Nothing to me,
All lights but yours nothing to me.
Let the memory of tongues not unnerve me so that I stumble or quake.

But lead me at times beside the still waters;
There when I crouch to drink let me catch a glimpse of your image
Before it is obscured with my own.

Preserve my eyes, which are irreplaceable.
Preserve my heart, veins, bones
Against the slow death building in them like hornets until the place is entirely
    theirs.
Preserve my tongue and I will bless you again and again.

Let my ignorance and failings
Remain far behind me like tracks made in a wet season,
At the end of which I have vanished,
So that those who track me for their own twisted ends
May be rewarded only with ignorance and failings.
But let me leave my cry stretched out behind me like a road
On which I have followed you.
And sustain me for my time in the desert
On what is essential to me.

                                                —W. S. MERWIN

LEONARDO DA VINCI'S

        Saint Jerome and his lion,
            in that hermitage
        of walls half gone,
            share sanctuary for a sage—
joint frame for impassioned, ingenious
        Jerome versed in language,
and for a lion like one on the skin of which
        Hercules' club made no impression.

        The beast, received as a guest—
            although some monks fled—
        with its paw dressed
            that a desert thorn had made red,
stayed as guard of the monastery ass,
        which vanished, having fed
its guard, Jerome assumed. The guest, then, like an ass,
        was made carry wood and did not resist,

        but, before long, recognized
            the ass and consigned
        its terrorized
            thieves' whole camel train to chagrined
Saint Jerome. The vindicated beast and
        saint somehow became twinned;
and now, since they behaved and also looked alike,
        their lionship seems officialized.

Pacific yet passionate—
for if not both, how
could he be great?—
Jerome, reduced by what he'd been through,
with tapering waist no matter what he ate,
left us the Vulgate. That in Leo
the Nile's rise grew food, checking famine, made
lion's-mouth fountains appropriate,

if not universally
at least not obscure.
And here, though hardly a summary, astronomy—
or pale paint—makes the golden pair
in Leonardo da Vinci's sketch seem
sun-dyed. Blaze on, picture,
saint, beast—and Lion Haile Selassie, with household
lions as symbol of sovereignty.

—MARIANNE MOORE

A LESSON IN HANDWRITING

Try first this figure 2,
how, from the point of the pen,
clockwise it unwinds itself
downward to the line,
making itself a pedestal to stand on.
Watch now. Before your eyes it becomes a swan
drifting across the page, its neck so carefully
poised, its inky eye
lowered in modesty.
As you continue, soon,
between the thin blue lines,
swan after swan sails beautifully past you,
margin to margin, 2 by 2 by 2—
a handwritten swirl of swans.
Under them now unroll
the soft, curled pillows of the 6's,
the acrobatic 3's, the angular 7's,
the hourglass 8's, and the neat tadpole 9's,
each passing in review
on stilts or wheels or platforms
in copybook order.

Turn the page, for now
comes the alphabet, an eccentric
parade of odd characters. If at first you tangle,
now and again, in a loop or a twirl,
no matter. Each in time will dawn
as faces and animals do, familiar,
laughable, crooked, quirky.
Begin with the letter S. Already
it twists away from the pen like a snake or a watch spring,
coiled up and back to strike. SSSS, it says,
hissing and slithering off into the ferns of the F's.
Follows a line of stately Q's floating
just off the ground, tethered by their tails,
over the folded arms of the W's
and the akimbo M's. Open-eyed, the O's
roll after them like bubbles blown away.
Feel how the point curls round them lovingly
after the serious three-tongued E's.
See now how the page fills up
with all the furniture of writing—the armchair H's,
the ladders and trestles of A's and Y's and X's,
the T-shaped tables and the upholstered B's.
The pen abandons a whole scaffolding
of struts and braces, springs and balances,
on which will rest eventually
the weight of a written world, storey on storey
of words and vows, all the long-drawn-out telling
that pens become repositories of.
These are now your care, and you may give them
whatever slant or human twist you wish
if it should please you. But you will not alter
their scrawled authority, durable
as stone, silent, grave, oblivious
of all you make them tell.

Tomorrow, words begin.

                                        —ALASTAIR REID

A LETTER

I have been wondering
What you are thinking about, and by now suppose
It is certainly not me.
But the crocus is up, and the lark, and the blundering
Blood knows what it knows.
It talks to itself all night, like a sliding, moonlit sea.

Of course, it is talking of you.
At dawn, where the ocean has netted its catch of lights,
The sun plants one lithe foot
On that spill of mirrors, but the blood goes worming through
Its warm Arabian nights,
Naming your pounding name again in the dark heartroot.

Who shall, of course, be nameless.
Anyway, I should want you to know I have done my best,
As I'm sure you have, too.
Others are bound to us, the gentle and blameless
Whose names are not confessed
In the ceaseless palaver. My dearest, the clear and bottomless blue

Of those depths is all but blinding.
You may remember that once you brought my boys
Two little woolly birds.
Yesterday the older one asked for you upon finding
Your thrush among his toys.
And the tides welled about me, and I could find no words.

There is not much else to tell.
One tries one's best to continue as before,
Doing some little good.
But I would have you know that all is not well
With a man dead set to ignore
The endless repetitions of his own murmurous blood.

—ANTHONY HECHT

A LETTER FOR ALLHALLOWS

I am still hurt, Plin,
by your desertion. Now and again,
between rains, or among
sagged syllables on a page,
I am stopped by your grinning, lantern-jawed,
monkey-eared, beautiful face.
And I am hurt
because you went to war
and died right in the middle of your letters,
and never said goodbye.
And then your father followed you,
at a respectful distance,
and the great house on the hill
went for a Trappist monkery.

I hope those monks
have veneration for the juniper
and the blackberries and the frog pond
and the dust of toy soldiers in the attic
where we warred long November afternoons;
above all, for the black road that,
if I listen on All Souls' Eve, will clatter
to the gait of you riding home from the white woods
on Diamond, your horse.
The glue is long since dry
they made of him. But we mark well
he was the last of the historic horses:
Revere rode him, and Sheridan,
and Sitting Bull.
I hope the monks treat you gently, shades
galloping alongside the empty meadows,
from Concord and Lexington,
the fords of the Shenandoah,
forks of the Little Bighorn.
Surely they would not be unmerciful
and frighten away with signs and bells and torches
so young an old soldier and his friend,
who, one way or another, were made ghosts
in all their country's wars.

—Peter Kane Dufault

LETTER TO P.

Help me to help your life
and so help mine.

Words! Words!

Your needs are children of a past
so strewn with murdered desires
that you must want and want
murderously.

I am willing to be
only a tongue speaking sincerely
the praise your life grows tall on,

the mirror necessary
to render your face its beauty,

your body its splendor,

a sun to light your moon
that otherwise rolls, cold stone,
in darkness, infinitely.

But where I stand
—outside your any recognition of me
who also need
a tongue, a mirror, and a sun—
I cannot help you.

Help me to help you.
I do not utter now
the word "love."

—Robert Friend

LETTER WRITTEN ON A FERRY
CROSSING LONG ISLAND SOUND

I am surprised to see
that the ocean is still going on.
Now I am going back
and I have ripped my hand
from your hand as I said I would
and I have made it this far
as I said I would
and I am on the top deck now,
holding my wallet, my cigarettes,
and my car keys
at two o'clock on a Tuesday
in August of 1960.

Dearest,
although everything has happened,
nothing has happened.
The sea is very old.
The sea is the face of Mary,
without miracles or rage
or unusual hope,
grown rough and wrinkled
with incurable age.

Still,
I have eyes.
These are my eyes:
the orange letters that spell
"ORIENT" on the life preserver
that hangs by my knees,
the cement lifeboat that wears
its dirty canvas coat,
the faded sign that sits on its shelf
saying "KEEP OFF."
Oh, all right, I say,
I'll save myself.

Over my right shoulder
I see four nuns
who sit like a bridge club,
their faces poked out
from under their habits,
as good as good babies who
have sunk into their carriages.

Without discrimination,
the wind pulls the skirts
of their arms.
Almost undressed,
I see what remains:
that holy wrist,
that ankle,
that chain.

Oh, God,
although I am very sad,
could you please
let these four nuns
loosen from their leather boots
and their wooden chairs
to rise out
over this greasy deck,
out over this iron rail,
nodding their pink heads to one side,
flying four abreast
in the old-fashioned side stroke,
each mouth open and round,
breathing together
as fish do,
singing without sound.

Dearest,
see how my dark girls sally forth,
over the passing lighthouse of Plum
    Gut,
its shell as rusty
as a camp dish,
as fragile as a pagoda
on a stone,
out over the little lighthouse
that warns me of drowning winds
that rub over its blind bottom
and its blue cover—
winds that will take the toes
and the ears of the rider
or the lover.

There go my dark girls;
their dresses puff
in the leeward air.
Oh, they are lighter than flying dogs
or the breath of dolphins;
each mouth opens gratefully,
wider than a milk cup.
My dark girls sing for this:
They are going up.

Here are my four dark girls.
See them rise
on black wings, drinking
the sky, without smiles
or hands
or shoes.
They call back to us
from the gauzy edge of paradise,
good news, good news.

—ANNE SEXTON

THE LIFEGUARD

In a stable of boats I lie still,
From all sleeping children hidden.
The leap of a fish from its shadow
Makes the whole lake instantly trem-
     ble.
With my foot on the water, I feel
The moon outside

Take on the utmost of its power.
I rise and go out through the boats.
I set my broad sole upon silver,
On the skin of the sky, on the moon-
     light,
Stepping outward from earth onto
     water
In quest of the miracle

This village of children believed
That I could perform as I dived
For one who had sunk from my sight.
I saw his cropped haircut go under.
I leapt, and my steep body flashed
Once, in the sun.

Dark drew all the light from my eyes.
Like a man who explores his death
By the pull of his slow-moving shoul-
     ders,
I hung head down in the cold,
Wide-eyed, contained, and alone
Among the weeds,

And my fingertips turned into stone
From clutching immovable blackness.
Time after time I leapt upward
Exploding in breath, and fell back
From the change in the children's
     faces
At my defeat.

Beneath them, I swam to the boat-
     house
With only my life in my arms
To wait for the lake to shine back
At the risen moon with such power
That my steps on the light of the rip-
     ples
Might be sustained.

Beneath me is nothing but brightness
Like the ghost of a snow field in sum-
     mer.
As I move toward the center of the
     lake,
Which is also the center of the moon,
I am thinking of how I may be
The savior of one

Who has already died in my care.
The dark trees fade from around me.
The moon's dust hovers together.
I call softly out, and the child's
Voice answers through blinding water.
Patiently, slowly,

He rises, dilating to break
The surface of stone with his forehead.
He is one I do not remember
Having ever seen in his life.
The ground that I stand on is trem-
bling
Upon his smile.

I wash the black mud from my hands.
On a light given off by the grave,
I kneel in the quick of the moon
At the heart of a distant forest
And hold in my arms a child
Of water, water, water.

—James Dickey

THE LIFE OF . . .

I

"So there we were stuck
in Alassio all that rotten winter
in a rented house, no one around
but puffed-up Germans, and nothing
to read but two men I can't abide,
Boswell and Johnson, the latter worse
than his crony.

And nothing to do
but struggle on through that wretched
'Life of . . .'. How I loathed it!"

II

"Ah, my friend," I say, "that's what,
more or less, it always comes to:
one book to a customer.

Oh, some are luckier than the rest—
richer text, pictures colored
every second page.

But all of us
are stuck in our own Alassio,
like it or not, waiting
there, flopped open."

III

"Actually,"
my friend's wife now breaks in, "after
the first two summer months, after
the Germans left, the gaudy decora-
tions
hung on the shops for them
pulled down,

and the Italians

gradually appearing, we grew to love
the town, rotten winter and all—
admit it—

our garden with its crazy,
tangled blooming—roses, geraniums,
and the rest—through shattered bot-
tles,
cans, and every kind of litter,

the narrow, dark, malarial streets
at the end of which, on our long walks,
the sea glittered like a blaze burst
through a tunnel,

the forlorn little
fishing-fleet going out each night
as we went to bed and, at dawn,
returning as we woke,

threw open
the shutters, and watched behind it
a red heaped up on the creamy water,
the sun rising, as though, towed
in, part of the catch . . .

later, too,
the mountain that we loved to climb,
looming over the town and high
enough
with its paths twisting to the top
so that one seemed to see—

a new day
previewed there, just as it was forging
forth—eye to eye with the moon."

—Theodore Weiss

THE LIFE OF SERVICE

Service, or Latin *sorbus*, European—
More especially English—shadbush or small tree,
Asks all the shade the fancier can find
In a walled garden. This is no plebeian
Of cottage plots, though coarse in leaf and rind.

Planted, it is persistent, of a thick
Skin, and grows strong the more it's trodden on—
Or afterward, as an established upas,
Thrives all the better for each welcomed nick
Of aggrieved knives wielded by interlopers.

By this indeed it knows itself. Self-thwarted,
It welcomes parasites, for playing host
To what insults and saps it is its virtue
And its fulfillment. Flourishing contorted,
All its long-suffering's overbearing, too.

Some cultivators hold that it repays,
By its small edible fruit (in favored species,
Of a vinous taste), its culture. It does not;
All saner growth abhors it, and the bays
Wither, affronted, in the poisoned plot.

—Donald Davie

LINES ON THE SEA

The sky's lip and the sea's lip shut in peace.
The horizontal is the line of calm.
Masts move across it: pygmy verticals.
Speeding diagonals of leaning sails
startle awake the eye that's drowsed with trust.
All's well, the horizon says. Peace—peace.
Time and more time is man's, whether for commerce
or purely for being, and knowing that he is.

But there's an unseen perpendicular
from the horizon, and every drowned man slides
down it to such an everlasting peace
as skyline never speaks of to the nerves.
Sane, living men refuse it. Every ship
keeps watch against that hanging rope. The sailor
would rather think the ocean wide than deep.

Thus he moves horizontally. His eyes
narrow for panoramas. His glance goes
laterally, to the land, where verticals
are skyscrapers and silos, towers, trees,
and even the little vertical of man
is blocked out solid in a capital I.

—DILYS BENNETT LAING

LINES WRITTEN IN OREGON

Esmeralda! Now we rest
Here, in the bewitched and blest
Mountain forests of the West.

Here the very air is stranger.
Damsel, anchoret, and ranger
Share the woodland's dream and dan-
ger.

And to think I deemed you dead!
(In a dungeon, it was said;
Tortured, strangled.) But instead—

Blue birds from the bluest fable,
Bear and hare in coats of sable,
Peacock moth on picnic table.

Huddled road signs softly speak
Of Lake Merlin, Castle Creek,
And (obliterated) Peak.

Do you recognize that clover?
Dandelions, *l'or du pauvre?*
(Europe, nonetheless, is over.)

Up the turf, along the burn,
Latin lilies climb and turn
Into Gothic fir and fern.

Cornfields have befouled the prairies
But these canyons laugh! And there
is
Still the forest with its fairies.

And I rest where I awoke
In the sea shade—*l'ombre glauque*—
Of a legendary oak.

Where the woods get ever dimmer,
Where the Phantom Orchids glim-
mer—
Esmeralda, *immer, immer.*

—VLADIMIR NABOKOV

A LISTENER'S GUIDE TO THE BIRDS

(AFTER A BINGE WITH ROGER TORY PETERSON IN HIS FAMOUS GUIDEBOOK)

Wouldst know the lark?
Then hark!
Each natural bird
Must be seen *and* heard.
The lark's "Tee-ee" is a tinkling entreaty,
But it's not always "Tee-ee"—
Sometimes it's "Tee-titi."
So watch yourself.

Birds have their love-and-mating song,
Their warning cry, their hating song;
Some have a night song, some a day song,
A lilt, a tilt, a come-what-may song;
Birds have their careless bough and teeter song
And, of course, their Roger Tory Peter song.

The studious oven-bird (pale pinkish legs)
Calls, "Teacher, teacher, teacher!"
The chestnut-sided warbler begs
To see Miss Beecher.
    "I wish to see Miss Beecher."
(Sometimes interpreted as "Please please please ta meetcha.")

The red-wing (frequents swamps and marshes)
Gurgles, "Konk-la-reeee,"
Eliciting from the wood duck
The exclamation "Jeeee!"
    (But that's the *male* wood duck, remember.
    If it's his wife you seek,
    Wait till you hear a distressed "Whoo-eek!")

Nothing is simpler than telling a barn owl from a veery:
One says, "Kschh!" in a voice that is eerie,
The other says, "Vee-ur," in a manner that is breezy.
    (I told you it was easy.)
On the other hand, distinguishing between the veery
And the olive-backed thrush
Is another matter. It couldn't be worse.
The thrush's song is similar to the veery's,
Only it's in reverse.

Let us suppose you hear a bird say, "Fitz-bew,"
The things you can be sure of are two:
First, the bird is an alder flycatcher (*Empidonax traillii traillii*);
Second, you are standing in Ohio—or, as some people call it, O-hee-o—
Because, although it may come as a surprise to you,
The alder flycatcher, in New York or New England, does not say, "Fitz-bew,"
It says, "Wee-be'-o."

"Chu-chu-chu" is the note of the harrier,
Copied, of course, from our common carrier.
The osprey, thanks to a lucky fluke,
Avoids "Chu-chu" and cries, "Chewk, chewk!"
    So there's no difficulty there.

The chickadee likes to pronounce his name;
It's extremely helpful and adds to his fame.
But in spring you can get the heebie-jeebies
Untangling chickadees from phoebes.
The chickadee, when he's all afire,
Whistles, "Fee-bee," to express desire.
He should be arrested and thrown in jail
For impersonating another male.
   (There's a way you can tell which bird is which,
   But just the same, it's a nasty switch.)
Our gay deceiver may fancy-free be
But he never does fool a female phoebe.

Oh, sweet the random sounds of birds!
The old squaw, practicing his thirds;
The distant bittern, driving stakes,
The lonely loon on haunted lakes;
The white-throat's pure and tenuous thread—
They go to my heart, they go to my head.
How hard it is to find the words
With which to sing the praise of birds!
Yet birds, when *they* get singing praises,
Don't lack for words—they know some daisies:
   "Fitz-bew,"
   "Konk-la-reeee,"
   "Hip-three-cheers,"
   "Onk-a-lik, ow-owdle-ow,"
   "Cheedle cheedle chew,"
And dozens of other inspired phrases.
            —E. B. WHITE (gray cheeks, inconspicu-
            ous eye-ring; frequents bars and glades)

LITTLE EXERCISE AT 4 A.M.

Think of the storm roaming the sky uneasily
like a dog looking for a place to sleep in,
listen to it growling.

Think how they must look now, the mangrove keys
lying out there unresponsive to the lightning,
in dark, coarse-fibred families,

where occasionally a heron may undo his head,
shake up his feathers, make an uncertain comment
when the surrounding water shines.

Think of the boulevard and the little palm trees
all stuck in rows, suddenly revealed
as fistfuls of limp fish skeletons.

It is raining there. The boulevard
and its broken sidewalks, with weeds in every crack,
are relieved to be wet, the sea to be freshened.

Now the storm goes away again in a series
of small, badly lit battle scenes,
each in "Another part of the field."

Think of someone sleeping in the bottom of a rowboat
tied to a mangrove root or the pile of a bridge;
think of him as uninjured, barely disturbed.

                                —ELIZABETH BISHOP

LITTLE GIRL, MY STRINGBEAN, MY LOVELY WOMAN

My daughter, at eleven
(almost twelve), is like a garden.

Oh, darling! Born in that sweet birth-
      day suit
and having owned it and known it for
      so long,
now you must watch high noon enter—
noon, that ghost hour.
Oh, funny little girl—this one under a
      blueberry sky,
this one! How can I say that I've
      known
just what you know and just where
      you are?

It's not a strange place, this odd
      home
where your face sits in my hand
so full of distance,
so full of its immediate fever.
The summer has seized you,
as when, last month in Amalfi, I saw
lemons as large as your desk-side
      globe—
that miniature map of the world—

and I could mention, too,
the market stalls of mushrooms
and garlic buds all engorged.
Or I think even of the orchard next
      door,
where the berries are done
and the apples are beginning to swell.
And once, with our first back yard,
I remember I planted an acre of yel-
      low beans
we couldn't eat.

Oh, little girl,
my stringbean,
how do you grow?
You grow this way.
You are too many to eat.

I hear
as in a dream
the conversation of the old wives
speaking of *womanhood*.
I remember that I heard nothing my-
      self.
I was alone.
I waited like a target.

Let high noon enter—
the hour of the ghosts.
Once the Romans believed
that noon was the ghost hour,
and I can believe it, too,
under that startling sun,
and someday they will come to you,
someday, men bare to the waist,
        young Romans
at noon where they belong,
with ladders and hammers
while no one sleeps.
But before they enter
I will have said,
Your bones are lovely,
and before their strange hands
there was always this hand that
        formed.

Oh, darling, let your body in,
let it tie you in,
in comfort.
What I want to say, Linda,
is that women are born twice.

If I could have watched you grow
as a magical mother might,
if I could have seen through my magi-
        cal transparent belly,
there would have been such ripening
        within:
your embryo,
the seed taking on its own,
life clapping the bedpost,
bones from the pond,
thumbs and two mysterious eyes,

the awfully human head,
the heart jumping like a puppy,
the important lungs,
the becoming—
while it becomes!
as it does now,
a world of its own,
a delicate place.

I say hello
to such shakes and knocking and high
        jinks,
such music, such sprouts.
such dancing-mad-bears of music,
such necessary sugar,
such goings on!

Oh, little girl,
my stringbean,
how do you grow?
You grow this way.
You are too many to eat.

What I want to say, Linda,
is that there is nothing in your body
        that lies.
All that is new is telling the truth.
I'm here, that somebody else,
an old tree in the background.
Darling,
stand still at your door,
sure of yourself, a white stone, a good
        stone—
as exceptional as laughter
you will strike fire,
that new thing!

                                        —ANNE SEXTON

LITTLE LULLABY

Dark-time. The little ones like bees
Have stolen your light, packed it away
In their healthy mandibles, and gone off.
Rest, little soul, of your lithe cunnings,
Of your tattling tattoo undressed. They

Have taken the daylight in their keeping;
Safe in the hive, hidden, it will not chide
You if you are silent. At last, listen:
Under the fallow, sad song of your neighbor's
Life, or the blood waltzing in your ear,
Dispossessed, uncharming, enormous
Bodies approach; they wish to fulfill you.

—IRVING FELDMAN

A LITTLE MORNING MUSIC

The birds in the first light twitter and whistle,
Chirp and seek, sipping and chortling; weakly, meekly, they speak and bubble
As cheerful as the cherry would, if it could speak when it is cherry ripe or cherry
    ripening.

And all of them are melodious, erratic, and gratuitous,
Singing solely to heighten the sense of morning's beginning.

How soon the heart's cup overflows, how soon it is excited to delight and elation!

And in the first light the cock's chant, roaring,
Bursts like rockets, rising and breaking into fragments of brilliance;
As the fields arise, cock after cock catches on fire,
And the pastures loom out of vague blue shadow,
The red barn and the red sheds rise and redden, blocks and boxes of slowly bloom-
    ing wet redness;
Then the great awe and splendor of the sun comes nearer,
Kindling all things, consuming the forest of darkness, lifting and lighting up
All the darkling ones who slept and grew
Beneath the petals, the frost, the mystery and mockery of the stars.

The darkened ones turn slightly in the faint light of the small morning,
Grow gray or glow green—
        They are gray and green at once
        In the pale cool of blue light;
They dream of that other life and that otherness
        Which is the darkness going over
Maple and oak, leafy and rooted in the ancient and famous light,
In the bondage of the soil of the past and the radiance of the future.

But now the morning is growing, the sun is soaring, all
That lights up shows, quickly and slowly, the showering plenitude of fountains,
And soon an overflowing radiance, actual and dazzling, will blaze and brim over all
        of us,

Discovering and uncovering all color and all kinds, all forms and all distances, ris-
    ing and rising higher
        and higher, like a stupendous bonfire of consciousness,
Gazing and blazing, blessing and possessing all vividness and all darkness.

                                —DELMORE SCHWARTZ

LIVING IN SIN

She had thought the studio would keep itself—
No dust upon the furniture of love.
Half heresy, to wish the taps less vocal,
The panes relieved of grime. A plate of pears,
A piano with a Persian shawl, a cat
Stalking the picturesque, amusing mouse
Had been her vision when he pleaded "Come."
Not that, at five, each separate stair would writhe
Under the milkman's tramp; that morning light
So coldly would delineate the scraps
Of last night's cheese and blank, sepulchral bottles;
That on the kitchen shelf among the saucers
A pair of beetle eyes would fix her own—
Envoy from some black village in the moldings. . . .
Meanwhile her night's companion, with a yawn,
Sounded a dozen notes upon the keyboard,
Declared it out of tune, inspected, whistling,
A twelve hours' beard, went out for cigarettes,
While she, contending with a woman's demons,
Pulled back the sheets and made the bed and found
A fallen towel to dust the tabletop,
And wondered how it was a man could wake
From night to day and take the day for granted.
By evening she was back in love again,
Though not so wholly but throughout the night
She woke sometimes to feel the daylight coming
Like a relentless milkman up the stairs.

                    —ADRIENNE CECILE RICH

LOBSTERS IN THE WINDOW

First, you think they are dead.
Then you are almost sure
One is beginning to stir.
Out of the crushed ice, slow
As the hands on a schoolroom clock,
He lifts his one great claw

And holds it over his head;
Now he is trying to walk.

But like a run-down toy;
Like the backward crabs we boys
Waded for in the creek,

Trapped in jars or a net,
And then took home to keep.
Overgrown, retarded, weak,
He is fumbling yet
From the deep chill of his sleep

As if, in a glacial thaw,
Some ancient thing should wake
Sore and cold and stiff,
Struggling to raise one claw
Like a defiant fist,
Yet wavering, as if

Starting to swell and ache
With that thick peg in the wrist.

I should wave back, I guess.
But still in his permanent clench,
He's fallen back with the mass
Heaped in their common trench
Who stir, but do not look out
Through the rainstreaming glass,
Hear what the newsboys shout,
Or see the raincoats pass.

—W. D. SNODGRASS

THE LONG WATERS

I

Whether the bees have thoughts we cannot say,
But the hind part of the worm wriggles the most,
Minnows can hear, and butterflies, yellow and blue,
Rejoice in the language of smells and dancing.
Therefore I reject the world of the dog,
Though he hear a note higher than C
And the thrush stopped in the middle of its song.

And I acknowledge my foolishness with God,
My desire for the peaks, the black ravines, the rolling mists
Changing with every twist of wind,
The unsinging fields where no lungs breathe,
Where light is stone.

I return where fire has been,
To the charred edge of the sea,
Where the yellowish prongs of grass poke through the blackened ash
And the bunched logs peel in the afternoon sunlight,
Where the fresh and salt waters meet
And the sea winds move through the pine trees—
A county of bays and inlets, and small streams flowing seaward.

II

Mnetha, Mother of Har, protect me
From the worm's advance and retreat, from the butterfly's havoc,
From the slow sinking of the island peninsula, the coral efflorescence,
The dubious sea change, the heaving sands, and my tentacled sea cousins.

But what of her
Who magnifies the morning with her eyes—

That star winking beyond itself
(The cricket voice deep in the midnight field,
The blue jay rasping from the stunted pine)?

How slowly pleasure dies!
The dry bloom splitting in the wrinkled vale,
The first snow of the year in the dark fir.
Feeling, I still delight in my last fall.

III

In the time when the trout and young salmon leap for the low-flying insects,
And the ivy branch, cast to the ground, puts down roots into the sawdust,
And the pine, whole with its roots, sinks into the estuary,
Where it leans, tilted east, a perch for the osprey,
And a fisherman dawdles over a wooden bridge,
These waves, in the sun, remind me of flowers:
The lily's piercing white,
The mottled tiger, best in the corner of a damp place,
The heliotrope, veined like a fish, the persistent morning-glory,
And the bronze of a dead burdock at the edge of a prairie lake,
Down by the muck shrinking to the alkaline center.

I have come here without courting silence,
Blessed by the lips of a low wind,
To a rich desolation of wind and water,
To a landlocked bay, where the salt water is freshened
By small streams running down under fallen fir trees.

IV

In the vaporous gray of early morning,
Over the thin, feathery ripples breaking lightly against the irregular shoreline—
Feathers of the long swell, burnished, almost oily—
A single wave comes in like the neck of a great swan
Swimming slowly, its back ruffled by the light cross-winds,
To a tree lying flat, its crown half broken.

I remember a stone breaking the eddying current,
Neither white nor red, in the dead middle way,
Where impulse no longer dictates, nor the darkening shadow,
A vulnerable place,
Surrounded by sand, broken shells, the wreckage of water.

V

As light reflects from a lake, in late evening,
When bats fly, close to slightly tilting brownish water,
And the low ripples run over a pebbly shoreline,
As a fire, seemingly long dead, flares up from a downdraft of air in a chimney,

Or a breeze moves over the knees from a low hill,
So the sea wind wakes desire.
My body shimmers with a light flame.

I see in the advancing and retreating waters
The shape that came from my sleep, weeping:
The eternal one, the child, the swaying vine branch,
The numinous ring around the opening flower,
The friend that runs before me on the windy headlands,
Neither voice nor vision.

I, who came back from the depths laughing too loudly,
Become another thing;
My eyes extend beyond the farthest bloom of the waves;
I lose and find myself in the long waters;
I am gathered together once more;
I embrace the world.

—THEODORE ROETHKE

LOOKING WEST

When I burned our leaves, a wind from the dark
trailed flakes of fire over the garden,
catching at the last of the beans and sparkling
far away like meteors or a gust of stars.
In the maple tree one falling star caught,
and glowed a long time before it went out.

—WILLIAM STAFFORD

LOST

In the six-acre field,
Heimbacher's smallest children
move like men among the grain.
Each has a sharpened sickle
and each swings at the wild mustard
that blazes fitfully from the green.
They are no higher than the paper flame
of the weed they bend to cut.
No, they might not be there at all
but that one sees the flames go out.

—MILLEN BRAND

THE LOST JEWEL

Who on your breast pillows his head now,
Jubilant to have won
The heart beneath on fire for him alone,

At dawn will hear you, plagued by nightmare,
Mumble and weep
About some blue jewel you were sworn to keep.

Wake, blink, laugh out in reassurance,
Yet your tears will say,
"It was not mine to lose or give away.

"For love it shone, never for the madness
Of a strange bed—
Light on my finger, fortune in my head."

Roused by your naked grief and beauty,
For lust he will burn:
"Turn to me, sweetheart! Why do you not turn?"

—ROBERT GRAVES

LOST SILVERTIP

Standing on the mountaintop,
he chews the fire tower's metal strut,
lips freezing to its zinc

and cries for his lost Silvertip
roasted away from her pines and
    streams.
How many trout did they share?
How much sweet honey nuzzle?

The char sifts down
like black soap flakes

over the cooked ribs of bears,
and their ebony claws
blued by flame.

The streams have boiled,
inferno,
the trout poached and
pines gone into coal,
another life;

the honey crystallized,
and the honey-lover   smoke.

—J. D. REED

A LOST WORLD

"Dear love, why should you weep
   For time's remorseless way?
Though today die in sleep
   And be called yesterday,
     We love, we stay."

"I weep for days that died
   With former love that shone
On a world true and wide
   Before this newer one,
     Which yours shines on."

"Is this world not as true
    As that one ever was,
Which now has fled from you
    Like shadows from the grass
    When the clouds pass?"

"Yet for that world I weep
    Kindly, before we kiss;
Love has a faith to keep
    With past felicities
    That weep for this."

—ROBERT GRAVES

THE LOVED ONE

Understand, he is naked in the sea,
And no child, either, and no champion;
Middle-aged, bald and bellied, cold and white,
And the tide black and restless, very strong,
Lashing his thin legs round with kelp,
And the boat broken on the rocks, the oars
Dangerously adrift and spinning, perched
Upon by hunched and gale-exhausted gulls;
Understand, he has put out many times
For the far shore or, failing that, for minor
Island triumphs, and repeatedly
Has been washed back, washed back;
And then imagine how, each time, he feels,
Confronted by the wife and kids, lined up
Along the jetsamed shore and smiling, smiling,
While out his mother wades—lavender-shawled,
White-haired, glasses agleam—bearing, in soft,
Soap-scented hands, another birthday card.

—JOSEPH HANSEN

LOVE FOR A HAND

Two hands lie still, the hairy and the white,
And soon down ladders of reflected light
The sleepers climb in silence. Gradually
They separate on paths of long ago,
Each winding on his arm the unpleasant clew
That leads, live as a nerve, to memory.

But often, when too steep her dream descends,
Perhaps to the grotto where her father bends

LOVERS IN WINTER

The posture of the tree
  Shows the prevailing wind;
And ours, long misery
  When you are long unkind.

But forward, look, we lean—
  Not backward as in doubt—
And still with branches green
  Ride our ill weather out.

—ROBERT GRAVES

LOVE'S STRATAGEMS

All these maneuverings to avoid
    The touching of hands,
These shifts to keep the eyes employed
    On objects more or less neutral,
As honor, for the time being, commands,
    Will hardly prevent their downfall.

Stronger medicines are needed.
    Already they find
None of their stratagems have succeeded,
    Nor would have, no,
Not had their eyes been stricken blind,
    Arms cut off at the elbow.

—DONALD JUSTICE

LUMBER OF SPRING

The images that hurt and connect . . . —W. H. Auden.

All the materials of a poem
Are lying scattered about, as in this garden
The lovely lumber of Spring.
All is profusion, confusion: hundred-eyed
The primulae in crimson, pink, and purple,
Gold at the pupil;
Prodigal the nectarine and plum
That fret their petals against a rosy wall.
Flame of the tulip, fume of the blue anemone,
White Alps of blossom in the giant pear tree,
Peaks and glaciers, rise from the same drab soil.

Far too much joy for comfort.
The images hurt because they do not connect:
No poem, no possession, therefore pain.

And struggling now to use
These images that bud from the bed of my mind,
I grope about for a form,
As much in the dark, this white and dazzling day,
As the bulb at midwinter; as filled with longing,
Even in this green garden,
As those who gaze from the cliff at the depths of sea
And know that they cannot possess it, being of the shore
And severed from that element for ever.

—ANNE RIDLER

LYING AWAKE

This moth caught in the room to-
    night
Squirmed up, sniper-style, between
The rusted edges of the screen;
Then, long as the room stayed light,

Lay here, content, in some cornerhole.
Now that we've settled into bed,
Though, he can't sleep. Overhead,
He throws himself at the blank wall.

Each night, hordes of these flutterers
    haunt
And climb my study windowpane;
Fired by reflection, their insane
Eyes gleam; they know what they
    want.

How do the petulant things survive?
Out in the fields they have a place
And proper work, furthering the race;

Why this blind, fanatical drive
Indoors? Why rush at every spark,
Cigar, head lamp, or railroad warning,
Break a wing off and starve by
    morning?
And what could a moth fear in the
    dark

Compared with what you meet inside?
Still, he rams the fluorescent face
Of the clock, thinks that's another
    place
Of light and families, where he'll hide.

We ought to trap him in a jar,
Or come like the white-coats with a
    net
And turn him out toward living. Yet
We don't: we take things as they are.

—W. D. SNODGRASS

M

MAD DAY IN MARCH

Beaten like an old hound
Whimpering by the stove,
I complicate the pain
That smarts with promised love.
The oilstove fails; the rain,
Forecast, licks at my wound;
Ice forms, clips the green shoot,
And strikes the wren house mute.

Those promises we heard
We heard in ignorance;
The numbered days we named,
And, in our innocence,
Assumed the beast was tamed.
On a bare limb, a bird,
Alone, arrived, with wings
Frozen, holds on and sings.

—Philip Levine

MADNESS

(TIME: SPRING. PLACE: VIRGINIA. A DOMESTIC DOG WANDERS FROM THE HOUSE,
IS BITTEN BY A RABID FEMALE FOX, RUNS MAD HIMSELF, AND HAS TO BE HUNTED
DOWN, KILLED, AND BEHEADED.)

Lay in the house mostly living
With children when they called   mostly
Under the table begging for scraps lay with the head
On a family foot
Or stretched out on a side,
Firesided. Had no running
Running, ever.
Would lie relaxed, eyes dim

With appreciation, licking the pure contentment
Of long   long notched
Black lips. Would lap up milk like a cat and swim clear
In brown grateful eyes. That was then, before the spring
Lay down and out
Under a tree, not far but a little far and out
Of sight of the house.
Rain had sown thick and gone

[407]

From the house where the living
Was done, where scraps fell and fire banked full
On one sleeping side of the spirit
Of the household
                         and it was best
To get up and wander
Out, out of sight. Help me was shouted
To the world of females   anyone will do
To the smoking leaves.

Love could be smelt. All things burned deep
In eyes that were dim from looking
At the undersides of tables   patient with being the god
Of small children. In spring it is better with no
Doors which the god
Of households must beg at   no locks where the wind blows
The world's furry women
About in heat. And there

She lay, firesided, bushy-tailed, her head
On the ground wide open, slopping soap.
Come   come close
She said like a god's
Wild mistress said come
On boy, I'm what you come

Out here in the bushes for. She burned alive
In her smell, and the eyes she looked at burned
With gratitude, thrown a point-eared scrap
Of the world's women, hot-tailed and hunted; she bit down
Hard on a great yell
To the house being eaten alive
By April's leaves. Bawled; they came and found.
The children cried

Helping tote to the full moon
Of the kitchen   "I carried the head"   Oh, full of eyes
Heads kept coming across, and friends and family
Hurt   hurt
The spirit of the household, on the kitchen
Table being thick-sewed   they saying it was barbed
Wire looked like
It got him, and he had no business running

Off like that. Black lips curled as they bathed off
Blood, bathed blood. Staggered up under

The table making loud
A lowborn sound, and went feeling

For the outer limits
Of the woods   felt them break and take in
The world   the frame turn loose and the house
Not mean what it said it was. Lay down and out
Of sight and could not get up
The head, lying on God's foot firesided
Fireheaded   formed a thought
Of spring   of trees in wildfire
Of the mind speeded up   and put all thirst

Into the leaves. They grew
Unlimited. Soap boiled
Between black lips; the house
Spirit jumped up beyond   began to run   shot
Through the yard and bit down
On the youngest child. And when it sprang down
And out across the pasture, the grains of its footprints leapt
Free, where horses that shied from its low

New sound were gathered, and men swung themselves
Up to learn what spring
Had a new way to tell, by bringing up
And out the speed of the fields. A long horn blew
Firesided   the mad head sang
Along the furrows   bouncing and echoing from earth
To earth through the body
Turning   doubling back
Through the weather of love running wild and the horses full

Of strangers coming after. Fence wire fell and rose
Flaming with messages as the spirit ran
Ran with house-hair
Burr-picking madly   and after came

Men   horses   spirits
Of households leaping crazily beyond
Their limits, dragging their bodies by the foaming throat through grass
And beggar-lice and by the red dust
Road where men blazed and roared
With their shoulders   blew it down and apart where it ran
And lay down on the earth of God's
One foot and the foot beneath the table kicked
The white mouth shut. This was something

In spring in mild brown eyes   as strangers
Cut off the head and carried and held it
Up, blazing with consequence   blazing
With freedom saying   bringing
Help   help   madness   help.

—JAMES DICKEY

THE MAGIC FLUTE

TO JANICE

Far in the woods my stealthy flute
Had jailed all gaudy feathered birds
And brought their songs back true to
    life;
Equipped with lime and quick salt,
    fruit,
And fifty linking nets of words,
I went to whistle up a wife.

My mouth was padlocked for a liar.
Losing what old hands never seek

To snare in their most cunning art,
I starved till my rib cage was wire
Beneath a towel. I could not speak
To hush this chattering, blue heart.

I beat about dead bushes where
No song starts and my cages stand
Bare in the crafty breath of you.
Night's lady, spreading your dark hair,
Come take this rare bird into hand;
In that trim cage, he might sing true.

—W. D. SNODGRASS

THE MAKERS

Discipline is not bad. . . . It is at least a beginning.
—From "Monsieur Teste," by Paul Valéry.

"What could I make," Socrates might have asked,
"And remain myself?" The master of dialectic
Would have groaned, knowing all works are tasked—
And all creators—to become the eclectic,
Ever-changing things observers observe;
Yet he, whose self, in utter consciousness,
Composed itself of others', had he the nerve,
Might have remarked the granite, immortal mess
Ideas become, stopped by the speaker's death,
And used the body, of which he highly spoke,
To build as well, breath by exquisite breath,
A granite heap, and called the joke a joke.

Cheops, who ordered built that master tomb,
His fixed idea, knowing the lightest craft
Must shortly float him into a vaster gloom,

Well may have wept, more probably have laughed,
To see his design dwarfed by a cruder one
Whereby frail flesh moved mountainous blocks from the Nile,
And learned that from each master plan is spun
Something quite different. Yet, there is that trial—
To show the tenacity of some designs—
Which Medici set for Michelangelo,
Who carved in snow who knows what perfect lines,
Which chilled their patron as they began to flow.

Loving the finished work, yet knowing well
How it excludes other aims of the mind,
Reb Löw married within his creative hell
Ideal to the Absurd, and what strode blind,
Obeying, often as not, the rabbi's leaning,
Wrought not much more either of good or evil
Than clay that reasons, twisting the Tablets' meaning.
Da Vinci's diverse modes betrayed upheaval
(By facile perfections, too professional sketches)
Of one lost among forms. "All . . . in each score!"—
Beethoven, too, among those divine wretches
The Wind of Being sucked to spew once more.

"Thou resemblest nothing, yet do not lack a shape."
Yeats might have nodded, laid low by early fame,
Disowning himself, his works, readers—his rape
Of Reason birthing an audience none can name,
Heroic, moral, which he then emulated
To compose verses deserving of its applause;
By this deception his best poems were created.
Valéry's mind each dawn danced through its laws
Of Pure Becoming, whereby a ship was scaled
From one's knowing the sea—its every part
Fashioned by waves perhaps—though this entailed
Replacing the sea. He made that craft his art.

—DAVID GALLER

MAN ALONE

It is yourself you seek,
In a long rage
Scanning through light and darkness
Mirrors, the page,

Where should reflected be
Those eyes and that thick hair,
That passionate look, that laughter.
You should appear

Within the book, or doubled,
Freed, in the silvered glass.
Into all other bodies
Yourself should pass.

The glass does not dissolve;
Like walls the mirrors stand.

The printed page gives back
Words by another hand;

And your infatuate eye
Meets not itself below:
Strangers lie in your arms,
As I lie now.

—Louise Bogan

THE MAN IN THE MIRROR

I walk down the narrow
carpeted hall.
The house is set.
The carnation in my buttonhole

precedes me like a small
continuous explosion.
The mirror
is in the living room.

You are there.
Your face is white, unsmiling, swollen.
The fallen body of your hair
is dull and out of place.

Buried in the darkness of your pockets,
your hands are motionless.
You do not seem awake.
Your skin sleeps

and your eyes lie in the deep
blue of their sockets,
impossible to reach.
How long will all this take?

I remember how we used to stand,
wishing the glass
would dissolve between us,
and how we watched our words

cloud that bland,
innocent surface,

and when our faces blurred,
how scared we were.

But that was another life.
One day you turned away
and left me here
to founder in the stillness of your
        wake.

Your suit floating, your hair
moving like eelgrass
in a shallow bay, you drifted
out of the mirror's room, through the
        hall

and into the open air.
You seemed to rise and fall
with the wind, the sway
taking you always farther away, far-
        ther away.

Darkness filled your sleeves.
The stars moved through you.
The vague music of your shrieking
blossomed in my ears.

I tried forgetting what I saw;
I got down on the floor,
pretending to be dead.
It did not work.

My heart bunched in my ribcage like
        a bat,

blind and cowardly,
beating in and out—
a solemn, irreducible black.

The things you drove me to!
I walked in the calm of the house,
calling you back.
You did not answer.

I sat in a chair
and stared across the room.
The walls were bare.
The mirror was nothing without you.

I lay down on the couch
and closed my eyes.
My thoughts rose in the dark
like faint balloons,

and I would turn them over,
one by one, and watch them shiver.
I always fell into a deep
and arid sleep.

Then out of nowhere, late one night,
you reappeared—
a huge vegetable moon,
a bruise coated with light.

You stood before me,
dreamlike and obscene,
your face lost
under layers of heavy skin,

your body sunk in a green
and wrinkled sea of clothing.
I tried to help you,
but you refused.

Days passed
and I would rest
my cheek against the glass,
wanting nothing but the old you.

I sang so sadly
that the neighbors wept

and dogs whined with pity.
Some things I wish I could forget.

You didn't care,
standing still while flies
collected in your hair
and dust fell like a screen before your
    eyes.

You never spoke
or tried to come up close.
Why did I want so badly
to get through to you?

It still goes on.
I go into the living room and you are
    there.
You drift in a pool
of silver air

where wounds and dreams of wounds
rise from the deep
humus of sleep
to bloom like flowers against the glass.

I look at you
and see myself
under the surface.
A dark and private weather

settles down on everything.
The dreams wither.
The air is cold.
You stand

like a shade
in the painless glass—
frail, distant, older
than ever.

It will always be this way.
I stand here scared
that you will disappear,
scared that you will stay.
                              —MARK STRAND

A MANTELPIECE OF SHELLS

The crimp and whorl of conch,
Serrated slot of cowries, stropped
Edge of razors, cup of nautilus,
Fan of the scallop, the sundial's
Coiled watch spring and the scrolled
Edge of the olives. The sound of surf
In the gastropod cupped to the ear.

But more than this. The memory
Recalls the short turf by the Scottish shores;
The anvil of the thrush, where Helix,
Sparsely nourished on the dune bents,
Was broken; the New England roads
Where, bomberwise, the hungry gull
Exploded the quahog; the seed scallop

Thicker than sand along the shores
After the storm; the flushed cowries
Of the Firth of Clyde and the rough coast
Of Northumberland; and jingle shells,
Tangerine, peach, and lemon, sparkling
The beach at Vineyard Haven; and vines
Festooned plumply with *escargots*.

Then, too, the truck on Eighth Street
Crammed with conchs—suffused
Pinks, purples, and browns peddled
For a quarter—stripped of the green moss
That covered those from Menemsha Pond;
Cockles by silver sand on Barra;
Black whelks from a stall in a London street;

Piddocks and angel's wings, borers;
And barnacles on driftwood—acorns
Of legendary geese. The disarray
Of an oyster against the precise flare
The scallop with the turquoise eyes presents;
The limpet's gyre, and the slipper's shelf.
These are the shells that I have known.

But that pink murex on the mantelshelf,
From Florida via Chicago's Shedd,
Japanese treasures from Brentano's,
Cuban land snails from Central Park West
Hold out their promises of places

Still to see, of seas to hear, and order
To observe. The spiral towers

Still hide the great adventure:
The Sargasso of the mind welcomes
Such symmetry among its tangled wrack.
Listen once more, to shell from near or far:
The surf still rolls these empty houses
Over the shingle and the sand,
Still breaks them on the granite rocks,

And still the sight and sound recall
Places known and places still to know.
The mind hankers for the angel's wings
And borer's skill, to learn the architecture
That can make so much perfection
From a little lime and silicate.
Listen, the ebbing tide has turned:

These dead, still shells are whispering
Of summer. In the museum cases,
Muted by glass for the moment, lies the roar
Of all the surf that beats up beaches
Round the world; the Aegean lies
In this that made the Tyrian purple.
Here are the more than seven seas

And more than seventy thousand sounds
Distinguishing the shores where, cast
By storm, discarded by the tide,
The makers of the shells wither and vanish,
Leaving the shells themselves to bleach,
To powder down again, to be absorbed
Into the vast spiral that will throw up others.

                                        —RUTHVEN TODD

MANUELZINHO

(BRAZIL. A FRIEND OF THE WRITER IS SPEAKING.)

Half squatter, half tenant (no
    rent)—
a sort of inheritance; white,
in your thirties now, and supposed
to supply me with vegetables,

but you don't; or you won't; or you
    can't
get the idea through your brain—
the world's worst gardener since Cain.
Tilted above me, your gardens

ravish my eyes. You edge
the beds of silver cabbages
with red carnations, and lettuces
mix with alyssum. And then
umbrella ants arrive,
or it rains for a solid week
and the whole thing's ruined again
and I buy you more pounds of seeds,
imported, guaranteed,
and eventually you bring me
a mystic three-legged carrot,
or a pumpkin "bigger than the baby."

I watch you through the rain,
trotting, light, on bare feet,
up the steep paths you have made—
or your father and grandfather made—
all over my property,
with your head and back inside
a sodden burlap bag,
and feel I can't endure it
another minute; then,
indoors, beside the stove,
keep on reading a book.

You steal my telephone wires,
or someone does. You starve
your horse and yourself
and your dogs and family.
Among endless variety,
you eat boiled cabbage stalks.
And once I yelled at you
so loud to hurry up
and fetch me those potatoes
your holey hat flew off,
you jumped out of your clogs,
leaving three objects arranged
in a triangle at my feet,
as if you'd been a gardener
in a fairy tale all this time
and at the word "potatoes"
had vanished to take up your work
of fairy prince somewhere.

The strangest things happen, to you.
Your cow eats a "poison grass"
and drops dead on the spot.

Nobody else's does.
And then your father dies,
a superior old man
with a black plush hat, and a mus-
        tache
like a white spread-eagled sea gull.
The family gathers, but you,
no, you "don't think he's dead!
I look at him. He's cold.
They're burying him today.
But you know, I don't think he's
        dead."
I give you money for the funeral
and you go and hire a *bus*
for the delighted mourners,
so I have to hand over some more
and then have to hear you tell me
you pray for me every night!

And then you come again,
sniffing and shivering,
hat in hand, with that wistful
face, like a child's fistful
of bluets or white violets,
improvident as the dawn,
and once more I provide
for a shot of penicillin
down at the pharmacy, or
one more bottle of
Electrical Baby Syrup.
Or, briskly, you come to settle
what we call our "accounts,"
with two old copybooks,
one with flowers on the cover,
the other with a camel.
Immediate confusion.
You've left out the decimal points.
Your columns stagger,
honeycombed with zeros.
You whisper conspiratorially;
the numbers mount to millions.
Account books? They are Dream
        Books.
In the kitchen we dream together
how the meek shall inherit the
        earth—
or several acres of mine.

With blue sugar bags on their heads,
carrying your lunch,
your children scuttle by me
like little moles aboveground,
or even crouch behind bushes
as if I were out to shoot them!
—Impossible to make friends,
though each will grab at once
for an orange or a piece of candy.

Twined in wisps of fog,
I see you all up there
along with Formoso, the donkey,
who brays like a pump gone dry,
then suddenly stops.
—All just standing, staring
off into fog and space.
Or coming down at night,
in silence, except for hoofs,
in dim moonlight, the horse
or Formoso stumbling after.
Between us float a few
big, soft, pale-blue,
sluggish fireflies,
the jellyfish of the air. . . .

Patch upon patch upon patch,
your wife keeps all of you covered.

She has gone over and over
(forearmed is forewarned)
your pair of bright-blue pants
with white thread, and these days
your limbs are draped in blueprints.
You paint—heaven knows why—
the outside of the crown
and brim of your straw hat.
Perhaps to reflect the sun?
Or perhaps when you were small,
your mother said, "Manuelzinho,
one thing: be sure you always
paint your straw hat."
One was gold for a while,
but the gold wore off, like plate.
One was bright green. Unkindly,
I called you Klorophyll Kid.
My visitors thought it was funny.
I apologize here and now.

You helpless, foolish man,
I love you all I can,
I think. Or do I?
I take off my hat, unpainted
and figurative, to you.
Again I promise to try.
                              —ELIZABETH BISHOP

THE MAP

Composed, generally defined
  By the long sharing
Of contours, continents and oceans
  Are gathered in
The same imaginary net.
  Over the map
The portioned air, at times but
  A continuance
Of boundaries, assembles in
  A pure, cloudless
Canopy of artificial calm.
  Lacking the haze,
The blurred edges that surround our
    world,

  The map draws
Only on itself, outlines its own
  Dimensions, and waits,
As only a thing completed can,
  To be replaced
By a later version of itself.
  Wanting the presence
Of a changing space, my attention
    turns
  To the world beyond
My window, where the map's colors
  Fade into a vague
Afterimage and are lost
  In the variable scene

Of shapes accumulating. I see
  A group of fields
Tend slowly inland from the breaking
  Of the fluted sea,
Blackwing and herring gulls, relaxed
  On the air's currents,
Glide out of sight, and trees,
  Cold as stone
In the gray light of this coastal eve-
    ning,
  Grow gradually
Out of focus. From the still
  Center of my eyes,

Encompassing in the end nothing
  But their own darkness,
The world spins out of reach, And yet,
  Because nothing
Happens where definition is
  Its own excuse
For being, the map is as it was:
  A diagram
Of how the world might look could we
  Maintain a lasting,
Perfect distance from what is.

            —MARK STRAND

THE MAPMAKER ON HIS ART

After the bronzed, heroic traveller
Returns to the television interview
And cocktails at the Ritz, I, in my turn,
Set forth across the clean, uncharted paper.
Smiling a little at his encounters with
Savages, bugs, and snakes, for the most part
Skipping his night thoughts, philosophic notes,
Rainy reflections, I translate his trip
Into my native tongue of bearings, shapes,
Directions, distances. My fluent pen
Wanders and cranks as his great river does,
Over the page, making the lonely voyage
Common and human. This, my modest art,
Brings wilderness well down into the range
Of any budget. Under the haunted mountain
Where he lay in delirium, deserted
By his safari, they will build hotels
In a year or two. I make no claim that this
Much matters (they will name a hotel for him,
Not me), yet, lest in the comparison
I should appear a trifle colorless,
I write the running river a rich blue
And—let imagination rage!—wild green
The jungles with their tawny meadows and swamps
Where, till the day I die, I will not go.

            —HOWARD NEMEROV

MARCH 1ST

Coming out of the house on a fresh March morning,
I saw February still meandering around
like laundry caught in a Bendix. Stray shreds
of cloud, like pillow slips, were rent from
her large endlessness. Outdated,
her decrepit body garlanded itself dis-
gracefully with powder. She luxuriated in old age.
Even her graying sheets were still there,
tattered, heaped carelessly on the street,
bearing the indentation of someone's huge body
and furred with a fine fringe of soot.
She had been plump, she had been heavy, sitting
on top of us since January. Winter, you
old clothes hamper, what mildew
still molders inside you before March
dribbles a bit, dries up, and is done for?

—KATHLEEN SPIVACK

MARCH, UPSTATE

Paint-flaken, it is paint-flaken,
and the barns are tense with sagging.
The broken orchards prop themselves.

Brush-wild, it is brush-wild
and elm-tangled, and the yards
are trashed with litter of many years,

as the house fronts and the business
    blocks

are dowdy with bare pretensions
where pity jumbles shame and show.

Road-gashed, it is road-gashed
and wire-strung. What green,
what sun, shall flesh and warm the
    flesh?

Loved land, unlovely, none can fit
you, for you have no shape—
mirror in March my human face.

—WILLIAM BRONK

MARCH WEATHER

I have believed too long in one thing.
It has grown dumpy with much believing.
And I? With a winter's fat in the mind.
Thank God, March is here and the March wind.
It tossed off the soft miniver snowstorm,
Put a crow, in its place, with a worm—
An end to the white white uniform.

March is here, thank God, and the March wind
Lashes in black branches, is curt and unkind
To all that slept, hid, cowered, snow-blind.
Time for the eel to slip out of the black
River, under dun leaves, starting his sleek,
Headlong, utterly limber fall to the sea.
Time too for a crack in that pewtery
Salver of heaven. Out of a crack, blue
Magnificent, hurrying birds sail through.
Clouds loom and topple. There's a sharp cheer
Hacking at columns of the atmosphere.
The devil has a hand in it. God stands.
We hear this excellent whipping of the winds.

—Jon Swan

A MARE

Lovely Fia was the summer queen
And the sun-bodied light of winter: she so slender
Of pastern, fine of cannon, sloped in the shoulders
To all perfection, with that gazelle head set
Arched beneath the drawn bow of her neck;
She who rose blazing from the dusky stall
And lunged on the snaffle, who reared on high white stockings,
Light-mouthed, light-footed, blasting her loud whinny,
Saying among the oak trees, "Ha ha!" She was a mirror
Of flame, and when she ran, then she ran burning,
Swift as the falcon that stoops through the windless sky.

Fiamma, who can tell of all your richness?
You were a dragon horde, gold-red and willful.
How dark the winter rains are falling now!
I cannot find your peer in any pasture.

—Kate Barnes

MARIN

Marin
saw how it feels:
the first raw shock
of Labrador current,
the surfacing gasp
at jut of rock,
bent sails, and wedged
trees. He wrote it—
Stonington, Small
Point, and Cape Split—
through a pane so
cracked by the lode-
star sun that he
swam back, blinded,

into himself, to
sign the after-
image: initialled
mountains, ledged
towns white as
Machias after
the hayrake rain,
sun-splintered
water, and written
granite—dark light
unlike what you

ever saw, until,
inland, your own
eyes close and, out
of that sea change,
islands rise thick,
like the riptide
paint that, flooding,
tugs at your vitals,
and is more Maine
than Maine.

—PHILIP BOOTH

THE MARRIAGE OF HEAVEN AND EARTH

Firelight in sunlight, silver-pale
Streaming with emerald, copper, sap-
    phire
Ribbons and rivers, banners, foun-
    tains—
They rise, they run swiftly away.

Now apple logs unlock their sunlight
In the many-windowed room to meet
New sunlight falling in silvered gold
Through the fern-ice forest of the
    glass
Whose tropic surface light may pierce
But not the eye. Oh, early world,
Still Daphne of the stubborn wood
Singing Apollo's song in light;
Oh, pulsing constancies of flame
Warping a form along the log's
Slowly disintegrating face,

Crackled and etched, so quickly
    aged—
These are my mysteries to see
And say and celebrate with words
In orders until now reserved.

For light is in the language now,
Carbon and sullen diamond break
Out of the glossary of earth
In holy signs and scintillations,
Release their fiery emblems to
Renewal's room and morning's room
Where sun and fire once again
Phase in the figure of the dance
From far beginnings here returned,
Leapt from the maze at the forest's
    heart,
Oh, moment where the lost is found!

—HOWARD NEMEROV

THE MARROW

I

The wind from off the sea says nothing new.
The mist above me sings with its small flies.
From a burnt pine the sharp speech of a crow
Tells me my drinking breeds a will to die.
What's the worst portion in this mortal life?
A pensive mistress and a yelping wife.

II

One white face shimmers brighter than the sun
When contemplation dazzles all I see;
One look too close can take my soul away.
Brooding on God, I may become a man.
Pain wanders through my bones like a lost fire;
What burns me now? Desire, desire, desire.

III

Godhead above my God, are you there still?
To sleep is all my life. In sleep's half-death,
My body alters, altering the soul
That once could melt the dark with its small breath.
Lord, hear me out, and hear me out this day:
From me to Thee's a long and terrible way.

IV

I was flung back from suffering and love
When light divided on a storm-tossed tree;
Yea, I have slain my will, and still I live;
I would be near; I shut my eyes to see;
I bleed my bones, their marrow to bestow
Upon that God who knows what I would know.

—THEODORE ROETHKE

THE MATIN PANDEMONIUMS

Begin before birth with swept-back fins.
Among animals and birds there are no echoes;
They live in an exorbitancy of orchestration.
It is the greatness of nature rides up the air
With such rich morning calls. The fleet shepherd
Lives in love of action; the goat has delicate steps;
The swan is the lord of all he surveys.
He surveys golden pheasant, accomplished tortoise.

One sees from the porch of the imagination
Fabulous oncome and arising of the world,
The get of jets, choiring high and rangy.
What is this talk of separation and anguish,
Where is there deeper secret revelation than among
The early morning pandemoniums of the birds?

—RICHARD EBERHART

MATLOCK BATH

From Matlock Bath's half-timbered
    station
  I see the black dissenting spire,
Thin witness of a congregation,
  Stone emblem of a Handel choir.
In blest Bethesda's limpid pool
Comes treacling out of Sunday
    School.

By cool Siloam's shady rill—
  The sounds are sweet as strawberry
    jam.
I raise mine eyes unto the hill,
  The beetling Heights of Abraham;
The branchy trees are white with rime
In Matlock Bath this winter time.

And from the whiteness, gray uprear-
    ing,
  Huge cliffs hang sunless ere they
    fall,
A tossed and stony ocean nearing
  The moment to o'erwhelm us all;
Eternal Father strong to save
How long wilt thou suspend the
    wave?

How long before the pleasant acres
  Of intersecting Lover's Walks

Are rolled across by limestone break-
    ers,
  Whole woodlands snapp'd like cab-
    bage stalks?
O God our help in Ages past
How long will Speedwell Cavern last?

In this dark dale I hear the thunder
  Of houses folding with the shocks,
The Grand Pavilion buckling under
  The weight of the Romantic Rocks,
And hardest Blue John ashtrays seem
To melt away in thermal steam.

Deep in their Nonconformist setting,
  Shivering children wait their doom,
The father's whip, the mother's pet-
    ting,
  In many a coffee-colored room,
And attic bedrooms shriek with fright
For dread of Pilgrims of the Night.

Perhaps it's this that makes me shiver
  As I traverse the slippery path
High, high above the sliding river
  And terraces of Matlock Bath—
A sense of doom, a dread to see
The Rock of Ages cleft for me.

—JOHN BETJEMAN

MAYBE ALONE ON MY BIKE

I listen, and the mountain lakes
hear snowflakes come on those winter wings
only the owls are awake to see.

And I have thought (maybe alone
on my bike, quaintly on a cold
evening, pedalling home), Think!
The splendor of our life, its current unknown
as those mountains, the scene no one sees . . .

Oh, citizens of our great amnesty,
we might have died! We live. Marvels
coast by, great veers and swoops of air
so bright the lamps waver in tears,
and I hear in the chain a chuckle I like to hear.

—William Stafford

THE MAY DAY DANCING

The kindergarten children first come forth
In couples dressed as little brides and grooms.
By dancing in, by dancing round and out,
They braid the Maypole with a double thread;
Keep time, keep faith, is what the music says.

The corporal piano now leads out
Successively the older boys and girls,
Grade after grade, all for the dancing paired,
All dressed in the fashion of forgotten folk;
Those nymphs and shepherds, maybe, never were.

And all the parents standing in a ring,
With cameras some, and some with only eyes,
Attend to the dancing's measurable rule,
Bemused, or hypnotized, so that they see
Not seven classes of children, but only one—

One class of children, seven times again,
That ever enters on the dancing floor
One year advanced in its compliant skill,
To patterns ever with more varied styles
Clothing the naked order of the bass.

Some here relate the May with wanton rites,
Some with the Haymarket Riot, some with nothing
Beyond the present scene and circumstance,
Which, by the camera's thin, incisive blade,
They hope to take a frozen section of,

Keeping their child with one foot on the ground
And one foot off, and with a solemn face
Or one bewildered between grin and tears,
As many times repeating time and faith
He follows the compulsions of the dance

Around the brilliant morning with the sun—
The dance that leads him out to bring him home,
The May Day dance that tramples down the grass
To raise the dust, that braids a double thread
Around the pole, in the great room of the sun.

—HOWARD NEMEROV

MAY 10TH

I mean
the fiddleheads have forced their babies,
blind topknots first, up from the thinking rhizomes,
and the shrew's children, twenty to a teaspoon,
breathe to their own astonishment
in the peephole burrow.

I mean
a new bat hangs upside down in the privy;
its eyes are stuck tight, its wrinkled pink mouth twitches,
and in the pond, itself an invented puddle,
tadpoles quake from the jello
and come into being.

I mean walk softly.
The maple's little used-up bells are dropping
and the new leaves are now unpacking,
still wearing their dime-store lacquer,
still cramped and wet from the journey.

—MAXINE W. KUMIN

MEDITATION AT OYSTER RIVER

I

Over the low, barnacled, elephant-colored rocks
Come the first tide ripples, moving, almost without sound, toward me,
Running along the narrow furrows of the shore, the rows of dead clamshells;
Then a runnel behind me, creeping closer,
Alive with tiny striped fish, and young crabs climbing in and out of the water.

No sound from the bay. No violence.
Even the gulls quiet on the far rocks,
Silent, in the deepening light,
Their cat-mewing over,
Their child-whimpering.

At last one long undulant ripple,
Blue black from where I am sitting,
Makes almost a wave over a barrier of small stones,
Slapping lightly against a sunken log.
I dabble my toes in the brackish foam sliding forward,
Then retire to a rock higher up on the cliffside.

The wind slackens, light as a moth fanning a stone—
A twilight wind, light as a child's breath,
Turning not a leaf, not a ripple.

The dew revives on the beach grass;
The salt-soaked wood of a fire crackles;
A fish raven turns on its perch (a dead tree in the river mouth),
Its wings catching a last glint of the reflected sunlight.

II

The self persists like a dying star,
In sleep, afraid. Death's face rises afresh,
Among the shy beasts—the deer at the salt lick,
The doe, with its sloped shoulders, loping across the highway,
The young snake, poised in green leaves, waiting for its fly,
The hummingbird, whirring from quince blossom to morning-glory—
With these I would be.

And with water: the waves coming forward without cessation,
The waves, altered by sandbars, beds of kelp, miscellaneous driftwood,
Topped by cross-winds, tugged at by sinuous undercurrents,
The tide rustling in, sliding between the ridges of stone,
The tongues of water creeping in quietly.

III

In this hour,
In this first heaven of knowing,
The flesh takes on the pure poise of the spirit,
Acquires, for a time, the sandpiper's insouciance,
The hummingbird's surety, the kingfisher's cunning.

I shift on my rock, and I think:
Of the first trembling of a Michigan brook in April,
Over a lip of stone, the tiny rivulet;
And that wrist-thick cascade tumbling from a cleft rock,
Its spray holding a double rainbow in early morning,
Small enough to be taken in, embraced, by two arms;
Or the Tittabawasee, in the time between winter and spring,
When the ice melts along the edges in early afternoon
And the mid-channel begins cracking and heaving from the pressure beneath,

The ice piling high against the ironbound spiles,
Gleaming, freezing hard again, creaking at midnight,
And I long for the blast of dynamite,
The sudden sucking roar as the culvert loosens its debris of branches and sticks—
Welter of tin cans, pails, old bird's nests, a child's shoe riding a log—
As the piled ice breaks away from the battered spiles
And the whole river begins to move forward, its bridges shaking.

IV

Now, in this waning of light,
I rock with the motion of morning;
In the cradle of all that is,
I'm lulled into half sleep
By the lapping of waves,
The cries of the sandpiper.

Water's my will and my way,
And the spirit runs, intermittently,
In and out of the small waves,
Runs with the intrepid shore birds—
How graceful the small before danger!

In the first of the moon,
All's a scattering,
A shining.

—THEODORE ROETHKE

A MEETING

Meeting the first time for many years,
What do they expect to see
Of the beings they made once, for better and worse,
Of each other—he and she?

A shrine to lost love? A hovel for guilt?
A vacant historic pile?
Something in ruins? Something rebuilt
In a grand or a makeshift style?

Whatever is here to be freshly scanned,
Their view will be overcast;
Though they'll encounter, smile, shake hands,
They can only meet in the past,

Meet at the point where they parted, in
The house of what once they were,
Haunted by ghosts of what they might have been
Today, had they lived on there.

The life they had fashioned long ago
Seemed close as a honeycomb;
And if anything couples these strangers now,
Who were each other's home,

It is grief that the pureness and plenitude of
Their love's long-flowering day
Could, like baser, flimsier stuff,
Corrupt or melt away.

Nothing left of the cells they stored
With joy, trust, charity
For years? . . . Nature, it seems, can afford
Such wastefulness—not we.

—C. DAY LEWIS

THE MEETING

For years I thought I knew, at the bottom of the dream,
Who spoke but to say farewell,
Whose smile dissolved, after his first words
Gentle and plausible.

Each time I found him, it was always the same:
Recognition and surprise,
And then the silence, after the first words,
And the shifting of the eyes.

Then the moment when he had nothing to say
And only smiled again,
But this time toward a place beyond me, where I could not stay—
No world of men.

Now I am not sure. Who are you? Who have you been?
Why do our paths cross?
At the deepest bottom of the dream you are let in,
A symbol of loss.

Eye to eye we look, and we greet each other
Like friends from the same land.
Bitter compliance! Like a faithless brother
You take and drop my hand.

—LOUISE BOGAN

THE MEETING

It never occurred to me, never,
That you were attached to your universe,
Standing on a corner, waiting for a bus,
While the thought-trees grew above your head
And a meadow stretched its rambling sward
All the way up Fifth Avenue.
I was thinking of myself thinking of water,
Of how, each day I went about my job,
I missed one break in the Atlantic Ocean,
Of how I might have been here or there,
Fishing off the coast of Mexico,
Turning the sailboat round the bay,
Or, my chin resting on the concrete edge
Of a swimming pool, I could survey a hill,
The cows' soft blotches stranded in the grass.
Maybe it was that, that last green thing,
That led me into your deepening meadow,
That made me turn among the giant stones
To look one minute into your mind,
To see you running across a field,
The flowers springing up where you had touched.
It was there, I think, we finally met.

—HOWARD MOSS

MEMO

Now we have always with us men—these men!—
Who have gone down into the savage pit,
Down where old atom has his cliff perpetual.
The courage of lizards for the abyss is theirs
And God Almighty's joy in the brink of things,
And thus they drove the genius of matter
From its ghastly cell. They are the men
Who made time tremble and draw back.
We shall never forget them. What are their names?

Unspeakable evil, unspeakable good.
To what end do they shave their skulls
And appear as saints—whose shadows have the posture
Intense of Satans? There is no help here.
Will they give their brains, a burnt offering,
To exorcise the dread that fouls
    The immaculate theorem?
Make a passionate note of this. Never expect it.
You may wish, in weak elegance of pity and hope,
    To pray for these men,
    To pray for them.

                              —HILDEGARDE FLANNER

MEMORANDUM

You'll see sometime—half
of the world will fracture,
or you will come out on a cold
ridge, flashed into knowing, and find
how all over our state, better
than we deserved, stories
went on, millions of unbound
sagas the wise were too dumb
to find: the shivering wolves
aflame in their savagery, hedges
that wove God's lost garlands
around abandoned fields.

Maybe a man lived somewhere—
    consider—

down in his yard, vicious, in the trash
and low schemes, but all of his life
by his door, unmerited, a fir tree
grew; at the top whole generations
of beautiful birds lived and sang.

All over our state, all over
the world, spiders are weaving,
rodents pause, whole forests
lean at once. And only some of the
things that shine are mean.

                              —WILLIAM STAFFORD

MERLIN ENTHRALLED

In a while they rose and went out aimlessly riding,
Leaving their drained cups on the table round.
Merlin, Merlin, their hearts cried, where are you hiding?
In all the world was no unnatural sound.

Mystery spied them riding glade by glade.
They saw it darkle from under leafy brows.
But leaves were all its voice, and squirrels made
An empty fracas in the ancient boughs.

Once by a lake-edge something made them stop,
Yet what they found was the thumping of a frog,

Bugs skating on the shut water-top,
Some hairlike algae bleaching on a log.

Gawen thought for a moment that he heard
A whitethorn breathe "Niniane." That Siren's daughter
Rose in a fort of dreams and spoke the word
"Sleep," her voice like dark, diving water;

And Merlin slept, who had imagined her
Of water-sounds and the black unsoundable swell,
A creature to bewitch a sorcerer,
And lay there now within her towering spell.

Slowly the shapes of searching men and horses
Escaped him as he dreamt on that high bed.
History died; he gathered in its forces;
The mists of time condensed in the still head

Until his mind, as clear as mountain water,
Went ravelling toward the deep transparent dream
Who bade him sleep. And then the Siren's daughter
Received him as the sea receives a stream.

Fate would be fated; dreams desire to sleep;
This the forsaken cannot understand.
Arthur upon the road began to weep
And said to Gawen, "Remember when this hand

Once haled a sword from stone; now no less strong
It cannot dream of such a thing to do."
Their mail grew quainter as they clopped along.
The sky became a still and woven blue.

—RICHARD WILBUR

ME TO YOU

Summer's gone brown, and, with it,
our wanderings in the shires, our ways.
Look at us now.
A shuttered house drips in Moroccan rain.
A mill sits ghostly in the green of France.
Beaches are empty now of all but pebbles.
But still, at crossroads, in seignorial gardens,
we meet, sleep, wrangle, part, meet, part,
making a lodging of the heart.

Now that the sea begins to dull with winter,
and I so far, and you so far
(and home farther than either),
write me a long letter,
as if from home.

Tell me about the snowfalls
at night, and tell me how we'd sit in firelight,
hearing dogs huff in sleep, hearing the geese
hiss in the barn, hearing the horse clop home.
Say how the waterfall sounds, and how the weeds
trail in the slithering river.
Write me about the weather.

Perhaps
a letter across water,
something like this, but better,
would almost take us strangely
closer to home.

Write, and I'll come.

—ALASTAIR REID

METROPOLITAN NIGHTMARE

It rained quite a lot, that spring. You woke in the morning
And saw the sky still clouded, the streets still wet,
But nobody noticed so much, except the taxis
And the people who parade. You don't, in a city.
The parks got very green. All the trees were green
Far into July and August, heavy with leaf,
Heavy with leaf and the long roots boring and spreading,
But nobody noticed that but the city gardeners,
And they don't talk.
                         Oh, on Sundays perhaps, you'd notice:
Walking through certain blocks, by the shut, proud houses
With the windows boarded, the people gone away,
You'd suddenly seen the queerest small shoots of green
Poking through cracks and crevices in the stone
And a bird-sown flower, red on a balcony,
But then you made jokes about grass growing in the streets
And the end of the depression—and there were songs
And gags and a musical show called "Hot and Wet."
It all made a good box for the papers. When the flamingo

Flew into a meeting of the Board of Estimate,
Mayor O'Brien acted at once and called the photographers.
When the first green creeper crawled upon Brooklyn Bridge,
They thought it was ornamental. They let it stay.

That was the year the termites came to New York
And they don't do well in cold climates—but listen, Joe,
They're only ants and ants are nothing but insects.
It was funny and yet rather wistful, in a way
(As Heywood Broun pointed out in the *World-Telegram*),
To think of them looking for wood in a steel city.
It made you feel about life. It was too divine.
There were funny pictures by Steig and Peter Arno
And Macy's ran a terribly clever ad:
"The Widow's Termite" or something.
                                        There was no
Disturbance. Even the Communists didn't protest
And say they were Morgan hirelings. It was too hot,
Too hot to protest, too hot to get excited,
An even, African heat, lush, fertile, and steamy,
That soaked into bone and mind and never once broke.
The warm rain fell in fierce showers and ceased and fell.
Pretty soon you got used to its always being that way.

You got used to the changed rhythm, the altered beat,
To people walking slower, to the whole bright
Fierce pulse of the city slowing, to men in shorts,
The new sun helmets from Best's and cops' white uniforms
And the long noon rest in the offices, everywhere.

It wasn't a plan or anything. It just happened.
The fingers tapped the keys slower, the office boys
Dozed on their benches, the bookkeeper yawned at his desk.
The A. T. & T. was the first to change the shifts
And establish an official siesta-room,
But they were always efficient. Mostly it just
Happened like sleep itself, like a tropic sleep,
Till even the Thirties were deserted at noon
Except for a few tourists and one damp cop.
They ran boats to see the lilies on the North River,
But it was only the tourists who really noticed
The flocks of rose-and-green parrots and parrakeets
Nesting in the stone crannies of the Cathedral.
The rest of us had forgotten when they first came.

There wasn't any real change, it was just a heat spell,
A rain spell, a funny summer, a weatherman's joke

In spite of the geraniums three feet high
In the tin-can gardens of Hester and Desbrosses.
New York was New York. It couldn't turn inside out.
When they got the news from Woods Hole about the Gulf Stream,
The *Times* ran an adequate story,
But nobody reads those stories but science cranks.

Until, one day, a somnolent city editor
Gave a new cub the termite yarn to break his teeth on.
The cub was just down from Vermont, so he took the time.
He was serious about it. He went around.
He read all about termites in the Public Library
And it made him sore when they fired him.
                                So, one evening,
Talking with an old watchman, beside the first
Raw girders of the new Planetopolis Building
(Ten thousand brine-cooled offices, each with shower),
He saw a dark line creeping across the rubble
And turned a flashlight on it.
                                "Say, buddy," he said.
"You better look out for those ants. They eat wood, you know.
They'll have your shack down in no time."
                                The watchman spat.
"Oh, they've quit eating wood," he said, in a casual voice,
"I thought everybody knew that"
                                —and, reaching down,
He pried from the insect jaws the bright crumb of steel.

                                —Stephen Vincent Benét

ME UP AT DOES

Me up at does

out of the floor
quietly Stare

a poisoned mouse

still who alive

is asking What
have i done that

You wouldn't have
                                —E. E. Cummings

MICROMUTATIONS

A million years of death some star
Required to fling its lies this far,
Where two shocked children in a car
Fumble and cling and kiss each other,
The blind in terror of the blind.
A million years. Why did they bother,
Fire-blossoming everlastingnesses,
To drift down here, of all God's
    places?

No matter, now. The instant they
Glitter in view they drift away:
Dark, blighted seeds that might as
    well
Keep company with the rest of us
Who took a million years to die,
Drift, cling, drift, cling, sky below sky,
Till we struck stone at last, to lie
Here on the frozen floor of hell.

—JAMES WRIGHT

MIDSUMMER

(COVENTRY, CONNECTICUT)

That the high sheen of death could
    blot
This green away, or life survive
The great ice age, is almost not

To be believed. Clearly, today's
Raw sunlight ripens into grass
And grazing cows, as though always

It has been so. Still, glacial rock,
Like giant bone, breaks through the
    earth
And weighs the age-old walls that
    block

These fields, the livestock locked
    within.
A herd of browns and whites and
    blacks,
The cows browse in oblivion,

All muscle dancing under veils
Of gaudy, violet-winged black flies
Aswarm their hides, and swish their
    tails—

Thickset, but limber as bullwhips
Perpetually in motion, long
Quick lengths unravelled at the tips—

From side to side. Apart, a brace
Of mules made fast to buried stakes
Stand stock-still. And out through
    space,

At times, too far away to hear,
A jet plane's sabre-flash transcends
The mules, the massive cows—a mere

Machine-tooled slip of silver light—
And wakes a ghostly rainbow arc
Flatly across far hills, its slight

Exhaustion burning through the blue
Useless sky, trailing away,
Its destination out of view.

The glacier's gone. The cows assent
Grassward, earmarked with metal
    tags,
Delicacies of ornament

That glint and tick away the sun
As their ears twitch, as they remain
One rhythmic mass—as if each one

Had undergone the bull, the calf,
Cold sheets of rain, and now held out
For nothing less than life itself:

Such middle-aging gaiety
As knows not what it was, nor is,
Nor what it is about to be,

Nor cares that space thins out, goes
        dumb,
That time may cease to come—as if,

Rock-bound, this were the kingdom
        come,

And the hunched fields were crystal-
        clear
Jerusalem, and life was just
Vibration in the summer air.

—JAMES SCULLY

THE MIND, INTRACTABLE THING

even with its own axe to grind, sometimes
helps others. Why can't it help me?

O imagnifico,
wizard in words—poet, was it, as
Alfredo Panzini defined you?
Weren't you refracting just now
on my eye's half-closed triptych
        the image, enhanced, of a glen—
"the foxgrape festoon as sere leaves fell"
on the sand-pale dark byroad, one leaf adrift
        from the thin-twigged persimmon; again,

a bird—Arizona
caught-up-with, uncatchable cuckoo
after two hours' pursuit, zigzagging
road runner, stencilled black
in stripes all over, the tail
        windmilling up to defy me?
You understand terror, know how to deal
with pent-up emotion, a ballad, witchcraft.
        I don't. O Zeus and O Destiny!

Unafraid of what's done,
undeterred by what looks like defeat,
you, imagnifico, unafraid
of disparagers, death, dejection,
have out-wiled the Mermaid of Zennor,*
        made wordcraft irresistible:
reef, wreck, lost lad, and "sea-foundered bell"—
as near a thing as we have to a king—
        craft with which I don't know how to deal.

—MARIANNE MOORE

* "The Ballad of the Mermaid of Zennor," by Vernon Watkins, New Directions.

MINE

(AFTER THE RIOTS)

A stranger it was never meant for
(years and years after the night raids
set it there), bathing offshore, or
crawling through caves, uncovered it,

nipples intact. Perhaps he thought
the odd shape rock, or hunk of coral
off a sunken reef; maybe a human
artifact tossed overboard, or lost.

Eventually, it gave itself away,
the nipples, the roundish cast, what
few links remained, and a fastening.

Alert to the folk wisdom of his day,
he called the police, who warned,
Don't Touch, Or Breathe, Don't Move
Too Close, and keep people away
until they arrive to disarm the thing.

I know what to think: no one should
lose an arm, stumble on death, be
blown apart. I wish no harm. But, my
heart is with the deep thing that

ticks in secret, and surfaces to speak.

—FRANK POLITE

MIRROR

I am silver and exact. I have no preconceptions.
Whatever I see I swallow immediately
Just as it is, unmisted by love or dislike.
I am not cruel, only truthful—
The eye of a little god, four-cornered.
Most of the time I meditate on the opposite wall.
It is pink, with speckles. I have looked at it so long
I think it is a part of my heart. But it flickers.
Faces and darkness separate us over and over.

Now I am a lake. A woman bends over me,
Searching my reaches for what she really is.
Then she turns to those liars, the candles or the moon.
I see her back, and reflect it faithfully.
She rewards me with tears and an agitation of hands.
I am important to her. She comes and goes.
Each morning it is her face that replaces the darkness.
In me she has drowned a young girl, and in me an old woman
Rises toward her day after day, like a terrible fish.

—SYLVIA PLATH

MISE EN SCÈNE

The last light muffles itself in cloud and goes
Wildly in silence to the west
Beyond the rough ridge and the pasture snows.

How pale it turns away, like a madman's guest,
Or the queen in the tragedy drawn back
To her luminous height with the sickness in her breast,

Leaving us weak as before to murmur "Alack"—
Though here is but nature turning to night,
Nor angel nor fury glides in the planet's track.

We own no powers in heaven, though well we might
Crave such company of the air
To make majestic our harrowing and our fright.

By what grand eye were these images summoned there?

—ROBERT FITZGERALD

MISERY

Misery is a good thing if misery is spread,
One hurt at a time, so relief feels good;
One grief to a long street,
A wrist burn a woman had,
A girl waiting for a letter, a dollar lost
By a child going to the store, and his slow return;
But we say so at no real cost.
We can always endure misery this way.

Or, if we think to, we can exult every day;
Any one of us can say,
Not this time, not me.
That is another way to talk about misery.

But when misery begins to bite bone,
And the sweet marrow is my own,
Then misery is nothing to talk about.
Misery must be killed and thrown out.

Kill it? But it will not die.
Losing it is not easy, either. No one knows why.

I have walked fast a long time on a dark night,
Turning the corner at every other street light,
And come back home, and found misery there.

I am not well, but misery is well.
Misery is in excellent health everywhere.
The worst about misery I know
Is that it can go anywhere anyone can go.
The worst about misery I shall tell
Is that some who find ways to put it to sleep
Cherish the cure, as if it were good to keep.

—JOHN HOLMES

THE MISSING PERSON

He has come to report himself
A missing person.

The authorities
Hand him the forms.

He knows how they have waited
With the learned patience of barbers

In small shops, idle,
Stropping their razors.

But now that these spaces in his life
Stare up at him blankly,

Waiting to be filled in,
He does not know where to begin.

Afraid
That he cannot answer even

To a description of himself,
He asks for a mirror.

They reassure him
That he can be nowhere

But wherever he finds himself
From moment to moment,

Which, for the moment, is here.
And he might like to believe them,

But in the mirror
He sees what is missing.

It is himself
He sees there emerging

Slowly, as from the dark
Of a furnished room,

Only when it is dark,
One who receives no mail

And is known to the landlady only
For keeping himself to himself,

And for whom it will be years yet
Before he can trust to the light

This last disguise, himself.

—-DONALD JUSTICE

MISTRAL

Percussive, furious, this wind
Sweeps down the mountain and,
Under its pennon of skirling air,
Blows through each red-tiled house as if
Nothing were there: Mistral,
Quartz-clear, spread-eagle,
Falls on the sea.
Gust upon gust batters
The surface—darkening blue—
Into a thousand scalloped fans. Where
Shall our noontime friends,
Cicada, hummingbird,
Who stitched the air with sound and speed,
Now hide? All rocks, islands, peninsulas
Draw near, hitch up their chairs,
Companions in this clearer, clean
Air, while inland fields are stripped of soil.
As I start home, a coven
Of winds is let loose at every corner;
Alone in a howling
Waste, figurehead sculptured in air,
Bent low, deafened, I plunge
On, blind in the face of the storm.

—BARBARA HOWES

THE MOCKINGBIRD

Look one way and the sun is going down,
Look the other and the moon is rising.
The sparrow's shadow's longer than the lawn.
The bats squeak, "Night is here;" the birds cheep, "Day is gone."
On the willow's highest branch, monopolizing
Day and night, cheeping, squeaking, soaring,
The mockingbird is imitating life.

All day the mockingbird has owned the yard.
As light first woke the world, the sparrows trooped
Onto the seedy lawn; the mockingbird
Chased them off shrieking. Hour by hour, fighting hard
To make the world his own, he swooped
On thrushes, thrashers, jays, and chickadees—
At noon he drove away a big black cat.

Now, in the moonlight, he sits here and sings.
A thrush is singing, then a thrasher, then a jay—
Then, all at once, a cat begins meowing.
A mockingbird can sound like anything.
He imitates the world he drove away
So well that, for a minute, in the moonlight,
Which one's the mockingbird? Which one's the world?

—RANDALL JARRELL

MOLES

Every day that their sky droops down,
they shrug before it can harden
and root for life, rumpling along
toward the green part of the garden.

Every day the moles' dirt sky
sags upon their shoulders,

and mine too sags on many a day,
pinned by heavy boulders.

We get tired, the moles and I,
toiling down our burrows.
They shrug dirt along their way,
and I rumple on through sorrows.

—WILLIAM STAFFORD

THE MOMENT

We passed the ice of pain,
And came to a dark ravine,
And there we sang with the sea;
The wide, the bleak abyss
Shifted with our slow kiss.

Space struggled with time;
The gong of midnight struck

The naked absolute.
Sound, silence sang as one.

All flowed: without, within;
Body met body, we
Created what's to be.

What else to say?—
We end in joy.

—THEODORE ROETHKE

THE MOMENTS HE REMEMBERS

The moments he remembers? They are those
In the dog part of him, the sleeping nose,

The animal awakened in him once—
Decrepit the old hound, yet how he hunts

Through the moist lands of youth! Or then he did—
Remembering what time almost has hid:

The hour at sunset when the ball and glove,
Hot with the play, exhaled a leather love,

And his left hand, withdrawn to wipe his eyes,
Sweetened the whole air with musk surprise—

The sweat of horses, tempered with his own,
And the rubbed oil that lingered on alone.

The animal, awakening once more,
Almost can live; except his bones are sore,

And the sunk valleys of his mind can save
Only a few more moments from the grave—

As when the boy, in January wind,
Ran till his face was nipped and scarlet-skinned;

Then stopped, and all of winter like a bell
Rang in his nostrils, soundless. Or the spell—

He can remember, suddenly, his trance
When feet upon the lawn had ceased to dance,

And his small cheeks, enamored of the bruise,
Lay pressed in grass the way sky-witches use,

Straining upon earth's arc, to enter in;
He entered it, the odor—now so thin,

So struggling now, so faint across the ground,
To the old man and the nearsighted hound.

—MARK VAN DOREN

MONDAY

Awake, like a hippopotamus with eyes bulged
from the covers, I find Monday, improbable
as chair legs, camped around me, and God's terrible
searchlight raking down from his pillbox on Mount Hood,
while His mystic hammers reach from the alarm clock
and rain spangles on my head.

Cliff at my back all week I live, afraid
when light comes, because it has deep whirlpools
in it. I cross each day by the shallow part but
have often touched the great hole in the sky
at noon. I close my eyes and let the day
for a while wander where all things will, and then
it settles in a fold of the north.

At the end, in my last sickness, I think I will travel
north, if well-meaning friends will let me—to bush,
to rock, to snow—have nothing by me, fall
on the sky of earth in the north, and let my heart
finally understand that part of the world
I have secretly loved all my life—the rock. But now
I gradually become young, surge from the covers,
and go to work.

—WILLIAM STAFFORD

MONSOON

A snake emptied itself into the grass.
A lizard wriggled out of a cup of ferns.
The pebbles, quiet, but nudging to follow the dust
Downwind, struggled with consciences,
Vaulting back as the gust, passing, kinked the long grass.
Then first we heard it, the long rush and rake
Abrading, stripping the earth's back, as the rain,
Trailing its millions of wires, and voiding first
The lecture hall, the library and bungalows,
All the gardens springing taut and the tennis courts
Smudged like wrecks at sea, the downpour came,
Caving its seething wall onto our verandas,
Submerging the whole house. And we froze,
Like water spiders clenched in their sacs of breathing,
Crouched, dry and firm in the damp, close mouth of the wind,
As the tropics snapped and tore at our moderate blood.

Then, after an hour, the ground steamed openly.
The rain, flickering northward into the shallow hills
Left little puddles behind, rubies aflame
In the fattened grasses drinking the sunset down,
Deep, through stem and root, and into the cave of stone
Where the scorpion hungers, carrying his bruise down.

—DAVID WEVILL

MONTANA ECLOGUE

I

After the fall drive, the last
horseman humps down the trail south;
High Valley turns into a remote, still cathedral.
Stone Creek in its low bank turns calmly
through the trampled meadow. The one scouting
thunderhead above Long Top hangs to watch,
ready for its reinforcements due in October.

Logue, the man who always closes down the camp,
is left all alone at Clear Lake, where
he is leisurely but busy, pausing to glance across
the water toward Winter Peak. The bunkhouse
will be boarded up, the cookshack barricaded
against bears, the corral gates lashed shut.
Whatever winter needs it will have to find
for itself, all the slow months the wind owns.

From that shore below the mountain, the water
darkens; the whole surface of the lake livens;
and, upward, high miles of pine tops bend where a storm
walks the country. Deeper and deeper, autumn
floods in. Nothing can hold against that current
the aspens feel. And Logue, by being there, suddenly
carries for us everything that we can load on him,
we who have stopped indoors and let our faces
forget how storms come. That lonely man works for us.

II

Far from where we are, air owns those ranches
our trees hardly hear of—open places
braced against cold hills. Mornings, that
news hits the leaves like rain, and we
stop everything time brings, and freeze that one,
open, great, real thing, the world's gift—day.

Up there, air like an axe chops, near timberline,
the clear-cut miles the marmots own. We
try to know, all deep, all sharp, even while
busy here, that other; gripped in a job,
aimed steady at a page, or riffled by distractions,
we break free into that world of the farthest coat—air.

We glimpse that last storm when the wolves
get the mountains back, when our homes will flicker

bright, then dull, then old; and the trees
will advance, knuckling their roots or lying in
windrows to match the years. We glimpse
a crack that begins to run down the wall,
and, like a blanket over the window at night,
that world is with us and those wolves are here.

III

Up there, ready to be part of what comes, the high lakes
lie in their magnificent beds; but men,
great as their heroes are, live by their deeds
only as a pin of shadow in a cavern their thought
gets lost in. We pause, we stand where
we are meant to be, waver as foolish as
we are, tell our lies with all the beautiful grace
an animal has when it runs:

Citizen, step back from the fire and let night
have your head. Suddenly you more than hear
what is true so abruptly that God is cold—
winter is here. What no one saw has
come. Then everything the sun approved could
really fail? Shed from your back, the years
fall one by one, and nothing that comes
will be your fault. You breathe a few breaths
free at the thought—things can come so great
that your part is too small to count,
if winter can come.

Logue brings us all that. Earth took
the old saints, who battered their hearts,
met arrows, or died by the germs God sent;
but Logue, by being alone and occurring to us,
carried us forward a little,
and on his way out for the year will
stand by the shore and see winter in,
the great, repeated lesson every year.
A storm bends by that shore and
one flake at a time teaches
grace, even to stone.

—WILLIAM STAFFORD

THE MOON AND THE YEW TREE

This is the light of the mind, cold and planetary.
The trees of the mind are black. The light is blue.
The grasses unload their griefs on my feet as if I were God,
Prickling my ankles and murmuring of their humility.
Fumey, spiritous mists inhabit this place
Separated from my house by a row of headstones.
I simply cannot see where there is to get to.

The moon is no door. It is a face in its own right,
White as a knuckle and terribly upset.
It drags the sea after it like a dark crime; it is quiet
With the O-gape of complete despair. I live here.
Twice on Sunday, the bells startle the sky—
Eight great tongues affirming the Resurrection.
At the end, they soberly bong out their names.

The yew tree points up. It has a Gothic shape.
The eyes lift after it and find the moon.
The moon is my mother. She is not sweet like Mary.
Her blue garments unloose small bats and owls.
How I would like to believe in tenderness—
The face of the effigy, gentled by candles,
Bending, on me in particular, its mild eyes.

I have fallen a long way. Clouds are flowering,
Blue and mystical over the face of the stars.
Inside the church, the saints will be all blue,
Floating on their delicate feet over the cold pews,
Their hands and faces stiff with holiness.
The moon sees nothing of this. She is bald and wild.
And the message of the yew tree is blackness—blackness and silence.

—Sylvia Plath

THE MOON IN YOUR HANDS

If you take the moon in your hands
and turn it round
(heavy, slightly tarnished platter),
you're there;

if you pull dry seaweed from the sand
and turn it round

and wonder at the underside's bright
amber,
your eyes

look out as they did here
(you don't remember)
when my soul turned round,

perceiving the other side of every-
    thing,
mullein leaf, dogwood leaf, moth wing,
and dandelion seed under the ground.
                                    —H. D.

MOONTAN

The bluish, pale
face of the house
rises above me
like a wall of ice

and the distant
solitary
barking of an owl
floats toward me.

I half close my eyes.

Over the damp
dark of the garden,
flowers swing
back and forth
like small balloons.

The solemn trees,
each buried
in a cloud of leaves,
seem lost in sleep.

It is late.
I lie in the grass,
smoking,
feeling at ease,
pretending the end
will be like this.

Moonlight
falls on my flesh.
A breeze
circles my wrist.

I drift.
I shiver.
I know that soon
the day will come
to wash away the moon's
white stain,

that I shall walk
in the morning sun
invisible
as anyone.
                —Mark Strand

MORELS

A wet gray day—rain falling slowly, mist over the
    valley, mountains dark circumflex smudges in the distance—

Apple blossoms just gone by, the branches feathery still
    as if fluttering with half-visible antennae—

A day in May like so many in these green mountains, and
    I went out just as I had last year

At the same time, and found them there under the big maples—
    by the bend in the road—right where they had stood

Last year and the year before that, risen from the dark duff
   of the woods, emerging at odd angles

From spores hidden by curled and matted leaves, a fringe of
   rain on the grass around them,

Beads of rain on the mounded leaves and mosses round them,

Not in a ring themselves but ringed by jack-in-the-pulpits
   with deep eggplant-colored stripes;

Not ringed but rare, not gilled but polyp-like, having
   sprung up overnight—

These mushrooms of the gods, resembling human organs
   uprooted, rooted only on the air,

Looking like lungs wrenched from the human body, lungs
   reversed, not breathing internally

But being the externalization of breath itself, these
   spicy, twisted cones,

These perforated brown-white asparagus tips—these morels,
   smelling of wet graham crackers mixed with maple leaves;

And, reaching down by the pale green fern shoots, I nipped
   their pulpy stems at the base

And dropped them into a paper bag—a damp brown bag (their
   color)—and carried

Them (weighing absolutely nothing) down the hill and into
   the house; you held them

Under cold bubbling water and sliced them with a surgeon's
   stroke clean through,

And sautéed them over a low flame, butter-brown; and we ate
   them then and there—

Tasting of the sweet damp woods and of the rain one inch
   above the meadow:

It was like feasting upon air.

                                                —WILLIAM JAY SMITH

MORNING, NOON, AND . . .

Easter dawn!
From early church unwalled,
taking fresh breath,
our voices join the bird
that earlier called
the day to life,
never having heard
any word of death.

East's Easter
lily spreads its pistils
over a world
of windows silvering

lintels to sills,
in heaven's hand—
above parading
Noon—is later held.

Latest, on
a western window ledge,
light-beggared Dark
slips the expended cup
a penny's edge
of afterglow
before it turns up-
side down with the lark.

—HAWLEY TRUAX

MORNING ON THE ST. JOHN'S

(THE CHINESE CHARACTER FOR LANDSCAPE IS MOUNTAINS-AND-WATER. A
JAPANESE IMAGE OF HEAVEN IS FUJI REFLECTED IN A POOL.)

This is a country where there are no mountains:
At dawn the water birds like lines of rain
Rise from the pencilled grasses by the river
And slantwise creak across the growing light.
The sky lifts upwards and the breath of flowers
Wakes with the shadows of the waking birds.

The shadows of the birds, the dancing birds!
With so much freedom, who could ask for mountains?
The heron stands here ankle-deep in flowers,
Wet hyacinths that burn more blue with rain,
And waves of smaller wings hurl wide the light
All up and down the horizontal river.

And now the sun shakes blue locks in the river
And rises dripping-headed while the birds
Go wild in curves of praise at sudden light.
The fire that would flash suddenly off mountains
Bathes this round world in dew as dark as rain
And then strikes green and gold among the flowers.

The dropping heads, the smooth and shaken flowers!
Among the grasses, blue eyes by the river,

And in the garden, fires after rain.
Under umbrella leaves the mockingbirds
Still nestle and trill quietly of mountains,
Then whistle Light!—cadenza—Light! and Light!

While higher and higher streams the opening light,
A rose corona like an opening flower,
More pure than snow at dawn among the mountains;
Paler than any color by the river,
Beyond the reach of eye-fall, flight of birds,
It floods a sky swept innocent by rain.

The assault of sun, the long assault of rain!
Look how our darkness is made true by light!
Look how our silence is confirmed by birds!
The mind that pastured ankle-deep in flowers
Last night must wake to sunrise on the river,
Graze wide and then grow vertical as mountains.

For even a glimpse of mountains fogged with rain
Or mirrored in a river brings delight
And shakes a man as dawn shakes birds and flowers.

—JANE COOPER

THE MORNING TRACK

Beginning in half darkness,
The horses up for hours with the men,
The quick slush of riding hoofs comes easily
Sounding around the muddy track, distantly
Fading into nearness and out of it again.
The high hum of singing from the gangling grooms
Beats a morning blues harmony, modified for years
By the endless running hoofs.
In the green morning—with the light
Mist of dawn rolling with the horse's breath
And the drifting ground smoke of fires
Built for water- and hand-warming—
Moving under the young sun,
The horse with his quick slush comes sounding
Easily off the track, snorting at the groom's
Caressing, cool hand.
                    Easy, easy, baby boy—
He loves the dumb horse with the dumbness
Of his cool hands upon him, rubbing down

The hard-veined animal powered by slim,
Brainy legs, poised delicately under the heaving body,
Like mobiles of bones and tendon, wired beautifully,
Just this side of stillness and of death.

—EDWARD PARONE

THE MOVEMENT OF FISH

No water is still, on top.
Without wind, even, it is full
Of a chill, superficial agitation.
It is easy to forget,
Or not to know at all

That fish do not move
By means of this rippling
Along the outside of water, or
By anything touching on air.
Where they are, it is still,

Under a wooden bridge,
Under the poised oar
Of a boat, while the rower leans
And blows his mistaken breath
To make the surface shake,

Or yells at it, or sings,
Half believing the brilliant scan
Of ripples will carry the fish away
On his voice like a buried wind.
Or it may be that a fish

Is simply lying under
The ocean-broad sun,
Which comes down onto him

Like a tremendous, suffusing
Open shadow

Of gold, where nothing is,
Sinking into the water,
Becoming dark around
His body. Where he is now
Could be gold mixed

With absolute blackness.
The surface at mid-sea shivers,
But he does not feel it
Like a breath, or like anything.
Yet suddenly his frame shakes,

Convulses the whole ocean
Under the trivial, quivering
Surface, and he is
Hundreds of feet away,
Still picking up speed, still shooting

Through half-gold,
Going nowhere. Nothing sees him.
One must think of this to under-
          stand
The instinct of fear and trembling,
And, of its one movement, the depth.

—JAMES DICKEY

MOVIES FOR THE HOME

I see the map of summer, lying still,
Its edges under water, blue, fragile.
You cannot hear, of course, from here
The Pacific's portable orchestra—

A kind of shimmery marimba music—
But if you follow all those lines of light,
The nerve-nets of connection, coast to coast,
That screened the days and nights from east to west,
You'll come upon their visions and their sounds:
The dawn's fine print when ink has leaked away,
And a radio turned off still tuned to play
Invisible music. Riding in that car,
I think that where we were is where we are.

The towns the distance fired into being
(By dint of light diagonally drawn
Downward to strike a steeple with a star)
Became fool's gold the closer we came near,
Assembling into lassitudes of palms,
The fresh rot of the wharfs, the hunchbacked hills,
But none of those visions we were driving for.
They drained away, strip cities come and gone,
As if we stayed while we went driving on,
Or they remained where they had never been,
Before us and behind us. They disappeared,
And what at first was flame at last was char.
One wheel turns or another, and there you are.

By supple deviations, twisting on,
The Snake River bent its shapely mail
In moonlight, enlarged and palpable.
The Tetons capped by a display of snow
Refreshed four lakes of summer far below
(Thimblefuls of a barbarian sky);
We dipped our fingers in their sunburnt water
To dribble waterdrops back into blue.
Telegraph wires stitched themselves to trees,
Then dropped away, somewhere in the Rockies.
The pictures pass. We are what we need.
If I remember rightly, we were lost.
We lost the way, being the way we are.

A beautifully painted abstract speed
Lacquered the windshield's cemetery
Of wing and smear so factually there
It seemed the factual was arbitrary
But natural. In those swift ends we saw
The wreckage of ourselves, our wheels in air . . .
Transparent vacancies attack the brain
At one point or another, as if a train
Should smash into a moving mirror of itself

Point-blank high up upon a mountain pass
And the snow, not even disturbed, give back
Its glacial white indifference to the wreck.
And there, where imagination ends, we are.

Where are we? In a country of lakes?
A Switzerland of Self through which we ski,
Dropping down a lighted scoop of valley
That soon transforms itself into the sea?
(And thus we might arrive at the Impossible:
That place where there is nothing left to see.)
Now we are standing on a wooden pier
Watching the Pacific stun itself on rocks;
If the camera stopped, if you could stare
Out far enough, the Orient, over there,
Might have the excitement of intense boredom.
Our house in Berkeley? You turn the corner there,
Go left and down the hill, and there you are.

Alongside water all the afternoon,
The sea so far below we could not fall,
What threatened ending rose from its abyss
To rattle in the tin can of the car?
Was it the blue that flaked away to cloud,
The green that flew away on either side,
The white-lined serpent of the road ahead,
Intense as distance in its silences,
That colored what we thought until we thought:
The color of the distance is the color bled
Out of the time it takes to get us there?
The pictures pass. We are the way we were.
Being here and there is what we are.

By going forward we were coming back.
When the film rewinds, you'll see what I mean.
In the woods, that lipsticked drinking cup,
Stuck in the drying margins of the stream,
Turns up again in the desert coming up
Quite soon in malignant iodine and green.
Now we are looking at an estuary
Whose waters gently poach an evening star
Whose spidery edges are collapsing down
As far as the eye can see, but just so far.
I wonder if you can go as far as far
And still not see things as they really are,
Only as they were, if that is where you are.

—Howard Moss

MOVIES, LEFT TO RIGHT

The action runs left to right,
Cavalry, the water-skiers—
Then a five-hour film, "The Sleeper,"
A man sleeping for five hours
(In fifteen sequences),
Sleeping left to right, left to right
Cavalry, a love scene, elephants.
Also, the world goes left to right,
The moon and all the stars—sex, too,
And newspapers, catastrophe.

In bed, my wives are to my left.
I embrace them, moving left to right.
I have lived my life that way,
Growing older, moving eastward—
The speedometer, the bank balance,
Architecture, good music.
"All that is most real moves left to right,"
Declares my friend the scenarist,
Puffing on a white cigar, eating
The *Herald Tribune*, the *New Republic*.

My life is a vision, a mechanism
That runs from left to right. I have lived badly.
Water-skier, I was until recently
In the U.S. Cavalry. Following that,
I played elephant to a lead by Tarzan.
Later, I appeared in a film called "The Sleeper."
Till today, standing on the edge of things,
Falling and about to fall asking "Why?,"
I look back. Nowhere. Meanwhile, one or more wives
Go on stilts for the mail.

—ROBERT SWARD

MR. ELIOT'S DAY

(IMPRESSIONS UPON PERUSING
"THE COMPLETE POEMS AND PLAYS OF T. S. ELIOT")

At 8:00 he rises, bathes, and dresses,
And very privately confesses.

At 9:00 he breaks fast with his host
On *café noir* and thin dry toast.

At 10:00, as one who bears the Grail,
A maid brings him his morning mail.

At 11:00, town. He offers thanks
At one old church and two old banks.

At 12:00, still in the mood of prayer,
He drops into a deep club chair.

At 1:00 he's lunching with a bishop
On spring lamb garnished with true hyssop.

At 2:00 the poet starts to nod,
Now toward, and now away from, God.

At 3:00 he wakes and makes repair
Of the strict parting of his hair.

At 4:00, back at his host's estate,
He picks a rose and ponders fate.

At 5:00, over a cocktail glass,
He is reminded of the Mass.

At 6:00 he and his favorite cat
Hold a brief, metaphysical chat.

At 7:00, with a distinguished sinner
And well-known saint, he faces dinner.

At 8:00 the three men still converse
On why the world is so much worse.

At 9:00, for lighter recreation,
They play charades on In-car-na-tion.

At 10:00, alone, robed in a jaunty
Dressing gown, he's deep in Dante.

11:00 strikes. Now hoots the owl.
He leaves the house for a deep, dark prowl.

At 12:00 he mounts, with measured tread,
The penitential stairs to bed.

—ROBERT FRANCIS

THE MUD TURTLE

Out of the earth beneath the water,
Dragging over the stubble field
Up to the hilltop in the sun,
On his way from water to water,
He rests an hour in the garden,
His alien presence observed by all:
His lordly darkness decked in filth
Bearded with weed like a lady's favor.
He is a black planet, another world
Never till now appearing, even now
Not quite believably old and big,
Set in the summer morning's midst,
A gloomy gemstone to the sun op-
    posed.
Our measures of him do not matter—
He would be huge at any size—
And neither do the number of his
    years;
The time he comes from doesn't
    count.

When the boys tease him with sticks,
He breaks the sticks, striking with
As great a suddenness as speed;
Fingers and toes would snap as soon,
Says one of us, and the others shud-
    der.

Then when they turn him on his back
To see the belly heroically yellow,
He throws himself fiercely to his feet,
Brings down the whole weight of his
    shell,
Spreads out his claws and digs himself
    in
Immovably, invulnerably,
But for the front foot on the left,
Red-budded, with the toes torn off.
So over he goes again, and shows
Us where a swollen slug is fastened
Softly between plastron and shell.
Nobody wants to go close enough
To burn it loose; he can't be helped
Either, there is no help for him
As he makes it to his feet again
And drags away to the meadow's edge.
We see the tall grass open and wave
Around him; it closes; he is gone
Over the hill toward another water,
Bearing his hard and chambered hurt
Down, down, down, beneath the
    water,
Beneath the earth beneath. He takes
A secret wound out of the world.

—HOWARD NEMEROV

MULES

In warm war-sun they erupt
in frontier towns, hard-
hoofed in a dark, cobbled yard,
waiting for what is apt:
cartridge cases, cordite, shells.

Always the sight of them compels
the memory of what we are.
A newsreel of a distant war
that flickers in our room recalls
a savage, wasting sense in us;

eyes that stare from skirmishes
a continent away propound
the pith of life our lives have dulled.
A braying in the silences
beyond those Asian leaves betrays

some close, restless agency,
half detected, feared, unseen
in unfamiliar terrain,
marauding, like the lurking spy
that snipes us from the wilderness

of dreams. We know ourselves wise,
mastering violence; but sometimes,
dimly, we sense other wisdoms—
he totally lives who dies
imminently; those eyes

only that see with terror see.
We do not say we would have gone
gladly, scrabbling screes to melon-
smelling foothill towns to be
quickened with fear; nor would these

wide-eyed soldiers fail to lob
grenades at the sniper's nest.
It will be time enough to test
our doctrines when our cancers throb.
But, as we watch the mules trot past,

we muse on how, in time of peace,
their withers twitch to flies
as, listlessly, they laze
neglected in corrals, or pace
at tether, shabby and unkempt.

—TED WALKER

THE MURDERED GIRL IS FOUND ON A BRIDGE

Hammerstroke and
hammerstroke and
hammerstroke de-
stroyed me—

that mallet
(or what you call it)
pounding away.
My thighs betrayed me.

The noise! The cries!
I cracked like a bell
forcing a chime
and came

or went.
At any rate I'm here
over streets that bear,
easily, giant trees;

here where the air's
absorbed my blood
into white light,
silence a bell,

an odor all about,
the smell of
oranges or
something growing.

—JANE HAYMAN

THE MURDERER

As the used anger drips from his hands like blood,
and the green canary bends an expectant eye
on that new-fashioned thing (its screeching done),
he feels the strange achievement of defeat.
As if squeezed out between his fingers, she
had risen into a mocking sky like smoke
and left him with his hate, robbed of its end,
still pressing in like some old torture room,
and from that flaccid bundle upward cast
the blank, constrictive shade in which he'd live.

—PAUL PETRIE

MUSICIAN

Where have these hands been,
By what delayed,
That so long stayed
Away from the thin

Strings which they now grace
With their lonely skill?
Music and their cool will
At last interlace.

Now, with great ease, and slow,
The thumb, the finger, the strong
Delicate hand plucks the long
String it was born to know.

And under the palm, the string
Sings as it wished to sing.

—Louise Bogan

MUSIC IN VENICE

Dismiss the instruments that for your pleasure
Have played allegro all through Italy.
Pay the musicians. Even let the poet
    Have part his pay.
For there is Venice—floating, and suspended
From purple ropes. Dismiss the music school!
Here anyone at all can play the fool
    In his own way.

Then thread the labyrinth of narrow streets,
Bridges, canals, windows of lace and glass,
High lattices that spill the scent of almonds.
    And the Minotaur
That lurks in this maze is Love. An Aschenbach
Round every corner is pursuing Eros.
"Love!" cry the naked offspring of the heroes
    On the wet stone floor.

It's night in the Piazza. Lighted space
Burns like your brandy. Violins and brass
Play waltzes, fox trots. On a cloud, St. Mark's
    Winged lion perches;
High palaces go sailing to the moon,
Which, as advertised, is perfectly clear.
The lovers rise, moon-struck, and whisper their
    Arrivedercis.

A prince of Venice, tangled in the eyes
Of a young courtesan, once staged a masque,
"The Banishment of Love." A boy like Eros
    Was rowed in chains,

Weeping, down the canal. The merchant's Venice
Splintered the Turk and swept him from her shores.
But Eros came, Eros with many oars,
    And Eros reigns.

Venice, the city built on speculation,
Still stands on it. Love sails from India
And Sweden—every hanging cloud pours out
    A treasure chest.
It's love on the Rialto, news of love,
That gives Antonio his golden life,
Even to Envy, sharpening a knife,
    His interest.

                       —LOUIS SIMPSON

MUSSEL HUNTER AT ROCK HARBOR

I came before the water-
colorists came to get the
good of the Cape light that scours
sand grit to sided crystal
and buffs and sleeks the blunt hulls
of the three fishing smacks beached
on the bank of the river's

backtracking tail. I'd come for
free fish bait: the blue mussels
clumped like bulbs at the grass-root
margin of the tidal pools.
Dawn tide stood dead low. I smelt
mud stench, shell guts, gulls' leavings;
heard a queer crusty scrabble

cease, and I neared the silenced
edge of a cratered pool bed.
The mussels hung dull blue and
conspicuous, yet it seemed
a sly world's hinges had swung
shut against me. All held still.
Though I counted scant seconds,

enough ages lapsed to win
confidence of safe-conduct
in the wary otherworld
eying me. Grass put forth claws;

small mud knobs, nudged from under,
displaced their domes as tiny
knights might doff their casques. The
    crabs

inched from their pygmy burrows
and from the trench-dug mud, all
camouflaged in mottled mail
of browns and greens. Each wore one
claw swollen to a shield large
as itself—no fiddler's arm
grown Gargantuan by trade,

but grown grimly, and grimly
borne, for a use beyond my
guessing of it. Sibilant
hordes, mass-motived, they sidled
out in a converging stream
toward the pool mouth, perhaps to
meet the thin and sluggish thread

of sea retracing its tide-
way up the river basin.
Or to avoid me. They moved
obliquely with a dry-wet
sound, with a glittery wisp
and trickle. Could they feel mud
pleasurable under claws

as I could between bare toes?
That question ended it—I
stood shut out, for once, for all,
puzzling the passage of their
absolutely alien
order as I might puzzle
at the clear tail of Halley's

comet, coolly giving my
orbit the go-by, made known
by a family name it
knew nothing of. So the crabs
went about their business, which
wasn't fiddling, and I filled
a big handkerchief with blue

mussels. From what the crabs saw,
if they could see, I was one
two-legged mussel picker.
High on the airy thatching
of the dense grasses, I found
the husk of a fiddler crab,
intact, strangely strayed above

his world of mud—green color
and innards bleached and blown off
somewhere by much sun and wind;
there was no telling if he'd
died recluse or suicide
or headstrong Columbus crab.
The crab face, etched and set there,

grimaced as skulls grimace—it
had an Oriental look,
a samurai death mask done
on a tiger tooth, less for
art's sake than God's. Far from sea—
where red-freckled crab backs, claws,
and whole crabs, dead, their soggy

bellies pallid and upturned,
perform their shambling waltzes
on the waves' dissolving turn
and return, losing themselves
bit by bit to their friendly
element—this relic saved
face, to face the bald-faced sun.

—SYLVIA PLATH

MY FATHER IN THE NIGHT COMMANDING NO

My father in the night commanding No
Has work to do. Smoke issues from his lips;
    He reads in silence.
The frogs are croaking and the street lamps glow.

And then my mother winds the gramophone—
The Bride of Lammermoor begins to shriek—
    Or reads a story
About a prince, a castle, and a dragon.

The moon is glittering above the hill.
I stand before the gateposts of the King—
    So runs the story—
Of Thule, at midnight when the mice are still.

And I have been in Thule! It has come true—
The journey and the danger of the world,
    All that there is
To bear and to enjoy, endure and do.

Landscapes, seascapes . . . Where have I been led?
The names of cities—Paris, Venice, Rome—
    Held out their arms.
A feathered god, seductive, went ahead.

Here is my house. Under a red rose tree
A child is swinging; another gravely plays.
    They are not surprised
That I am here; they were expecting me.

And yet my father sits and reads in silence,
My mother sheds a tear, the moon is still,
    And the dark wind
Is murmuring that nothing ever happens.

Beyond his jurisdiction as I move,
Do I not prove him wrong? And yet, it's true
    They will not change
There, on the stage of terror and of love.

The actors in that playhouse always sit
In fixed positions—father, mother, child
    With painted eyes.
How sad it is to be a little puppet!

Their heads are wooden. And you once pretended
To understand them! Shake them as you will,
    They cannot speak.
Do what you will, the comedy is ended.

Father, why did you work? Why did you weep,
Mother? Was the story so important?
    "Listen!" the wind
Said to the children, and they fell asleep.
              —Louis Simpson

MY FATHER, MY SON

I

Father,
        one day longer on this earth than you,
I want you home—not
as a sage arthritic in red silks
to whom I proffer
                birds of jade
& berries on a stick—not

as a totem with a spittled lip,
forked beard
            blown sidewise & Assyrian—
not as a democrat of rhetoric,
                        calligraphy,
astride bowlegged Chippendale—but
just as the man you were
                        in dull Glen plaid,
high collar, homburg hat,
                Kodak'd
beside our bathtub of a Hupmobile.
Your new estate is mine;
                    & if, at first,
I treat you like a well-scrubbed foreigner
to whom one gives a suit of clothes,
                        five dollars
& a map of the city,
accept the circumstance: I need
help in the yard,
                a hand with heavy things,
someone to keep the books.

                        II
Flames I've not eaten
                I have quashed
with a small cap of silver—yet
what was it like when,
                    clacking west,
you heard the waters hiss & part,
                        & saw
the sun rise cold as cash?
                    Your eyes
like plums in fifty watts
                        of washroom light,
you shaved, halfway across Ontario,
with a straight razor & your braces down.
Bandbox fresh,
                whisked to your high-topped shoes,
when you stepped from a Grand Trunk sleeping car,
what was it like to be,
                    emblazoned in your tracks,
one man alive,
                Gladstone in hand?
Those boom-town dollar bills—were they
not barbarous as they were absurd?
When, Sunday afternoons,
                .
                        they showered

out of canvas biplanes onto
                              lots for sale,
& craven girls, knee-deep
in goldenrod & Queen Anne's lace,
picked them like lettuce,
                              was not history,
finally, a subdivision of brown bungalows,
                                            a small
down payment on the Middle West,
& good clean fun?
                    On the Tashmoo boat,
its splashy paddle wheels
                            walking the water,
did I not watch
                  the snake dance
                                    deck to deck
of realtor & typist,
                      branch manager & clerk?
Your hands outstretched,
                          your fingertips upon
a boozy woman's pin-striped back,
                                    two other
hands on yours,
                  et cetera—*Yes!* you sang,
your flint face mesmerized,
                              Yes!
we have no bananas,
we have no bananas today!

III

Set down in our raw suburb
                            Mother wept,
her old life now a province in a mist
where military bands,
                        caged in an iron wedding cake,
played Humperdinck & Grieg
                            to the King's swans;
& years of calling cards,
                            laid in a silver dish,
tallied the last turns in the vestibule
of waltzing osprey & high-stepping fox.
                                        You must
have understood,
                  though you would not,
the vast leer of our Morris chair,
the desolations of Caruso on the console,
                                          the ache

of Maxfield Parrish's blue dawn
above a five-foot shelf of books,
                                        glassed in.
Why was she crying?
Where did she hurt?
                        Shrunk in the threat
of something still more awful
                                than the oven eyes
of grizzlies,
                chained,
                        snarling, to a pole,
that wanted to get at me,
                                I lay, eyes shut, awake.
"He's not asleep."
                        Her sob
broke like a bubble on a pink geranium.
"He's a good actor. Jack, see what you can do."
Shoshonis gobbling at the sight of him,
                                Buffalo Bill,
that worn-out hero of your one-man repertoire,
skirmished across my bed.
                        What a brute!
I think you thought so too.

IV

Father,
        what do I do with years
still hovering like a castle quarried to its floors,
wrapped,
            piece by piece in burlap,
                                stacked away
in some red warehouse just outside of town?
To whom can I show off?
                            Where now can I talk big?
Blood on my hockey stick,
                            I limped home
pitifully.
            Marbles in my mouth,
I got my message through to Garcia,
                                & stalked
the dining room for liberty or death.
Erasmus redivivus,
I fell asleep in the encyclopedia.
                            When you
told your one joke
                    (Irate Diner: Waitress—what is
this fly doing in my soup?
                        Waitress: Why—it does look like

the breaststroke, sir.)
                    I laughed
louder than anyone. I said
your Friday haircut was the cat's pajamas.
I said
          So's *your old man!*
                          & bit my tongue.
You pondered *The Outline of History,*
                          you took up golf.
I sulked & fasted,
                told my beads,
                          slammed
out to Mass at dawn.
                The simplest form
of tyranny, I learned,
                    is holiness.
Remember our most delicate of interviews?
I had to know what it was all about;
                          you had to say.
My eyes outstaring yours—
                    yours fixed,
first on my saints, all smiles in their blue lights,
then on my 2 for 25¢ photographs
                          of Bebe Daniels & Ben Lyon,
then on the water-falling tails
                    of birds of paradise
you'd painted on my walls—
                    you began
at the beginning, you told it all.
                    Hushed
by great news, I sat stock-still as,
                    surfacing
from 20,000 leagues,
                you lit a Camel
& then studied it. "Do you think you understand?"
I nodded,
          completely in the dark.
                    That's where I stayed
until,
      one morning in a field,
                    instructed
by a playmate grown up fast,
I thought my head, like a boiled egg,
was sliced off at the top.

                    V

You couldn't bear it,
              yet every June

you'd pack us off, dolls in a box,
to summer in the Maritimes.
                                ."Hon,"
you wrote from the East Side Y.M.C.A.,
"I don't think I can stand it.
                                I eat
at some dog wagon near the office,
read *Liberty*, take in a show."

Stalled like a whale,
                                her hawsers loose,
the S. S. Berengaria
lay sidling at the Ocean Terminal.
                                At noon,
her deck rails lined with duchesses,
she churned the harbor skidding in her bells,
then dropped her tugs
                                & slid
basso profundo out to sea.

                                I still
had graves to dig:
                                a cricket skewered on a pin,
a grasshopper dismantled to its knees.
I put them
                side by side,
                                a few
limp dandelions for one,
purple clover for the other,
                                a matchstick
cross for each. I had no sympathy.

                                VI
Up in the smoke of 1929 went your big deal.
Grass withered in the cleats
                                of your golf shoes.
You closed the office,
                                hocked your turnip watch,
replaced the lining in your overcoat.
Across a neighborhood of rotting mortgages
you saw your future out of sight.
They even tried to repossess the car!
Thank God,
                                you still had brushes & a union card.
You climbed a ladder,
                                you began to paint
a painted desert, streets in Trinidad,
a salmon-colored *auberge* in a forest where,

descending,
      weightless,
            from a tulip coach,
Lucrezia Bori,
        like a walking tent,
embraced the full measure of illicit joy.
                 Back
in overalls, you made good money
               & you grew morose.
What could you do with a kid afraid of heights,
half-crocked on Proust,
          tooling a sonnet
on the very day the Tigers clinched the pennant?

VII

Father,
     riddle me this:
            If I'm not half
the man you were,
         what fortune makes you
all I am?
You gave me your car keys.
I put you on the shelf.
           What did you know
of Tzara, Aschenbach, Barbusse?
How could you stomach Hitler & Republic Steel?
Out all night,
        my fingers mimeo'd
with U.A.W. strike bulletins,
I made the breakfast nook my drumhead court.
Charged with murder,
           you sat still.
Hectored out of conscience, you,
with crypto-fascist nonchalance,
           ate two
fried eggs,
     a slice of ham,
         & dolloped
cream into your coffee. You had to see a man,
you said, about a dog,
        then wiped your lips
& handed me a week's allowance.

VIII

Cranking a winch one working day,
          your hands went white.
A stippled garden shuddered to the stage.

So much to say,
                    I couldn't get there fast enough.

Time eats you in that box I bought
next morning in a sort of catacomb
on Jefferson near East Grand Boulevard.

Tailgating your black Packard to Mount Olivet,
lights on,
              we ran the lights,
                              stopped dead
in a charred grove &,
                    ill at ease,
                              stood witness
to your last embarrassment.
                          Traffic with insane
persistence scratched the hedges.
                              Overhead,
like pterodactyls sitting on the wind,
Ford Tri-Motors snored importantly
                              & side-slipped home.
Broken at the wrist,
                    the hand you never shook
hung at my side.
                    I can't remember—
did the rain hold off?

In your collar box I found
                          love poems—
Love poems! When had you written them? To whom?
Your heart, you said, it "burned,"
                              it "yearned."
You said, "You make the winter rains seem glad, my dear.
    The sky above me smiles when you are near."

They were so bad I cried.

                              —JOHN MALCOLM BRINNIN

MY MANY-COATED MAN

Under the scarlet-licking leaves,
through bloody thought and bubbly
    shade,
the padded, spicy tiger moves—
a sheath of swords, a hooded blade.

The turtle on the naked sand
peels to the air his pewter snout
and rubs the sky with slotted shell—
the heart's dismay turned inside out.

The rank red fox goes forth at night
to bite the gosling's downy throat,
then digs his grave with panic claws
to share oblivion with the stoat.

The mottled moth, pinned to a tree,
woos with his wings the bark's disease

and strikes a fungoid, fevered pose
to live forgotten and at ease.

Like these, my many-coated man
shields his hot hunger from the wind,
and, hooded by a smile, commits
his private murder to the mind.

—LAURIE LEE

MY MOTHER ONCE TOLD ME

My mother once told me
Not to sleep with flowers in the room.
Since then I have not slept with flowers.
I sleep alone, without them.

There were many flowers.
But I've never had enough time.
And persons I love are already pushing themselves
Away from my life, like boats
Away from the shore.

My mother said
Not to sleep with flowers.
You won't sleep.
You won't sleep, mother of my childhood.

The bannister I clung to
When they dragged me off to school
Is long since burnt.
But my hands, clinging,
Remain
Clinging.

—YEHUDA AMICHAI

(Translated from the Hebrew by Assia Gutmann)

MY NAME AND I

The impartial Law enrolled a name
  For my especial use;
My rights in it would rest the same
Whether I puffed it into fame
  Or drowned it in abuse.

Robert was what my parents guessed
  When first they peered at me,
And *Graves* an honorable bequest,
  With Georgian silver and the rest,
  From my male ancestry.

They taught me: "You are *Robert
    Graves*
(Which you must learn to spell),
But see that *Robert Graves* behaves,
Whether with honest men or knaves,
    Exemplarily well."

Then, though my I was always I,
    Illegal and unknown,
With nothing to arrest it by—
As will be obvious when I die
    And *Robert Graves* lives on—

I cannot well repudiate
    This noun, this natal star,
This gentlemanly self, this mate

So kindly forced on me by fate,
    Time, and the registrar;

And therefore hurry him ahead
    As an ambassador
To fetch me home my beer and bread
Or commandeer the best green bed,
    As he has done before.

Yet, understand, I am not he
    Either in mind or limb;
My name will take less thought for
    me,
In worlds of men I cannot see,
    Than ever I for him.

                    —ROBERT GRAVES

MYSTIC

The air is a mill of hooks—
Questions without answer,
Glittering and drunk as flies
Whose kisses sting unbearably
In the fetid wombs of black air under pines in summer.

I remember
The dead smell of sun on wood cabins,
The stiffness of sails, the long salt winding sheets.
Once one has seen God, what is the remedy?
Once one has been seized up

Without a part left over—
Not a toe, not a finger—and used,
Used utterly, in the sun's conflagrations, the stains
That lengthen from ancient cathedrals,
What is the remedy?

The pill of the Communion tablet,
The walking beside still water? Memory?
Or picking up the bright pieces
Of Christ in the faces of rodents,
The tame flower-nibblers, the ones

Whose hopes are so low they are comfortable—
The humpback in her small, washed cottage
Under the spokes of the clematis?

Is there no great love, only tenderness?
Does the sea

Remember the walker upon it?
Meaning leaks from the molecules.
The chimneys of the city breathe, the window sweats,
The children leap in their cots.
The sun blooms, it is a geranium.

The heart has not stopped.

—SYLVIA PLATH

MYSTIC RIVER

I

The dirty river by religious explorers
Named Mysticke and recorded forever into its future
Civilization of silt and sewerage recovers
The first sweet moon of time tonight. A tremor
More thought than breeze, more exhalation than motion
Stirs the gold water totem, Snake of the Moon.

"A most pleasynge gentle and salubrious river
Wherein lieth no hindraunce of rock nor shoal
To the distresse of nauvigation, but ever
Aboundaunce of landynge and of fisherie, and withal
Distillynge so sweet an air thorough its course
Sith it runneth salt from the sea, fresh from its source

And altereth daily thorough its greater length
Thus chaungynge and refreshynge the valleys breath,
That," wrote the Gods, "God grauntynge strength
We took up launds, and here untill oure death
Shall be oure hearthes, oure labour, and oure joy."
But what the Gods will have they first destroy.

Still Mystic lights the wake of Gods—the moon
Dances on pollution, the fish are fled,
Who had a finer instinct of revulsion
Than Gods had. And the Gods are dead,
Their sloops and river rotted, and their bones,
Which scrubbed old conscience down like holystones,

Powdered imperceptibly. Their land
Is an old land where nothing's planted
Beside the rollerdrome and hot-dog stand—

Still Mystic lights the wake of Gods, still haunted
By the reversing moon: "Let me be clean,"
It cries and cries, but there are years between.

II

And I have stoned and swum and sculled them all:
Naked behind the birches—at the cove
Where Winthrop built a landing and a yawl
And tabloids found a famous corpse of love
Hacked small and parcelled into butcher's paper—
Joe La Conti stumbled on an old pauper

Dying of epilepsy or D.T.s,
And I came running naked to watch his fit.
We had to dress to run for the police.
But did we run for help or for the joy of it?
And who was dying at the sight of blood?
Weeks long we conjured its traces in the mud.

And there was no trace. Later, above the cattails,
A house frame grew, and another, and then another.
Our naked bank bled broken tiles and nails.
We made a raft and watched the alewives smother;
But there our play drank fever, and Willie Crosby
Went home from that dirty water and stayed to die.

III

So I know death is a dirty river
At the edge of history, through the middle of towns,
At the backs of stores, and under the cantilever
Stations of bridges, where the moon drowns
Pollution in its own illusion of light.
O rotten time, rot from my mind tonight!

Let me be richly lit in this one stir,
And where the Gods grew rich and positive
From their ruinous landing, I'll attend disaster
Like night birds over a wake, flying and alive
Above the shuttered house, and beautifully
Wheel on the wing, find food in flight, and be

Captured by light, drawn down and down and down
By moonshine, street lamps, windows, moving rays,
By all that shines in all the caved-in town
Where Mystic in the crazy moon outstays
The death of Gods, and makes a life of light—
That breaks, but calls a million birds to flight.

—JOHN CIARDI

N

THE NAKED AND THE NUDE

For me, the naked and the nude
(By lexicographers construed
As synonyms that should express
The same deficiency of dress
Or shelter) stand as wide apart
As love from lies, or truth from art.

Lovers without reproach will gaze
On bodies naked and ablaze;
The Hippocratic eye will see
In nakedness, anatomy;
And naked shines the Goddess when
She mounts her lion among men.

The nude are bold, the nude are sly
To hold each treasonable eye.
While draping, by a showman's trick,
Their dishabille in rhetoric,
They grin a mock-religious grin
Of scorn at those of naked skin.

The naked, therefore, who compete
Against the nude may know defeat,
Yet when they both together tread
The briary pastures of the dead,
By Gorgons with long whips pursued,
How naked go the sometime nude!

—ROBERT GRAVES

NAKED IN BORNEO

(FROM A PAINTING BY TOBIAS)

They wear air
or water like a skin,
their skin the smoothest suit.
Are tight and loose
as the leopard, or sudden
and still as the moccasin.
Their blouse is black

shadows of fronds
on a copper vest of sun.
Glossy rapids are
their teeth and eyes
beneath straight harsh blonds
of rained-on grain that thatch
their round head-huts.

Long thongs their bodies, bows
or canoes. Both tense and lax
their bodies, spears
they tool, caress, hoard, decorate
with cuts. Their fears
are their weapons. Coiled or
straight, they run up trees

and on jungle thorns; their feet
are their shoes, fierce hair
their hats that hold off sun's hate.
They glide, muscles of water
through water, dark oil-beads
pave their lashing
torsos. Are bare in air,

are wind-combed, armpit and groin;
are taut arrows turned sinuous reeds
for dancing on drumskin ground.
Rasped by the sun's tongue, then
        moon-licked
all their slick
moist feathered shafts
in the hammocks of tangled thighs

the silks of night plash among.
Their joys, their toys, are their chil-
        dren
who as kittens ride
their mother's neck, or wrestle
with the twins of her breasts
where she squats by the meal pot.
At hunter's naked side

little hunter stalks fix-eyed,
his miniature poison-dart
lifted, learning the game—
young pointer in the bush,
fish-diver in the river,
grave apprentice in the art
of magic pain

when the blood pines
to be let a little,
to sharpen the friction of Alive,
in the feckless skin
leave some slits and signs
that old spirit leaked out,
new spirit sneaked in.

—MAY SWENSON

NAPKIN AND STONE

Fire-kindled satellite,
Passing the bounds
Of the cold moon in flight
From the pool's hounds,
Midwife to ecstasy
Silver and thrilling free,
Where is your place of rest
Ending an aeon's quest,
Shot from the catalyst
Of the world's wounds?

Fast from this rock of earth
Spring waters run.
Here, till I bring to birth
Daughter or son,
How should I emulate
You in your loss of weight?
All those encircling rings
Fire into distance flings,
Touch not the hour that brings
Labor begun.

Darkness encloses light;
Light pushes free.
Brilliant, abounding night,
Think of this tree.
Swathed in the swaddling silk
Under galactic milk,
You that ascending fly
Through the transfigured sky,
When shall the infant lie
Safe on my knee?

Ponder the secret hearth,
Manger and cow,
You whose dynamic path
Crosses the Plough.
Sucked by unconscious night
Into the speed of light,
What can you know of this
Falling from Genesis
Into the pulse of bliss
Near to me now?

Wheel upon wheel in flight,
Whines the far sound.
Napkin and stone are white
In the moon's round.
Midwife to ecstasy

Silver and thrilling free,
While they conspire to break
Silence for wonder's sake,
Wonder itself I make—
Here it is found.

—VERNON WATKINS

NAPLES AGAIN

The hills yet hills, and still the yellow town
declines into the sea by particles.
Six years: so many grams of dust dispersed,
so many repetitions of the sky,
so many skins of spring sloughed off, and snows
melted, to move the dial of days
to February of a similar year,
myself to the same stance and place.

By the long bay I walked, where fishermen
of Mergellina thrash their crusted nets
in shallow water to shake loose the mud.
Where the balloonman piped, and the slow sea
smothered a colony of rocks with weeds
—abundant, rust-colored, and rank—
patterns of change and sameness filmed my mind
like oil slick in the pitted bank.

Six years, what have I never learned—like silt
to shake free or be shaken in good time?
Like the high, unaccommodating rock
to bear with dignity the yoke of grass?
Even the salt wash whispers in reproach;
see how insinuation speeds
my lightness to the limit of the beach,
beyond the rocks, beyond the weeds.

Here then the unsought accidence of place
and the false glass of nature warp me. Hills
borrow the furled brows of the lately dead,
the sky the wide eyes of the living. Bent
by the conviction of analogy,
the credulousness of a dumb thing,
the tired mind buckles and the stripped will
relaxes its questioning.

See with what unconcern the tides demesne
each to its niche: crayfish and pebble, shells

by the unshelled, and chip by parent block—
such as it is, the natural effect,
the disposition of all patiently
predictable as the sea,
undifferentiated, dumb. Silt, stones, and froth—
am I and all things less than these?

But the wind's wisdom comes too easy now,
and reason wriggles on its string like bait,
and again life is more than metaphor.
Up on the hill the starved and savage cats
swallow their nature to take milk at hand
and wail all night to charm it back.
Haphazard children in the shadowed slums
torture their narrow eyes with chalk

and beg in the great squares; and some men pay
and some will not; and there is no design.
I and the waterfront must draft our peace
if what I learn is not what the earth learns,
if what I doubt is all my discipline;
for earth persists, and in good time
—when I am the same silent element—
may set its simpler meaning over mine.

—ARTHUR FREEMAN

NATURA NATURANS

Veil upon veil,
Petal and shell and scale
The dancer of the whirling dance lets fall.

Visible veils the invisible
Reveal, conceal
In bodies that most resemble
The fleeting mind of nature never still.

A young princess,
Sealed in the perfect signature of what she was,
With her grave lips of silent dust imparts a mystery
Hidden two thousand years under the Appian Way—

A frond in the coal,
An angel traced upon a crumbling wall,
Empty chrysalids of that bright ephemerid the soul.

—KATHLEEN RAINE

NATURE

A cycle sings
Within the wings;
The wings inscribe the wild.
The small birds sing from flower and stalk
While, from his stump, the sparrow hawk
Strikes at the sparrow's child.

Within a wave,
The sea's wet grave
Receives the shrinking lands;
The wet nurse gathers to her breast
A hillock or an Everest
Dissolving in her glands.

In setting forth,
Man's pole was north;
Polaris marked the air.
But time, while man evolves from ape,
Will beat the Dipper out of shape
And point his pole elsewhere.

From hawks to seas
To galaxies
All Nature is pursual;
But men, whose brothers love each other
(As Cain loved Abel), find their mother
Unfathomably cruel.

And Nature spares
No glance, no tears
For those who loved her best.
They thought themselves her secret child
But found themselves beguiled, beguiled
By her indifferent breast.

—WALTER STONE

NATURE STUDY, AFTER DUFY

When a friend accused him [Dufy] of playing fast and loose
with nature, he replied: "But nature, my dear Sir, is only an
hypothesis."—*From the section on "Fauvism" by Maurice Ray-
nal in "The History of Modern Painting."*

I must remember to dismiss
These wintry skies that seem to me
Not gray, like an hypothesis,
But silver, like reality—
This arguable wind that stirs
So plausibly the conifers.

From postulates of days, unwary,
By seeming snows preoccupied,
I have conjectured January
And whiteness in the countryside,
Presumed the starlings in the holly.
I must remember now as folly

What earlier instants of surmise?
(The earth, one green and passing
      minute;
The poplar, gold before my eyes;
The summer beech with sunlight in it—
These that by leaflessness of bough,
By empty fields, are proven now

Untenable, as soon must be,
With the first inference of spring,
This crystal world, this theory?)
I must be quick in questioning
The look of April, after this,
When it, too, is hypothesis.

—Helen Bevington

THE NAUGHTY PREPOSITION

I lately lost a preposition;
    It hid, I thought, beneath my chair;
And angrily I cried, "Perdition!
    Up from out of in under there!"

Correctness is my vade mecum,
    And straggling phrases I abhor,
And yet I wondered, "What should he come
    Up from out of in under for?"

—Morris Bishop

NEARING WINTER

Two pairs of mallards, tandem,
swim the pond in a soundless
march. The males in white collars
search through the dusk of rain,
their motives cold as silence,
their hens brown as November drizzle.

Of such adroit inconsequence,
which is easier to say:

that time stoops down from the affairs
of suns and planets, from the hush
of light-years, to become four feathers

balancing on an eyedrop,
or that this moment listens
to forgive an earth that shakes so
with savage important noise?

—Ernest Sandeen

A NECESSARY MIRACLE

This shall be called the laying on of hands,
For only touch gives healing
After acquittal.
Words may not succor or belittle,
And never more may body comfort body,
But gentle fingers can erase
An old malignancy,
Cell, as it were, by cell,
And touch can work the necessary miracle.
This shall be called the laying on of hands
And a farewell.

—Eda Lou Walton

NEWS FROM THE CABIN

I

Hairy was here.
He hung on a sumac seed pod.
Part of his double tail hugged the crimson
    scrotum under cockscomb leaves—
    or call it blushing lobster claw, that swatch—
    a toothy match to Hairy's red skull patch.
Cried *peek!* Beaked it, chiselled the drupe.
His nostril I saw, slit in a slate whistle.
White-black dominoes clicked in his wings.
Bunched beneath the dangle he heckled with holes,
    bellysack soft, eye a brad, a red-flecked
    mallet his ball-peen head, his neck its haft.

II

Scurry was here.
He sat up like a six-inch bear;
    rocked on the porch with me—
    brought his own chair, his chow-haired tail.
Ate a cherry I threw.
Furry paunch, birchbark-snowy. Pinecone-brown back,
    a jacket with sleeves to the digits.
Sat put, pert, neat, in his suit and his seat, for a minute,
    a frown between snub ears, bulb-eyed head
    toward me sideways, chewed.
Rocked, squeaked. Stored the stone in his cheek.

Finished, fell to all fours, a little roan couch;
    flurried paws loped him off, prone-bodied,
    tail turned torch, sail, scarf.

III

Then Slicker was here.
Dipped down—cobalt and turquoise brushes
    fresh as paint. Gripped a pine tassel,
    folded his flaunts, parted his pointed nib, and scrawled
    jeeah! on the air.
Japanned so smooth, his head peak and all his shaft
    (harsh taunts from that dovey shape, soft tints)—
    nape and chin black-splintered, quill tip white-lashed.
Javelin-bird, he slurred his color;
    left his ink-bold word here; flashed off.
Morning prints his corvine noise elsewhere,
    while that green toss still quivers with his equipoise.

IV

And Supple was here.
Lives nearby at the stump.
Trickled out from under, when the sun struck there.
Mud-and-silver-licked, his length—a single spastic muscle—
    slid over stones and twigs to a snuggle of roots, and hid.
I followed that elastic—loose
    unicolored knot, a noose he made as if unconscious—
    until my shadow touched him. Half his curd
    shuddered, the rest lay chill.
I stirred. The ribbon raised a loop;
    its end stretched, then cringed like an udder;
    a bifid tongue, his only rapid, whirred
    in the vent; vertical pupils lit his hood.
That part, a groping finger, hinged, stayed upright.
Indicated what? That I stood
    in his light? I left the spot.

                                   —MAY SWENSON

NEWS FROM THE HOUSE

Love, I have warmed the car,
the snow between us lies

shaking at the sound of my wheels
pawing the ground, my radio

snorting through its shimmering
nostrils.
            I

have command of the seats,
the trunk has been blessed

by Eskimos, and the hood
(or British Bonnet) anointed
with a stern steam.
                          There

is no time like the present,
send for me.

                  Love, over
what dark miles do I come, shall I,
dark

as the wind round the house
I lie in,

the great bed, the long
night draining me,
                          Love,
in what season may it, tell me
the green date mice may

swear by, and the vast
branches spread dizzy those
distances my eyes too well
see through this winter. What
I have done that you

weep, what you have
worked that I
pace continually

this most sad house, meals
of its emptiness in every
corner, that the wind
                          sounds,

the house refusing to be musical,

in the sheerest dark. Tell me
the previous times, hear my

greed for you. Under it all
and the cold ground
                          we
sleeping you said, and ending,
the April waking, that trap
sprung.
            Love, in my
solitude my hands
garrisoned, hear them

nightly beside me muttering
of freedoms they were

warm in. How
on these nights the house
refusing to be musical
                          I

lie stone, seed-
cold, kernel of this
husked house, the white
miles between us

coiled soft as roads inside
me, my walls the blood
of rabbits, the bathroom
                          a lodge for hunters,
the bath

of fur and stained.
                          Love,

in what season, tell

me, I may unwrap this house
from me, these walls

remove, from my pockets
these stairs, drink

such dark no more
        nor wear ever

this most sad hat of shadows. Tell

me, make me instructions,
send them like news
from a dairy.
            I will feed

no more on this print and milk,
wait, crouch, mad in the sad house

refusing to be musical,
though I sing it each night the notes
my longest body is learning.

                                    —MICHAEL DENNIS BROWNE

NEXT DAY

Moving from Cheer to Joy, from Joy to All,
I take a box
And add it to my wild rice, my Cornish game hens.
The slacked or shorted, basketed, identical
Food-gathering flocks
Are selves I overlook. Wisdom, said William James,

Is learning what to overlook. And I am wise
If that is wisdom.
Yet somehow, as I buy All from these shelves
And the boy takes it to my station wagon,
What I've become
Troubles me even if I shut my eyes.

When I was young and miserable and pretty
And poor, I'd wish
What all girls wish: to have a husband,
A house and children. Now that I'm old, my wish
Is womanish:
That the boy putting groceries in my car

See me. It bewilders me he doesn't see me.
For so many years
I was good enough to eat: the world looked at me
And its mouth watered. How often they have undressed me,
The eyes of strangers!
And, holding their flesh within my flesh, their vile

Imaginings within my imagining,
I too have taken
The chance of life. Now the boy pats my dog
And we start home. Now I am good.

The last mistaken,
Ecstatic, accidental bliss, the blind

Happiness that, bursting, leaves upon the palm
Some soap and water—
It was so long ago, back in some Gay
Twenties, Nineties, I don't know. . . . Today I miss
My lovely daughter
Away at school, my sons away at school,

My husband away at work—I wish for them.
The dog, the maid,
And I go through the sure unvarying days
At home in them. As I look at my life,
I am afraid
Only that it will change, as I am changing:

I am afraid, this morning, of my face.
It looks at me
From the rearview mirror with the eyes I hate,
The smile I hate. Its plain, lined look
Of gray discovery
Repeats to me, "You're old." That's all, I'm old.

And yet I'm afraid, as I was at the funeral
I went to yesterday.
My friend's cold made-up face, granite among its flowers,
Her undressed, operated-on, dressed body
Were my face and body.
As I think of her I hear her telling me

How young I seem; I *am* exceptional;
I think of all I have.
But really no one is exceptional,
No one has anything, I'm anybody,
I stand beside my grave
Confused with my life, that is commonplace and solitary.

—RANDALL JARRELL

A NICE PART OF TOWN

One would never assume, from the toy bulldogs taking the air
Or the doorman's smart salute at the entrance to the hotel

Or the attendant pushing the elderly invalid in the wheel chair
Or the pedestrian with the cornflower in his coat lapel

Or the general ease or the attention paid to the fingernails
Or the burden of the conversation on the slatted green bench

Or the seeming safety that guards the children and their sand pails
Or the pick-and-shovel men lunching in the open sewer trench,

That under the feet of these people the crust of the known world breaks
And the transformation of the familiar into something monstrous has begun.

Because they have governed or been governed by the blank check
And the French telephone and the memo scribbled on the small pad

Or have seen the ocean only as advertised from the steamer's deck
And the antitoxin has always been close at hand and so easily had

And the intricate and combined services of power and heat and light
Have fed them through tubes and mains for so long and so well,

They cannot conceive now of a world powerless and without light
Or a world in which, when the button is pressed, they shall not hear the bell.

So the uninjured imagination, limited to a tabloid's idea of disaster
And perhaps luckily seeing only what the camera allows to be seen—

Something with smoke in it and possibly flame and fallen timbers and plaster
But the firemen there on time and the brief caption describing the scene—

Walks out into the safe afternoon, where charged ferocities hang,
Full of real death and enormous explosions that actually go bang.

                                                    —ALFRED HAYES

NIGHT JOURNEY

Now as the train bears west,
Its rhythm rocks the earth,
And from my Pullman berth
I stare into the night
While others take their rest.
Bridges of iron lace,
A suddenness of trees,
A lap of mountain mist
All cross my line of sight,
Then a bleak wasted place,
And a lake below my knees.
Full on my neck I feel
The straining at a curve;
My muscles move with steel,
I wake in every nerve.
I watch a beacon swing
From dark to blazing bright;
We thunder through ravines
And gullies washed with light.
Beyond the mountain pass
Mist deepens on the pane;
We rush into a rain
That rattles double glass.
Wheels shake the roadbed stone,
The pistons jerk and shove,
I stay up half the night
To see the land I love.

                                                    —THEODORE ROETHKE

THE NIGHT MIRROR

What it showed was always the same—
A vertical panel with him in it
Being a horrible bit of movement
At the edge of knowledge, overhanging
The canyons of nightmare. And when the last
Glimpse was enough—his grandmother,
Say, with a blood-red face, rising
From her Windsor chair in the warm lamplight
To tell him something—he would scramble up,
Waiting to hear himself shrieking, and gain
The ledge of the world, his bed, lit by
The pale rectangle of window, eclipsed
By a dark shape, but a shape that moved
And saw and knew and mistook its reflection
In the tall panel on the closet door
For itself. The silver corona of moonlight
That gloried his glimpsed head was enough
To send him back into silences (choosing
Fear in those chasms below), to reject
Freedom of wakeful seeing, believing,
And feeling, for peace and the bondage to horrors
Welling up only from deep within
That dark planet head, spinning beyond
The rim of the night mirror's range, huge
And cold, on the pillow's dark side.

—JOHN HOLLANDER

NIGHT THOUGHT

Trying to fall asleep
is like trying to catch
yourself unawares, or trying
not to think of something,
or trying to fall
in love or out of love.
Some things will not yield.
Trying not to think of something
is like trying to fall
asleep, or trying to catch
yourself unawares, or trying
to fall in or out of love
with someone who will not yield.
Yielding is like not thinking
of something or someone,
and without yielding
there is no catching yourself
unawares, and no falling
in love or out of love,
and trying to yield
is like trying to fall
asleep, or trying not to.

—GERALD JONAS

NIGHT THOUGHTS IN AGE

Light, that out of the west looked back once more
Through lids of cloud, has closed a sleepy eye;
The heaven of stars bends over me its silence,
A harp through which the wind of time still whispers
Music some hand has hushed but left there trembling—
Conceits of an aging man who lies awake
Under familiar rafters, in this leafy,
Bird-singing, haunted, green ancestral spot
Where time has made such music! For often now,
In this belovèd country whose coastal shores
Look seaward, without limit, to the south—
Land of flung spume and spray, sea winds and voices,
Where the gull rides the gale on equal wing
With motionless body and downward-bending head,
Where, in midsummer days, offshore, the dolphin
Hurdles the water with arching leap and plunge—
I meditate, lying awake, alone,
On the sea's voice and time's receding music,
Felt ebbing in the heart and shrunken vein—
How time, that takes us all, shall at the last,
In taking us, take the whole world we are dreaming:
Sun, wind, and sea, whisper of rain at night,
The young, hollow-cheeked moon, the clouds of evening
Drifting in a great solitude—all these
Shall time take away, surely, and the face
From which the eyes of love look out at us
In this brief world, this horror-haunted kingdom
Of beauty and of longing and of terror,
Of phantoms and illusion, of appearance
And disappearance, magic of legerdemain,
Trick of the prestidigitator's wand—
The huge phantasmagoria we are dreaming—
This shall time take from us, and take forever,
When we are taken by that receding music.
O marvel of things, fabulous dream, too soon,
Too soon will the wild blood cry out and death
Quell, with one blow, the inscrutable fantasy!
Shall prayer change this? Youth is the hour for prayer,
That has so much to pray for; a man's life,
Lived howsoever, is a long reconcilement
To the high, lonely, unforgiving truth,
Which will not change for his or any prayer,
Now or hereafter; in that reconcilement
Lies all of wisdom. Age is the hour for praise,
Praise that is joy, praise that is acquiescence,

Praise that is adoration and gratitude
For all that has been given and not been given.
Night flows on. The wind, that all night through
Quickened the treetops with a breath of ocean,
Veers inland, falls away, and the sea's voice,
Learned in lost childhood, a remembered music,
By day or night, through love, through sleep, through dream,
Still breathing its perpetual benediction,
Has dwindled to a sigh. By the west window,
In the soft dark, the leaves of the sycamore
Stir gently, rustle, and are still, are listening
To a silence that is music. The old house
Is full of ghosts, dear ghosts on stair and landing,
Ghosts in chamber and hall; garden and walk
Are marvellous with ghosts, where so much love
Dwelt for a little while and made such music,
Before it too was taken by the tide
That takes us all, of time's receding music.
Oh, all is music! All has been turned to music!
All that is vanished has been turned to music!
And these familiar rafters that have known
The child, the young man, and the man, now shelter
The aging man who lies here, listening, listening—
All night, in a half dream, I have lain here listening.

—JOHN HALL WHEELOCK

NIGHT WALK

Flintlike, her feet struck
such a racket of echoes from the steely street,
tacking in moon-blued crooks from the black
stone-built town, that she heard the quick air ignite
its tinder and shake

a firework of echoes from wall
to wall of the dark, dwarfed cottages.
But the echoes died at her back as the walls
gave way to fields and the incessant seethe of grasses
riding in the full

of the moon, manes to the wind,
tireless, tied, as a moon-bound sea
moves on its root. Though a mist-wraith wound
　up from the fissured valley and hung shoulder-high
　　ahead, it fattened

to no family-featured ghost,
nor did any word body with a name
the blank mood she walked in. Once past
　the dream-peopled village, her eyes entertained no dream,
　　and the sandman's dust

lost lustre under her footsoles.
The long wind, paring her person down
to a pinch of flame, blew its burdened whistle
　in the whorl of her ear, and, like a scooped-out pumpkin crown,
　　her head cupped the babel.

All the night gave her, in return
for the paltry gift of her bulk and the beat
of her heart, was the humped, indifferent iron
　of its hills, and its pastures bordered by black stone set
　　on black stone. Barns

guarded broods and litters
behind shut doors; the dairy herds
knelt in the meadow, mute as boulders;
　sheep drowsed stoneward in their tussocks of wool; and birds,
　　twig-sleeping, wore

granite ruffs, their shadows
the guise of leaves. The whole landscape
loomed absolute, as the antique world was
　once, in its earliest sway of lymph and sap,
　　unaltered by eyes,

enough to snuff the quick
of her small heat out. But before the weight
of stones and hills of stones could break
　her down to mere quartz grit in that stony light,
　　she turned back.

—Sylvia Plath

NO MOON, NO STAR

Sky is such a softness, is such dark,
Mat as the pelt of a black panther is
In his den's night. Under the mat soft black
Flows—a moving mirror of that pure dark—
The river. Sparse lights debate or affirm a farther shore.
But darkness is at flood where, slow, black moves upon black
Yet lifts two lanterns
A boat's length apart; they kindle the water
To brief life, moving down the river.
And vanish.

—BABETTE DEUTSCH

NORTH PHILADELPHIA, TRENTON, AND NEW YORK

Thin steel in paired lines, forever mated, cuts,
forks, and crosses—catches blue light, threads a station and a yard,
finds a bridge across the winter Schuylkill lithograph,
slips by the winter boardings, the chimney pots, the dirty
windowpanes and chimneys, cut aslant for factories
on either side.

The prison steps into your window square, runs beside,
and drops away. The nunnery, the monastery after it,
fleetly shine, dip, recover, and are gone,
as houses in precise, astonished rows come out,
solidify, stare, and are politely wheeled away.
Under bridge and under wheel the Delaware floats down
ice cakes, watched by the gilt glitter of the Capitol.

North, now: Sky change on earth angle altering,
color of iron blooms on spinneys, Breughel snow, and brown tree.

In North Jersey—flat, endlessly
arranged in silver gas cylinders, shine of plane wing—deep,
dirty, and deliberate rivers grope between meadows
where the catkins keep good order and the posters march beside you,
and the turnpike, loping on legs of iron, stays to race you,
and the hill with houses slides to meet you.

The tunnel: You are gone,
and the bright winter sky as from a tube of indigo is squeezed away.

—RICHMOND LATTIMORE

NOTES FOR THE CHART IN 306

The bubbles soar and die in the sterile bottle
Hanging upside down on the bedside lamppost.
Food and drink
Seep quietly through the needle strapped to the hand.
The arm welcomes the sting of mosquito hypodermic—
Conveyor of morphia, the comforter.
Here's drowsiness, here's lassitude, here's nothingness,
Sedation *in excelsis.*
The clouded mind would stray into oblivion
But for the grackle-squawk of the box in the hall,
The insistent call for a faceless goblin horde
Of sorcerers, vivisectionists, body-snatchers.
Dr. Polyp is summoned,
Dr. Gobbo and Dr. Prodigy,
Dr. Tortoise, Dr. Sawdust, and Dr. Mary Poppins,
La belle dame sans merci.
Now it's Dr. Bandarlog and Dr. Bacteria,
And last of all, the terrifying one,
Dodger Thomas.
And there is no lock on the door.
On the third day, the goblins are driven off
To the operating room beneath the hill.
Dr. Vandeleur routs gibbering Bandarlog,
Bacteria flees before swarthy Dr. Bagderian.
Sawdust and Polyp yield to Saunders and Pollitt,
And it's Porter instead of Tortoise who knocks at the door.
He will test the blood, not drain it.
The eerie impostors are gone, all gone but one—
Dodger Thomas.
I know he is lurking somewhere in a shadow.
Dodger Thomas.
I've never met him, but old friends have.
I know his habit:
He enters without knocking.

                                               —OGDEN NASH

NOTES ON A LIFE TO BE LIVED

I STARGAZING

The stars are only a backdrop for
The human condition, the stars
Are brilliant above the black spruces,
And fall comes on. Wind

Does not move in the star stillness, wind
Is afraid of itself, as you have been afraid in
Those moments when destruction and revelation
Have spat at each other like cats, and the mirror
Showed no breath, ha, ha, and the wind,

Far off in arctic starlight, is afraid
To breathe, and waits, huddled in
Sparse blackness of spruce, black glitter in starlight, in
A land, north, where snow already is, and waits;

And the girl is saying, "You do not look
At the stars," for I did not look at
The stars, for I know they are there, know
That if I look at the stars, I

Will have to live over again all I have lived
In the years I looked at stars and
Cried out, "O reality!" The stars
Love me. I love them. I wish they

Loved God, too. I truly wish that.

II DRAGON TREE

The faucet drips all night, and will not stop.
A cat, *in coitu*, squalls like Hell's honeymoon.
A child is sick. The doctor coughs.
Do you feel, in your heart, that life has turned out as once
                                        you expected?

Spring comes early; ice
Groans in the gorge; water, black, swirls
Into foam like lace white in fury. The gorge boulders boom.
When you hear, in darkness, the gorge boulders boom, does your
                                heart say, "No comment"?

Geese pass in dawn light, and the news
From Asia is bad, and the Belgians sure mucked up
The Congo. Human flesh is yet eaten there, often uncooked.
Have you sat on a hillside at sunset and eaten the flesh of
                                your own heart?

The world drives at you like a locomotive
In an archaic movie. It whirls off the screen,
It is on you, the iron. You hear, in that silence, your heart.
Have you thought that the headlines are only the image of your
                                own heart?

Some study compassion. Some, confusing
Personal pathology with the logic of history, jump
Out of windows. Some walk with God, some by rivers, at twilight.
Have you tried just to sit with the children and tell a tale
                                  ending in laughter?

Oh, tell the tale, and laugh, and let
God laugh—for your heart is the dragon tree, the root
Feels, in earth-dark, the abrasive scale, the coils
Stir. But look! The new leaf, in sunlight, flaps
                     gilt. Birds sing.

III COMPOSITION IN GOLD AND RED-GOLD

Between the event and the word, golden
The sunlight falls, between
The brown brook's braiding and the mountain it
Falls, in pitiless plenitude, and every leaf
On the ruined apple tree is gold, and the apples all
Gold, too, especially those

On the ground. The gold of apples
That have fallen flushes to flame, but
Gold is the flame. Gold
Goes red-gold, and the scene:

A chipmunk is under the apple tree, sits up
Among gold apples, is
Golden in gold light. The chipmunk
Wriggles its small black nose
In the still center of the world of light.

The hair of the little girl is as brown-gold as
Brook water braiding in sunlight.

The cat, crouching by the gray stone, is gold, too.
The tail of the cat, half Persian, weaves from side to side,
In infinite luxury, gold plume
Of seaweed in that tide of light.
That is a motion that puts
The world to sleep.

The eyes of the cat are gold, and

I want to sleep. But
The event: the tiny

Shriek unstitches the afternoon, the girl
Screams, the sky
Tingles crystalline like a struck wineglass, and you
Feel the salt thickening, like grit, in your secret
                                blood. Afterward

There is a difference in the quality of silence.
Every leaf, gold, hangs motionless on the tree, but
There is a difference in the quality of
Motionlessness: unverbed, unverved, they
Hang. On the last day will the sun
Explode? Or simply get too tired?

The chipmunk lies gold among
The gold apples. It
Is prone and totally relaxed like ripe
Fruit fallen, and,
Upon closer inspection, you can see
The faint smear of flame-gold at the base
Of the skull. This effect
Completes the composition.

The little girl
Holds the cat in her arms,
Crooning, "Baby, oh, baby." She weeps under
The powerful flood of gold light.

Somewhere, in the shade of alders, a trout
Hangs steady, head against a current like ice.

The eagle I had earlier seen climbing
The light above the mountain is
Now beyond sight.
                          —ROBERT PENN WARREN

NOTE TO WANG WEI

How could you be so happy, now some thousand years
dishevelled, puffs of dust?
It leaves me uneasy at last,
your poems tease me to the verge of tears,
and your fate. It makes me think.
It makes me long for mountains & blue waters.

Makes me wonder how much to allow.
(I'm reconfirming, God of bolts & bangs,
of fugues & bucks, whose rocket burns & sings.)
I wish we could meet for a drink
in a "freedom from ten thousand matters."
Be dust myself pretty soon; not now.

—JOHN BERRYMAN

NOVEMBER POPPIES

I walked with you this eleventh in the coppice,
Harry, to see what late blooms we could find.
We combed the grass for the last eyes of autumn
Opening to see the leaves fall in the wind.
But the only flowers I found were November poppies
Springing all over the sad mud of my mind.

Three years before my birth that seed was scattered
By a hand of bones, broadcast on a foreign plot.
I grew up in the rumors of that sowing,
All the red cries they cropped; like weeds they shot
And through my growing dreams they were always blowing,
With paper petals like telegrams people had got.

They were centered with the yellowing photo faces
Of musical Uncle George and Uncle Hugh,
The dasher with his leg over the traces;
A child, I heard them talked of, never knew.
They stood in serge, in silver frames, on pianos.
The youngest of them now would be sixty-two

Only, a man I could talk with, lunch with, stay with,
And would have bred me cousins. By that default
I grew up friendless, in a two-minute silence.
On knotted roots like barbed wire out of the vault
The poor gnarled poppies waver; if you break them,
Not sleepy juices but what wakes with salt.

No matter what blooms may fail, it is never those ones.
We picked no posy at all, the year gone sour;
But all over England, dotted round shire memorials,
In back-yard runs or under the noble tower,
Every November the thin red legions are mustered
And they flower like clockwork in her bitterest hour.

—HILARY CORKE

NOVEMBER THROUGH A GIANT COPPER BEECH

This almost bare tree is racing,
taut in the wind, leaves flaring,
jet fire fed by a hurrying
keen whistling bird, against

hundred-limbed elephant branches
steadied in wrinkled gray molten
antediluvian skin
wrapped tight to stay where it is.

Think of sheer endlessness, beauty
patient in form, forever
uncrumbled between time's nickering
teeth—oh brutal necessity!

Think of the still and the flowing—
Heraclitus's *everything passes*,
the one-eyed conviction against
the rockheaded *everything dozes*.

On this bleary white afternoon,
are there fires lit up in heaven
against such faking of quickness
and light, such windy discoursing?

While November numbly collapses,
this beech tree, heavy as death
on the lawn, braces for throat-
cutting ice, bandaging snow.

—Edwin Honig

NOW DOES OUR WORLD DESCEND

now does our world descend
the path to nothingness
(cruel now cancels kind;
friends turn to enemies)
therefore lament, my dream
and don a doer's doom

create is now contrive;
imagined, merely known
(freedom: what makes a slave)
therefore, my life, lie down
and more by most endure
all that you never were

hide, poor dishonoured mind
who thought yourself so wise;
and much could understand
concerning no and yes:

if they've become the same
it's time you unbecame

where climbing was and bright
is darkness and to fall
(now wrong's the only right
since brave are cowards all)
therefore despair, my heart
and die into the dirt

but from this endless end
of briefer each our bliss—
where seeing eyes go blind
(where lips forget to kiss)
where everything's nothing
—arise, my soul; and sing

—E. E. Cummings

O

OBIT ON PARNASSUS

Death before forty's no bar. Lo!
  These had accomplished their feats:
Chatterton, Burns, and Kit Marlowe,
  Byron and Shelley and Keats.

Death, the eventual censor,
  Lays for the forties, and so
Took off Jane Austen and Spenser,
  Stevenson, Hood, and poor Poe.

You'll leave a better-lined wallet
  By reaching the end of your rope
After fifty, like Shakespeare and Smollett,
  Thackeray, Dickens, and Pope.

Try for the sixties—but say, boy,
  That's when the tombstones were built on
Butler and Sheridan, the play boy,
  Arnold and Coleridge and Milton.

Three score and ten—the tides rippling
  Over the bar; slip the hawser.
Godspeed to Clemens and Kipling,
  Swinburne and Browning and Chaucer.

Some staved the debt off but paid it
  At eighty—that's after the law.
Wordsworth and Tennyson made it,
  And Meredith, Hardy, and Shaw.

But, Death, while you make up your quota,
  Please note this confession of candor—
That I wouldn't give an iota
  To linger till ninety, like Landor.

—F. Scott Fitzgerald

OF HISTORY MORE LIKE MYTH

(THE CONQUEST OF PERU)

They guided birds and came to hear their story
At that astounding hour sacred to birds
When mirthful on light's nourishment they go
Wild with tournaments of cries upon the air—
At wing feats are as angels, light as flowers
That glide and skate the upbeats and whirl down
With that velocity that only air allows.
They dreaded most the still hour when all went,
Cut of a sudden by some quick response
To that which flares no longer bird-blood up.

They guided birds and were at one with birds,
At one with lizards gloating in the sun,
Feverish and dry, their little throats swollen,
Nor had time bells nor wheels, nor did they count
Sands that ran through the glass relentlessly.
Time simply set the sun and swung with seas;
In the rare mountains it was not at all,
Nor had the self a shadow save of wings.

And was their life an abundance as of birds?
Had they for blood a bird-blood sad and gay?
We do not know. What questions caged
Birds in their thickets till they sang no more?
The wiry air was free with its whole light,
The sun a potency they understood,
And by it got great harvests and as well
From earth a curious sun-like thing
From which they made gold gardens for their One,
And disks to mirror the round sun's ruddy head,
And light was in this instance fixed and firm.

And time was as the shadows of the birds
Declining and arising in their play.
In time they learned by study of the stars
To read of those first waters of immensity
By which unfevered stars arose, and birds;
And patient seeds they set flowered into grain.
The birds were masters of transparency
And they were heavy with a thing not born.

Until those enemies and foes of birds,
Self-seeking, ravening, and mad for gold,
Thrust through the thickets of the long blue days.

Then all fell down: the birds in headlong droves,
The realm divided, taken prisoner,
The gold brought in to fill a room or more
To please another One back home,
Bird-self sent underground, bird-blood
In harness, bird-blood taxed
To pay an invalid thing, and stillness came—
The thing they'd learned to dread, and reigned.

—JEAN GARRIGUE

OLD AMUSEMENT PARK

BEFORE IT BECAME LA GUARDIA AIRPORT

Hurry, worry, unwary
visitor, never vary
    the pressure till nearly bat-blind.
    A predicament so dire could not
    occur in this rare spot—

where crowds flock to the tramcar
rattling greenish caterpillar
    as bowling-ball thunder
    quivers the air. The park's elephant
    slowly lies down aslant;

pygmy replica then rides
the mound the back provides.
    Jet black, a furry pony sits
    down like a dog, has an innocent air—
    no tricks—the best act there.

It's all like the never-ending
Ferris-wheel ascending
    picket-fenced pony-rides (ten cents).
    A businessman, the pony-paddock boy
    locks his equestrian toy—

flags flying, fares collected,
shooting gallery neglected—
    half-official, half-sequestered,
    limber-slouched against a post,
    and tells a friend what matters least.

It's the old park in a nutshell,
like its tame-wild carrousel—
  the exhilarating peak
    when the triumph is reflective
    and confusion, retroactive.
                        —MARIANNE MOORE

AN OLD FIELD MOWED

My loud machine for making hay
Mutters about our work today;
Through bushes and small trees it
    flails—
Blueberry, sumac, cherry, bay.

I lay the little woods in swales
And burn them as the daylight fails,
For no surviving horse or cow
Is fed such crazy salad bales.

They fall like jackstraws, anyhow,
Or like the forest, trunk and bough,

That harder hands and will than these
Burned once, where it is meadow
    now.

I side with meadow against trees
Because this woodsmoke freights the
    breeze
With ghosts and ghostly woods—
    though both
Would find us puny enemies,
Second growth and second growth.
                        —WILLIAM MEREDITH

OLD GRAMOPHONE RECORDS

(DISCOVERED IN AN OLD ALBUM AT CORSHAM COURT, ENGLAND)

On these ancient discs, smooth-backed, severe,
And thick as slates, we trace the grooves
Our grandparents' needles pricked, and hear—
How far away!—the hoarse echoes of their Edwardian loves.

O "Songs Round the Piano"! Edison Bell! His Master's Voice!
Those were the days when, unscratched still, with well-bred style
The plush-hung, stiff-lipped lieder singer's choice
Vibrato matched her rolling eye, her bust, her top-note smile.

Here are the absurdity and brass-band charm
Of Auber, "Zanetta" Overture; and Meyerbeer,
The march from "Le Prophète;" "Jerusalem
The Golden," chorused by the Mixed Church Choir.

A gloomy contralto, Mme. L. Dews,
Neighs, moos, and bleats above a quailing
Pianoforte accompaniment in "The Promise
Of Life" and "Three Fishers Went Sailing."

Mr. John Harrison (tenor) renders
"I Know a Lovely Garden" (the composer
Guy d'Hardelot—a *lady* to those in the know) and the splendors
And miseries of "A Love Song" by Kaiser.

Bel canto Caruso! Karl Jörn (Kgl. Hofopernsänger)
Nobly delivers, with a voice like velvet and gold braid,
The "Preislied" from the "Meistersinger."
Mme. Amy Castles gives us Gounod's "Serenade."

The darling of the musicale, Dame Nellie Melba,
Promises, from her gold-signed salmon label, "Caro Nome."
Then, in a lingering farewell, the same divine and only diva,
Emotional and rapt, laments the "Old Folks at Home."

Hurrah! The spluttering sound box, big as a samovar,
The exotic gold-and-orange trumpet, like a hothouse plant,
Bawl out "Pale Hands I Loved Beside the Shalimar;"
Patti in "La Calesera" screams; a silver band thumps out von Suppé's "Peasant."

We smile, for we cannot explain the sadness these voices cast.
And the turntable turns on a ghost of the ghosts of the past.

—JAMES KIRKUP

OLD PAINTINGS ON ITALIAN WALLS

Who could have thought that men and women could feel,
With consciousness so delicate, such tender secret joy?
With finger-tips of touch as fine as music,
They greet one another on viols of painted gold
Attuned to harmonies of world with world.
They sense, with inward look and breath withheld,
The stir of intangible presences
Upon the threshold of the human heart alighting—
Angels winged with air, with transparent light,
Archangels with wings of fire and faces veiled.
Their eyes gleam with wisdom radiant from an invisible sun.

Others contemplate the mysteries of sorrow:
Some have carried the stigmata, themselves icons
Depicting a passion no man as man can know,
We being ignorant of what we do;
And painted wounded hands are by the same knowledge formed
Beyond the ragged ache that flesh can bear
And we with blunted mind and senses dulled endure.

Giotto's compassionate eyes, rapt in sympathy of grief,
See the soul's wounds that hate has given to love,
And those that love must bear
With the spirit that suffers always and everywhere.

Those painted shapes stilled in perpetual adoration
Behold in visible form invisible essences
That hold their gaze entranced through centuries; and we
In true miraculous icons may see still what they see,
Though the sacred lineaments grow faint, the outlines crumble,
And the golden heavens grow dim
Where the Pantocrator shows in vain wounds once held precious.
Paint and stone will not hold them to our world
When those who once cast their bright shadows on those walls
Have faded from our ken, we from their knowledge fallen.

—KATHLEEN RAINE

THE OLD ROOM

I am in the old room across from the synagogue
a dead chief hangs in the wallpaper
he is shrinking into the patch of street light
with its waves and nests and in the silence that follows
his death
the parade is forming again
with the street car for its band
it is forming I hear the shuffling the whispers
the choking then the grinding starts off
slowly as ice melting
they will pass by the house

closed ranks attached to the iron trolley
dragged on their backs
the black sleeves the fingers waving like banners
I am forbidden to look
but the faces are wrapped except for the eyes
darkness wells from the bandages
spreads
its loaves and fishes while on the curbs
the police the citizens
of all ages beat the muffled street with bars

what if I call *It is not me* will it stop
what if I raise an arm
to stop it
I raise an arm the whole arm stays white
dry as a beach

little winds play over it
a sunny and a pleasant place I hold it
out it leaves me it goes toward them
the man in charge is a friend of the family
he smiles when he sees it he takes its hand
he gives it its bar
it drops it
I am forbidden to look

I am in the old room across from the stone star
the moon is climbing in gauze
the street is empty
except for the dark liquid running
in the tracks of ice
trying to call
W*ait*
but the wires are taken up with the election
there is a poll at the corner I am not to go in
but I can look in the drugstore window
where the numbers of the dead change all night on the wall
what if I vote *It is not me* will they revive
I go in my father has voted for me
I say no no I will vote in my own name
I vote and the number leaps again on the wall

I am in the old room across from the night
the long scream is about to blossom
that is rooted in flames
if I called *It is not me* would it reach
through the bells

—W. S. MERWIN

THE OMELET OF A. MACLEISH

I

And the mist: and the rain in the west: and the wind steady:
There were elms in that place: and graven inflexible laws:
Men of Yale: and the shudder of Tap Day: the need for a man to
  make headway

MacLeish
breaks an
egg for his
omelet.

Winning a way through the door in the windowless walls:
And the poems that came easy and sweet with a blurring of Masefield
(The same that I later denied): a young man smooth but raw

Eliot alarmed me at first: but my later abasement:
And the clean sun of France: and the freakish but beautiful fashion:
Striped bathhouses bright on the sand: Anabase and The Waste Land:

He puts
plovers' eggs
and truffles
into his om-
elet.

These and the Cantos of Pound: O how they came pat!
Nimble at other men's arts how I picked up the trick of it:
Rode it reposed on it drifted away on it: passing

Shores that lay dim in clear air: and the cries of affliction
Suave in somniferous rhythms: there was rain there and moons:
Leaves falling: and all of a flawless and hollow felicity:

He slips in
a few prizes
for philoso-
phers.

In that land there were summer and autumn and nighttime and noon
But all seemed alike: and the new polished planets by Einstein:
And a wind out of Valéry's graveyard but it never blew anything loose:

And the questions and questions
                                    questioning
                                                What am I? O
What shall I remember?
                        O my people
                                        a pensive dismay
What have I left unsaid?
                        Till the hearer cried:

The omelet
becomes a
national in-
stitution and
gets into
Fanny Far-
mer.

"If only MacLeish could remember if only could say it!" . . .
And young girls came out: they were innocent strong in the tendons
Hungry for all that was new: and hearing their eyelids were hazy with

Tears and delight: and the campuses brown in November:
Hey but white shirt fronts pink faces: the prizes won:
The celluloid tower with bold intonations defended:

He experi-
ments with
a new kind
of pepper-
corn.

And the mean tang of Cummings turned saltless and sleek on the
        tongue:
And a Dante gone limp: and a shimmer and musical sound
That gleamed in the void and evoked approbation and wonder

That the poet need not be a madman or even a bounder.

II

He seems
likely to lose
his invest-
ment in his
omelet.

And at last I drew close to a land dark with fortifications:
Men shrieking outlandish reproaches till all my blood tingled:
It was ragged and harsh there: they hated: heart horribly quaked in me:
Then I thought "I have staved off the pricking of many a sting:
These perchance I may placate too": I put in at that place:
I met them with scorn and good-natured agreement mingled:

Their fierce cries of "Aesthete!" and "Fascist!": and like them I
        railed at the
Bankers and builders of railroads: I said "Social Credit":
(He's a tough lad under the verse mister all the same!):

He is obliged
to reopen his
omelet and
put a little
garlic in.

And the Polacks and Dagoes and Hunkies undoubtedly dead:
And behold these savage and sybarite-baiting strangers
Had many among them like me well-mannered well-fed

Bubbling over with schoolboy heroics: their line had been changing:
And long in that plentiful land I dwelt honored in peace:
And then schoolboys from Britain came over us flying like angels:

Them too I courted: and labored to roughen the sweet
To stiffen the wilt of a style that seemed lax in that land:
A starch of Greek tragedy: stark Anglo-Saxon the beat of it:

He is
doomed to
go on doc-
toring his
omelet.

Stock-market talk: still my numbers as mawkishly ran:
(Señora, I could go on like this forever:
It is a strange thing to be an American):

I was wired for sound as I started again down the river:
And my colons went out on the air to the clang of a gong:
O when shall I ring with the perilous pain and the fever?

A clean and clever lad
                    who is doing
                                his best
                                    to get on. . . .
                                    —EDMUND WILSON

ON A BOUGAINVILLAEA VINE IN HAITI

Under the sovereign crests of dead volcanoes,
See how the lizards move in courtly play;
How when the regnant male
Fills the loose bagpipe of his throat with air,
His mate will scale
Some vine portcullis, quiver, halt, then peer—
Eyes sharp as pins—
At that grandee posed stiff with self-esteem,
His twiglike tail acurve.

What palaces lie hid in vines! She sees
Chameleon greenrooms opening on such
Elite boudoirs,
Flowers as bright as massacres; should she
Not try their spiring tendrils
That like string
Hammocks are slung upon the open air?
Tensing his tiny jaw, he seems to smile;

And while all nature sways,
Lightly rides his delicate trapeze.

A virid arrow parts
The leaves—she's at
His side. Then darts away; he following,
They lose themselves within the redolent shade. . . .
Quiet the palace lies
Under the sun's green thumb,
As if marauding winter would never come.

—BARBARA HOWES

ON A CHILD WHO LIVED ONE MINUTE

Into a world where children shriek like suns
sundered from other suns on their arrival,
she stared, and saw the waiting shape of evil,
but could not take its meaning in at once,
so fresh her understanding, and so fragile.

Her first breath drew a fragrance from the air
and put it back. However hard her agile
heart danced, however full the surgeon's satchel
of healing stuff, a blackness tiptoed in her
and snuffed the only candle of her castle.

Oh, let us do away with elegiac
drivel! Who can restore a thing so brittle,
so new in any jingle? Still I marvel
that, making light of mountainloads of logic,
so much could stay a moment in so little.

—X. J. KENNEDY

ON AESTHETICS, MORE OR LESS

I moved, to keep the moon
in its matrix of elm boughs un-
closeting into faint aigrettes
and stars like some thirty-ton
poised peacock or heron,

but both of them got away:
the moon into clear sky,
elm into darkness. Per-

haps, on analysis, I
was reminded of Hokusai—

some print of profiling hill,
with moon in an interval
of catkin and twig—like him,
or like Joshua in the vale
of Ajalon wanting a full

grasp of this opposition,
since elms will be sawdust soon
of the beetle that's at the heart,
and the moon's privileged, an-
cient halo could yet wink on

-off for COLA or GASOLINE.
But I think it was merely a sane
satisfaction by contraries.
They do say only the lun-
atic stares at the bare moon.

—PETER KANE DUFAULT

ON APPLES

One is not hale until one inhales
The russet of these apples—
Their rosy smell . . .
As from cleft hearts there rises
The green
Veridical stem.

Thus in Cézanne one sees
The stillness of utter rest: an electric calm
Of placement; the apple transcendent—
Flat: cool: the virtual assumed
As real . . .

Anne once refused to have
An apple; yet she held it
And sat there like another, or the first
Eve, who again rejected
Pleasure for the pleasure of a cusp,
Self-worried; the famous prerogative
Of feminine indecision . .

The apple need not be eaten; must be had.
I recall at the end of the road, where rampant boys lived,
Green apples on the ground, ant-laden, brown, abscessed—
We'd chuck them at each other, or at trees.
Hit in the ribs, it hurt.
Ted Mingo showed me.

And sometimes near Cooper Union, peddlers buff
Pippins upon their rusty
Winter sleeves;
Reset each polished crimson
On their cart.

McIntosh are best
Unpeeled, for rosy apple sauce,
For eating, as for fragrance . . .
            Try them—
But you must smell them.

—DAVID ROSS

ON A RECENT PROTEST AGAINST SOCIAL CONDITIONS

The maples have turned. Fire snaps on my tongue,
Veined in red, a brief felicity
Which hangs in balance between speech and silence,
Trembling toward a word whose simplicity,
Like wind, everyone has heard.

I want to write a petition, make a prayer,
Get somebody punished, rewarded.
But the birds in this academy
Refuse to sing by ear, they take cover,
Since light is an approximate hope.

The Dean can tell dates, balance a budget,
Explain education. Although his nerves are on edge,
He is clear about what needs to be done:
You must know facts. The sun
Has nothing to do with these.

The Dean would not like shifting among shadows.
You speak against injustice; it alters
Before the mind can hold its shape.
Imagine a crooked elm disguised by sun,
A tree that rots in blossom.
The hue and cry must be begun again.

And after all, what is it but a tree,
Always almost impossible to describe,
Pleasant in summer,
In winter barely visible on dark days.
Do you call a tree an injustice?

I see in the branches ignorance, corruption,
Murder in its season.
There are other names for the cold wind
And the uncertain color of leaves.
It is not knowledge that knows.

Truth will drive the scientist to prove
His facts before the elements agree, and love
Can find a definition
In all sorts of weather. We die together,
Caught in the roots of evil.

Suffering was never an exact science.
So I speak when I'm hurt or when
You are, though I don't know the reason
And cannot be sure there ever was an answer.
Only the dead say nothing,
Even then not in fear of error.

—David Posner

ON DISCOVERING A BUTTERFLY

I found it in a legendary land
all rocks and lavender and tufted grass,
where it was settled on some sodden sand
hard by the torrent of a mountain pass.

The features it combines mark it as new
to science: shape and shade—the special tinge,
akin to moonlight, tempering its blue,
the dingy underside, the checkered fringe.

My needles have teased out its sculptured sex;
corroded tissues could no longer hide
that priceless mote now dimpling the convex
and limpid teardrop on a lighted slide.

Smoothly a screw is turned; out of the mist
two ambered hooks symmetrically slope,
or scales like battledores of amethyst
cross the charmed circle of the microscope.

I found it and I named it, being versed
in taxonomic Latin; thus became
godfather to an insect and its first
describer—and I want no other fame.

Wide open on its pin (though fast asleep)
and safe from creeping relatives and rust,
in the secluded stronghold where we keep
type specimens it will transcend its dust.

Dark pictures, thrones, the stones that pilgrims kiss,
poems that take a thousand years to die
but ape the immortality of this
red label on a little butterfly.

—Vladimir Nabokov

ON EDITING SCOTT FITZGERALD'S PAPERS

Scott, your last fragments I arrange tonight,
Assigning commas, setting accents right,
As once I punctuated, spelled, and trimmed
When, passing in a Princeton spring, now dimmed—
A quarter-century ago and more—
You left your "Shadow Laurels" at my door.
That was the tale of one who sang and shone,
Lived for applause but had his life alone,
In some beglamoured, shimmering, bluish-green,
Imagined Paris wineshop of nineteen;
Who fed on drink for weeks, forgot to eat,
"Worked feverishly," nourished on defeat
A lyric pride, and lent a lyric voice
To all the tongueless, knavish tavern boys,
The liquor-ridden, the illiterate;
Got stabbed one midnight by a tavern mate—
Betrayed, but self-betrayed by stealthy sins—
And faded to the sound of violins.

Tonight, in this dark, long Atlantic gale,
I set in order such another tale,
While tons of wind that take the world for scope
Rock blackened fathoms where marauders grope
Our blue and bathed-in Massachusetts ocean;
The Cape shakes to the depth bomb's dumbed concussion;
And guns can interrupt me in these rooms,
Where now I seek to breathe again the fumes
Of iridescent drinking dens, retrace
The bright hotels, regain the eager pace
You tell of. . . . Scott, the bright hotels turn pale;
The pace limps or stamps; the fumes are stale;
The horns and violins blow faint tonight.
A rim of darkness that devours light
Runs like the wall of flame that eats the land;
Blood, brain, and labor pour into the sand;
And here among our comrades of the trade
Some buzz like husks, some stammer, much afraid,
Some mellowly give tongue and join the drag
Like hounds that bay the bounding anise bag,
Some swallow darkness and sit hunched and dull,
The stunned beast's stupor in the monkey skull.

I climbed, a quarter-century ago and more
Played out, the college steps, unlatched my door,

And, creature strange to college, found you there—
The pale skin, hard green eyes, and yellow hair—
Intently cleaning up before a glass
Some ravage wrought by evenings at the Nass;
Nor did you stop abashed, thus pocked and blotched,
But kept on peering while I stopped and watched.
Tonight, from days more distant now, we find,
Than holidays in France were, left behind,
Than spring of graduation from the fall
That found us grubbing below City Hall,
Through storm and darkness, time's contrary stream,
There gleams surprisingly your mirror's beam
To bring before me still, in graver guise,
The glitter of the hard and emerald eyes;
The cornea tough, the aqueous chamber cold,
Those glassy optic bulbs that globe and hold,
They pass their image on to what they mint,
Suffuse your tales of summer with their tint,
And leave us to turn over, iris-fired,
Not the great, Ritz-sized diamond you desired
But jewels in a handful, lying loose:
The opal's green chartreuses, shifting blues,
Its shadowy-vivid vein of red that flickers,
Tight phials of the spirit's light mixed liquors;
Some zircons livid, tinsel rhinestones; but
Two emeralds, green and lucid, one half cut,
One cut consummately—and both take place
In Letters' most expensive Cartier case.

And there I have set them out for final show,
And come to the task's dead end, and dread to know
The eyes struck dark, dissolving in the wrecked
And darkened world, the light of intellect
That spilled into the spectrum of tune, taste,
Scent, color, living speech is gone, is lost;
And we must dwell among the jagged stumps,
With owls digesting mice to gruesome lumps
Of skin and gristle, monkeys scared by thunder,
Great buzzards that descend to grab the plunder.
And I, your scraps and sketches sorting yet,
Can never thus relight one sapphire jet,
However close I look, however late,
But only spell and point and punctuate.

                                            —EDMUND WILSON

ONE MORE NEW BOTCHED BEGINNING

Their voices heard, I stumble suddenly.
Choking in undergrowth, I'm torn,
Mouth pressed against the thorns
     remembering
Ten years ago here in Geneva—
I walked with Merleau-Ponty by the lake.
Upon his face I saw his intellect.
The energy of the sun-interweaving
Waves, electric, danced on him. His eyes
Watched with their smiling logic through
Black coins thrown down from leaves. He who
Was Merleau-Ponty that day is no more
Irrevocable than the I that day who was
Beside him—though I'm living.

Also that summer
My son stayed up the valley in the mountains.
One day I went to see him, and he stood
Not seeing me, watching some hens.
Doing so, he was absorbed
In their wire-netted world. He danced
On one leg. Leaning forward, he became
A bird-boy. I am there
Still seeing him. To him,
That moment—unself-knowing even then—
Is drowned in the oblivious earliness. . . .
     Such pasts
Are not diminished distances, perspective
Vanishing points, but doors
Burst open suddenly by gusts
That seek to blow the heart out.
     Today, I see
Three undergraduates standing talking in
A college quad. They show each other poems—
Louis MacNeice, Bernard Spencer, and I.
Louis caught cold in the rain, Bernard fell
From a train door. Both died within ten days.
Their lives are now those poems that were
Pointers to the poems to be their lives.
We read there in the college quad. Each poem
Is still a new beginning. If
They had been finished, though, they would have died
Before they died. Being alive

Is when each moment's a new start, the past
And future shuffled between fingers
For a new game. I'm dealing out
My hand to them, one more new botched beginning
Where we still stand talking in the quad.
—STEPHEN SPENDER

104 BOULEVARD SAINT-GERMAIN

(FOR A BRITISH TRAVELLER IN PARIS)

In a basement just off Saint-Michel
there are windows that look onto the street,
revealing to those at the gooseneck lamps below
disembodied pairs of moving feet.

Stand back as you pass some afternoon,
observe the rows of sullen boys
assembling surgical instruments and yawning,
sequestered from idleness and the city's noise.

Stand long enough in your rush from the Louvre
to Notre Dame and you will find
that the lit faces lift at last and return your gaze,
squinting at your shadow, as though half blind.

Then comes the moment, not recorded
in any of the travel books,
that opposes your trim suit and your camera
to their open collars, dark eyes, and grave looks.

You will think of zoos, or aquariums,
or of hothouse plants behind squares of glass,
but it will be you, surely, who are on display
in that exchange of glances before you pass.

Go on to the next sight, whatever it is,
for at five o'clock they will come forth
to the permanent freedom of embraces and laughter
that you long for but deny, in your chaste North.
—KENNETH PITCHFORD

ON FALLING ASLEEP BY FIRELIGHT

The wolf and the lamb shall feed together, and the lion shall
eat straw like the bullock, and dust shall be the serpent's meat.
—Isaiah 65:25.

Around the fireplace, pointing at the fire,
As in the prophet's dream of the last truce,
The animals lie down; they doze or stare,
Their hoofs and paws in comical disuse;
A few still run in dreams. None seems aware
Of the laws of prey that lie asleep here, too,
The dreamer unafraid who keeps the zoo.

Some winter nights impel us to take in
Whatever lopes outside, beastly or kind;
Nothing that gibbers in or out of mind
But the hearth bestows a sleepy sense of kin.
Promiscuous hosts, we bid the causeless slime
Come in; its casualness remains a crime,
But metaphysics bites less sharp than wind.

Now, too, a ghostly, gradually erect
Company lies down, weary of the walk—
Parents with whom we would, but cannot, talk,
Beside them on the floor their artifacts:
Weapons we gave them, which they now bring back.
If they see our privilege, they do not object,
And we are not ashamed to be their stock.

All we had thought unkind were all the while
Alike, the firelight says, and strikes us dumb;
We dream there is no ravening or guile
And take it kindly of the beasts to come
And suffer hospitality; the heat
Turns softly on the hearth into that dust
Isaiah said would be the serpent's meat.

—WILLIAM MEREDITH

ON INSTALLING AN AMERICAN KITCHEN
IN LOWER AUSTRIA

Should the shade of Plato
Visit me, anxious to know
How Anthropos is, I could say to him, "Well,
We can read to ourselves, our use

Of holy numbers would shock you, and a poet
        May lament 'Where is Telford,
Whose bridged canals are still a Shropshire glory?
        Where Muir, who, on a Douglas spruce,
Rode out a storm and called an earthquake noble?
        Where Mr. Vynian Board,
Thanks to whose lifelong fuss the hunted whale now suffers
        A quicker death?' without being
Called an idiot, though none of them bore arms or
        Made a public splash." Then "Look!"
    I would point out, for a dig at Athens. "Here
        Is the place where we cook."

        Though built last May in Austria,
            Do-it-yourself America
        Prophetically blueprinted this
            Palace kitchen for kingdoms
Where royalty would be incognito, and an age when
        Courtesy would think, "From your voice
And the back of your neck I know we shall get on,
        But cannot tell from your thumbs
Who is to give the orders." The right note is harder
        To hear than in the Age of Poise,
When She talked shamelessly to her maid and sang
        Noble lies to Him, but struck
It can be still in New Cnossos, where if I am
        Banned by a shrug it is my fault,
    Not Father's, as it is my taste whom
        I put below the salt.

        The prehistoric hearthstone,
            Round as a birthday button
        And sacred to Granny, is as old
            Stuff as the bowel-loosening,
Nasal war cry, but this all-electric room,
        Where ghosts would feel uneasy,
A witch at a loss, is numinous and again
        The center of a dwelling,
Not, as lately it was, an abhorrent dungeon
        Where the warm, unlaundered meinie
Belched their comic prose and from a dream of which
        Chaste Milady awoke blushing.
House-proud, deploring labor, extolling work,
        These engines politely insist
    That banausics can be liberals,
        A cook a pure artist

Who moves everyman
At a deeper level than
Mozart, for the subject of the verb
To *hunger* is never a name;
Dear Adam and Eve had different bottoms,
    But the neotene who marches
Upright and can subtract reveals a belly
    Like the serpent's, with the same
Vulnerable look. Jew, Gentile, or pygmy,
    He must get his calories
Before he can consider her profile or
    His own, attack you or play chess,
And take what there is, however hard to get down.
    Then surely those in whose creed
God is edible may call a fine
    Omelette a Christian deed.

The sin of Gluttony
Is ranked among the Deadly
Seven, but in murder mysteries
    One can be sure the gourmet
Didn't do it; children, brave warriors out of a job,
    Can weigh pounds more than they should
And one can dislike having to kiss them, yet,
    Compared to the thin-lipped, they
Are seldom detestable. Some waiter grieves
    For the worst dead bore to be a good
Trencherman, and no wonder chefs mature into
    Choleric types, doomed to observe
Beauty peck at a master-dish, their one reward
    To behold the mutually hostile
Mouth and eyes of a sinner married
    At the first bite by a smile.

The houses of our City
Are real enough, but they lie
Haphazardly scattered over the earth,
    And her vagabond forum
Is any space where two of us happen to meet
    Who can spot a citizen
Without papers. So, too, can her foes. Where the
    Power lies remains to be seen;
The force, though, is clearly with them. Perhaps only
    By falling can She become
Her own vision, but we have sworn under four eyes
    To keep Her up. All we ask for,

Should the night come when comets blaze and meres break,
  Is a good dinner, that we
May march in high fettle, left foot first,
  To hold her Thermopylae.

                      —W. H. AUDEN

ON LAKE PEND OREILLE

All day the wind has made love
to the lake and tonight the water
takes up its bruises and moves
away to a safer distance.

I am listening for the small
sounds of another departure.

Summer is leaving
as if she could afford the trip.

She stands by the road
in her ragged coat and fumbles
for her keys in the darkness.

At her pathetic signal
the aristocracy of leaves
will begin to let go.

                      —RICHARD SHELTON

ONLY THE DEAD

Only the dead have manners; they alone
Are never trapped between The Lady and The Door,
Never drop The Spoon and never need be shown
How to slice The Blancmange, or what The Sauce is for.

Only the dead are nice. Where they go
They never pass the careful line that cuts
Good Taste from Show,
Nothing from Too Much.

Only the dead are heroes; they alone
Achieve that final Elegance, that last
Umpty of grim Gallantry unknown
To those who must exonerate their past.

Wiser than the living, they have shown
How true Nobility is bred in The Bone.

                      —REED WHITTEMORE

ON SCAFELL PIKE

Beyond the last gate, where I made my first halt,
The last of darkness still clung on the rock
Though a ladder of sun leaned on a further mountain.
The valley below was a vellum of mist,
For all of August's hung thunder among it.
Glad for rests, I watched—refuting the cold
That carried in the shifting damp of the air—
A buzzard rise slowly over the steaming peat.
Mine, else, the mountain was, whose skylarks
Slept, hidden in the wax and shrub of bilberry.
Across the long bog I was to cross, no sheep
Moved in its mesh of black runnels. Water,
The very water, was dazed, fumbling, unpurposeful.

Once I had left it behind, the formality
Of standing a moment alone on top of England
Would take an hour, no more. But for the buzzard,
Lazing just within sight on a ledge of wind,
I might have claimed as mine, as won, there and then,
That total, boundless tundra of solitude
I came before dawn to be on the mountain for.
Cairn by cairn, I watched him with his sort of eye,
And passed each rug by slashed and shrivelling rug
Of emptied carcass. I felt how flicking a blunt wing
Sufficed to steady the sun or to turn a rock face;
Fingers warmed as they would had I held him
Shot in all the amazement of his needless beauty.

Once begun—the final pitch, my back to slab
For a mooring against the thrown stacks of gust,
My calves flexed from the nudge of my wondering
Whether any flinching creature could keep there
And not be torn across the insubstantial rock,
Hurled to the grit-faced crags of the wind—
To go on, on into the mountain's shifting now,
On, or back, would have been to ride lightning.
And into the afternoon I kept to a crouch,
A whitened gristle of ravelled fear, mindless
Of wonder, beauty, desire, or of solitude,
Being the wind's thing, helpless as the mountain,
A harsh, dry rattle assembling within my craw.

—TED WALKER

ON SEEING MY BIRTHPLACE FROM A JET AIRCRAFT

The nursery boast •
Among the teacups uttered, as the hunt
Went squelching over fields of buttered toast:
Someday I'll fly about with magic power.
Someday I'll wear a peak cap back to front
And travel at five hundred miles an hour.

O brave halloing huntsmen, lost to me,
While at five hundred miles an hour I fly!
O boastful rattle of a nursery tea,
Lost while I cruise a new suburban sky!

Come, little ghost,
Come, pressurized in this brief dream. Swoop down
To justify the solemn nursery boast.
Follow the lost line of the magic hunt
Over the butter fields all turned to town.
Imagine that your cap's on back to front.

—JOHN PUDNEY

ON THE CURVE-EDGE

From the thick cover of unknowingness
Breaking a little farther than the beast,
We children of the formless, slow to wake,
From that serene circumference delivered
To gale and tumult and the razor's edge,
Cast up and wincing, pick our way down shingle—

On the curve-edge of oblivion to live,
In the shadow of extinction, like the last
Fierce spark that burns on the black rim of the sun
Before the eclipse sweeps over, in the shade
Of a mounting threat to snatch our crumb of joy.

Then do we well to live? Yes, we do well.
Doom halts to topple, but we living lie
Awake in the dark, under terror rich in our peace,
Who have drawn breath for this little, knowing we are,
Relishing life, sucking the honeycomb.

—ABBIE HUSTON EVANS

ON THE DEATH OF AN EMPEROR PENGUIN
IN REGENT'S PARK, LONDON

A proletarian, unlikely bird, no monarch,
Whose northern relation, the garefowl or great auk,
One hundred years has been extinct on these islands;
An ugly, blubber-jacketed, wingless giant
Laboriously transported from his desert of ice,
His house of hurricanes (uncomfortable birthplace!
Cold and insanitary, where ocean hardens!),
Has perished in the Zoological Gardens.
Tell, masochistic martyr, what ailed you?
Here there is care and comfort; what can have killed you?
Speak, shade! Were your keepers neglecting your welfare?
Did you lack anything purchasable with silver?
O stupid, ungrateful bird! Blubber and feather!
To die of desire for freedom and bad weather,
For a perch where you, pegged to a glacier's bitter stone,
Outlast an antarctic unending cyclone,
And watch, neither superb nor able, from below
A smashed world whirl away in stinging snow.

—DAVID WRIGHT

ON THE ISLAND

To an isle in the water
With her would I fly.
—W. B. *Yeats.*

I. FRIDAY NIGHT

We issue from the meat of Pineapple Street,
Skipping in unison in the jet rain to
The cadence of our footsteps left behind
Just momentarily as we bound on
To water, laughing, soaked, four-legged and
Three-armed, two-hearted, Siamese, unique,
And fifty put together. On the Heights,
We embrace like trenchcoats on a rack at Brooks.
You taste like lipstick, wine, and cigarettes
(And, now quite irrecoverably, you:
A tear in the material of memory
No reweaver can match. Nevertheless,
I feel your rainy face against mine still,
Hear your low laugh join boat hoots in the night
—One Song, one Bridge of Fire! Is it Cathay?—
And see, just past the corner of your eye,
Our city momentarily at bay).

II. SATURDAY MORNING

Starting for Paumanok from Remsen Street,
Taking my Buick, leaving your LaSalle,
Putting the top down in the false-spring light
Of February 2nd, following
The "27" signs—Atlantic Ave.,
Rockaway Parkway, Linden Boulevard,
And Sunrise Highway finally at noon—
We leave the city we did sometime seek
In favor of the fish-shaped fastnesses
Due east, beyond the sounding wave
Of outer suburbs rushing up the shore
To flood the flat potato country with
The family of man. Past Babylon,
We run at last aground on the prewar
Simplicities and complications: farms
Looked down on by great houses in the style
Of Insull, piles of those who made a pile
In Motors, Telephone, and Radio
And dropped it all down the defile
Between decades, where all our fortunes go.

III. SATURDAY AFTERNOON

Patchogue, my dear, harbors a white-faced bar
With a black heart. In its interior,
You are more beautiful than you really are,
More *dégagée*, more *jeux sont faits*, world-wearier.
That artificial night, with evident aim,
Plinks out my daylit thoughts and goes to black,
Where, in the tarry sky, the Bull, the Swan
Couple illegally till dawn
With lavish princesses and Spartan queens,
As I autistically do
With you, while you invent a terrible drink—
A pilot biscuit drowned in Gin and It,
Dubbed a Wet Blanket, in a whiskey glass—
Before my wondering eyes. With a bright crack,
A back door opens and the atmosphere
Of night blows out as sharply as a tire,
Revealing a slack rank of garbage cans
Out back and a red carpet underfoot.
You look yourself again; I start to feel
Like death in the afternoon. Let us be gone.

IV. SATURDAY EVENING

Night, like a funeral, comes marching in
On muffled heels, its west-bent coffin met

By gathering naked bulbs and neon tubes
Along Sag Harbor's streets. Beyond the pale
Pearl light of day's regrettable demise,
The whalers' churches and town halls rise up like white
Whales surfacing, their sugarloaves of white
Mammalian clapboards sailing on a gray
Calm main of mud. These Puritanic arks,
Fane and profane, holy and secular,
Divide their flocks into white Sunday sheep
Ripe to be fleeced of grace, and weekday goats
Alert to steal their wool. A vesper bell,
Like a late bird, sings curfew to the town,
Turning our steps to where, in tongues of fire,
A stammering sign defines the Grande Hotel.

V. Saturday Night

Now, wearing my discounted wedding ring
Still foggy with disuse, you face the desk,
Where the Korean War loudly bombards
The *Daily News* with black. The manageress,
A human hatchet in a florid dress,
Takes five from me for her best double. We
Go up and up to that sidereal
Address, where all the bentwood furniture,
The stunted metal bed, the chiffonier
Graced with our pint of Partners' Choice, but scarred
By all the post-coital cigarettes
Of sadder, wiser transients, the ashtray
("Momento of Peconic Bay"), the tin
Wastebasket lithographed with pennants—yours
Included—all call time and freeze till we
Move on. The four-light window, featuring
A huge streetlamp dead center, resonates
To the first wave of onshore rain as we
Resume our elevating, ludicrous
Posture of love. Dear Jane, the prize is far
Too near for me to melt with laughter now,
But there's a whoop down in my throat. Later
And cooler, rubbing Lucky Strike ash in-
To my bare chest, I'll tell you what I mean:
The fact that I, unhandsome, awkward, pale,
And you, Vassar or no, too ample for
An age of skin and bone, should tumble for
Love seven stories high, with eyes as blue
As tropospheres, with dazzling teeth the size
Of cornerstones, and noses straight as dies—
The cliché of the first-class citizens.

VI. Monday Morning

The party's over now. In a tense white
Ruffed blouse, you look as different from last night
As day. I swallow the last scratchy crumbs
Of my last baking-powder biscuit and
Leave your place, touching for the first time now,
Noting my fingermarks on the front door.
Once more unto the breach: at the St. George,
We sound the hellmouth of the I.R.T.
And ride the hissing, green, Draconic train
Under the river. *Wicker, wicker* goes
The air compressor at a stop. You sit
On shiny wicker, looking at my feet;
I hang from a chipped white enamel strap
Marked "Rico Type 11." Soon, at Wall
Street, we get off. Now, leaving Trinity
Out of the corner of my eye, I spin
Behind you into the loud lobby of your tower,
Where banks of Gothic elevators rise,
Absurd, on high. You turn and face me now,
All Bala-Cynwyd in your Peter Pan
Collar and single string of pearls, dear Jane.
"It's no go, Lou." "But wait—" "But why?" "But I—"
"I know, but it won't ever work. You know
That I have some traditions—" "Pouring tea."
"Yes, pouring tea. And you just don't, that's all.
You just don't care." "But I can try." "Unh-uh.
Look, Lou, let's stop this." "Can't I see you once?
Just one more time? Tonight?" "No. I'll be late
For work upstairs. Goodbye." Now that I know
I won't see you again, an awful pain
Of deprivation twists my abdomen.
The lancet doors squeeze shut between us, and
Lights track your progress overhead as you
Devise me to myself. Jane, for the gift
Of you at first, then us, and lastly me,
My thanks, since even such off-islanders
As I can profit by a visit to
The fish-shaped island, population two.

—L. E. Sissman

ON THE TWENTY-FIFTH OF JULY

On the twenty-fifth of July
there was no mail, not
even a bill, leaving my
being high and dry on
a screened porch, pen between
my lips to write a sister
I never had, compiling
condolences for a man
who is not yet dead, but
who ambles by, stick in hand,
slashing at Japanese beetles,
his glasses hanging mad.

There is no need to write
the letter, to fulfill
the wish, to amplify
any yearning, there is no
need to reach up and pull
the air flight back that
did not take me off; yet
at the rear of my house,
the hound, rooting deep
to bury a bone, finds
a message I sent to
the beetles of Japan.

—DAVID CORNEL DEJONG

ON THE WELSH MARCHES

The farmer's eyes are dark; he speaks in song,
In whom the Iberian rises, though long slain.
He points to Skyrrid falling all day long
Upon its side where Satan entered Hell.
He smiles through darkness, telling it again—
A myth of Merlin, Christianized, confused
Like his own blood, where Welsh and English dwell.
His English laughs; his Welsh is not amused.
Hedgerows more ancient than his Norman deed
Mark out his land; he keeps them with his toil.
A motte and bailey in his garden feed
His cabbages their patiently worked soil.
Upon the hill a Roman legion sleeps
Among the Celts they killed and married there.
A church of Norman stone, whose belfry keeps
Satan in Skyrrid, calls his eyes to prayer.

Whatever Druid gods, what Saxon charms
Make his mind's climate, his composite weather,
In him all enemies lay down their arms;
Saxon and Celt at last asleep together
Have reconciled their legends. What he fears
He has no choice to fear or not to fear—
His hedgerows run beyond philosophy
Into the ancient dark; he trims as he
Was taught; he hears with his ancestral ears.

Wide as the Roman road, an American's car
Pauses before the church. A camera whirs.
Behind his hedge he greets the conquerors
Mildly, though memory opens like a scar
And in his depths the first Iberian stirs.

—WALTER STONE

OPERATIVE NO. 174 RESIGNS

The subject was put to bed at midnight, and I picked him up again at 8 A.M.
I followed, as usual, while he made his morning rounds.
After him, and like him, I stepped into taxis, pressed elevator buttons, fed nickels
into subway turnstiles, kept him under close surveillance as he dodged through
heavy traffic and pushed through revolving doors.

We lunched very pleasantly (though separately) for $1.50, plus a quarter tip.
(Unavoidable expense.)
Then out again. For twenty minutes on the corner the subject watched two
shoeshine boys fish for a dime dropped through a subway grating. (No dice.)
And then on. We had a good stare into a window made of invisible glass.
Another hour in a newsreel movie—the usual famine, fashions, Long Beach
bathing, and butchery. Then out again.
I realized, presently, that the subject was following a blonde dish in blue he had
seen somewhere around.
(Nothing, ultimately, came of this.)
And shortly after that a small black pooch, obviously lost, attached himself to
your operative's heels.
(Does he fit into this picture anywhere at all?
It doesn't matter. In any case, I resign.)

Because the situation, awkward to begin with, swiftly developed angles altogether
too involved.
Our close-knit atomic world (to be dispersed by night) became a social structure,
and then a solar system with dictates of its own.
We had our own World's Fair in a pinball arcade. The blonde had her picture
taken in a Photomat.
And so (whether by law or by magnetism) did we.
But still there was nothing, in any of this, essentially new to report.

Except I began to think of all the things the subject could have done but did
not do.
All the exciting scenes he might have visited but failed to visit.
All the money I might have watched him make or helped him spend; the murders
he might have committed, but somehow he abstained.
What if he met a visiting star from the Coast (and she had a friend)?
Or went to Paris, or the South Sea Islands? Did my instructions (with expenses)
cover the case?
But none of this happened. Therefore, I resign.

I resign, because I do not think this fellow knew what he was doing.
I do not believe the subject knew at all clearly what he was looking for, or from
what escaping.
Whether from a poor man's destiny (relief and the Bellevue morgue), or a
middle-class fate (always the same job with a different firm), or from a
Kreuger-Musica denouement.
And then, whose life am I really leading? Mine or his? His or the blonde's?

And finally, because this was his business, all of it, not mine.
Whatever vices or virtues were his, whatever conscience, boredom, or penal justice
he sought to escape, it was his business, not mine in the least. I want no
part of it.
I have no open or concealed passion for those buttons we pressed together, those
doors we opened, those levers, slots, handles, knobs.
Nor for the shadow of a bathing beauty on a screen. Nor any interest in possible
defects shown by invisible glass.

I mean, for instance, I do not (often) feel drawn toward that particular type of
blonde in that particular shade of blue.
And I have no room to keep a dog.

Therefore, this resignation.
Whether signed in a Turkish bath with a quart of rye, or in a good hotel, sealed
with a bullet, is none of your business. None at all.
(There is no law compelling any man on earth to do the same, second-hand.)
I am tired of following invisible lives down intangible avenues to fathomless ends.
Is this clear?
Herewith, therefore, to take effect at once, I resign.

—KENNETH FEARING

AN ORDINARY EVENING IN CLEVELAND

I

Just so it goes—the day, the night,
what have you. There is no one on TV.
Shadows in the tube, in the street.
In the telephone, there are echoes and mumblings,
the buzz of hours falling through wires.

And hollow socks stumbling across
the ceiling send plaster dust sifting down
hourglass walls. Felix the cat has
been drawn on retinas with a pencil of light.
I wait, gray, small in my cranny,

for the cardboard tiger on the
kitchen table to snap me, shredded, from
the bowl.

II

Over the trestle go
the steel beetles, grappled tooth-to-tail—over and
over and over, there, smokestacks

lung tall hawkers into the sky's
spittoon. The street has a black tongue. Do you
hear him, Mistress Alley, wooing
you with stones? There are phantoms in that roof's trousers;
they kick the wind. The moon, on a

ladder, is directing traffic
now. You can hardly hear his whistle. The
oculist's jeep wears horn-rimmed wind-
shields, the motor wears wires on its overhead valves.
Grow weary, weary, sad siren,

you old whore. It's time to retire.

III

The wail of the child in the next room quails
like a silverfish caught in a
thread. It is quiet now. The child's sigh rises to
flap with a cormorant's grace through

the limbo of one lamp and a
slide-viewer in your fingers. I cannot
get thin enough for light to shine
my color in your eyes. There is no frame but this for
the gathering of the clan. Words

will stale the air. Come, gather up
our voices in the silent butler and
    pour them into the ashcan of
love. Look, my nostrils are dual flues; my ears are
    the city dump; my eyes are the

    very soul of trash; my bitter
tongue tastes like gasoline in a littered
    alley.

IV

    The child cries again. Sounds
rise by the riverflats like smoke or mist in time's
    bayou. We are sewn within seines

    of our own being, thrown into
menaces floating in shadows, taken
    without volition like silver
fish in an undertow down the river, down time,
    and smogs of evening.

V

                            The child cries.

VI

    Do you hear the voice made of wire?
    Do you hear the child swallowed by carpets,
        the alley eating the city,
rustling newsprint, in the street, begging moonlight with
        a tin cup and a blindman's cane?

VII

    The lamps are rheumy in these tar
avenues. Can you sense the droppings of
    flesh falling between walls falling,
the burrowing of nerves in a cupboard of cans?
    Can you hear the roar of the mouse?

VIII

    There is nothing but the doorway
sighing; here there is nothing but the wind
    swinging on its hinges, a fly
dusty with silence, and the house, on its back, buzzing
    with chimneys, walking on the sky

like a blind man eating fish in an empty room.
                            —LEWIS TURCO

ORIGINAL SIN

I remember now how first I knew what death was.
I remember the air rifle, the Daisy pump gun,
Smelling of 3-in-One oil, and stiff in action.
Fire at random. Fire at a flying crow.
Aim at his yellow beak. While the bullet flies,
The heart of the crow will fly to where the beak was.

Fire at a perch in water, but remember
How the oar bends along the line of sight,
Making a sliding joint upon the surface.
Remember that, and aim below the perch.
Fire at a tin can, which the BB shot
Can puncture if the muzzle of the air gun
Is almost touching. Fire at a stone, sharp angled,
And hear the tsing, the ricochet, the whining
Snip of the torn bullet, tearing the oak leaves.

Do not fire at a chipmunk, or a pigeon.
Fire at a crow, fire at an English sparrow.
Use up the little money rolls of shot.
Fire at the sharp rat-noses in the holes
Under the chicken coop. Life dodges quickly.

And then the day came when I knew what death was—
The day when life, intent on feather-preening,
Was late in lunging upward from the twig.

Warm in the hand, its flight forever ended,
Death was a fallen sparrow, with chipmunk markings,
And a small blue bubble of lead under the skin.

                                        —ALEXANDER LAING

OUT IN THE COLD

All day today the sea gulls cried.
All day they cried, if not because of you,
then not at least because I asked them to.
I've got enough poor bastards on my side;
I'm not a Greek, I can be satisfied
to share a chorus with the shrill sea mew
without pretending it's an interview
with souls plucked from the shipwrecked as they died.

I've got enough cold company: the guys
you used to tell me how you used to see
before I came along and you got wise.
Where are they now, in what capacity—
those dear, well-meant, unsatisfactory
approximations of the eventual me?

—GEORGE STARBUCK

THE OUTLANDERS

The Channel moon went down, as ignorance,
They say, looks down before the eye of light.
We watched upon the deck from dawn to noon
And Dover passed the left and stared at France.
The sunken relics of the war, upright,
And spars bright orange, like the shoots of June
Sprang up as though the plough had scratched that field
That swelled and wrinkled, ebbed, and gaped, and healed.

A boding mood, a summer of the vein,
Had stopped us all like Venus on her shell;
We called ourselves serene but did not sleep.
We looked at Belgium with a kind of pain;
Her hotels swam in light, a part of Hell
Whose windows flare, whose people suffer, weep,
Endure in cells of silence—or was God
The awe before which not a fly could nod?

The captain watched us from the bridge bent out,
Charon's bloodshot orbs of bead his eyes.
It was as though he took our obolus
For transport to the shade. We sank in doubt,
Pale penitents of our temerities,
In groups along the rail. Blank over us,

The wind made spiral plans, the sky glared blue,
We felt the tressilation of the screw.

The distance, like a shopman's Christmas light,
Made bastard prodigies of sights we knew.
The land drew in, we ventured up the Scheldt:
Columbuslike, we proved our guess was right—
The world was round—but like the wandering Jew,
Were half at home; half of what we felt
Was new world doubt if good or guile were there
In all the level stare that met our stare.

—ANDREW GLAZE

OUTWARD

The staff slips from the hand,
Hissing, and swims on the polished floor.
It glides away to the desert.

It floats like a bird or lily
On the waves, to the ones who are arriving.
And if no god arrives,

Then everything yearns outward.
The honeycomb cell brims over
And the atom is broken in light.

Machines have made their god. They walk or fly.
The towers bend like Magi, mountains weep,
Needles go mad, and metal sheds a tear.

The astronaut is lifted
Away from the world, and drifts.
How easy it is to be there!

How easy to be anyone, anything but oneself!
The metal of the plane is breathing;
Sinuously it swims through the stars.

—LOUIS SIMPSON

OVER BRIGHT SUMMER SEAS

Quick! Hoist the jib and cast us off, my son.
The racing fleet maneuvers for the gun,
And we shall stand offshore to give them leeway—
Eventually they'll crowd us from the seaway.
The handsomest and yet profanest sport
Summons bright argosies from every port,
A dazzling zodiac of racing types,
Stars, Comets, Lightnings, Meteors—and Snipes,
White on the sunlit blue, and whiter still
Against the shoreline of a shadowed hill,
Mechanical, precise, well disciplined,
Yet, like ourselves, dependent on the wind.

Lord of the wind-torn or the windless sail,
To whom Odysseus prayed without avail,
Mad Aeolus! But how much madder grown
Since weather bureaus claimed you as their own.
The squalls they are too haughty to announce
Swirl east with unpremeditated pounce
And rip the spinnaker's ballooning bubble,
Splinter the heaven-reaching spars to stubble,
Only to add an overdose of balm
And leave all drifting on an oily calm.
Meanwhile, our able sloop pursues her way,
Swift without haste, and calm without delay.

Pleased with four knots, incredulous of five,
The cruising sailor does at least arrive,
And somewhere else than where he started from,
Breathes deep quiescence of the night to come,
Then hears but echoes underneath the stars
Of disputations in the yacht-club bars,
The race re-raced with expletives of wrath
Like flotsam of the tempest's aftermath.
At last no light is showing but his own,
On shore one voice dies out in monotone,
And, free from disappointment or success,
He slips the mooring of his consciousness.

—ROBERT HILLYER

OVID ON THE DACIAN COAST

Publius Ovidius Naso relegatus non exsul.—The Decree of Banishment.

Airs from the sea blown back,
  The salt wind dense with sedge,
In the surf the sea wrack,
  And rocks ground at the world's
    edge.

With shells, with bits of quartz,
  With flints, with fragment bones,
Castaway, by dolphin arts,
  He starts, translates the stones.

The marsh birds wheel and shriek
  Above him, as he takes

Word after word from their bleak
  Coast of love: his heart breaks.

In place of gold, he sets
  A banished life between
Driftwood, and out of fish nets
  Roofs his loss with sea green.

Thus lives unexiled, though
  Abandoned, stranded, scanned
By the Dog Star only, for so
  Based, his poems are his own land.

—DUNSTAN THOMPSON

OWL

In the unnavigable dusk, when
it is neither day nor dark,
when pilots of small planes flick
running lights on and hurry down,
and in the town
it is supper—
then onto the shadow of the world
launches the owl.

Up there over the reservoir,
between ice rafts and stars,
the hunched silhouette goes
a slanting, silent mile
to a blurred hill,
there to lurk
alone, muffled in gray drift
of his imponderable down.

No innocence could seem soft to
    touch
as that lynx-of-the-wind who
tramples no twig, rustles no
dry grass or leaf, whose wings stroke

lightly as smoke
when,
with ubi-loquial hoot,
he dissolves from a limb.

Yet all the while he hoots, floats,
vague as pod-puff or moon-gall,
in velvetest sockets curl
the ironic grapples that posit
dying rabbit,
plucked grouse.
In his own way the owl
is definite. Gloved

in the generality of dusk
deepening over reservoir,
talons are, making the poor
loon dive from nothing, the rat
hesitate.
How dare disbelieve
the Indians' orenda, or the Greeks'
Athene, the Owl?

—PETER KANE DUFAULT

OXYGEN

Bearer of finches and clouds, pale atmosphere
Holds it, a rose in a bouquet of daisies,
Although odorless, the one-fifth of each breath
That keeps flesh firm on the bone, the old blood warm,

Thought bright as young fish in the brain. Botanists
Say that plants exhale this element, push it
Out through olive skin. But who can say whether
It is this calm expiration or merely

Twilight and the first dew when, bending above
Vinca, hovering over viburnum leaves,
Underneath wide maples, we fill our nostrils
With a cool abundance of what gives us life?

—JOAN SWIFT

P

PAPERMILL GRAVEYARD

NORTH BENNINGTON, VERMONT

In that country of thresholds we move like vandals,
overturning birth dates, death dates, necrologies, Bartlett's
Familiar Quotations, the exorbitant rhetoric
of compliment, spelling hard names, looking for pictures
under the blackboards of a child's stone library
of aphorisms. In the runt gardens and the greenhouse
"arrangements"—pinwheels of laurel in plastic, jelly jars
crammed with wildflowers not meant to outlast
an homage, the rancid memoranda of the very poor—
all is remembered. Each gives to each in the ghastly
plenty: the intimacy of a terminal cough
recalled in formaldehyde and licorice, a bull's-eye of death trance,
the husband's abandoned spasm in a barrow of granite,
endearments, betrayals. The tribal successions of the unexceptional man
are plausible here. Even the destitute scribble their heraldries.
The soldier schooled in a captive security, mistrusting the living,
salutes the interrogator with name, rank, and serial number.
Under the chintzy flags, holidays, holocausts, individual
deaths, the unlucky recruit, blinded by chevrons, is caught
in the scintillation of family keepsakes, a rabbit's foot
crossing the spaces in search of savory greens. All
remains minimal: footlockers of Government Issue
cut frugally to size, berry boxes for the stillborn,
mortuary cabinets indexed under Urgent Business
in an Erechtheum of furnished pillars
where death begets death and nothing comes of nothing.

Having nothing to memorize but an expatriate spirit,
her chemist-husband married, unmarried, remarried, the epithalamial rasp
of a cello string, and the kindness of friends who covered her loss
with a willow, I forage for trifles—the maggot's hammer blow,
a lawnmower's blade in the chicory, my face on the bevel
of granite glazed over "Mother" and "Father."
                    But this is no trifle.

Jeanne Butler, Jeanne Butler, Jeanne Butler, how strangely you lean
toward the heel of my hand, still living on your nerves, severe in your Breton
cheekbones, repeating the uvular "r" for schoolgirls from Cambridge, settling
your napery while our teacups bitter in a garden
over pitted persimmons broken and eaten together, and a changing wind
works in the wafer's paste, hardens the knife's edge, and delivers
our unhaunted world to the Prince of Darkness!

—BEN BELITT

PAPHOS

The sea limps up here twice a day,
And, sigh by leaden sigh, deposes
Crude granite hefts and sponges
Sucked smooth as foreheads or as
          noses;
No footprints dove the laboring sand,
For terrene clays bake smooth
But coarse as a gypsy's hand.

A rose in an abandoned well,
The sexless babble of a spring,
A carob's torn and rosy flesh,
A vulture sprawling on a cliff
Will tell the traveller nothing.

The double axe, the double sex,
The noble mystery of the doves
Before men sorted out their loves
By race or gender chose
One from these dying groves.

This much the sea limps in to touch
With old confiding foam-born hand,
While lovers seeking nothing much
Or hunting the many through the
          one
May taste in its reproachful roar
The ancient relish of her sun.

—LAWRENCE DURRELL

THE PARACHUTIST

Then the air was perfect. And his descent
to the white earth slowed.
                              Falling
became an ability to rest—as

the released breath
believes in life. Further down it snowed,

a confusion of slow novas
which his shoes touched upon, which seemed,
as he fell by,

to be rising. From every
small college and rural town,
 · the clearest, iced blossoms of thought,

but gentle.
          Then the housetops

of friends, who
he thought had been speaking of his arrival,
withdrew, each from another.

He saw that his friends
lived in a solitude they had not ever said aloud.

Strangely he thought this good.

 The world, in fact,
which in these moments he came toward,
seemed casual.

   Though not new.
Had he been thinking this all along?
 A life
where he belonged—having lived with himself

always—as a secret friend?

A few may have seen him then. In evidence:
the stopped dots
of children and dogs, sudden weave

 of a car—
acquaintances circling up
into the adventure they imagined. They saw him drop

through the line breaks
and preciousness of art

down to the lake
which openly awaited him.
   Here the thin
green ice allowed him in.

Some ran, and were late.
These would
forever imagine tragedy

(endless descent,
his face floating among the reeds, by the fish
unrecognized), as those

who imagine the silence of a guest
to be mysterious, or wrong.
      —JON ANDERSON

PARADISE

There is a walled garden where the flowers never pale or turn dark,
A fiery dream couched in sunlight where the rose
Burns redly over her seeds and the water lily breaks
A surface of deep lake without strain;
Her fire is white and many-petalled with a golden spark
(Caught from the sun?) in its well-guarded core; only one floating root shows

Red—crimson of the clear sort. There is nothing opaque
In her, not even that singular most curious vein
Which must once have leaped in a long arc
To the sun!   Enclose
Your self and seek the inmost gold,
The rose, the lily—

Put your arms around me. Our winter is real.

—E. N. Sargent

PARALLAX

Mr. Vanessa took the phone
    His secretary proffered him;
His office windows faced upon
    Boötes and Triangulum.

The chrome-light building cleft the shock
    Of levin down its fluted scroll;
Its weight was anchored in the rock
    That turns upon the Gallup Pole.

His suit was uniformly serge,
    His tie was neat, his smile conventioned.
As the earth slithered toward the verge
    His name was prominently mentioned.

"This is the call, I beg you note,
    I hoped yet dreaded to receive."
He drew his heart from out his coat
    And pinned it on his dexter sleeve.

"Cancel today's appointments. Call
    My wife." His words were clipped and terse.
"I must be ready by the fall
    With blueprints for a universe."

Armed with a slide rule and a plumb,
He paced the aching firmament,
Finding the stress by rule of thumb
And taking soundings as he went.

* * *

Now, wetted finger in the air,
He tests the wind. As he proceeds
He checks each step by questionnaire
And follows after those he leads.
The end is neither here nor there.
Aloft, secure, he runs and reads.

It will take more to overawe
That steady eye, that level brow,
Than light that left Andromeda
Nine hundred thousand years ago.

—MAXWELL ANDERSON

THE PASSENGERS

Who are they
they come by train by car
they won't stand still
we see them underground
through windows
by lamplight
they read they speak they eat
they move their hands
their breath is on the glass
is moving

        toward a fruit tree
beside a river
beside a stone lion on the steps
        toward a field of white
           stones

sit on the floor
eat fish place salt upon your tongue
throw in pine cones and pieces of
      cedar

throw in kleenex and coffee grounds
and the remnants of shoes
raise a lament of white scarves

in a field of white stones
cultivated by the wind
among white pebbles in a light rain
      we cast
          a shadow
that moves over the ground
like the shadow of a bird

every single thing contains all things

the pebble in your mouth its blue
      flame
the feather its blood
your hand falling releases the light
that your hand rising encloses
the shadow of pain in your eyes
the shadows of clouds over water

in principle your eyes
could annihilate the earth
with their shadow

the fruit tree moves its branches be-
 side the river
the stone lion licks salt from its eyes

a building at the bottom of a lake
between me and the sun
gives back the light
particulate petals of the flower
a window an orange a shadow of an
 odor.

      —David Antin

PASTORAL

The afternoon wears on,
The river wears her swan,
And a canoe, moored to the jetty
Below the sewage farm,
Nuzzles herbage growing
On a lip of Avon.

Mortal upon water,
A boy's eye regards
A panoply of summer:
Trees with a crush of leaves,
The bottom of a cloud
Written on molten water.

The afternoon is still,
So still the waters are,
A dead but floating leaf has hardly
Dawdled an inch toward
The sea to which it moves
Upon a fated voyage.

I look back at a boy.
The afternoon is calm.
So still the waters are.

He does not move, nor do
The engines of his harm
On reaches of Avon.

Gales rage; it is autumn,
And half stripped beeches thrash
A flying moon or sun
Across a sky half clouded,
And I feel winter press
A vision on the land,

Yet this is the same scene—
Only another season.
I look back at a boy
On a day of no date
In summer by Avon,
Watching his light boat float,

A swan reflect, the sun
Glitter on the black rim
Of the now savage beeches,
Some midges pulse and thrum,
And the round earth turn a shoulder
Into mustering gloom.

      —David Wright

PATRIOTIC TOUR AND POSTULATE OF JOY

Once, once, in Washington,
D.C., in June,
All night—I swear it—a single mockingbird
Sang,
Sang to the Presidential ear,
Wherein it poured

Such criticism and advice as that ear
Had rarely had the privilege to hear.

And sang to every senator
Available,
And some, as sources best informed affirm,
Rose,
Rose with a taste in the throat like bile,
To the bathroom fled
And spat, and faced the mirror there, and while
The bicarb fizzed, stared, feet cold on tile.

And sang to Edgar Hoover, too,
And as it preached
Subversion and all bright disaster, he
Woke,
Woke and then kissed Mom's photo, so heard
No more. But far,
Far off in Arlington, the heroes stirred
And meditated on the message of that bird.

And sang—oh, merciless!—to me,
Who to that place
And to that massive hour had moved, and now
Rose,
Rose naked, and shivered in moonlight, and cried
Out in my need
To know what postulate of joy men have tried
To live by, in sunlight and moonlight, until they died.

—Robert Penn Warren

A PAUSE FOR BREATH

Having taken her slowly by surprise
For eighty years,
The hills have won; their ring is closed.

The field-walls float their pattern
Over her eye,
Whether she looks outward or inward.

Nothing added, nothing taken away.
Year after year, the trout in the pools
Grow heavy and vanish without ever emerging.

Foxglove, harebell neither protest nor hope
By the steep lane where she climbs.
Out of nothing she grew here simply,

Also suffering to be merely flowerlike
But with the stone agony growing in her joints
And eyes, dimmed with losses, widening for losses.

—Ted Hughes

PEASANT

A PRAYER TO THE POWERS OF THIS WORLD

All those years that you ate and changed
And grew under my picture
You saw nothing
It was only when I began to appear
That you said I must vanish

What could I do I thought things were real
Cruel and wise
And came and went in their names
I thought I would wait I was shrewder but you
Were dealing in something else

You were always embarrassed by what fed you
And made distances faster
Than you destroyed them
It bewitched my dreams
Like magazines I took out with the sheep
That helped to empty the hours
I tried to despise you for what you did not
Need to be able to do
If I could do it
Maybe I could have done without you

My contempt for you
You named ignorance and my admiration for you
Servility
When they were among the few things we had in common
Your trash and your poses were what I most appreciated
Just as you did

And the way you were free
Of me
But I fought in your wars
The way you could decide that things were not

And they died
The way you had reasons
Good enough for your time

When God was dying you bought him out
As you were in a position to do
Coming in the pale car through the mud and fresh dung
Unable to find the place though you had been there
Once at least before
Like the doctor
Without a moment to lose
I was somewhere
In the bargain

I was used to standing in the shade of the sky
A survivor
I had nothing you
Could use

I am taking my hands
Into the cleft wood assembled
In dry corners of abandoned barns
Beams being saved
For nothing broken doors pieces of carts
Other shadows have gone in there and
Wait
On hewn feet I follow the hopes of the owls
For a time I will
Drift down from the tool scars in a fine dust
Noticeably before rain in summer
And at the time of the first thaws
And at the sound of your frequent explosions
And when the roofs
Fall it will be a long while
Since anyone could still believe in me
Any more than if I were one of the
Immortals

It was you
That made the future
It was yours to take away
I see
Oh thousand gods
Only you are real
It is my shame that you did not
Make me
I am bringing up my children to be you

—W. S. MERWIN

THE PEASANT

Six times faster than the fool can weep,
His passions trick him. When he's dry,
The urban peasant kills his tender sheep,
Which, softly, on his pillow, pass him by.

This much Manhattan does. The bulky swain,
In Harris tweed, takes more than can be borne,
Until he howls at night because his brain
Is undervalued and his nerves are worn.

He counts his goods or counts the throats of sheep
Or murmurs to his soul, "My soul, be still."
But there's no gully deep enough to keep
The helpful yearlings that his passions kill.

An average man, the pavement where he walks
Is tough and bearable, but every night
The city slicker on his pillow balks
Before the switch that must turn out the light.

Barefoot and trembling, he will not be held
Accountable for murder in his sleep;
"It is not I," his country cousin yelled,
"Who cut the gentle jugulars of sheep!"

—LEONARD WOLF

PENNY TRUMPET

I had a dog like a love.
And once I had a cruel
Dream: she was a milk-pool
Around a penny trumpet.

I bought button-candy, bright
As bulbs on a high marquee.
My mind was like a movie
Of myself eating until—

Deep in the box—a penny
Trumpet like a lost light!
I stayed outside that night
In woods which were stained black,

And when the first light hauled
Itself up on its back, I heard
Proclaiming clock and bird,
And played my penny trumpet.

And then I never stopped.
I played in every mood.
Till once, grass sang in my blood
While touching foot to top

With a girl who had no ear
For song and was not good
(Or so I understood).
The penny trumpet stayed

In my pocket like a boat
Sunk, trying to surface
Aright. Her face's
Remote, encircling lines

Broke in bars of light.
And her hard, feverish blooms—
Lips, breasts—led me to rooms
Where trumpets play all night.

—RAPHAEL RUDNIK

PENTAGONIA

(THOUGHTS OF A BEMUSED TRAVELLER IN A STRANGE LAND, WITH STOPS AT WASH-
INGTON, D.C., FONTANA, N.C.; OAK RIDGE, TENN.; AND NEW LONDON, CONN.)

This is the Pentagon Building.

This is the river that had to be dammed
Because of the plan that the men had planned
Who work in the Pentagon Building.

This is the village, in mountains wild,
To house the worker (and wife, and child)
Who dammed the river that had to be dammed
Because of the plan that the men had planned
Who work in the Pentagon Building.

This is the project the dam is for,
To light a city or win a war,
And this is the town that a great magician
Has caused to rise from nuclear fission
To house the worker (and wife, and child)
Who wields the power from the mountains wild
That comes from the river that had to be dammed
Because of the plan that the men had planned
Who work in the Pentagon Building.

This is the ship that shows no smoke
From its radioactive isotope
Whose chain reactions secure our coasts
With the armored might of atomic hosts
That was forged on the forge that rose on the plain
To be stoked by the snows and the dews and rain
That came from the river that had to be dammed
Because of the plan that the men had planned
Who work in the Pentagon Building.

These are the men of the Pentagon brand
Who sail a ship with a pen in hand,

Who split an atom or build a home
Or dam a river by telephone
So that space and time may be swiftly spanned
Because of the plans that the men have planned
Who work in the Pentagon Building.

—G. E. Bates

PEREGRINE'S SUNDAY SONG

When I have grown foolish
And ripe for my grave,
O, I'll be a mulish
And stubborn old knave!

I'll open my coffer
That's gilt and engraved;
Only those who suffer
Shall share what I've saved.

I'll build a great castle
In the heart of the town,
Like a long golden tassel
The clouds have let down.

I'll spread a broad table
Where thieves may repair;
There'll be oats in my stable
For the murderer's mare.

Most brightly on one day
My lamp shall be lit,
And Sunday, Sunday,
Is the sad name of it.

For then to the churches
The gentlefolk come,
But the sinner searches
Bare streets for a crumb;

O, bare but for sparrows,
And these eating dung!
On his breast-bone his sorrows
Like mill-stones are hung.

The saved and the shriven
Have consecrate meat,

But the poor unforgiven
Get nothing to eat.

While bells from the steeple
Rain silver on grief,
I'll call wicked people
To pudding and beef.

To plum-cake and liquor,
To sugary buns;
O, I shall call quicker
The wickeder ones!

If my hand should be hostile
To these hungry friends
I'll climb fire and frost till
My pilgrimage ends.

If I held me their better
By the very least part
Of a hair, 'twere a fetter
That rusted my heart.

O, few merry-makers
Will come to my board;
No salt in the shakers
I'll need to afford.

Much weeping will season
The viands with salt,
But I'll give none a reason
To grieve for his fault.

Eve shall not eat apples
Nor Cain wheaten bread
While something yet dapples
His white hand with red.

His thanks none shall owe me
Save for courtesy's sake;
I'll let the young Salome
Cut slices of cake,

Which she'll bring on a platter
To everyone,
For why should it matter
To me about John?

None shall be so rude as
To show pity or pride;
Broken-necked Judas
Shall sit by my side.

My tables and trestles
May fall down accursed,
But I'll have filled vessels
To charity first.

"How got you this jam?" ask
The prudenter sort;
"This silver and damask?
This pastry and port?"

"By murder? By arson?
By stabbing a knight?
By strangling a parson?"
Perhaps they are right.

Now I sing this fasting
By an elder tree;
Life everlasting
Is not for me.

I've leave to squander
What I never can keep,
However I wander
Or walk in my sleep.

—ELINOR WYLIE

PERSONAL

Cultured gentleman, mature, congenial, refined,
Philosophical background, idealistic by nature,
Fond of music, sense of humor, scintillating mind,
Introspective, shy, shy as some small forest creature,
Invites exchange of views with feminine counterpart,
Discerning, amiable, unselfish young lady who shares
His deep interests and, in communing with a lonely heart,
Will not be frightened off by a few gray hairs.

Middle-aged woman, personable, gracious, loving fun and life,
Sophisticated, independent, with unslacked curiosity,
Partial to the pursuit of happiness, having had enough
Of convention and Lenten fare, unencumbered, fancy-free,
Seeks adventure via correspondence,
Easement, margin where time now cramps and pinches,
Diversion, experience, warmth, abundance
Where life has denied, sitting on its thin haunches.

Solitary young introvert, disillusioned, cynical,
Educated beyond endurance, bored, bored, bored,
Versatile, intelligent, creative, highly original,
Hopeful of striking responsive chord,
Desires letters from fellow-iconoclast,

Seeks escape from tedium's dominion,
Invites the piquant, the provocative, the unexpressed,
Desires—*Arcades ambo*—a lost soul's companion.

Invites, seeks, desires—the sleazy words stick in the craw!
Where are the desperate words, the words to compel and enjoin?
Alas, those victims of a kind of Gresham's law
Have been driven into hiding by this debased coin.
Seeks, invites, desires! Will these words penetrate,
Touch, arouse? Oh, will someone hear
Before *too late, too late, too late, too late,*
Becomes a deafening clamor in the ear?

—SAMUEL YELLEN

PETER

Peter sleep-walks.
And is my brother.

Not knows why. But does.
Not knows why. But is.

Because my father and my mother.

And this night in pyjamas,
Barefoot,
Left the house and walked
Five hundred yards to my sister's
    house
And knocked
To be let in.

Let me in. I knock.
Let me in.

And walked back,
Saying he did not remember.

I knock. Let me in.
I am asleep.

He was.

O let us in.
We are all asleep.
We are asleep, let us in.

—MICHAEL DENNIS BROWNE

THE PHENOMENON

How lovely it was, after the official fright,
To walk in the shadowy drifts, as if the clouds,
Saturated with the obscurity of night,
Had died and fallen piecemeal into shrouds.

What crapes there were, what sables heaped on stones,
What soft shakos on posts, tragically gay!
And oil-pool-flooded fields that blackly shone
The more black under the liquid eye of day!

It was almost warmer to the touch than sands
And sweeter-tasting than the white, and yet,
Walking, the children held their fathers' hands
Like visitors to a mine or parapet.

Then black it snowed again, and while it fell,
You could see the sun, an irritated rim
Wheeling through smoke; each from his shallow hell
Perceived gunpowder-blackened seraphim.

But one day all was clear, and one day soon,
Sooner than those who witnessed it had died,
Nature herself forgot the phenomenon,
Her faulty snowfall brilliantly denied.

—Karl Shapiro

PHILATELIC LESSONS: THE GERMAN COLLECTION

The Zollverein was hardly neutral. One recalls
The brick-towered walls of Hamburg (puce and green)
And all the feuding marches that lay between
Mecklenburg-Strelitz and the Rhine River falls;
Or that in cold Nassau at the War of Sixty-six
Grand Duke Adolf, kinsman to the Dutch king,
Slept in his uniform to dramatize the *Ding
An Sich* of discipline; or that the *Rix-
Thaler* dropped out of use there soon after
This altercation. What follows are petty points
Affixed with glue and hinges at the creaky joints
Of stiff confederations to provoke our laughter,
While further still, if one patiently collates
Bavarian pre-cancels, one will usually find
Variations in the ink and casts in the blind
Stare of Prince Luitpold—he mocked the fates
That pull taxes and imposts from each page.
But to get on (the map was always wrong):
Red post horns blow a tinny kind of song
About the borders like an antique rage,
While in Saxony the one-*Groschen* stamp
Shows John the First within a rose medallion
Pointing his chin at some corpulent battalion,
The watermark faint and his gummed backside damp.
The colors begin to run and odd shapes perhaps
Tire the eye more than we know or care
To know. I have learned Henry of Reuss lacked hair;
The Prussian boundaries were drawn by Polish chaps.

—Lawrence P. Spingarn

PIANO PRACTICE

I

Such splendid icecaps and hard rills, such weights
And counterweights, I think I scale the heights
When pentatonic Chinese crewmen start
Up in a cold sweat from the bottom of the keyboard
Only to arrive at some snow-stormed valley
To dissolve in steam-holes and vanish out of sight.

II

The left hand's library is dull, the books
All read, though sometimes, going under velvet,
An old upholsterer will spit out tacks,
Turn them into sparks and smartly hurl them
Up and down the loudest bowling alley—
His pressure of effects can last all night.

III

Two bird notes endlessly repeat themselves.
Or are they fish scales—iridescent, hard?
Mica into marble back to mica?
No images in trills. They're formal. Take
Your foot off the pedal. You're in a wood
Near the sea. And every tree and wave is fake.

IV

An underwater haircut by Debussy?
Oh, that's too easy. Astringent lotions
Let the swimmer down by easy stages
Down among the flashy soda fountains
Down to the bottom where the light bulbs waver
Down where all the mirrors eat their hearts out.

V

Grammar becoming poetry is what
You're after—say, a rational derangement
Requiring that you forget technique
And concentrate on what is harder like
A fireplace that burns pine needles only,
Before which spills the gore of Persian rugs.

VI

A vial of antiseptic meant for Schubert,
One modest, flat, meticulous translation
Of Chopin's lightning undercurrent Spanish—
These are the mere necessities of travel.

Someone you must meet is Dr. Czerny.
Then, through him, Domenico Scarlatti.

VII

Seizures are occurring. Despite snow-lightning,
The black keys are bent on mountain climbing—
All of it against a doctor's warning.
Soon they're descending like the black dots of
A wirephoto in transmission. An
Erotic black wing hovers up above.

VIII

Bach is more like opening an ember
And digging hard into the heart of fire.
The heart of fire is another fire.
When it comes to Mozart, just say nothing.
Think of it as milk, and drink it slowly.
Slowly you will taste the cream of angels.

IX

This black and white's deceptive. Underneath
The spectrum rages. Did you ever see
The calmest waters quickly come to life
Because a minnow's tinfoil flash in sun
Had rent them suddenly? It came. And went.
We take two thousand takes before we print.

X

Don't try to catch that lion by Rousseau.
Before you wake, he'll eat you up. If you
Should meet the sleeping gypsy, let her sleep.
Tomorrow they'll be gone without a trace,
Half fact and half enigma. Now your hands
Are on the mysteries of the commonplace.

—HOWARD MOSS

PIGEONS

On the crooked arm of Columbus, on his cloak,
they mimic his blind and statuary stare,
and the chipped profiles of his handmaidens
they adorn with droppings. Over the loud square,
from all the arms and ledges of their rest,
only a bread crust or a bell unshelves them.
Adding to Atlas' globe, they dispose themselves
with a portly propriety and pose as garlands

importantly about his burdened shoulders.
Occasionally a lift of wind uncarves them.

Stone becomes them; they, in their turn, become it.
Their opal eyes have a monumental cast,
and, in a maze of noise,
their quiet *croomb croomb* dignifies the spaces,
suggesting the sound of silence. On cobbled islands,
marooned in tantrums of traffic, they know their place—
the faithful anonymity of servants—
and never beg, but properly receive.

Arriving in rainbows of oil-and-water feathers,
they fountain down from buttresses and outcrops,
from Fontainebleau and London,
and, squat on the margin of roofs, with a gargoyle look,
they note from an edge of air, with hooded eyes,
the city slowly lessening the sky.

All praise to them who nightly in the parks
keep peace for us; who, cosmopolitan,
patrol and people all cathedraled places,
and easily, lazily haunt and inhabit
St. Paul's, St. Peter's, or the Madeleine,
the paved courts of the past, pompous as keepers—
a sober race of messengers and preservers,
neat in their international uniforms,
alighting with a word perhaps from Rome.
Permanence is their business, space and time
their special preservations, and wherever
the great stone men we save from death are stationed,
appropriately on the head of each is perched,
as though forever, his appointed pigeon.

—Alastair Reid

PINEY WOODS

Teeth on the saw,
Teeth on the rake,
Trout in the brook,
Pine in the brake . . .

The big trees sing to the little trees
In the pine-crowded brake,
"Here is a twigful of sky," they sing,

"That we will stretch out our limbs and take.
Here is a seep of rain to drink
And moldering leaves to yeast our bread.
Give us the last of your earth," they sing,
"That our great roots may spread."

> Gorging on mold,
> Engrossing the sky,
> The big trees grow.
> The little trees die.

—MALCOLM COWLEY

PIT VIPER

A slow burn
in cold blood
is all snake
muscle does.
The nerves drone
their dull-red
test pattern
for days. Days.

The eyes, black
push buttons,
are just that.
On each side
a fixed dish
antenna
covers the
infrared.

The ribs, like
a good set
of stiff twin
calipers,
lie easy
and don't take
measure of
what's not there.

The skin's dim
computer-
control-board
arrangement
of massed lights
betrays no
least motion.
But watch out.

A strike force
is no more
than its parts,
but these parts
work. Dead-game
defense-work
specialists,
they die well.

The point is
they don't *choose*
livings: they
don't *choose* Death.
God save them,
they aren't small-
time haters
that joined up.

—GEORGE STARBUCK

PLAINNESS

The garden's grillwork gate
opens with the ease of a page
in a much thumbed book,
and, once inside, our eyes
have no need to dwell on objects
already fixed and exact in memory.
Here habits and minds and the private language
all families invent
are everyday things to me.
What necessity is there to speak
or pretend to be someone else?
The whole house knows me,
they're aware of my worries and weakness.
This is the best that can happen—
what Heaven perhaps will grant us:
not to be wondered at or required to succeed
but simply to be let in
as part of an undeniable Reality,
like stones of the road, like trees.

—JORGE LUIS BORGES
(*Translated from the Spanish
by Norman Thomas Di Giovanni*)

PLANE GEOMETER

A water strider skates upon the brook
Toward micro-landfalls shimmery with sun.
Boulders cleave the current, but his nook
Is eddyless, a shallow-shady one.

His water-window lights the channelled chamber,
Sandy at bottom, laced with feeler roots;
A little squaretail trout, congealed in amber,
Deflects the shadow-bullets that he shoots.

Perpetual saucers sliding under feet,
From point to point his motor impulse seems,
By aberration of the drowsy heat,
To box the crazy compass of bad dreams.

—DAVID McCORD

THE PLEADERS

What are you going to do with us, who have
No edges, no talents, no discriminations,
Who hear no inner voices, who perceive
No visions of the future, no horizons?
We are among you; we are going to stay.

We crush, we drag, we heave, we draw the water
For you to spill. We gather together to listen
To your speeches, though your tongues run on so fast
We cannot follow, and your jokes dart in and out
Too quickly for our laughter to form itself.
We are your children, whom you treat like horses.

When crowds surge out into the streets
You have invited them; we run with them.
You give us order, speak on our behalf,
For we speak up too slowly to interrupt you.
We are the numbers ranked on your computers.
We are among you; we are going to stay.

If we knew how to pray to you, we'd pray
That you could listen long enough to listen
To what it is we think we want. We know
That what you think we want stands far away
From anything that has occurred to us.
We are your children, whom you treat like horses.

We are the eyes your eyes have never met.
We are the voice you will not wait to hear.
We are the part of you you have forgotten
Or trampled out, or lost and wept to lose.
We are your children, whom you treat like horses.
We are among you; we are going to stay.

—Peter Davison

PLEA FOR A CAPTIVE

Woman with the caught fox
By the scruff, you can drop your hopes;
It will not tame though you prove
    kind,

Though you entice it with fat ducks
Patiently to your fingertips
And in dulcet love enclose it,
Do not suppose it will turn friend,

Dog your heels, sleep at your feet,
Be happy in the house.

                    No,

It will only trot to and fro,
To and fro, with vacant eye;
Neither will its pelt improve
Nor its disposition, twisting
The raw song of its debasement

Through the long nights, and in your
        love,
In your delicate meats, tasting
Nothing but its own decay
(As at first hand I have learned).

                            Oh,

Kill it at once or let it go.
                    —W. S. Merwin

THE PLEIADES

They are heard as a choir of seven
shining voices; they descend
like a flock of wild swans to the
        water.

The white wing-plumage folds;
they float on the lake—seven
stars reflected among the reeds.

Tonight, the Seven Little Sisters,
daughters of the Moon, will come
        down
to bathe or wash their summer
        dresses.

They wear costumes of the seven
rainbow colors; they wear feather
mantles they can lift in sea winds

raised by their singing, and so rise
flying, soaring, until they fade
as the moon dawns; their voices dwin-
        dle

and die out in the North Woods,
        over
Australian bush, from Spartan
dancing grounds and African beaches.

They have returned to the sky
for the last time, and even
Electra's weeping over Troy is stilled.

What girl or star sings now
like a swan on the Yellow River?
                    —Mary Barnard

POEM ABOUT MORNING

Whether it's sunny or not, it's sure
To be enormously complex:
Trees or streets outdoors, indoors whoever you share,
And yourself, thirsty, hungry, washing,
An attitude toward sex.
No wonder half of you wants to stay
With your head dark and wishing
Rather than take it all on again—
Weren't you duped yesterday?
Things are not orderly here, no matter what they say.

But the clock goes off, if you have a dog,
It wags, if you get up now, you'll be less
Late. Life is some kind of loathsome hag
Who is forever threatening to turn beautiful.
Now she gives you a quick toothpaste kiss
And puts a glass of cold cranberry juice,
Like a big fake garnet, in your hand.
Cranberry juice! You're lucky, on the whole,
But there is a great deal about it you don't understand.

—WILLIAM MEREDITH

POEM AT EQUINOX

Pale darts still quivering, crocuses
    pin the ground down,
but underneath them falls and rises,
    like breasts under a gown,
a breathing land, and through its dreams,
    below the grass,
phantoms of flowers and phantoms
    of fruit pass—

as if in sleep sighing, fretting,
    when the unsleeping
ghost in the brain shoots shadows, setting
    the limbs leaping,
or as a canvas, in a crass wind
    pegged down,
catches the gust regardless and
    bellies around.

Heavy façades and factories, will you
    be heavy enough?
Or will the push unseat you until you
    shudder in half?
For crescent and clock tower, already
    huddling aloof,
feel all the heady thrusting ready
    to raise the roof,

and bells in the stone spires, swinging
    forth back and forth,
sense in their black crypts wriggling,
    snuffling earth

hump like a bear to get up; douce graves
    clamp down their dead
stricter than ever—and, oh, how the lark raves
    wild in the head

of whoever walks the tenements seeing
    sewer and slum
toss on a sea of returning being
    and the spring come
· and from under the cracked paving everywhere
    the tall sap shove
green bubbles bursting in the powdery air
    for love!

—HILARY CORKE

A POEM TO EXPLAIN EVERYTHING ABOUT
A CERTAIN DAY IN VERMONT

Fifty wizards working in the wind
And one tall wizard standing in their rear
Made a quick sheen to lacquer all Vermont.
Up leapt the sun. The air was far and near.

The weeds, the grass, the corn, the slipping river
Made wizard-quiet. My noon-sleepy deer
Whisked in the shade, saw winsome sun go over,
And still those wizards brewed the atmosphere.

The lone tall wizard opened up the west.
Sunset made its exit beryl and sheer.
Those wizards leapt like acrobats, swinging free,
Hung their thin capes upon cold Vega's spear . . .

Galaxies were thick, weather was clear.

—GENEVIEVE TAGGARD

POEMS TO A BROWN CRICKET

I

I woke
Just about daybreak and fell back
In a drowse.
A clean leaf from one of the new cedars
Has blown in through the open window.

How long ago—a huge shadow of wings pondering and hovering leaned down
To comfort my face.
I don't care who loved me.
Somebody did, so I let myself alone.
I will stand watch for you, now.
I lay here awake a long time before I looked up
And found you sunning yourself asleep
In the Secret Life of Jakob Boehme
Left open on the desk.

II

Our friends gave us their love
And this room to sleep in.
Outside now, not a sound.
Instead of rousing us out for breakfast,
Our friends love us and grant us our loneliness.
We shall waken again
When the courteous face of the old horse David
Appears at our window
To snuffle and cough gently.
He, too, believes we may long for
One more dream of slow canters across the prairie
Before we come home to our strange bodies
And rise from the dead.

III

As for me, I have been listening,
For an hour or so, now, to the scampering ghosts
Of Sioux ponies, down the long road
Toward South Dakota.
They just brought me home, leaning forward, by both hands clinging
To the joists of the magnificent dappled feathers
Under their wings.

IV

As for you, I won't press you to tell me
Where you have gone.
I know. I know how you love to edge down
The long trails of canyons.
At the bottom, along willow shores, you stand, waiting for twilight,
In the silence of deep grass.
You are safe there, guarded, for you know how the dark faces
Of the cliffs forbid easy plundering
Of their beautiful pueblos:
White cities concealed delicately in their chasms
As the new eggs of the mourning dove
In her ground nest

That only the spirit hunters
Of the snow can find.

V

Brown cricket, you are my friend's name.
I will send back my shadow for your sake, to stand guard
On the solitude of the mourning dove's young.
Here, I will stand by you, shadowless,
At the small golden door of your body till you wake
In a book that is shining.

—JAMES WRIGHT

THE POETS OF HELL

Poe, a very sick man in Baltimore,
Moaned, "Lord have mercy on my soul," and died.
Charles Baudelaire kept at his deathbedside
His mother's silver crucifix to adore.
Arthur Rimbaud, third of the poets of Hell,
And newly brought back from the sinful East,
Called for white linen, candles, and the priest
—Or so reports his sister Isabelle.

In Heaven three spirits with a single voice
Ceaselessly sing and pray for a lost lamb,
The brilliant Irish novelist James Joyce,
Who from the steps of Purgatory cries
"All or not at all. *Non serviam!*"
And spits into the constellated skies.

—KARL SHAPIRO

A POET SPEAKS FROM THE VISITORS' GALLERY

Have Gentlemen perhaps forgotten this?—
We write the histories.

Do Gentlemen who snigger at the poets,
Who speak the word professor with guffaws—
Do Gentlemen expect their fame to flourish
When we, not they, distribute the applause?

Or do they trust their hope of long remembrance
To those they name with such respectful care—

To those who write the tittle in the papers,
To those who tell the tattle on the air?

Do Gentlemen expect the generation
That counts the losers out when tolls the bell
To take some gossip-caster's estimation,
Some junior voice of fame with fish to sell?

Do Gentlemen believe time's hard-boiled jury,
Judging the sober truth, will trust again
The words some copperhead who owned a paper
Ordered one Friday from the hired men?

Have Gentlemen forgotten Mr. Lincoln?

A poet wrote that story, not a newspaper,
Not the New Yorker of the nameless name
Who spat with hatred like some others later
And left, as they will, in his hate his shame.

History's not written in the kind of ink
The richest man of most ambitious mind
Who hates a president enough to print
A daily paper can afford or find.

Gentlemen have power now and know it,
But even the greatest and most famous kings
Feared and with reason to offend the poets
Whose songs are marble
                and whose marble sings.
                  —ARCHIBALD MACLEISH

THE POND

With nets and kitchen sieves they raid the pond,
Chasing the minnows into bursts of mud,
Scooping and chopping, raking up frond after frond
Of swollen weed after a week of flood.

Thirty or forty minnows bob and flash
In every jam jar hoarded on the edge,
While the shrill children with each ill-aimed splash
Haul out another dozen as they dredge.

Choked to its banks, the pond spills out its store
Of frantic life. Nothing can drain it dry

Of what it breeds; it breeds so effortlessly,
Theft seems to leave it richer than before.

The nostrils snuff its rank bouquet—how warm,
How lavish, foul, and indiscriminate, fat
With insolent appetite and thirst, so that
The stomach almost heaves to see it swarm.

But trapped in glass the minnows flail and fall,
Sink, with upended bellies showing white.
After an hour I look and see that all
But four or five have died. The greenish light

Ripples to stillness, while the children bend
To spoon the corpses out, matter-of-fact,
Absorbed—as if creation's prodigal act
Shrank to this empty jam jar in the end.
                              —ANTHONY THWAITE

A POOL

This is a pool which bears deep looking into
Beneath moon-shadow trees, beneath the mud
I imagine at its bottom, and beneath
All its appearances as just a pool.
It is a special pool because the train
I am in has stopped indefinitely beside it.
I am the National Limited standing still.
I am the pool my eyes are stopped beside.
I am all Ohio deep in night and snow.
I am midway somewhere. Where, I do not know.
                              —THOMAS WHITBREAD

THE POPLAR'S SHADOW

When I was little, when
the poplar was in leaf,
its shadow made a sheaf:
the quill of a great pen
dark upon the lawn
where I used to play.

Grown, and long away,
into the city gone,

I see the pigeons print
a loop in air and, all
their wings reversing, fall
with silver undertint
like poplar leaves, their seams
in the wind blown.

Time's other side, shown
as a flipped coin, gleams

on city ground
when I see a pigeon's feather;
little and large together,
the poplar's shadow is found.

Staring at here,
and superposing then,

I wait for when.
What shapes will appear?
Will great birds swing
over me like gongs?
The poplar plume belongs
to what enormous wing?
—MAY SWENSON

POROUS

Cattail fluff
blows in
at the bank door,

and on wings
of chance
the money floats out,

lighter than a dream,
through the heavy walls
and vanishes.
—WILLIAM CARLOS WILLIAMS

THE "PORTLAND" GOING OUT

Early that afternoon, as we keep
Remembering, the water of the harbor
Was so smooth you wanted to walk on it—
It looked that trustworthy: glassy and black,
Like one of those pools they have in the lobbies
Of grand hotels. And, thinking back, we say
That the same bells we had heard telling
Their shoals and hours since we were children
Sounded different, as though they were
Moving about the business of strangers. By
Five, it was kicking up quite a bit,
And the greasiest evening you ever saw.
We had just come in, and were making fast,
A few minutes to seven, when she went
Down the harbor behind us, going out,
Passing so close over our stern that we
Caught the red glow of her port light for
A moment on our faces. Only
When she was gone did we notice

That it was starting to snow. No, we were
Not the last, or even nearly the last,
To see her. A schooner that lived through it
Glimpsed her, at the height of the storm,
In a clear patch, apparently riding it;
That must have been no more than minutes
Before she went down. We had known storms
Before almost as brutal, and wrecks before
Almost as unexplained, almost
As disastrous. Yet we keep asking
How it happened, how, and why Blanchard sailed,
Miscalculating the storm's course. But what
We cannot even find questions for
Is how near we were—brushed by the same snow,
Lifted by her wake as she passed. We could
Have spoken, we swear, with anyone on her deck,
And not had to raise our voices, if we
Had known anything to say. And now,
In no time at all, she has put
All of disaster between us—a gulf
Beyond reckoning. It begins where we are.

—W. S. Merwin

POSSIBILITIES

Three pigeons down-swing
through a chimney of air
onto Black Tom—a rock
in the Sound's shallows, bare
but for gulls' dung
and clams' broken crocks.
There is no food there—

not even a flotsam weed
from high tide. No food.
Unless you're a rock-dove
that maybe eats rocks; or brood
of the Roc, and feed
on imponderables—plasm of
lost time, dreamt magnitude.

Time plasm. There's a neat
notion, if lunatic,

like— Who was it who said
our souls make an aspic
for the moon to eat?
He saw Man as aphid
in an ant-heap zodiac.

Well, who knows what stocks
of men the moon needs?
She does drag out of us
dreams, longings, certain tides
in the blood, paradox—
being Ishtar, libidinous,
and Dian, light-of-maids.

Maybe time's the stuff
a moon eats. The white
meat of desire, the dark
of regret, a meat

Universe had none of
till mind reached fore and back—
and, to immortals, sweet.

Something is ranching us!
We wax in numbers; all
our plagues, wars, genocides
don't dent the capital
stock, the increasing mass

cracking on all sides
our spherical corral;

and always we strew in wake
of the planet—and cast ahead—
cobwebs of time. To the moon,
maybe, or some dread
Draco? A chance we take,
till pigeons settle in
their pigeonholes for good.

—Peter Kane Dufault

THE POSTMAN'S BELL IS ANSWERED EVERYWHERE

God and the devil in these letters,
stored in tin trunks, tossed in wastebaskets,
or ticketed away in office files:
love, hate, and business, mimeograph sheets, circulars,
bills of lading, official communiqués,
accounts rendered. Even the anonymous letter says,
Do not forget.

And in that long list, Dean Swift to Stella,
Walpole to Hannah More, Carlyle to Jane—
and what were Caesar's "Gallic Wars" other than letters
of credit for future empire?
                    Do not forget me.
I shall wear laurels to face the world;
you shall remember the head in bronze,
profile on coin.

As the bell rings, here is the morning paper and more letters,
the post date 10 P.M. "It is an effort
for me to write; I have grown older.
I have two daughters and a son, and business prospers,
but my hair is white; why can't we meet for lunch?
It has been a long time since we met;
I doubt if you would know me if you glanced quickly
at my overcoat and hat, and saw them vanish
in a crowded street. . . ."

Do not forget. . . . "Oh, you must not forget
you held me in your arms while the small room
trembled in darkness; do you recall the slender, violet
light between the trees next morning through the park?

Since I'm a woman, how can I unlearn
the arts of love within a single hour,
how can I close my eyes before a mirror,
believe I am not wanted, that hands, lips, breast
are merely deeper shadows behind the door
where all is dark? . . ."

Or, "Forgive me if I intrude; the dream I had
last night was of your face; it was a child's face,
wreathed with the sun's hair, or pale in moonlight,
more of a child than woman; it followed me
wherever I looked, pierced everything I saw,
proved that you could not leave me, that I am always
at your side. . . ."

Or, "I alone am responsible for my own death." Or,
"I am White, Christian, Unmarried, 21." Or, "I am happy
to accept your invitation." Or, "Remember that evening at the
Savoy-Plaza?" Or, "It was I who saw the fall of France."

As letters are put aside, another bell
rings in another day; it is, perhaps, not too late to remember
the words that leave us naked in their sight,
the warning,
                "You have not forgotten me;
these lines were written by an unseen hand
twelve hours ago. Do not reply at this address; these are the last
words I shall write."

—Horace Gregory

POWWOW

(TAMA RESERVATION, IOWA, 1949)

They all see the same movies.
        They shuffle on one leg,
                Scuffing the dust up,
        Shuffle on the other.
They are all the same:
        A Sioux dance to the spirits,
        A war dance by four Chippewa,
        A Dakota dance for rain.
                We wonder why we came.

Even tricked out in the various braveries—
    Black buffalo tassels, beadwork, or the brilliant
    Feathers at the head, at the buttocks—
Even in long braids and the gaudy face paints,
        They all dance with their eyes turned
    Inward, like a woman nursing
A sick child she already knows
    Will die. For the time, she nurses it
    All the same. The loudspeakers shriek;
        We leave our bleacher seats to wander
    Among the wickiups and lean-tos
In a search for hot dogs. The Indians
        Are already packing; have
    Resumed green dungarees and khaki,
    Castoff combat issues of World War II.
        (Only the Iroquois do not come here;
They work in structural steel; they have a contract
        Building the United Nations
    And Air Force installations for our future wars.)
These, though, have dismantled their hot-dog stand
        And have to drive all night
To jobs in truck stops and all-night filling stations.
        We ask directions and
    They scuttle away from us like moths.
        Past the trailers,
    Beyond us, one tepee is still shining
Over all the rest. Inside, circled by a ring
        Of children, in the glare
    Of one bare bulb, a shrunken fierce-eyed man
Squats at his drum, all bones and parchment,
        While his dry hands move
    On the drumhead, always drumming, always
Raising his toothless, drawn jaw to the light
    Like a young bird drinking, like a chained dog,
Howling his tribe's song for the restless young
        Who wander in and out.
        Words of such great age,
Not even he remembers what they mean.
        We tramp back to our car,
    Then nearly miss the highway, squinting
Through red and yellow splatterings on the windshield,
    The garish and beautiful remains
        Of grasshoppers and dragonflies
That go with us, that do not live again.

                —W. D. SNODGRASS

PRELUDE

Woman, woman, let us say these things to each other
as slowly as if we were mill-stones in a field
with centuries of rain in which to say them,
let us say in the morning
        "we do not hear each other"
and in the evening
        "we do not hear each other"
and let us be bewildered by the yes and no,
the plus and minus, the where and there,
the hour in the thistledown, the acre in the seed,

and walk distracted in the world of men,
bow to all voices,
see ourselves in the mirrors of all minds,
smile at all faces,
and in the beneficent evening, once more, always,
sleep in all peacefulness.

—Conrad Aiken

PRELUDE TO COMMENCEMENT

The air's advice is all
Young birds are guided by:
Fly and you will not fall,
Or fall and you will fly.

Love and you will be wise,
Be wise and you will love,

Heaven's designs advise
The young owl, the young dove.

You of a stranger feather,
More powerful in flight
Than all the birds together,
Cannot get off so light.

—Marie de L. Welch

A PRIMER OF THE DAILY ROUND

A peels an apple, while B kneels to God,
C telephones to D, who has a hand
On E's knee, F coughs, G turns up the sod
For H's grave; I do not understand,
But J is bringing one clay pigeon down,
While K brings down a nightstick on L's head,
And M takes mustard, N drives into town,

O goes to bed with P, and Q drops dead,
R lies to S, but happens to be heard
By T, who tells U not to fire V
For having to give W the word
That X is now deceiving Y with Z,
  Who happens just now to remember A
Peeling an apple somewhere far away.

—HOWARD NEMEROV

THE PRIVATE DINING ROOM

Miss Rafferty wore taffeta,
Miss Cavendish wore lavender.
We ate pickerel and mackerel
And other lavish provender.
Miss Cavendish was Lalage,
Miss Rafferty was Barbara.
We gobbled pickled mackerel
And broke the candelabara,
Miss Cavendish in lavender,
In taffeta, Miss Rafferty,
The girls in taffeta lavender,
And we, of course, in mufti.

Miss Rafferty wore taffeta,
The taffeta was lavender,
Was lavend, lavender, lavenderest,
As the wine improved the provender.
Miss Cavendish wore lavender,
The lavender was taffeta.

We boggled mackled pickerel,
And bumpers did we quaffeta.
And Lalage wore lavender,
And lavender wore Barbara,
Rafferta taffeta Cavender lavender
Barbara abracadabra.

Miss Rafferty in taffeta
Grew definitely raffisher.
Miss Cavendish in lavender
Grew less and less stand-offisher.
With Lalage and Barbara
We grew a little pickereled,
We ordered Mumm and Roederer
Because the bubbles tickereled.
But lavender and taffeta
Were gone when we were soberer.
I haven't thought for thirty years
Of Lalage and Barbara.

—OGDEN NASH

THE PRIVATE MEETING PLACE

I saw three withered women limp across
The burdock field, softly, before you came.
One of them chuckled, one was weaving moss,
And one made silly rhymes about your name.

How could I mock them? I believed their truth.
They have plucked away my loves from time long gone
And wagged their fingers at my comic wrath,
Danced in a ring, and faded back to stone.

You should have hurried here before those three
Measured this meeting place, and left their mark
(Your name scarred naked on a shrivelling tree),
And hobbled into the rocks to wait for dark.

Over your hair, I spy one humorous witch
Soundlessly gobbling berries, grapes, and wings,
And another dancing, waving a willowy switch,
And another murmuring inconceivable things.

Look in my eyes, love, let your eyelids close.
Lean to my whisper, seek for nothing more.
Cradled and rocked in drifts of woven moss,
Those hags remember I have died before,

Aghast at snow and time. They, too, will die,
Long after we lie grieved of them, and dumb.
Then we might mock their ashes where they lie,
We angry ghosts. But now the winter's come.

—JAMES WRIGHT

THE PRODIGAL

The brown enormous odor he lived by
was too close, with its breathing and thick hair,
for him to judge. The floor was rotten; the sty
was plastered halfway up with glass-smooth dung.
Light-lashed, self-righteous, above moving snouts,
the pigs' eyes followed him, a cheerful stare—
even to the sow that always ate her young—
till, sickening, he leaned to scratch her head.
But sometimes mornings after drinking bouts
(he hid the pints behind a two-by-four),
the sunrise glazed the barnyard mud with red;
the burning puddles seemed to reassure.
And then he thought he almost might endure
his exile yet another year or more.

But evenings the first star came to warn.
The farmer whom he worked for came at dark
to shut the cows and horses in the barn
beneath their overhanging clouds of hay,
with pitchforks, faint forked lightnings, catching light,
safe and companionable as in the Ark.
The pigs stuck out their little feet and snored.

The lantern—like the sun, going away—
laid on the mud a pacing aureole.
Carrying a bucket along a slimy board,
he felt the bats' uncertain staggering flight,
his shuddering insights, beyond his control,
touching him. But it took him a long time
finally to make his mind up to go home.

—ELIZABETH BISHOP

THE PROGRESS OF FAUST

He was born in Deutschland, as you would suspect,
And graduated in magic from Cracow
In 1505. His portraits show a brow
Heightened by science. The eye is indirect,
As of bent light upon a crooked soul,
And that he bargained with the Prince of Shame
For pleasures intellectually foul
Is known by every court that lists his name.

His frequent disappearances are put down
To visits in the regions of the damned
And to the periodic deaths he shammed,
But, unregenerate and in Doctor's gown,
He would turn up to lecture at the fair
And do a minor miracle for a fee.
Many a life he whispered up the stair
To teach the black art of anatomy.

He was as deaf to angels as an oak
When, in the fall of 1594,
He went to London and crashed through the floor
In mock damnation of the playgoing folk.
Weekending with the scientific crowd,
He met Sir Francis Bacon and helped draft
"Colours of Good and Evil" and read aloud
An obscene sermon at which no one laughed.

He toured the Continent for a hundred years
And subsidized among the peasantry
The puppet play, his tragic history;
With a white glove he boxed the Devil's ears
And with a black his own. Tired of this,
He published penny poems about his sins,
In which he placed the heavy emphasis
On the white glove which, for a penny, wins.

Some time before the hemorrhage of the Kings
Of France, he turned respectable and taught;
Quite suddenly everything that he had thought
Seemed to grow scholars' beards and angels' wings.
It was the Overthrow. On Reason's throne
He sat with the fair Phrygian on his knees
And called all universities his own,
As plausible a figure as you please.

Then back to Germany as the sages' sage
To preach comparative science to the young
Who came from every land in a great throng
And knew they heard the master of the age.
When for a secret formula he paid
The Devil another fragment of his soul,
His scholars wept, and several even prayed
That Satan would restore him to them whole.

Backwardly tolerant, Faustus was expelled
From the Third Reich in 1939.
His exit caused the breaching of the Rhine,
Except for which the frontier might have held.
Five years unknown to enemy and friend
He hid, appearing on the sixth to pose
In an American desert at war's end
Where, at his back, a dome of atoms rose.

—KARL SHAPIRO

THE PROMONTORY MOMENT

Think of only now, and how this pencil,
tilted in the sand, might be a mast,
its shadow to an ant marking the sun's place;
little and vast are the same to that big eye
that sees no shadow.

Think how future and past, afloat on an ocean
of breath, linked as one island,
might coexist with the promontory moment
around the sun's disc—for that wide eye
knows no distance or divide.

Over your shoulder in the circular cove, the sea,
woven by swimmers' gaudy heads, pulses an indigo
wing that pales at its frothy edge;
and, far out, sails, as slow as clouds,
change bodies as they come about.

Look at the standing gull, his pincered beak
yellow as this pencil, a scarlet streak beneath the tip,
the puff of his chest bowl-round and white,
his cuff-button eye of ice and jet
fixed on the slicing waves; shingle-snug, his gray wing
tucked to his side; aloft, that plumpness,
whittled flat, sits like a kite.

Turn to where fishermen rise from a neck
of rock, rooted and still, rods played like spouts
from their hips, until, beneath the chips of waves,
a cheek rips on the barb, a silver soul is flipped
from the sea's cool home into fatal air.

Close your eyes and hear the toss of the waves'
innumerable curls on the brow of the world—
that head is shaggy as Samson's, and three-fourths
furred. And *now* is eternal in beard and tress
piled green, blown white on churned sand,
the brand of the past an ephemeral smutch
of brown seaweed cast back to the sucking surf.

Tomorrow the marge is replaced
by a lace of shells, to be gathered again
by the hairy sea when it swells; here nothing is built
or grown, and nothing destroyed; and the buoyed
mind dares to enmirror itself,
as the prone body, bared to the sun,
is undone of its cares.

The eye, also a sun, wanders,
and all that it sees it owns;
the filled sail, tacking the line between water
and sky, its mast as high as this pencil,
becomes the gull's dropped quill, and the fleece
of the wave, and the sea robin's arc
now stilled on the rock.

—MAY SWENSON

PRO PATRIA

On a green island in the Main Street traffic
is a granite arch to the dead of the Civil War—
in the Eastlake style, all cubes and tetrahedrons,
each end of the passage barred by an iron-lace door.

They are always locked, though the space between is empty—
from door to door it isn't much over a yard;
break open one, you could almost touch the other.
Nobody knows what the locks were meant to guard.

East and west, the head of a blank-eyed lion
hisses an arc of spray to the pool below,
with a faint, persistent sound, an endless whisper,
steady under the traffic's stop and go.

On top of the monument stands a gilded lady
casting a wreath forever into space;
her carven robes are decent and concealing;
there is no emotion graven on her face.

Words are cut in the stone above the arches—
"THEY JOINED THE MORTAL STRUGGLE AND WENT DOWN"—
and on every quoin is written the name of a battle
that bloodied creek and landing, bluff and town,

now dry and hard in history and granite.
In summer the sun lies hot upon the stone,
and the bums and the drunks and the old men and the pigeons
take over the little island for their own.

The old men sit on a bench, with nuts and bread crusts
for the birds to eat from their hands; the ne'er-do-wells
sprawl on the grass and drowse and boast and argue;
the drunks discourse like statesmen and oracles,

while the birds skim over their heads with a cardboard clatter
of wings, or mince on the pavement at their feet.
They are all of them tolerant of one another
in this world like a bubble, this island in the street.

The sun is warm, the lions hiss, and the faithful
loaf in their places, lazy and benign,
a little hierarchy who inherit
this plot of earth, this obsolescent shrine.

Who can recall the day of that war's ending?
Think of our own time, then—the summer night
when the word came, and all the church bells sounded
the end of the dark and the coming of the light.

How many times how many towns have seen it,
the light, the hope, the promise, after the dark—
seen it, and watched it flicker and ebb and vanish,
leaving no trace except some little park

where no one recalls that dream, that disillusion,
and a monument to death is only known
as a place where the harmless unambitious gather
and the doves come down for bread on the sun-warmed stone.

—CONSTANCE CARRIER

THE PROPHETS

I keep pushing this
wheelbarrow full of ambition
down a bruised road
toward blind decisions like roadsigns
in a language I cannot read

with my brother the general
and my frenzied companion
the inner voice I have come a long
    way

but the dead do not
wait they do not give a damn
about any of us

I search for their lost faces
in a field of broken mirrors and find
only my eyes shattered
as usual vacant as usual

and all this time the dead
know what they are doing
they attend classes in forgetting
and come out with diplomas of si-
    lence

from nests in their ripe mouths
the aisles of teeth open like wings
and fly away

I shout to them across the distance I
tell them the worst thing
that can happen has happened

but they rise out of themselves
laughing silently watching
their fingers drip from their hands
letting them go

—RICHARD SHELTON

PROTHALAMION

The far court opens for us all July.
Your arm, flung up like an easy sail bellying,
comes down on the serve in a blue piece of sky
barely within reach, and you, following,
tip forward on the smash. The sun sits still
on the hard white canvas lip of the net. Five-love.
Salt runs behind my ears at thirty-all.
At game, I see the sweat that you're made of.
We improve each other, quickening so by noon
that the white game moves itself, the universe
contracted to the edge of the dividing line
you toe against—limbering for your service,
arm up, swiping the sun time after time—
and the square I live in, measured out with lime.

—MAXINE W. KUMIN

THE PRUNED TREE

As a torn paper might seal up its side,
Or a streak of water stitch itself to silk
And disappear, my wound has been my healing,
And I am made more beautiful by losses.
See the flat water in the distance nodding
Approval, the light that fell in love with statues,
Seeing me alive, turn its motion toward me.
Shorn, I rejoice in what was taken from me.

What can the moonlight do with my new shape
But trace and retrace its miracle of order?
I stand, waiting for the strange reaction
Of insects who knew me in my larger self,
Unkempt, in a naturalness I did not love.
Even the dog's voice rings with a new echo,
And all the little leaves I shed are singing,
Singing to the moon of shapely newness.

Somewhere what I lost I hope is springing
To life again. The roofs, astonished by me,
Are taking new bearings in the night, the owl
Is crying for a further wisdom, the lilac

Putting forth its strongest scent to find me.
Butterflies, the sailboat's grooves, are winging
Out of the water to wash me, wash me.
Now, I am stirring like a seed in China.

—HOWARD MOSS

PSYCHOANALYSIS

How can one tell what Love may be about
In his uncharted waters, where the mines
Entice the summer swimmers as they shout
And fishermen reel in tremendous lines?

The marker buoys bob lightly in slow motion
And near the ports the fish are known by schools—
But not the monsters of the deeper ocean
Or those unclassified in the rock pools.

With clarity and elegance of style
Cartographers trace maps—till one forgets
That in the teeming sea, mile after mile,
The biggest fish are still outside the nets.

—GAVIN EWART

PUER AETERNUS

A little child
Enters by a secret door, alone,
Was not, and is,
Carrying his torch aflame.

In pilgrim cloak and hood
Many and many come,
Or is it the one child
Again and again?

What journey do they go,
What quest accomplish, task fulfill?
Whence they cannot say,
Whither we cannot tell,
And yet the way they know.

So many innocents,
Reflections in a torrent thrown—
Can any on these treacherous waters
        cast,
Unmarred, unbroken,
Image the perfect one?

All things seem possible to the new-
        born;
But each one story tells, one dream
Leaves on the threshold of unbounded
        night,
Where all return
Spent torch and pilgrim shroud.

—KATHLEEN RAINE

PUERTO RICO SONG

Well, God is
love,
so love me.

God
is love, so
love me. God

is
love, so love
me well.

Love, the sun
comes
up in

the morning,
and
in

the evening—
zippe, zappe!—
it goes.

—WILLIAM CARLOS WILLIAMS

Q

THE QUEEN

Always before, we sped in the same direction,
not even aware we moved until the opposite train
swayed alongside. Then we saw
how full of arcs and spirals the course
webbed out before us: one train dipping
as the other rose out of sight to reappear
on the other side, so that we sat a foot apart,
peering into each other's lives.

Sometimes, when I regained the upper air,
I might look about expecting to see you
ascending the stair a second later,
but we met only underground,
both our trains hissing as though to strike
our illusory, single destination
just ahead in the darkness,
like the intertwining bodies of two snakes.

We met thus often. You never read
a paper or book or even the curved advertisements
of my time's madness above us,
always wearing the same unpleated blue,
wheat-colored hair drawn back by a single comb.
Whenever I saw you, you were already looking
into my gaze as long as the trains allowed.
Perhaps we invented each other. Neither smiled.

Here, this first winter day, I see you motionless
on the other platform, waiting as I,
but now for a train that runs the other way.
Again, you have already seen me when I notice,
but neither goes to the stairway that would lead
to the other's landing. We only stand and cast
a spider web of intersecting gazes,
less beautiful than those our courses wove.

I spin your history, sister, Persephone,
still wearing the color of your fields and skies,
making a stately progress across the river
into the kingdom of sleepless sleep. And yet,
I wonder why you rode so long beside me
and break away forever now, at the season's turning.
I could not be your king, except where dreams erupt
through an uprooted aconite in a field

real trains never reach. As a hiss of brakes
heralds our cars' arrival,
and our brittle net shatters in sympathy,
we wave goodbye, our only recognition,
until our trains curve back upon each other a last time,
you on the way to our impossible meadow
where the springtime's bridegroom waits,
I on my last descent into the dark.

—KENNETH PITCHFORD

THE QUEENS

The solemn whip-poor-will
That sang the dusk away grew still again.
Now from the summer night most still
Moth after moth comes feathery to the pane.

Now we have filled our kitchen with cold fire,
The salamandrine bird of Araby
Refreshed upon his pyre
Had no such incandescence as have we.

Enchanted by that dazzle and driven wild
From the wood, on powdered wings,
So lightly made and of a stuff so mild,
Come the soft beating things.

We see them on the black night, blind with love,
Flutter and cling, wings down.
Each one has ermine or satin robes, and bears above
A wand and crown.

—ROBERT FITZGERALD

THE QUEST

In pasture where the leaf and wood
Were lorn of all delicious apple,
And underfoot a long and supple
Bough leaned down to dip in mud,
I came before the dark to stare
At a gray nest blown in a swirl,
As in the arm of a dead girl
Crippled and torn and laid out bare.

On a hill I came to a bare house,
And crept beside its bleary windows,
But no one lived in those gray hol-
 lows,
And rabbits ate the dying grass.
I stood upright, and beat the door,
Alone, indifferent, and aloof
To pebbles rolling down the roof
And dust that filmed the deadened
 air.

High and behind, where twilight chewed
Severer planes of hills away,
And the bonehouse of a rabbit lay
Dissolving by the darkening road,
I came, and rose to meet the sky,
And reached my fingers to a nest
Of stars laid upward in the west;
They hung too high; my hands fell
 empty.

So, as you sleep, I seek your bed
And lay my careful, quiet ear
Among the nestings of your hair,
Against your tenuous, fragile head,
And hear the birds beneath your eyes
Stirring for birth, and know the world
Immeasurably alive and good,
Though bare as rifted paradise.

—JAMES WRIGHT

QUESTION IN A FIELD

Pasture, stone wall, and steeple,
What most perturbs the mind:
The heart-rending homely people,
Or the horrible beautiful kind?

—LOUISE BOGAN

R

THE RACER'S WIDOW

The elements have merged into solicitude.
Spasms of violets rise above the mud
And weed, and soon the birds and ancients
Will be starting to arrive, bereaving points
South. But never mind. It is not painful to discuss
His death. I have been primed for this—
For separation—for so long. But still his face assaults
Me; I can hear that car careen again, the crowd coagulate on asphalt
In my sleep. And watching him, I feel my legs like snow
That let him finally let him go
As he lies draining there. And see
How even he did not get to keep that lovely body.

—Louise Glück

THE RADIO UNDER THE BED

Why was a radio sinful? Lord knows. But it was.
So I had one
That I kept locked in a strongbox under my bed
And brought forth, turned on, tuned, and fondled at night,
When the sneaky housemaster slept and vice was all right.

The music played in my ear from the Steel Pier,
Knob Hill, the Astor, and other housemasterless
Hebrides where (I heard) the loved lived it up.
I listened myself to sleep, the sweet saxes
Filtering into my future, filling my cup.

All prohibitions have vanished. Radios bore me,
As do the two-step debauches I used to crave.
But the songs still remain, the old vulgar songs, and will play me,
Tum-te-tum, tum-te-tum, tum-te-tum, into my grave.

—Reed Whittemore

[583]

RAIN AT WILDWOOD

The rain fell like grass growing
upside down in the dark,
at first—thin shoots,
short, crisp, far apart—

but, roots in the clouds,
a thick mat grew
quick, loquacious, lachrymose blades
blunt on the tent top.

The grass beneath ticked,
trickled, tickled like rain
all night, inchwormed
under our ears,

its flat liquid tips slipping
east with the slope.
Various tin plates
and cups and a bucket filled

up outside,
played, plinked, plicked,

plopped till guttural.
The raccoon's prowl was almost

silent in the trash,
soggy everything but eggshells.
No owl called.
Waking at first light

the birds were blurred,
notes and dyes of jay and towhee
guaranteed to bleed.
And no bluing in the sky.

In the inverted V
of the tent flaps,
muddy sheets of morning
slumped among the trunks,

but the pin oaks' viridian,
dripping, raggedy leaves
on the wood's floor released
tangy dews and ozones.

—MAY SWENSON

RAKING LEAVES

Packed with woodpeckers, my head knocks,
Coaxing the drum of the tree to make its sap speak—
My sap, my boned branches, my veined leaves
Staining the wind, dizzying down
Amid a busyness of birds.

And she, in the bedroom, hands warm with work,
Smoothes out the wrinkles from the sheets,
That last night's tumbled sleep may once again
Grow young, that habit, unfolded back
Into desire, may heat the purposed place
Where body's music's sung. Unknown
Even to herself, as they
Who do not live by words, she sings
This place whose memories are birds,
And, as she turns away, back
Into her noon of bells, in her flown eyes

Nothing like gratitude remains;
There are no debts in her farewells.

Raking, taking time quickly,
I watch my own feet move in the ragged shade
Of the shagbark hickory, burly in the blood
Of my own speed, my own strength, now smack
In the sun, barbarously bright (sight
For closed eyes), and up, out again, to seek,
To take, to make what I will, skill of delight
I am not author of. Above, no missing God
I miss; high, satisfying sky, though; and, below,
Chrysanthemums in garb of gaiety,
Little serious clowns—and look, beyond the brook,
The fat grouse bumps across the field
And jumps for berries in the honeysuckle.

Not here, not now, one world goes down,
And not in my head the serious men
Chronicle its going. I cannot tell them
I am raking leaves. This day is hers;
This is my time; with us together
Two chores away, all rocking hours
Support this hour, all knocking days
Repeat this day.

—Robert Pack

RANDOM REFLECTIONS ON A SUMMER EVENING

All day the bird-song here has seemed
The praise and description of this sunny countryside;
Now, with the coming of the stars—
Revelation of the mournful depths of heaven,
Revelation of the truth—those gay voices
Falter, fall silent; a pensive silence,
Soundless as dew, a vague malaise descends,
Quieting all. No matter. In the early morning,
While yet the weather holds, while yet the planet Venus
Sparkles like a jewel on the breast of dawn,
Let us go walk in the woods; the wind
Stirs the top leaves, they rustle, they murmur together,
They clash, like waves of the sea, are still
As the wind stills; a crow rises, cawing,
And fades out of the copse like an evil thought,

Or a hermit-thrush, very far away,
From some towering oak lets fall
His bell-like music.
                        How good it is to ramble
Through leaf-green woods; or in autumn,
Before the trees turn bald, when the colors
Of autumn still flame on the boughs; in winter, too,
Under the tracery of bare branches,
While down the face of the rock
The waterfall hangs mute, and the tender brooks
Wear a new skin of ice—the mountain
Will mirror your voice there, as a mirror echoes
Your face.
                        How good it is to walk
By the strict sea, by void extension
Pressed to the point of absurdity; such vastness
Is supernatural, you await
Almost the feet of an angel treading the blue
Floor of trampling waves—he is
Your dead child-brother, and comes,
With averted face, not to blind you, and folded wings,
Over the level plain, the huge hollow of heaven
Would serve as his canopy. But, of course,
No miracle occurs; better
The loved, familiar things:
Soft ocean odors, space, light, rustling subsidence,
Whisper and hush of fawning waters
Along the shore that terns
Travel with downward head as if cogitating
Their scribbled hieroglyphs there, cast shells, driftwood,
Detritus, old sea-wreckage—the sandy beach
Flows, lion-colored, evenly on
Between the green of the dunes and the changing
Blue-green of the sea. The sea
Can be tragic when roused, has a longer memory
Than that of the wind; their encounter ended,
The wind will hush and the stars come out; not so easily
The sea forgets—hear then, long after,
The restless cry of waters passion-worn
Pleading for rest.
                        How strange the world is!
In the evening, the moon—whose orbit
Feeds parasitic upon earth's ampler orbit—
The gaunt skull of the moon, peers out
Or hides in hurrying cloud; bats
With their lopsided flight cut figures on the air,
Slipping and sliding like the town drunkard,

Tom Swain, who swears he saw,
At dawn, the clouds playing leapfrog and got so excited
He lost the way home.   Thunder
Growls in the west.
                        Now, in sky-crowding cities,
Under the neon's glare, under
The calcium light's demented moonlight, down
Canyons that cleave and rim
The city's massive rock, the sluggish
Man-swarm moves, the sluggish
Traffic, like impeded blood
In senile arteries, moves.   Here man
Has elected to dwell among his engines, here
Man's cleverness is all, he lives
In the shadow of monster shapes,
Created by him, that belittle him.
Strange beauty is here, sinister
Beauty that is man's own—see, from some towering mass,
As from some tower of time, watchful,
Two solemn eyes of light
Look seaward with incorrigible stare,
Questioning heaven.
                        In Kennedy
The fan-jet rouses, slowly
Trundling its ponderous body, the span of enormous wings
Rigidly spread, the stiff machine,
Ungainly on the ground as an albatross, rumbles
Toward the runway—wheels,
Manoeuvring for position—vibrates like an angry
Hornet, races the runway, is airborne, climbs,
Enters the palace of pure light,
The soundless, shadeless empyrean
Above earth's filth and tumult.   Soon
We are over the arctic highlands; wolves
Howl in the forest; in Africa,
The elephant trumpets his desolate call, the panther's
Scream tortures the night.   Oh, this animal lamentation
Heard round the planet—cries
Wrung out of rage, out of lust, out of hunger—only
The birds make music for joy, only
The insect orchestras draw their bows
Over the thighs of longing, only
The deer,.the rabbit, the snake comprehend
The value of reticence, the fish
The vanity of words; in the cool crystal
Of inland streams, in the dusky
Underworld ocean forests or dark

Quiet of deeper waters, oblivion
Of the hushed sea, they drift in silence
Or devour one another with remarkable rapidity, indifferent
To all but survival; in warmer waters
The octopus, a bald upside-down head,
With tentacles writhing like the Medusa's hair,
Hangs motionless, the grinning
Shark turns over to attack.
                              How beautiful
The clouds are: the great thunderheads
Piled one on the other; the lesser clouds hastening
Like messengers through heaven; clouds
Kindled by dawn or sunset—abysses of flame, portals
Opening on blue paradise; chiaroscuro
Of darkening cloud; luster
Of cloud around the moon; the upper strata,
Sand-ribbed or scaled like fish; whorls,
Flourishes, shreds of cloud unravelled by wind; high
Peace of exalted cirrus. How strangely
Clouds, at a certain moment, in a certain light, perhaps,
Will rouse us as to remembrance of something lost
That yet was there always, a sense
Of how we are part of things—stars, grass, earth—
And they of us. Oh, to move
Among the clouds and above them, to pass through the universe
As a god might, and taste
The whole of it in its splendor, to discover
New worlds and new races on them, beings
That have some kinship with us, and so break
Our long solitude here, upon
This lonely planet!
                              Where
Are they that are yet to be? Alicia,
Dear unborn child, your face
Haunts the darkness before birth. What generations
Lurk there, or speak to us
In wind or water, riffle of leaves, what millions
Wait in that dark and silence to which
The dead return! Truly,
Our home is among the unborn; there we find refuge
After this temporal dream. To each,
One taste of it, one life,
One only. No foreknowledge,
No memory after. It shall *not* have been.
The moment here is all.
                              How strange a thing time is,
Forever going and coming: the prow of the ship

And the stern of the ship move in separate waters
Yet are one ship and always
Travel the same water, and we, who live
Outside of time in dreams, live also
In a past and a future that form
The ever-continuing present. Dreamlike, the past is present
In the memories of an old man: the face of the mother
Bending over his cot; the first day at school,
Its pride, its terror; the first
Kiss of solemn first love—the grave eyes
Burning, so near, beyond him; faces of women
From the after-days; faces
Of friends, living or dead; face
Of the darling friend and more than friend, belovèd
Face, by half-light known, glimmer
Of cloudy breast, pale thigh—oh, nevermore
Between the dear body and the stars to confide
Life's sorrowful secret, never
Throughout all time again to share
The incommunicable moment!
                        How full of sadness the world is,
How full of evil and horror! At the jungle's edge,
The python slowly subdues
The body of the struggling fawn; the spider
Kisses the moth to sleep, and sucks
The life from her paralyzed victim; foul
Diseases dry up the sap
In the blossoming tree, the marrow
In the bones of a child—the lower
Preys on the higher, the bacillus would bring down
A Mozart, no favors are shown,
Catch-as-catch-can is the rule—whirlwinds and earthquakes
Devastate earth; well-reasoned
Insanities are abroad; in hidden vaults are ranged
The eggs that shall hatch death, his bombers
Are on the alert, the brute
Fury of violated matter shall be unleashed
Against mankind; our galaxy
Is rushing, almost with the speed of light,
Nowhere; there is, we are told,
No sense in things. But in our woods
There are pheasants, young ones—listen, beyond the thicket,
The tender cluck of the hen pheasant urging them on.

—John Hall Wheelock

RAVENGLASS RAILWAY STATION, CUMBERLAND

The up-line platform bridges a metal road
That slopes unwalled to salt and sand, and boats
Anchored in green-webbed goosefoot and sea aster,
Tarred spars and bendwaters, the cockly trod
Of stumps that mark the ebb track of the ford.
Here when a straight-from-Nova Scotia storm
Chivies in autumn the tide through the bar of the dunes,
Annexing tar and tarmac for the Irish Sea,
Children, waiting for a train, and nosing
End to end of a station long as a Blackpool pier,
Can drop their pennies between the wooden planks
Full splash into the water. The storm
Rolls up and over like a drum, leaving
The little auk and the fork-tailed petrel
Brained against telegraph poles; shore-side chimneys
Breathe heavy as horses into the mist; each tree,
Back jacked to the wind, arms high from the shoulder,
Twists in a tatter and tangle of brown,
Like a boy pulling his jersey over his head.
Here camped the Romans, sweating in thermal saloons,
Bragging their autobiographies like dice
(A raped virgin beats a burnt town),
Then in the exilic not-quite-dark, they ambled
Down past the boundary ditch to the huts and the girls,
Warm beds and Welsh voices, while yonder
The dunes, as now, drifted in the purple rain.
Here, too, in the winter of war the children came,
A Tyneside tang smoking from the stretched larynx,
And here the gold and graphite of the Tate,
Crated and stacked like lemons.
The wagons twitch their toes, the engine blows its nose,
Wheels, rods, and pistons bulge and blur in the spray,
And eighty tons of steel float easily away,
Light as suds in the breath of a child. But here
In the fog-sodden fields, under the rain-eaten
Dish-clout of the dykes, among the wrack and rubble
Of the gull-rummaged estuary, or hidden behind
The one-eyed wink of the ticket-seller's window—here
Is the root of a race, clamped tight to the rock,
Wringing from the earth its few last drops of green
Long years after the once tall trunk is down.

—NORMAN NICHOLSON

READING THE BROTHERS GRIMM TO JENNY

Jenny, your mind commands
kingdoms of black and white:
you shoulder the crow on your left,
the snowbird on your right;
for you the cinders part
and let the lentils through,
and noise falls into place
as screech or sweet roo-coo,
while in my own, real, world
gray foxes and gray wolves
bargain eye to eye,
and the amazing dove
takes shelter under the wing
of the raven to keep dry.

Knowing that you must climb,
one day, the ancient tower
where disenchantment binds
the curls of innocence,
that you must live with power
and honor circumstance,
that choice is what comes true—
oh, Jenny, pure in heart,
why do I lie to you?

Why do I read you tales
in which birds speak the truth
and pity cures the blind,
and beauty reaches deep
to prove a royal mind?
Death is a small mistake
there, where the kiss revives;
Jenny, we make just dreams
out of our unjust lives.

Still, when your truthful eyes,
your keen, attentive stare,
endow the vacuous slut
with royalty, when you match
her soul to her shimmering hair,
what can she do but rise
to your imagined throne?
And what can I, but see
beyond the world that is,
when, faithful, you insist
I have the golden key—
and learn from you once more
the terror and the bliss,
the world as it might be?

—LISEL MUELLER

READ ME, PLEASE!

If, as well may happen
    On an autumn day
When white clouds go scudding
    And winds are gay,

Some earth-bound spirit,
    A man lately dead
(Your fellow-clerk), should take it
    Into his crazed head

To adopt a more venturesome
    Shape than a dead leaf
And wish you a good morning,
    Abrupt and brief,

He will come disguised
    As a sheet of newspaper
Charging across the square
    With a clumsy caper,

To flatten himself out
  Across your shins and knees
In a suppliant posture:
  "Read me, please!"

Then, scanning every column
  On both sides, with care,

You will find the clerk's name
  Printed somewhere—

Unless, perhaps, in warning
  That sheet comes blown
And the name which you stumble on
  Is, alas, your own.

                                —ROBERT GRAVES

REAR VISION

The cars in the mirror come swiftly forward,
While I, in thought, move slowly back;
Time past (reflected) seems to wind
Along the boundaries of mind,
A highway cold, distinct, and black.
Who knows to what the years have led,
And at which turning up ahead—
On the white-stitched road reflected back—
The furies gather in a pack,
While all the sky above burns black,
Unwinding still the darkening thread?

                        —WILLIAM JAY SMITH

RECALL

But for an hour's sleep in a filthy bed
And a couple of stops for coffee, you have been driving
Steady since yesterday noon—for your country,
Your scoundrel country, suddenly cause
Of all that afflicts you: weather, a cold, a cough, and some psychic malaise
From not being where you should be, wherever that is.

But here at last is the Base; at the gate you exhibit
Your terrible summons, are passed, and pass on, in
To that old familiar wasteland of barracks and mess halls,
Where nothing, nothing has changed, could change, and no soldier,
No matter how daintily dandled and distanced by time,
Could think himself anywhere but (though unhappily) home.

You report to an insolent CQ reading the funnies.
You report to an empty supply room for sheets and blankets.
You report and report, sign your name, sign your name, and the forms
Lengthen, the files fatten, and lazily

The paperwork army marches, marches, marches
Through file-case crevasses, in-and-out-box morasses, everlastingly,

To chow. And the years come back.
Chow, time's goal, time's grail, is again before you,
A mirage from out of your past in maybe a dozen
States and countries: hundreds of heavy
Days dragging toward hundreds of lunches and suppers,
And not a step further.

It all comes back.
And you, falling in, march too, again, toward chow,
Having lost in one tedious morning five or six years
Of something that ailed you, and found the old remedy:
"Hip, hip. Eyes front. Chin up," to the tick
Of the marvellous stomach clock.

—REED WHITTEMORE

THE RED COW IS DEAD

Isle of Wight (AP)—Sir Hanson Rowbotham's favorite Red
Polled cow is dead. Grazing in the lush pastures of the Wellow
Farm, she was bitten on the udder by an adder.—*The Herald
Tribune.*

Toll the bell, fellow,
This is a sad day at Wellow:
Sir Hanson's cow is dead,
His red cow,
Bitten on the udder by an adder.

Spread the bad news! What is more sudden,
What sadder than udder stung by adder?
He's never been madder, Sir Hanson Rowbotham.

The Red Polled cow is dead.
The grass was lush at very last,
And the snake (a low sneak)
Passed, hissed,
Struck.

Now a shadow goes across the meadow,
Wellow lies fallow.
The red cow is dead, and the stories go round.
"Bit in the teat by a dog in a fit."

"A serpent took Sir Hanson's cow—
A terrible loss, a king's ransom."

A blight has hit Wight:
The lush grass, the forked lash, the quick gash
Of adder, torn bleeding udder,
The cow laid low,
The polled cow dead, the bell not yet tolled
(A sad day at Wellow),
Sir Hanson's cow,
Never again to freshen, never again
Bellow with passion—
A ruminant in death's covenant,
Smitten, bitten, gone.
Toll the bell, young fellow!

—E. B. WHITE

THE REMAINS

I empty myself of the names of others.
I empty my pockets. I empty my shoes and leave them beside
the road. At night I turn back the clocks; I open the family
album and look at myself as a boy.

What good does it do? The hours have done their job.
I say my own name. I say goodbye.
The words follow each other downwind.
I love my wife but send her away.

My parents rise out of their thrones
into the milky rooms of clouds. How can I sing?
Time tells me what I am. I change and I am the same.
I empty myself of my life and my life remains.

—MARK STRAND

REMEMBERING ALTHEA

When you came out of your house
and put your hand on the August day,
walls of the barn, delicate in the light,
began the season that would ribbon away
all that we saw and blow it past the world,

For after we contended at school, we had
our war, sought outward for enemies, awarded
each other greatness; and you were left
forgotten a while. Why touch what was
already ours, when there was more—cities, glory?

For you held no power, Althea,
according to any of us; but after the others
asserted, claimed their place, posed for
every storm, your true beam found all. That
August day is yours, and every honor

You gave away. I remember Jeff,
who always won, and Ben, and his sister,
that whole class. They are only your chorus,
because you waved, and it was far and the end,
you knew, delicately, through amber, that August day.

—WILLIAM STAFFORD

THE REPLY

Bird, bird don't edge me in;
  I've had enough today
  Of your fine-honèd lay
That prickles my coarse skin.

I'm neither out nor in
  Before that simple tune
  As cryptic as a rune,
  As round and pure as the moon,
And fresh as salt-drenched skin.

This shivers me; I swear
  A tune so bold and bare,
  Yet fine as maidenhair,
Shakes every sense. I'm five
Times five a man; I breathe
  This sudden random song,
  And, like you, bird, I sing,
  A man, a man alive.

—THEODORE ROETHKE

REPLY TO THE PROVINCES

He writes from the provinces: It is
Shuttered and desolate there; will I please
Every so often sit on a bench for him
In the Luxembourg Gardens? So now,
In the elegant autumn, to regard and guess:

The sea-eyed children watching their sloops
Angling on the flood? Expectant in their books
The delicate young women? The would-be
Casters-off of expectation? The hands-in-hands?
The Algerians, Americans, English, Danes,
Giving the Gardens their Parisian character?   ·
Fountained light streaming on the wind?
The fellow shucking chestnuts for his girl?
Surely these, and things of this kind—
Whatever is human. Also, I marvel at the leaves
Yellow on the sky, and there, on the grass,
Where the leaves overlap, yellow, the yellow sun
Forcing the hidden glowing from the earth.
I, like an ape on a branch, on a bench
Swing and peer in the jungle of mankind,
Closer, closer, I think, to the earth—its
Secret throes—than the swinging beast itself.

In the provinces, maybe he has walked from town.
In a city of leaves, he may have found her already.
Perhaps they are lying among the leaves, laughing,
Pointing out for each other the brown faces in the leaves.

—GALWAY KINNELL

THE REPORT

I

When I wake up again, when I wake up
Ready for small talk and a coffee cup,
Hearing the noise of time and break of dawn
In distinct alarms and a common yawn,
I wonder how those days will pass that do,
Though seldom exactly as I want them to;
And rise again and drink and eat and go
Down the hall, down the elevator and, so,
Out. Buildings stand out, a pigeon-gray,
And a gray street climbs the hill to Broadway.
I climb it. I slip into the people
And, like a lot of them, pick the hole
At Ninety-sixth Street to walk into.
And down, leaving the sky behind, we go—
Swallowed up without a bite
By a mouth without an appetite.

II

I come up seeing the same pigeons and different people
Or the same people and different pigeons that I left uptown.
They seem inescapable, grumpy or affable,
Brown, gray, plump, gray or brown.
The same things still seen on the same level.
We are not used to change.

In my office building there are four ranks of elevators.
Lobby captains, the idle brass of automation, stand
Ready for the nothing that usually occurs,
Looking alert, lost, grand,
As if I were a guest, they the waiters.
At what strange banquet, pray?

There are others. We go up in a scattered, speechless cluster,
Swung up in the humming air. The machine is impatient,
Closing its rubber-lipped doors anxiously after
Each of us has left—sent,
Delivered to our proper floor,
To open our own black door.

I open my own black door, walk in feeling rather dapper,
Feeling at home almost, master in that cubicle,
Free enough to sit and finish the morning paper,
And wheel my swivel
To the window where the flat skyscraper
Is half of what I see.

Two-thirds of the other half is equally fat and tall.
Hundreds of windows and a continual repetition
Of straight lines and the buildings are interchangeable.
The miscalculation
Of the sky stands out, blue, against that wall—
The park, a gap of green.

Tell me whether, when you, when you look out on such a scene,
The windows all the same and each repeating the same hard gaze
That yours repeats to them, you too feel there must be one
Behind which stares a face
And sits a body in all ways like your own,
That turns now as you turn.

I turn to work, to do what others in my building do.
I hear—through walls that are thin, dun, easily removable—
Others at work, as perhaps I am intended to.

Perhaps it makes us feel
As one—this listening, being listened to—
Although we rarely meet.

We see each other in a corridor. The smiles come.
Ride up together to another floor. What is there to say?
We live together, minor, in a gigantic home.
We criticize. We stay.
It is a world within a world for some.
For most, security.

And yet on evenings when I stay till ten, almost alone,
Saunter the halls and pay the automat that, hit, spits coffee
In a cup—there's a high-pitched, keen, whistling overtone
As elevators, empty,
Their affable, bland music playing on,
Rise in their shafts and fall,

Ecstatically mechanical, as if, if that place
Had a spirit, it rode there singing in the emptiness.
I listen, drink, and then return to my office,
Where, by night, I feel less
Single than during the days, when faces
Have voices and the rooms hum.

III

I shall not stay forever. I will go,
Someday, when I can afford to go,
Will leave that stiff, repetitive view
That still suggests there is another who,
With a similar, patient irony,
With the same wishes and glasses, looks at me
As I look out my window, as I wait
For him to move before it grows too late
To move, and walk, decisive, down the hall
To push the button and wait to fall,
And so continue, travelling in air,
Suspended, but moving downward in there,
Stepping out when the quick doors yawn
That close the minute we are gone—
Like a mouth without an appetite.
And, after the subway, walk up to the night.

—JON SWAN

REPORT FROM CALIFORNIA

I

In California,
ankle-high animals occupy the tablelands.
How many, going and coming from behind each other,
                    I cannot verify
(some ranging with insolence anywhere,
                    some never moving)
because my heart with its whips grows tired of pursuing
those creatures it cannot know it cannot know.

II

Men packed in slickers profess expertise
            off the coasts of California.
Some say the sinking rain is a whole thing,
            torn when they get to it.
Some say it's a handful of random parts
            falling toward nomination.

III

Our heads are not pleased with these provisions;
bells ring, guns ring, rains strike simultaneities,
but we are not amused.
We say this place, where nothing is sacrilege, is no fun—
we want a better odds.
We want a sky clear again,
with a yellow hemisphere, of which
the rest can be guessed and the whole called MOON.

IV

In California,
the opposite of one hundred suns is none
                    (and of one, too).
No wonder we feel we have things in common here.
We cry out, "Count us, Father, we are the same.
Do not distinguish—how could you?
We're a funnel of numbers; at the bottom is zero,
at the top eight hundred thousand. Count us!"

V

Sometimes in California they say
            the earth is flat (meaning it's tasteless),
or they say it's round (meaning it's not flat),
and under the slender stone-game-of-rain it rolls
and relieves the air of instabilities.

VI

But our heads are not pleased with these divisions
                              in California.
Where our eyes drift aimlessly over the ground,
they're like wild ideas.
To what shall we apply them? To nothing for long,
for truly they are soothed with drifting.

                                        —Lois Moyles

THE REPORTS COME IN

A country Gulliver
staked down on these plains,

rusted Kaisers and hot
Buicks race out my limbs,
trailing dust like overhead shots
in comic books.

Inspected by grocers
and tiny druggists,
I down twenty hogsheads of syrup,
wagonloads of meatloaf.

The reports come in:

young men with .22s
blast roadsigns.

Mosquito bumps,
a stuffed trout shudders dust
on the patrons of a roadhouse,

and somewhere in the lamplight
my country lurches from
its cot like a combine lurching
over a field of oats,

and scratching in its underwear,
fumbles for a heritage.

                                        —J. D. Reed

RESCUE

I have looked at this photograph
Of you at rest in that rowboat
For hours, but can't see your face.
When my eyes finally go slack,
The dark space
Between your white shirt and hat
Becomes a hole in the bay
Behind you, and I fall in.
I am no better swimmer
Now than I was at five,

And the past is more treacherous water
Than the creek you fished me from
Then, finding me by the bubbles
That were the chain of my breath.
Going down again, lifesaver,
Where it is darker and deeper,
I leave the same trail,
Believing that where you've been
Is the only depth I'll sound
That may save me from myself.

                                        —Dabney Stuart

THE RESCUE

I doubt if you knew,
my two friends,
that day the tips
of the boats' white wings
trembled over the capped,
brilliant lake
and fireboats at the regatta
rocketed their giant streams
blue and white and green
in the sun just off the shore,
that I was dying there.

Young jets were play-
ing over the lake,
climbing and falling back
with a quick, metallic sheen
(weightless as I am
if I dream),
sound coming after the shine.
They rose and ran and
paused and almost touched,
except for one,

who seemed to hang back in the air
as if from fear.

I doubt if you know,
my two beloved friends—
you with the furious black beard,
your classical head
bobbing bodiless above the waves
like some just appearing god,
or you: brown, lean, your bright
face also of another kind,
disembodied
when you walked upon your hands—

That as you reached for me
(both) and helped my graying bulk
up out of the lake
after I wandered out too far
and battered weak along the pier,
it was my self you hauled
back from my despair.

—JOHN LOGAN

RESOLUTION

Back of the door the child is playing that
Piano drawn on a piece of paper
He keeps to the black notes it
Gets dark
He moves to the white notes it gets
Too dark I can't hear him any more

As I was

The customs men multiply between

He takes with him
Memory leaking feathers
If he knew what I
Know now in the same X-ray

The pictures turn to the walls here is
Death the same taste in

A different color
Thinks I will say it

The scars
Grow leaves the feeling
Runs ahead and hides in bushes with its
Knives painted out
I know

Thinks I will say
It say it
As the hole climbs the sky

               Oh let it be yesterday surely
       It's time

       Never

Never

A usage I'm learning a beak at my ear
I hear

The hearts in bottles
The dice lying awake

The clock dropping its shoes and
No floor

              —W. S. MERWIN

THE RETURN

    After the light has set,
First I imagine silence; then the stroke
As if some drumbeat outside has come in.
And in the silence I smell moving smoke
And feel the touch of coarse cloth on my skin.
    And all is darkness yet
Save where the hot wax withers by my chin.

    When I had fallen (bone
Bloodying wet stone) he would lead me back
Along the street and up the corkscrew stair
(Time running anticlockwise, fingers slack)

And open windôws to let in fresh air
And leave me stretched alone
With sunken cheeks drained whiter than my hair.

Then I was young. Before
Another stroke he will come back in bone
And thin my heart. That soot-black hill will break
And raise him in his clay suit from the stone
While my chalk-ridden fingers dryly ache
And burn. On this rush floor
He will come striding hotly. When I wake

The stroke will have been tolled
And I shall take his crushed purse in my hand
And feel it pulse (warm, empty) on my wrist.
Blood floods my temples. Clay man, from what land
Have you come back to keep your freezing tryst
With someone grown so old?
Soldier, forgive me. Candles die in mist.

And now a cold wind stirs
Inside the shuttered room. I feel his hand
Brushing the stale air, feeling for my place
Across the phlegm-soaked pillows. I am sand
Threading a glass with slow and even pace
And dying in my furs.
My father turns, with tears on his young face.

—GEORGE MacBETH

RETURNING FROM HARVEST

It is always so: the declining
Daylight touching the edge
Of a window quickens knowledge,
Whets the invisible wing

Of thought, as the mist-hazed hummer
Michaelmas patterns weaves.
The stream understands the leaves
Better than in high summer.

And however the intellect
Predict the pattern of days,

It is never repeated. Always
A change we did not expect

Interprets the sickle gleaning
High sheaves for a sheltered place.
A young moon hangs in space
But shines with a different meaning.

Evening never deceives
Man, as the wagon swings
Back from migrating wings
To his mud-encrusted eaves.

They are gone before the stoat
In the iron track dawn-fires smelt
Changes his chestnut pelt
For the white of the ermine's coat.

O freshness of the precise
Season, frost-clear sky,
Full harvest tilted high
In the ruts of tomorrow's ice.

—VERNON WATKINS

THE RETURN TO WORK

Promenading their
skirted galleons of sex,
the two office assistants

one
(as I follow slowly
in the trade wind

rock unevenly
together
down the broad stairs,

of my admiration)
gently
slapping her thighs.

—WILLIAM CARLOS WILLIAMS

RILLONS, RILLETTES

R I L L E T T E S
Hors d'oeuvre made up of a mash of pigmeat, usually highly
seasoned. Also used for making sandwiches. The *Rillettes* enjoy-
ing the greatest popularity are the *Rillettes* and *Rillons de Tours*,
but there are *Rillettes* made in many other parts of France.

R I L L O N S
Another name for the *Rillettes*, a pigmeat *hors d'oeuvre*. The
most popular *Rillons* are those of Blois.
    —"*A Concise Encyclopaedia of Gastronomy*," *edited by André
    L. Simon.*

Rillons, Rillettes, they taste the same,
And would by any other name,
And are, if I may risk a joke,
Alike as two pigs in a poke.

The dishes are the same, and yet
While Tours provides the best *Ril-
    lettes,*
The best *Rillons* are made in Blois.
There must be some solution.
                    Ah!—

Does Blois supply, do you suppose,
The best *Rillettes de Tours*, while
        those
Now offered by the chefs of Tours
Are, by their ancient standards, poor?

Clever, but there remains a doubt.
It is a thing to brood about,
Like non-non-A, infinity,
Or the doctrine of the Trinity.

—RICHARD WILBUR

RISE AND SHINE

At the big trumpet, we must all put on
our dentures, tie old strings to knees, adjust
shank upon socket, wig to cranium, bust
on ribbed architrave, fastidiously don
our properties, and blink to face the sun.
Farewell, dream image, cankered in our dust,
and sweets shrunk in the brain, farewell, we trust.
Uprise, O fragment brethren! We have won—
For, hallelujah, these dry graves are torn!
Thin bugles crash the valley of our bones
to rock the vultures wide away and scare
the griffin from his precipice as, worn
and damp, we crawl like grubs from under stones
to scarf our loves in paradisial air.

—RICHMOND LATTIMORE

THE RITUALISTS

In May, approaching the city, I
saw men fishing in the backwash
between the slips, where at the time
no ship lay. But though I stood

watching long enough, I didn't see
one of them catch anything
more than quietness, to the formal
rhythms of casting—that slow dance.

—WILLIAM CARLOS WILLIAMS

THE RIVER

The lifeguard's whistle organized our swimming
Around the anchored raft at summer camp,
Saving us from the tricky channel current.
When he blew it, we gave in to the system,
Each raising his buddy's hand in the sudden quiet
To be reckoned, officially, among the living.
Half a pair meant someone might have drowned
Or, more likely, not checking out, gone back
To his cabin where no one made him buddy,
Where, if he wished, he could desert the raft,

The restricting whistle, all practiced safety,
And, dreaming the channel's bottom, sound
That deep cut, the rocks' dark hollows, and the cold.

I have been back once, when no one was there,
And poked around in the empty cabins
Boarded against vandals as if something valuable
Were left to steal, where no one was dreaming.
Yet, as if in a dream, I saw a name
The same as mine printed in faded chalk
On a wall, and I took a dented canteen
With a torn case from a nail rusted with rain.
It lay on the beach with my clothes while I went swimming
Where the channel cuts deep across from the steady raft,
Without a buddy. In over my head,
I finned to the bottom, expelling breath
Until the cold pressure cracked in my ears,
Then fought that pressure upward with my arms
And shot, like a dolphin, high
Into the weightless air
Over and over again, each time higher,
Until I could use the bottom as a springboard.
However high I went, there was always bottom.

After, I took the canteen to the springs
Which feed the river, and filled it.
It hangs now on a nail in my room,
And when the season's dry and the city liquid
Tastes too much of metal and the system
That pumps it to my taps,
I drink that water, and find it cool and clear.

—DABNEY STUART

RIVER GOD'S SONG

My eyes are white stones
That shine through water
As the moon shines
Through a glistening mist,
My limbs the supple ripples
That part like a fan
Or fuse into one,
Wrinkle and fade
As lines erased
On a carbon pad.
The racing weed
Is my green hair.
Stare in the pool—
My wraith is there
In a wreath of water
Around a rock;

Look for long,
It will disappear.

My name is Evenlode,
Windrush, or Dove;
Or else Alpheus,
Ladon, Leucyanias:
Water as dark
As a night with glittering
Stars of the frogbit;
Water so clear
That the peering fish
Fear their own shadows;
As sleek as oil,

Or boiling down
In white cascades
And braids of glass.
Choose my name
And paint my scene
After your choice,
I am still the river.
You passers by
Who share my journey,
You move and change,
I move and am the same;
You move and are gone,
I move and remain.

—Anne Ridler

THE RIVERMAN

A man in a remote Amazonian village decides to become a
sacaca, a witch doctor who works with water spirits. The river
dolphin is believed to have supernatural powers; Luandinha is
a river spirit associated with the moon; and the *pirarucú* is a fish
weighing up to four hundred pounds. (These and many other
details on which this poem is based are from "Amazon Town," by
Charles Wagley. The *sacacas* named were famous fifty years ago.)

I got up in the night
for the Dolphin spoke to me.
He grunted beneath my window,
hid by the river mist,
but I glimpsed him—a man like my-
    self.
I threw off my blanket, sweating;
I even tore off my shirt.
I went through the window naked.
My wife slept and snored.
Hearing the Dolphin ahead,
I went down to the river
and the moon was burning bright
as the gasoline-lamp mantle
with the flame turned up too high,
just before it begins to scorch.
I went down to the river.

I heard the Dolphin sigh
as he slid into the water.
I stood there listening
till he called from far outstream.
I waded into the river
and suddenly a door
in the water opened inward,
groaning a little, with water
bulging above the lintel.
I looked back at my house,
white as a piece of washing
forgotten on the bank,
and I thought once of my wife,
but I knew what I was doing.

They gave me a shell of *cachaça*
and decorated cigars.

The smoke rose like mist
through the water, and our breaths
didn't make any bubbles.
We drank *cachaça* and smoked
the green cheroots. The room
filled with gray-green smoke
and my head couldn't have been diz-
      zier.
Then a tall, beautiful serpent
in elegant white satin,
with her big eyes green and gold
like the lights on the river steamers—
yes, Luandinha, none other—
entered and greeted me.
She complimented me
in a language I didn't know;
but when she blew cigar smoke
into my ears and nostrils
I understood, like a dog,
although I can't speak it yet.
They showed me room after room
and took me from here to Belém
and back again in a minute.
In fact, I'm not sure where I went,
but miles, under the river.

Three times now I've been there.
I don't eat fish any more.
There is fine mud on my scalp
and I know from smelling my comb
that the river smells in my hair.
My hands and feet are cold.
I look yellow, my wife says,
and she brews me stinking teas
I throw out, behind her back.
Every moonlit night
I'm to go back again.
I know some things already,
but it will take years of study,
it is all so difficult.
They gave me a mottled rattle
and a pale-green coral twig
and some special weeds like smoke.
(They're under my canoe.)
When the moon shines on the river,
oh, faster than you can think it

we travel upstream and downstream,
we journey from here to there,
under the floating canoes,
right through the wicker traps,
when the moon shines on the river
and Luandinha gives a party.
Three times now I've attended.
Her rooms shine like silver
with the light from overhead,
a steady stream of light
like at the cinema.

I need a virgin mirror
no one's ever looked at,
that's never looked back at anyone,
to flash up the spirits' eyes
and help me recognize them.
The storekeeper offered me
a box of little mirrors,
but each time I picked one up
a neighbor looked over my shoulder
and then that one was spoiled—
spoiled, that is, for anything
but the girls to look at their mouths
      in,
to examine their teeth and smiles.

Why shouldn't I be ambitious?
I sincerely desire to be
a serious *sacaca*
like Fortunato Pombo,
or Lúcio, or even
the great Joaquim Sacaca.
Look, it stands to reason
that everything we need
can be obtained from the river.
It drains the jungles; it draws
from trees and plants and rocks
from half around the world;
it draws from the very heart
of the earth the remedy
for each of the diseases—
one just has to know how to find it.
But everything must be there
in that magic mud, beneath
the multitudes of fish,

deadly or innocent,
the giant *pirarucús*,
the turtles and alligators,
tree trunks and sunk canoes,
with the crayfish, with the worms
with tiny electric eyes
turning on and off and on.
The river breathes in salt
and breathes it out again,
and all is sweetness there
in the deep, enchanted silt.

When the moon burns white
and the river makes that sound
like a primus pumped up high—
that fast, high whispering
like a hundred people at once—
I'll be there below,
as the turtle rattle hisses
and the coral gives the sign,

travelling fast as a wish,
with my magic cloak of fish
swerving as I swerve,
following the veins,
the river's long, long veins,
to find the pure elixirs.
Godfathers and cousins,
your canoes are over my head;
I hear your voices talking.
You can peer down and down
or dredge the river bottom
but never, never catch me.
When the moon shines and the river
lies across the earth
and sucks it like a child,
then will I go to work
to get you health and money.
The Dolphin singled me out;
Luandinha seconded it.

—Elizabeth Bishop

THE ROAD BACK

The car is heavy with children
tugged back from summer,
swept out of their laughing beach,
swept out while a persistent rumor
tells them nothing ends.
Today, we fret and pull
on wheels, ignore our regular loss
of time, count cows and others,
while the sun moves over
like an old albatross
we must not count or kill.

There is no word for time.
Today, we will not think
to number another summer
or watch its white bird into the ground.
Today, all cars,
all fathers, all mothers, all
children and lovers will
have to forget
about that thing in the sky
going around
like a persistent rumor
that will get us yet.

—Anne Sexton

ROBINSON

The dog stops barking after Robinson has gone.
His act is over. The world is a gray world,
Not without violence, and he kicks under the grand piano,
The nightmare chase well under way.

The mirror from Mexico, stuck to the wall,
Reflects nothing at all. The glass is black.
Robinson alone provides the image Robinsonian.

Which is all of the room—walls, curtains,
Shelves, bed, the tinted photograph of Robinson's first wife,
Rugs, vases, panatelas in a humidor.
They would fill the room if Robinson came in.

The pages in the books are blank,
The books that Robinson has read. That is his favorite chair,
Or where the chair would be if Robinson were here.

All day the phone rings. It could be Robinson
Calling. It never rings when he is here.

Outside, white buildings yellow in the sun.
Outside, the birds circle continuously
Where trees are actual and take no holiday.

—WELDON KEES

ROBINSON AT HOME

Curtains drawn back. The door ajar.
All winter long it seemed a darkening
Began. But now the moonlight and the odors of the street
Conspire and combine toward one community.

These are the rooms of Robinson.
Bleached, wan, and colorless this light, as though
All the blurred daybreaks of the spring
Found an asylum here, perhaps for Robinson alone,

Who sleeps. Were there more music sifted through the floors
And moonlight of a different kind,
He might awake to hear the news at ten,
Which will be shocking, moderately.

This sleep is from exhaustion, but his old desire
To die like this has known a lessening.
Now there is only this coldness that he has to wear.
But not in sleep. Observant scholar, traveller,

Or uncouth bearded figure squatting in a cave,
A keen-eyed sniper on the barricades,
A heretic in catacombs, a famed roué,
A beggar on the streets, the confidant of popes—

All these are Robinson in sleep, who mumbles as he turns,
"There is something in this madhouse that I symbolize—
This city—nightmare—black—"

                                    He wakes in sweat
To the terrible moonlight and what might be
Silence. It drones like wires far beyond the roofs,
And the long curtains blow into the room.

                                    —WELDON KEES

THE ROOM

The room a dying poet took
at nightfall in a dead hotel
had both directories—the Book
of Heaven and the Book of Bell.

It had a mirror and a chair,
it had a window and a bed,
its ribs let in the darkness where
rain glistened and a shop sign bled.

Not tears, not terror, but a blend
of anonymity and doom,
it seemed, that room, to condescend
to imitate a normal room.

Whenever some automobile
subliminally slit the night,
the walls and ceiling would reveal
a wheeling skeleton of light.

Soon afterward the room was mine.
A similar striped cageling, I

groped for the lamp and found the
          line
"Alone, unknown, unloved, I die"

in pencil, just above the bed.
It had a false quotation air.
Was it a she, wild-eyed, well-read,
or a fat man with thinning hair?

I asked a gentle Negro maid,
I asked a captain and his crew,
I asked the night clerk. Undismayed,
I asked a drunk. Nobody knew.

Perhaps when he had found the
          switch
he saw the picture on the wall
and cursed the red eruption which
tried to be maples in the fall?

Artistically in the style
of Mr. Churchill at his best,

those maples marched in double file
from Glen Lake to Restricted Rest.

Perhaps my text is incomplete.
A poet's death is, after all,
a question of technique, a neat
enjambment, a melodic fall.

And here a life had come apart
in darkness, and the room had grown
a ghostly thorax, with a heart
unknown, unloved—but not alone.

—Vladimir Nabokov

A ROOM IN THE VILLA

What is the mirror saying with its O?
What secret does the still, untroubled surface lock?
What terror told by chair, by unmade bed and bedclothes?
Now the clock is speaking; hear the clock.

Hear it tensely ask: Is someone coming?
Did someone just then step into the hall below?
Is someone there upon the stairway, whistling, humming?
The solemn mirror's mottled, mocking O,

Like some black lake, absorbs all things in silence.
A tattered curtain flaps; the coals within the grate
Are kindled to a brief and unremarked refulgence
While, patient in the eaves, the shadows wait.

—William Jay Smith

THE ROSE

I

There are those to whom place is unimportant,
But this place, where sea and fresh water meet,
Is important—
Where the hawks sway out into the wind
Without a single wingbeat,
And the eagles sail low over the fir trees,
And the gulls cry against the crows
In the curved harbors,
And the tide rises up against the grass
Nibbled by sheep and rabbits.

A time for watching the tide,
For the heron's hieratic fishing,
For the sleepy cries of the towhee—

The morning birds gone, the twittering finches,
But still the flash of the kingfisher, the wingbeat of the scoter,
The sun a ball of fire coming down over the water,
The last geese crossing against the reflected afterlight,
The moon retreating into a vague cloud shape
To the cries of the owl, the eerie whooper.
The old log subsides with the lessening waves,
And there is silence.

I sway outside myself
Into the darkening currents,
Into the small spillage of driftwood,
The waters swirling past the tiny headlands.
Was it here I wore a crown of birds for a moment
While on a far point of the rocks
The light heightened,
And below, in a mist out of nowhere,
The first rain gathered?

II

As when a ship sails with a light wind—
The waves less than the ripples made by rising fish,
The lacelike wrinkles of the wake widening, thinning out,
Sliding away from the traveller's eye,
The prow pitching easily up and down,
The whole ship rolling slightly sideways,
The stern high, dipping like a child's boat in a pond—
Our motion continues.

But this rose, this rose in the sea-wind,
Stays,
Stays in its true place,
Flowering out of the dark,
Widening at high noon, face upward,
A single wild rose, struggling out of the white embrace of the morning glory,
Out of the briary hedge, the tangle of matted underbrush,
Beyond the clover, the ragged hay,
Beyond the sea pine, the oak, the wind-tipped madroña,
Moving with the waves, the undulating driftwood,
Where the slow creek winds down to the black sand of the shore
With its thick grassy scum and crabs scuttling back into their glistening craters.
And I think of roses, roses,
White and red, in the wide six-hundred-foot greenhouses,
And my father standing astride the cement benches,
Lifting me high over the four-foot stems, the Mrs. Russells, and his own elaborate
        hybrids,

And how those flowerheads seemed to flow toward me, to beckon me, only a child,
    out of myself.

What need for Heaven, then,
With that man, and those roses?

III

What do they tell us, sound and silence?
I think of American sounds in this silence:
On the banks of the tombstone, the wind harps having their say,
The thrush singing alone, that easy bird,
The killdeer whistling away from me,
The mimetic chortling of the catbird
Down in the corner of the garden, among the raggedy lilacs,
The bobolink skirring from a broken fencepost,
The bluebird, lover of holes in old wood, lilting its light song,
And that thin cry, like a needle piercing the ear, the insistent cicada,
And the ticking of snow around oil drums in the Dakotas,
The thin whine of telephone wires in the wind of a Michigan winter,
The shriek of nails as old shingles are ripped from the top of a roof,
The bulldozer backing away, the hiss of the sandblaster,
And the deep chorus of horns coming up from the streets in early morning.
I return to the twittering of swallows above water,
And that sound, that single sound,
When the mind remembers all,
And gently the light enters the sleeping soul,
A sound so thin it could not woo a bird.

Beautiful my desire, and the place of my desire.

I think of the rock singing, and light making its own silence,
At the edge of a ripening meadow, in early summer,
The moon lolling in the close elm, a shimmer of silver,
Or that lonely time before the breaking of morning
When the slow freight winds along the edge of the ravaged hillside,
And the wind tries the shape of a tree,
While the moon lingers,
And a drop of rain water hangs at the tip of a leaf
Shifting in the wakening sunlight
Like the eye of a new-caught fish.

IV

I live with the rocks, their weeds,
Their filmy fringes of green, their harsh
Edges, their holes
Cut by the sea-slime, far from the crash
Of the long swell,

The oily, tar-laden walls
Of the toppling waves,
Where the salmon ease their way into the kelp beds,
And the sea rearranges itself among the small islands.

Near this rose, in this grove of sun-parched, wind-warped madroñas,
Among the half-dead trees, I came upon the true ease of myself,
As if another man appeared out of the depths of my being,
And I stood outside myself,
Beyond becoming and perishing,
A something wholly other,
As if I swayed out on the wildest wave, alive,
And yet was still.

And I rejoiced in being what I was:
In the lilac change, the white reptilian calm,
In the bird beyond the bough, the single one,
With all the air to greet him as he flies,
The dolphin rising from the darkening waves;

And in this rose, this rose in the sea-wind,
Rooted in stone, keeping the whole of light,
Gathering to itself sound and silence—
Mine and the sea-wind's.

—THEODORE ROETHKE

A RUNE FOR C.

Luck? I am upset. My dog is ill.
I am now in that gray shuttling trains go in for;
The sky clouds; it is hard to believe dawn will

Ever show up.—I look for omens:
Not birds broken, not Fords lashed around trees,
But some item showing that fate is open. . . .

Sometimes, far far down in the magical past
Of us all, in something that stutters, something that rises,
There is an intimation of luck just

Swinging over our way: a cat's paw loose
In the banister, a long train-run, and then,
Square and oil-shambled, blue between elms, the caboose!

—BARBARA HOWES

RUNES FOR AN OLD BELIEVER

The wolves of evening will be much abroad—
Hold to the sprig of rowan
When we are near the evening of the world.

The weather darkens; wilderness and wood
Thicken with stalkers; when the sun goes down,
The wolves of evening will be much abroad.

They creep toward fold and barn, across the field,
Gaunt-gray or shagbark-brown,
When we are near the evening of the world.

The herd their meat, their smell the smell of blood,
The ground their ground, the bolted house their own,
The wolves of evening will be much abroad.

The body, like the oak, is bent and gnarled,
The shallow-rooted mind is overthrown,
When we are near the evening of the world.

If iron fails, and salt, and Aaron's rod,
Hold to the twig of rowan.
When we are near the evening of the world,
The wolves of evening will be much abroad.

—ROLFE HUMPHRIES

S

SACRIFICE OF A RED SQUIRREL

Leaping from oak to oak, tangled-up in the woods,
    Gray squirrels and reds
Scrambled in elegant furs with nuts in their heads.
That was their life; they didn't know any other.
    Spring, once arrayed
In sun-checkered flowers, stood in its climate of shade,
      Crying
    Squirrels, beware, beware;
      Red squirrel, run!
The fixed ideas are coming to hunt you down.

Three boys strolled up to the woods from neighboring farms
    With a twenty-two gun.
They wanted a red squirrel fur. Red squirrel, run!
That was their life. Why should they learn of another?
    Quick targets in trees
Were trophies of summer, red squirrels the rarest of these,
      Crying
    Squirrels, beware, beware;
      Red squirrel, run!
The fixed ideas are coming to hunt you down.

Bang went the gun. Gray squirrels ran into their holes;
    And red squirrel now,
With a front leg flapping, clung to the uppermost bough,
Quivering with life. If he would know of another
    Some instinct must hide
An eye of himself around on the opposite side,
      Crying
    Squirrels, beware, beware;
      Red squirrel, run!
The fixed ideas are coming to hunt you down.

Red was the sheen of his coat; then it glistened in sun
    Redder than red.

Teetering high on his claws, he chattered and bled
And hung to his home. How could he cling to another?
      Then up came a stone
And tickled the paw of the leg with the bullet-hung bone,
        Crying
    Squirrels, beware, beware;
      Red squirrel, run!
The fixed ideas are coming to hunt you down.

Then up came showers of stones and bangs from the gun,
      Shouts from the boys,
And the green home trembled over that chaos of noise.
Alive to this life, and not having known any other,
      Red squirrel, come down!
Crawl at their feet and ride in their sack to the town,
        Crying
    Squirrels, beware, beware;
      Red squirrel, run!
The fixed ideas are coming to hunt you down.

And now in their halls he hangs on a missile of skins,
      While mere boys comb
The wing-diving furs that flew in the airiest home.
And that is their life; they still do not know any other.
      Oh, wild riddled woods,
Autumnal with reds, quake in your great green hoods
      And cry
    Squirrels, beware, beware;
      Red squirrel, run!
The fixed ideas are coming to hunt you down.

                —JOSEPH LANGLAND

SAILING, SAILING

It is the sea's edge lubbers love,
Where sand, the mirror, slurs their
    faces,
And the surf's smash completes the
    cove,
At least from an observer's basis.

Such people like the harbor's hull
That rides so steady in the swell
And never lists or pitches. Lull,
Not squall, for them, means sailing well.

But we have known some sailors who,
In a seaway mauled around,
Didn't dream of Malibu
Or catboats on Long Island Sound.

A lot of commodores in whites
Foundered on the yacht-club shoals
While Captain Slocum's riding lights
Danced a jig between the poles.

                —GRAY BURR

SAILORS

When the last star breathes like a rose
On the stem of the mast,
A woman appears on deck.

In her shy look the sailors
Inhale the perfume of swamp roots
And certain dark streets of Marseille.

She stands still in a shadow
While the bow cleaves the dawn
And waves slap the laboring hull.

Voices of children rising from the
    sea,
Air bells and flowers . . .
Or maybe she is thinking of a house,

One of those little streets in Paris
Where lovers twitter like canaries
And yellow sunlight stripes the wall.

Or maybe it's a forest

Where birds and dreams go drifting
    through the leaves.
On Sundays you can hear hosannas.

All this, and more, the sailors
Think of while she stands,
One hand lightly resting on the rail.

In the morning light, a line
Stretches and the star fades.
Farewell, my old pine forest!

I might have lived there for a thou-
    sand years.
She turns and descends,
Carrying their lives with her. The bell
    strikes,

And the muscular sailors
Face the day heat, with blades of
    anger
Threshing the salt green sea.

—Louis Simpson

SAINT NICHOLAS,

might I, if you can find it, be given
a chameleon with tail
that curls like a watch spring; and vertical
on the body—including the face—pale
tiger-stripes, about seven
    (the melanin in the skin
        having been shaded from the sun by thin
            bars; the spinal dome
                beaded along the ridge
                    as if it were platinum)? *

If you can find no striped chameleon,
might I have a dress or suit—
I guess you have heard of it—of *qiviut?*
And, to wear with it, a taslon shirt, the drip-dry fruit

* Pictured in *Life*, September 15, 1958, with a letter from Dr. Doris M. Cochran, Curator
of Reptiles and Amphibians, National Museum, Washington, D.C.

of research second to none,
    sewn, I hope, by Excello,
    as for buttons to keep down the collar-points, no.
      The shirt could be white—
        and be "worn before six,"
      either in daylight or at night.

But don't give me, if I can't have the dress,
a trip to Greenland, or grim
trip to the moon. The moon should come here. Let him
make the trip down, spread on my dark floor some dim
    marvel, and if a success
      that I stoop to pick up and wear,
        I could ask nothing more. A thing yet more rare,
          though, and different,
            would be this: Hans von Marées'
          St. Hubert, kneeling with head bent,

    form erect—in velvet, tense with restraint—
hand hanging down; the horse, free.
Not the original, of course. Give me
a postcard of the scene—huntsman and divinity—
    hunt-mad Hubert startled into a saint
      by a stag with a Figure entined.
    But why tell you what you must have divined?
      Saint Nicholas, O Santa Claus,
        would it not be the most
        prized gift that ever was!
                                    —MARIANNE MOORE

ST. VALENTINE,

permitted to assist you, let me see . .
    If those remembered by you
are to think of you and not me,
      it seems to me that the memento
      or compliment you bestow
should have a name beginning with "V,"

such as Vera, El Greco's only
    daughter (though it has never been
proved that he had one), her starchy
      veil, inside chiffon; the stone in her

ring, like her eyes; one hand on
her snow-leopard wrap, the fur widely

dotted with black. It could be a vignette—
  a replica, framed oval—
bordered by a vine or vinelet.
    Or give a mere flower, said to mean the
    love of truth or truth of
love—in other words, a violet.

Verse—unabashedly bold—is appropriate;
  and always it should be as neat
as the most careful writer's "8."
    Any valentine that is *written*
Is as the *vendange* to the vine.
    Might verse not best confuse itself with fate?

                              —MARIANNE MOORE

SALAMIS

A treatise of the Subtle Body,
Dark van of winter-pledging stars,
Spearheads of the advancing deep
Of seas whose soft commotions keep
The tracery of ships' lace spars.
Another island: another small eternity;
Many tonight must smell the thunder,
Look up uneasily from yellowing books—
Is the work of art really a work of nature
To mobilize the sense of wonder,
Revise all time's nomenclature?

On the dark piers to roam, to anonymize,
A blue rust dusted to tones of soots,
Plum dark, the countenances move in mist
And the seaman's ironshod boots
On the wet quays loiter and list,
And some lost tug hoots and hoots.

A night of leave-takings and summaries,
Inventory of the capes unwinding
In their old smoke and cursing spray,
In scarves of smoking suds—
Never to leave, perhaps, never to go away,
And yet, past the heart's reminding,
See the soft underthrust of water sway

The spending loin come combing out
Ringlets washed back from a dead sea-king's
Face, a helm of gold, a mask
In the autumnal water's writhing.
To remain and realize were the harder task.

—LAWRENCE DURRELL

SANDPIPER

The roaring alongside he takes for granted,
and that every so often the world is bound to shake.
He runs, he runs to the south, finical, awkward,
in a state of controlled panic, a student of Blake.

The beach hisses like fat. On his left, a sheet
of interrupting water comes and goes
and glazes over his dark and brittle feet.
He runs, he runs straight through it, watching his toes.

—Watching, rather, the spaces of sand between them,
where (no detail too small) the ocean drains
rapidly backwards and downwards. As he runs,
he stares at the dragging grains.

The world is a mist. The world is marvellously
minute and vast and clear. The tide
is higher or lower. He couldn't tell you which.
His beak is focussed; he is preoccupied,

looking for something, something, something.
Poor bird, he is obsessed!
The millions of grains are black, white, tan, and gray,
and mixed with quartz grains, rose and amethyst.

—ELIZABETH BISHOP

SCALA COELI

We do not see them come,
Their great wings furled, their boundless forms infolded
Smaller than poppy seed or grain of corn,
To enter the dimensions of our world
In time to unfold what in eternity they are,
Each a great sun, but dwindled to a star
By the distances they have travelled.

Higher than cupola their bright ingress;
Presences vaster than the vault of night,
Incorporeal mental spaces infinite,
Diminished to a point and to a moment brought.
Through the everywhere and nowhere invisible door
By the many ways they know,
The thoughts of wisdom pass;
In seed that drifts in air or on the waters' flow,
They come to us down ages long as dreams
Or instantaneous as delight.

As from seed tree, flower, and fruit
Grow and fade like a dissolving cloud,
Or as the impress of the wind
Makes waves and ripples spread,
They move unseen across our times and spaces.
We try to hold them, trace on walls
Of cave, cave-temple or monastic cell their shadows cast:
Animal-forms, warriors, dancers, winged angels, words of power
On precious leaves inscribed in gold and lapis lazuli,
Or arabesques in likeness of the ever-flowing.
They show us gardens of Paradise, holy mountains
Where water of life springs from rock or lion's mouth,
Walk with us unseen, put into our hands emblems,
An ear of corn, pine cone, lotus, looking glass or chalice;
As dolphin, peacock, hare or moth or serpent show themselves,
Or human-formed: a veiled bride, a boy bearing a torch,
Shrouded or robed or crowned, four-faced,
Sounding lyre or sistrum, or crying in bird-voices.

Water and dust and light
Reflect their images as they slowly come and swiftly pass.

We do not see them go
From visible to invisible like gossamer in the sun;
Bodies by spirit raised
Fall as dust to dust when the wind drops,
Moth-wing chrysalis.
Those who live us and outlive us do not stay
But leave empty their semblances, icons, bodies
Of long-enduring gold or the fleet golden flower
On which the Buddha smiled.
In vain we look for them where others found them,
For by the vanishing stair of time immortals are forever departing;
But while we gaze after the receding vision
Others are already descending through gates of ivory and horn.

—Katlheen Raine

SCENE OF A SUMMER MORNING

Scene of a summer morning: my mother walking
To the butcher's, I led along. Mountains
Of feathers. My breath storms them. Angry feathers.
Handfuls. The warm gut windings stinking.
Here, chickens! Yankel, the bloody storeman—
Daringly he takes the live animals
In vain. Yankel, a life for a life! Eternal
Morning too young to go to school. I get
A hollow horn to keep. Feathers, come down!
Gone. The world of one morning. But somewhere,
Sparkling, it circles a sunny point.

Incredible the mazes of that morning,
Where my life in all the passages at once
Is flowing, coursing, as in a body
That walked away, went.
                        Who writes these lines
I no longer know, but I believe him
To be a coward, the only one who escaped.
The best and bravest are back there still,
All my Ten Tribes wandering and singing
In the luminous streets of the morning.
Unsounded the horn! And silence shudders
In the center of the sunny point,
Heartstopping at dawn.
Enormous my thieving hand in the ancient sunlight
No longer mine. Littering through my fingers,
Drifting, the Ten Tribes there, lost forever.

                                —IRVING FELDMAN

THE SEA BIRDS

No light except the stars, but from the cliff
I saw in motion, out on the rolling waves,
The white sea birds that swim beyond the surf.

Their movements made a pattern on the mauve,
Contorted stretch of dark, corrosive water,
Where even the images of stars dissolve.

When I had thought the birds were fixed in order,
I saw the swimming rim of their starlit ring
Minutely swerve and spiral toward the center;

The birds that had been swimming in between
Were shuttled outward on a wheel of light,
Reflecting, like the sea, the stars' design.

I paused, and looked, and saw a star burn out
And sink back into space as through a fissure.
It was an ancient word without a thought.

Perhaps birds love the pattern for the measure
It imposes on the ruptured waves at night;
Perhaps they spiral purely for their pleasure.

While I was trying to untie this knot,
A motion in the motion of the weather
Turned, and the birds turned, too, and tore the net

I knitted for them. (A star had torn another
I had knitted for stars.) I saw them climb the gale
That drove small arrows in through every feather—

One by one they spread their flapping sails.
I think the stars are moving in a school
With restless birds above a freezing pool,
And no one shall put salt on their bright tails.
                                        —VAN K. BROCK

SEA BURIAL FROM THE CRUISER "REVE"

She is now water and air,
Who was earth and fire.

"Reve" we throttled down
Between Blake's Point and Western Isle,

Then, oh, then, at the last hour,
The first hour of her new inheritance,

We strewed her ashes over the waters,
We gave her the bright sinking

Of unimaginable aftermaths,
We followed her dispersed spirit

As children with a careless flick of wrist
Cast on the surface of the sea

New-cut flowers. Deeper down,
In the heavy blue of the water,

Slowly the white mass of her reduced bones
Waved, as a flag, from the enclosing depths.

She is now water and air,
Who was earth and fire.

—RICHARD EBERHART

THE SEA FOG

It was sudden.
From that slightly heaving hotel of the folder,
we watched through the glass a blood-orange ball
just diving, a pure blue desert of dusk
on the other horizon; a motion, the symbol of seas,
carried our music, our drinks, the relative facets
of latitude, longitude, steward and poster, and sun disc
just hidden.

The ship spoke
with a minotaur sound from around and under,
and we raised our eyes; but the sea was gone—
sub-sun, space darkening, the swelling shift
of dunes of water, our precious image of movement—
gone, gone, clean gone. The fog was at the pane.
No shore behind us; ahead, in the breathy drift,
no port.

Supported
by shore and port, now we had neither.
There was only here. The ship was here
in the fog. The ship roared and the fog blotted
us into itself and fumed into its rifts,
and the sealess, skyless fear—and there was fear—
had nothing to do with sinking; at least, not
into water.

Worse:
when we went below, at the familiar turn,
a bulkhead reared instead, metal and huge,
and, trapped, we turned from that hulk and hastened
through stranger stairs and came from a different angle

to a cabin stiller and smaller, though none of its objects had moved.
But the mirror stirred like fog when we looked
at the fastened face.

We crept
through fog all night, but it closed behind us,
around, and very close above.
Only down down in the black, the self-lit fishes
passed ignorantly among the wracks of wrecks,
and all the water held its tongue and gave
no password; and so, sealed in our motionless passage,
we slept.

The bell
for the bulkhead doors to open woke us.
Everything had been reconnected: sun to the sea,
ship to the sun, smiles to our lips, and our names related
to our eyes. Who could—in that brassy blue—
have stillness to harbor the memory
of being relative to nothing; isolated;
responsible?

—JOSEPHINE JACOBSEN

SÉANCE

Now, suddenly, the table rocks, a bell
Rings savagely, a high-pitched Cockney voice
Close to the ceiling cries, "Lor' love a duck,
But many a narsty secret I could tell."

Miss Sloane, at the piano, bangs the hymn once more;
The widow from Roslindale chokes back a sob.
In the sweating darkness we are brothers and sisters,
Nearer to terror than we'd bargained for.

It is our immense ennui, we claim, that keeps
Us here, in this rented room, with its smell of gin
And formalin, among the red serge hangings.
It is to amuse us that the table leaps.

Then why, when the bell was silent, did you press
My hand and shudder? Why, when that voice said,
"Ducky, it's love you're wanting," did you cry out,
As though I were not beside you, "Yes! Oh, yes!"

—WILLIAM ABRAHAMS

SEA SCHOOL

This afternoon I swam with a school of fish.
Waiting in shallow water for the tide to change,
They swept at leisure through their green pleasance,
Turning at will as one, or at some private
Signal all felt;
White and delicate, each one bedizened
By an ochre spot behind his sickle of gill,
Pale translucent fish they were, divided
By the hair-thin mustache-line of backbone.

We plied our way along, taking our ease
In concert, as a school,
Feeling the flickering lozenges of light—
Chicken wire of sunlight grazing us
As we passed up and down under its stroke.
So for an hour, an age, I swam with them,
One with the rhythm of the sea, weightless,
Graceful and casual in our schoolhood,
Within our coop of light,
One with a peace that might go on forever. . . .
Till, of a sudden, quick as a falling net,
Some thought embraced them. I watched them go
Tidily over the reef, where I could not follow.

—Barbara Howes

THE SEASONS

All the seasons are riders.—*From "Carried Wide," by Mike Fagan.*

They all are riders: Spring on a two-year-old,
A chestnut colt, with a green way of going,
Azure and saffron halves, with pink cross sashes,
And a whip with blossoms on it, forsythia-gold.

Summer, all green, blue cap, on a distance runner
In a good field, dark bay or black or brown,
Getting the distance handily, well-lathered,
Yet coming back ears forward, far from blown.

Autumn in scarlet coat, a tanned outrider
On a fat piebald pony, whom they all

Troop after in parade, in bright decorum,
Toward the last race of all.

And Winter a hollow-cheeked, gaunt, grizzled jockey—
Forcing an old gray jumper, whose white breath
Steams on the air, over the black rail fences,
Across the snow—in at the fox's death.

—ROLFE HUMPHRIES

SECOND GLANCE AT A JAGUAR

Skinful of bowls, he bowls them,
The hip going in and out of joint, dropping the spine
With the urgency of his hurry
Like a cat going along under thrown stones, under cover,
Glancing sideways, running
Under his spine. A terrible, stump-legged waddle,
Like a thick Aztec disemboweller
Club-swinging, trying to grind some square
Socket between his hind legs round,
Carrying his head like a brazier of spilling embers,
And the black bit of his teeth—he takes it
Between his back teeth, he has to wear his skin out,
He swipes a lap at the water trough as he turns,
Swivelling the ball of his heel on the polished spot,
Showing his belly like a butterfly,
At every stride he has to turn a corner
In himself and correct it. His head
Is like the worn-down stump of another whole jaguar,
His body is just the engine shoving it forward,
Lifting the air up and shoving on under,
The weight of the fangs hanging the mouth open,
Bottom jaw combing the ground. A gorged look,
Gangster, club tail lumped along behind gracelessly,
He's wearing himself to heavy ovals,
Muttering some mantra, some drum song of murder
To keep his rage brightening, making his skin
Intolerable, spurred by the rosettes, the Cain brands,
Wearing the spots off from the inside,
Rounding some revenge. Going like a prayer wheel,
The head dragging forward, the body keeping up,
The hind legs lagging. He coils, he flourishes
The blackjack tail as if looking for a target,
Hurrying through the underworld, soundless.

—TED HUGHES

SEDIMENT

You are such a well-rounded sponge
from head to foot that I have made
        myself
a lake for you, not to see you shrivel
        up,
and I have surrounded you with trees
and a distant view of a mountain,
calm sky above. No rain comes
while you and I float together,

your reflection in me; but then slowly
you settle down, filled. I think
you are going to drown
and I will go dry, utterly absorbed in
        you,
my mud and rock showing. I worry
about us, you swollen and out of
        shape
and I tasting of sediment.

—DAVID IGNATOW

SEMMES IN THE GARDEN

Semmes waited under the still trees;
Shadow lay dead across his knees.
Europe was half a world away
From that burnt September day,
But fortress, city, armed frontier
Were near as now and close as here;
For all the bright abstract terrain
Was vivified in Semmes's brain,
And he, the modern Hercules,
Supported Europe on his knees,
Where the colored map was spread.
In the still trees above his head,

Crouched upon a lower limb,
A panther lay regarding him;
Piston thigh and razor tooth
Concentrated on his youth.
Between the panther and the map,
Semmes waited in a balanced trap.
The panther, watching from the
        shade,
Tightened for his leap, delayed,
And poised with muscles taut, intent
Upon the passionless descent.

—GEORGE MARION O'DONNELL

THE SENSE OF SMELL

Smells—how many
Evocative, poignant,
Hypnotic, pervading
Smells: the beanfield
(May's carousal),
The bonfire (autumn's
Mart of memory);
Turf smoke for Ireland,
Wine for France;
Moss rose, jasmine
For love, and violets;
Homesick rosemary,
Lavender, mint,
Buddleia (loud

With bees), and clover;
Trees in rain;
Tar for travel.

And the smells indoors:
Pantry and kitchen—
Chicken in casserole,
Baking bread,
Cheddar, cinnamon,
Herring and mackerel,
Coffee in the morning,
Oil and garlic.
Each of the rooms
A different blend—

Beeswax, hyacinth,
And burning logs;
Leather and pipe smoke;
Trunks and damp;
French fern soap
And bath powder;
Witch hazel, talc,
Laundered linen;
Smells of domestic
Peace, routine.

Social smells:
Office and warehouse,
Factory and train;
Smut and soot
And Diesel oil.
Smell of a church:
Hassocks and prayer books,
Varnished pews
And brass polish,
Odor of sanctity,
Gas and mortar.
Smells of hotels:
Cigars and soap.
Smells of the cinema:
Real and fancied—
The fancy sweet
With the spice of China,
Attar of summer
And Arabian wafts;
Plush and cheap
Scent and stale
Smoke the reality.
Smell of the work gang:
Coke in a brazier,
Sweat, corduroy,
Shirts they sleep in,
Beer and shag,
Cement, tarpaulin.
Smells of the rich:
Blend of indulgence—
Turkish tobacco,
Punch and gin,
Perfumed women
And men's barbers,
Eau de cologne
And Harris tweed.

Smells of shops:
Heterogeneous—
Clamor of groceries,
Candles, fish,
Methylated spirits,
Rolls of carpets.
Smell of the roads:
Of hedge and moor,
Gasoline, rubber,
Asphalt, carbon,
Flax and pinewood,
Tar and wind.
Smell of the ports:
Bales and pitch,
Crates of oranges,
Anthracite,
Terra Incognita,
Foreign flesh.
Smells of farms:
Goats and cow dung,
Hay and gaiters,
Udder and crupper,
A wet dog lying
On the parlor floor,
Hanging halters,
Mash and bran.

And whatever the place,
At whatever time,
The smells we cannot
Name, but known
Smells, and some
Unknown, but ours.

And how many others
Linked for different
People with different
Times and people,
Historic, exotic
Chains and fountains;
Smells that become
Picture and music,
Prayer and communion,
Challenge and anthem,
Ghost and angel,
Dissolving the present
Moment and changing

Season and tone
Back to a vanished
April, an ended
Voyage, a picnic
On grass that now
Is pavement; sweeping
Us back to islands
That are off the map,
To forbidden bedrooms
In demolished houses,
Homes we left
Or ports we touched at,
Back to a walled
Garden or a wood,
To a street or a field,
To nursery or *bistro*,
To unusual or usual
Days, to forgotten

Slang, to abandoned
Habits, to men
And women and children.

Smells—how many
Tricky, deceiving,
Luminous will-
O'-the-wisps, Aladdin's
Lamps that are lost
When hardly lit,
Bricked-up arches
Suddenly open,
Revealing roads
Or woodland alleys,
But bricked-up arches
Before we enter.
How many delights?
How many adieus?

—Louis MacNeice

SEPARATE PARTIES

(for my daughter)

While your great-grandmother and her sons
Champagned her eightieth birthday
Into a timeless, elegant disguise,
You stayed aloof, kept away
From their brave oblivion,
Hugging your two-year generation like a prize.
No one would guess
The silent fact to which you gestured *Yes*.

Divorced, I see you seldom, a legal sleight
Of hand, making you seem, when you appear, a trick,
Or a conjurer getting into the act.
This time, your voice a wand, you called the olives grapes,
Discovered a river under the tablecloth,
Spoke into pleasing shapes
The gargoyles on the mantel,
Saved a wayward moth
From the deadly candle.

Simply by word of mouth,
Unfallen angel, you hung a world
Out in the sun to glisten.

It had its own light, too, like a pearl.
All I had to do was listen.
Yet, deserting your role,
You called me by my name—
I'd rather
Have been that metaphor, your father.

Now you've gone home. Alone in this dark house,
Where light is artificial but itself,
I sink in a cushy chair, pelf
From the estate
Of a man I couldn't change, just hate,
Whose blood I get to save
For the transforming grave,
And think of nothing special.

The taste of my cigarette
Stales in my mouth. I think of this debt
Neither money nor self-spite
Has power to set right.
For supper, I can have bread or water
With my inheritance. I'm not partial.
Child, though magician, elf, you're not
My imagination but my daughter.

—DABNEY STUART

THE SEQUEL

I

Was I too glib about eternal things,
An intimate of air and all its songs?
Pure aimlessness pursued and yet pursued
And all wild longings of the insatiate blood
Brought me down to my knees. O who can be
Both moth and flame? The weak moth blundering by.
Whom do we love? I thought I knew the truth;
Of grief I died, but no one knew my death.

II

I saw a body dancing in the wind,
A shape called up out of my natural mind;
I heard a bird stir in its true confine;
A nestling sighed—I called that nestling mine;
A partridge drummed; a minnow nudged its stone;
We danced, we danced, under a dancing moon;

And on the coming of the outrageous dawn,
We danced together, we danced on and on.

III

Morning's a motion in a happy mind:
She stayed in light, as leaves live in the wind,
Swaying in air, like some long water weed.
She left my body, lighter than a seed;
I gave her body full and grave farewell.
A wind came close, like a shy animal.
A light leaf on a tree, she swayed away
To the dark beginnings of another day.

IV

Was nature kind? The heart's core tractable?
All waters waver, and all fires fail.
Leaves, leaves, lean forth and tell me what I am;
This single tree turns into purest flame.
I am a man, a man at intervals
Pacing a room, a room with dead-white walls;
I feel the autumn fail—all that slow fire
Denied in me, who has denied desire.

—THEODORE ROETHKE

THE SHADOWGRAPHS

Image comes down to live as fact, and turns
in the same motion, and is memory. The process
climbs my long gallery, jogs the score, and burns
in points of color, fancy, and—ah yes!—
love. For the same finesse
that changed my copper counters into gold
falters not, sleeps not ever, nor grows old.

What then have I not done, what have I done
with *sometimes, not,* and *never,* how to list
my loss against my gain when all are one
and on the vision's glad and deceived mist
the blond illusionist
performs before my captured audience
her same and golden chores of innocence?

Here is a march of fictions down the road
to nowhere and forever. Did I live
these dolls of faith or die that episode

of fury? Who knows now? Pale, through a sieve,
drained days combine to give
substance of what? Who knows? Never goodbye
while the deft hand is sweeter than the eye.
                                        —RICHMOND LATTIMORE

THE SHARK'S PARLOR

Memory: I can take my head and strike it on a wall   on Cumberland Island
Where the night tide came crawling under the stairs   came up the first
Two or three steps   and the cottage stood on poles all night
With the sea sprawled under it   as we dreamed of the great fin circling
Under the bedroom floor. In daylight there was my first brassy taste of beer
And Payton Ford and I came back from the Glynn County slaughterhouse
With a bucket of entrails and blood. We tied one end of a hawser
To a spindling porch-pillar and rowed straight out of the house
Three hundred yards into the vast front yard of windless blue water
The rope outslithering its coil   the two-gallon jug stoppered and sealed
With wax   and a ten-foot chain leader   a drop-forged shark-hook nestling.
We cast our blood on the waters   the land blood easily passing
For sea blood   and we sat in it for a moment with the stain spreading
Out from the boat   sat in a new radiance   in the pond of blood in the sea
Waiting for fins   waiting to spill our guts also in the glowing water.
We dumped the bucket, and baited the hook with a run-over collie pup. The jug
Bobbed, trying to shake off the sun as a dog would shake off the sea.
We rowed to the house   feeling the same water lift the boat a new way,
All the time seeing where we lived rise and dip with the oars.
We tied up and sat down in rocking chairs, one eye on the other responding
To the blue-eye wink of the jug. Payton got us a beer and we sat

All morning sat there with blood on our minds   the red mark out
In the harbor slowly failing us   then   the house groaned   the rope
Sprang out of the water   splinters flew   we leapt from our chairs
And grabbed the rope   hauled   did nothing   the house coming subtly
Apart   all around us   underfoot   boards beginning to sparkle like sand
With the glinting of the bright hidden parts of ten-year-old nails
Pulling out   the tarred poles we slept propped-up on   leaning to sea
As in land-wind   crabs scuttling from under the floor   as we took turns about
Two more porch-pillars   and looked out and saw   something   a fish-flash
An almighty fin in trouble   a moiling of secret forces   a false start

Of water   a round wave growing   in the whole of Cumberland Sound the one
      ripple.
Payton took off without a word   I could not hold him either

But clung to the rope anyway   it was the whole house bending
Its nails that held whatever it was   coming in a little and like a fool
I took up the slack on my wrist. The rope drew gently   jerked   I lifted
Clean off the porch and hit the water   the same water it was in
I felt in blue blazing terror at the bottom of the stairs and scrambled
Back up looking desperately into the human house as deeply as I could
Stopping my gaze before it went out the wire screen of the back door
Stopped it on the thistled rattan   the rugs I lay on and read
On my mother's sewing basket with next winter's socks spilling from it
The flimsy vacation furniture   a bucktoothed picture of myself.
Payton came back with three men from a filling station   and glanced at me
Dripping water   inexplicable   then we all grabbed hold like a tug-of-war.

We were gaining a little   from us a cry went up   from everywhere
People came running. Behind us the house filled with men and boys.
On the third step from the sea I took my place   looking down the rope
Going into the ocean, humming and shaking off drops. A houseful
Of people put their backs into it   going up the steps from me
Into the living room   through the kitchen   down the back stairs
Up and over a hill of sand   across a dust road   and onto a raised field
Of dunes   we were gaining   the rope in my hands began to be wet
With deeper water   all other haulers retreated through the house
But Payton and I on the stairs   drawing hand over hand on our blood
Drawing into existence by the nose   a huge body   becoming
A hammerhead   rolling in beery shallows   and I began to let up
But the rope strained behind me   the town had gone
Pulling-mad in our house   far away in a field of sand they struggled
They had turned their backs on the sea   bent double   some on their knees
The rope over their shoulders like a bag of gold   they strove for the ideal
Esso station across the scorched meadow   with the distant fish coming up
The front stairs   the sagging boards   still coming in   up   taking
Another step   toward the empty house   where the rope stood straining
By itself through the rooms   in the middle of the air. "Pass the word,"
Payton said, and I screamed it   "Let up, good God, let up!"   to no one there.
The shark flopped on the porch, grating with salt-sand   driving back in
The nails he had pulled out   coughing chunks of his formless blood.
The screen door banged and tore off   he scrambled on his tail   slid
Curved   did a thing from another world   and was out of his element and in
Our vacation paradise   cutting all four legs from under the dinner table
With one deep-water move   he unwove the rugs in a moment   throwing pints
Of blood over everything we owned   knocked the buckteeth out of my picture
His odd head full of crashed jelly-glass splinters and radio tubes   thrashing

Among the pages of fan magazines   all the movie stars drenched in sea-blood.
Each time we thought he was dead   he struggled back and smashed
One more thing   in all coming back to die   three or four more times after death.
At last we got him out   logrolling him   greasing his sandpaper skin
With lard to slide him   pulling on his chained lips as the tide came,
Tumbled him down the steps as the first night wave went under the floor.
He drifted off   head back   belly white as the moon. What could I do but buy
That house   for the one black mark still there   against death   a forehead-
      toucher in the room he circles beneath   and has been invited to wreck?
Blood hard as iron on the wall   black with time   still bloodlike
Can be touched whenever the brow is drunk enough. All changes. Memory:
Something like three-dimensional dancing in the limbs   with age
Feeling more in two worlds than one   in all worlds the growing encounters.

—JAMES DICKEY

SHE THAT IS MEMORY'S DAUGHTER

She that is memory's daughter,
Looking at running water,
Pauses, aware of other
Words that the water teaches.
Time lets the stream soon falling
Stray among reeds where gather,
One to another calling,
Birds in the upper reaches.

Silence is there renewing,
Losing and still pursuing
Songs of an age forgotten,
So it compels her wonder.

Rain from an ancient mountain
Writes what is unbegotten,
Seen in the playing fountain,
Heard in the cataract's thunder.

Under the river racing
Bridegroom and bride embracing
Fall from the girl whose vision
Plunging divines a constant.
Circle on circle spinning
Fly from her hand's impression
Seeking her true beginning
Fixed in the tranquil instant.

—VERNON WATKINS

THE SHE WOLF

The old ridiculous partner is back again
who speaks my mind before me, singing me now
fonder than ever, my embarrassing vancourier.

I am her fool, the noisy one to follow
years at a time, and know her for my other,
who sounds my superstition like a bagpipe.

I am her acrobat and, altogether
lacking an answer loud enough, I
somersault to her tune, how sick soever.

I left her once
for seven years long;
then she piped
and I did not dance.

Little I gained that
seven long years
I wept not
although she mourned,

since she is back again and the mood is on.

So must I bear my old she wolf who once
suckled the rising moon
to blow her pipes when I will dance again.

—MURIEL SPARK

A SHIP BURNING AND A COMET ALL IN ONE DAY

When the tide was out
And the sea was quiet,
We hauled the boat to the edge,
On a fair day in August,
As who, all believing,
Would give decent burial
To the life of a used boat,
Not leave a corpse above ground.

And some, setting fires
On the old and broken deck,
Poured on the kerosene
With a stately quietude,
Measuring out departure,
And others brought libations
In red glasses to the sea's edge,
And all held one in hand.

Then the Captain arose
And poured spirit over the prow
And the sparks flew upward
And consigned her with fierce
Cry and fervent prayer
To immortal transubstantiation.
And the pure nature of air
Received her grace and charm.

And evening came on the sea
As the whole company
Sat upon the harsh rocks
Watching the tide come in
And take the last debris,
And when it became dark
A great comet appeared in the sky
With a star in its nether tail.

—RICHARD EBERHART

THE SHUDDER

The foot of death has printed on my chest
Its signature, and I am rattled free
Of time and its dimensions and the rest
Of the hard outlines of identity.
Now minutes mix with centuries as if
Time were an undeciphered hieroglyph,
   For someone has walked on my grave.

O someone, walk in other places, please,
Whoever, when, or where your self may be,
That I may deal with near anxieties,
In fear of now and not eternity:
That future where you wander without guilt
Over the grass my private body built,
   For someone has walked on my grave.

"Grandfather Fool, thin voice I sometimes hear
Like scratches on a crystal radio,
Nothing I do will make death disappear
Or let your shudder or your knowledge go.
See the world whole, and see it clearly then—
A globe of dirt crusted with bones of men.
   If we walk, we walk on graves."

—DONALD HALL

THE SICKNESS OF FRIENDS

Do I give off in the wee
small hours a phosphorescent
glow, perhaps, like rotting wood?

Am I in the Yellow Pages?
I am sick of that sickness
within me that so lures them

to their phones when the night comes
to a dead calm: "H'llo." It's Dick,

who can't bear to be alone;

or Jane, who needs a father;
or Spot, who leads a dog's life.
Even the operator

has twin raw scars on her wrists,
but I'm fine, unmarked, floating
in the bath of their self-love.

—HENRI COULETTE

SISYPHUS

When Sisyphus was pushing the stone up the mountain,
Always near the top
As you remember, at the very tip of the height,
It lapsed and fell back upon him,
And he rolled to the bottom of the incline, exhausted.

Then he got up and pushed up the stone again,
First over the grassy rise, then the declivity of Dead Man's Gulch,
Then the outcroppings halfway, at which he took breath,
Looking out over the rosy panorama of Helicon;
Then finally the top

Where the stone wobbled, trembled, and lapsed back upon him,
And he rolled again down the whole long incline.
Why?
He said a man's reach must exceed his grasp,
Or what is Hades for?

He said it's not the goal that matters but the process
Of reaching it, the breathing joy
Of endeavor, and the labor along the way.
This belief damned him, and damned, what's harder,
The heavy stone.

—JOSEPHINE MILES

SIX POETS IN SEARCH OF A LAWYER

Finesse be first, whose elegance deplores
All things save beauty, and the swinging doors;
Whose cleverness in writing verse is just
Exceeded by his lack of taste and lust;
Who lives off lady lovers of his verse
And thanks them by departing with their purse;
Who writes his verse in order to amaze,
To win the Pulitzer, or *Time's* sweet praise;
Who will endure a moment, and then pass,
As hopeless as an olive in his glass.

Dullard be second, as he always will,
From lack of brains as well as lack of skill.

Expert in some, and dilettante in all
The ways of making poems gasp and fall,
He teaches at a junior college where
He's recognized as Homer's son and heir.
Respectable, brown-suited, it is he
Who represents on forums poetry,
And argues to protect the libelled Muse,
Who'd tear his flimsy tongue out, could she choose.

His opposite is anarchistic *Bomb*,
Who writes a manifesto with aplomb.
Revolt! Revolt! No matter why or when,
It's novelty—old novelty again.
Yet *Bomb*, if read intently, may reveal
A talent not to murder but to steal:
First from old Gone, whose fragmentary style
Disguised his sawdust Keats a little while;
And now from one who writes at very best
What ne'er was thought and much the less expressed.

Lucre be next, who takes to poetry
The businessman he swore he would not be.
Anthologies and lecture tours and grants
Create a solvency that disenchants.
He writes his poems, now, to suit his purse,
Short-lined and windy, and reserves his curse
For all the little magazines so fine
That offer only fifty cents a line.
He makes his money, certainly, to write,
But writes for money. Such is appetite.

Of *Mucker* will I tell, who tries to show
He is a kind of poet men don't know.
To shadowbox at literary teas,
And every girl at Bennington to seize,
To talk of baseball rather than of Yeats,
To drink straight whiskey while the bard creates—
This is his pose, and so his poems seem
Incongruous in proving life a dream.
Some say, with Freud, that *Mucker* has a reason
For acting virile in and out of season.

Scoundrel be last. Be deaf, be dumb, be blind,
Who writes satiric verses on his kind.

                                        —DONALD HALL

SKIMMERS

When the sun begins to throw
between boulders darknesses
and the skimmers gather shells
at the edge of amber pools,
he follows his long shadow
through the sea-wall buttresses.

He stands by the longest groin
in a black and flapping coat,
watching a boy make a mound
of oyster shells on the sand,
hurl them up the wind and on,
curving, curling, lying flat

in the windfall, falling fast
to the dark Decembered bark
that lists by the low-tide mark.
Too old for the skimming now,
still he advises, will boast
of the skill he once had, how

as a boy he used the wind
to lob a cockleshell over
trees as high as a rook flies.

So he flings his memories
again and again, never
disbelieved. His tales soar and

are caught awhile in the breath
of a boy's brief innocence.
When he comes here wanting death
but not the dying of it,
watching wind in water
white in the seas of winter,

his eyes weep truths of summers
when crops of poppies were blown
like paper parasols back
and wings of yellowhammer
hovered on the white chalk rock.
And when he moves on alone,

shuffling up the pea-beach track
on shores of his mind's making,
he does not stop to look back
at the long rollers breaking
or at the boy that he knows
at a distance follows.

—TED WALKER

THE SKIN DIVERS

Up and down the beach
gritty as grindstone pound
ball ball ball
heel and splay toe
of the beachball players.

Fitful as hot pigs
snuggling into the sand
the red sunbathers drowse.
Ball Ball Ball
hoofs it over them all.

It's the hungover Sun
treading their eyes, the Sun
hunkering closer down,
having a green wine
ball ball ball.

It's ball ball ball
in the beach-pavilion bars,
a polyrhythm riff
for washboard and brushed traps
thundering under the pier

and gone. The minuscule
ball ball ball
of our breaths arises. Still
deeper we settle, cool
as perfectly matched pearls

while up and down the beach
and over the waves and on,
ball ball ball
throbs the dissolving call
of the beachball players.

—GEORGE STARBUCK

SKIN DIVING IN THE VIRGINS

Alfonso was his name; his sad cantina
leaned against a palm. Over my head,
he scanned a coastline only he could see
and took my order in cuneiform.

My water gear, like loose connections
from some mild machine, dripped on the table. What
a good morning! The wreck I'd shimmied through—
a sunken vessel, like Alfonso, some-
what Spanish in the stern—still weighed its gold,

while angelfish and sunfish still made mouths
to tell me nothing. That kind of poetry
one is, in principle, against. But what
sweet swarms of language to be silent in!
I tasted salt, half dreaming back and down.

All of a sudden came the pelicans:
crazy old men in baseball caps, who flew
like jackknives and collapsed like fans . . .
They'd zeroed in, Alfonso said, on fish
that shark or barracuda'd chased inshore.
Hitting the water, bull's-eye on bull's-eye,
they'd sit there rocking, naked in their smiles.

Those birds ate well.
Was there some new conclusion to be drawn
from such vast hunger without appetite?
In the next rising wave,
I saw a barracuda standing on its tail,
clear as a sea horse in a paperweight.

Alfonso, listing, brought me canned corned beef
and a cool wet Amstel winking in the bottle.
Beware of irony, I thought, and swigged my beer,

seek depths where irony cannot descend.
The bald sun rolled in the bland sky. One clown,
cartwheeling pell-mell to the kill, just missed
another floating off, his big pouch full.
                            —JOHN MALCOLM BRINNIN

SLAVE QUARTERS

In the great place the great house is gone from   in the sun
Room, near the kitchen of air   I look across at low walls
Of slave quarters, and feel my imagining loins

Rise with the madness of Owners
To take off the Master's white clothes
And slide all the way into moonlight.

Let me stand as though moving

At midnight, now at the instant of sundown
When the wind turns

From sea-wind to land, and the marsh grass
Hovers, changing direction.
                            There was this house
That fell before I got out. I can pull
It over me where I stand, up from the earth,
Back out of the shells
Of the sea,
            become with the change of this air

A coastal islander, proud of his grounds,
His dogs, his spinet
From Savannah, his pale daughters,
His war with the saw-grass, pushed back into
The sea it crawled from. Nearer dark, unseen,
I can begin to dance
Inside my gabardine suit
As though I had left my silk nightshirt

In the hall of mahogany, and crept
To slave quarters to live out
The secret legend of Owners. Ah, stand up,
Blond loins, another

Love is possible! My thin wife would be sleeping
Or would not mention my absence.

                                   The moonlight

On these rocks can be picked like cotton
By a crazed Owner dancing-mad
With the secret repossession of his body,

Phosphorescent and mindless, shedding
Blond-headed shadow on the sand,
Hounds pressing in their sleep
Around him, smelling his footblood
On the strange ground that lies between skins.
Who seeks the other color of his body,

His loins giving off a frail light
On the dark lively shipwreck of grass,   sees
Water live where
The half-moon touches,
The moon made whole in one wave.

                                   I come past

A sand crab pacing sideways   his eyes out
On stalks   the bug-eyed vision of fiddler
Crabs sneaking a light on the run
From the split moon   holding in it a white man stepping
Down the road of clamshells and cotton   his eyes out
On stems   the tops of the sugar
Cane soaring   the saw-grass walking.

                                   I come past

The stale pools left
Over from high tide   where the crab in the night-sand
Is basting himself with his claws   moving ripples outward,
Feeding on brightness
                    and above
A gull also crabs slowly,
Tacks, jibs   then turning the corner
Of wind   glides down upon his reflection.

My body has a color not yet freed.
In that ruined house let me throw
Obsessive gentility off,
Let Africa rise upon me like a man
Whose instincts are delivered from their chains
Where they lay close-packed and wide-eyed
In muslin sheets

As though in the miserly holding
Of too many breaths by one ship. Now

Worked in silver   their work lies all
Around me   and I pass through the ghost of a slave
Born in this place of a white man   the fields dissolving
Into the sea   I stoop to the soil   working
Gathering   moving to the rhythm of a music
That has crossed the ocean in chains,

In the grass the great singing void of slave

Labor about me   the moonlight bringing
Sweat out of my back as though   the sun
Changed skins upon me   some other
Man moving near me on horseback   whom I look in the eyes
Once a day.
                    But now I am here
In slave quarters,   am white   and know what I came for.
There in that corner

Her bed turned to grass. Unsheltered by these walls,
The outside fields form slowly
Anew, in a kind of barrelling blowing,
Bend in all the right places. How take on the guilt

Of slavers? How shudder like one who made
Money from buying a people
To work as ghosts
In this blowing solitude?
I only stand here upon shells   dressed poorly
For nakedness   poorly
For the dark wrecked hovel of rebirth,

Picking my way in thought
To the black room
Where starlight blows off the roof
And the great beasts that died with the minds
Of the first slaves stand at the door, asking
For death, asking to be
Forgotten: the sadness of elephants,
The visionary pain in the heads
Of incredibly poisonous snakes
Lion   wildebeest   giraffe   all purchased also
When one wished only
Labor
          those beasts becoming

For the white man the animals of Eden,
Emblems of sexual treasure   all beasts attending
Me now   my dreamed dogs snarling at the shades
Of eland and cheetah
On the dispossessed ground where I dance
In my clothes beyond movement.

In nine months she would lie
With a knife between her teeth to cut the pain
Of bearing
A child who belongs in no world   my hair in that boy
Turned black   my skin
Darkened by half   his, lightened
By that half exactly   the beasts of Africa reduced
To cave-shadows flickering on his brow
As I think of him.   A child would rise from that place
With half my skin. He could for an instant
Of every day   when the wind turns   look
Me in the eyes. What do you feel when passing

Your blood beyond death
To another in secret: into
Another who takes your features   and adds
A misplaced Africa to them,
Changing them forever
As they must live? What happens
To you   when such a one bears
You after your death into rings
Of battling light   a heavyweight champion
Through the swirling glass of four doors,
In epauletted coats   into places
Where you learn to wait
On tables   into sitting in all-night cages
In parking lots   into raising
A sun-sided spade in a gang
Of men on a tar road working
Until the crickets give up?
What happens when the sun goes down

And the white man's loins still stir
In a house of air   still draw him toward
Slave quarters? When the moon begins to come
Apart on the water
And two hundred years are turned back
On with the headlights of a car?
When you learn that there is no hatred
Like love in the eyes

Of a wholly owned face? When you think of what
It would be like   what it has been,
What it is to look once a day
Into an only
Son's brown, waiting, wholly possessed
Amazing eyes, and not
Acknowledge, but own?

—JAMES DICKEY

THE SLEEPING GIANT

(A HILL, SO NAMED, IN HAMDEN, CONNECTICUT)

The whole day long, under the walking sun
That poised an eye on me from its high floor,
Holding my toy beside the clapboard house
I looked for him, the summer I was four.

I was afraid the waking arm would break
From the loose earth and rub against his eyes
A fist of trees, and the whole country tremble
In the exultant labor of his rise;

Then he with giant steps in the small streets
Would stagger, cutting off the sky, to seize
The roofs from house and home because we had
Covered his shape with dirt and planted trees;

And then kneel down and rip with fingernails
A trench to pour the enemy Atlantic
Into our basin, and the water rush
With the streets full and all the voices frantic.

That was the summer I expected him.
Later, the high and watchful sun, instead,
Walked low behind the house, and school began,
And winter pulled a sheet over his head.

—DONALD HALL

SLEEPING WITH ONE EYE OPEN

Unmoved by what the wind does,
The windows
Are not rattled, nor do the various
Areas
Of the house make their usual racket—
Creak at
The joints, trusses, and studs.
Instead,

They are still. And the maples,
Able
At times to raise havoc,
Evoke
Not a sound from their branches'
Clutches.
It's my night to be rattled,
Saddled
With spooks. Even the half moon
(Half man,
Half dark), on the horizon,
Lies on
Its side, casting a fishy light,
Which alights
On my floor, lavishly lording

Its morbid
Look over me. Oh, I feel dead,
Folded
Away in my blankets for good, and
Forgotten.
My room is clammy and cold,
Moonhandled
And weird. The shivers
Wash over
Me, shaking my bones, my loose ends
Loosen,
And I lie sleeping with one eye open,
Hoping
That nothing, nothing will happen.
—MARK STRAND

THE SLEEPWALKER

circling upon his star
is awakened by
the white feather of morning—
the bloodstain on it reminds him—
startled, he drops
the moon—
the snowberry breaks
against the black agate of night
sullied with dream—

No spotless white on this earth—
—NELLY SACHS
(*Translated from the German by Michael Hamburger*)

A SMALL BOY, DREAMING

A spin, a hardy spin, and here's the globe
In the schoolroom reeling—seas and countries,
Purples and greens and pinks and azures fly
On the puzzled axis of futurity.
With lazy, catlike attitudes, the curled
And lounging students fix a half-bored eye
Upon their teacher, and otherwise prefer
Hot dreams of football to her history
Droning above their heads, while one, whose eyes

With swift evasion slide in a small, wild face,
Hair scribbled about in tangled snarls of lace,
Veers to a future none of them may know.

There where the darkness and the undertow
Of Africa and the cliffs of Tenerife
Reel with the stars, where tart, alluvial spray
And sea salt darken his rebellious way,
He travels to an unknown ocean, gone
Into a world that's calmer and more alone
Than any schoolroom. He is lost within
Sea attitudes, which gather as his mind
Spills out in oceans cooler and more kind.

"Here's where *we* are!" the teacher snaps. He nods.
Of course she is not right; and he is not here,
Though companions all surround him with the clear,
Flutelike, piping voices of the still unsure.
The schoolroom fades, its teacher fades, the sea
Slips in its foam, skids to oblivion
Her world, the future;
And he is lost in oceans while he thinks,
They'll never find me here. And he is right;
Neither the sea bird nor the bird-ringed liner
Nor Crusoe's raft nor any imploring gesture
Of thoughtful love shall ever find him here.

                                        —ALBERT HERZING

SMALL SAD SONG

I am a lady
three feet small.
My voice is thin,
but listen, listen:
Before I die
my modest death,
tell me what gentlemen
do with great ladies,
for thigh-high now
are the thoughts I think.

Once, as a girl,
I knew how to smile.
My world stayed small

as my playmates mountained.
Dogs plagued me.
My mother mocked me.
Now I am doomed
to dwell among elephants.
Sometimes I fall
in love with a bird.

I move amongst
donkeys and monkeys.
Dwarfs paw me
with stubby hands.
I cannot look at them.
There are no friends

of a suitable size.
Giants tease me.
Men do not choose me.
A hunchback loves me.

If someone moved me,
I might make
a monstrous poem,

wild as my dreams,
but what can come
from a thumbnail lady?
Words like watch ticks,
whispers, twitterings,
suitable tinkles,
nothing at all.

—ALASTAIR REID

SMOKE

Nicky, the word has come to the West
    Coast
Of how you
Shuffled your feet, stammered,
And slipped out the back door

When no one was looking.
What did you have in mind?

*   *   *

I picture myself back there,
In the kitchen, peering out
Through the glass, then through the
    orchard, your shirt

A small red dot among
The apple trees that run down
The long slope; the water
Glitters and flashes in

The cold sunlight; I try
To open the window, to tell you
To wait, to come back, but
It is too late, too
Late in the day; already

The boat is adrift; it is
On fire; the flames
Splash at the gunwales; and you
Are smoke, Nicky, you are smoke.

—CHARLES WRIGHT

SNAKE

I saw a young snake glide
Out of the mottled shade
And hang, limp on a stone;
A thin mouth, and a tongue
Stayed, in the still air.

It turned; it drew away;
Its shadow bent in half;

It quickened, and was gone.

I felt my slow blood warm.
I longed to be that thing,
The pure, sensuous form.

And I may be, some time.

—THEODORE ROETHKE

SNOW

Plentiful snow deepens the path to the woods.
Jay, hawing, shakes the juniper,
Gray squirrel and titmouse trick in hectic moods,
Fluff buffeters of down and fur.
Jay skates on ice-blue air with bluer flight,
Dives in down-soft whirl and comes up light.
The dried and dead hackberry dangles white.
Tall trees droop down while ground grows up,
And the powder-white snuff blows from the wind's lip,
Sneezing the world. Still the old lady shakes her puff
In the well of the wind, and feathers fly from the rip.

—RUTH STONE

SNOW BY MORNING

Some for everyone,
plenty,
and more coming—

fresh, dainty, airily arriving
everywhere at once,

transparent at first,
each faint slice—
slow, soundlessly tumbling;

then quickly, thickly, a gracious fleece
will spread like youth, like wheat,
over the city.

Each building will be a hill,
all sharps made round—

dark, worn, noisy narrows made still
wide, flat, clean spaces;

streets will be fields,
cars be fumbling sheep;

a deep, bright harvest will be seeded
in a night.

By morning we'll be children
feeding on manna,
a new loaf on every doorsill.

—MAY SWENSON

THE SNOW CURLEW

Snow has fallen all night
Over the cliff. There are no paths.
All is even and white.
The leaden sea ebbs back, the sky is not yet light.

Hidden from dawn's gray patch
Behind frosted windows, ash ticks out faded hearths.

How quickly time passes. There is no mark
Yet upon this manuscript of snow.
Where water dripped, ice glitters, sheaved and stark.
The pen has fallen from the hand of dark.
White are lintel and latch.
Earth has forgotten where her dead go.

Silence. Then a curlew flutes with its cry
The low distance, that throbbing spring call,
Swifter than thought. It is good-bye
To all things not beginning, and I must try,
Making the driftwood catch,
To coax, where the cry fades, fires which cannot fall.

—Vernon Watkins

SNOWFALL: FOUR VARIATIONS

Basic White

Angels
might fall that way,
caught at their harmless
passionate war
by the street's electric light.

Stilled syllables,
flakes,
locked in the dead
heat of that debate,
steer a dazed
formal dance through cold halos.

The Shadows

Driving the known roads
of New Jersey, at night,
I flinch inside as the blurred arrows
        die

into the windshield. . . .
Accusations—
the white poisonous thoughts
of tracer bullets hurled from the last
        war.

No. This is a delicate
invasion. The ghosts are my own.
Drops that have grown so cold
they flower, cling
to the blind shapes of this world.

Station Break

In the dark bedroom, a girl
shrugs off her mohair sweater.
What is this shocked
blue crackling
if not some abstract god
that cares, desperately,

for the shape and feel of her human
shoulders?

Static.
A cold fact.

NEWS OF THE WORLD

The snow is cold, factual, a mind
battering static which proliferates
at windows and litters my TV screen
with dandruff, heroin,

flaked ash from the ovens of the
Third Reich. . . .

I think of all the established remedies
we've bought but can never pay for.

Angels, pale barbarians,
this is the white plague.
Sugary, insect faces
continue to fall
into the eyes of lit cities
out of the dark ages of the sky.

—GEORGE AMABILE

THE SOMERSET DAM FOR SUPPER

She tells us an interminable story, from television,
Through the fried potatoes, hamburg, and coleslaw. She is five.
She uses her mother's voice, voices and names from school life,
To be the only one talking. Her mother watches me for signs of impatience.
I am her father, I conceal my impatience, and for his own good
Silence her brother, restless at monologue not his own. He is nine.
It ends with only bread left, coffee coming for the grownups.

I begin the true story of the long trip to Somerset Dam in 1912
With my father, by train from North Cambridge to Hoosac Tunnel,
By narrow-gauge to Mountain Mills where log booms filled a sawmill lake,
By gas car to the bunkhouse end of the line. A berry-eating bear
Plunged into the bushes along the tracks. Excitement. A real bear?
A real bear. What color? Brown, I say, but didn't really see.
I am the only one talking, and tell them now about the flat-bed wagon
To the engineers' house at the base of the big earth dam.
He and she and their mother never heard this story. I have more.

But he runs to my desk, brings back a photograph of the dam;
Maybe his grandfather's boy, I think, as he turns my table story
Into an explanation of the dam's construction, the borrow pits,
The dump cars on the bare log trestles. I begin again,
Remembering when my father took me, and my sister and brother,
To see the steam shovels at the east borrow pit. A shouted
Warning, we ducked behind a small rock and a forked birch,
And Boom, and Roar, went the dynamite,
Rock raining all around us, but no one hit.
He likes this part. He is nine.

My father was chief engineer—and important, I knew, when the foreman,
Helmeted and scared, came running to see if he had killed any of us.
But we shouldn't have been there, and my father couldn't be angry.
Later my mother said, "What were you thinking of, taking the children there?"
He had no excuse for that, either. This part is for my wife.
I have more story, but no more dynamite. Time for ice cream.

Our son's unusual silence has earned him his turn now.
He begins a riddle, anything to be talking: There were seven pine trees—
His sister says, "Acorns!," and he storms out of the room; the giveaway
Ruins it. We all call at once to come back, shut up, sit down, stop crying.
The ice cream is brought. He comes back, gets a grip on himself, starts again.
I try to multiply seven pine trees times seven branches times seven
Twigs on each, times seven acorns on each twig, and can't.
None, is the answer. Now he has the center of attention. Climax.

Time to clear the supper table. The first storyteller
Feels it has been too long since her performance, wants to repeat,
But we carry away dishes, and in the kitchen my wife
Washes the glass of the framed photograph of Somerset Dam, 1912
(My father's square lettering in Higgins' Black Ink for draughtsmen),
And I hang it under a shelf there. None of them knows it,
But I intend to tell about the berry-eating bear and the dynamite
Again tomorrow, and go on from there.
                                        It's a long story,
As I think of the fisherman who, pulling a trout from the river,
Snagged a low-flying young hawk for a double catch,
And the morning ritual of rain gauge and thermometer,
And the half-Indian cook who came with a knife to collect
What he'd won playing cards with our cook.
                                        I'll outtalk them.
I'm the father, and at fifty-six I know more, that's all.

—JOHN HOLMES

SOME TIPS ON WATCHING BIRDS

This is not poetry, he said;
Here are no Grecian glimpses of lost birds
Exotically entrancing and entranced
In well-kept gardens where they soar and sing.
This chitter is not song.

There isn't room for nightingales
Upon this perch where spring can only be the hope

That hope will spring;
But as a bird watcher I would like to say
That one bright cardinal cocked
Is not exactly worth a score of finches.

Beauty cannot be banded,
But is found sometimes
In the most unlikely treetops; the poets now
Are not all brain-bewildered.
Because the phoenix sways a moment
On some clothesline does not mean
Old flames are finally dying.

The trick is seeing, and binoculars
Are certainly no better than the eye
For anyone with faulty vision—
The bird will always fly before he finds it,
And there has never been
A Field Guide to the heart of anything.

A would-be watcher must begin to wait
Even as aviaries of the mind are emptied
Of sparrows and those nondescript small birds
That nothing but love
Can quite identify for sure.

                                        —DEATT HUDSON

SOMEWHERE THE EQUATION BREAKS DOWN

between the perfect
                    (invisible, Plato said)
and the imperfect
                    that comes at you on the street—
                    stench and cloth and fried eyes—
between the wired bones of the dead
                                        stuttering, shamed,
and the marvellous lucid spirit
                        that moves in the body's spaces—
                        a rainbow fish behind glass—
            decide. Oh, coincide!

                                        —DANIEL BERRIGAN

SONG

Say this city has ten million souls;
Some are living in mansions, some are living in holes,
Yet there's no place for us, my dear, yet there's no place for us.

Once we had a country and we thought it fair;
Look in the atlas and you'll find it there.
We cannot go there now, my dear, we cannot go there now.

In the village churchyard there grows an old yew;
Every spring it flowers anew.
Old passports can't do that, my dear, old passports can't do that.

The Consul banged the table and said,
"If you've got no passport, you're officially dead."
But we are still alive, my dear, but we are still alive.

Went to a Committee; they offered me a chair,
Asked me politely to return next year.
But where shall we go today, my dear, where shall we go today?

Came to a public meeting; the speaker stood up and said,
"If we let them in, they will steal our daily bread."
He was talking of you and me, my dear, he was talking of you and me.

Thought I heard the thunder, rumbling in the sky.
It was Hitler over Europe, saying, "They must die."
O we were in his mind, my dear, O we were in his mind.

Saw a poodle wearing a jacket, fastened with a pin;
Saw a door open and a cat let in.
But they weren't German Jews, my dear, but they weren't German Jews.

Went down to the harbor and stood upon the quay;
Saw the fish swimming as if they were free,
Only ten feet away, my dear, only ten feet away.

Walked into a wood; saw the birds in the trees,
They had no politicians and sang at their ease.
They weren't the human race, my dear, they weren't the human race.

Dreamt I saw a building with a thousand floors,
A thousand windows, and a thousand doors.
Not one of them was ours, my dear, not one of them was ours.

Ran down to the station to catch the express;
Asked for two tickets to Happiness,
But every coach was full, my dear, but every coach was full.

Stood on a great plain in the falling snow;
Ten thousand soldiers marched to and fro
Looking for you and me, my dear, looking for you and me.

                                        —W. H. AUDEN

SONG

This is the song of those who live alone,
who, when the boat has sailed, the plane has flown,
the train is gone,
turning from an open space to a closed one,
are confronted by other visitors—
promiscuous affection, impotent devotion.

Too little and too late! Too much and much too soon.
When the heart has lost its wisdom,
how shall it be educated?
How, living in a room of more than ordinary view,
can the view be delimited
or the room contain two—
not one and a multitude?

Watchers from behind curtained windows,
receivers of a monthly letter,
lingerers under the arches of bridges,
driftwood and fine-editions collectors,
artists, all of you, in all save living,
pariahs and saints—this song is for you.

                                        —WILLIAM JUSTEMA

SONG

Sweet beast, I have gone prowling,
    a proud, rejected man
who lived along the edges,
    catch as catch can;
in darkness and in hedges
    I sang my sour tone,

and all my love was howling,
conspicuously alone.

I curled and slept all day
    or nursed my bloodless wounds
until the squares were silent

where I could make my tunes
singular and violent.
  Then, sure as hearers came,
I crept and flinched away.
  Girl, you have done the same.

A stray from my own type,
  led along by blindness,

my love was near to spoiled
  and curdled all my kindness.
I find no kin, no child,
  only the weasel's ilk.
Sweet beast, cat of my own stripe,
  come and take my milk.

—W. D. SNODGRASS

SONG FOR THE LAST ACT

Now that I have your face by heart, I look
Less at its features than its darkening frame
Where quince and melon, yellow as young flame,
Lie with quilled dahlias and the shepherd's crook.
Beyond, a garden. There, in insolent ease
The lead and marble figures watch the show
Of yet another summer loath to go
Although the scythes hang in the apple trees.

Now that I have your face by heart, I look.

Now that I have your voice by heart, I read
In the black chords upon a dulling page
Music that is not meant for music's cage,
Whose emblems mix with words that shake and bleed.
The staves are shuttled over with a stark
Unprinted silence. In a double dream
I must spell out the storm, the running stream.
The beat's too swift. The notes shift in the dark.

Now that I have your voice by heart, I read.

Now that I have your heart by heart, I see
The wharves with their great ships and architraves;
The rigging and the cargo and the slaves
On a strange beach under a broken sky.
O not departure, but a voyage done!
The bales stand on the stone; the anchor weeps
Its red rust downward, and the long vine creeps
Beside the salt herb, in the lengthening sun.

Now that I have your heart by heart, I see.

—LOUISE BOGAN

SONG FROM A TWO-DESK OFFICE

Randal Groveling works where I work.
Randal does the tasks that I shirk.
He irks me and I'm sure I irk
    Randal Groveling.

Randal Groveling eats where I eat.
Randal's meat, though, is not my meat.
He treats me and sometimes I treat
    Randal Groveling.

Randal Groveling drinks when I drink.
Ale for Randal; Scotch is my drink.
Gladly in his ale would I sink
    Randal Groveling.

Randal's dull and hard to bear with,
Hard to travel everywhere with.
Why must I this short life share with
    Randal Groveling?
              —Byron Buck

SONG OF RESIGNATION

I

I resign!

My son has my father's eyes,
My mother's hands,
And my own mouth.
There is no further need of me. Many thanks.
The refrigerator is beginning to hum toward a long journey.
An unknown dog sobs over the loss of a stranger.

I resign!

II

I paid my dues to so many funds.
I am fully insured.
Let the world care for me now;
I am knotted and tied with it and all of them.
Every change in my life will cost them cash.

Every movement of mine will hurt them.
My death will dispossess them.
My voice passes with clouds.
My hand, stretched out, has turned into paper. Yet another contract.
I see the world through the yellow roses
Someone has forgotten
On the table near my window.

III

Bankruptcy!
I declare the whole world to be a womb.
And as of this moment
I appoint myself,
Order myself
At its mercy.
Let it adopt me. Let it care for me.

I declare the President of the United States to be my father,
The Chairman of the Soviet Union to have my power of attorney,
The British Cabinet to be my family,
And Mao Tse-tung to be my grandmother.

I resign!
I declare the heavens to be God.
They all together go ahead and do those things
That I never believed they would.

—Yehuda Amichai
(*Translated from the Hebrew by Assia Gutmann*)

SONG OF THE QUEEN BEE

"The breeding of the bee," says a United States Department of Agriculture bulletin on artificial insemination, "has always been handicapped by the fact that the queen mates in the air with whatever drone she encounters."

When the air is wine and the wind is
    free
And the morning sits on the lovely lea
And sunlight ripples on every tree,
Then love-in-air is the thing for me—
    I'm a'bee,
    I'm a ravishing, rollicking, young
        queen bee,
    That's me.

I wish to state that I think it's great,
Oh, it's simply rare in the upper air,
    It's the place to pair
    With a bee.
Let old geneticists plot and plan,
They're stuffy people, to a man;
Let gossips whisper behind their fan.
    (Oh, she *does?*
    Buzz, buzz, buzz!)

My nuptial flight is sheer delight;
I'm a giddy girl who likes to swirl,
  To fly and soar
  And fly some more,
    I'm a bee.
And I wish to state that I'll *always*
    mate
  With whatever drone I encounter.

There's a kind of a wild and glad ela-
    tion
In the natural way of insemination;
Who thinks that love is a handicap
Is a fuddydud and a common sap,
For I am a queen and I am a bee,
I'm devil-may-care and I'm fancy-free,
The test tube doesn't appeal to me,
  Not me,
  I'm a bee.
And I'm here to state that I'll *always*
    mate
  With whatever drone I encounter.

Let mares and cows, by calculating,
Improve themselves with loveless mat-
    ing,
Let groundlings breed in the modern
    fashion,
I'll stick to the air and the grand old
    passion;
I may be small and I'm just a bee
But I *won't* have Science improving
    me,
  Not me,
  I'm a bee.
On a day that's fair with a wind that's
    free,
Any old drone is the lad for me.

I have no flair for love *moderne*,
It's far too studied, far too stern,
I'm just a bee—I'm wild, I'm free,
  That's me.
I can't afford to be too choosy;
In every queen there's a touch of
    floozy,
  And it's simply rare
  In the upper air

And I wish to state
  That I'll *always* mate
With whatever drone I encounter.

Man is a fool for the latest move-
    ment,
He broods and broods on race im-
    provement;
What boots it to improve a bee
If it means the end of ecstasy?
  (He ought to be there
  On a day that's fair,
  Oh, it's simply rare
    For a bee.)
Man's so wise he is growing foolish,
Some of his schemes are downright
    ghoulish;
He owns a bomb that'll end creation
And he wants to change the sex rela-
    tion,
He thinks that love is a handicap,
He's a fuddydud, he's a simple sap;
Man is a meddler, man's a boob,
He looks for love in the depths of a
    tube,
His restless mind is forever ranging,
He thinks he's advancing as long as
    he's changing,
He cracks the atom, he racks his
    skull,
Man is meddlesome, man is dull,
Man is busy instead of idle,
Man is alarmingly suicidal,
  Me, I'm a bee.

I am a bee and I simply love it,
I am a bee and I'm darned glad of it,
I am a bee, I know about love:
You go upstairs, you go above,
You do not pause to dine or sup,
The sky won't wait—it's a long trip
    up;
You rise, you soar, you take the blue,
It's you and me, kid, me and you,
It's everything, it's the nearest drone,
It's never a thing that you find alone.
  I'm a bee,
  I'm free.

If any old farmer can keep and hive me,
Then any old drone may catch and
    wive me;
I'm sorry for creatures who cannot pair
On a gorgeous day in the upper air,
I'm sorry for cows who have to boast
Of affairs they've had by parcel post,
I'm sorry for man with his plots and
    guile,
His test-tube manner, his test-tube
    smile;

I'll multiply and I'll increase
As I always have—by mere caprice;
For I am a queen and I am a bee,
I'm devil-may-care and I'm fancy-free,
Love-in-air is the thing for me,
    Oh, it's simply *rare*
    In the beautiful air;
      And I wish to state
      That I'll *always* mate
With whatever drone I encounter.

—E. B. WHITE

SONNETEERING MADE EASY

I

With hyphens, clip off endings that don't fit;
We call this "Hyper-Technic Line Expan-"
It has a certain rhythmic swing to it
That can't be got with ordinary scan-

Pentameter, iambic, is the rule
They teach in every other Sonnet School;
But we have found it simpler, if not nea-
To take occasional liberties with me-

Three quatrains and a couplet is the length
Of Shakespeare's sonnets, and of those by Mil-
It's standardized, like cheese from Brie or Stil-
The only difference being in the strength.

So now that we have settled length and ti-
Our Lesson Number II involves the rhy-

II

You'll note the scheme, "a," "b," "a," "b," above
In Quatrain One; that's perfectly O.K.
If something different's what you're thinking of,
See Quatrain Three, with its "a," "b," "b," "a."

For mittel quatrains we prefer to reck-
With what the Germans, in their "schonnet-sprech-"

Employ: "a," "a," "b," "b;" ja, that's correct;
No German schonnet's e'er been besser sprecht.

So mix your "a"s and "b"s, your "b"s and "a"s
To suit your own convenience; any son-
Will have our professorial blessings on
If it is rhymed in one of these three ways.

The metre, length, and rhyme scheme now are def-
La porte est ouverte—simply put la clef.

III

The only item still to be discussed
Is subject matter, and we think you'll find
That Love is one that you can always trust
(Though Milton did quite well On Being Blind).

So Love it is, the simplest of all top-
Like "Frozen Love" or else "Love in the Trop-"
If you feel good, try "Love Is Here to Stay,"
And if you don't, there's "Love Has Gone Away."

Love's hot or cold; it moves like a thermom-
It's in, it's out, it's either up or down;
It's in the country or it stayed in town—
A Fair or Stormy, Wet or Dry barom-

So get a pencil and a piece of pa-
And you're all set to start "The Sonnet Ca-"

—S. B. Botsford

SOUTHBOUND ON THE FREEWAY

A tourist came in from Orbitville,
parked in the air, and said:

The creatures of this star
are made of metal and glass.

Through the transparent parts
you can see their guts.

Their feet are round and roll
on diagrams or long

measuring tapes, dark
with white lines.

They have four eyes.
The two in the back are red.

Sometimes you can see a five-eyed
one, with a red eye turning

on the top of his head.
He must be special—

the others respect him
and go slow

when he passes, winding
among them from behind.

They all hiss as they glide,
like inches, down the marked

tapes. Those soft shapes,
shadowy inside

the hard bodies—are they
their guts or their brains?
—MAY SWENSON

THE SOUTHERNER

He entered with the authority of politeness
And the jokes died in the air. A well-made blaze
Grew round the main log in the fireplace
Spontaneously. I watched its brightness
Spread to the altered faces of my guests.
They did not like the Southerner. I did.
A liberal felt that someone should forbid
That soft voice making its soft arrests.

As when a Negro or a prince extends
His hand to an average man, and the mind
Speeds up a minute and then drops behind,
So did the conversation of my friends.
I was amused by this respectful awe,
Which those hotly deny who have no prince.
I watched the frown, the stare, and the wince
Recede into attention, the arms thaw.

I saw my Southern evil memories
Raped from my mind before my eyes, my youth
Practicing caste, perfecting the untruth
Of staking honor on the wish to please.
I saw my honor's paradox:
Grandpa, the saintly Jew, keeping his beard
In difficult Virginia, yet endeared
Of blacks and farmers, although orthodox.

The nonsense of the gracious lawn,
The fall of hollow columns in the pines—
Do these deceive more than the rusted signs
Of Jesus on the road? Can they go on
In the timeless manner of all gentlefolk
There in a culture rotted and unweeded,
Where the black yoni of the South is seeded
By crooked men in denims thin as silk?

They do go on, denying still the fall
Of Richmond and man, who gently live
On the street above the violence, fugitive,
Graceful, and darling, who recall
The heartbroken country once about to flower,
Full of black poison, beautiful to smell,
Who know how to conform, how to compel,
And how from the best bush to receive a flower.

—KARL SHAPIRO

SPANISH BLUE

They wore it walking Sunday, three small men
with wine jugs jogging at their thighs, and flat
black hair, their faces copper in the light.

And it would be impossible but here—
the color that they bore—at Malaga,
the foreground sea clear to its flickered floor,
the other sea floating a deepest blue
far off and moving in—the pines, the palms,
the peaks, the roses, and the frailest sky.
They wore it walking Sunday by the rocks,
walking the sea road where the slender gnats
hovered and sang with all their silent voice,
figuring hammered fugues against the sun
(clear songs from windows where the washing-girls
moved in their rooms of shade this afternoon):

blue of all distance in a March of leaves,
and where the dust is still, is still, is still.

—HERBERT MORRIS

THE SPANISH LIONS

Guarding the doors of the Hispanic Society
At a Hundred and Sixty-fifth near Riverside,
Two lions sit, so charged with natural piety
(In the Virgilian sense), so filled with pride,
They seem less carved from rock than from the spirit
Of Spain. Oh, these are lords of the Spanish law,
Castilian lions, gilt-edged and eighteen-carat,
Hidalgos from rearing head to rigorous paw.

They are leaner than wasps. Yet neither thirst nor hunger
Possesses them. They thrive on honor alone,
Like granite exemplars, as if when time was younger
All lions were haughty and Spanish and made of stone.
They look down their high-bred noses. Their manes are jaunty
As a matador's queue. They stare on nothing at all—
Not even the bas-relief of Rosinante,
Posed with his Knight astride, on the opposite wall.

—PHYLLIS McGINLEY

SPARROWS AMONG DRY LEAVES

The sparrows
by the iron fence post—
hardly seen

for the dry leaves
that half
cover them—

stirring up
the leaves, fight
and chirp

stridently,
search
and

peck the sharp
gravel to
good digestion

and love's
obscure and insatiable
appetite.

—WILLIAM CARLOS WILLIAMS

A SPARROW'S FEATHER

There was this empty bird cage in the garden.
    And in it, to amuse myself, I had hung
pseudo-Oriental birds, constructed of
        glass and tin bits and paper, that squeaked sadly
as the wind sometimes disturbed them. Suspended
    in melancholy disillusion, they sang
of things that had never happened, and that never
        could in that cage of artificial existence.
The twittering of these instruments lamenting
        their absent lives resembled threnodies
torn from a falling harp, till the cage filled with
        engineered regret like moonshining cobwebs,
as these constructions grieved over not existing.
        The children fed them with flowers. A sudden gust
and, without sound, lifelessly, one would die,
        scattered in scraps like debris. The wire doors
always hung open against their improbable
        transfiguration into, say, chaffinches
or even more colorful birds. Myself, I found
        the whole game charming, let alone the children.
And then, one morning—I do not record a
        matter of cosmic proportions, I assure you,
not an event to shake the Volscian dovecotes—
        there, askew among these artificial images,
like a lost soul electing to die in Rome,
        its feverish eye transfixed, both wings fractured,
lay—I assure you, Catullus—a young sparrow.
        Not long for this world, so heavily breathing
one might have supposed this cage his destination
        after laboring past seas and holy skies
whence he had flown, death not being known there.
        Of course, there was nothing to do. The children
brought bread crumbs, brought water, brought bright eyes,
        perhaps to restore him, that shivering panic
of useless feathers, that tongue-tied little gossip,
that lying flier. So there, among its gods
that moaned and whistled in a little wind,
flapping their paper anatomies like windmills,
wheeling and bowing dutifully to the
        divine intervention of a child's forefinger,
there, at rest and at peace among its monstrous
        idols, the little bird died. And, for my part,
I hope the whole unimportant affair is
        soon forgotten. The analogies are too trite.

                              —GEORGE BARKER

SPINDRIFT

1

On this tree thrown up
From the sea, its tangle of roots
Letting the wind go through, I sit
Looking down the beach: old
Horseshoe crabs, broken skates,
Sand dollars, sea horses, as though
Only primeval creatures get destroyed,
At chunks of sea mud still quivering,
At the light as it glints off the water
And the billion facets of the sand,
At the soft, mystical shine the wind
Blows over the dunes as they creep.

2

Sit down
By the clanking shore
Of this bitter, beloved sea,

Pluck sacred
Shells from the icy surf,
Fans of gold light, sunbursts,

Lift one to the sun
As a sign you accept to go,
As bid, to the shrine of the dead,

And as it blazes
See the lost life within
Alive again in the fate-shine.

3

This little bleached root
Drifted from some foreign shore,
Brittle, cold, practically weightless,

If anything is dead, it is
This castout worn
To the lost grip it always essentially
was.

If it has lost hold,
It at least keeps the wild
Shape of what it held,

And it remains the hand
Of that gravel, one of the earth's
Wandering icons of "to have."

4

I sit listening
To the surf as it falls,
The power and inexhaustible fresh-
ness of the sea,

The suck and inner boom
As a wave tears free and crashes back
In overlapping thunders going away
down the beach.

It is the most we know of time,
And it is our undermusic of eternity.

5

I think of how I
Sat by a dying woman,
Her shell of a hand
Wet and cold in both of mine,
Light, nearly out, existing as smoke,
I sat in the glow of her wan, absorbed
smile.

6

Under the high wind
That moans in the grass
And whistles through crabs' claws,
I sit holding this little lamp,
This icy fan of the sun.

Across gull tracks
And wind-ripples in the sand
The wind seethes. My footprints
Slogging for the absolute
Already begin vanishing.

7

What does he really love,
That old man,
His wrinkled eyes
Tortured by smoke,

Walking in the ungodly
Rasp and cackle of old flesh?

The swan dips her head
And peers at the mystic
In-life of the sea,
The gull drifts up
And eddies toward heaven,
The breeze in his arms . . .

Nobody likes to die
But an old man
Can know
A kind of gratefulness
Toward time that kills him,
Everything he loved was made of it.

In the end
What is he but the scallop shell
Shining with time like any pilgrim?

—GALWAY KINNELL

SPIRITS, DANCING

Having put yourself on the way,
it is inevitable that you
should reach here. If in
your thoughts you've had
the notion of reward
as you fought to come this far,
banish them. And,
as penalty for entering,
shed the attitudes of worldly men
regarding us and this
celestial sphere, where now
you spirit begs to enter.

From the extremity
to which you've come, you see
us sway as in a dance.
It is no sign that we
are happy. To be happy
is being a step removed
from happiness. Which we
never are. Nor are we sad.
Sorrow is man in the world,
and we, the total expression
and awareness of his state,
are sorrowful.

What seems to you,
who were taught to feel
we must fulfill
where the world has failed,
must turn to good the bad,
must invoke permanence
for material whose law
and will it is to die—
what seems to you, driven here
by urgency, a dance
is nothing but the pain in the world
which we like a mirror contain.

To sway is to depart,
as branches from a stem,
as shadows from foliage
thick and dark—
and to depart is what is pain.
What you must know before
you enter this domain
and learn the ways of which
we shall not speak is this
first truth of what you are:
a sorrow, a sorrow
begging for home. Or you
would not have come this far.

—ARTHUR GREGOR

SPIRIT'S SONG

How well you served me above ground,
Most truthful sight, firm-builded sound.

And how you throve, through hunger, waste,
Sickness and health, informing taste;

And smell, that did from dung and heather
Corruption, bloom, mix well together.

But you, fierce delicate tender touch,
Betrayed and hurt me overmuch,

For whom I lagged with what a crew
O far too long, and poisoned through!

—Louise Bogan

THE SPOILS OF LOVE

When all is over and you march for home,
The spoils of war are easily disposed of;
Standards, weapons of combat, helmets, drums
May decorate a staircase or a study
While lesser gleanings of the battlefield—
Coins, watches, wedding rings, gold teeth, and such—
Are sold anonymously for solid cash.

The spoils of love present a different case
When all is over and you march for home;
That lock of hair, those letters, and the portrait
May not be publicly displayed; nor sold;
Nor burned; nor returned (the heart being obstinate)—
Yet never trust them to a strong-room safe
For fear they burn a hole through two-foot steel.

—Robert Graves

SPORTIF

Prescott, press my Ascot waistcoat—
Let's not risk it
Just to whisk it:
Yes, my Ascot waistcoat, Prescott.

Worn subfusc, it's
Cool and dusk: it
Might be grass-cut
But it's Ascot,

And it fits me like a gasket—
Ascot is *the* waistcoat, Prescott!
Please get
Off the spot of grease. Get
Going, Prescott—
Where's that waistcoat?
It's no task at
All, an Ascot:
Easy as to clean a musket

Or to dust an ivory tusk. It
Doesn't take a lot of fuss. Get
To it, Prescott,
Since I ask it:
We can't risk it—
Let's not whisk it.
That's the waistcoat;
Thank *you*, Prescott.

—DAVID MCCORD

SPRING SONG

For a toad enjoys a finer prospect than another creature to compensate his lack . . . For there are stones, whose constituent particles are toads.—*Christopher Smart.*

B'york! but it's lovely under the leaf—
cool, green, slimy, sleeping,
quietly breathing at all my pores—
a jade toad in a rainy garden.

Down here, ceiling zero,
pulse steady, breathing slow,
heart smiling under his harness,
brain grinning behind the bone,

down here, in the dead of winter,
nothing happens, honey of time
slowly, sweetly melts and oozes
in the vein.

Tall in the saddle, hulking stranger,
looking for trouble, blind with anger,

you who think to stand between
the sun and me: think again.

Ten feet up, you cannot see
further than your bleeding fist;
blows leap out from every tree,
the night is your antagonist.

Sad Goliath, gloomy champion,
lost in an unfriendly wood,
riding high, riding handsome,
ten feet up from where my gleaming
stones can do you any good,

far away your love is sleeping,
far away your king is dead,
your eye is almost shut with weeping,
your foot is bruised against my head.

—DONALD FINKEL

SQUARING THE CIRCLE

A bear cub, chained and tethered to a stake,
Prowled in a Humble service-station yard
In a rubble of popcorn, apple cores, dumped cars,
And tourists giving him 7-Up to drink.
He swept in a centrifuge, arc over arc

Like a windshield wiper, and his chain and collar clanked,
Four paces left—does freedom die that hard?—
Four paces right, till the center wound him back.

Beyond the dump, meadow and swamp meet trees
Grown dark as they crawl the Appalachian chain;
Ahead, the freeway flumes the traffic east,
Scatters sunlight, and dips to the Gulf of Maine,
Where the lobsterman prowls the hundred-fathom curve
And the yacht swings on her mooring like a slave.

—LOUIS O. COXE

A STAR

Above the violent park,
Where only men with knives walk bright as air,
She drifts in peace
Too rich in light for darkness to make way
Beyond her screens. No drop of night
Filters through windows where the ice of day
Mingles through mirrors with the muted white
Of all her walls. She moves through golden fleece
Out of the rain, past chair piled high on chair,
Into the womb of dark,

Alone. Above the park,
I see the flaming oriole of her hair
Swing like a fleece
Flirting with air. In silent love I sway
By temples whose cold locks hang tight
Against my fingers that would loose and play
Through all her flames. I taste their burning white
On my raw lash. Alas, there is no peace
Unless I shed her brilliance from my chair
And lose her in the dark.

See, where the dying park
Erupts with light! With knives they strip her bare
And part her fleece
And lay her in the ground and make their way
Where no help comes. I sense thick light
Swirl in the windows. The broad fin of day
Swims to the surface. Edged with flirting white,
She veers toward me. If I break my peace,

And flow to meet her, cool night-scented air
     Will fill the world. Such dark

          Has never been. The park
Opens its willows to the morning air
          Where all her fleece
Echoes and burns to nothing. Far away,
     There comes a sound whose leaves are white
For all her silver cloisters and her sway
Of Southern fire. This is my tree tonight
That listens for the wind within the fleece
And sings in flame. O tree, sing through her hair
          As she sways into dark!
                         —GEORGE MACBETH

THE STARRY NIGHT

Faraway hands are folded and folded
or pick at the threads in the lap of blackness
or spool and spool at the tenantless tangle
of blackness, of blackness, of emptiness.

They are the stars; you can see them flash
like the bonewhite fingers of finical ladies;
and far and away the depth of their cunning
is distance—a tissue of distances.

Their heads are down; they are plummeting downwards;
we cling to our millwheel meadows; their heads
are bowed to the task; no comet commotion
of gazes effaces the emptiness.

In chairs of the rest home at paranoid random
great-aunt and great-grandmother jaw like fates
till we wish them to heaven and wake to our wishes
and cling to the earth and each other's flesh.

And ours is the flaw in the nets of blackness.
And theirs is the task by the great sea wall:
the mending, the mending, the never-mending
of blackness, of blackness, of emptiness.
                         —GEORGE STARBUCK

STATUES

They more than we are what we are:
Serenity and joy
We lost or never found,
The forms of heart's desire,
We gave them what we could not keep;
We made them what we cannot be.

Their kingdom is our dream, but who can say
If they or we
Are dream or dreamer, signet or clay?
If the most perfect be most true,
These faces pure, these bodies poised in thought
Are substance of our form
And we the confused shadows cast.

Growing toward their prime they take our years away,
And from our deaths they rise
Immortal in the life we lose.
The gods consume us, but restore
More than we were:
We love, that they may be,
They are, that we may know.

—KATHLEEN RAINE

STAYING ALIVE

Staying alive in the woods is a matter of calming down
At first and deciding whether to wait for rescue,
Trusting to others,
Or simply to start walking and walking in one direction
Till you come out—or something happens to stop you.
By far the safer choice
Is to settle down where you are, and try to make a living
Off the land, camping near water, away from shadows.
Eat no white berries;
Spit out all bitterness. Shooting at anything
Means hiking further and further every day
To hunt survivors;
It may be best to learn what you have to learn without a gun,
Not killing but watching birds and animals go
In and out of shelter
At will. Following their example, build for a whole season:
Facing across the wind in your lean-to,

You may feel wilder,
And nothing, not even you, will have to stay in hiding.
If you have no matches, a stick and a fire-bow
Will keep you warmer,
Or the crystal of your watch, filled with water, held up to the sun
Will do the same, in time. In case of snow,
Drifting toward winter,
Don't try to stay awake through the night, afraid of freezing—
The bottom of your mind knows all about zero;
It will turn you over
And shake you till you waken. If you have trouble sleeping
Even in the best of weather, jumping to follow
With eyes strained to their corners
The unidentifiable noises of the night and feeling
Bears and packs of wolves nuzzling your elbow,
Remember the trappers
Who treated them indifferently and were left alone.
If you hurt yourself, no one will comfort you
Or take your temperature,
So stumbling, wading, and climbing are as dangerous as flying.
But if you decide, at last, you must break through
In spite of all danger,
Think of yourself by time and not by distance, counting
Wherever you're going by how long it takes you;
No other measure
Will bring you safe to nightfall. Follow no streams: they run
Under the ground or fall into wilder country.
Remember the stars
And moss when your mind runs into circles. If it should rain,
Or the fog should roll the horizon in around you,
Hold still for hours
Or days, if you must, or weeks, for seeing is believing
In the wilderness. And if you find a pathway,
Wheel rut, or fence wire,
Retrace it left or right—someone knew where he was going
Once upon a time, and you can follow
Hopefully, somewhere,
Just in case. There may even come, on some uncanny evening,
A time when you're warm and dry, well fed, not thirsty,
Uninjured, without fear,
When nothing, either good or bad, is happening.
This is called staying alive. It's temporary.
What occurs after
Is doubtful. You must always be ready for something to come bursting
Through the far edge of a clearing, running toward you,
Grinning from ear to ear
And hoarse with welcome. Or something crossing and hovering

Overhead, as light as air, like a break in the sky,
Wondering what you are.
Here you are face to face with the problem of recognition.
Having no time to make smoke, too much to say,
You should have a mirror
With a tiny hole in the back for better aiming, for reflecting
Whatever disaster you can think of, to show
The way you suffer.
These body signals have universal meaning: If you are lying
Flat on your back with arms outstretched behind you,
You say you require
Emergency treatment; if you are standing erect and holding
Arms horizontal, you mean you are not ready;
If you hold them over
Your head, you want to be picked up. Three of anything
Is a sign of distress. Afterward, if you see
No ropes, no ladders,
No maps or messages falling, no searchlights or trails blazing,
Then, chances are, you should be prepared to burrow
Deep for a deep winter.

—DAVID WAGONER

STEALING TROUT

I park the car half in the ditch and switch off and sit.
The hot astonishment of my engine's arrival
Sinks through 4 A.M. silence and frost.
At the end of a long gash,
An atrocity through the lace of first light,
I sit with the smoking instrument.
I am on delicate business.
I want the steel to be cold instantly,
And myself secreted three fields away,
And the farms, back under their blankets, supposing a plane passed.

Because this is no wilderness you can just rip into.
Every leaf here is plump and well-married,
Every grain of the soil of known lineage, well-connected,
And the gardens like brides are fallen asleep
Before their weddings have properly begun,
The orchards, the hushed maids, fresh from convent—

It is too hushed, something improper is going to happen.
It is too ghostly-proper, all sorts of liveried listenings
Tiptoe along the lanes and peer over hedges. . . .

I listen for the eyes jerked wide on pillows,
Their dreams washed with sudden ugly petroleum.
(They need only look out at a sheep;
Every sheep within five miles
Is nailing me accurately down
With its hellishly shaven, starved-priest expression.)

I emerge. The air, after all, has forgotten everything.
The sugared spindles and wings of grass
Are etched on great goblets. A pigeon falls into space.
The earth is coming quietly and darkly up from a great depth,
Still under the surface. I am unknown,
But nothing is surprised. The tarmac of the road
Is velvet with sleep, the hills are out cold—
A new earth still in its wrapper
Of gauze and cellophane,
The frost from the storage still on its edges;
My privilege to poke and sniff.
The sheep are not much more than the primroses.
And the river there, amazed with itself,
Flexing and trying its lights,
And unused fish that are rising
And sinking for the sheer novelty
As the sun melts the hill's spine and the spilled light
Flows through their gills. . . .

My mind sinks, rising and sinking,
And the opening arms of the river forget me
Into the buried tunnel of hazels. There
My boot dangles down till a thing black and sudden
Savages it, and the river is heaping under,
Alive and malevolent,
A coiling glider of shock, the space-black
Draining off there under the hazels—
But I drop and stand square in it, against it.
Then it is river again, washing its soul,
Its stones, its weeds, its fish, its gravels,
And the rooty mouths of the hazels clear
Of the discolorings bled in
Off plowlands and lanes—wanting the pure peat whiskey
Fed from the breast on Dartmoor.

For minutes, I can hardly look at it—
The riding tables, the corrugated shanty roofs tightening

To braids, boilings where boulders throw up
Gestures of explosion, black splitting everywhere
To drowning skirts of whiteness, a slither of mirrors,
Where the bundled hazel rods, hugging each other,
Lean over and peer in and cannot
Make up their minds. Here it is shallow,
Ropes my knees, lobbing fake boomerangs,
A drowned woman loving each ankle,
But I'm heavier and wade with them upstream,
Flashing my blue minnow
Up the open throats of water,
And across through the side of the rush
Of alligator, escaping along there
Under the beards of the hazels, and I slice
The wild nape-hair off the bald bulges,
Till the tightrope of my first footholds
Tangles away downstream
And my boot soles move as to magnets.

Now I deepen. And here comes the mob
Of voices and hurriers, piling down
And tumbling past me. I am missing a panic—
This army of river is a rout
Of tumbrils and gun carriages, rags and metal,
All the funeral woe-drag of some overnight disaster
Mixed with planets, electrical storms, and darkness
On a high mapless moorland of granite,
Trailing past me with all its frights, its eyes
With what they have seen and still see.
They drag the flag off my head, a dark insistence
Tearing the spirits from my mind's edge and from under.
To pull me clear takes the strike and strong spine
Of one of the river's genuine members—
Thoroughly made of dew, lightning, and granite
Very slowly over three years. A trout, a foot long,
Lifting its head in a shawl of water,
Fins banked stiff like a schooner,
Forces the final curve wide, getting
A long look at me. So much for the horror:
It has changed places.
                    Now I am a man in a painting
(Under the scabby stuffed head of a fox)
Painted circa 1905,
Where the river steams and the frost relaxes
From the pear blossoms. The brassy wood pigeons
Bubble their colorful voices and the sun
Rises upon a world well-tried and old.

                              —TED HUGHES

STILES

I doubt if the wind in your boots
Would make you walk this mile,
The full meadow stretch of love,
From that to this stile.

A dally of dew on your hair,
The arching sun on your spine

Keep you idly perched on your stile,
A mile from mine.

I doubt if the wind in your boots,
Or a song in your cuff,
Or news of me cutting my throat
Would move you enough.

—JOHN PUDNEY

STILL-LIFE

Outcrop stone is miserly

With this wind. Hoarding its nothing,
Letting wind run through its fingers,
It pretends to be dead of lack.
Even its grimace is empty,
Warted with quartz pebbles from the sea's womb.

It thinks it pays no rent,
Expansive in the sun's summerly reckoning.
Under rain, it gleams exultation blackly,
As if receiving interest.
Similarly, it bears the snow well.

Wakeful and missing little, and landmarking
The flylike dance of the planets,
The landscape moving in sleep,
It expects to be in at the finish,
Being ignorant of this other, this harebell

That trembles, as under threats of death,
In the summer turf's heat-rise,
And in which—filling veins
Any known name of blue would bruise
Out of existence—sleeps, recovering,

The maker of the sea.

—TED HUGHES

STILL POND, NO MORE MOVING

I

They have taken the maps and spread
    them out
And parted from each other,
Have slipped the rivers into their veins
And pocketed the sandy beaches,
Have gone walking through slow
    trains
Across where the Mississippi bends,
Have gone in even slower freighters
Down the irregular coastlines—
The inlet's curve, the island's nest
Lure them along a dotted line
Back or forward, forward or back,
And some have settled at an address.

Above them all the same sky
Shapes the mountain or meets the
    shore,
And some—now undecided why
They chose one or the other—stare
Out of a crooked window from
A ramshackle cabin on a dune
At the slow rollers coming in,
The sheets hung out on a clothesline,
While the children's disparate cries
Rise up from the hard shore,
And someone is looking up
Wishing that he were where
The pines soar to the mountaintop
Or stop at the snowline.

II

Is it water they want, water,
The sea changingly in,
Or, cool to the tilted diver
Ringed round by quarry walls,
The stills of deep water
That make him weightless, blind,
As he soars back to the beginning,
That spring without a mind?
Or the highest mountain places
Where the sudden shaded lake

Refreshes the eye because
No two lakes are alike?

And sometimes by its absence—
Or by its opposite—
Water is strangely felt:
In New Mexico, appearance
Conceived as existence springs
Forward into the distance
In vanishing parallels
Of skylines of lighted cliffs
That race up to the hills;
The desert, its own mirage,
Breaks in wave on wave
Between the bloodied mountains
At the running out of day,
And when the sun says it is
Life and death at once,
There, in the few trees,
Water stands up to dance.

III

And some are far out at sea.
The horizon is growing dark.
Someone is taking a walk
On the deck of a dipping hull
Or the deck awash in a storm—
Barely holding on—
While some at the ship's bar
Sit while an arm extends
Their gin and their caviar,
And find with the first sip
The seepage of doubt begin—
Oh, what did I come for?
What am I doing here?
Supposing the lights went off
And we stopped right where we are?

IV

Who is painting the barn door?
Who is painting the painter there,
Summer after summer,
The summer plucked from the year?

But there is that one summer
When old age, like a stick
Thrown for a retriever
Who does not bring it back,
Keeps drifting farther out
Till it's no longer seen—
One mountainside slides down,
One city street slams shut,
A piece of the sea is gone.

V

Is it Hythe or Rockaway?
Or the Puerto Rican waves
That roll in in the same way?
Or Rosarita Beach
Where the sulphur of the sand
Is marked by the horse's hoof,
And the Moorish hotel stands,
A white elephant, aloof,
Where once the gamblers jammed
The tables, and now one goes
Into almost empty rooms
And the four guitarists come
To the table to serenade?

VI

I know some landscapes where
Intensity comes late,
And, deepening in light,
Brings such an inner peace

That floating by in the gold
The world is half dissolved
And the last birds cry farewell
To the day and the shadows seem
To lean on the trees in the wood.

And others where morning comes
Spun out on a crystal web,
And innocence is abroad
And drinks in the new-made world,
And nothing appears to be
Violent or amiss,
And silence would be a tree,
Except that the wind is.

VII

Someone is bitterly thinking
The innermost's not said:
Where is the great theme?
Whoever saw the world
At once and saw it whole?
In New England now,
Here where the water is,
Here where the red barn
Is an advocate of hills,
Time rigs up famous shapes,
The white whales, the white ships,
Yet in summer's lapse
The drunken sea bards come
To lounge on all its Capes.

—HOWARD MOSS

STOIC

I, a slave, chained to an oar of poem,
Inhabiting this faraway province where
Nothing happens. I wouldn't want it to.
I have expressly deprived myself of much:
Conversation, sweets of friendship, love. . . .
The public women of the town don't appeal.
I wouldn't want them to. There are no others,
At least for an old, smelly, covetous bookman.
So many things might have fed this avocation,
But what's the point? It's too late.

About the matter of death I am convinced,
Also that peace is unattainable and destiny

Impermeable to reason. I am lucky to have
No grave illness, I suppose, no wounds
To ache all winter. I do not drink or smoke.
From all these factors I select one, the silence
Which is that jewel of divine futility,
Refusal to bow, the unvarnished grain
Of the mind's impudence: you see it so well
On the faces of the self-reliant dead.

                              —LAWRENCE DURRELL

THE STONE

The stone found me in bright sunlight
around 9th and Stuyvesant Streets and
found, if not a friend, at
least a travelling companion.
Kicking, we crossed
Third Avenue, then Cooper Square, a-
voiding the traffic in our oblique and
random way, a cab almost got him, and I had
to wait a few seconds, crowding
in from the triangular portion edged about
with signs, safety island, crossed
Lafayette, him catching between the cobbles, then
with a judicious blow
from the toes of my foot (right), well, a
soccer kick aiming for height, we cleared
the curb and turned left down Lafayette,
that long block,
with a wide sidewalk and plenty of room to maneuver
in over metal cellar doorways or swinging
out toward the curb edge. The low worn
curb at 4th was a cinch to make, and
at Great Jones Street the driveway into a
gas station promised no impediment. But
then he rolled suddenly to the right
as though following an old gentleman in a long
coat, and at the same time I was addressed
by a painter I know and his girl on their way
to Washington Square, and as I looked up to
answer,
I heard the small sound. He had fallen
in his run, into water gathered in a sunken
plate which they lift to tighten or loosen
something to do with the city water supply I think,
and sank out of sight.
I spoke to Simeon and Dee

about a loft it turned out he hadn't gotten, but
felt so desolate at having lost him they didn't
stay long, I looked at the puddle, explained
we'd come all the way from beyond Cooper Square,
they hurried away.
I suppose I could have used my hands, picked him
out and continued, he'd have been dry by the time
we got home, but just as I decided to abandon him
the sun disappeared.
I continued on down Bleecker finally,
a warm front moving in from the west, the
cirrus clotting into alto-cumulus, sun seeping through
as the front thickened, but not shining, the air turned
cool, and there were pigeons
circling
over the buildings at
West Broadway, and over them a gull, a
young man with a beard and torn army jacket walked
a big mutt on a short leash teaching him to heel.
The mutt was fine, trotting alongside, nuzzling
lightly at his master's chino pants, the young
man smiled, the dog smiled too, and on they went.
They had each other.
I had left him there in the puddle, our game
over, no fair using hands I had told myself.
Not that he could have smiled.
The sun gone in.
He had been shaped like a drunken pyramid, ir-
regularly triangular.
I liked him.

—PAUL BLACKBURN

STONE HORSE SHOALS

"To wade the sea mist, then to wade the sea
At dawn, let drift your garments one by one,
Follow the clean stroke of a sea gull's wing
Breast-high against the sun;
Follow a sail to sunward, slowly nearing
The lazy lobster boats at Stone Horse Shoals,
And pass them silent, on a strong ebb tide,
Into an ocean empty to the poles."

The tall man clenched his eyes against the world;
His face was gray and shook like a torn sail.
"I have lived," he said, "a life that moved in spirals

Turned inward like the shell of a sea snail.
I have been the shadow at the heart of shadows.
I have stared too many years at my own face.
On Stone Horse Shoals, among the lobster boats,
I will shed my carapace.

"Something will die there, something move and watch
Its shadow fathoms downward on the sand,
Summer and winter. In another season
Another man comes wading to the land,
Where other blossoms fade among the dunes
And other children. . . . I am tired," he said,
"But I can see a naked body climbing
A naked seacoast, naked of the dead,

"Naked of language. There are signs inscribed
On stones and trees, familiar vocables;
I hope to rise out of the sea as white,
As empty and chalk-smooth as cockleshells.
And children digging naked in the sand
Will find my shell and on it scratch new words
That soon will blossom out," he said, "and bear
New fruit, strange to the tongue of men and birds."

—MALCOLM COWLEY

THE STORM

Because you have increased my hurt,
I will not mention what occurs to me now
In this rainstorm, the green curtains
Soaked at the bottom, heavily flapping
Out time, the shadows of clouds moving
Across the sides of buildings, shapes
Everywhere changing, the words to use
Changing, thoughts to refer to, changing
Too, and now, in the rain, whatever you do
Hurts me, hurts me, and makes me wait for
The next thing you think of, the next thing
You do.

What makes memory, I wonder, what makes
It whole and what makes it part?
What eliminates feeling in time
And what makes it real,
And why, when the rain is falling,
And the wind is raging,

And the curtains allow in no light,
And the cat is asleep in dreams,
And the walls shift and the dust is wet,
Why is there no feeling
For what happens,
As it rains, as one sleeps?

I shudder and make myself small
By drawing up my legs to my chest
And take the covers off me and watch myself
In a long mirror, a body a ball on a white sheet,
Rocking slightly, and he is pink and brown,
And she is waiting to say something
That hurts him, embarrassing the stewards
In his house, caressing his coachman,
Stealing lovely looks at the air . . .
To whom, darling, can it be directed,
This heart, and
How to maintain it?

Will you stop hurting me, will you stop saying
Things which make me sick,
Which make me mad in the stark, raving moonlight?
                                   —ROBERT DAVID COHEN

THE STORM

Noonlight is sudden full of the spirits
of dead butterflies moving
like a holiday—
surely, all that have ever been!
They are like flowers in the bushy pine,
on hedges, trees; fluttering
knee-deep in the fields; flailing
out of a sky thick with them as if with
          snow.
I go up on the roof to see them.
The landscape is a blizzard of hues,
farms going under—
wingbeats, petals, flakes—

they come in at my lips and eyelids,
they fly in the currents of my blood;
friendly, they kill with such gentle
          wings:
knives stroking as softly as eyelashes.
The day hums in their overshadow-
          ings;
they will cover the electric lines;
even the mountains will be buried
in this colored Pompeii,
in these deep, bright ashes.
                                   —ROBERT WALLACE

A STORM FROM THE EAST

Their house faces east, is protected by trees
From winds from the Gulf, which (the weatherman says) prevail
In that section. But a correction
Is due (of the thesis, or maybe the house),
Since, for three days, from the east a preëminent gale
Has frozen, through sweaters and sweaters, both husband and spouse.

They have an unspoken agreement that they will be surly
Unto each other, and any intruders,
For the duration. And they have kept it—
One refusing to talk, cook, or sweep the place,
The other composing briefs for his side of the case
And watching gulls fight for dead fish, as the wind blows.

They have children, too, but are keeping them properly cowed
Until the storm drops (or the children), at which time the patter
Of tiny feet will again be allowed
And the oldest may even stop asking what is the matter.

They have love, too—put away, put away, while they fret
About the injustices done them: life, and no mail.
Oh, when will the wind die down, weatherman, and let
What is so be so, what prevails prevail?

—REED WHITTEMORE

A STORM OF LOVE

Nightsea and violet wave,
The Negroes at the pump,
Uneven storms that have
The ship gripped by the lamp—
Vain dizzy striving:
Rude oblivion,
You ride the whitecaps and are
Close heart to every scuttling star.

Crouch in the shrouds then; safety is
Only a land hypothesis;
The bearing element
Is broken liquid strings that do not hold.
Water and air are one fire.
Spire and crackle of heaven hellbent

Fold on the gloom-broached parapet,
Doom beyond use of tackle
Or spending of black sweat.

Easy for me who have done my time
On roller coasters; but you where the sea's detritus
Has turned land had built your stone house
Only in earshot of the shingle-knock
That lulled your night-hours.
That dull rhyme and cradle-rock
I have brought you out of into this carouse.
So we go down together. In God's name.
No pity for you and for me no blame!

—Hilary Corke

THE STREET

The street climbs upward steeply,
hiding its ascent sometimes
in sudden angles, abrupt
twistings, the cobbles ahead
darting off into shadow.
Where the sunlight is brightest,
an iron shutter seems rung
down on the street where it turns;
the blackness dazzles between
houses that are stepping out
into space or are hugging
one another, teetering
like drunkards, but not falling.
This one sees, after a while.
When one has hesitated
at the turn, the feeling is
not of the street going on,
but of a new encounter,
vaguely threatening. The street's
blackness is like the blackness
of the dogs who lie across
one's path inevitably
in these mountain villages—
dogs that bring one to a stop
each time, though they sleep on and
seem as passive as puddles.
Looking up an unexplored
stretch of the street, one senses
a cul-de-sac that is not

there; in fact, there is likely
to be only a single
street that travels back upon
itself through its leisurely
mazes, attaining perhaps
a square with well or fountain,
but breaking at once into
a flight of stone steps trotting
forward to gather dimness.
To turn with one's camera
is to find that one has come,
as it were, from a blank wall,
on which a rooftop has set
its geometric shadow,
making an abstract painting;
but when one resumes the way,
one climbs the streets of countless
pictures in hotel bedrooms
at home. But there is never
a campstool here, no paintbox
or easel. Austerities
of light and shade are all—cube
upon cube mounting the sky's
blue perspectives. There is no
view. (What have they done with it?)
Doors and windows are holes
in the light. The street staggers
onward, lurching its cobbles
to the next elevation.

The masonry swells under
red rooftops, through the tiers of heat.
One climbs, it seems, uselessly,
feeling the straining in thighs
and calves, following one's feet.
At yet another turning,

the figure of a woman is revealed—
a peasant dressed in black, bent
forward, her face averted,
she hurries past and downward.
She is noiseless on the stones.

—GENE BARO

THE STREET OF NAMED HOUSES

(135TH STREET, HARLEM)

My Sun,
You smile at the granite of Milton,
Glare on the windows, dazzle the doors,
Dancing on this universe of five floors,
Shining your face around the place.
No matter what you have done,

My Wind,
The birds of Howard's ledges don't mind
That you preen with little wind the black crown
Of feathers, disturb the mild down
At the bead eyes, surprise the dark seeds
At the beak. Young girls find,

My Rain,
What is silent and small with Lorraine—
That is the fine spray. The hands,
Palm up, reach as divining wands;
To know your warm water, they bathe the wrists, arms,
And skirts. Corinne cannot contain,

My Snow,
Her women. At the doors and every window
They appear, and in all your cold they talk
And frost the glass; they note the men that walk
Past, in and out. They comb the white hair, wear
Flowers on a housecoat. I know,

My Moon,
Now that sleep is coming soon;
Dreams are to touch all eyes. Sweet Helen
Falls asleep again.
Light of your face, slow shadows
Singing on a wall, come to dance. Soon, soon,

My Love.

—ROBERT DAVID COHEN

STUTTERER

Courage: your tongue has left
its natural position in the cheek
where eddies of the breath
are navigable calms. Now
it locks against the glottis or
is snapped at by the teeth
in mid stream: it must be work
to get out what you mean:
the rapids of the breath
are furious with belief
and want the tongue, as blood
and animal of speech,
to stop it, block it, or come clean
over the rocks of teeth
and down the races of the air,
tumbled and bruised to death.
Relax it into acting, be
the air's straw-hat
canoeist with a mandolin
yodelling over the falls.
This is the sound advice
of experts and a true despair:
it is the toll to pass the locks
down to the old mill stream
where lies of love are fair.

—ALAN DUGAN

SUBJECTIVITY AT SESTOS

To Hero nightly, wet and rather cold,
    Leander came at last from the dark sea,
A little breathless, if the truth be told,
    And needing towels and a pot of tea.
    But she, purblind to the low comedy,
Rated her own reaction at its cost,
    Finding him more than man-size because she
Seven times since sunset had assumed him lost.

Conversely, parting, she assumed him home,
    And slept. Myself, in spite of what is said,
    I think he sank seeking the Asian shore.
Next night she cried because he did not come,
    Not knowing, when at dawn she found him dead,
    He had in fact been drowned the night before.

—P. M. HUBBARD

SUBURBAN WIFE'S SONG

When you are gone, I lie upon your bed
And you are there, dark as the light of stars,
Closer than measurements of heart, and loud
With the silences of all our daily years;

And then the door key, lights in the living room,
The slamming wood, the briefcase on the floor,
The way you say, "Where's everyone? I'm home"—
And do not know how far away you are.

—ROBERT HUTCHINSON

SUBURB HILLTOP

Withdrawn from layers of upper air, ice-blue and clear,
the city wrinkles down under its mist
as if in fear,
as if it wished to hide
under those smoky threads which twist
up in the winter afternoon.
They've spun a huge, bruise-colored cocoon
with all the city's larval movements there inside.

I watch a trolley like a worm explore,
halting, over the valley floor,
the lice of traffic and, far away,
black-feelered freighters squatting on the bay . . .
The smoke's cocoon, half curled
back, shows me this new wriggling world,
framed
where my eye has aimed
and pinned it to the valley floor,
visible through my metaphor.

My urban larva, bared to the sharp view
of such iced weapons and the skies,
what will we do
now? Flutter into butterflies?

—RICHARD MOORE

THE SUMMER LANDSCAPE
OR, THE DRAGON'S TEETH

On the stone terrace, underneath the shade
Of the perfect maple, I watch the summer scene.
Beyond the strip of lawn, the strip of garden,
Tall flowers, yellow and blue and red and orange,
Day lilies, bergamot, and coreopsis,

Delphinium, phlox, and marigold and foxglove
And low alyssum, white against the green.

The side hill falls away, and a point of woods
Comes in from the right, and a little farther down
Another from the left; then rolling hills,
The colored counties, corn and oats and wheat,
Dark green, light green, light brown;
One or two red barns, no sign of a town,
Far to the north, the lone blue line of mountain.

I am alone, do nothing but sow my fancies;
I am alone, and the afternoon is long.

And the light darkens and the color changes,
Turns livid green or cyanotic blue.
And I am less alone now, for a throng
Of people is coming out, a twilight crew,
Who spring, like the men of Cadmus, from the ground.
I sowed them earlier in the afternoon:

    The ugly and mean, who sit in grim dejection
And speak no word nor utter any sound,
Self-pitiers flinging themselves face down in tears,
Matricides and murderers in the bushes,
Cowards whose bowels loosen at every noise,
Voyeurs who watch for animals to couple,
And when the act occurs, their heartbeats pound,

Schoolgirl seducers, lovers of little boys,
Impotent suicides hanging themselves on trees,
Adulterers hunting women whose open kiss
Has a taste like that of water in a jar
Where flowers have stood too long—all of them are
Thick around house and orchard, brothers, fighting,
Slaying and slain; and I am all of these.

—Rolfe Humphries

SUMMER'S EARLY END AT HUDSON BAY

The old sandpiper contemplates his age
As one only can, with ignorant unease,
And the scene imparts a mood of sad alarm.
A steady wind bends the thin grass,
And the sunlight, too, streams thinly, distantly;

The first ice gleams on the water,
Embracing the rocks and reeds with brittle strength.
The flock is nervous; like clockwork toys, the shapes
Mill and bob, a confusion of white and gray;
A hundred dances of anxiety
And fluttering movements begin and flare
And subside. The old one, too, turns on his rock,
Round and round with ceremonial steps,
His eyes wary for the others; and this old land
That had been so alien once
And then so familiar is alien again—
A point of coldness.
The imperfect young are fledged or dead,
Scarcely remembered now.
Upon the evidences of the scene
Mount tremors, warnings, subtle arguments
That urge his shivering nerves and awkward wings—
The other land is an impulse he must keep.
Into the uncertain air, on painful wings,
The aging migrant labors,
Dull to the image of the other land
And to the storms that prowl
The long seas of Brazil.

—Hayden Carruth

THE SUN

I have heard of fish,
coming up for the sun,
who stayed forever
shoulder to shoulder—
avenues of fish that never got back,
all their proud spots and solitudes
sucked out of them.

I think of flies
who come from their foul caves
out into the arena.
They are transparent at first.
Then they are blue with copper wings.
They glitter on the foreheads of men.
Neither bird nor acrobat,
they will dry out like small black shoes.

I am an identical being.
Diseased by the cold and the smell of
the house,
I undress under the infinite bulk.
My skin flattens out like sea water.
O yellow eye,
let me be sick with your heat,
let me be feverish and frowning.
Now I am utterly given.
I am your daughter, your sweetmeat,
your priest, your mouth, and your bird,
and I will tell them all stories of you
until I am laid away forever,
a thin gray banner.

—Anne Sexton

SUNDAY EVENINGS

All this indigo, nonviolent light will triumph.

Uneven shadows have fallen out of the darkness that waits,
Continuously created there, as in the whiteness
Of the kitchen, two rooms away, ice cubes are being made
With a humming of generation. Whether, earlier, it had been
Fine, with sunlight infusing the hints of ice incipient
In the blue air, with promises of gleaming winters
Already trumpeting through the blood and singing *"l'Avenir!"*
Unheard, but pounding somewhere within the inner ear,
Or whether the delaying rains and the two-day-old
Grayness of sky, grayness of generality, had
Spoiled the earlier day for being outside an apartment,
Outside a self—no matter. With night unfolding now
In every corner wherever walls meet or dust collects,
What has just been is obscured. The trickle of time and loss
Condenses along the outsides of things: this icy glass
Sweats drops of terror not its own; this room diffuses
Tiny patches of light through its half-shaded windows
Into the winking, myriad galaxies of all
New York on clear October nights—bits of a brightness
It doesn't have, let alone can give. This world inside
These walls, condensing on the outside of my mind,
Has corners and darkenings quite unimaginable,
But visible as Presences in gray and purple light
At this time of day, of week, of year, of life, of time.

Even the usual consolations of Sunday become
A part of all its general threat: symphonic music
On heavy afternoons; the steam heat, blanketing
A brown couch and a bridge lamp and dark bookshelves;
No need for a meal, and too much newspaper to be read;
Rooms around this one, full of what is still undone
And what may never be; the glimpses out at tiny,
Unwise revelations of light from rooms as high up as this,
Several blocks away. And to put an end to the near-
Darkness would hurt too much—a senseless, widening light
From an unfrosted lamp would do it.
                                        But then what?
Why, blinking. Then numbing to the icy fire of incandescence.
Lidded blinds lowering over the windows that overlook
Darknesses of the Park, this room being all the light
In the world now. And then, perhaps, Sunday will have been over.

But then what? Oh yes, once, perhaps, in a month of Sundays,
The exciting stars against a clear, cold, black sky

Shone down like promising, wise, and truthful splinters of mirror.
We saw that the light was good, and meteored across
The starlight of high Manhattan to ordered arrangements of taxis
And blocks of apartments, and parties of frosty eyes like wide,
Entire mirrors, reflecting in joy the twinkling, burning
High overhead at the end of some windy afternoon.

But then what? The next week was full of itself, and ended,
Inevitably, in the darkening late afternoon, indoors,
On Sunday? Ended? Or was it merely the new week's beginning
Come to a bad end? No matter. Whatever ends up like this—
The day, week, year; the life; the time—can't be worth much.

On Sunday afternoons, one can have followed the blackening
Water of the river from eyes along the Drive
And then climbed up a concrete hill to one's own walls
And quietly opened a vein. *"It would be no crime in me*
To divert the Nile or Danube from its course, were I able
To effect such purposes. Where then is the crime
Of turning a few ounces of blood from their natural channel?"
Or the crime of emptying this late-afternoon room
Of all its indigo, not by the light of common
Illumination but by a long pouring of darkness?
Yes, if it is permitted, everything is. So let it
Be. And let it be night now, at very long last,
A night outside the cycle of light and dark and Sunday,
A night in despite of fiery life or icy time
That starts its chilling-out of the heart each week at five
Or five-thirty or so on Sunday, when the big, enlightening myths
Have sunk beyond the river and we are alone in the dark.

—JOHN HOLLANDER

SUNKEN EVENING IN TRAFALGAR SQUARE

The green light floods the city square—
  A sea of fowl and feathered fish,
    Where squalls of rainbirds dive and splash
And gusty sparrows chop the air.

Submerged, the prawn-blue pigeons feed
  In sandy grottoes round the Mall,
    And crusted lobster-buses crawl
Among the fountains' silver weed.

There, like a wreck, with mast and bell,
  The torn church settles by the bow,

And phosphorescent starlings stow
Their mussel shells along the hull.

The oyster-poet, drowned but dry,
    Rolls a black pearl between his bones;
    The mermaid, trapped by telephones,
Gazes in bubbles at the sky.

Till, with the dark, the shallows run,
    And homeward surges tide and fret—
    The slow night trawls its heavy net
And hauls the clerk to Surbiton.
                              —LAURIE LEE

THE SUN-WITCH TO THE SUN

He wakens from the clover rick
And somersaults the woodlot gate,
He sprouts the corn and warms the
        chick,
He plunges in the timberthick.

Green is his pasture in the East,
He bids the stallion and his mate,
The cloven-hoof and hornèd beast
To crop the carpet of his feast.

His slender fingers comb the briar
And search between the spiny leaves
And liberate the starling choir
To cry the curfew of his fire.

The rick, the hill, the trees do move,
I think the very graveyard heaves,
To bask in such a generous love,
Which only I share nothing of.

The birds aspire, the herds agree
In adoration of his heat,
He turns the earth, except for me
The pivot in Eternity.

Reject me not who all alone
Attend my failing cannel grate,
Though they call me heart-of-stone
And whisper of the Evil One.

Thou art God that kissest so
To blanch or quicken all a hill,
To wrap it in the secret snow
Or bare it that the corn may grow.

I veil my face in curtain lace,
I shiver at the miracle;
Burn me in the same embrace,
Spin me in the heavenly chase;

In meetinghouse though I be mute
My heart is forty acres wide
And thirsty as the poplar root;
Let me bear my woman-fruit,
O Sun, my lover deified,
Thou the bridegroom, I the bride!
                              —GEORGE HOWE

SUPPER

I supped where bloomed the red rose,
   And the bird in the tree
Looked on my sweet white bread and
     whistled
    Tunes to me.

And a wasp prowled in the golden
    light,

My honey all about;
And the martin to her sun-baked nest
   Swept in and out.

I sat so still in the garden
   That wasp and leaf and bird
Seemed as I dreamed the only things
   That had ever stirred.

          —WALTER DE LA MARE

SURPRISED BY ME

(TO STEPHEN MOONEY)

I

Let the wood be pulled,
Tree by tree, out of the underground.
Secret veins, like the splayed tissue of moss, will run
Spring waters through the grain.
Let the fountains of spilled green be pine.

Out of the ground-skinned hill
Let grass perspire like an oozing passion.
Rocks will grow humorous and round,
Concealing red worms.
Birds in their lofty blue, complaining
Of a private joke, will pluck snacks of beetles.
Crickets will be their mimics.

And the lake, let it be
A languid body, mother of all seasons.
Let baby-skinned fishes hover
Where the weed dips in, making curious O's
And nipples.
The pine and the hill will fall
Asleep in her swelling, settling,
And a fly skirr over the clouds.

II

This world should be free of timeless renewals.
Let it be immortal.

On a lacquered plain, the hedgerows gather
To a point out of sight.

The cerulean bell-like dome that rings
The plain is arrayed with mosaic light,
White-gold and white.

There the cupola of chinaberry tree,
Its dangling, tinkling green glass,
Tints a circle of brocade,
An onyx beetle pinned to the grass,
And a bee of brass.

Wind, with the incense of song,
Breathes into everything its glory,
Sways the silver platter lake
That sudden mysteries make starry
And the wax scene flowery.

III

But neither that.
Art of the still present is surpassed
By Creation's
Reawakened world of the dying.
Let everything begin to end with:

The adoration of oaks
In the constant elevation of sacrifice
Causes the deer to contemplate its fall;
The hidden birds cry *where where*
And sunflowers gaze—

So much are the eyes and ears,
Tongue and hands
Of the wild world struck
By morning and my arrival.

The arms of the outspread East
Receive
What I must give and give.

—WALTER DARRING

THE SURVIVORS

Quite rightly, we remained among the living;
Managed to hoard our strength; kept our five wits;
So far as possible, withheld our eyes
From sights that loosen keystones in the brain.
We suffered, where we had to, thriftily,

And wasted nothing on the hopeless causes,
Foredoomed escapes, symbolic insurrections.

So it is we, not you, who walk today
Under the rebuilt city's raw façades,
Who sit upon committees of selection
For the commemorative plaque. Your throats
Are dumb beneath the plow that must drive on
To turn the fields of wire to fields of wheat.
Our speeches turn your names like precious stone,

Yet we can pay our tax and see the sun.
What else could we, what else could you, have done?
                                    —ADRIENNE CECILE RICH

SWEENEY TO MRS. PORTER IN THE SPRING

In Prospect Street, outside the Splendid Bar
And Grill, the Pepsi generation—
The beardless, hard-eyed future of our nation—
Rolls casually south out of the slum
From which it will go far,
Leaving an old country where spring has come.

It is not obvious about the spring.
You have to know the signs: a hoist of wash
On every back-piazza line, a sash
Propped open with an empty pint of cream,
A comic softening
Of the wind's blade to rubber, an old dream

Of something better coming soon for each
Survivor who achieves the shores of May—
Perhaps a legacy, a lucky play
At dogs or numbers, or a contest prize.
Lady Luck, on the beach
Between assignments, does not hear their cries—

"Me! Me!," like gulls'. She never will. The old
Diminish steadily in all but years
And hope, which, uncontrollable as tears,
Racks them with life. Just look at Mrs. Porter,
Preparing to unfold,
In the dark bar, a letter from her daughter,

A beauty operator in Ladue,
And to remasticate the lovely tale

Of ranch and Pontiac, washed down with ale
Cold from the Splendid bowels, while waiting for
Her unrefined but true
Love's shape to shade the frosted-glass front door.

Meanwhile, Sweeney, Medallion 83
(A low old-timer's number), wheels his hack,
In Independent livery, past a back-
Projected process shot of Central Square,
To where his love will be,
Impatient to resume their grand affair.

She, like a pile of black rugs, stirs to hear
His two-tone horn just outside, heralding
The coming of both Sweeney and the spring.
Inside, he greets her as before, "Hi, keed,"
While Wilma lays his beer
And whiskey down between them and gets paid.

His knotty fingers, tipped with moons of dirt,
Lock on the shot of Seagram's, which he belts
And chases with a swig of Knick. Nobody else
Could comfort them except their old selves, who
Preserve, worn but unhurt,
The common knowledge of a thing or two

They did together under other moons.
Now the Splendid night begins again,
Unkinking cares, alleviating pain,
Permitting living memories to flood
This country for old men
With spring, their green tongues speaking from the mud.
                                             —L. E. SISSMAN

SWIMMING BY NIGHT

A light going out in the forehead
Of the house by the ocean,
Into warm black its feints of diamond fade.
Without clothes, without caution

Plunging past gravity—
Wait! Where before
Had been floating nothing, is a gradual body
Half remembered, astral with phosphor,

Yours, risen from its tomb
In your own mind,
Haunting dexterity, glimmerings a random
Spell had woken. So that, illumined

By this weak lamp
The evening's alcohol will feed
Until the genie chilling bids you limp
Heavily over stones to bed,

You wear your master's robe
One last time, the far break
Of waves, their length and sparkle, the spinning globe
You wear, and the star running down his cheek.

—JAMES MERRILL

A SYMPATHY, A WELCOME

Feel for your bad fall how could I fail,
poor Paul, who had it so good.
I can offer you only this world like a knife.
Yet you'll get to know your mother,
and, humorless as you do look, you will laugh,
and *all* the others
will not be fierce to you, and loverhood
will swing your soul like a broken bell
deep in a forsaken wood, poor Paul,
whose wild bad father loves you well.

—JOHN BERRYMAN

T

THE TALE OF JORKYNS AND GERTIE
OR, VICE REWARDED

Jorkyns was great; he labored in the City
    And had an office fifty feet by thirty.
His heart was quite unvisited by pity,
Yet he admired his typist; she was pretty,
    And hailed from Hackney, and her name was Gertie.

Poor, simple Gertie had a widowed mother
    (Her father was a fallen window cleaner);
Likewise she had a little orphaned brother
Whom no one had been wise enough to smother,
    A downcast eye, and a reserved demeanor.

Yet how could she resist the cruel temptation
    Of Jorkyns, with his furs and pearly brooches?
On pin-striped knees he swore his adoration.
Poor Gertie could not bear with resignation
    Her widowed mother's voluble reproaches;

Mink-clad, she fled from the abode parental
    Through snow and fog, and landed up at Putney.
Abandoned, desolate, and slightly mental,
She took a flatlet at a modest rental
    And lived awhile on bread and bottled chutney.

Ere long the mink was sold, the pearls were bartered,
    And Jorkyns found her, sapped of all resistance.
Although her attitude was slightly martyred,
He bore her, in a plane that he had chartered,
    To some green island in the sunbathed distance.

And there they dwelt till, wearied of his quarry,
    Proud Jorkyns left her, stranded, on the beaches,
Flew back to Town (nor said that he was sorry)

And took a fancy to a girl called Florrie—
   A plump one, with a skin like cream and peaches.

Gertie, her eyes indomitably wiping,
   Worked as a waitress at the Carlton-Splendid.
She liked it better, on the whole, than typing,
And married a Marine with scarlet piping,
   Which isn't how the story should have ended.

—R. P. Lister

A TALE TOLD BY A HEAD

Proud of my pride,
I grew fat and romantic,
I grew rich in revenge and loved animals.
A nature walk was a kind of
      Belgian bestiary brought with me
where one tapestried foot at a time
      was woven to the ground,
where my hounds followed face down
like surface swimmers unable to drown,
      and I knew I'd brought
it all with me—
all already there in the restless bodies of my eyes
rolling in their oval recesses.

I liked my nature green and
didn't care how it got that way.
It's a mistake to always ask,
    Is it alive, is it dead? Where's the heart?

I crushed the feeding grass
feeding, feeding—what egotism!—until it fails
    in a whole field of feeding.
How can I know when it dies anyway?
Except that nothing's refreshed
      that doesn't die a little.

It was a place like this, I suppose,
where the original nudes, wrong in their
      kindness to each other,
suffered their great loss at the hands of an adder,
and the four darknesses converged on them

and the black tenderness
    began digesting them horribly.

But this is all a tale told by a head to a head
of how the weeds came up like animals out of the dirt
and grew larger—
    their chief act, in fact—
        and how they found me
like a prey to an older prey
whose reverence for reverence grows bigger each day
and less fastidious.

                    —LOIS MOYLES

TANK TOWN

On the forgotten si-
ding, weeds grow, between
sway-backed boxcars, drop-
sical gondolas dripping
gray dust. Who needs
empty, red, slatted hop-
per cars used for shipping
exhausted ore? Bees
hum, and Ramón Gonzá-
lez thinks, sitting on
his wooden steps, in Mex-
ican. I can't call
to him be-

cause here comes the main line's living shriek
and clatter with a swaying swoosh, the sun flash-
ing from eighty windows; white, blind grub faces,
in hermetically sealed glass, click-clack past.

Fishing-pole grass
grows on the dead
spur track where Ra-
món's house is anchored
fast; rusty wheels spread
among the thistles sa-
bre sharp and stacks
of ties where crickets sing;
a grave of names on red
neglected cars on the si-
ding, ding, ding.

                  —JOHN ATHERTON

TECHNOLOGIES

On Commonwealth, on Marlborough,
the gull beaks of magnolia
were straining upward like the flocks
harnessed by kings in storybooks
who lusted for the moon. Six days
we mooned into each other's eyes
mythologies of dune and dawn—
naked to the Atlantic sun—
loving and loving, to and fro
on Commonwealth, on Marlborough,
our whole half hours. And where our
　　　bloods
crested, we saw the bruise-red buds

tear loose the white impeded shapes
of cries. And when our whitest hopes
tore at the wind with wings, it seemed
only a loony dream we dreamed
on Commonwealth, on Marlborough.
They do the trick with atoms now,
with methodologies of steel,
with industry, or not at all.
But so, sweet love, do those white
　　　trees
that dare play out their lunacies
for all they are, for all they know
on Commonwealth, on Marlborough.

　　　　　　　　　　—GEORGE STARBUCK

TELL ME, TELL ME

　　　where might there be a refuge for me
　　　　　from egocentricity
　and its propensity to bisect,
　misstate, misunderstand,
　　　　　and obliterate continuity?
　　　　　Why, oh why, one ventures to ask, set
　flatness on some cindery pinnacle
　as if on Lord Nelson's revolving diamond rosette?

　　　It appeared; gem, burnished rarity,
　　　　　and peak of delicacy—
　in contrast with grievance touched off on
　any ground—the absorbing
　　　　　geometry of a fantasy:
　　　　　a James, Miss Potter, Chinese
　"passion for the particular," of a
　tired man who yet, at dusk,
　　　　　cut a masterpiece of cerise—

　　　for no tailor-and-cutter jury,
　　　　　only a few mice to see—
　who "breathed inconsistency and drank
　contradiction," dazzled
　　　　　not by the sun but by "shadowy
　　　　　　possibility." (I'm referring

to James, and Beatrix Potter's tailor.)
I vow, rescued tailor
    of Gloucester, I am going

    to flee; by engineering strategy—
      the viper's traffic knot—flee
to metaphysical new-mown hay,
honeysuckle, or woods fragrance.
    Might one say or imply T.S.V.P.—
      Taisez-vous? "Please" does not make sense
to a refugee from verbal ferocity; I am
perplexed. Even so, "deference,"
    yes, deference may be my defense.

A *précis?*
    In this told-backward biography
      of how the cat's mice, when set free
by the tailor of Gloucester, finished
the Lord Mayor's cerise coat,
    the tailor's tale ended captivity
      in two senses. Besides having told
of a coat which made the tailor's fortune,
it rescued a reader
    from being driven mad by a scold.

          —MARIANNE MOORE

TEMPERATURE

When the sun shone hot the girl's arm was detected
    by the temperature changes, either by a drop
    when the girl walked into his shadow
or by a rise when the sun shone hot upon her
    as she neared the sun. The sun also became
    part of love's odors which could be detected.

It was odorless indoors, but the arm
    gave off a distinct taste of lemon like the sun
    when the sun struck the edge
of the girl's arm out-of-doors.
    He could tell by the sense of smell
    and the temperature changes alone when he was near her.

On a cloudy day, or when the sun was just a sun,
    the girl's arm was lacking his attention.
    The boy was also lacking on a cloudy day,
but the recess of the sun behind his head

did not immediately bring about a cessation of the odor,
  or the temperature changes on the girl, from the sun.

Any of these temperature changes was at times sufficient
  for the perception of the girl. Like a blind man,
the boy grasped at the odors that would serve him.
Though the odors from the wind, or the arm,
  and the sun were at times sufficient, they
  were neither necessary nor always present.

                  —GERARD MALANGA

THANKSGIVING FOR A HABITAT

(FOR GEOFFREY GORER)

Nobody I know would like to be buried
  with a silver cocktail shaker,
a transistor radio, and a strangled
  daily help, or keep his word because

of a great-great-grandmother who got laid
  by a sacred beast. Only a press lord
could have built San Simeon; no unearned income
  can buy us back the gait and gestures

to manage a baroque staircase, or the art
  of believing footmen don't hear
human speech. (In adulterine castles,
  our half-strong might hang their jackets

while mending their lethal bicycle chains—
  luckily, there are not enough
crags to go round.) Still, Hetty Pegler's Tump
  is worth a visit, so is Schönbrunn,

to look at someone's idea of the body
  which should have been his, as the flesh
Mum formulated shouldn't. That whatever
  he does or feels in the mood for—

stocktaking, horseplay, worship, making love—
  he stays the same shape disgraces
a royal I. To be overadmired is not
  good enough; although a fine figure

is rare in either sex, others like it
  have existed before. One may

be a Proustian snob or a sound Jacksonian
    democrat, but which of us wants

to be touched inadvertently, even
    by his beloved? We know all about graphs
and Darwin, enormous rooms no longer
    superhumanize, but earnest

city planners are mistaken: a pen
    for a rational animal
is no fitting habitat for Adam's
    sovereign clone. I, a transplant

from overseas, at last am dominant
    over three acres and a blooming
conurbation of country lives, few of whom
    I shall ever meet and with fewer

converse. Linnaeus recoiled from the Amphibia
    as a naked gruesome rabble;
arachnids give me the shudders, but fools
    who deface their emblem of guilt

are germane to Hitler—the race of spiders
    shall be allowed their webs. I should like
to be to my water brethren a spell
    of fine weather; many are stupid

and some, maybe, are heartless, but who is not
    vulnerable, easy to scare,
and jealous of his privacy? I am glad
    the blackbird, for instance, cannot

tell if I'm talking English, German, or
    just typewriting, that what he utters
I can enjoy as alien rigmarole. I ought
    to outlast the limber dragonflies

as the muscle-bound firs are certainly
    going to outlast me. I shall not end
down any esophagus, though I may succumb
    to a filter-passing predator,

shall, anyhow, stop eating, return my smidge
    of nitrogen to the World Fund
with a drawn-out *Oh* (unless, at the nod
    of some jittery commander,

I be translated in a nano-second
   to a c.c. of poisonous nothing
in a giga-death). Should conventional
   blunderbuss war and its routiers

invest my bailiwick, I shall of course
   assume the submissive posture,
but men are not wolves and it probably
   won't help. Territory, status,

and love, sing all the birds, are what matter.
   What I dared not hope or fight for
is, in my fifties, mine, a toft and croft
   where I needn't, ever, be at home *to*

those I am not at home *with*, not a cradle,
   a magic Eden without clocks,
and not a windowless grave, but a place
   I may go both in and out of.

                    —W. H. AUDEN

THAT SUMMER

That summer, the red may and the white may made
Glorious the garden wall, and bees burdened
The golden air with their carrying, till it hung
Heavy, a canopy over our heads
As we lay on the lawn and dreamed our way
Through jungles of tangled marrow shoots.
Foxgloves and campanulas swayed in the borders
And God bloomed over all, a benevolent sun.
Only the doves, like feathered augurs
Brooding in thatch, suspected time.

That year, snow came in April and again
In May, and the pony died in his harness;
But in summer, under the whitewashed trees,
A girl in a white dress gave me an apple.
I fitted my teeth in the marks her teeth
Had made; so we were one. Then dusk
Moved slowly among the trees like a blue
Smoke at night, and I cried that joy
Could come so easily, for then I knew
It must break with as little warning.

                    —HENRY TREECE

THEME AND VARIATION

Coleridge caused his wife unrest,
Liking other company best;
Dickens, never quite enthralled,
Sent his packing when she palled;
Gauguin broke the marriage vow
In quest of Paradise enow.
These things attest in monochrome:
Genius is the scourge of home.

Lady Nelson made the best of
What another took the rest of;
Wagner had, in middle life,
Three children by another's wife;
Whitman *liked* to play the dastard,
Boasting here and there a bastard.
Lives of great men all remind us
Not to let their labors blind us.

Each helped to give an age its tone,
Though never acting quite his own.
Will of neither wax nor iron
Could have made a go with Byron;
Flaubert, to prove he was above
Bourgeois criteria of love,
Once took a courtesan to bed
Keeping his hat upon his head.

But mine is off to Johann Bach,
For whom my sentiment is *"Ach!"*
Not once, but twice, a model spouse,
With twenty children in the house.
Some fathers would have walked away
In what they call a fugue today;
But he left no one in the lurch,
And played the stuff he wrote in church.

—Peter De Vries

THEIR PARTY, OUR HOUSE

Into our empty room
One by one they come,
Making themselves at home,
Opening window, door,
Demanding we make more
Space for them and for
Friends they insisted come,
Expecting a vaster room,
Expecting, in short, a home,
Not for ourselves, for them.

They enter and possess us
Cheerfully and by surprise,
Guests whose faces all are strange,
And we apologize.
They inhabit and expand
Us, adding wings, for their ease,
Whose new dimensions only
Slowly suit them, nearly please.
Though we, in our own house,
Now seem clumsy, incapable

Of knowing quite where we are,
They grow more comfortable
And less complaining, show few
Signs of leaving, and divert
Themselves regardless ·of our mood.
Some are heard to assert
(While they enjoy our furniture
And we endure the floor)
They never have felt, or seldom,
So at home before.

Yet when at last they rise,
Remembering themselves
Or long-neglected businesses,
Drift out the door, and cry
Their vanishing goodbye,
If only we left, as they,
This house grown theirs and bare!
But visit it, tier by tier,
Superfluous as the furniture,
The very ghost of what we were.

—Jon Swan

THERE IS NO OPERA LIKE "LOHENGRIN"

But one Apocalyptic Lion's whelp (in flesh
called William Lyon Phelps) purrs: After all,
there is no opera like "Lohengrin"!
My father, a Baptist preacher, a good man,
is now with God—and every day is Christmas.
Apart from questions of creative genius,
there are no gooder men than our good writers.
Lyman Abbott and I, who never can read Dante,
still find cathedrals beautifully friendly.
Hell is O.K.; Purgatory bores me; Heaven's dull.
There is no opera like "Lohengrin"!
Miss Lulu Bett's outline is a Greek statue.
Augustus Thomas' "Witching Hour" 's a masterpiece;
Housman's Second Volume is a masterpiece;
Anglo-Americans well know Ollivant's
masterpiece, "Bob, Son of Battle," that masterpiece!
There is no opera like "Lohengrin"!
In verse, these masterpieces are worth reading:
"The Jar of Dreams," by Lilla Cabot Perry;
"Waves of Unrest," by Bernice Lesbia Kenyon.
(O Charlotte Endymion Porter! Percy Bysshe Shelley?
Helen Archibald Clark! O women with three names!)
Anna Hempstead Branch read all the Bible
through in a few days. Speaking of Milton,
bad manners among critics are too common,
but gentlemen should not grow obsolete.
Often we fall asleep—not when we're bored,
but when we think we are most interesting.
There is no opera like "Lohengrin"!
I sometimes think there are no persons who
can do more good than good librarians can.
American books grow easier to hold;
dull paper and light weight is the ideal.

—JOHN WHEELWRIGHT

THEY SING

(A DYING MAN SPEAKS)

All women loved dance in a dying light.
The moon's my mother—how I love the moon!
Out of her place she comes, a dolphin one,
Then settles back to shade and the long night.

A beast cries out as if its flesh were torn,
And that cry takes me back where I was born.

Who thought love but a motion in the mind?
Am I but nothing, leaning toward a thing?
I'll scare myself with sighing, or I'll sing;
Descend, O gentlest light, descend, descend.
O sweet field far ahead, I hear your birds;
They sing, they sing, but still in minor thirds.

I've the lark's word for it, who sings alone:
What's seen recedes; *forever's* what we know—
Eternity defined, and strewn with straw,
The fury of the slug beneath the stone.
The vision moves, and yet remains the same.
In heaven's praise, I dread the thing I am.

The edges of the summit still appall
When we brood on the dead or the beloved;
Nor can imagination do it all
In this last place of light. He dares to live
Who stops being a bird, yet beats his wings
Against the wide abyss, the gray waste nothingness of things.

—THEODORE ROETHKE

THEY WERE ALL LIKE GENIUSES

The lunchroom bus boy who looked like Orson Welles,
Romeo, Brutus, and a man from Mars in his two eyes,
the bellhop who was Joe Louis to the life,
the Greek fruit peddler who in church on Sundays
was a lightning-struck dead image of J. P. Morgan,
the Italian barber who in a mirror was more like
John Barrymore than Barrymore himself,
the Woolworth demonstration cold-cream girl
who was Garbo at a glance, only more real,
the shoe clerk who in midnight rain outside of Lindy's
should have been Clark Gable,
the Second Avenue ex-Baptist minister
who was born to have a face like Cordell Hull's—
why do they look at me like that,
why do they stare,

                                sleepwalking through my dreams?
What was the big mistake?

They looked like power and fame,
like love, like everything you need;
and you would think their looks would put them where
they could dictate a letter or run a bank
or kiss a microphone or float a yacht or sleep in
a genuine imitation Marie Antoinette bed
or get somewhere before they die
instead of dropping into dreams too deep
to tell themselves who, what, or where they are
until a fire turns them out into the street
or a shot is heard and the police are at the door.

                                —HORACE GREGORY

A THIN FAÇADE FOR EDITH SITWELL

WHEN
Dr.
Edith (Hon. D. Litt. [Leeds], Hon. D. Litt. [Durham])
Descends in Mayfair from her brougham
Tall as a chimney stack,
Her
     straight
          back
Encased in a pelisse as black
As cloven Lucifer's silk sack,
She
Enters a bluestockinged club
And, through the Grub Street antics
Of best-selling Corybantes
Who
From castles and from hovels
Meet to contemplate their novels,
Elicits sudden hushes
'Mongst the pudding-colored plushes.

Her hat is a black wheel,
With six spokes of tempered steel,
From her swan's neck hang medallions
Brought from Tenerife in galleons,
And her fingers are afire
With cut amethyst, sapphire,
When
At ease with duke and Cockney,

A transmigratory Procne,
She folds her flutt'ring wing and tail
And perches on the Chippendale.

Yet in that grace marmoreal,
Mantilla'd and Escorial,
Deep
As the sea
On which sails the slant Chinee
She
Sounds the mad note of Ophelia,
The sad organ of Cecilia,
The song of Dian as, a-hunting,
She outraced the brute and grunting
Dryads of the lewd and moody wood.
Up to no good!

She orders Martinis
And quick as Houdinis
The waiters in gaiters return in a trice.
They know as well as we
It
   —was
        she
Who took a verse a-dying
And with her sweet bazooka
Sent its fusty fragments flying.
Encircled by critics
Benign and mephitic,
By poets long dead and *nouveaux*,
She blesses, caresses, and what she dismisses
She kills with the dart of a *mot*.
So.
At lunch as the bards nip
Mutton and parsnip,
The homage like fromage
Comes in with the fruit.
"Ah, laureate lady,"
Says one as he reaches
Toward apples and peaches,
"Once cottoned and bent to,
Your tones *quattrocento*,
Who then could descend to
The deserts of prose?"

"You are sweet," says she
(Purring and stirring the oolong),

"To admit you've been smitten
                    By these bits that I've written."
          "Not at all," says he,
"For the charm, don't you see,
Is a matter, *à fond*, of English *esprit:*
When
Bertie and Harry,
Dirty and hairy,
Loaf by the docks of the gull-splattered sea
In Plymouth and Harwich and Dover,
Who's to oppose their sordid repose,
Who's to amuse them but you?"
          "Lunch is over!" says she.

                    —John Malcolm Brinnin

THINGS KEPT

From the years
when cars were worth looking at,
when they sat the road with dignity and aplomb,
a hint of nautical danger in their construction,
now a parade of ten, a dozen
elegant dragons
moves down the street under its own deliberate power,
with wire wheels spinning, or immensely solid wheels
painted in sulphur yellow,
with collapsible roofs thrown back
like elbows akimbo, resting in thorough ease.

Even in the most empty day
creation can happen, and the ancient cars—
the Pyramids on wheels, the ruins of the Forum mobile,
a sudden fragment of Minoan Greek translated—
shine forth in the pure faith of restoration,
spin merrily forward with the wholesome noise
of intimate, personal engines.
Red on red,
deep blue picked out with brass,
polished beyond fear of time or road stains,
they lavish in undecided weather
the beauty of making and keeping.

I can remember
sitting, reading a book, in early summer
on a stone terrace, at my right hand a weir,

and looking up to a ring of inquisitive peacocks,
six tame peacocks, trailing their tails in sequence,
tilting to one side their blue anachronous heads;
behind them, over the narrow, ruffled water,
on a small island, a stern stone lion, crowned,
remembering back toward the pulse of royal ages.
Their questions about me satisfied, the peacocks
took heavily to air, long trains depending,
and slowly flew through the pale sun to join him.

Objects, beings that have
the passion and flower of beauty caught about them,
the great design, rising, of peacock feathers,
the sculptured wheel of the maker's admiration,
the bold brass headlamp, the lion, defying night
and the dull years' ability to extinguish,
stand like right faith on their undoubted islands,
or move as gods move, powerful, of clear color,
meaning themselves and the virtue of their being,
bright coachwork tuned, wheels flashing, hackles raised
to hold strongly their inheritance of distinction,
blood relics of an ampler dispensation,
pure peacock blue, brass glory, furious stone.

—WILLIAM DICKEY

THOMAS IN THE FIELDS

The cow walks away from him,
gives up her immensity, letting it die
                    before his very eyes,
and acquires a new smallness that fits her nature perfectly.
And in Aquinas,
what dies also are those details of udder and eyelid
to be changed, while he watches, into legs and head.
                    But he cannot leave it yet.
To be forced to forsake the end
without foreseeing the beginning, it's impossible!
And this middle, which he wishes to keep, and yet
is not yet complete
but will be added to every minute, until it, too,
is destroyed.

For he shall not be able to imagine it when he leaves here:
the rain that falls on the rock
                    (that hurts the foot)
                              seems harder than

the rain that falls on the grass.
Recognition of rock and of cow, too,
                    are mixed together, but to predict
what shall move away and what shall stay fixed,
he must separate them again: the cow to move out
mixed with the rain
                    and the rock to remain.

And the face of this field is acre needed
to furnish a place over which its time may pass
and against which its ticking may be heard.
It's the fixity that speaks!
Its rocks resting like Roman numerals, without which
hands could move in space forever, unreadable.

Thomas, seeing himself in the little pond as wavy,
guesses his original is straight but not seen
                    standing nearby.
In the water or on it, he sees the water, too,
and separates out the wonder from the wet
                    and names its cause.

                                        —LOIS MOYLES

THE THOUGHT-FOX

I imagine this midnight moment's
        forest:
Something else is alive
Beside the clock's loneliness
And this blank page where my fingers
        move.

Through the window I see no star;
Something more near,
Though deeper within darkness,
Is entering the loneliness:

Cold, delicately as the dark snow,
A fox's nose touches twig, leaf;
Two eyes serve a movement that now,
And again now, and now, and now,

Sets neat prints into the snow
Between trees, and warily a lame
Shadow lags, by stump and in hollow,
Of a body that is bold to come

Across clearings, an eye,
A widening deepening greenness,
Brilliantly, concentratedly,
Coming about its own business

Till, with a sudden sharp hot stink of
        fox,
It enters the dark hole of the head.
The window is starless still; the clock
        ticks;
The page is printed.

                                        —TED HUGHES

A THOUGHT IN TIME

Elinor Wylie fell in love with Shelley,
   Amy Lowell fell in love with Keats,
Byron posthumously does so well he
   Can hardly count his valentine receipts.
Die early, poets, if you would adorn
The boudoirs of young ladies yet unborn.

Nobody ever fell in love with Shakespeare,
   Nobody ever fell in love with Blake.
A poet must be Lancelot of the Lake's peer
   Yet perish young and fair for Beauty's sake.
I'm far too old myself, at fifty-three;
No one will ever fall in love with me.

(But hold! a saving thought, a ray of hope!
Edith Sitwell fell in love with Pope.)
                   —ROBERT HILLYER

THE THOUSAND AND SECOND NIGHT

I. RIGOR VITAE

Istanbul. 21 March. I woke today
With an absurd complaint. The whole right half
Of my face refuses to move. I have to laugh
Watching the rest of it reel about in dismay

Under the double burden while its twin
Sags on, though sentient, stupefied.
I'm here alone. Not quite—through fog outside
Loom wingèd letters: PAN AMERICAN.

Twenty-five hundred years this city has stood between
The passive Orient and our frantic West.
I see no reason to be depressed;
There are too many other things I haven't seen,

Like Hagia Sophia. Tea drunk, shaved and dressed . . .
Dahin! Dahin!

The house of Heavenly Wisdom first became
A mosque, is now a flame-
less void. The apse,
Militantly dislocated,
Still wears those dark-green epaulets

On which (to the pilgrim who forgets
His Arabic) a wild script of gold whips
Has scribbled glowering, dated
Slogans: "God is my grief!" perhaps,
Or "Byzantine,
Go home!"
Above you, the great dome,
Bald of mosaic, senile, floated
In a gilt wash. Its old profusion's
Hypnotic shimmer, back and forth between
That of the abacus, that of the nebula,
Had been picked up from the floor,
The last of numberless handfuls,
By the last 18th century visitor.
You did not want to think of yourself for once,
But you had held your head erect
Too many years within such transcendental skulls
As this one not to feel the usual, if no
Longer flattering, kinship. You'd let go
Learning and faith as well, you too had wrecked
Your precious sensibility. What else did you expect?

Outdoors. Uprooted, turban-crested stones
Lie side by side. It's uglier than I feared.
The building, desperate for youth, has smeared
All over its original fine bones

Acres of ochre plaster. A diagram
Indicates how deep in the mudpack
The real façade is. I want *my* face back.
A pharmacist advises

. . . THE HAMAM

After the hour of damp heat
One is addressed in gibberish, shown
Into a marble cell and thrown
On marble, there to be scrubbed clean,
Is wrapped in towels and a sheet
And led upstairs to this lean tomb
Made all of panes (red, amber, green)
With a glass star hung in the gloom,

Here sits effaced by gemlike moods,
Tastes neither coffee nor loukoum,
And to the attendant who intrudes

(Or archeologist or thief)
Gravely uptilts one's mask of platinum
Still dripping, in a sign of life.

And now what? Back, I guess, to the modern town.
Midway across the bridge, an infantile
Memory promises to uncramp my style.
I stop in deepening light to jot it down:

On the crest of her wrist, by the black watered silk of the
watchband, his grandmother had a wen, a large mauve
bubble up from which bristled three or four white hairs.
How often he had lain in her lap and been lulled to a
rhythm easily the whole world's then—the yellowish
sparkle of a ring marking its outer limit, while in the fore-
ground, silhouetted like the mosque of Suleiman the Mag-
nificent, mass and minarets felt by someone fallen asleep
on the deck of his moored caïque, that principal land-
mark's rise and fall distinguished, from any other, her
beloved hand.

Cold. A wind rising. An entire city
Dissolved by rhetoric. And out there, past
The mirror of the Bosporus, what black coast
Reflecting us into immobility?

On this side, crowds, a magic-lantern beam—
Belgians on bicycles, housewives with red hair,
Masts, cries of crows blown high in the rose-blue air,
Ataturk's tailcoat . . . It is like a dream,

The "death-in-life and life-in-death" of Yeats'
Byzantium; and, if so, by the same token,
Alone in the sleepwalking scene, my flesh has woken
And sailed for the fixed shore beyond the straits.

II. The Cure

The doctor recommended cortisone,
Diathermy, vitamins, and rest.
It worked. These months in Athens, no one's guessed
My little drama; I appear my own

Master again. However, once you've cracked
That so-called mirror of the soul,

It is not readily, if at all, made whole.
("Between the motion and the act

Falls the Shadow"—T. S. Eliot.)
Part of me has remained cold and withdrawn.
The day I went up to the Parthenon
Its humane splendor made me think, *So what?*

One May noon in the Royal Park, among
The flora of l'Agneau Mystique—
Cypress, mimosa, laurel, palm—a Greek
Came up to name them for me in his tongue.

I thanked him; he thanked me, sat down. Peacocks
Trailed by, hard gray feet mashing overripe
But bitter oranges. I knew the type:
Superb, male, raucous, unclean, Orthodox

Ikon of appetite feathered to the eyes
With the electric blue of days that will
Not come again. My friend with time to kill
Asked me the price of cars in Paradise.

By which he meant my country, for in his
The stranger is a god in masquerade.
Failing to act that part, I am afraid
I was not human either—ah, who is?

He is, or was; had brothers and a wife;
Chauffeured a truck; last Friday broke his neck
Against a tree. We have no way to check
These headlong emigrations out of life.

Try, I suppose, we must, as even Valéry said,
And said more grandly than I ever shall—
Turning shut lids to the August sun, and all
Such neon figments (amber, green, and red)

Of incommunicable energy
As in my blindness wake, and at a blink
Vanish, and were the clearest hint, I think,
Of what I have been, am, and care to be.

III. CARNIVALS

Three good friends in as many months have complained,
"You were nice, James, before your trip. Or so
I thought. But you have changed. I know, I know,
People do change. Well, I'm surprised, I'm pained."

Before they disappeared into the night
Of what they said, I'd make a stab at mouthing
Promises that meant precisely nothing
And never saved my face. For they were right.

These weren't young friends, what's more. Youth would
        explain
Part of it. I have kept somewhere a page
Written at sixteen to myself at twice that age,
Whom I accuse of having become the vain,

Flippant, unfeeling monster I now am—
To hear them talk—and exhorting me to recall
Starlight on an evening in late fall,
1943, and the walk with M.,

To die in whose presence seemed the highest good.
I met M. and his new wife last New Year's.
We rued the cold war's tainted atmospheres
From a corner table. It was understood

Our war was over. We had made our peace
With—everything. The heads of animals
Gazed in forbearance from the velvet walls.
Great drifts of damask cleaned our lips of grease.

Then L.—her "Let's be friends" and her clear look
Returned in disbelief. I had a herd
Of *friends*. I wanted love, if love's the word
On the foxed spine of the long-mislaid book.

A thousand and one nights! They were grotesque.
Stripping the blubber from my catch, I lit
The oil-soaked wick, then could not see by it.
Mornings, a black film lay upon the desk

. . . Where just a week ago I thought to delve
For images of those years in a Plain Cover.
Some light verse happened as I looked them over:

POSTCARDS FROM HAMBURG, CIRCA 1912

The ocelot's yawn, a sepia-dim
Shamelessness from nun's coif to spike heels,
She strokes his handlebar who kneels

To do for her what a dwarf does for him.
The properties are grim,

Are, you might want to say, unsexed
By use. A divan covered with a rug,
A flat Methusalem of Krug
Appear from tableau to tableau. The next
Shows him with muscle flexed

In resurrection from his underwear,
Gaining an underworld to harrow.
He steers her ankles like—like a wheelbarrow.
The dwarf has slipped out for a breath of air,
Leaving the monstrous pair.

Who are they? What does their charade convey?
Maker and Muse? Demon and Doll?
"All manners are symbolic"—Hofmannsthal.
Here's the dwarf back with cronies . . . oh I *say!*
Forget about it. They,

In time, in pain, unlearned their tricks.
Only the shrouded focusser of the lens
May still be chasing specimens
From his lone bathysphere deep in the Styx.
St. Pauli's clock struck six;

Sighing, "The death of sin is wages,"
He paid his models, bade them dress and go,
Earthlings once more, incognito
Down swarming boulevards, the contagious-
ly easy, final stages,

Dodged even by the faithful, one of whom
(Morose Great-Uncle Alastair)
Brought back these effigies and would shortly bear
Their doctrine unconfessed, we may assume,
Into his brazen tomb.

We found the postcards after her divorce,
I and Aunt Alix. She turned red with shame,
Then white, then thoughtful. "Ah, they're all the same—
Men, I mean." A pause. "Not you, of course."

And then: "We'll burn them. Light the fire." I must
Meanwhile have tucked a few into my shirt.

I spent the night rekindling with expert
Fingers—but that phase needn't be discussed. . . .

"The soul, which in infancy could not be told from the
body, came with age to resemble *a body one no longer
had,* whose transports went far beyond what passes, now,
for sensation. All irony aside, the libertine *was* 'in search
of his soul;' nightly he labored to regain those firelit lodg-
ings. . . . Likewise, upon the Earth's mature body we
inflict a wealth of gross experience—drugs, drills, bombard-
ments—with what effect? A stale *frisson,* a waste of re-
sources all too analogous to our own. Natural calamities
(tumor and apoplexy no less than flood and volcano) may
at last be hailed as positive reassurances, perverse if you
like, of life in the old girl yet."

—Germaine Nahman

". . . faced with such constant bickering, Cynthia would
have to pinch herself to recall how warmly and deeply
those two did, in fact, love one another."
—A. H. Clarendon, "Psyche's Sisters"

Love. Warmth. Fist of sunlight at last
Pounding emphatic on the gulf. High wails
From your white ship: The heart prevails!
Affirm it! Simple decency rides the blast!—
Phrases that, quick to smell blood, lurk like sharks
Within a style's transparent lights and darks.

The lips part. The plume trembles. You're afloat
Upon the breathing, all-reflecting deep.
The past recedes and twinkles, falls asleep.
Fear is unworthy, say the stars by rote;
What destinations have been yours till now
Unworthy, says the leaping prow.

O skimmer of deep blue
Volumes fraught with rhyme and reason,
Once the phosphorescent meshes loosen
And the objects of your quest slip through,
Almost you can overlook a risen
Brow, a thin, black dawn on the horizon.

Except that in this virgin hemisphere
One city calls you—towers, drums, conches, bells
Tolling each year's more sumptuous farewells

To flesh. Among the dancers on the pier
Glides one figure in a suit of bones,
Whose savage grace alerts the chaperones.

He picks you out from thousands. He intends
Perhaps no mischief. Yet the dog-brown eyes
In the chalk face that stiffens as it dries
Pierce you with the eyes of those three friends.
The mask begins to melt upon your face.
A hush has fallen in the market place,

And now the long adventure

. . . Let that wait.
I'm tired, it's late at night.
Tomorrow, if it is given me to conquer
An old distrust of imaginary scenes,
Scenes not lived through yet, the few final lines
Will lie on the page and the whole ride at anchor.

I'm home, of course. It's winter. Real
Snow fills the road. On the unmade
Brass bed lies my adored Scheherazade,
Eight-ninths asleep, tail twitching to the steel

Band of the steam heat's dissonant calypso.
The wind has died. Where would I be
If not here? There's so little left to see!
Lost friends, my long ago

Voyages, I bless you for sore
Limbs and mouth kissed, face bronzed and lined,
An earth held up, a text not wholly undermined
By fluent passages of metaphor.

IV.

Now if the class will turn back to this, er,
Poem's opening section, I shall take
What little time is left today to make
Some brief points. So. The rough pentameter

Quatrains give way, you will observe, to three
Interpolations, prose as well as verse.
Does it come through how each in turn refers
To mind, body, and soul (or memory)?

It does? Good. No, I cannot say offhand
Why this should be. I find it vaguely satis—

Yes please? The poet quotes too much. Hm. That is
One way to put it. Mightn't he have planned

For his own modest effort to be seen
Against the yardstick of the "truly great"
(In Spender's phrase)? Fearing to overstate,
He lets *them* do it—lets their words, I mean,

Enhance his— Yes, what now? Ah. How and when
Did he "affirm"? Why, constantly. And how else
But in the form. Form's what affirms. That's well
Said, if I do—[*Bells ring.*] Go, gentlemen.

V.

And when the long adventure reached its end,
I saw the Sultan in a glass, grown old,
While she, his fair wife still, her tales all told,
Smiled at him fondly. "O my dearest friend,"

Said she, "and lord and master from the first,
Release me now. Your servant would refresh
Her soul in that cold fountain which the flesh
Knows not. Grant this, for I am faint with thirst."

And he: "But it is I who am your slave.
Free me, I pray, to go in search of joys
Unembroidered by your high, soft voice,
Along that stony path the senses pave."

They wept, then tenderly embraced, and went
Their ways. She and her fictions soon were one.
He slept through moonset, woke in blinding sun,
Too late to question what the tale had meant.

—JAMES MERRILL

THREE GREEN WINDOWS

Half awake in my Sunday nap,
I see three green windows
in three different lights—
one west, one south, one east.
I have forgotten that old friends are
     dying.
I have forgotten that I grow middle-
     aged.
At each window such rustlings!

The trees persist, yeasty and sensuous,
as thick as saints.
I see three wet gargoyles covered with
     birds.
Their skins shine in the sun like leather

I'm on my bed as light as a sponge.
Soon it will be summer.
She is my mother.

She will tell me a story and keep me
    asleep
against her plump and fruity skin.
I see leaves—
leaves that are washed and innocent,
leaves that never knew a cellar,
born in their own green blood
like the hands of mermaids.

I do not think of the rusty wagon on
    the walk.
I pay no attention to the red squirrels
the leap like machines beside the
    house.
I do not remember the real trunks of
    the trees
that stand beneath the windows

as bulky as artichokes.
I turn like a giant,
secretly watching, secretly knowing,
secretly naming each elegant sea.

I have misplaced the Van Allen belt,
the sewers and the drainage,
the urban renewal and the suburban
    centers.
I have forgotten the names of the lit-
    erary critics.
I know what I know.
I am the child I was,
living the life that was mine.
I am young and half asleep.
It is a time of water, a time of trees.

                      —ANNE SEXTON

THE THRIFTY ELEPHANT

In my rudyard-kipling-simple years I read
Of mid-jungle where the elephants go to die.
Old bulls know, and, rather than death by herd,
Wait alone, and add to the fabulous ivory.

My uncle had a wiry chicken yard, and told
Me in my chicken-childish time that one,
Bleeding or sick, would be pecked and killed
By hens terrified silly of the different hen.

Into the big ears of children wisdom goes,
Out of the mouths of grown-up men it comes—
The hencoop-jungle myths turned into laws
For one another, and given longer names.

Man's in his second childhood now. He'll take
As gospel anything barnyard-rudyard speaks.
What flurry of feathers and hysterical squawk
All around me, and deadly incessant beaks,

The sick healing the sick with the sickness.
The last of hens will peck at itself, cluck,

Flop in the gravel, and die of uniqueness.
The thrifty elephant saves even his neck.

A health of dying. An anguish without rant.
Who's seen an old bull elephant lately, old
Red-eyed, foot-dragging, single-minded blunt-
Tusk, lugging his bones to the bones piled?

—JOHN HOLMES

TIME PASSES

Once I was a boy and I sat in a meadow with flowers in it;
  I sat for hours in it,
Enjoying the sun and the brave birds in the heaven,
  When I was approximately seven.

Later I was a long and learned stripling,
  Reading Kipling,
And nothing I heard but the factory hooters blowing,
  While time was remorselessly flowing.

The hours they fly me by with astonishing celerity;
  I have not the temerity
To remember the hours that have gone by, unnumbered,
  While often I slumbered.

I have sat in the pubs and seen the rings of froth on the glasses,
  And thought to myself, Time passes.
They brought me a pint of mild, but I asked for bitter,
  Thinking it fitter.

For life, as it lumbers by, unwieldily hastening,
  Is a matter most chastening;
Too seldom have we laughed in the morning with the larks on the mountain,
  Or leaned on the fountain

Watching the waves and the neat-clad ducks in a huddle,
  Or, kneeling beside a puddle,
Beheld the leather-legged insects jumping in jubilation
  Or pausing in sudden indignation;

It is a strange error that keeps us such things ignoring,
  In studies insensately snoring,
While the hands of the rude, insatiate clock
  Go tick, tock, tick, tock.

—R. P. LISTER

TO AN ARTIST, TO TAKE HEART

Slipping in blood, by his own hand, through pride,
Hamlet, Othello, Coriolanus fall.
Upon his bed, however, Shakespeare died,
Having endured them all.

—LOUISE BOGAN

TO ARIAKE KAMBARA

(1876–1952)

(WHO PUBLISHED FOUR BOOKS OF POEMS, THE LAST AT THE AGE OF 32, AND FOR
THE NEXT FORTY-FOUR YEARS OCCUPIED HIMSELF IN REVISING THEM)

Ariake, Japanese friend, I regard
Your ghost, your fine print, with
    amazement.
How could you do it, brother?
The sheer courage, the humor,
The intensity of your pen!

And what, after all, is the poem
But the constant threading of a needle?
You have used the same thread
Over and over, sewing clouds, sewing

A damaged heart, perfecting the things
You knew well.

          It is quite possible,
Dear Ariake, we are old at thirty,
And would be wiser to close our doors
After one last swift year of the senses.
Seen once, felt once, the world should
Persist as the image of a breast,
As the hand's perfection, as flame—
As love is recalled to us, once
Having been so blinded.

—NORMAN ROSTEN

TO A SALESGIRL, WEARY OF ARTIFICIAL HOLIDAY TREES

The clock shows nearly five.
Girls are not evergreen,
And most gray women are gone,
Exhausted, from the store.
You, who have seen them go,
Wonder whether they live
Or scatter and grow old.
Past floor, past mezzanine,
You mourn the illusory green
Of every tree you sold.
Young, you endure the change.
Green daylight ripples past.

You lounge in daylight, strange,
And the seasons die at last.
I love you, proud up there
On the balcony, soft of face,
Your curious mouth, your hair,
Your hands' immobile grace.
The soft noon of your face
Glances over my stare.
The casual sun falls down.
You do not care for the sky.
The weathered wives go by.
Whether they live or die,

You rise, you brush your knees,
And one last year of leaves
Flutters beyond your sleeves.
The first moon of the year

Outside is lost in trees.
You draw your muffler on,
The last girl of the year,
And one more year's far gone.

—JAMES WRIGHT

TO CARRY THE CHILD

To carry the child into adult life
Is good? I say it is not.
To carry the child into adult life
Is to be handicapped.

The child in adult life is defenseless
And, if he is grown up, knows it,
And the grownup looks at the childish
    part
And despises it.

The child, too, despises the clever
    grownup,
The man-of-the-world, the frozen,
For the child has the tears alive on his
    cheeks,
And the man has none of them,

As the child has colors, and the man
    sees no
Colors or anything,

Being easy only in things of the mind;
The child is easy in feeling—

Easy in feeling, easily excessive,
And, in excess, powerful,
For instance, if you do not speak to
    the child,
He will make trouble.

You would say the man had the upper
    hand
Of the child (if a child survive),
But I say the child has fingers of
    strength
To strangle the man alive.

Oh, it is not happy, it is never happy,
To carry the child into adulthood.
Let children lie down before full
    growth
And die in their infanthood,
And be guilty of no one's blood.

—STEVIE SMITH

TO HIS CHI MISTRESS

I

It's spring; the City, wrapped
in unaccustomed grace,
goes scarlet where they slapped
a garden in her face,
right in the sunken place
she found her rotten set

of ivory towers gapped
when the last Fair pulled out.

We look out at the Park
from Iris and Rose's Bar.
Watching the dancers bare
their little almost-all,

letting the whiskey work,
lusty and lachrymal,
has primed us—it's not far;
it might as well befall.

II

The elms along the drag,
so mop and yet so fag—
these pigeon-breasted hags
with their fans above their bags
along the runway of
iris and roses, love—
sad sex in long black gloves,
have sent away their doves.

Bare ruined chorus-lines,
for what they are, they stand.
The winos give them a hand.
Where amber light refines
an audience of flowers
to wax, it may be hours
before some bluecoat shines
his hunger onto ours.

III

Well, we didn't come to Walt's,
we didn't come to Dan's,
we come to Rose and Iris's,
Iris's, man.
Their shapes may be piracies,
their colors may be false,
but you know you've seen a dance
when they shake that schmaltz.

IV

Winds of morning sift
down through the heavy wires

and branches, like a gift
of tongues. Our voices drift
lazily on a wash
of motors, brushes, tires—
street-cleaning—the soft flush
of a cat house after hours.

We'll make it—worlds of time;
even the winos seem
posted to see us home.
And shoring up the elms,
shoring up the el,
lighting up an L & M
butt, these fragments will
sustain us pretty well.

V

Behind us, the gates lock.
The iron rolling stock
of the bankrupt CTA
jolts, and gets under way.
This is the only Rock:
give with your knees, and sway
close to the very wreck
they had here yesterday.

Back of the yellowed laces
flaunting past our faces,
dispirited embraces
weary a spavined bed.
With some who will curse bread,
with some who will free races,
the Sooty Slut replaces
her defeated dead.

—GEORGE STARBUCK

TO JANET

Goodbye
Until such time as bobolinks do dine
On courses of blue pasture,
And water-horses whine
Across the grainfields' brine,

Canter and posture.

Then loosed will be forever
The goose-quill feathers
Of the friendly willow

Tickling the ticklish grass,
And the pond's brown glass,
And the blown flower-pillow.

Heaped in a hum of sun,
The bees will gun
It to new honey—odd fellows
Lunching on rose-carpets

In cool encampments,
Wild in a blur of yellows.

And we? We will play
A game of catch with poems,
As we did, one May,
In those other homes,
When grief was on holiday.

—RALPH POMEROY

TO KATE, SKATING BETTER THAN HER DATE

Wait, Kate! You skate at such a rate
You leave behind your skating mate.
Your splendid speed won't you abate?
He's lagging far behind you, Kate.
He brought you on this skating date
His shy affection thus to state,
But you on skating concentrate
And leave him with a woeful weight
Pressed on his heart. Oh, what a
     state
A man gets into, how irate
He's bound to be with life and fate
If, when he tries to promulgate
His love, the loved one turns to skate
Far, far ahead to demonstrate
Superior speed and skill. Oh, hate

Is sure to come of love, dear Kate,
If you so treat your skating mate.
Turn again, Kate, or simply wait
Until he comes, then him berate
(Coyly) for catching up so late.
For, Kate, he *knows* your skating's
     great,
He's *seen* your splendid figure eight,
He is not here to contemplate
Your supersonic skating rate—
That is not why he made the date.
He's anxious to expatiate
On how he wants you for his mate.
And don't you want to hear him,
     Kate?

—DAVID DAICHES

TOM FOOL AT JAMAICA

Look at Jonah embarking from Joppa, deterred by
the whale; hard going for a statesman whom nothing could detain,
     although one who would not rather die than repent.
     Be infallible at your peril, for your system will fail,
and select as a model the schoolboy in Spain
     who, at the age of six, portrayed a mule and jockey
          who had pulled up for a snail.

" 'There is submerged magnificence,' as Victor Hugo
said." *Sentir avec Ardeur;* that's it; magnetized by feeling.
     Tom Fool "makes an effort and makes it oftener
          than the rest"—out on April 1st, a day of some significance
in the ambiguous sense—the smiling

Master Atkinson's choice, with that mark of the champion, the extra
  spurt when needed. Yes, yes. Chance

is "a regrettable impurity;" like Tom Fool's
left white hind foot—an unconformity; although judging by
  results, a kind of cottontail to give him confidence.
      Up in the cupola comparing speeds, Signor Capossela keeps his head.
"It's tough," he said, "but I get 'em, and why shouldn't I?
  I'm relaxed, I'm confident, and I don't bet." Sensational. He does not
    bet on his animated

valentines—his pink-and-black striped, sashed, or dotted silks.
Tom Fool is "a handy horse," with a chiselled foot. You've the beat
  of a dancer to a measure—the harmonious rush
of a porpoise at the prow where the racers all win easily—
    like centaurs' legs in tune, as when kettledrums compete;
  nose rigid and suède nostrils spread, a light left hand on the rein, till
    well—this is a rhapsody.

Of course, speaking of champions, there was Fats Waller
with the feather touch, giraffe eyes, and that hand alighting in
  "Ain't Misbehavin'." Ozzie Smith and Eubie Blake
    ennoble the atmosphere; you recall the Lipizzan school;
the time Ted Atkinson charged by on Tiger Skin—
  no pursuers in sight—cat-loping along. And you may have seen a monkey
    on a greyhound. "But Tom Fool . . ."

                                              —MARIANNE MOORE

TO MY BROTHER

KILLED: CHAUMONT WOOD, OCTOBER, 1918

O you so long dead,
You masked and obscure,
I can tell you, all things endure:
The wine and the bread;

The marble quarried for the arch;
The iron become steel;
The spoke broken from the wheel;
The sweat of the long march;

The haystacks cut through like loaves,
And the hundred flowers from the seed.

All things indeed,
Though struck by the hooves

Of disaster, of time due,
Of fell loss and gain,
All things remain,
I can tell you, this is true,

Though burned down to stone,
Though lost from the eye,
I can tell you, and not lie—
Save of peace alone.

                                              —LOUISE BOGAN

TO MY FELLOW-MARINERS, MARCH, '53

That odyssey? We three left Amherst late
Saturday morning, got to the Met late
In Isolde's narrative (and also late
In Traubel's Bing career), had dinner late,
And kept on going, going. Two A.M.,
Hagerstown, gas stop. Then, till eight, one snoozed
In back two hours, one drove, one death-sat
And kept awake to keep the driver awake.
Morn, Roanoke, speedometer cable broke.
Afternoon, Blue Ridge Parkway, sinuous sloth
Through sloshing fogs, our car sea-serpenting
Past Scenic Vistas, Scenic Overlooks,
Overlooked, unseen, passed at no miles per hour.
Late afternoon finally down and out
To solid rain, red rutted soil, green grass,
And spring vacation on a mountain near
The house where, two years earlier, we three
Discovered west North Carolina and
World's Edge, whereoff winds menacingly swept
Into a funnel valley down beneath
The quaking house that safely held us, where,
One leading, all three reading parts aloud,
Two of us first read and loved "The Dead."
We found the house had burned. It still survives
Only in ashes, ashes of our lives.

—THOMAS WHITBREAD

TO MY FRIENDS

Holding its huge life open to the sky,
snow fringes the scaly cones on this hilltop;
I can see it cupped and pierced by the rich needles.
This far from the city, it takes weeks to melt,
and nothing passes on the road that reaches me here
at the back of my house, planted above the river
of headlights. Do you remember that sad movie
where Bogart loses everything and begins
a new life after his plane takes off through the fog,
where he becomes an underground fighter, and poor?
It haunts me tonight because I am not myself
and, wedged between ceilings and floors,
I can feel the tight path of my hands over the keys
get wider. Because those bare, lasting pines

are understandable, because I am here
and not here, because of the silent breath
rising from different lungs,
because these hands are yours, I remember
something no one will ever tell us. Our life,
more like those trees than we are, is the snow;
the stars know it, the dirt road says it again
each time I stop for a minute and listen to the strange
human words of the hedges scraping together, and go in
where the moonlit weedy spaces continue.

—STEPHEN BERG

TO MYSELF, AFTER FORTY YEARS

Terence, if I could return
My drear tideway to your bright burn,
If we could meet where I once
        strayed,
The betrayer and the betrayed,
If we could win back in time's de-
fiance,
Would you be afraid of me, ten-year-
old Terence?

No, you would not fear.
You would love, trust,
Cherish, admire
This tedious dust.

For, oh, we were all brimming once
With the sun-sparkled dew.
One heart could have loved this hulk—
The ignorant heart of you.

—T. H. WHITE

TO THE LAST WEDDING GUEST

"Eat my cake, eat," cried the young,
Newly won, enraptured, smiling bride.
"It is here to eat
As your eyes glide
Between the folds of my white veils"—
Silks, satins flowing
Among quick limbs in whiteness held,
Sweetness in white.

"Eat of my cake
Brought by the caterer in white,
The cake in a glass bell, flowered,
Snow-crystalled, starred
In silver light
On cloth and plate."

"Eat of my secret,"
She might well have said,
For it is there
Among the secrets of the wedding night—
All that is white-limbed, young, and fair
Shall know its sign;
As the white rose flushes with a drop of blood,
So is this secret spread.

The gifts bestowed in white
Turn as a prism turns
Within the waiting eye
Of faces greeting
The downward-stepping, ever-descending stair:
See how the groom gleams
In a golden spiral
As the bride's gaze, turning inward to his sight,
Shall find her body held within his arms,
There to be caught and held as all joys are,
Wordless in the brief silence after prayer,
Held in the blue-reflected summer sky
Before the coming of a darkening wind,
Before the waking of increasing winter storms.

As the cake is cut
For guests to eat,
See in that light
The bridal wreath lean over earth,
The tremulous, shaken
Bough, leaf, and flower
Piercing the hour
Of bell-chiming fragrance within a summer night,
Echo and leaf and bough
To reappear
Through seventy winters of deepening ice and snow.

The lacquered car, the floating bridal suite
Wait at the embrace
Of the wedding-night hotel;
Even the belated guest who has missed the bride
Stands in the hall,
Sees in its light the reflection of her face,
Hears lips that say, "Eat of my cake;
It has been my life; it is why you came;
It is everything that I have left behind,
Even to the last fragment on a covered plate;
It is yours to take."

—HORACE GREGORY

TOURISTS

Cramped like sardines on the Queens, and sedated,
The sittings all first, the roommates mismated,

Three nuns at the table, the waiter a barber,
Then dumped with their luggage at some frumpish harbor,

Veering through rapids in a vapid *rapido*
To view the new moon from a ruin on the Lido,

Or a sundown in London from a rundown Mercedes,
Then high-borne to Glyndebourne for Orféo in Hades,

Embarrassed in Paris in Harris tweed, dying to
Get to the next museum piece that they're flying to,

Finding, in Frankfurt, that one indigestible
Comestible makes them too ill for the festival,

Footloose in Lucerne, or taking a pub in in
Glasgow or Belfast, or maudlin in Dublin, in-

sensitive, garrulous, querulous, audible,
Drunk in the Dolomites, tuning a portable,

Homesick in Stockholm, or dressed to toboggan
At the wrong time of year in too dear Copenhagen,

Generally being too genial or hostile—
Too grand at the Grand, too old at the Hostel—

Humdrum conundrums, what's to become of them?
Most will come home, but there will be some of them

Subsiding like Lawrence in Florence, or crazily
Ending up tending shop up in Fiesole.

—HOWARD MOSS

TO WAKEN A SMALL PERSON

You sleep at the top of streets
Up which workmen each morning
Go wheeling their bicycles

You must be dreaming these tears
Wake up please open yourself
Like a little umbrella

Your eyes are like the windows
Of some high attic the one
The very one you sleep in

Hurry the sidewalks need you
The awnings not one is up
And the patient bicycles

They're shut it's raining the rain
Falls on the streets of the town
As it falls falls through your sleep

Halted at intersections
They need you they are confused
The colors of traffic lights

Are bleeding bleeding wake up
The puddles of parking lots
Cannot contain such rainbows
—DONALD JUSTICE

TRAVELLER'S GUIDE TO ANTARCTICA

Here we can observe the superior mi-
        rages,
distortions, dreams, repeated rainbows,
false sunsets and deceptive sunrises,
ships overturned yet serenely riding
the high abyss as if to some anchor
hung between Polaris and the Goat.

The wisest visitors have been misled,
followed the wrong image, found
        themselves
trapped in a hall of carnival mirrors
where the glassy air's inverted lens
reflects an insupportable landscape,
makes grotesque the simplest being,
and holds the golden oasis forever
one inch away from the scheming
        hand.

Even at the gate where the first floes
        drift
like dead messengers from some wrin-
        kled tomb,
the fata morgana magnifies and lifts

the wind's debris into steeples,
hoists cathedrals against the sky,
erects such cities a pilgrim imagines
Atlantis risen with all its green tow-
        ers,
garlands, and women, and stalks
        through the crystal
into the darkness behind every mir-
        ror.

Early explorers followed a mirage
twisting with angels and horny fires,
recorded phantoms as veritable flesh,
pursued illusion beyond the round
        edge
of experience and the orbiting world,
believed the wind was turned by a
        fist
so faceted, jewelled, encumbered with
        light,
mortals must be blinded by a glimpse
of one radiant knuckle. Other voy-
        agers,
the cold still creaking in their hair,
reported an unimaginable forehead,

eyeless, Neanderthal, sloping into
        heaven
from the loud jaws of a gaping sea.

Some, circumnavigating this circle,
flee what they find, leave it for saints
or merchants to conquer, retire to rest
        homes,
diseases, games. Others go through
to that crevasse where the last mirror
        hangs
and the staring self dangles in its worn
        harness

over a void, while breath crashes
like a blue, falling window.

Only the mirage lives through these
        winters,
and the boneless wind sniffing at
        tracks
fixed like a wreath, where the most re-
        cent traveller
has pitched his blind, enduring tent.
                            —Adrien Stoutenburg

TRAVELLING BACKWARD

First, the scene endlessly diminishes.
Trees and houses flinch away, struck off from
the rapping and tapping rails. A steady
swaying lulls one's disbelief when the clouds
keep up, walking the sky like mountains, or
when the mountains themselves heave into view,
distance shaping them against the swarthy
window. They shimmer bluely or sit like
fists on the land. Still, plains and prairies are
the hardest part of this journey, until,
with the telegraph wires, they are eaten
by twilight, or trail into it, a broad
sea, or a glimmering snail's wake of green
and gold. This rushing into the night, this
racketing away from it, hangs the face
a perfect moment on the glass, a pensive
snapshot, out of focus as the evening
lights spark on; stations and farms like fireflies
swim through the head; one enters an orchard's
depths and sees the globes of light, a dazzling
fruit in the nodding dark. Sleep—but under
the eyelid the train curves away, scything
a night grown shoulder high. One wakes to see
toward the zenith the new moon skirmishing
upward and on the far ridges a quick-
silver trace. Then, the night unrolls tunnels
of itself; there is nothing to watch but
trembling hulks of luggage, newspapers read
blank, a thin face wearying the window.
There is the night, of course, carbon

copying itself, returning only
its black looks. Where are the stations, the sad
shunting yards under toffee lamps? Where are
the towns scrubbed with soot, the abandoned streets
inky with rain? In the morning, buildings
will lurch from behind, sheds and factories
jumble along the roadway. In the first
light, the auto junkyards will mimic hills
thick with suburbs. But the city harvests
its stones. The sun will fly to perch among
aerials. Standing in the station, facing
forward at last, will be a figure caught
in the crowd that is caught and whirled away
in the crowd that has pressed beyond the gates.

—GENE BARO

THE TRAVELLING OUT

I wonder, since we are both travelling out,
If we may go together? Thank you.

You may be sure you will be alone
And private as though I were no one.
God knows, I do not wish to increase your burden.
Naturally, these airports, blinding cities,
And foundry lights confuse you, make you
More solitary than the sight of one lost lamp
Across a bare land promising life there—
Someone over that field alone and perhaps
Waiting for you. That used to be the way.

Feel perfectly free to choose how
You will be alone, since we are going together.
Of course, I never move, I merely hold you
In my mind like a prayer. You are my way
Of praying, and I have chosen you out of hordes
Of travellers to speak to silently, on my own.
I will be with you, with your baffled anger
Among fuming cities, with your grief
At having lost dark fields and lamplight.
It is my way of moving, or praying—

Oh, not to give you someone like me,
That's all over, impossible, I go nowhere;
And besides, nothing is given, absolutely
Nothing and no one, only white sermons among

The white of a billion bulbs. No,
Sitting here behind my shutters at twilight,
I am stretching over the blazing lanes,
The dazed crowds jostled and razed
By light, only to join your mind and guide you
Gently, leading you, not, alas, to my own lamp
Across the fields of the world, or to a cozy last
Prayer of lamplight blessing the fields of the air,
But out into hordes of stars that move away
As we move, and for which your travelling
Prepares you to go out a little more boldly,
All alone as I am alone.

—LUCILE ADLER

TREES

I asked the holly, "What is your life if . . . ?"
There was a rustle of answer—dark,
Dark, dark, a gleamer recoiling tensely backward
Into a closing nest of shattered weapons
Like a squid into clouds of protection.
I plucked a spiny leaf. Nothing protested.
Glints twitched, watched me.

I asked the birch, "How can you . . . ?"
My breath crept up into a world of shudderings.
Was she veiled?
Herself her own fountain,
She pretended to be absent from it, or to be becoming air,
Filtering herself from her fingertips
Till her bole paled, like a reflection on water,
And I felt the touch of my own ghostliness;
Like a ghost I tried to fade.

I moved on, looking neither way,
Trying to hear
The outcry that must go with all
Those upflung maidenly gestures, that arrested humpback rout
Stumbling in blackberries and bracken—

Silence.

Trees, it is your own strangeness, in the dank wood,
Makes me so horrifying
I dare not hear my own footfall.

—TED HUGHES

THE TRUEST POETRY IS THE MOST FEIGNING
OR, ARS POETICA FOR HARD TIMES

By all means sing of love, but if you do,
Please make a rare old proper hullabaloo:
When ladies ask *How much do you love me?*
The Christian answer is *Così-così*,
But poets are not celibate divines;
Had Dante said so, who would read his lines?
Be subtle, various, ornamental, clever,
And do not listen to those critics ever
Whose crude provincial gullets crave in books
Plain cooking made still plainer by plain cooks,
As though the Muse preferred her half-wit sons;
Great poets have a weakness for bad puns.

Suppose your Beatrice be, as usual, late,
And you would tell us how it feels to wait,
You're free to think, what may be even true,
You're so in love that one hour seems like two,
But write—*As I sat listening for her call,*
Each second longer darker seemed than all
(Something like this, but more elaborate still)
Those raining centuries it took to fill
That quarry whence Endymion's love was torn:
From such ingenious fibs are poems born.
Then, should she leave you for some other guy,
Or ruin you with debts, or go and die,
No metaphor, remember, can express
A real historical unhappiness:
Your tears have value if they make us gay;
O happy grief! is all sad verse can say.

The living girl's your business (My! what sorts
Have been an inspiration to men's thoughts):
Yours may be old enough to be your mother,
Or have one leg that's shorter than the other,
Or play lacrosse, or do the Modern Dance—
To you that's destiny, to us it's chance;
We cannot love your love till she take on,
Through you, the wonders of a paragon.
Sing her triumphant passage to our land,
The sun her footstool, the moon in her right hand,
And seven planets blazing in her hair,
Queen of the Night and Empress of the Air;
Tell how her fleet by nine king swans is led,
Wild geese cut magic letters overhead,

And hippocampi follow in her wake
With Amphisbaena, gentle for her sake;
Sing her descent on the exultant shore
To bless the vines and put an end to war.

If, halfway through such praises of your dear,
Riot and shooting fill the streets with fear,
And overnight, as in some terror dream,
Poets are suspect with the new regime,
Stay at your desk and hold your panic in;
What you are writing can still save your skin.
Resex the pronouns, add a few details,
And, lo, a panegyric ode which hails
(How is the Censor, bless his heart, to know?)
The new potbellied Generalissimo.
Some epithets, of course, like *lily-breasted*—
That's easy—must be changed to *lion-chested*,
A title *Goddess of Wrynecks and Wrens*
To *Great Reticulator of the Fens*,
But in an hour your poem qualifies
For a state pension or his annual prize,
And you will die in bed (which he will not;
That silly sausage will be hanged or shot).
Though honest Iagos, true to form, will write
Shame! in the margin, *Toady! Hypocrite!*,
True hearts, clear heads will hear the note of glory
And put inverted commas round the story,
Thinking *Old slyboots! We shall never know
Her name or nature. Well, it's better so.*

For, given man, by birth, by education,
Imago Dei who forgot his station,
The self-made maker who himself unmakes,
The only creature ever made who fakes,
With no more nature in his loving smile
Than in his theories of a natural style,
What but tall tales, the luck of verbal playing,
Can trick his lying nature into saying
That love, or truth in any serious sense,
Like orthodoxy, is a reticence.

                                    —W. H. AUDEN

A TRYST IN BROBDINGNAG

In this terrible agitation of mind I could not forbear thinking of Lilliput.

My Glumdalclitch, come here and sit with me,
And let us speak of that which may not be.
I, on your dewy palm, will tailorwise
Arrange myself the nearer to your eyes,
Those pearly bulbs enclosed with beds of fern,
Whose tears I dare not drink, so hot they burn.
And I shall scan each dimpled vale and crease
Of that sublime topography, your face,
Hoping to read some tenderness therein
You save for me and keep from grosser men.

My sweet colossus, though with me and you
There's coquetry, here's what we may not do:
I cannot charge the grotto of your ear
With whispers; all persuasions I must roar.
And if you answer in too eager voice,
My head will splinter at the darling noise.
I cannot with a daring hand caress
The damask skin beneath your heaving dress,
Lest, unawares, you blow me like a fly
Upon the gale of one ecstatic sigh.

If still to Gulliver you would be kind,
Keep passion delicate and zest refined.
Take but the daintiest of token sips,
Lest, taking even this, you bruise his lips.
Nor think your love was always such a creature,
Too fragile for the mightier ways of nature.
Once, huge against the tower-needled air,
I turned an empire into miniature,
Held Ministers in my palm and, laughing, blew
Confusion on the fleets of Blefuscu!

      —ADRIENNE CECILE RICH

TULIPS

The tulips are too excitable; it is winter here.
Look how white everything is, how quiet, how snowed-in!
I am learning peacefulness, lying by myself quietly
As the light lies on these white walls, this bed, these hands.
I am nobody; I have nothing to do with explosions.

I have given my name and my day-clothes up to the nurses
And my history to the anesthetist and my body to surgeons.

They have propped my head between the pillow and the sheet-cuff
Like an eye between two white lids that will not shut.
Stupid pupil, it has to take everything in.
The nurses pass and pass; they are no trouble;
They pass the way gulls pass inland in their white caps,
Doing things with their hands, one just the same as another,
So it is impossible to tell how many there are.

My body is a pebble to them; they tend it as water
Tends to the pebbles it must run over, smoothing them gently.
They bring me numbness in their bright needles, they bring me sleep.
Now I have lost myself, I am sick of baggage—
My patent-leather overnight case like a black pillbox,
My husband and child smiling out of the family photo.
Their smiles catch onto my skin, little smiling hooks.

I have let things slip, a thirty-year-old cargo boat
Stubbornly hanging onto my name and address.
They have swabbed me clear of my loving associations,
Scared and bare on the green plastic-pillowed trolley,
I watched my tea set, my bureaus of linen, my books
Sink out of sight, and the water went over my head.
I am a nun now; I have never been so pure.

I didn't want any flowers, I only wanted
To lie with my hands turned up and be utterly empty.
How free it is, you have no idea how free!
The peacefulness is so big it dazes you,
And it asks nothing—a name tag, a few trinkets.
It is what the dead close on, finally; I imagine them
Shutting their mouths on it, like a Communion tablet.

The tulips are too red in the first place; they hurt me.
Even through the gift paper I could hear them breathe
Lightly, through their white swaddlings, like an awful baby.
Their redness talks to my wound, it corresponds.
They are subtle: they seem to float, though they weigh me down,
Upsetting me with their sudden tongues and their color,
A dozen red lead sinkers round my neck.

Nobody watched me before; now I am watched.
The tulips turn to me and the window behind me,
Where, once a day, the light slowly widens and slowly thins,
And I see myself, flat, ridiculous, a cut-paper shadow
Between the eye of the sun and the eyes of the tulips,

And I have no face. I have wanted to efface myself.
The vivid tulips eat my oxygen.

Before they came, the air was calm enough,
Coming and going, breath by breath, without any fuss.
Then the tulips filled it up like a loud noise.
Now the air snags and eddies round them the way a river
Snags and eddies round a sunken rust-red engine.
They concentrate my attention that was happy
Playing and resting without committing itself.

The walls, also, seem to be warming themselves.
The tulips should be behind bars, like dangerous animals;
They are opening like the mouth of some great African cat,
And I am aware of my heart: it opens and closes
Its bowl of red blooms out of sheer love of me.
The water I taste is warm and salt, like the sea,
And comes from a country far away as health.

—SYLVIA PLATH

TULIPS AND ADDRESSES

The Museum of Modern Art on West Fifty-third Street
Is interested only in the flower not the bulb.
After the Dutch tulips finished blooming in the garden last year,
They pulled them up and threw them away—that place has no heart.
Some fortunately were rescued and came into my possession.

I kept them all winter in a paper bag from the A. & P.—
At first where I was living then, on the West Side,
Until the next-door tribe of Murphys drove me out with rock 'n' roll,
Then at Thompson Street in the Village where, overhead,
A girl and her lover tromped around all night on each other.

And that wasn't the end of it. I shlepped those bulbs around
For two months from place to place, looking for a home,
All that winter, moving, oy—although this was nothing new to me,
Coming as I do from a wandering race,
And life with its twelve plagues making me even more Jewish.

Now I am living on Abingdon Square—not the Ritz exactly, but a place,
And I have planted the tulips in my windowbox.
Please God make them come up, so that everyone who passes by
Will know I'm there, at least long enough to catch my breath,
When they see the bright, red, beautiful flowers in my window.

—EDWARD FIELD

TUNE FOR A LONESOME FIFE

Merry the green, the green hill shall be merry.
Hungry, the owlet shall seek out the mouse,
And Jack his Joan, but they shall never marry.

And snows shall fly, the big flakes fat and furry.
Lonely, the traveller shall seek out the house,
And Jack his Joan, but they shall never marry.

Weary the soldiers go, and come back weary—
Up a green hill, and down the withered hill—
And Jack from Joan, and they shall never marry.

—Donald Justice

TWINK DRIVES BACK, IN A BAD MOOD, FROM
A PARTY IN MASSACHUSETTS

I slump in the bucket seat.
You coax a barely believable roar
From the pint-sized motor. My head is sore.
This chilled air runs me through.
Only a witch could drive these hills this late.
Or a revved-up blonde like you.

Your small white fists and wry
Foresight straighten out every curve
The road can throw. You've got more nerve
Than skill, I think, although
The way you pull out hard and shift to high
It's difficult to know.

In shades of whiskied sleep,
I watch your features turn to soft
Iron, your hair to fog. You drift
Away from me. Away.
My feelings poke around in some old slag heap
Until the smell of hay

Filters in to lead
Me back. You've changed. The early light
Builds faint lustres in your hair and the slight

Smile you offer me is filled
With the kind of sun I need.
Shadows dissolve. The sun outside
Has turned lead-colored lakes into pure gold.

—GEORGE AMABILE

TWO

There was that fall the fall of desire
And in the senseless night a sense of wires
Cut, plugs pulled from the darkened switchboard—
And then the silent cold like sudden swords,
And then the snow silencing depths and heights.
Together we walked alone the white-twigged night
Followed by our desperate, disparate tracks,
Which even to us were lost when we looked back.

—WINFIELD TOWNLEY SCOTT

TWO CAMPERS IN CLOUD COUNTRY

ROCK LAKE, CANADA

In this country there is neither measure nor balance
To redress the dominance of rocks and woods,
The passage, say, of these man-shaming clouds.

No gesture of yours or mine could catch their attention,
No word make them carry water or fire the kindling
Like local trolls in the spell of a superior being.

Well, one wearies of the Public Gardens; one wants a vacation
Where trees and clouds and animals pay no notice—
Away from the labelled elms, the tame tea roses.

It took three days' driving north to find a cloud
The polite skies over Boston couldn't possibly accommodate.
Here on the last frontier of the big, brash spirit

The horizons are too far off to be chummy as uncles;
The colors assert themselves with a sort of vengeance.
Each day concludes in a huge splurge of vermilions

And night arrives in one gigantic step.
It is comfortable, for a change, to mean so little.
These rocks offer no purchase to herbage or people;

They are conceiving a dynasty of perfect cold.
In a month we'll wonder what plates and forks are for.
I lean to you, numb as a fossil. Tell me I'm here.

The Pilgrims and Indians might never have happened.
Planets pulse in the lake like bright amoebas;
The pines blot our voices up in their lightest sighs.

Around our tent the old simplicities sough
Sleepily as Lethe, trying to get in.
We'll wake blank-brained as water in the dawn.

—SYLVIA PLATH

U

THE UMBRELLA

It is a kind of shadow,
Not shaded but in mind,
That settles down the pole
And runs its transit wide
Over the rocks and sand
To make them private land.

Towels, the picnic hamper,
The canvas leaned upon
Are furnishings for summer,

Small porches of the sun.
In the shore's summer care
Our needs grow shallower.

Space gives formality.
The spokes expand through air.
The swimmers from the sea
Shake the wet from their hair,
Toward its blue circle come,
And suddenly are home.

—ANN STANFORD

UNALTERABLES

Mistakes are dredged up again,
not mine but before mine began,
of figures I never knew,
and those I did know gone,
except that, since what had
been done to them is carried on
through me, they lurk about,
unwelcome presences unseen
but evident like something

moving beneath dead leaves.
I thought I was done with them.
What need had I of faceless crea-
    tures,
agitation in their hair,

uttering unalterables
in languages I refused to hear?
Other sayings filled my ears,
other directions shook me—signs
that led to gates and guards who kept

the doom promoters out. I realized,
when I returned, that doom or past
were unthinkable behind those gates,
but learned that they come back,
figures of my old mistakes,
who, in spite of where I have been,
what I have found and seen,
want me to dance with them
their old, disordered dance.

—ARTHUR GREGOR

[751]

THE UNBLINDING

(FOR MY STUDENT, UPON THE ANNIVERSARY OF THE OPERATION
THAT RESTORED HIS SIGHT)

When I think of my fear
of moving through my dreamed
life into the tough, unknown, real
images that burn my senses and mind
more fiercely than human
events that stick

in the craw of biographies,
when I shy away
from the incandescent moments that
     fall
into my hands unsought, un-
deservedly given or lent
to me, visions,

so to say, that can—and do
on occasion—sweep me off into their
     own
orbits, shattering my known self
into ill-fitting puzzle
pieces, and grinding
each fragment to smithereens,

leaving me numb to objects,
to the feel of a thing, to all identities
clogged, hopelessly blocked, I find
I try again, taught
by my student, Robert Beegle,
who was here today

leaning sail on a puff
of wind five thousand miles out from
     Cal-
ifornia to say hello   here
I am   fully bearded   one hundred
     years
younger than the eighteen-year-old
death-of-me you met

two years ago   Mr. Lieberman.
And it is true.

He has grown younger more quickly
than anyone old I have
known. When I first
fastened my twenty-twenty two eyes
     on two

totally blinded at age
four in a traffic
mishap, two stillborn egg yolks
immobile in vacant
sockets, I saw a being sunk
within and drilling

deeper, as the innermost rings
in the trunk of a withered
sycamore, dying inward.
In the front row
next to the door (at his feet, the see-
     ing-
eye German shepherd, head

on his paws, licking
and snuffling toward bell-time,
often mistaking a distant horn or whis-
     tle
for the hour-gong), the handicapped
listener shivered his lips
to decipher braille

that flew past shortwave
of fingertips,
the lips racing to overtake the fingers,
casting about within for broken
tape-ends of emotions
straggling from reels of earliest

childhood. I felt my eyes
clamber into hollowness, opening
in him like a bottomless
pit. Once exposed, it overflowed his
     face

and spread around the class,
like a skin

tightening. We could not breathe.
He shut his eyes.
Words failed—our voices
drawn into declivities of his nose
and mouth—
the room becoming an abyss

over which we teetered
dizzily. I looked and looked. Where
I had seen clearly
before grew blind spots
now. I saw too near,
too far, sight

locked. I had
to try not to see him,
to lay violent hands upon the light,
to make it bend
around his chair and twist
over his clenched,

sight-slaying face.
My skull bones grew
in weight,

converging on the delicate
flesh of eyeballs. Then, for days,
I walked shakily,

one foot stretched
before me, hunting anchorage (safe
lodging) like the tip of a white
cane, tapping. . . . One morning, I
        glanced
about, dazedly—he stood
beside me, no one

I have ever seen before
outside his dog's
life, extending the pink absence slip
for my O.K. I saw (powerless
to believe) he saw my face,
smiling his first

look of me, the words
loosening from his tongue
as sparrows from a shaken clothes-
        line.
One flick of a surgeon's knife
struck long-idle retinas
into perfect sight.

—LAURENCE LIEBERMAN

UNDER THE WINDOW: OURO PRETO

(FOR LILLI CORREIA DE ARAÚJO)

The conversations are simple: about food,
or, "When my mother combs my hair it hurts."
"Women." "*Women!*" Women in red dresses

and plastic sandals, carrying their almost
invisible babies—muffled to the eyes
in all the heat—unwrap them, lower them,

and give them drinks of water lovingly
from dirty hands, here where there used to be
a fountain, here where all the world still stops.

The water used to run out of the mouths
of three green soapstone faces. (One face laughed
and one face cried; the middle one just looked.

Patched up with plaster, they're in the museum.)
It runs now from a single iron pipe,
a strong and ropy stream. "Cold." "Cold as ice,"

all have agreed for several centuries.
Donkeys agree, and dogs, and the neat little
bottle-green swallows dare to dip and taste.

Here comes that old man with the stick and sack,
meandering again. He stops and fumbles.
He finally gets out his enamelled mug.

Here comes some laundry tied up in a sheet,
all on its own, three feet above the ground.
Oh, no—a small black boy is underneath.

Six donkeys come behind their "godmother"
—the one who wears a fringe of orange wool
with woolly balls above her eyes, and bells.

They veer toward the water as a matter
of course, until the drover's mare trots up,
her whiplash-blinded eye on the off side.

A big new truck, Mercedes-Benz, arrives
to overawe them all. The body's painted
with throbbing rosebuds and the bumper says

HERE I AM FOR WHOM YOU HAVE BEEN WAITING.
The driver and assistant driver wash
their faces, necks, and chests. They wash their feet,

their shoes, and put them back together again.
Meanwhile, another, older truck grinds up
in a blue cloud of burning oil. It has

a syphilitic nose. Nevertheless,
its gallant driver tells the passersby
NOT MUCH MONEY BUT IT IS AMUSING.

"She's been in labor now two days." "Transistors
cost much too much." "For lunch we took advantage
of the poor duck the dog decapitated."

How talkative are the seven ages of man,
how soiled and thirsty!
                 Oil has seeped into
the margins of the ditch of standing water

and flashes or looks upwards brokenly,
like bits of mirror—no, more blue than that:
like tatters of the *Morpho* butterfly.
               —Elizabeth Bishop

AN UNFINISHED HISTORY

We have loved each other in this time twenty years
And with such love as few men have in them even for
One or for the marriage month or the hearing of

Three nights' carts in the street but it will leave them:
We have been lovers the twentieth year now:
Our bed has been made in many houses and evenings:

The apple tree moves at the window in this house:
There were palms rattled the night through in one:
In one there were red tiles and the sea's hours:

We have made our bed in the changes of many months—and the
Light of the day is still overlong in the windows
Till night shall bring us the lamp and one another:

Those that have seen her have no thought what she is:
Her face is clear in the sun as a palmful of water:
Only by night and in love are the dark winds on it. . . .

    I wrote this poem that day when I thought
    Since we have loved we two so long together
    Shall we have done together—all love gone?

    Or how then will it change with us when the breath
    Is no more able for such joy and the blood is
    Thin in the throat and the time not come—
        the time not come to us for death. . . .
               —Archibald MacLeish

THE UNICORN AND THE LADY

(IMPROVISATION ON THE THEME OF THE TAPESTRIES AT THE MUSÉE DE CLUNY)

Christ! These are her angels!
Frighten us not with seven heads on a stalk!
They guard her sleep in a parable of flowers,
The plumed porcupine
And he of the great horn in the middle of his head,
Who paws with laughing modesty the rose standard,
Or, in a pavilion, wears armorial bearings,
Goat-bearded, his breast broader than day,
Breasting the pennant more white than she
Whose skin sheds light as she bathes white in a pool
Where the flutist blows

By a field of blue upon the rose, rose-red,
And flowers, her simple flowers, degrees of rose,
Where, on the dark blue, he of the red-stocking'd legs proffers
The small heart split at the top that the fingers hold;

And flowers, her simple flowers that print the day,
Her Michael-fighting pennant, rose and gray,
And major beasts and lesser beasts, those winged stags
Exultant as deities, whiteness, her rose,
Over which a pennant emblazoned with three moons,
More formal and more salient than the sea,
Sails out to greet the swollen-bellied ship
That flaunts with answering streamers in the bay.

By this, Primavera, in the morning of the year,
And by daisies, the arbiters of justice and goodness,
Is she appointed to her destiny,
And the red heart burns like a jewel, or a fire;
We are held by the heart as he hands it,
Not to be played with or eaten by his lady.
The flowers revolve with the beasts around it,
While from the knee joints of armor stare faces,
And the lion is clasped by his fetlock,
His spanieled feet and arched tongue flared
Like the backward foil of the lily—

While the unicorn without pasture or fence
Beholds his face stitched in the glass,
Who, white as day, lights up dark speech,
Maintaining the lion's valor. Though he looks
In a glass at his image, he need not;
He suffers, he, singular, needing none other,

Though in the herbage you may see him again,
Reduced in stature.
Need not look in the glass
(Being of the glass, lord of the maze and enigma,
Where each thing to its degree
Is beheld in its entity,
Such as Reynard, such as the dove, and the wolf
Fallen headfirst into a trap, and the porcupine
Plumed, it would seem, or his quills supine),
Who is quintessential,
Toute Belle,
Pursuivant to all that was hunted for,
Who glides inwoven in flowers, himself the pulled thread,
Infinite relations in his train
In the *perceforest* of shadow.
Who gives a scripture to smiling eyes,
To the small mouth that sweetly psalms,
Being all signs and figures of love.

Blood and the whiteness of day,
She of the sole desire, dogs, deer,
Stupendous bear embracing,
The hare that leaps against a stretched rope
In the season of venery,
Each with his part in the thirsty quest,
Subjects all of the single objective;
Truly they, like the planets, whirl in an earth order!
Truly here, in a fresh candor,
The bather bathes in the parapets of lilies,
And earth bears everywhere the upstanding flower,
Fruit wood with yellow quince clearly,
Clearly in a fresh candor conceived.
The vair-rose trumpet that her Michael blows,
He jams the dragon to its knees,
And the small heart sparkles amidst the leaves
Of the one thousand flowers, and flares.

—Jean Garrigue

THE UNINVITED

There is never an open door to the wild beasts' home,
And stepstones leading to their secret wood
Are watched by snails with horns and ants with wings.
You are tripped by little things: a spider's thread
That rings a hundred lead bells down their trails;
A twig will break and some old inching worm

Will turn his head, concerned because of all
The needless noise you make. Your anxious shadow,
Like a nosing hound, will race with deer mice
To their grassy nests, and, headlong on the path you found,
It will invade the deeper shade where partridge rest
And send them shuddering across the disturbed hill.
You will be seen from mounds where hooded woodchucks cull
Their gravel acre; where, from lonely cells, they come
To work their sparse monk gardens for their fare;
Where all the braided briars and underbrush
Guard the low runs used by the fox and hare.
"There! There is the open door!" you'll say,
Pointing to where a wide space runs,
An open corridor through pillared trees.
Then you will know that squirrels claim the place
By sudden show and chatter, and, as though
To mock your thought, they'll stir a noisy whirlwind
In the leaves. Always you'll walk announced
To hedgehog hovels. Your pace will be regarded
From each wildcat lair. Your hour of coming
Will be drummed through all the forest rooms.
Your show of strength will be considered
From each hilltop tower. Your journey will be timed
By beasts beyond your sight, and, should you follow,
Though moving cautiously, the wary host, like startled deer
In flight, will all go bounding back, until at last
They move into the trackless cover of the night.

—William D. Mundell

THE UNKNOWN CITIZEN

TO

SOCIAL SECURITY ACCOUNT NUMBER 067-01-9818
THIS MARBLE MONUMENT IS ERECTED BY THE STATE

He was found by the Bureau of Statistics to be
One against whom there was no official complaint,
And all the reports on his conduct agree
That, in the modern sense of an old-fashioned word, he was a saint,
For in everything he did he served the Greater Community.
Except for the war, till the day he retired
He worked in one factory and never got fired,
But satisfied his employers, Fudge Motors, Inc.,
Yet was neither a scab nor odd in his views,
For his Union reports that he paid his dues
(Our report on his Union says it was sound),

And our Social Psychology workers found
He was popular with his mates and liked a drink.
The Press are convinced that he bought a paper every day,
And that his reactions to advertisements were normal in every way.
Policies taken out in his name prove that he was fully insured,
And a certificate shows that he was once in hospital but left it cured.
Both *Producer's Research* and *High Grade Living* declare
He was fully sensible to the advantages of the Installment Plan,
And had everything necessary to the Modern Man—
A victrola, a radio, a car, and a frigidaire.
Our investigators into Public Opinion are content
That he held the proper opinions for the time of year;
When there was peace, he was for peace; when there was war, he went.
He was married and added five children to the population,
Which, our eugenist says, was the right number for a parent of his generation,
And our teachers report that he never interfered with their education.
Was he free? Was he happy? The question is absurd;
Had anything been wrong, we should certainly have heard.

—W. H. AUDEN

V

VAIN ADVICE AT THE YEAR'S END

The shadows blown from trees
Lie easy, vague of form.
Twilight revises these
To flowing twig and bough.
The only waves that flow
Against a maple's arm
Are dripping dew and rain
Thrown to the air and down.

Even the shadow cast
By a man on autumn ground
Lies clear till he goes past;
Then the dark legs run forth
And race the sun to death,
Dark fingers close around
Apple and cat-tail shade;
The dark lips breathe, and fade.

Today I came, balked, at last,
Where all the shade lay still
And the air froze up, past
The barn, the barren hill;
The riven trees, the stars,
And everything I knew
Would huddle up and die
Under the winter fires.

Only, behind the waste,
I saw one boulder fill
The sky from east to west,
It hung so close and full.
The flesh the body wears
For wind to hack and hew
Is broken under the sky,
Racked on its own desires.

Dear love, be stony breast,
Be rock, and crack the flail
Of heaven, woo the dust
For room to sink and fall;
Only the pure stone bears
The nagging rain, the dew
That nibbles life away.
Only the dead endures.

And I know you will not hear
Whatever I plead to you;
You will gather the residue
Of loveliness out of the air
And flaunt it under the blast
Of wind on stones and fires
As long as the light words last,
And darkening winter stars.

—JAMES WRIGHT

VAINLY

Vainly
the epistles burn
in the night of nights
on the pyre of flight
for love winds itself out of its thornbush

[761]

flogged in martyrdom
and with its tongue of flames
is beginning to kiss the invisible sky
when vigil casts darknesses on the wall
and the air
trembling with premonition
prays with the noose of the hunter
blowing in with the wind:

Wait
till the letters have come home
from the blazing desert
and been eaten by sacred mouths
Wait
till the ghostly geology of love
is torn open
and its millennia
aglow and shining with blessed pointing of fingers
have rediscovered love's word of creation:
there on the paper
that dying sings:

It was
at the beginning
                    It was
                        My beloved
                                It was—
                            —NELLY SACHS
            (*Translated from the German by Michael Roloff*)

A VALEDICTORY TO STANDARD OIL OF INDIANA

In the darkness east of Chicago, the sky burns over the plumbers' nightmares
Red and blue, and my hometown lies there loaded with gasoline.
Registers ring like gas pumps, pumps like pinballs, pinballs like broken alarm
    clocks,
And it's time for morning, but nothing's going to work.
From cat-cracker to candle shop, from greaseworks along the pipeline,
Over storage tanks like kings on a checkerboard ready to jump the county,
The word goes out: With refined regrets,
We suggest you sleep all day in your houses shaped like lunch buckets
And don't show up at the automated gates.
Something else will tap the gauges without yawning
And check the valves at the feet of the cooling-towers without complaining.

Standard Oil is canning my high-school classmates
And the ones who fell out of junior high or slipped in the grades.

What should they do, gassed up in their Tempests and Comets, raring to go
Somewhere, with their wives scowling in front and kids stuffed in the back,
Past drive-ins jammed like car lots, trying to find the beaches
But blocked by freights for hours, stopped dead in their tracks
Where the rails, as thick as thieves along the lake front,
Lower their crossing gates to shut the frontier? What can they think about
As they stare at the sides of boxcars for a sign,
And Lake Michigan drains slowly into Lake Huron,
The mills level the Dunes, and the eels go sailing through the trout,
And mosquitoes inherit the evening while toads no bigger than horseflies
Hop crazily after them over the lawns and sidewalks, and the rainbows fall
Flat in the oil they came from? There are two towns now,
One dark, one going to be dark, divided by cyclone fences;
One pampered and cared for like pillboxes and cathedrals,
The other vanishing overnight in the dumps and swamps like a struck sideshow.
As the Laureate of the Class of '44—which doesn't know it has one—
I offer this poem, not from hustings or barricades
Or the rickety stage where George Rogers Clark stood glued to the wall,
But from another way out, like Barnum's "This Way to the Egress,"
Which moved the suckers when they'd seen enough. Get out of town.

—DAVID WAGONER

THE VALLEY

Once I was jealous of lovers. Now I am
jealous of things that outlast us—the road
between Route 28 and our house, the bridge
over the river, a valley of second-growth trees.
Under the birches,
vines, the color of wolves, survive a winter
ten below, while the unpicked apples turn black
and the picked fruit is red in the basket.
I am not sure that the hand of God
and the hand of man ever touch, even by chance.

—STANLEY MOSS

VARIATIONS FOR TWO PIANOS

There is no music now in all Arkansas.
Higgins is gone, taking both his pianos.

Movers dismantled the instruments; away
Sped the vans; the first detour untuned the strings.

There is no music now in all Arkansas.

Up Main Street, past the cold shopfronts of Conway,
The brash, self-important brick of the college,

Higgins is gone, taking both his pianos.

Warm evenings, the windows open, he would play
Something of Mozart's for his pupils, the birds.

There is no music now in all Arkansas.

How shall the mockingbird mend her trill, the jay
His eccentric attack, lacking a teacher?

Higgins is gone, taking both his pianos.
There is no music now in all Arkansas.

                                        —DONALD JUSTICE

VARITALK

When Very was a celibate,
It meant "in high degree;"
Its emphasis was moderate
But quite enough for me.
It never thumped its little chest
Or raised its voice unduly,
And always looked its level best
When flanked by Yours and Truly.

But in an age of shrill extremes
One adverb's ineffective,
So now the Verys trot in teams
To gain the same objective,

And no one can be mortified,
Or sad, or shy, or merry,
Unless the mood is fortified
By Very comma Very.

I hope this twosome will suffice
For purposes emphatic.
But mated words may breed like mice
Sequestered in an attic
And thus produce a corollary
—the intensified intensive—
A triple threat that makes me Very,
Very, *Very* apprehensive.

                                        —WEARE HOLBROOK

V. B. NIMBLE, V. B. QUICK

SCIENCE, PURE AND APPLIED, by V. B. Wigglesworth, F.R.S.,
Quick Professor of Biology in the University of Cambridge.
—*A talk listed in the B.B.C. Radio Times of February 2, 1955.*

V. B. Wigglesworth wakes at noon,
Washes, shaves, and very soon
Is at the lab; he reads his mail,
Swings a tadpole by the tail,
Undoes his coat, removes his hat,

Dips a spider in a vat
Of alkaline, phones the press,
Tells them he is F.R.S.,
Subdivides six protocells,
Kills a rat by ringing bells,

Writes a treatise, edits two
Symposia on "Will Man Do?,"
Gives a lecture, audits three,
Has the Sperm Club in for tea,
Pensions off an aging spore,

Cracks a test tube, takes some pure
Science and applies it, finds
His hat, adjusts it, pulls the blinds,
Instructs the jellyfish to spawn,
And, by one o'clock, is gone.

—JOHN UPDIKE

A VIEW

A silence of our watching, waiting springs
A net between ourselves and what's out there.
A powdery landscape rises and floats free,
As if Paul Klee had willed it to appear.
Some elements of church and wharf appear
To twinkle in it. Irresistibly

The lights drift up and tug the sky with toy
Machinery, my room turns as the stars regroup
Themselves. My room, desk, lamp extend, float past
Through window frames and windowpanes. My shelves
Are empty. And still my feet hold fast.

—BEVERLY QUINT

THE VIEW

Under his view the wind
Blows shadows back and forth
Across the lawn beneath
The blowing leaves. And now
Into his silent room
Noon whistles, or a cry
Comes from the road where to
Is fro. Inquietude!
He walks from room to room,
From empty room to room
With the white curtains blowing.
He goes down to the kitchen
And takes from the cold tap
A glass of water pale
As glass. In the long hall
He stares into the mirror
And wills that it should break
Under his image, but

It does not break. Once more
He comes to stand before
The window and the screen,
Framing, dividing coarse
And fine, his view of flowers,
Of fields beyond the flowers,
The hanging hill, the blue
Distance that voids his vision,
Though not as tears might do.
He has no tears, but knows
No one will come, there's no
Comfort, not the least
Saving discrepancy
In a view where every last thing
Is rimed with its own shadow
Exactly, and every fall
    Is once for all.

—HOWARD NEMEROV

VIEW FROM THE GORGE

(CUERNAVACA)

Doré knew this overhang—
            he cut
his cortège for the damned, on those levels,
to carom on the magnets and springs, in the banging
of gongs and the lights of his pinball *commedia.*
In his black-and-white
world, the ascents and descents of the Gorge,
the roots like a fistful of entrails, the hachure
of pitchblende and acid that abuts
on that ordered logistics for sinners
lead to a fall or a forge.
                The odds
are already well known: electric displays for the winners,
and the damned circling down toward the hammers.

What holds me today
is the purgatorial moment, seen small on the opposite side,
on the tilt of the slope where the gardeners
move in the marzipan whiteness squared off
like a waffle. Quicklime
has dazzled the glass of the greenhouses there,
sugared the ovens of Hänsel and Gretel
where a work of redemption begins
in the alternate lines of the cuttings—bougainvillaea
and palm, on the ledges—blazing giddily in buckets and tins.

Some loving solicitude has motioned the mannikins there
to hover like dragonflies and settle like seeds in the air—
to balance all day
on a long foot, for purchase, with the shorter
doubled into their shoulders—penitential, half mantis,
half angel, on a causeway of manna and boulders.

And the moment suffices.
What lies plane at the top,
like a sponge-rubber glaze for an architect's table
or a primitive frieze for a ceiling,
what we guess from below, in the clot of the mangroves:
the generations of Rahab, the fires and the basalt of Dante, the bones
of the beast of Apocalypse, Quetzalcoatl
and Grendel in the offal and trash of our sins—
these were an earlier fable.

Inbetween, go the gardeners, with the grace of the hummingbird's
balance, who bend to the slope
in the quicklime and flowers, planting knowns
and unknowns, because sun shines exceedingly there
and the spirit is willing.

—BEN BELITT

VIOLENT STORM

Those who have chosen to pass the night
Entertaining friends
And intimate ideas in the bright,
Commodious rooms of dreams
Will not feel the slightest tremor
Or be wakened by what seems
Only a quirk in the dry run
Of conventional weather. For them,
The long night sweeping over these trees
And houses will have been no more than one
In a series whose end
Only the nervous or morbid consider.
But for us, the wide-awake, who tend
To believe the worst is always waiting
Around the next corner or hiding in the dry,
Unsteady branch of a sick tree, debating
Whether or not to fell the passerby,
It has a sinister air.
How we wish we were sunning ourselves
In a world of familiar views
And fixed conditions, confined
By what we know, and able to refuse
Entry to the unaccounted for. For now,
Deeper and darker than ever, the night unveils
Its dubious plans, and the rain
Beats down in gales
Against the roof. We sit behind
Closed windows, bolted doors,
Unsure and ill at ease
While the loose, untidy wind,
Making an almost human sound, pours
Through the open chambers of the trees.
We cannot take ourselves or what belongs
To us for granted. No longer the exclusive,
Last resorts in which we could unwind,
Lounging in easy chairs,

Recalling the various wrongs
We had been done or spared, our rooms
Seem suddenly mixed up in our affairs.
We do not feel protected
By the walls, nor can we hide
Before the duplicating presence
Of their mirrors, pretending we are the ones who stare
From the other side, collected
In the glassy air.
A cold we never knew invades our bones.
We shake as though the storm were going to hurl us down
Against the flat stones
Of our lives. All other nights
Seem pale compared to this, and the brilliant rise
Of morning after morning seems unthinkable.
Already now the lights
That shared our wakefulness are dimming
And the dark brushes against our eyes.

—MARK STRAND

VISION

I

Two hummingbirds as evanescent as
Themselves
Startled me at my study window
As sea bells

Heard slipping through the fog,
Or yells
Of children down the block.

Phenomena,
Prolegomena,
They were

So sensitively sent
Beyond my pane,
Seen through it,

I thought the hummingbirds were an-
gels
In a world of morning
And flowers
Soon invisible.

II

Again they come
Two hummingbirds,

But my eye,
Prejudiced to angelic vision,

Saw them not as brown,
Which they were, brown machines;

They riffle and rifle the flowers,
Sense-drenched in September;

Sense-drenched I exult
In their lithe bodices—

Where will they go, above
The frail duration of a flower,

Powerful in frailty,
Come October, come November?

III

The hummingbirds of hope!
Hope they are of all
That is exquisite and beautiful,

Small, round, and smooth,
Burke's three categories for the beau-
    tiful,
Held in an instant

Before the eye which triumphs

In realization and sings
Insistence all through the being

Of the rich delight of this seeing,
Sings of purity and power,
And hope that is highest

When visions of the earth
Like intuitions before birth
Sing, sing with the hummingbirds.

—RICHARD EBERHART

VIVALDI

I

In the dark church of music,
Which never is of land or sea alone
But blooms within the air inside the mind,
Patterns in motion and in action—successions
Of processionals, moving with the majesty of certainty
To part the unparted curtains, to bring the chandeliers
Into the sarabande of courtiers who have bowed and curtsied,
Turned somersaults in circuses, climbed masts and towers,
Or dived as from a glistening tower toward a glittering lake,
Springing, daring and assured, fearless and precise—
Find, in the darkness of the dark church
That music is: This is what music is:
It has no meaning and is possessed by all meaning,
For music says,

> *Remorse, here is the scar of healing.*
> *Here is a window, curiosity!*
> *And here, O sensuality, a sofa!*
> *Behold, for ambition's purposeless energy,*
> *Mountains rising beyond mountains*
> *More tense and steep than any known before.*

Devout
The processional (having a solemn majesty,
Though childlike acrobats like flowers decorate
With flourishes and *entrechats* the passage to success,

As queens serene, crowned by poise, slowly
Are drawn in cars by dragons domesticated in the last of wars)
Is uttered again, freshly and fully, newly and uniquely,
Uniquely and newly, fully and freshly uttered again.

II

O clear soprano like the morning peal of bluebells!
O the water colors of the early morning,
Con amore and *vivace*, dancing, prancing, galloping, rollicking!

This is the surrender to the splendor of being's becoming and being!
Here are all the flowers and the images of faces as flowers, of fear and hope, long-
          ing and despair;
Here is the hour of the new blue flower
Dissolved, consumed in this being that is the being of beings.
So we are to be contained, so we are to be consumed—
The iron petal of the flute possesses morning's intuition;
The cellist is as Gautama Buddha, curved like an almond;
The first violinist is St. Francis of Assisi,
Blessing the trees, the cats, the birds, calling to them, and calling them his
          brothers and his sisters;
The full orchestra responds to the virtuoso's cadenza:
"Love is the dark secret of everything,
Love is the open secret of everything,
An open secret as useless as the blue!"

Music is not water, but it moves like water;
It is not fire, but it soars as warm as the sun.
It is not rock, it is not fountain,
But rock and fountain, clock and mountain
Abide within it, bound together
In radiance, pulsing, vibrating, and reverberating,
Dominating the domination of the weather.

III

The music declares
"Is this what you want? Is this the good news for which you have been here con-
          vened—
To be, to become, and to participate in the sweet congress of serene attention,
Silent, attentive, motionless, waiting,
Save for the heart clutching itself and the hushed breathing?"

The answered question is: Our being. Our presence. Our surrender.
Consciousness has consented, is consumed, has surrendered, to hear only the
          players playing.
Consciousness has become only and purely listening;

The vivid world has been barred,
  The press of desire shut out.
This is the dark city of the innermost wish,
  The motion beyond emotion,
  The power beyond and free of power.
This is the dark city of the hidden innermost wish,
This is the immortality of mortality, this
Is supreme consciousness, the grasped reality of reality, moving forward,
  Now and forever.

—DELMORE SCHWARTZ

THE VOICE

(ON A FRIEND IN A SANITARIUM)

All Virgil's idylls end in sunsets; pale
With death, the past of Dante opens deep;
The men of Shakespeare do not break, they fail;
And Joyce's dreamers always drift asleep.

—Her loved American laughter, male and clear,
That rang so young in London or in Rome—
A quarter-century gone, my fortieth year—
Is mute among those living ghosts at home.

And I have been among them, and I know
The spirit shrunken to its shuttered cell;
And hear no laughter—only, piercing low,
This voice that always says, "Farewell! sleep well!"

I heard it, dulled with love against your breast;
I heard it in our peace of summer suns;
I heard it where the long waves of the West
Retard the dark with loud suspended guns;

And even in the white bark of that wood,
Those mountains roped and broken by our race,
Beside those high streams where the horses stood
And watched our strange and desperate embrace.

—EDMUND WILSON

VOW

(ON DISCOVERING ONESELF LISTED ON THE BACK OF A CONCERT PROGRAM AS A
"MUSEUM FRIEND OF EARLY MUSIC")

May I forever a Muse-
um Friend of Early Music be;
And may I never cease to thrill
When three-stringed rebecs thinly
    trill,
Or fail to have a lumpish throat
When crumhorns bleat their fuzzy
    note.
I'll often audit, with *ma femme*,
Duets of psaltery and shawm;
Cross flutes of pre-Baroque design
Shall twit our eardrums as we dine,
And Slavic guslas will, forsooth,

In harsh conjunction with the crwth
(Which is a kind of Welsh vielle,
As all us Friends know very well),
Lull both of us to sleep. My love,
The keirnines (Irish harps) above
Tune diatonically, and lyres
Augment august celestial choirs
That plan to render, when we die,
"Lamento di Tristano" by
Anonymous. With holy din
Recorder angels will tune us in
When we have run our mortal race
From sopranino to contrabass.

          —JOHN UPDIKE

W

WALDEN IN JULY

The clouds were fishbone
high. Downwind.
From the pond,
water color rose toward the sun
like heat, and voices
carried from a boat.
Four feet from shore,
two executive bass
meandered by,
bored by bait
and waiting.

Armed,
a crawfish backed
from underneath a rock;
a boy amused his girl
by skipping stones
across the cove;
a lone Canada goose
dove under; some cloven crows
flapped out of a pine
like a frayed black bow
untying.

Summer had closed
in. At dusk,
the waterfront began
to clear; tiptoeing
bathers crossed the gravel
to their cars. Kibbies
cupped their noses
up for flies and
popped the watertop. A band
of Negroes with a banjo
settled in.

The smell
of warm fresh water
wafted toward the shore;
across the cove, where
Thoreau built his
hut, seventy frogs
were bulling
"chug-a-rum,
chug-a-rum."
The night was opening
like a cotyledon.

—DONALD JUNKINS

WALES VISITATION

White fog lifting & falling on mountain-brow
    Trees moving in rivers of wind
            The clouds arise
  as on a wave, gigantic eddy lifting mist
    above teeming ferns exquisitely swayed
            along a green crag

glimpsed thru mullioned glass in valley raine—

Bardic, O Self, Visitacione, tell naught
    but what seen by one man in a vale in Albion,
        of the folk, whose physical sciences end in Ecology,
           the wisdom of earthly relations,
    of mouths & eyes interknit ten centuries visible,
        orchards of mind language manifest human,
   of the satanic thistle that raises its horned symmetry
   flowering above sister grass-daisies' small pink
           bloomlets angelic as lightbulbs—

Remember 160 miles from London's symmetrical thorned tower
    & network of TV pictures flashing bearded your Self
  the Lambs on the tree-nooked hillside this day bleating
      heard in Blake's old ear, & the silent thought of Wordsworth in
          eld Stillness
   clouds passing through skeleton arches of Tintern Abbey—
     Bard Nameless as the Vast, babble to Vastness!

All the Valley quivered, one extended motion, wind
        undulating on mossy hills
  a giant wash that sank white fog delicately down red runnels
          on the mountainside
  whose leaf-branch tendrils moved asway
        in granitic undertow down—
and lifted the floating Nebulous upward, and lifted the arms of the trees
    and lifted the grasses an instant in balance
      and lifted the lambs to hold still
   and lifted the green of the hill, in one solemn wave.

A solid mass of Heaven, mist-infused, ebbs thru the vale,
    a wavelet of Immensity, lapping gigantic through Llanthony Valley,
the length of all England, valley upon valley under Heaven's ocean
           tonned with cloud-hang,
     Heaven balanced on a grassblade,
Roar of the mountain wind slow, sigh of the body,
    One Being on the mountainside stirring gently
    Exquisite scales trembling everywhere in balance, one motion
      on the cloudy sky-floor shifting through a million
          footed daisies,
     pheasant croaking up steep meadows,
one Majesty the motion that stirred wet grass quivering
   to the farthest tendril of white fog poured down
      through shivering flowers on the mountain's
          head—

No imperfection in the budded mountain,
   Valleys breathe, heaven and earth move together,
  daisies push inches of yellow air, vegetables tremble,
    green atoms shimmer in grassy mandalas,
sheep speckle the mountainside, revolving their jaws with empty eyes,
    horses dance in the warm rain,
  tree-lined canals network through live farmland,
    blueberries fringe house walls
      on hills nippled with white rock,
    meadow-bellies haired with fern—

Out, out on the hillside, into the ocean sound, delicate
        gusts of wet air,
Fall on the ground, O great Wetness, O mother, No harm on your body!
Stare close, no imperfection in the grass,
    each flower Buddha-eye, repeating the story,
       the myriad-formed soul—
Kneel before the foxglove raising green buds, mauve bells drooped
   doubled down the stem trembling antennae,
  look in the eyes of the branded lambs that stare
  breathing stockstill under dripping hawthorn—
I lay down mixing my beard with the wet hair of the mountainside,
  smelling the brown vagina-moist ground, harmless,
   tasting the violet thistle-hair, sweetness—
One being so balanced, so vast, that its softest breath
   moves every floweret in stillness on the valley floor,
   trembles lamb-hair hung gossamer rain-beaded in the grass,
  lifts trees on their roots, birds in the great draught
   hiding their strength in the rain, bearing same weight,

Groan thru breast and neck, a great Oh! to earth heart
      Calling our Presence together
   The great secret is no secret
    Senses fit the winds,
     Visible is visible,
  rain-mist curtains wave through the bearded vale,
    gray atoms wet the wind's Kaballah
Crosslegged on a rock in dusk rain,
   rubber-booted in soft grass, mind moveless,
  breath trembles in white daisies by the roadside,
    Heaven breath and my own symmetric
  Airs wavering thru antlered green fern
  drawn in my navel, same breath as breathes thru Capel-y-Ffn,
   Sounds of Aleph and Aum
      through forests of gristle,
  my skull and Lord Hereford's Knob equal,
      All Albion one.

What did I notice? Particulars! The
        vision of the great One is myriad—
    smoke curls upward from ash tray,
            house fire burned low,
The night, still wet & moody black heaven
                starless
    upward in motion with wet wind.

                                    —ALLEN GINSBERG

A WALK BY THE CHARLES

Finality broods upon the things that pass.
Persuaded by this air, the trump of doom
Might hang unsounded while the autumn gloom
Darkens the leaf and smokes the river's glass,
For nothing so susceptible to death
But on this forenoon seems to hold its breath:
The silent single oarsmen on the stream
Are always young, are rowers in a dream;
The lovers underneath the chestnut tree,
Though love is over, stand bemused to see
The season falling where no fall could be.

You oarsmen, when you row beyond the bend,
Will see the river winding to its end.
Lovers that hold the chestnut bur in hand
Will speak at last of death, will understand,
Foot-deep amid the ruinage of the year,
What smell it is that stings the gathering air.

From our evasions we are brought at last,
From all our hopes of constancy, to cast
One look of recognition at the sky,
The unimportant leaves that flutter by.
Why else upon this bank are we so still?
What lends us anchor but the mutable?

O lovers! Let the bridge of your two hands
Be broken like the mirrored bridge that bends
And shivers on the surface of the stream.

Young oarsmen, who in timeless gesture seem
Continuous, united with the tide,
Leave off your bending to the oar, and glide
Past innocence, beyond these aging bricks,
To where the Charles flows in to join the Styx.

—ADRIENNE CECILE RICH

A WALK IN WÜRZBURG

Passing a dull red college-block
Of the bygone, full-fed, Kaiser time,
When the tribal mercury welled up
Ready to burst, is to wonder if inside
That institute some intent and balding head,
Bored by the strut of the showoff turkey cock,
Used at that time, through steel-rimmed ovals, perhaps
To peer with love, pure love, of finding out;

Is to wonder who now may be tunnelling there
For an unknown vein, or perhaps with the sifting hand
Of an archeologist-in-reverse
Dredging toward a treasure the future hides.
Bombs broke the wigged Baroque only yards away,
But his thoughtful back would be that of a sage
Averted from fractured dreams, unhealable wounds,
Revenges, ruined walls, undruggable nerves.

By chance to see an inconspicuous plaque
On that otherwise unadorned wall is to learn
That here, right here, a miracle struck
Which altered us all—as Gutenberg did,
Daguerre, or Freud; is to feel what the pious feel,
Quite carried away to find they face
Unawares a place of sublime prestige,
Where a saint flared out of the chrysalid stage.

Not to have known about this! That here—
That nowhere else in the wasteful, willful,
Death-wishing world—here Röntgen focussed his ray
And the eye first saw right through the skin,
So that now without knives we see what is wrong
Or is going to be wrong. We still need a ray
To coax the delicate wings from the commonplace husk
And detect why the horde we are destroys itself.

—WILLIAM PLOMER

WALKING TO SLEEP

As a queen sits down, knowing that a chair will be there,
Or a general raises his hand and is given the field-glasses,
Step off assuredly into the blank of your mind.
Something will come to you. Although at first
You nod through nothing like a fogbound prow,
Gravel will breed in the margins of your gaze,
Perhaps with tussocks or a dusty flower,
And, humped like dolphins playing in the bow-wave,
Hills will suggest themselves. All such suggestions
Are yours to take or leave, but hear this warning:
Let them not be too velvet green, the fields
Which the deft needle of your eye appoints,
Nor the old farm past which you make your way
Too shady-lintelled, too instinct with home.
It is precisely from Potemkin barns,
With their fresh-painted hex-signs on the gables,
Their sparkling gloom within, their stanchion-rattle
And sweet breath of silage, that there comes
The trotting cat whose head is but a skull.
Try to remember this: what you project
Is what you will perceive; what you perceive
With any passion, be it love or terror,
May take on whims and powers of its own.
Therefore a numb and grudging circumspection
Will serve you best—unless you overdo it,
Watching your step too narrowly, refusing
To specify a world, shrinking your purview
To a tight vision of your inching shoes,
Which may, as soon you come to think, be crossing
An unseen gorge upon a rotten trestle.
What you must manage is to bring to mind
A landscape not worth looking at, some bleak
Champaign at dead November's end, its grass
As dry as lichen, and its lichens gray—
Such glumly simple country that a glance
Of flat indifference from time to time
Will stabilize it. Lifeless thus, and leafless,
The view should set at rest all thoughts of ambush.
Nevertheless, permit no roadside thickets
Which, as you pass, might shake with worse than wind;
Revoke all trees and other cover; blast
The upstart boulder which a flicking shape
Has stepped behind; above all, put a stop
To the known stranger up ahead, whose face
Half-turns to mark you with a creased expression.

Here let me interject that steady trudging
Can make you drowsy, so that without transition,
As when an old film jumps in the projector,
You will be wading a dun hallway, rounding
A newel post, and starting up the stairs.
Should that occur, adjust to circumstances
And carry on, taking these few precautions:
Detach some portion of your thought to guard
The outside of the building; as you wind
From room to room, leave nothing at your back,
But slough all memories at every threshold;
Nor must you dream of opening any door
Until you have foreseen what lies beyond it.
Regardless of its seeming size, or what
May first impress you as its style or function,
The abrupt structure which involves you now
Will improvise like vapor. Groping down
The gritty cellar steps and past the fuse-box,
Brushing through sheeted lawn-chairs, you emerge
In some cathedral's pillared crypt, and thence,
Your brow alight with carbide, pick your way
To the main shaft through stopes and rubbly tunnels.
Promptly the hoist, ascending toward the pit-head,
Rolls downward past your gaze a dinted rock-face
Peppered with hacks and drill-holes, which acquire
Insensibly the look of hieroglyphics.
Whether to surface now within the vast
Stone tent where Cheops lay secure, or take
The proffered shed of corrugated iron
Which gives at once upon a vacant barracks,
Is up to you. Need I, at this point, tell you
What to avoid? Avoid the pleasant room
Where someone, smiling to herself, has placed
A bowl of yellow freesias. Do not let
The thought of her in yellow, lithe and sleek
As lemonwood, mislead you where the curtains,
Romping like spinnakers which taste the wind,
Bellying out and lifting till the sill
Has shipped a drench of sunlight, then subsiding,
Both warm and cool the love-bed. Your concern
Is not to be detained by dread, or by
Such dear acceptances as would entail it,
But to pursue an ever-dimming course
Of pure transition, treading as in water
Past crumbling tufa, down cloacal halls
Of boarded-up hotels, through attics full
Of glassy taxidermy, moping on

Like a drugged fire-inspector. What you hope for
Is that at some point of the pointless journey,
Indoors or out, and when you least expect it,
Right in the middle of your stride, like that,
So neatly that you never feel a thing,
The kind assassin Sleep will draw a bead
And blow your brains out.

                                   What, are you still awake?
Then you must risk another tack and footing.
Forget what I have said. Open your eyes
To the good blackness not of your room alone
But of the sky you trust is over it,
Whose stars, though foundering in the time to come,
Bequeath us constantly a jetsam beauty.
Now with your knuckles rub your eyelids, seeing
The phosphenes caper like St. Elmo's fire,
And let your head heel over on the pillow
Like a flung skiff on wild Gennesaret.
Let all things storm your thought with the moiled flocking
Of startled rookeries, or flak in air,
Or blossom-fall, and out of that come striding
In the strong dream by which you have been chosen.
Are you upon the roads again? If so,
Be led past honeyed meadows which might tempt
A wolf to graze, and groves which are not you
But answer to your suppler self, that nature
Able to bear the thrush's quirky glee
In stands of chuted light, yet praise as well,
All leaves aside, the barren bark of winter.
When, as you may, you find yourself approaching
A crossroads and its laden gallows tree,
Do not with hooded eyes allow the shadow
Of a man moored in air to stain your forehead,
But lift your gaze and stare your brother down,
Though the swart crows have pecked his sockets hollow.
As for what turn your travels then will take,
I cannot guess. Long errantry perhaps
Will arm you to be gentle, or the claws
Of nightmare flap you pathless God knows where,
As the crow flies, to meet your dearest horror.
Still, if you are in luck, you may be granted,
As, inland, one can sometimes smell the sea,
A moment's perfect carelessness, in which
To stumble a few steps and sink to sleep
In the same clearing where, in the old story,

A holy man discovered Vishnu sleeping,
Wrapped in his maya, dreaming by a pool
On whose calm face all images whatever
Lay clear, unfathomed, taken as they came.
—RICHARD WILBUR

WALKING WITH LULU IN THE WOOD

The wood is a good place to find
the other road down to that hollow
which rocks a little with the same
motion as my soul. Come on, Lulu,
follow me and be careful of the rain
washed leaves. But you were always gentle.
Now that you're dead you can come more silently.
I'll be quiet, too, and we won't disturb
the raccoons or any of the other animals.
I want to talk with the god here, Lulu.
This is a grove where he must be hiding,
and here is a pool for a small water god
to swim in. Let's talk with the god, Lulu.

The sun makes a great splash and you
are the one who is hiding in the tall grass
just the way you used to. Lulu,
you are the color of sand in a certain light,
like the shadow of light. The sun
is embracing me; the shadow also
means death. It is the god's word
in the language he speaks. He says
you are small again, that you have chosen it.
He says your reflection will be in the pool
forever, a blue resemblance, a startled joy.
He says this is your world now, this night
of tall trees, this cave of silences.
He says he loves you, too; he watches you sleep.

Is the grove real? Is this your heaven, Lulu,
that you have let me enter? This glade,
the winter ivories?—the season you missed
by dying in the fall. Are these your jewelled
stones, your curled-up animals, your grass?
And your god, the secret splash in the water
that you always seemed to be listening for?

Is it the god's way—the mouth in the wood,
the opening to paradise?

God of animals and children, separations, loss.
Goodbye. Goodbye, sweet girl, again.
The days pass like oranges tossed
from hand to hand. Then one will drop
and it will be my turn. Wait for me here.
I hope to be fortunate, to come back and share
this winter wood with you, the dark hollow,
the snow-dusted face of the god.

                                        —NAOMI LAZARD

THE WALTZ

Out of brightness, a brightness out of brightness,
The brightness clustered about the outer rim,
Rim of the slippery space that's glassy-sanded,
One detaches and lightly
One detaches and with such gentleness
As falling leaves that touch in air are gentle with
They close.

By what hands chosen or by what
Mind or regardless wind
Picked of the shaking and the shining aspen,
Twined lights, twined and twinned,

As under the baton the world begins to spin
Her brightness now not only a part of brightness
Clears with the dizzying of the rim
(First jerky then all smooth where blue and orange,
Blue as the leaf of orange, and crimson and color of tin
Blur in a melting gray),
Clears and detaches and brightly
Detaches and with such radiance
As the day-dashed shield of the aspen is radiant with
She goes,

She goes or rather stays as all is going?
Who knows?
Who says?

But all the world's the brightness of one face,
And all that face the brightness of two eyes
She shows him naked, steady heart of wheel
From which their spokes strike out to feel that rim;
Yes more than naked, dressed in not even skin.

—HILARY CORKE

THE WALTZER IN THE HOUSE

A sweet, a delicate white mouse,
A little blossom of a beast,
Is waltzing in the house
Among the crackers and the yeast.

O the swaying of his legs!
O the bobbing of his head!
The lady, beautiful and kind,
The blue-eyed mistress, lately wed,
Has almost laughed away her wits
To see the pretty mouse that sits
On his tiny pink behind
And swaying, bobbing, begs.

She feeds him tarts and curds,
Seed packaged for the birds,
And figs, and nuts, and cheese;
Polite as Pompadour to please
The dainty waltzer of her house,
The sweet, the delicate, the innocent
	white mouse.

As in a dream, as in a trance,
She loves his rhythmic elegance,
She laughs to see his bobbing dance.

—STANLEY KUNITZ

THE WASP

It was a wasp, or an imprudent bee,
Against my skin, underneath my shirt,
That stung as I was trying to set it free.
Art is perhaps too long, or life too short.

Ignorant of entomology,
I watched it at the crumbs of my dessert,
Numbered its stripes, curious what sort
Of wasp it was, or what tribe of bee,

While bored, aware that it was watched, maybe,
Buzzing, it appeared to pay me court,
And darted in where I could not see
It, against my skin, underneath my shirt,

There, in the sweaty twilight next to me,
Its amorous antennae to disport,
But always armed. The minute, golden flirt
Stung as I was trying to set it free.

So it escaped, but died eventually,
An event exceeding its desert,
While I, stung as I deserved to be . . .
But art is perhaps too long, or life too short.

Trivial, scarce worthy of report,
Wonderful, the wounds of love should be
Occasion, none the less, for poetry.
Thus deaths, that is the deaths of others, hurt.

                     It was a wasp.

                   —DARYL HINE

THE WATCHER

The dog who knew the winter felt no spleen
And sat indoors; the birds made tracks all day
Across the blue-white crust; he watched the branches sway
Like grasping fingers mirrored on the snow.
The house was warm, and long ago the grass was green;
And all day long bones rattled in his head,
While seven withered apples swung like time,
So quick, so short the pendulum. The tree,
Cursing with wind, prayed mercy on its knee.
He saw the snow toward evening flush to red,
Stepped on his bowl of milk, licked up his crime,
Rolled on his cozy self and smelled his skin,
And snuffed the nighttime out around the bed.

                   —RUTH STONE

THE WATCHERS

It's going to rain
Across the avenue a crane
whose name is

           CIVETTA LINK-BELT

dips, rises and turns in a
       graceless geometry

      But grace is slowness   /   as
ecstasy is some kind of speed or madness   /
The crane moves slowly, that
much it is graceful   /   The men
      watch and the leaves

Cranes make letters in the sky
    as the wedge flies
        "The scholar's function is"

          Mercury, thief and poet,
          invented the first 7 letters,
          5 of them vowels, watching
          cranes · after got

The men watch and the rain does not come
              HC - 108B   CIVETTA LINK-BELT
In the pit below a yellow cat,
        CAT - 933
              pushes the debris
and earth to load CIVETTA HC - 108B
    Cat's name is PASCO and
    there is an ORegon phone number,
· moves its load toward 3 piles
"Let him leave the building to us"

    Palamedes, son of Nauplius,
    invented 11 more
          (consonant)
    Also invented the lighthouse, and
    measures, the scales, the disc, and
    "the art of posting sentinels"
    Ruled over the Mysians,
        Cretan stock, al-
        though his father was Greek
        Took part in the Trojan trouble on the
Greek side · "The scholar's function is fact · Let him
        quarry cleanly" · All

     THOSE INVENTIONS CRETAN
    so that a Greek / alpha-beta-tau
    based on a Cretan, not a Phoenician
        model
        Three different piles:

earth / debris / & schist, the stud / stuff of the island
    is moved by this
    PASCO
    CAT - 933
    ORegon 6-

it does not rain   ·   smoke, the
                          alpha-beta-tau

raised from   5   vowels,   13   consonants to
                   5   vowels,   15   consonants
                   (Epicharmus)   not
the Sicilian writer of comedies, 6th century B.C., but
his ancestor   /
the Aesculapius family at Cos, a couple are
mentioned in the Iliad as physicians to
the Greeks before the equipotent walls
of Troy

                          No, it does not rain, smoke
                          rises from the engines, the
                          leaves   ·   The men watch
                          before the walls of Troy

Apollo in cithaera ceteras literas adjecit

                          7   strings on that zither
                          & for each string a letter
                          Thence to Simonides,
native of Ceos in the service of Dionysus
which god also at home in Delphos
both gods of the solar year as were   /   Aesculapius
                                              & Hercules
                                              Let's
          get all of this into one pot, 6-700 years B.C.

Simonides, well-known poet, intro-
ducted into Athens   4   more letters   ·   the
          unnecessary double-consonants *PSI*
                              (earlier written Pi-Sigma)
          and *XI* (earlier written Kappa-Sigma)
plus   (plus)   two vowels   :   *OMEGA*, a distinction from

          the omicron Hermes conned
          from the 3 Crones, and
EPSILON, as distinct from their *Eta*
& that's the long & the short of it.

Cranes fly in V-formation & the
Tyrrhenians, or Etruscans, were

also of Cretan stock, held
the crane in reverence   /   The men watch
                    LINK-BELT move up its load, the
                    pile to the left near 24th St., the
                    permanent erection moves
                    slow-ly, almost sensually, al-most
                              gracefully
"The scholar's function   /   fact   ·   Let him quarry
cleanly   /   leave the building to us"   ·   Poems
nicked with a knife onto the bark of a stick (Hesiod)
        or upon tablets of clay

                    Perseus cuts off the Gorgon-head
                              (Medusa)
                    and carries it off in a bag   ·   But
the head's a ritual mask and a protection, we
frighten children with it
and trespassers
when we perform the rites   ·   It is
                    no murder,
                    she has given him power of sight
p o e t r y,
            the gorgons no pursuers
            are escort, and the mask
                        (his protection)
Hermes / Car / Mercury / Perseus / Palamedes / Thoth / or
        whatever his original name was,
winged sandals and helmet, you bet!
the swiftness of poetic thought   /   And the bag

THE ALPHABET'S IN THE BAG!

Almost sensually, almost
gracefully   ·   The men watch
and know not what they watch
The cat pushes   ·   the crane   ·   the bud
lifts upward   ·   above the

                    Pillars of Hercules, desti-
nation, where he is going, bringing the secret in the bag
                    The tree at Gades (Cádiz)
            principal city of Tartessus, the
Aegean colony on the Guadalquivir

F r o m   t h e r e   t h e   M i l e s i a n s   w i l l   t a k e   i t   t o   I r e l a n d ?
T h e   o l d e r   c i t y   i s   o n   t h e   w e s t e r n   s h o r e   w i t h   i t s
            Temple of Cronus   ·   island,

                    the island of the goddess,
                       Red Island   /   & Cronus
     god of the middle finger, the fool's finger   /   It is
             his father he kills not his mother, his mother
             gives him
                         the secret
                            "Scholar's function is"

                                                    The men watch

     Hercules' shrine set up by colonists, 1100 B.C.
     400 years before the Phoenicians
     coming from Tyre in painted ships
                 and their oracle
                         HERCULES = PALAMEDES (?)

     7   &   2
     9   steps to the goddess
     & everyone lives to 110 years
     5   years to a lustrum
                             (Etruscan)
     22   lustra   =   110
                             (alpha-beta-tau
     & the circumference of the circle when
             the diameter is   7   is
     22
     proportion known as π
     22   (plus)   over   7
     a neat recurrent sequence
     which does not work out because it never
     ends   /
     7   lustra is   35   years   ·   Maturity,
     or the age at which a man may be elected
     President of the United States   /   a convention
     or a Roman might be elected Consul   /   a convention
                         $$\frac{22}{7}$$
     These numbers no longer a secret   /   But in Crete
                                             or Spain . . .
     Spanish, the mother's family name
     still is set down last, and
     still in Crete descent is matrilineal
     The Greeks have accomplished nothing
                 but death   beauty
                     (Troy)

     The men watch the cat push
     keeping the piles discrete

e a r t h   /   d e b r i s   /   & s c h i s t
the stuff of the island, the crane, the bud
l i f t s   u p w a r d   ·   a b o v e   t h e

And at Cádiz, Caius Julius Hyginus,
a Spaniard and Ovid's friend,
curator of the Palatine Library,
exiled from the court of Augustus

sitting under a tree in Cádiz
over the problem, over a millennium later,
traces Greek letters in the spelt of wine at his table
watches the cranes fly over toward Africa
wedge in the sunset   /   set down the score:

Mercury (or the Fates)	7
Palamedes	11
Epicharmus	2
Simonides	4

Say that he used Etruscan sources,
      does that explain it?
"Let them quarry cleanly
      Let them leave"
Cranes winging over toward Africa
            a wedge
Hyginus traces π on the wooden table in wine spelt

The cat pushes, the crane, the bud
lifts upward   /   above the
rain comes finally
The watchers leave the construction site,
the men leave their machines
      At 323 Third Avenue,
      an old drunk (Hyginus)
sits in a doorway and downs a whole
pint of Sacramento Tomato Juice
            The watchers are the gods

            The leaves burgeon.
                              —PAUL BLACKBURN

(*To Robert Graves, his goddess*)

WATER COLOR

There are some quiet crossings in his city
    Where the wind holds up red kites
        In a sky of flaky whitewash.
The roads are black, like roads
    Drawn brusquely by a child.

Then suddenly the child decides that roads
    And kites are not enough; there must
        Be grass along the roads,
And there is grass. But this is red
    Grass, in windy weather.

Grass calls for sun, a red swirl in between
    The kites, which now require a boy
        To hold the strings. His jacket
And shoes and trousers must be red.
    All red he draws himself.

The roads are brusque and black because
    It has been raining. In skies like these,
        The wind can quickly bring another
Rain. So comes at once oblique
    Black rain into the whitewashed sky.

The black rain mixes with the white,
    And a wet-gray, rosy sky consumes
        The sodden roads and kites,
Consumes the rain itself, dissolves the child
    Who stands at the quiet crossing,

And a sheet of paper, solid gray, floats
On the water, which is also gray.
                                        —STEPHEN MOONEY

WATER COLOR OF GRANTCHESTER MEADOWS

(CAMBRIDGE, ENGLAND)

There, spring lambs jam the sheepfold. In air
Stilled, silvered as water in a glass,
Nothing is big or far.
The small shrew chitters from its wilderness
Of grassheads and is heard.

Each thumb-size bird
Flits nimble-winged in thickets, and of good color.

Cloud rack and owl-hollowed willows slanting over
The bland Granta double their white-and-green
World under the sheer water
And ride that flux at anchor, upside down.
The punter sinks his pole.
In Byron's pool
Cattails part where the tame cygnets steer.

It is a country on a nursery plate.
Spotted cows revolve their jaws, and crop
Red clover or gnaw beetroot,
Bellied on a nimbus of sun-glazed buttercup.
Hedging meadows of benign
Arcadian green,
The blood-berried hawthorn hides its spines with white.

Droll, vegetarian, the water rat
Saws down a reed and swims from his limber grove,
While the students stroll or sit
Rapt in the moony indolence of love—
Black-gowned, but unaware
How in such mild air
The owl shall stoop from his turret, the rat cry out.

—SYLVIA PLATH

WATER ISLAND

(TO THE MEMORY OF A FRIEND, DROWNED OFF WATER ISLAND, APRIL, 1960)

Finally, from your house there is no view;
The bay's blind mirror shattered over you
And Patchogue took your body like a log
The wind rolled up to shore. The senseless drowned
Have faces nobody would care to see,
But water loves those gradual erasures
Of flesh and shoreline, greenery and glass,
And you belonged to water, it to you,
Having built, on a hillock, above the bay,
Your house, the bay giving you reason to,
Where now, if seasons still are running straight,
The horseshoe crabs clank armor night and day,
Their couplings far more ancient than the eyes
That watched them from your porch. I saw one once

Whose back was a history of how we live;
Grown onto every inch of plate, except
Where the hinges let it move, were living things,
Barnacles, mussels, water weeds—and one
Blue bit of polished glass, glued there by time:
The origins of art. It carried them
With pride, it seemed, as if endurance only
Matters in the end. Or so I thought.

Skimming traffic lights, starboard and port,
Steer through planted poles that mark the way,
And other lights, across the bay, faint stars
Lining the border of Long Island's shore,
Come on at night, they still come on at night,
Though who can see them now I do not know.
Wild roses, at your back porch, break their blood,
And bud to test surprises of sea air,
And the birds fly over, gliding down to feed
At the two feeding stations you set out with seed,
Or splash themselves in a big bowl·of rain
You used to fill with water. Going across
That night, too fast, too dark, no one will know,
Maybe you heard, the last you'll ever hear,
The cry of the savage and endemic gull
Which shakes the blood and always brings to mind
The thought that death, the scavenger, is blind,
Blunders and is stupid, and the end
Comes with ironies so fine the seed
Falters in the marsh and the heron stops
Hunting in the weeds below your landing stairs,
Standing in a stillness that now is yours.

                                    —HOWARD MOSS

WATER OUZEL

Follow back from the gull's bright arc and the osprey's plunge,
Past the silent heron, erect in the tidal marsh,
Up the mighty river, rolling in mud. Branch off
At the sign of the kingfisher poised on a twisted snag.
Not deceived when the surface grows calm, keep on,
Past the placidity of ducks, the delusive pastoral dreams
Drawn down by the effortless swallows that drink on the wing.
With the wheat fields behind you, do not neglect to choose
At every juncture the clearest and coldest path.

Push through the reeds where the redwing sways,
Climb through the warnings of hidden jays,
Climb, climb the jostling, narrowing stream
Through the aspen sunlight into the evergreen darkness
Where chattering crossbills scatter the shreds of cones.
Here at last at the brink of the furthest fall,
With the water dissolving to mist as it shatters the pool below,
Pause beneath timber-line springs and the melting snow.
Here, where the shadows are deep in the crystal air,
So near a myriad beginnings, after so long a journey,
Expecting at least a golden cockatoo
Or a screaming eagle with wings of flame,
Stifle your disappointment, observe
The burgher of all this beauty, the drab
Citizen of the headwaters; struggle to love
The ridiculous ouzel, perched on his slippery stone
Like an awkward, overblown catbird deprived of its tail.

Not for him the limitless soaring above the storm,
Or the surface-skimming, or swimming, or plunging in.
He walks. In the midst of the turbulence, bathed in spray,
From a rock without foothold into the lunging current,
He descends a deliberate step at a time till, submerged,
He has walked from sight and hope. The stream
Drives on, dashes, splashes, drops over the edge,
Too swift for ice in midwinter, too cold
For life in midsummer, depositing any debris,
Leaf, twig, or carcass, along the way,
Wedging them in behind rocks to rot,
Such as these not reaching the ocean.

Yet, lo! The lost one emerges unharmed,
Hardly wet as he walks from the water.
Undisturbed by beauty or terror, pursuing
His own few needs with a nerveless will,
Nonchalant in the torrent, he bobs and nods
As though to acknowledge implicit applause.
This ceaseless tic, a trick of the muscles shared
With the solitary sandpiper, burlesqued
By the teeter-bob and the phoebe's tail,
Is not related to approbation. The dipper,
Denied the adventure of uncharted flight
Over vast waters to an unknown homeland, denied
Bodily beauty, slightly absurd and eccentric,
Will never attain acclaim as a popular hero.
No prize committee selects the clown
Whose only dangers are daily and domestic.

Yet he persists, and does not consider it persisting.
On a starless, sub-zero, northern night,
When all else has taken flight into sleep or the south,
He, on the edge of the stream, has been heard to repeat
The rippling notes of his song, which are clear and sweet.
                                —William H. Matchett

THE WAY TO THE RIVER

(for dido)

The way to the river leads past the names of
Ash the sleeves the wreaths of hinges
Through the song of the bandage vendor

I lay your name by my voice
As I go

The way to the river leads past the late
Doors and the games of the children born looking backwards
They play that they are broken glass
The numbers wait in the halls and the clouds
Call
From windows
They play that they are old they are putting the horizon
Into baskets they are escaping they are
Hiding

I step over the sleepers the fires the calendars
My voice turns to you

I go past the juggler's condemned building the hollow
Windows gallery
Of invisible presidents the same motion in them all
In a parked cab by the sealed wall the hats are playing
Sort of poker with somebody's
Old snapshots game I don't understand they lose
The rivers one
After the other I begin to know where I am

I am home

Be here the flies from the house of the mapmaker
Walk on our letters I can tell
And the days hang medals between us
I have lit our room with a glove of yours be

Here I turn
To your name and the hour remembers
Its one word
Now

Be here what can we
Do for the dead the footsteps full of money
I offer you what I have my
Poverty

To the city of wires I have brought home a handful
Of water I walk slowly
In front of me they are building the empty
Ages I see them reflected not for long
Be here I am no longer ashamed of time it is too brief its hands
Have no names
I have passed it I know

  Oh Necessity you with the face you with
  All the faces

  This is written on the back of everything

  But we
  Will read it together

         —W. S. MERWIN

WEATHER

    But swinging doesn't bend them down to stay.
    Ice storms do that.
       —*"Birches," Robert Frost.*

The elm is turned to crystal   The sentimental willows
The tamarack is glass   Weep with no green excuse
An iridescent boneyard
Has taken the place of grass   But the birch trees stricken double
             Cry to the sun click clack
Someone has piled old shakos   Ours are the only natures
Where there was pine and spruce   That you cannot give back.

             —WILLIAM MEREDITH

THE WEATHER OF SIX MORNINGS

I

Sunlight lies along my table
like abandoned pages.

I try to speak
of what is so hard for me—

this clutter of a life—
puritanical signature!

In the prolonged heat insects,
pine needles, birch leaves

make a ground bass of silence
that never quite dies.

II

Treetops are shuddering
in uneasy clusters

like rocking water
whirlpooled before a storm.

Words knock at my breast,
heave and struggle to get out.

A black-capped bird
pecks on, unafraid.

Yield then, yield
to the invading rustle of the rain.

III

All is closed in
by an air so rain-drenched

the distant barking of tied-up dogs
ripples to the heart of the woods.

Only a man's voice
refuses to be absorbed.

Hearing of your death
by a distant roadside

I wanted to erect some marker
though your ashes float out to sea.

IV

If the weather breaks
I can speak of your dying,

if the weather breaks,
if the crows stop calling

and flying low
(again today there is thunder

outlying . . .),
I can speak of your living,

the lightning-flash of meeting,
the green leaves waving at our windows.

V

Yesterday a letter
spoke of our parting—

a kind of dissolution
so unlike this sudden stoppage.

Now all the years in between
flutter away like lost poems.

And the morning light is so delicate,
so utterly empty . . .

at high altitude, after long illness,
breathing in mote by mote a vanished
world. . . .

VI

Rest.
A violin bow, a breeze

just touches the birches.
Cheep—a new flute

tunes up in a birch top.
A chipmunk's warning skirrs. . . .

Whose foot disturbs these twigs?
To the sea of received silence

why should I sign
my name?

—JANE COOPER

WE HAVE BEEN HERE BEFORE

I think I remember this moorland,
   The tower on the tip of the tor;
I feel in the distance another existence;
   I think I have been here before.

And I think you were sitting beside me
   In a fold in the face of the fell;
For Time at its work'll go round in a circle,
   And what is befalling, befell.

"I have been here before!" I asserted,
   In a nook on a neck of the Nile.
I once in a crisis was punished by Isis,
   And you smiled. I remember your smile.

I had the same sense of persistence
   On the site of the seat of the Sioux;
I heard in the tepee the sound of a sleepy
   Pleistocene grunt. It was you.

The past made a promise, before it
   Began to begin to begone.
This limited gamut brings you again. Damn it,
   How long has this got to go on?

—MORRIS BISHOP

«¡WELLCOME, TO THE CAVES OF ARTA!»

They are hollowed out in the see coast at the municipal ter-
minal of Capdepera, at nine kilometer from the town of Arta
in the Island of Mallorca, with a suporizing infinity of graceful
colums of 21 meter and by downward, wich prives the spectator
of all animacion and plunges in dumbness. The way going is
very picturesque, serpentine between style mountains, til the
arrival at the esplanade of the vallee called «The Spider». There
are good enlacements of the railroad with autobuses of excur-
sion, many days of the week, today actually Wednesday and
Satturday. Since many centuries renown foreing visitors have ex-
plored them and wrote thier eulogy about, included Nort-
American geoglogues.—*From a tourist leaflet.*

Such subtile filigranity and nobless of construccion
   Here fraternise in harmony that respiracion stops.
While all admit thier impotence (though autors most formidable)
   To sing in words the excellence of Nature's underprops,
Yet stalactite and stalagmite together with dumb language
   Make hymnes to God wich celebrate the stregnth of water drops.

¿You, also, are you capable to make precise in idiom
   Consideracions magic of ilusions very wide?
Already in the Vestibule of these Grand Caves of Arta
   The spirit of the human verb is darked and stupefyed;
So humildy you trespass trough the forest of the colums
   And listen to the grandess explicated by the guide.

From darkness into darkness, but at measure, now descending,
   You remark with what esxactitude he designates each bent:
«The Saloon of Thousand Banners», or «The Tumba of Napoleon»,
   «The Grotto of the Rosary», «The Club», «The Camping Tent».
And at «Cavern of the Organ» there are knocking streange formacions
   Wich give a nois particular pervoking wonderment.

¡Too far do not adventure, sir! For, further as you wander,
   The every of the stalactites will make you stop and stay.
Grand peril amenaces now, your nostrills aprehending
   An odour least delicious of lamentable decay.
It is some poor touristers, in the depth of obscure cristal,
   Wich deceased of thier emocion on a past excursion day.

                    —ROBERT GRAVES

WE SETTLED BY THE LAKE

We settled by the lake where reeds
Cloaked off the water from the shore.
The sun like a flashlight lit the church
In shady fields on the other side.
Black geese honked their wild way
    home;
Dead clouds absorbed the dripping
    sky;
An old man drove his limping mares
From what his children called the
    sea.

But we were taken up with time—
How all these years the land had
    stayed

Green and flat, the steeple had risen
But not the ground; the lake still lay
As smooth and tarnished as the tea
Left in a saucer after all
The old, perspired guests have gone.

The land is a museum—day
By day it builds its collection up
From wind-leavings. You can't avoid
Admiring it, although it says
"Not me" when in the waterfall
The heart cries out like a conductor
On a morning train, "Change! All
    change!"

—F. D. REEVE

WESTERN TOWN

Strange Western town at the round edge of night,
Into your sleep the broad-shouldered train
Gentles its way, absorbed in its thunderous quiet,
Shearing off porches of Carpenter's Gothic,
Gathering bulbs and crocuses of electricity.
Now the green blinds of country stores go down
And arches of gold lettering gleam
Like old asbestos in dead movie houses.

Heart-heavy in the cool compartments,
The travelling men turn over in their sleep
As the pale squares of light, newspaper thin,
Fall on their eyelids again and again and again,
Plunging the sleepers into a deeper sleep,
A deeper drift of linen than their dream.

Perhaps a single figure is let down
In the hometown dark, or maybe not;
Perhaps only the sleepy sacks of mail
Or a lone coffin come by rail
At rest now on a sketchy cart. Tomorrow,
Somewhere, a city will take the train apart.

—KARL SHAPIRO

THE WEST FORTIES: MORNING, NOON, AND NIGHT

But nothing whatever is by love debarred . . . —*Patrick Kavanagh.*

1. WELCOME TO HOTEL MAJESTY (SINGLES $4 UP)

On this hotel their rumpled royalties
Descend from their cross-country buses, loyalties
Suspended, losses cut, loves left behind,
To strike it lucky in the state of mind
That manufactures marvels out of mud.
Ensanguined by a bar sign selling Bud,
The early-Streamline lobby, in its shell
Of late-Edwardian ornament, with a bell-
Mouthed cupidon extolling every swag
On its tall, fruitful front (a stale sight gag
First uttered by the comic landsmen who
Compounded a Great White Way out of blue
Sky, gneiss, and schist a whole stone age ago,
Before time steeled the arteries we know)—
The lobby washes redly over guests
With rope-bound bags containing their one best
Suit, shirt, tie, Jockey shorts, and pair of socks,
Half-empty pint, electric-razor box,
Ex-wife's still smiling picture, high-school ring,
Harmonica, discharge, and everything.
Amid the alien corn and ruthless tares
I hear a royal cry of horseplayers
Winding their tin horns in a chant of brass,
Their voices claiming in the wilderness.

II. SAL'S ATOMIC SUBMARINES

The Puerto Rican busboy, Jesus, coughs
Above the cutting board where Sal compiles
An outbound order for the Abinger
Associates next door; then, carrying
A pantheon of heroes in a brown
Kraft-paper bag, he sidles by the chrome-
Formica-plastic dinette furniture
And gains the world, where anti-personnel
Gases from crosstown buses, vegetable
Soup simmering at Bickford's, and My Sin
Seeping from Walgreen's silently combine
To addle all outsiders. Only lithe,
Quick indigenes like Jesus (whose tan neck
Is thinner than my wrist) can long survive
And later even prosper in the air
Of these times' squares, these hexahedral hives
Where every worker drudges for his queen.

III. Stage-Door Johnny's

Silvana Casamassima, Vic Blad
(The talent agent), Lance Bartholomey,
Piretta Paul, Max Dove, A. Lincoln Brown,
Samarra Brown, Lil Yeovil, Beryl Cohn
(Theatrical attorney), Johnny Groen
(The owner), Merritt Praed, Morty Monroe,
Dame Phyllis Woolwich, Sir Jack Handel, Bart.,
Del Hector (the producer), Coquetel,
Fab Newcome, Temple Bell, Vanessa Vane,
Burt Wartman, C. R. Freedley, F.R.S.,
Alf Wandsworth (author of "Queer Street"), Mel Hess,
His Honor Judge Perutz, Merced McCall,
Tam Pierce, Jan Stewart, Tom Cobley, and all
The darlings, mirrored in their flourishing
Autographed caricatures on every wall,
Sail on, sealed in, important, bright, serene,
In league in Captain Nemo's submarine.

IV. Penny Arcadia

Like lava, rock erupts to fill the room
From each coäx- coäx- coäxial
Concentric speaker's throat, and rolls like doom
Over the unmoved pinball-playing boys
Whose jaws lightly reciprocate like long-
Stroke pistons coupled to the Tinguely loom
Of augmented electric music, strong
As sexuality and loud as noise,
Which keens across the dingy room at full
Gain and, its coin gone, as abruptly dies.

V. Meyer Wax Loans

Clear and obscure, elbows of saxophones
Shine out like sink traps in an underworld
Of pledges unredeemed—a spectral band
Of brass and nickel marching in the dark
Toward the morning and redemption, where
Known lips will kiss their reeds, familiar hands
Resume their old and loving fingering.
Unlikely. In a hundred rented rooms
From here to Ybor City, pledgers plan
What next to pawn: the Rolleicord, the ring,
The eight-transistor Victor radio,
The travelling alarm. Alarm creeps in-
To all their calculations, now the bloom
Is off their promise, now the honeymoon
Is over with a cry, and time begins

To whittle expectations to a size
Convenient for their carrying to pawn.

● VI. Lovemovie

Before the glazed chrome case where Lovelies Swim
Au Natural, and under the sly lights,
Which wink and bump and wink and grind, except
For those that have burned out, the singing strings
Of Madame Violin essay "Caprice,"
Not missing many notes, considering
How cold it is outside the Lovemovie.
Stray pennies in her tin cup punctuate
The music like applause. Play, gypsies! Dance!
The thin strains of a Romany romance
Undaunt the ears of each peajacketed
Seaman on liberty, and of each old
Wanderer slowly losing to the cold,
And of each schoolboy who has come to see
Life in the flesh inside the Lovemovie.
Beneath her stiff green hair, an artist's grin
Knits up the ravelled cheek of Madame Violin.

VII. The Argo Building: New Delman's Good Night

The last bone button in the old tin tea
Box of the Argo Building lastly sees
ɔᴎɪ⅄ᴧƎWƎᴚ Ǝ˥ᗺɪꙄɪ⅄ᴎɪ peeling off
His street-side window as he locks the door
Of 720 one more night and struts
His septuagenarian stuff down
The corridor, past Aabco Dental Labs,
Worldwide Investigations, Inc., Madame
Lillé, Corsetière, Star School of Tap,
Dr. O'Keefe, Franck Woodwind Institute,
Wink Publications, and Watch Hospital.
Up the wrought shaft, preceded by its wires
Ticking and twittering, the intrepid car
Rises like an old aeronaut to take
Its ballast-passenger aboard beneath
The pointed clear bulbs of its four flambeaux,
Sweetly attenuated Art Nouveau
Which was *vieux jeu* and is the rage, unknown
To old New Delman, whom it ferries down
In its black cage, funebrially slow,
To Stygian Forty-seventh Street below.

—L. E. Sissman

WET THURSDAY

A stiff wind off the channel
Linking the chimney's mutterings
With rain; the shaken trees,
Mile after mile, greening the sand.
Turn to the fire as the afternoon
Turns gray. Then, suddenly,
The locked door opens without sound,
Thunder shaking the sky, to usher in
A monstrous cat that seems
Far older than the oldest carp
In the waters under the earth,
Moving like a shadow over the floor
To warm its frozen paws
Before the fire. He turns,
Smiling into the woodbox,
And says, "*Felis libyca domestica*

They call me, kept by man for catch-
　　ing
Rats and mice. Of Eastern or
Egyptian origin. Now to be
Your spiteful and envenomed shadow.
　　Here
Will I live out my nine and evil lives
Before your very interesting fire.
And the days, months, years, are end-
　　less."

Wind pounds along the coast.
The trees bend double to the sand.
The cat sleeps like an old campaigner
During this season of the long rains.
　　　　　　　—WELDON KEES

WHAT HATH MAN WROUGHT EXCLAMATION POINT

(POEM SUITABLE FOR TRANSMISSION BY WESTERN UNION)

Amid Tibetan snows the ancient lama
Mutters his lifelong intercessions comma
Turns the unresting wheel of prayer a myriad
Times in its sacred circling period period
But hold comma what omen strange and dark
Is this on high interrogation mark
A giant bird has out of India stolen
To ravish holy Tibet semicolon
The plane soars upward comma tops the crest
Of the inviolate God of Everest
Period and the lama smote his wheel
Asunder semicolon with a peal
Of dreadful laughter he arose and cried
Colon quotation marks the God has died
Comma so worship man who dared and smote
Exclamation line of dots close quote
　　　　　　　—MORRIS BISHOP

WHAT THE EARTH ASKED ME

Why did you kiss the girl who cried
For lovers through her lonely mind,
Homely as sin and sick of pride?

In pity for my kind.

What good will pity do the lost
Who flutter in the driven wind,
Wild for the body, ghost on ghost?

No good, no good to me.

Why did you hammer with your fist
That beetle on the window blind,
Withered in summer's holocaust?

In pity for my kind.

What good will pity do the found
Who flutter in the driven wind,
Wild to be ghosts below the ground?

No good, no good to me.

The living and the dead together
Flutter before, flutter behind.
Why do you try to change the weather?

In pity for my kind.

What good will pity do the kiss
That shrivels on the mouth like grief?
Have you been calling me for this?

No good to me, no good to me.
—JAMES WRIGHT

"WHAT YOU SEE IS ME"

—*The Beatles.*

Cataclysmic if it were so
They want it to be so
To prove it *is* so
All the young who love dancing
Their long hair streaking
Wildly searching faces
Blind with the wish to see
Senseless with the wish
To feel themselves and the others

How simple

What you see

Words we've known
Since babyhood

Is me

But how cataclysmic
If it were so

They writhe their bodies
Shut their blind eyes tight
And make a closed circle
By holding hands
To keep out all

The old cold ones like us
Who've never
They think
Confronted one another
Comforted one another

This way the world gets on
By dreaming
What can't be possible
Believing that it is
Making it so

Open up your eyes now

They believe it
And for them it is so

But our cold tired eyes
Can open wider than theirs
We know a thing or two
They don't know
About the art of seeing
The song says

What you see is me

But we know that it's
Impossible
If what the song says
Were true
And we could all open our eyes at once
And see one another
Right then we'd be in heaven

—BARBARA GIBBS

WHEN THE VACATION IS OVER FOR GOOD

It will be strange
Knowing at last it couldn't go on forever,
The certain voice telling us over and over
That nothing would change,

And remembering, too,
Because by then it will all be done with, the way
Things were, and how we had wasted time as though
There was nothing to do,

When, in a flash,
The weather turned and the lofty air became
Unbearably heavy, the wind strikingly dumb,
And our cities like ash,

And knowing, also,
What we never suspected, that it was something like summer
At its most august, except that the nights were warmer
And the clouds seemed to glow,

And even then,
Because we will not have changed much, wondering what
Will become of things, and who will be left to do it
All over again,

And somehow trying,
But still unable, to know just what it was
That went so completely wrong, or why it is
We are dying.

—MARK STRAND

WHEN WE LOOKED BACK

The most present of all the watchers where we camped
were the animals that stood beyond the firelight,
being dark, but there, and making no sound.
They were the most remembered eyes, that night.

Tapestries of fern had taken them in
when we walked out in the morning along the track
their eyes had bored through the air. And the camp we left
was a little spot in the trees when we looked back.

—WILLIAM STAFFORD

WHERE

Monkeys in a forest,   Flowers in a parlor,
Beggarmen in rags,   Dunces in a school;
Marrow in a knucklebone,
Gold in leather bags;   Feathers in a pillow,
                              Cattle in a shed,
Dumplings in the oven,   Honey in a beehive,
Fishes in a pool,   And me in bed.

—WALTER DE LA MARE

WHITE GUARDIANS OF THE UNIVERSE OF SLEEP

white guardians of the universe of sleep

safely may by imperishable your
glory escorted through infinite countries be
my darling (open the very secret of hope
to her eyes, not any longer blinded with
a world; and let her heart's each whisper wear

all never guessed unknowable most joy)

faithfully blossoming beyond to breathe
suns of the night, bring this beautiful
wanderer home to a dream called time: and give
herself into the mercy of that star,
if out of climbing whom begins to spill
such golden blood as makes his moon alive

sing more will wonderfully birds than are
—E. E. CUMMINGS

WHITMONDAY

Their feet on London, their heads in the gray clouds,
The Bank (if you call it a holiday) Holiday crowds
Stroll from street to street, cocking an eye
For where the angel used to be in the sky;
But the Happy Future is a thing of the past, and the street
Echoes to nothing but their dawdling feet.
The Lord's my shepherd—familiar words of myth
Stand up better to bombs than a granite monolith.
Perhaps there is something in them. *I'll not want*—
Not when I'm dead. *He makes me down to lie*—
Death my christening and fire my font—
The quiet (Thames' or Don's or Salween's) *waters by.*
—LOUIS MACNEICE

WHO ARE YOU, LITTLE I

who are you, little i

(five or six years old)
peering from some high

window; at the gold

of november sunset

(and feeling: that if day
has to become night

this is a beautiful way)
—E. E. CUMMINGS

WHY THEY WAGED WAR

Out of all this, M. de Coquet only got one thing: that the
Trojan War took place despite all efforts to prevent it.—*From
a review in "Commune."*

It's clear, Trojan cried out to Greek,
You've chosen Troy as your prey.
Not at all, called back Agamemnon,
Your Paris took Helen away.

It is not wise, said Ulysses,
To have gods so covered with gold.
And worse, in his palace sighed Priam,
To be gilded and yet grow old.

—John Peale Bishop

THE WIDOW

How easily the ripe grain
Leaves the husk
At the simple turning of the planet

There is no season
That requires us

Masters of forgetting
Threading the eyeless rocks with
A narrow light

In which ciphers wake and evil
Gets itself the face of the norm
And contrives cities

The Widow rises under our finger-
nails
In this sky we were born we are born

And you weep wishing you were num-
bers
You multiply you cannot be found
You grieve

Not that heaven does not exist but
That it exists without us

You confide
In images in things that can be
Represented which is their dimension
you
Require them you say This
Is real and you do not fall down and
moan

Not seeing the irony in the air

Everything that does not need you is
real

The Widow does not
Hear you and your cry is numberless

This is the waking landscape
Dream after dream after dream walk-
ing away through it
Invisible invisible invisible

—W. S. Merwin

WILD (AT OUR FIRST) BEASTS UTTERED HUMAN WORDS

wild (at our first) beasts uttered human words
—our second coming made stones sing like birds—
but o the starhushed silence which our third's

—E. E. Cummings

WINTER IN ÉTIENBURGH

One imagines the lives of the Prince
And the principality
Will never be over,   ·
That they will go on forever
Into the next chapter
Simply by shifting tactics,
Making alliance
With all enemies, ancient
And modern,
In a mutually profitable defense.
So when, in his car, the Prince
Rides out into the early
Medieval morning
Of Étienburgh, the shops, the post
    office,
The casino, etc., wink
As he motors by;
From a thousand windows,
The sun, alternately gold and silver,
Flashes back over
The Mediterranean. Just so.

In the castle, unlike other princesses
In castles, the Princess is
A former Hollywood star
In an ordinary
Sleep—but she does not dream.
What would she dream
About, what would she wish for?
Some extraordinary
Dream in which she is ordinary?
She has let down her hair.
But there is nothing to be saved from,
Nothing to become.
Already her melodramas,
Or herself, among orange cabañas,

Are, to affectionate
Subjects, matters of fact.
The State rests. Old women
Beat clean their clothes
At the edge of the sea, which foams
Like Rinso, blue.

So Étienburgh prospers, under the
    Prince,
As if all nature has an interest.
The sea has come to terms,
Washing the beach
As white as confectioner's sugar
For the newly rich,
And as pure
For the fastidious.
Women, wearing bikinis,
Walk in the skins
Of the long wealthy.
Beach umbrellas
Lean like parched flowers.
Should evening come, the shops, the
    houses
Open wide their mouths.
Signs blink.
The casino beckons;
A visiting prince
Accelerates, in his black Lincoln,
Toward a night of heroic
Losses. All night,
The surf scrubs and mutters
Like an old servant
After the guests have retired.

The Prince and the principality
Are not without principle;

Perhaps the defense
Of accommodation is the best
Principle if the enemy
Attacks, if there is an enemy.
Who is to say?
Meanwhile, the sky warms,
The light
Is extravagant,
Everywhere there is
Music from hidden transistors.
Within the impeccable coach-

Work of a Porsche
Ride the Prince and the Princess.
If one knew what to do
One could stay here,
Opening, perhaps,
A little shop,
A business, some small concession,
If one knew what to do
With oneself
Here, for just a season,
Among these clever citizens.

—Stephen Parker

WINTER NIGHT

The circuit closes. House and heart
Must cut and save the heat they use.
A circuit closed by sleep shall start
The nightlong quarrel life must lose.

Ticking like deathwatches, my house
Stands up this night to ice once more,
Knowing at last it cannot rouse
That strength and sap it knew before.

The seasoned timbers of the stair
Creak to my weight; a dog outside
Howls windily. How should hearts prepare
To front a cold few beasts abide?

Padding the hall, I pause by doors
And listen to my children's breathing
While cold of night-fear and remorse
Puddles and curds for all the sheathing,

All the revetment I had tiered
To insulate from northern breath;
My house, for all the worst I feared
And bargained for, shall catch a death.

And lusts that spread today in sun,
Flattered in pride of life grown tall,
Shall clot, by gradual ice, to one
Standing with held breath in the hall.

—Louis O. Coxe

WINTER POND

(lake paran)

for j.v.f.

Lest the ripple deceive us
with its midsummer dazzle, a cat's-paw
of lustre on the shimmering weight of the water,
and the Heraclitean swimmer
dissolve into light, scarring the pond
with his passing—arm over arm in the herringbone ringed with a gas—
and no one believe us,

I stand in the March
of my mind in a winter perspective:
suds, scurf, and cobble—a sherbet of blackening ice
with a pylon inset on a lunar enormity, and beyond
it a tractor in characterless orange;
the lake like an adamant
drawing into the flint and the salt
all a planet's mobility—algae and perch,
the gelatinous hives of the frog, night crawlers,
the semen and freeze of a winter—until
all locks like a cluster of crystal,
lifts up in its basin in its perfect containment,
a monolith crowding the shale,
a troglodyte's hammer
pounding the weathers and pressing on obdurate matter
like the light on the pomegranate's rind
or the bones on the scales of a carp.

The seasons disclaim us. But a shock lives on in the air—
a pulse, like a forge in a cloud
that beats on the latent and makes the ambiguous bearable.
Facet by facet, we assemble a vanished relation—
the swimmer under the ice and the skater on water—
harden the edge of our world till our images name us,
and the possible touches the heart and declares what it saw:
an ice-floe that burned in the thaw,
the hailstone's precipitation
that opened a well for the noon of the fish and the flycaster,
set a bow on the ripple, recovered the spinner's vibration,
till all was motion and passion and presence, flashing as never before,

and the swimmer arose in his nakedness and called from the opposite shore.

—BEN BELITT

WINTER SONG

When I walk home through snow or
    slush
Under a dismal sky,
I do not seek to question much
The what and/or the why.
I am contented to observe
A wintry world. I keep my nerve.

I steer my course mid frozen rocks,
But I forbear to shiver;

Ice cubes as big as city blocks
Beckon me from the river.
I answer them as they deserve,
Displaying how I keep my nerve.

I tell the truth—I am no fibber—
And loudly cry to all
That though the ghouls of winter
    gibber
And mock the buried Fall,

From mental calm I do not swerve—
I swallow hard, but keep my nerve.

Why do they look at me askance
As though my nerve had failed?

I do not live in gloomy trance,
My cheek has never paled,
I shout to all, without reserve,
"*I keep my nerve, I keep my nerve!*"

—DAVID DAICHES

A WINTER'S TALE

It is a winter night. Fever and chill
Rummage the blind cars on Lover's Hill,
And rabbits shiver in the frozen grass.
Along the river, ice, like broken glass,
Clicks and flickers. For an hour we walk
The bank, and I half listen to your talk
Of kids and marriage. Here, piles of junk
Blaze with frost, and summer's juice is sunk
To the hidden root. But even as a bloom
Of ice melts in my hand, I think of a room
Warmed by summer moonlight. You are beside
Me on the bed. I turn. Your eyes grow wide
And darken as we kiss. Wild and sweet,
Your body whispers against me on the sheet.
But this is dream; for I have heard the west
Wind sigh down the dozing Berkshires, its past
Naming our future, the tide of its restlessness
Heaving through raw towns. It is not less
Than itself, this image. It summons me
Where breakneck houses spill toward a fresh sea.
And you, you are your father's child; your face
Tells me you will never leave this place,
His dead mills, the hope that they'll come back
To life. Downstream, they loom, crusted wrack
Jamming their floodgates, their bobbins wound
With the dust of years. Watchman and hound
Prowl the yards. But what is there to watch?
Tonight, your father warms his hopes with Scotch,
And pacing before the fireplace, stops, and turns
To stare at the *Wall Street Journal* as it burns.
Now, the town clock bells you home. But I
Draw you close. You smile a little and cry
Against my shoulder. We stand in this heavy air,
And stand, knowing all we'll ever share
Is this embrace. The sky above us palls,
And the blue snow melts about us as it falls.

—ROBERT PATRICK DANA

WINTER VERSE FOR MY SISTER

Moonlight washes the west side of the house
As clean as bone, it carpets like a lawn
The stubbled field tilting eastward
Where there is no sign yet of dawn.
The moon is an angel with a bright light sent
To surprise me once before I die
With the real aspect of things.
It holds the light steady and makes no comment.

Practicing for death, I have lately gone
To that other house
Where our parents did most of their dying,
Embracing and not embracing their conditions.
Our father built bookcases and little by little stopped reading,
Our mother cooked proud meals for common mouths.
Kindly they raised two children. We raked their leaves
And cut their grass, we ate and drank with them.
Reconciliation was our long work, not all of it joyful.

Now outside my own house at a cold hour
I watch the noncommittal angel lower
The steady lantern that's worn these clapboards thin
In a wash of moonlight while men slept within,
Accepting and not accepting their conditions,
And the fingers of trees plied a deep carpet of decay
On the gravel web underneath the field,
And the field tilting always toward day.

—WILLIAM MEREDITH

THE WITCH OF EAST SEVENTY-SECOND STREET

"I will put upon you the Telephone Curse," said the witch.
"The telephone will call when you are standing on a chair with a Chinese vase in
either hand,
And when you answer, you will hear only the derisive popping of corks."
But I was armed so strong in honesty
Her threats passed by me like the idle wind.

"And I will put upon you the Curse of Dropping," said the witch.
"The dropping of tiny tacks, the dropping of food gobbets,
The escape of wet dishes from the eager-grasping hand,
The dropping of spectacles, stitches, final consonants, the abdomen."
I sneered, jeered, fleered; I flouted, scouted; I pooh-pooh-poohed.

"I will put upon you the Curse of Forgetting!" screamed the witch.
"Names, numbers, faces, old songs, old joy,
Words that once were magic, love, upward ways, the way home."
"No doubt the forgotten is well forgotten," said I.

"And I will put upon you the Curse of Remembering," bubbled the witch.
Terror struck my eyes, knees, heart;
And I took her charred contract
And signed in triplicate.

—Morris Bishop

WOMAN, GALLUP, N.M.

The shadow of her profile lay stringent
Across the step of curb—
A styptic etch against his blood,

And he silent beside her,
Lesions pale in the scars
Of his limp hands.

The baby, against
The breathing of her breast,
Watched, with black eyes
From under a ruffled lamb-chop hat;

The bus passengers walk
Arranged oblivion in and out.

They did not talk.
She yielded him nothing but rigid back,
Her neck a carved anger of tendons
Where the black down murmured.

God, what had he done
That could not be darned with tears?

She sat lizard dry.
Road and railroad ran through her head.
The land ate red
To a frail mirage of mountains.

He raised his head
And with a gentleness of hand

Hesitant as settling dust
Stroked the curve of her neck.

His motion was only man to woman.
It was not enough.
Her silhouette, knifed out of sunlight,
Fell into the gutter.

The passengers walked over it,
And she was mute as snake skin.

If he had cast himself into his own
Shadow under the bus wheel
She would not have wept
Or cracked her parched profile

Until night erased it
Or the baby gummed a pale cry.

He reached out again,
A cramped consent of fingers
Down her shoulder.

His arm opening
To press the baby's head against
The hollow of her collarbone
Scythed back into his breath.

Across a red scorch to mountains
She shattered on the pavement.

—Karen Swenson

WORD

The word bites like a fish.
Shall I throw it back free
Arrowing to that sea
Where thoughts lash tail and fin?
Or shall I pull it in
To rhyme upon a dish?
—STEPHEN SPENDER

THE WORD

There's the field. I can see it.
Of course it's a dream, but I know it,
and still I see it: the big cardboard box
where we crouched and played house,

or the red roundhouse for streetcars
where the tracks ended and the cars stood,
quiet, no one in them, and the workmen
went their rounds carrying huge oil guns,

or the jump from a roof on a dare
into a pile of straw—I landed so hard
I almost bit my tongue off.
My tears were real, seemed to fall

of their own will; I was stunned
by knowledge, pain for the first time,
icicles or light playing over my tongue,
some word huge and black in my mouth.
—NEIL WEISS

WORDS SPOKEN ALONE

A WOMAN TO A MAN

To own nothing, but to be
like the vagrant wind that bears
faintest fragrance of the sea
or, in anger, lifts and tears
but hoards no property—

I praise that state of mind.
Wind, music, and you are such.
All the visible you find
(the invisible you touch),
alter, and leave behind.

To pure being you devote
all your days. You are your eyes,
seemingly near but remote.
Gone, now, the sense of surprise,
like a dying musical note.

Like fragrance, you left no trace.
Like anger, you came my way.
Like music, you filled the space
(by going, the more you stay).
Departures were in your face.

A WIFE TO A HUSBAND
Doth the music always flee?
Who kiss, that they may own,
sing happily, oh happily
of brick on brick till stone
keeps out both wind and sea.

So come back fast, come back slow;
I'll be distance and your home,
every symbol that I know—
church, tower, mosque, and dome—
then, by staying, the more you'll go.

Let me breathe in music where
I am nothing but your life—
your designs, directions share,
to be no mistress but a wife,
pluck your meanings from the air.

I'll be all things you would be—
the four wild winds, the seven wide
    seas—
you'll play with such a gaiety
devastating melodies
till music be my body.

—DANNIE ABSE

THE WORLD'S GREATEST TRICYCLE RIDER

The world's greatest tricycle rider
is in my heart, riding like a wildman,
no hands, almost upside down, along
the walls and over the high curbs
and stoops, his bell rapid-firing,
the sun spinning in his spokes like a flame.

But he is growing older. His feet
overshoot the pedals. His teeth set
too hard against the jolts, and I am afraid
that what I've kept from him is what
tightens his fingers on the rubber grips
and drives him again and again on the same block.

—C. K. WILLIAMS

WRITING

The cursive crawl, the squared-off characters,
these by themselves delight, even without
a meaning, in a foreign language, in
Chinese, for instance, or when skaters curve
all day across the lake, scoring their white

records in ice. Being intelligible,
these winding ways with their audacities
and delicate hesitations, they become
miraculous, so intimately—out there
at the pen's point or brush's tip—do world
and spirit wed. The small bones of the wrist
balance against great skeletons of stars
exactly; the blind bat surveys his way
by echo alone. Still, the point of style
is character. The universe induces
a different tremor in every hand, from the
check forger's to that of the Emperor
Hui Tsung, who called his own calligraphy
the "Slender Gold." A nervous man
writes nervously of a nervous world, and so on.

Miraculous. It is as though the world
were a great writing. Having said so much,
let us allow there is more to the world
than writing; continental faults are not
bare convoluted fissures in the brain.
Not only must the skaters soon go home;
also the hard inscription of their skates
is scored across the open water, which long
remembers nothing, neither wind nor wake.

                              —HOWARD NEMEROV

Y

YOU AND IT

Think what you like, but
It is really the same. Oh,
You can walk around on it
All right and, watching the speed
With which it falls back, fool
Yourself into thinking it changes,

Or, standing with your head
On it, think it above you,
With all the grass of summer
Hanging down, mindless
Birds at your feet, your blood
Rushing up to greet your shadow.

But move, and only the angle
It is regarded from changes.
Turn up the stones, and they

Reveal what has always been
Uppermost. Put them back?
And you are where you started.

You could go on for years
And never get close at all
To the obvious bottom of it.
A slave to a number of fictions,
You would learn of only your own
Deep-seated simplicity.

Perhaps, when you are tired,
You will stretch out on what
Can be thought its own level.
And, closing your eyes at last,
Catching the merest fraction
Of sleep, you will know what I mean.

—MARK STRAND

YOU DRIVE IN A CIRCLE

Slowly a hundred miles through the powerful rain.

Your clothes are towelled with sweat and the car glass sweats,
And there is a smell of damp dog.
Rain-sog is rotting your shoes to paper.

Over old hairy moors, a dark Arctic depth, cresting under rain,
Where the road topples, plunging with its crazed rigging
Like a rackety iron tanker

Into a lunge of spray, emerges again—
Through hard rendings of water,
Drowned eyes at the melting windshield,

Out above the swamped moor-wallows, the mist gulfs of no-thinking.
Down in there are the sheep, rooted like sponges,
Chewing and digesting and undeterred.

What could they lose, however utterly they drowned,
Already sodden as they are with the world, like fossils?
And what is not the world is God, a starry comforter of good blood.

Where are you heading? Everything is already here.
Your hardest look cannot anchor out among these rocks, your
                    coming days cannot anchor among
                    these torn clouds that
                    cannot anchor.

Your destination waits where you left it.

—TED HUGHES

YOU KNOW

You know those rose sherbets,
The gathering of evening around the leaves,
The suffusions of such tinctures of heavens
On the shorn meadows, the suèdes going gold,
And the delicious checkerboard squares
Taking on every strain of the light;
And you know how the shutters close,
How the rocks, wedged in between trees,
Turn rose,
And somebody blue in the grasses
Makes the gold leap, and how the washed skies
Glitter like scales.
So do cheeks, eyes, on fire
With the stilled clarity of the rose of air,
And we get on the bus,
Taking the last of it down with us.

—JEAN GARRIGUE

Index